The R

First-Time Africa

written and researched by
Emma Gregg and Richard Trillo

ROUGH
GUIDES

www.roughguides.com

Contents

◀◀ Locals playing bao, Tanzania ◀ Karo girls, Omo Valley, southwest Ethiopia

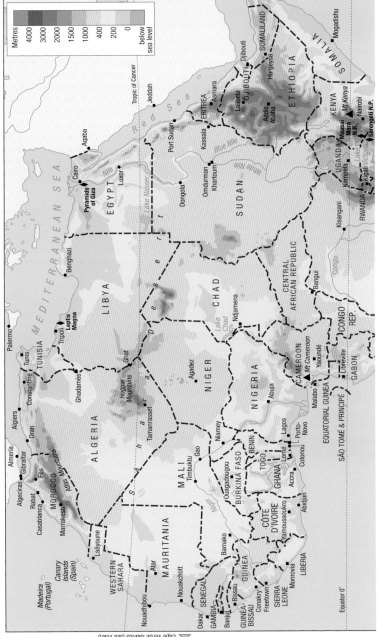

Metres	
4000	
3000	
2000	
1500	
1000	
400	
200	
0	
below sea level	

Tropic of Cancer

Equator 0°

MEDITERRANEAN SEA

Red Sea

Almería
Gibraltar
Algeciras
Oran
Algiers
Palermo
Tunis
Constantine
Benghazi
Cairo
Jeddah
Aqaba

Rabat
Fès
Casablanca
Marrakesh
Atlas Mountains
MOROCCO
Laâyoune

Madeira
(Portugal)

Canary
Islands
(Spain)

Nouâdhibou
Nouakchott
Atar

WESTERN
SAHARA

MAURITANIA

Dakar
SENEGAL
GAMBIA
Banjul
GUINEA-
BISSAU
Bissau
Conakry
GUINEA
SIERRA
LEONE
Freetown
Monrovia
LIBERIA

Bamako
MALI
Timbuktu
Gao

Nouadhibou

ALGERIA

TUNISIA
Tripoli
Leptis
Magna
Ghadamès
Ghat
Hoggar
Mountains
Tamanrasset

LIBYA

S a h a r a

D e s e r t

Agadez
NIGER
Niamey
BURKINA FASO
Ouagadougou
CÔTE
D'IVOIRE
Yamoussoukro
Abidjan
GHANA
Accra
TOGO
BENIN
Lomé
Cotonou
Porto-
Novo
Lagos

Niger

NIGERIA
Abuja

Lake
Chad

CHAD
Ndjamena

CAMEROON
Yaoundé
Mt Cameroon
Malabo
EQUATORIAL GUINEA
SÃO TOMÉ & PRINCIPE
Libreville
GABON

CENTRAL
AFRICAN REPUBLIC
Bangui

CONGO
REP.

Congo

EGYPT
Luxor
Pyramids
of Giza
Nile
Lake Nasser

Dongola
Omdurman
Khartoum

SUDAN

Port Sudan
Kassala
Blue Nile
White Nile

ERITREA
Asmara

Addis
Ababa
Lalibela
ETHIOPIA

DJIBOUTI
Djibouti
Hargeysa
SOMALILAND
Mogadishu
SOMALIA

UGANDA
Kampala
Lake
Victoria
RWANDA
Kigali
Kisangani

KENYA
Mt Kenya
Nairobi
Serengeti N.P.
Maasai
Mara
N.R.

Madeira
(Portugal)

Cape Verde Islands (see inset)

4

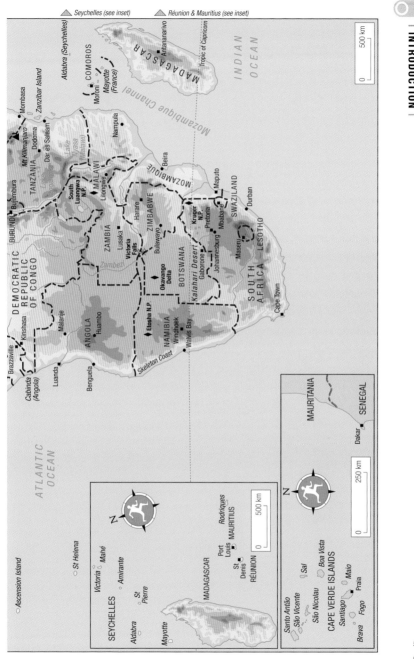

△ Seychelles (see inset)   △ Réunion & Mauritius (see inset)

ATLANTIC OCEAN

Ascension Island

St Helena

INDIAN OCEAN

Aldabra (Seychelles)

COMOROS
Moroni
Mayotte (France)

MADAGASCAR
Antananarivo

Tropic of Capricorn

Mozambique Channel

Zanzibar Island

Mombasa
Dar es Salaam
Dodoma
Mt Kilimanjaro
TANZANIA
BURUNDI
Bujumbura
Lake Nyasa (Malawi)
Nampula
MALAWI
South Luangwa N.P.
Lilongwe
Beira
MOZAMBIQUE
DEMOCRATIC REPUBLIC OF CONGO
ZAMBIA
Lusaka
Harare
ZIMBABWE
Maputo
SWAZILAND
Mbabane
Kruger N.P.
Pretoria
Johannesburg
Maseru
LESOTHO
Durban
Brazzaville
Kinshasa
Victoria Falls
Bulawayo
Zambezi
BOTSWANA
Gaborone
Kalahari Desert
SOUTH AFRICA
Cape Town
Cabinda (Angola)
Luanda
ANGOLA
Malanje
Huambo
Benguela
Okavango Delta
Etosha N.P.
NAMIBIA
Windhoek
Walvis Bay
Skeleton Coast

0   500 km

N

SEYCHELLES
Aldabra
Mayotte
St Pierre
Amirante
Victoria
Mahé

MADAGASCAR

Port Louis
Rodrigues
MAURITIUS
St Denis
RÉUNION

0   500 km

N

MAURITANIA
SENEGAL
Dakar

0   250 km

Santo Antão
São Vicente
São Nicolau
Sal
Boa Vista
Santiago
Maio
Fogo
Praia
Brava
CAPE VERDE ISLANDS

5

Introduction to

First-Time Africa

Africa is a compelling destination for adventurous travellers. Its roadless rainforests and radiant savannas are some of the world's most spectacular ecosystems and the wildlife extravaganza in the safari heartlands can be overwhelming, surrounding visitors with a panorama of animals, from elephants to lion prides and giant ostriches to brilliant weaverbirds. Yet while travellers may come mostly to witness Africa's natural assets, they often leave most impressed by its cultural ones: music and dance, remote communities, old kingdoms, traditional architecture and dress, and the sheer ebullience and good grace of people in the face of hardships that would crush most visitors. That spirit adds extra resonance to Africa's huge appeal: nothing can equate to your experiences here.

 Indeed, your first day or two may be rather intense, especially if you start in a city, as you adjust to the heat and the culture shock. It can be disturbing to come face to face with serious poverty in the shape of beggars and street children, jarring to find yourself in streets used as living spaces, laundries and toilets, and disconcerting to find that, being a relatively rich – and in some places highly unusual – visitor, you're the focus of attention wherever you go. Be prepared at the beginning to grit your teeth and put up with whatever each day brings.

As soon as you get out on the red earth roads and ribbons of tarmac, or start exploring Africa's wide, brown rivers, great lakes, deserts, alpine peaks and coral seas, you'll discover what hooks people about the continent. The sights, sounds and smells – of waking before dawn on the sandy banks of the Niger, spending a night in the Central African rainforest, stopping in the silent heat of the Sahara for prayers and a snack, waiting as the dry earth of the plains is quenched by a tropical downpour, watching shooting stars from the roof of a mud-brick house –

Will it break the bank?

African countries may be poor, but they're not particularly cheap. Try to visit with too little money and you'll be disappointed at the limitations imposed on what you can do. With careful planning, you can still travel affordably: just don't expect to do it on US$10 a day.

If, like many visitors, you book an organized trip, you'll quickly discover that the range of options and prices is mind-boggling. If you're based in the UK, then with just two weeks to play with, you could grab a Moroccan beach holiday for £400 (US$650), a Kenyan safari and beach trip for £1500 (US$2500) or a spot of rustic luxury in Mozambique for around £5000 (US$8000), including flights. Flying from North America will add significantly to prices – a return ticket can easily cost over US$1500.

Of course, you could make your own way around. We estimate minimum in-country budgets in *Where to go* (from p.225), but you may prefer to allow more, particularly if you're travelling on your own (the budgets are per person for two people travelling together) or if you'll be country-hopping or visiting the pricier areas in peak season. You'll often pay more in less-visited countries thanks to poor infrastructure and limited accommodation options, while popular destinations such as Morocco, Egypt and South Africa can be good value. Experiences such as gorilla-trekking or chilling out in a gorgeous eco-lodge, meanwhile, can cost a bomb – and be utterly unforgettable.

will stay with you for a lifetime. And the sheer diversity of peoples and languages can be hard to keep up with: you can pass, often in a matter of hours, from the tribal homeland of herders in traditional dress to densely cultivated farms

▲ The Mandara Mountains, Cameroon

populated by a different tribe, speaking a different language, to a lakeside district of fishing people and traders, speaking yet another language, and with equally different customs.

Coming from a homogenous society to this ethnic and cultural diversity can be intoxicating: many visitors soon find themselves trying out local languages and wanting to learn more about customs and history.

7

▼ Food stalls at Marrakesh's famous Djemaa el Fna

Planning the big trip

A s the authors of this book, we hadn't thought much about our first trips to Africa. One of us sketched out an epic, year-long adventure, aiming to take public transport from The Gambia right down to the south, but in the end West Africa proved so interesting that she spent her entire time there instead. The other took off from England one Friday with a plan to hitch-hike to Timbuktu, getting to the fabled city, and home again, largely by good luck and the kindness of others, having learned what a visa is, and what malaria feels like.

A different kind of safari

So you're hooked on natural history documentaries, and you're itching to see the real thing. You're not alone: a huge proportion of first-time visitors to Africa make wildlife-watching their primary focus.

There's absolutely nothing wrong with that – we sing the praises of Africa's superb safari scene in Chapter Eleven. But as well as your binoculars, make sure you bring your hiking shoes and swimming togs – the continent has some stunning walking and climbing country, thrilling places to snorkel or dive and beautiful beaches. You can explore ancient ruins, monuments and rock art sites, take guided tours of villages, townships and cities, and get swept away by the party spirit at traditional festivals and events. For some ideas, turn to Chapter Twelve.

To enhance your connection with the continent even more, you may want to find out about African culture (we give an introduction in Chapter Thirteen) and consider the impact your trip will have on the environments and the communities you visit (see Chapter Fourteen). Whichever approach you choose, common sense, good humour and, above all, an eagerness to try something new will set you on the right track.

Both of us could have done with reading a book like this. It is full of the practical advice and, we hope, wisdom absorbed from a combined fifty years of visiting Africa, studying its languages, cultures and wildlife, writing guidebooks and articles and travelling with our families. We haven't been absolutely everywhere, but between us we've covered most of Africa. And we keep going back for more, because the continent is endlessly absorbing and still full of mysteries.

▶ Banana Beach, Príncipe

This is a **trip-planning book**, intended to get you ready. You might take it − or pages from it − with you, but you'll need extra maps and guidebooks for the actual journey. The main idea here is to get you to the point where you know where you're going and what you're aiming to do.

The first half of the book, **The Big Adventure**, covers the practicalities of travelling in Africa, starting with stuff you'll be doing at home, from planning a route to deciding what to pack, before discussing transport, accommodation, food and drink, safaris and other activities, money, culture, responsible travel and staying safe. The second part of the book, **Where to go**, covers every country in Africa with the exception of Somalia. Each one starts with an

◀ The Okavango Delta, Botswana

Spotting cheetahs in the Maasai Mara

essential fact file, including an estimated minimum daily budget, followed by our take on the country's highlights, information about routes in and out of the country, and the lowdown on visas.

It's easy to describe Africa in broad brushstrokes, much harder to do it justice. Our **Directory**, at the back of the book, includes not just plenty of recommended travel and tour operator contacts, but hundreds of festivals and country-by-country listings of the books and websites we recommend: turn to them for more insight and inspiration. This continent of more than fifty nations and hundreds of different ethnic groups has provided bottomless inspiration for writers and other artists, both African and from overseas.

You'll have many memorable and unexpected **conversations**. Travel long enough and you'll meet out-of-luck hunters, negligent cattle herders, sardonic

Dugout canoes on the Sangha in Congo Republic

market ladies, fastidious shopkeepers and even helpful border guards. In this, the most rewarding, stirring and engaging place in the world, you'll travel with Berber women on mobile phones, Maasai warriors on motorbikes, Zulu police inspectors and Swahili TV presenters. Give yourself plenty of time, turn your personal thresholds up to eleven, and let the fun begin.

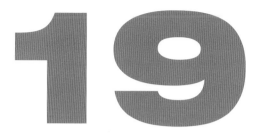

reasons to go

Africa offers such a dazzling array of experiences, sights and events that it would be impossible to see everything in your first trip, or even in a lifetime. What follows, in no particular order, is a selection of highlights, from classic wildlife adventures to unmissable cultural encounters, any of which are worthy of a place in your dream itinerary.

01 **Hear the thunder** Pages **393** & **397** • Victoria Falls is a wonder of the natural world – its raw power and shimmering rainbows have been captivating visitors since Livingstone's time.

02 **Party with the locals** Page **248** • Glam it up at Cape Verde's Mardi Gras Carnival, a sparkling occasion with parades, drums, feathers and sequins galore.

04 **Try something refreshing** Page **132** • Wake up at an Indian Ocean resort, and prepare to be dazzled by tropical treats – breakfast will never seem the same again.

05 **Get the lowdown** Page **235** • Learn about wetland habitats as you explore the Okavango Delta to a gentle chorus of bird calls and hippo grunts. It's one of Africa's most serene wilderness experiences.

03 **Spot a colourful character** Page **162** • You'll be glad you remembered your binoculars when you clap eyes on Africa's astonishing array of birds, from lugubrious hornbills to delightfully pretty bee-eaters.

06 **Take part in a ceremony** Page **289** • Traditional ceremonies take place across the continent: in Kumasi, Ghana, visitors can join crowds of *kente*-cloth draped courtiers at regular receptions held by the King of Asante.

07 **Float away** Page **180** • Get a fresh perspective on the wonders of Ancient Egypt by drifting over pyramids, temples and colossi in a hot air balloon.

08 **Climb Kilimanjaro** Pages **175** & **378** Though not a specialist climb, it will test every sinew. Make it all the way to the snowy peak, and you'll feel like a conquering hero.

09 Fall in love with the desert Page **337** • Best seen in the soft light of the early morning, the monumental dunes at Sossusvlei in Namibia are fun to climb and a hoot to run down.

10 Let your jaw drop Pages **299** & **377** • Feel like an extra in a classic wildlife documentary as you witness the annual epic that is East Africa's Great Migration.

11 Go on safari Page **154** • Hook up with an expert guide to head deep into the bush in the safari heartlands of East and southern Africa for wildlife encounters you'll never forget.

12 Witness an ancient ritual Page **278** • In some regions, intricate tribal customs survive intact; in rural Ethiopia you may be invited to watch a stick fight or a bull-jumping ceremony.

14 Have a night on the town • Sample Dakar's super-charged club scene (page **357**), jive to *kwaito* in Jo'burg (page **369**) or let yourself go at a fabulous festival (page **62**).

13 Meet the family Page **156** • Each day, a few dozen people hike through rainforest to spend an hour in precious proximity to the awe-inspiring gorillas of Central Africa.

15 Raft the rapids Page **177** • If you reckon you've got what it takes to tackle Africa's wildest waters, you'll love the Zambezi, the Victoria Nile and the Orange River.

16 Take a reality check •
Leave the conventional tourist trail behind by joining a township tour (page **181**) or a community voluntourism project (page **206**), or simply staying with a family (page **125**).

17 Explore the ocean Page
178 • Cast yourself adrift in the Red Sea or the Indian Ocean and you can swim through clouds of colourful fish or encounter whale sharks and mantas, harmless giants of the deep.

18 Splurge in an eco-lodge
Page **122** • To truly bond with nature, treat yourself to a stay in a gorgeous wilderness retreat with impeccable green credentials.

19 Pay homage Page **183** • The Great Mosque of Djenné, in Mali, and the mosques, churches and temples of North Africa and and Ethiopia count among the continent's most important and beautiful spiritual sites.

First-Time Africa

The Big Adventure

Planning your trip

A frica is big. Until you compare a map of your own country or state with the map of Africa, you don't realize how big: at more than thirty million square kilometres the continent is five times larger than Europe, four times the size of Australia, more than three times the size of the USA and seventy percent bigger than South America.

When choosing **where to go** on this vast landmass it's easy to bite off more than you can chew: even a few centimetres across the map can take weeks of arduous travel. Africa's landscape and climate is highly diverse – mountain ranges separate dense forest from plains, river basins from arid deserts. The **infrastructure** varies enormously too: there are countries, cities and regions where you can travel as easily as you can in Europe or North America using reliably scheduled public transport and decent roads to get from A to B pretty much at will. But these are the exceptions: in most parts of Africa, roads and transport are notoriously unreliable. Even if you plan on doing some or all of your trip as an organized tour (see p.51), remember that your tour operator has to contend with the same conditions. Not that this has to be a problem to grapple with, even if you could do anything about it – it's all part of the experience. It's just that you have to include respect for the unexpected in all of your plans.

During that planning stage, it's worth keeping the following thoughts in mind:

- **Stay informed** Decide why you're going and what you want to get out of the trip. Browse the book stores and libraries and read up on the areas you're interested in visiting; browse the specialist travel forums; subscribe to online news feeds from local papers; and tune in to internet radio (see p.153).

● **Be realistic** Give yourself time. The rewards get thinner the faster you go, and the point of being there can get lost in the pursuit of the next goal. If you've got a plane to catch, or a tour to check in with, that connection inevitably becomes your main focus. And enforced haste tends to lead to intolerance and irritation: visiting one country after another for just a week or two then becomes a blur of organization with precious few highlights.

● **Stay safe** Africa is not unchanging. Like everywhere, events can move swiftly and it's important not to overlook security issues when planning your route across the continent. Visit your country's government travel advisory website and take note of warnings about particular nations and regions. They're usually somewhat over-cautious (and occasionally months out of date on key areas), but at least you'll get some perspective. The British FCO and US State Department travel advisories are both detailed, but it's worth referring to the sites of several countries to build up a picture. See p.24 for our notes on no-go areas.

● **Choose a date** Find out about the climate and try to avoid the rainy season – each of our country profiles covers the best time to go. Setting off overland through West Africa at the start of the European summer, for example, will give you a view of much of the region under torrential rain. Equally, travelling during the rains in central or East Africa can be a washout. While main roads usually stay open, earth roads through the bush can be wiped out, making travel impossible. Travelling shortly after the rains, however, with fresh greenery and clear skies, can be wonderful. See p.53.

● **Stay healthy** It's important to look after yourself. In many parts of the continent you can be hours or even days away from the nearest medical staff. Plan your travel health meds well in advance, take enough anti-malarials for your trip, and don't travel when you're sick – if you suddenly get much worse you may not be able to find help. See p.68.

● **Stay longer** The urge to rush on to the next destination in your itinerary can mean missing out: don't let self-discipline trump flexibility. If staying on feels the right thing to do – for example because a festival or a wedding party is happening, or simply because you're enjoying yourself – then cancel your travel plans and relax. Staying in one place for a while is how to get the most out of your trip – and also gives you a chance to give something back (see p.199). You'll learn and see more, and begin to understand cultures and environments in a way that intercity travel can't deliver.

● **Change your mode of travel** It's good to be prepared to change your travel style if circumstances dictate. You might set off using public transport in West Africa and then decide you want more independence and buy a bicycle. Or you might have intended to travel solo on a low budget in East Africa for six months, but team up with another traveller and end up flying to Madagascar or Egypt. See p.93.

● **Stay at home if you don't have the funds** Give yourself the best budget you can achieve and don't set off if you can't afford the trip you've planned. Africa's countries may mostly be poor but they're rarely cheap, and there's nothing so frustrating as having to pass up on an experience because you don't have the funds. You risk spoiling the whole trip – and in a way you're also short-changing your hosts, to whom you represent huge wealth no matter how skint you feel. See p.137.

Africa in perspective

The various countries that make up Africa are part of major **regions** just as the countries of Europe have their regional characteristics. Never forget, however, that Africa is a continent, not a country – the name really refers only to the geographical entity – and only a few of Africa's countries are fully coherent nations. Their borders were fixed in place by the colonial powers in the 1950s, creating a mosaic of nation states that disguises an equally significant pattern of older indigenous nations often built over hundreds of years (see p.32).

Landscapes and wildlife

The popular impression of the African landscape may be a mix of **rainforest** and elephant-dotted **savanna**, but the truth is more diverse, more animated and often more urban than that. Central Africa still has room for the second biggest rainforest on earth after the Amazon, but beyond the grasslands to the north you traverse the dry **Sahel** – an Arabic word referring to the fringes of the desert – and then reach the Sahara itself, by far the worlds' biggest **desert**. Southern Africa also has large deserts in the shape of the Kalahari and the Namib. At the northern and southern extremities of the continent, in coastal Morocco and Algeria and in Western Cape province of South Africa, the climate and scenery are **Mediterranean**, similar in many ways to what you'd find in southern Spain or southern California.

Most of the continent is flat or rolling. Africa has no Andes, Himalayas or Rockies, but there are some serious **mountain ranges** – the glacier-capped Rwenzori range in Uganda and Democratic Republic of Congo, the Atlas mountains in Morocco and Algeria, the Drakensberg range in South Africa and Lesotho, and the highlands of Ethiopia and northern Cameroon. Towering above the plains in East Africa are the giant, free-standing former volcanoes of Kilimanjaro and Mount Kenya, and the still-active volcanoes of Fogo in the Cape Verde Islands, Karthala in the

Comoros Islands, and Mount Cameroon. All these peaks and ranges can be hiked and summited.

Africa's **rivers** have helped shape its history and culture. In West Africa, nine countries rely partly or entirely on the **Niger** for water and hydroelectricity. From its source in Sierra Leone, it flows north and opens into a giant inland delta that nurtured the Mali and Songhai empires, before flowing close to the edge of the Sahara, where sand dunes loom on the riverbank behind snorting hippos. It then turns back south and flows out into the Atlantic in Nigeria through a vast, spreading network of mangrove-fringed channels and meanders, peppered with the region's oil derricks.

The **Nile**, the world's longest river and lifeblood of ancient Egypt's Pharaonic civilization, has its two sources in Ethiopia and Rwanda, and provides hydroelectricity and water for another seven countries. In the heart of Africa, no fewer than ten countries are dependent on the **Congo**, which rises in Zambia and flows in an immense loop through savanna and rainforest, joined by huge tributaries on its way, eventually to surge through a series of rapids and emerge into the Atlantic. In southern Africa, the big river is the **Zambezi**, a source of water and hydroelectricity for eight countries – its dramatic plunge over the Victoria Falls is one of Africa's greatest sights. Although none of these great rivers have ferry services that fully exploit their potential, you can at least usually travel along them – even if it's in a plank canoe on the Niger, propelled by a man with a pole, or on a floating marketplace barge drifting and bumping down the Congo.

Visiting the thrillingly biodiverse **rainforests** of central Africa is an intoxicating experience, although they can be hard to access – Cameroon, Uganda and Rwanda are probably your best bet. The wildlife is there in abundance, though much of it is 30m up in the tree canopy and hard to see. You can, however, almost guarantee a close encounter with the world's biggest and rarest primate – the mountain gorilla – by signing up for a specialist trek to visit a habituated group.

Far easier and generally more affordable are the great savanna **parks** of East and southern Africa. Huge areas of Kenya, Uganda, Tanzania, Zambia, Botswana, Namibia and South Africa are given over to wildlife conservation, and most parks are well set up for safari tourism, with maintained dirt roads patrolled by rangers, permanent camps and lodges, and nature trails where you can leave your vehicle and walk. The parks are usually unfenced, leaving the animals free to come and go. In the most dramatic and photogenic examples of this, more than a million wildebeest make an annual migration in search of pasture from Tanzania's Serengeti National Park to Kenya's Maasai Mara National Reserve, while flocks of pink flamingos tens of thousands strong migrate, apparently randomly, from one shallow salt lake to another, creating a unique spectacle in the Rift Valley. For full details about wildlife and safaris, see p.154.

Africa's coastline

Africa's 26,000km **coastline** (surprisingly short for such a huge land mass) is as varied as its regions. Along the Mediterranean, Tunisia has most of the best beaches, while Morocco's busy seaside areas are along the rougher Atlantic coast, much of which, as far south as Senegal, is backed by dunes – the old Barbary Coast, swept by the chilly, fish-rich Canary Current. Rough seas and strong currents dominate much of the coastline of **West Africa** – at least where swampy creeks and mangroves don't make it completely inaccessible – but there are good beach areas, with some surf, particularly in Senegal and The Gambia, between Sierra Leone and Ghana, and on the Cape Verde Islands.

Central Africa has good, palm-fringed beaches and warm swimming in Cameroon, São Tomé and Príncipe and Gabon, but from here south the cold Benguela Current conspires against swimming until you reach the Indian Ocean, east of the Cape. In **southern Africa**, the best beaches are east of the Cape of Good Hope and especially up the eastern seaboard towards Mozambique. From here to Tanzania and Kenya and as far north as Egypt's Red Sea coast lies a succession of idyllic beaches, protected by offshore coral reefs and providing ideal conditions for snorkelling and diving.

Towns and cities

When you're in the more heavily populated regions, and even in central Africa and coastal West Africa, where the natural vegetation is dense forest, by far the commonest scenery today is a rather desolate, bush-stripped landscape in which dust and bare earth figure heavily. For decades, few of Africa's **cities** have been really compelling destinations in their own right – with the notable exceptions of the old trading cities of North and West Africa, such as Cairo, Kano and Marrakesh. But increasingly the modern cities are reinventing themselves: it's not always a pretty process, but there are windows of hope in the urban jungle, and for every blighted slum, there's a sprouting of affordable housing for the growing middle class and a succession of new malls and galleries, shops and internet cafés, cine-complexes and restaurants.

North Africa

Algeria, Egypt, Libya, Morocco & Western Sahara, Tunisia

They may be close to Europe – frequent car ferries shuttle across the Mediterranean – but parts of this region are as culturally exotic as much of the continent further south, with the addition, barely found in sub-Saharan Africa, of large, thousand-year-old cities still functioning as thriving metropolises, complete with souks and mobile phones, arched alleyways and DVD stores.

No-go areas and trouble spots

Don't assume this list will be as long (or as short) when you start your own trip, but at the time of writing the following countries were experiencing problems severe enough to give you pause for thought before contemplating a visit – either a visit of any kind to the country, or a visit to a particular region within these states. All but Somalia are, however, covered in our country profiles, and several of those in the list of countries with purely regional problems are mainstream tourist destinations that are safe outside the regions in question. Note that the terrorist threat in the Sahara (Mauritania, Algeria, Mali and Niger) appears to be growing, though it is hard to establish how many active members Al-Qaeda in the Maghreb (or AQIM) actually has. For further information see the relevant country profiles.

Countries

Algeria Extremists supporting Al-Qaeda continue to threaten foreigners visiting Algeria and have attacked and kidnapped tourists in the Sahara. Banditry, and kidnapping for ransom (not necessarily with any connection to AQIM), is also a serious problem on some desert routes. The danger extends south into parts of Mali, Mauritania and Niger.

Angola Away from the cities, the whole country suffers the legacy of its decades-long civil war through the enormous number of landmines still unexploded in the bush. Towns and busy routes are safe.

Central African Republic (CAR) The corrupt government's writ barely extends beyond the capital, Bangui. Domestic rebels, deserters from the military, and elements of Uganda's LRA rebel group are reasons to be exceptionally cautious when travelling anywhere outside the capital.

Chad As in CAR, the government in Ndjamena is fighting several rebel groups and unexploded mines are a problem in many districts.

Congo Republic As well as an anti-government rebellion in the Pool region, near Brazzaville, northern Congo has had to deal with refugees from conflicts in neighbouring CAR and DRC.

Democratic Republic of Congo (DRC) As well as complicated, ongoing conflicts between the Kinshasa government and various rebel groups, and ongoing ethnic conflict in the northeast, many parts of DRC are seriously contaminated by unexploded landmines.

Côte d'Ivoire In the aftermath of the civil war, the country is divided into south and north and a return to conflict is not out of the question. In the far west, near the border of Sierra Leone and Liberia, banditry is a serious problem.

Morocco or **Tunisia**, the most accessible countries, are cases in point: much of Tunisia feels as European as Naples and parts of Morocco are no less familiar than Marseille, but once you get off the beaten track (easy in Morocco, harder in Tunisia since there's not much that isn't beaten), the adventure kicks in. The markets and backstreets of the old cities of Fes and Marrakesh have an allure that has happily survived their emergence as weekend-break destinations. The high Atlas, the desert routes, or cautious explorations of the Rif mountains are highly recommended in Morocco, with warm and exuberant encounters with Berber

Mauritania Al-Qaeda-supporting extremists have attacked and kidnapped tourists and foreign residents in several parts of the country, threatening the only currently open West African overland route, from Morocco to Senegal.

Somalia Devastated by decades of civil war and more recently by Al-Shabaab, a terrorist group that controls much of the south, Somalia itself is off the map, even for most journalists or official visitors with armed protection. Two breakaway regions – Puntland and Somaliland – have established some security, but are in conflict with each other. The government of Somaliland declared independence in 1991 and has sought international recognition ever since. The capital, Hargeisa, is relatively prosperous and safe, and has some international flight connections, but overland travel around the rest of Somaliland is still subject to restrictions.

Regions

Egypt Mines left over from World War II are still a problem in the western desert; travel here is restricted as a result.

Kenya The northern districts bordering Ethiopia and Somalia have long been prone to banditry. Most vehicles travel in escorted convoys.

Mali Banditry and low-level, Al-Qaeda-supporting extremists make parts of the northeast unsafe (see Algeria, left).

Morocco and Western Sahara Western Sahara has been occupied by Morocco since 1975 and remains a highly militarized region with travel restrictions. Mines are a problem in the Mauritania border area.

Niger Banditry, an anti-government Tuareg rebellion, and Al-Qaeda-supporting extremists make much of the north and east unsafe (see Algeria, left).

Nigeria The Niger Delta has been a flashpoint for years, with guerrilla groups fighting for a share of the region's oil wealth and expat workers frequently kidnapped for ransom. Sporadic ethnic conflicts in Plateau State have not so far affected visitors.

Senegal Separatists in the southern region of Casamance sporadically attack government targets and vehicles. Off the main roads mines can be a danger in this region.

Sudan The war in Darfur has made travelling in that part of the country highly inadvisable and the likely emergence of South Sudan as a recognized independent state in 2011 or 2012 may also have repercussions on both sides of the new border, although the outlook for the south seems promising.

Uganda The remnants of the rebel Lord's Resistance Army still pose a threat to travel and security in pockets of northern Uganda, although the main road to Sudan seems to be generally safe.

families almost guaranteed and wonderful desert architecture, valleys and canyons to admire.

Algeria and **Libya** are slightly tougher destinations (along with Western Sahara, which has all but been rubbed out by the Moroccan occupation). While Libya is largely empty desert, and travel restrictions are a pain, the Roman ruins on the coast are outstanding and easily the equal of popular Carthage in Tunisia. Algeria also has a clutch of superb Roman sites in the northeast – Timgad, Djemila and Hippo Regius – but security remains a problem.

Religion

Although it's easy to see that **Islam**, **Christianity** and so-called **animism** – a catch-all term for traditional belief systems – are the three religions of Africa, the facts on the ground are more complicated. Islam or Christianity often overlies the older, local religion, with elements of both incorporated into religious practices. The tenets of traditional beliefs vary greatly between ethnic groups, but a distant supreme being is the norm, combined with a multitude of spiritual entities, represented by, or actually living in, parts of the natural world – animal and plant species, hills or caves, rivers and lakes. At the same time, people's ancestors are part of the community in a way that Westerners find hard to grasp. They have control over people's lives, and to ignore their needs – assuaged through regular sacrifices, celebrations and libations – is as risky as ignoring the requirements of a demanding grandfather or grandmother. See p.192 for a more detailed discussion of religion.

Egypt is as much a part of the Middle East as of Africa, though Cairo is a melting pot of old residents and African newcomers and it commands respect throughout the continent: biblical influences spread by missionaries may account for the widespread origin myth that this or that tribe came originally from Egypt. As a destination, Egypt is hugely popular, with the Pyramids and a cruise on the Nile on every travel wish list. With the development of tourism in the Sinai peninsula, including direct flights to Sharm el-Sheikh, diving and beach lounging are also now firmly on the list.

West Africa

Benin, Burkina Faso, Cape Verde, Côte d'Ivoire, The Gambia, Ghana, Guinea, Guinea-Bissau, Liberia, Mali, Mauritania, Niger, Nigeria, Senegal, Sierra Leone, Togo

This vast region of old trading kingdoms, forests and savanna extends deep into the Sahara and includes some of the earliest parts of sub-Saharan Africa to have had contact with Europe (the Portuguese were trading here by the end of the fifteenth century). Africa's third longest river, the Niger, sweeps through West Africa, linking its source in Sierra Leone with its mouth in Nigeria, via the ancient university town of Timbuktu.

Of West Africa's nine francophone colonies, the country most dominated by French culture and language is **Senegal**, which also has a decent infrastructure, making it an obvious starting point. **Côte d'Ivoire** (Ivory Coast) used to be the first choice in the region for French expat postings but it has been traumatized by its north–south civil war so you need to get advice before travelling much outside Abidjan.

Huge, land-locked **Mali** is blessed with the great inland delta of the Niger River and striking cultural contrasts – the old Islamic cities of Gao, Timbuktu and Djenné near the river, and the magnificent and fascinating Dogon country along the rocky Bandiagara escarpment.

Other francophone countries include the narrow strips of **Togo** and **Benin**, the latter being especially easy-going and full of interest, with its voodoo culture and historical sites; the laidback, former revolutionary republic of **Burkina Faso**, famous for its huge festival of African cinema; and the remote, dramatic expanses of **Mauritania** and **Niger**, both of which are currently dubious destinations because of security threats.

Perhaps the most impressive of the *pays francophones* is **Guinea**, with its low population density, beautiful landscapes and relatively thin intrusion of European culture. The plateau region of the Fouta Djalon is great hiking and biking country, with tumbling streams and steep mesas, and in the forested hills of the far southeast you'll find some of West Africa's best tracts of rainforest.

Four of West Africa's countries are former British colonies. **The Gambia**, despite its repressive government, makes a very accessible gateway to the region. **Ghana**'s distinctive, can-do personality and more open society make for an easy welcome and some flamboyant cultural experiences, especially in local festivals. The palm-lined coast, dotted with old European slave-trading forts and the country's handful of good wildlife sanctu-

Is this the way to Télimélé?

Hiking in the Fouta Djalon in Guinea, and not knowing which way to go, we decided, rather than head off in the wrong direction, to wait a little while for someone to pass and ask directions. As remote as we were, that might have been a bit optimistic but we could only give it a try. Finally, a car appeared and trundled to a stop in the road in a cloud of dust. I greeted the driver in French:

Hello there!
Hello.

Can you help us with directions?
Yes.

Good. Is Télimélé this way?
Yes.

How far is it?
Yes.

Okay. Is Télimélé that way?
Yes.

Which way is shorter?
Yes.

Where are you going yourself?
Yes.

Well thanks for the help!
Yes.

We tossed a coin. On reflection, perhaps he didn't speak French.

Yuri Horowitz

aries, make it one of West Africa's most popular destinations. **Sierra Leone** has put its years of civil war behind it and has emerged still boasting some of the best beaches in the world – only minutes away from the raffish tumble of Freetown. **Liberia** has been through civil war, too, but as one of Africa's older independent nations (1847) and now with the continent's first female head of state, the future looks promising. As in the 1980s, its forests could once again be targets for wildlife enthusiasts and, like Sierra Leone it has excellent beaches – and even a nascent surfing scene. **Nigeria** arguably has the continent's worst reputation, stemming largely from the workaholic zeal of Africa's biggest population and its inevitable share of crooks and scoundrels. But the travel incentives – including old Hausa cities in the north and wildlife reserves and dramatic mountains in the east – are a revelation, and even Lagos has its fans. If only the politicians could stick to their day jobs.

The former Portuguese colony of the **Cape Verde** islands is growing in popularity as a package holiday destination for European beach-lovers and watersports fans. But they only visit two of the least interesting islands. The islands further west – beguiling, volcanic outcrops in the mid-Atlantic – have unique scenery and a culture that mixes Portugal, Africa and Brazil. The other ex-Portuguese colony, **Guinea–Bissau**, has its own island highlights, the Bijagós – luxuriant green forests in the warm, inshore sea – but you need to be aware of its less inviting reputation as a staging post for the South American cocaine trade, which is close to throttling normal life here.

Central Africa

Cameroon, Central African Republic, Chad, Congo Republic, Democratic Republic of Congo, Equatorial Guinea, Gabon, São Tomé & Príncipe

Central Africa has had a hard time of it over the last two centuries, subject to the whims of Europe's monarchs, robber barons and politicians. Yet five hundred years ago, Central Africa was dominated by the Kongo kingdom, which traded on equal terms with the Portuguese. There are scant reminders of the old pre-colonial states in the Central Africa of today, but for hardy travellers the region's cultures – and its great rivers, forests and mountains – remain very much worth exploring.

Cameroon – which is English-speaking in the west and French-speaking elsewhere – blends stunning scenery and national parks with an extraordinarily rich culture, from "Pygmy" communities in the rainforest to Arabic-speaking trading towns. Cameroon, along with the little Portuguese-speaking island nation of **São Tomé & Príncipe**, is the most visited – and visitable – country in the region. **Gabon** is a growing eco-tourism destination, but its bureaucracy is obstructive, while just getting a visa for **Equatorial Guinea** requires a feat of ingenuity. Both countries, however, have masses of potential for rainforest visits.

For the rest of the huge region – which in some parts is literally unexplored in the sense that outsiders have rarely visited – war, refugees, infrastructure collapse and the pillaging of natural and mineral resources are the not very encouraging dominant themes. Much of **Central African Republic** and **Chad** are currently downright dangerous and not recommended – or easy – for the ordinary traveller to wander around in, which is a pity, because both countries need more paying visitors to bolster the fragile protection afforded to their rich and impressive national parks.

As for the two Congos, **Congo Republic** suffers from the aftermath of recent civil war and puts huge obstacles in the way of independent travellers – or in fact any visitor – wanting to see the fantastic richness of its rainforests. As for the so-called **Democratic Republic of Congo** (formerly Zaire), there are glimmers of hope for intrepid visitors in this giant country of rainforests and moist savanna – there's decent infrastructure around Goma in the east, for example, including gorilla visits in the Virunga National Park – but those chinks could just as easily close again with an upsurge of the sporadic inter-ethnic and government–rebel conflict that persists in eastern DRC.

East Africa

Burundi, Djibouti, Eritrea, Ethiopia, Kenya, Rwanda, Seychelles, Somalia, Sudan, Tanzania, Uganda

Parts of East Africa were first colonized a century ago in a way that much of the continent was not – by quite large numbers of European settlers arriving to lay claim to untilled (but not unoccupied) land. The fallout from that process is ongoing – with disputes over land owner-ship a critical issue in some areas – but colonization ensured that several countries were spotlighted as desirable destinations to live and travel in when they reclaimed their independence half a century later.

The tourist magnets in this region are Kenya, Tanzania and Uganda, with their solid infrastructures (relatively speaking: there's no high-speed rail or motorways), thriving market economies and more or less adequately functioning governments. Vitally for visitors, of course, they also have unforgettable scenery, an almost carnival-like variety of tribes and ethnic groups and the world's most famous safari parks.

Kenya has the most developed infrastructure in East Africa, with some busy parks and the slightly intimidating sprawl of Nairobi, but perhaps ninety percent of visitors tick off the same short list of destinations – Amboseli, Tsavo West and East, Maasai Mara and the coast – leaving much of the rest of the country off the tourist trails. The Aberdare range, Laikipia plateau and Mount Kenya itself, the northern Rift Valley lakes, the country around Lake Victoria, and the whole of the northern deserts are yours for the visiting.

The much larger country of **Tanzania** is fast catching up with Kenya in terms of popularity. In the northwest, a busy safari circuit takes in the Serengeti, Ngorongoro Crater and Lake Manyara, with Kilimanjaro not far to the east. On the coast, the biggest city, Dar es Salaam, is the gateway to the archipelago of Zanzibar, which is really a country in its own right. Venture further south and west into the heart of Tanzania and you'll leave the mainstream tourist industry behind.

Although **Uganda's** post-independence strife held it back for more than two decades, it has been making up rapidly for the lost years, and is now a hugely attractive country to travel in. Gorilla-tracking trips are its best-known asset, but the re-emerging game parks of the centre and west, the adrenaline-sports base of Jinja on the Victoria Nile, and Lake Victoria itself, are just the standouts in an embarrassment of natural riches, while the capital, Kampala, is East Africa's most user-friendly big city.

The increasingly popular travel destination of **Ethiopia** is close to joining the Kenya-Uganda-Tanzania triumvirate, though its large population and major historical sites such as the rock churches of Lalibela and the old city of Harar mean that culture just trumps nature in terms of visitor attractions – though Ethiopia's natural heritage of mountain parks is far from meagre. One area where culture and nature combine in still almost untouched harmony is the far southwest corner of the country along the valley of the Omo River. Here, some of Africa's most isolated, culturally intact and colourfully attired tribes coexist alongside wildlife-rich bush savanna.

Rwanda – renowned for its gorillas and post-genocide nation-building – is also edging towards mainstream popularity. Its neighbour, **Burundi**, has a way to go, but there are worse places to spend a few days than the beaches outside the pleasant little capital Bujumbura, on the shores of Lake Tanganyika. For a spell in Eden at a price, meanwhile, visit the natural history paradise of the **Seychelles**. Way out in the Indian Ocean with a population of less than 100,000, it is far removed from the problems facing most African countries.

In the Horn of Africa, those problems are paramount. Even if peace arrived tomorrow, it would be many years before **Somalia** could welcome visitors as it once did in the 1980s. **Djibouti** and **Eritrea** are more promising: Djibouti, because the French expat community and Foreign Legion garrison pump money into the economy; Eritrea for its security and natural and historical attractions (though its government seems hellbent on being Africa's most repressive).

Lastly, **Sudan** is northeast Africa's biggest unknown quantity. Renowned historical attractions in the north and the wonderful welcome extended to visitors – reinforced by the sheer safety of Khartoum – have to be weighed against the brutal regime in power and the fact that the country is likely to be split in two when the south votes for independence in a referendum in 2011. That could result in a new African nation, with vast natural assets, including tremendous migratory game areas, its capital in Juba – already the fastest growing city in Africa – and its economic and social horizons firmly oriented southwards towards East Africa.

Southern Africa

Angola, Botswana, Comoros & Mayotte, Lesotho, Madagascar, Malawi, Mauritius, Mozambique, Namibia, Réunion, South Africa, Swaziland, Zambia, Zimbabwe

Dominated by the sheer pulling power and size of **South Africa**, this region receives the lion's share of tourists to sub-Saharan Africa. South Africa's remarkable infrastructure can make it seem relatively bland – often enough you could be in the USA – but that has its merits for a first-time visit to Africa and the breadth of experiences available, from tracking big beasts in Kruger National Park to adrenaline sports and wine tours, cements its appeal. The landlocked kingdoms of **Lesotho** and **Swaziland** are South Africa's impoverished little siblings, havens for mountain pony treks and nature reserves respectively, and usually visited as excursions from South Africa itself.

The practicalities of travel – gas stations, campgrounds, B&Bs – are almost as easy in Namibia as in South Africa, and not much less so in Botswana and Zimbabwe; but in all three countries there are tribal areas that are more traditional than is usually the case in South Africa itself. The travel experience in these three is just a tier higher in terms of adventure and uncertainty, too, and together they encompass a collection of African highlights that could keep you travelling for months.

Huge and for the most part empty of human population, **Namibia** has one of Africa's premier natural sanctuaries in Etosha, a national park shaped around a vast salt pan, where wildlife stands photogenically on the level horizon. The other outstanding attraction is the Namib desert, with its towering, apricot-coloured sand dunes, desert-tolerant elephants and hardy oryx. Damaraland in the northwest is a good area for tracking black rhino, and the remote Caprivi strip has outstanding birdlife.

In **Botswana**, the vast Okavango Delta wetland is the biggest jewel in a crown of natural attractions that includes Chobe National Park (along the river of the same name), the Tsodilo Hills with their rock art and the endless expanse of the Kalahari desert. Long the preserve of upmarket safari-goers, Botswana still prices itself out of many budgets, but its pristine wilderness isn't completely exclusive and there is some modest and affordable community tourism.

The majestic plunge of the Zambezi River over **Victoria Falls** is one of Africa's iconic sights, and on a superficial level submerges the rest of **Zimbabwe**'s attractions – a fact compounded by the country's disappearance into international obscurity over the last decade as the elderly tyrant Robert Mugabe presided over the destruction of the economy. Thankfully, Zimbabwe's recent change of heart has seen the return of visitors, and once again the remarkable stone ruins of Great Zimbabwe, as well as superb parks such as Mana Pools, Matobo and Chimanimani – where hiking and game walks are encouraged – are on many trans-African itineraries.

When you travel into **Zambia**, you're on much more intrepid trails. It has superb wildlife areas – particularly renowned for guided walking safaris – and some of Africa's top adrenaline activities along the Zambezi River. On Zambia's eastern border, the shores of Lake Malawi, the main feature of **Malawi**, offer an obvious area to rest and recuperate, and although the country as a whole has a low-key wildlife reputation, Liwonde national park's wetland and woodland and Nyika national park's highland savanna are compelling ecosystems.

Angola is much more uncharted territory as far as travel and tourism are concerned. Huge and challenging, its infrastructure decimated by decades of civil war, this isn't a country where you follow the herd: there is still virtually no tourism, so you need to take advice about areas safe from mines, and make up your own travel plans – or join one of the few organized tours.

Mozambique, by contrast, hamstrung for so long by its equally bitter but even more senseless civil war, is today a gem of a destination, full of South African visitors enjoying its superb beaches and islands, diving and seafood – just as their parents did in the 1960s.

Southern Africa's Indian Ocean nations are well and truly topped by **Madagascar**'s magnificent natural heritage and mellow, musically rich culture. It's an increasingly popular eco-tourism destination, but quite a tough place to get around, so give yourself plenty of time. **Mauritius** and **Réunion** are fine beach and nature destinations, heavily influenced by their French connections (still umbilical in the case of Réunion).

The remote **Comoros Islands** have severed the link with Paris and are notoriously unstable politically for such a small and idyllic setting, but their natural history, like Madagascar's, makes them an irresistible target. Mayotte, the most southerly island in the archipelago, is still under French rule (by choice) and, again, a good target for keen wildlife and underwater enthusiasts.

Africa's tribes and cultures

Africa's **ethnic and cultural complexity** is hard to overstate. In a world where the norm may be seen as nation states of millions of people mostly speaking the same language, it is difficult at first to come to terms with a continent of 600 million people where the 53 states and territories are superimposed on hundreds of separate tribes, kingdoms, city-states and language communities. When you also reckon with the fact that until the late nineteenth century, most African societies transmitted their cultures without writing – through oral tradition, music, dance, architecture, woodcarving, metalwork and weaving – it's clear how hard it can be for outsiders to get to grips with who everyone is and where they fit in.

The most important determinant of identity in Africa is **language**, and most references to tribes and ethnic groups are talking about groups of people sharing the same mother tongue. But to complicate matters, most people in Africa speak at least two languages (often because their mother and father are from different tribes) and with European-style education, the norm is to speak at least three, including French, English or Portuguese, and often four, including a lingua franca – a language of trade and travel like Swahili, Hausa or Arabic.

The groups covered below are the main examples of the language groups you're likely to come into contact with. There are hundreds of others, many related linguistically and culturally to the ones listed here in the same way Spanish and Italian have much in common.

North Africa

From Morocco to Egypt, the dominant themes of Arabic and Islam are evident enough in **North Africa,** but there's a more subtle cultural geology underlying the social landscape.

- **Arabs** Arabic-speakers moved west from the Arabian Peninsula with their camel herds in a series of military conquests in the seventh and eighth centuries, soon after the foundation of Islam. They rapidly became dominant in the Nile Valley and intermarried with local Berbers along the shores of the Mediterranean, establishing thriving trading cities throughout the Maghreb – the countries from Libya to Morocco.

- **Bedouin** Also known as Badawi or Bedu, these Arabic-speakers are traditional

Taking the ghost train

I've travelled almost all Sudan's railways. First-class, second-class, third-class, roof-class, hanging-off-the-door-wishing I'd-found-a-handle-held-in-by-more-than-one-screw-class. Sitting-on-a-pile-of-watermelons-in-toilet-class. I think my all-time favourite was sitting-on-the-roof-of-a-truck-transported-on-a-flatcar-class.

But one train journey from Karima to Wadi Halfa was particularly memorable, as it entailed changing trains at a desert junction, which meant that there was no possibility of reserving a place, and the connecting train would inevitably be full. I arrived at the junction after dark, and when I eventually found someone to ask in the unlit station, I was told the next train was due the following morning. I attempted to settle down for the night, taking a sleeping pill to counter the scuttling sound of the rats and the whining of mosquitoes.

The next thing I knew the station master was shaking me. "Hurry up, the train is leaving in two minutes". I dutifully boarded, gave up any attempt to push through the crowds of people jamming the corridor, and promptly fell asleep where I was standing, jammed against the wall, rocked senseless by the motion.

I had the strangest dream. I was in a place filled with pulsing white light. Through white mist I could see stacks of bodies piled high, all in white robes with unearthly, white faces. After some time, I began to think maybe this wasn't a dream and hoped that I hadn't somehow died on the train and woken up in the afterlife. As I reached for my glasses and rubbed my eyes, I remembered where I was. The sun was just rising, creating a strobe effect through the missing slats on the wooden carriage walls. The carriage was full of people slumped asleep on top of each other, their skin and clothes covered in a fine white dust blowing in from the desert.

Peter Moszynski

nomads, culturally attuned to desert life, moving their sheep, goats and camels with the seasons. Although they are increasingly likely to be town-dwellers, you will still meet nomadic herders in places such as Egypt's Sinai peninsula and in scattered communities as far west as Morocco.

- **Berbers** The speakers of the Berber languages (which have had a single written form for at least two thousand years) dominated northwest Africa before the arrival of the Arabs. Although largely assimilated with Arab culture and religion, there are still districts where an older Berber identity persists and is sometimes championed – such as the mountainous Kabyle in Algeria, the Jebel Nafusa in Libya and the Souss valley in Morocco.

- **Moors** Though today mostly referring to the majority population of Mauritania, Moorish identity dates back to the expansion of Berber-Arab control from Morocco in the eleventh and twelfth centuries, forming the Almoravid (Morav: Moor) empire which stretched north into Spain and south across the Sahara and along the Atlantic coast as far as the Senegal River.

- **Tuareg** Tuareg is a European name – these Tamazight-speaking nomads call themselves Amazigh. Famous for their fierce independence, they stuck to their Berber roots when the Arabs arrived, adopting only the newcomers' camels and some of their religion, and moved deep into the Sahara with their herds. Which is where you will meet them today, especially around the towns of the southern Sahara in Algeria, Mali and Niger.

West Africa

West Africa is one of the world's most complex regions, with dozens of major languages and at least three hundred minor languages and dialects. Many peoples or tribes of the region can date their ethnic identity back for hundreds of years, and some of the continent's oldest and most powerful city-states and empires arose here.

- **Asante** The best-known of the Akan-speaking peoples, the Asante created an empire in the late seventeenth century, based at Kumasi, that spread over much of modern Ghana and beyond, and sold war captives and refugees as slaves to their Fante ethnic cousins on the coast, who passed them onto the Europeans in exchange for firearms. You can meet the current *asantehene* (king) at regular public appearances and see evidence of Akan culture all over Ghana, especially in the brilliant, woven *kente* cloth.

- **Bamana** Also called Bambara, this large Malian tribe, based around the river cities of Bamako and Ségou and the inland Niger delta, trace their roots back to the medieval Mali Empire. By the fourteenth century, rumours of the wealth of Mali had spread to medieval Europe as the myth of Timbuktu with its fabled pots of gold. Today, you're most likely to encounter Mande culture through its music – Salif Keita is a global exponent from a noble family.

- **Dogon** Although a small community, this Malian farming tribe are famous for their elaborate mythology and mask culture, played out in villages on the vertiginous Bandiagara escarpment – an immense rocky cliff that they moved to in the face of Islamic expansionism from the north. You can make an accompanied trek around Dogon country: choose your guide carefully, as unpicking the riddles of Dogon culture is half the experience.

- **Fon** In modern Benin you'll find the capital of the Fon kingdom of Dan-Homey at Abomey. Closely related to the Yoruba, the Fon were a slaving nation ruled by a succession of bloodthirsty kings, culminating in Ghezo, who preyed on his own people and conscripted six thousand women (the "Amazons" of European myth) into his army. The Fon are easy-going people today and their royal palace and museum are well worth visiting.

- **Fula** Like many African peoples, the Fula-speakers have a seemingly interminable list of alternative names, including Fulbe, Peulh and Pulaar. There are lots of cultural variations, too, from the farming Tukulor community of the Senegal valley (musician Baaba Maal's people) to the pastoralist Wodaabé of Niger. There are town Fula (who are in commerce) and country Fula (who herd livestock or trade); nearly all are Muslims, and most West and Central African countries have minority Fula populations, while in Guinea they are the largest ethnic group.

- **Hausa** Because of their success as traders, the Hausa language can be heard throughout West and central Africa. Their cultural roots, however, are in northern Nigeria and Niger, where their Seven States have a universally loved origin myth linking the people with the king of Baghdad and a story of rejection and wandering. The states in question all survive as commercial towns and you can still see wonderful traditional architecture in several of them, notably Zaria in Nigeria and Zinder in Niger.

- **Igbo** In the forests of southeast Nigeria, this trading and farming people are one of Nigeria's three dominant ethnic groups. Unlike the state-building Hausa and Yoruba, Igbo society was more egalitarian and clan-based. They fell victim to European slavery, but the lack of social impediments seems to have meant a quick absorption of colonial education and norms and they soon dominated Nigerian cultural life (the author Chinua Achebe is a notable Igbo), a fact which led to the stillborn Igbo republic of Biafra and the disastrous Nigerian civil war.

- **Wolof** The dominant people of Senegal, they converted relatively late to Islam, after their highly stratified mini-states were trapped in the seventeenth century between the slave-trading French and Muslim reformist preachers determined to stamp out slavery. In Senegal today, the language and culture of the Wolof is pervasive (Youssou N'Dour, with his *mbalax* music, is their most famous son) and fishing and trading have largely given way to the cultivation of vast fields of groundnuts (peanuts) and traditional beliefs to Islamic Sufi brotherhoods.

- **Yoruba** The people of Yorubaland, in the savanna of southwest Nigeria, built a powerful empire of allied city states, all of them still in existence as flourishing towns. One, Ife, became a major artistic centre, whose superb sculptures, cast in bronze, can be seen in the Ife museum and in some museums abroad. Yoruba slaves took their complex and beautiful Orisha religion to Brazil, Cuba and the USA, where it emerged as Santería, a synthesis of Christianity and traditional beliefs. The outspoken Nobel prize-winning writer Wole Soyinka often infuses his work with Yoruba mysticism.

Ramadan acts of kindness

Ramadan should be a time of maximum patience and consideration for others. It's also an opportunity to show a bit of generosity in the same spirit.

In The Gambia I was waiting for transport for the last six miles home, in the heat of the afternoon, and was tempted to take a taxi. I had no baggage that would justify the fare, so I hauled myself into the nearest bush-taxi instead – a converted minibus – and waited for it to fill up.

When the other seventeen passengers were on board and it set off, the lad at the back started collecting the fares. An idea struck me, and I immediately handed him enough to pay for twenty fares – everyone on board and the next two people along the road. It cost me no more than it would to take a regular taxi all to myself. "This is for Ramadan", I told them. That was two years ago. To my amazement, people in the village still remember it.

Peter Verney, Ⓦ sudanupdate.org

Central Africa

Central Africa's peoples are dominated by closely related ethnic groups speaking languages of the great Bantu family. The languages, and it's presumed most of the people who now speak them, originated in southeast Nigeria and Cameroon around 2500 years ago. Having developed innovative technologies in iron-making, fishing and boat-building, they were able to migrate across the rainforest, using the rivers as highways, chopping paths where they needed to, colonizing the river margins and forest clearings, and moving through the territories of the indigenous hunter-gatherers with nonchalant ease.

- **Kongo** The largest of the Bantu-speaking ethnic groups in central Africa, now spread along the coast from the Congo

Republic to Angola, the Kongo had coalesced into several small states by the fifteenth century, when the Portuguese first encountered them and began trading, initially for ivory and hides. Kongo dignatories arrived in Lisbon and there was widespread conversion to Christianity. The local divisions that resulted enabled the Portuguese to gain a toehold on the coast, ultimately resulting in the colony of Angola.

- **"Pygmies"** The original people of the rainforest, its sole human inhabitants for perhaps 20,000 years, are collectively known by a term that seems demeaning, and they are not always much smaller in stature than the Bantu-speaking peoples they live amongst. Known by a variety of different names to themselves – including Aka, Twa, Efe and Mbuti – they still live a largely subsistence lifestyle based on hunting and gathering in the forest, together with some paid work in Bantu communities along the roads and rivers. In a few areas, it's possible to hook up with local groups for guided walks, net and bow hunting, funny and haunting musical performances and invariably serious consumption of marijuana (see p.241, p.246, p.252, p.351 & p.390).

- **Tikar** In the verdant, savanna and forest-covered hills of western Cameroon, the villages house a complex web of linguistic and cultural connections. The Tikar (a so-called "semi-Bantu" people) have a series of chiefdoms all over this "Grassfields" region north of Bamenda, each with its own distinctive wood and thatch architecture. You're likely to witness local festivals, will be encouraged to buy crafts and can still visit the chiefs (or *fon*) as long as you remember an alcoholic gift.

East Africa

East Africa's peoples are dominated, like those of Central Africa, by Bantu-language speakers. In this part of Africa, the indigenous, pre-Bantu inhabitants were either wiped out or assimilated over the last thousand years, though a tiny group of hunter-gatherers, the Hadzabe, hang on in northern Tanzania.

- **Amharic-speakers** The majority language group of Ethiopia, numbering more than twenty million, are traditionally farmers of the highlands. Christians, with their own Ethiopian Orthodox Church (one of the world's oldest, dating back to the fourth century), they had a traditional royal line, whose most famous emperor was Haile Selassie, which ruled over a multi-ethnic population that included Muslims and Jews.

- **Baganda** The people of the Buganda nation in Uganda (who speak Luganda) are the biggest ethnic group in the country. They were already well established under their line of kings – the *kabakas* – when the first European explorers visited in the late nineteenth century, and they inevitably became the go-betweens in relations between the British and their colonial subjects. The Baganda royal tombs are a major attraction in Kampala.

- **Kalenjin** A group of small tribes in Kenya's Rift Valley province, all speaking closely related dialects of the Nandi language, the Kalenjin have had a disproportionate impact on national politics since one of their number, Daniel Arap Moi, became Kenya's second president (he was voted out of office in 2002). Much of their traditional herding lands have been settled by Kikuyu farmers displaced by colonial settlers.

- **Kikuyu** Kenya's dominant tribe in the run-up to independence lost much of their highland pastures and farmland to white settlement and later to military eviction during their Mau Mau anti-colonial rebellion in the 1950s. But the arrival of mission schools put them in the forefront of national politics and their most famous son, Jomo Kenyatta, became Kenya's first president, while another Kikuyu, Mwai Kibaki is the country's current, third, president.

- **Maasai** Hugely powerful in the early nineteenth century, the well-armed Maasai of Kenya and Tanzania – traditional pastoralists who moved securely among wild animals with their cattle herds – were split into separate districts by their own civil wars, livestock diseases, colonial land grabbing and the creation of national parks. Today, while impoverished, they still live a largely traditional lifestyle that depends less on their treasured cattle and increasingly on tourism. In many areas it's easy to spend a few hours on a Maasai nature trail or village visit, and some of the best safari lodges and camps are run with Maasai staff for the benefit of local schools, clinics and other services.

- **Swahili** When the early Bantu-speaking peoples of the coast of Tanzania and Kenya (ancestors of today's Giriama, Digo and others) traded with Arab merchant fleets who arrived with the annual northeast monsoon wind, the Arabs (who had to wait several months for the wind to change before going home) frequently married local women. So was born the Swahili language (Bantu grammar peppered with Arabic and other foreign words) and ultimately a seductive, urban culture that you can explore in towns such as Lamu, Mombasa and Zanzibar.

Southern Africa

Throughout southern Africa, Bantu-speaking ethnic groups are, again, dominant. The Bantu-speakers, whose particular languages were known as Nguni (but who adopted many of the click sounds from the indigenous Khoisan languages), moved steadily south out of the rainforests and across the savanna from around the sixth century, arriving in what is now South Africa around 1000 AD.

- **Khoikhoi** Established with their cattle herds in southwestern Africa more than two thousand years ago, the people disparagingly called Hottentot by Dutch settlers (who couldn't pronounce their "click" language) had been under pressure from Bantu-Nguni expansion for centuries and in the European era were decimated by a combination of eviction, smallpox and violence. Their remaining number, the Nama (or Namaqua) live in poverty but some dignity in the Richtersfeld Transfrontier Park on the South Africa-Namibia border, where community tourism makes contacts worthwhile for both sides.

- **San** The so-called "Bushmen" of the region are the hunter-gatherer peoples who, together with the Khoikhoi herders, formed the Khoisan group of languages. Hunted down and murdered to extinction through much of their homeland by Europeans in the nineteenth century, they survive only as the descendants of intermarriage throughout the region, and in several parts of Botswana, where they struggle to maintain their traditional lifestyle against government relocation policies.

- **Shona** Today Zimbabwe's largest ethnic group by far (Robert Mugabe is a Shona on his father's side), the Bantu-Nguni Shona nation has deep roots in southern Africa and dates back to at least the twelfth century, when the dry stone town of Great Zimbabwe was a trading partner of the Arabs on the east coast.

- **Tswana** The majority people of Botswana speak the Bantu-Nguni language Setswana, which is closely related to the Sotho languages of South Africa and Lesotho. The whole of Botswana's Tswana population is divided into large chiefdoms whose leaders sit in the country's legislature, though a larger part of the Tswana nation are actually South African citizens.

- **Xhosa** Part of the Bantu-Nguni-speaking wave of migrants, the Xhosa arrived in the far southeast of what is now South Africa in the sixteenth century. Three centuries later, they were pushed westwards as the expansionist Zulu nation to the north created turmoil in the region. Weakened and scattered, they began moving into the money economy of the white-ruled state earlier than most of the country's peoples and became politically active. Nelson Mandela and Desmond Tutu are both Xhosa.

- **Zulu** South Africa's most powerful and aggressive Bantu-Nguni-speaking nation defeated the British army at Isandlwana in 1879 under the leadership of King Cetshayo, the last Zulu king to exercise real

Maps and GPS

You won't regret having a good map or three, but first-class cartography of Africa is rare. **Michelin** publishes what have long been considered to be the best general travel maps, offering the whole continent at a scale of 1:4,000,000 (10mm on the map is equal to 40km on the ground, in other words 63 miles to the inch) on three big sheets, plus larger-scale maps of Morocco, Algeria and Côte d'Ivoire. Available worldwide from most booksellers, they're updated regularly but still suffer from inaccuracies (especially in the non-French-speaking parts of the continent) and that scale, while adequate for route planning, is just not sufficient for driving or getting off the beaten track. Fortunately, the German publisher **Reise-Know-How** now produces a superb range of maps, printed on rip-proof, waterproof paper, covering most of Africa. Several of these (Egypt, Kenya & Northern Tanzania, Morocco, South Africa) are published by **Rough Guides**. It's also worth checking out the French state publisher **Institut Géographique National**, which produces large-scale maps of many former French colonies, though unfortunately they aren't frequently updated.

The best pre-departure mapping resources are the indispensable **Google Earth** and **Google Maps**, with Google Street View inevitably rolling out (South Africa is already covered). If you have a laptop or suitable mobile phone you'll be able to fire up these resources as you need them – assuming you have a fast connection. More than any of the sparse conventional cartographic coverage of Africa, Google Earth enables you to go on virtual expeditions across huge parts of the continent, where the resolution is already good enough to spot vehicles and people captured on their latest satellite photos.

Portable **GPS units** (Sat Navs) are useful for keeping track of distance, altitude, direction and so on (they can prevent you from getting lost in the bush by enabling you to go back to your starting point, for example), but with the notable exceptions of South Africa and Morocco, navigable mapping to load onto them for driving is still limited in comparison with the detail you get in Europe or North America.

power (he was defeated by the British six months later). Today, the Zulu are prominent in every aspect of South African life (President Jacob Zuma is a Zulu) and their culture and history, from Zulu Wars battlefield tours to crafts villages and colourful festivals, are likely to figure conspicuously in your travels through Kwa-Zulu Natal.

Key overland routes

The whole of Africa is your oyster, more or less (see p.24) but the last half century – roughly the period that travellers have been visiting Africa in fairly large numbers – has, inevitably, seen the evolution of several arteries across the continent which now offer the main, and in some cases only, viable routes. If your Africa trip involves **cross-border travel** then the following summaries should help you to figure out the key routes and some of the travellers' crossroads where you have an odds-on chance of meeting up with other overlanders. Think of these routes, purely metaphorically, as Africa's motorways or interstate highways, allowing you to make somewhat predictable, reasonably rapid progress and the opportunity to stop at any point and explore the neighbourhood – usually an entire country. It's worth reading this section in conjunction with the chapter on getting around, especially rail travel, on p.101.

The most obvious "easy" route might appear to be from Morocco to Egypt or vice versa, via Algeria, Tunisia and Libya. Unfortunately making this **trans-North African** journey isn't possible unless you ferry-hop back to Europe once or twice or fly some of the way: the land border between Morocco and Algeria has been closed for decades, while the Egyptian–Libyan border is prone to closure at short notice. Algeria itself has some serious safety issues, while travel in Libya is usually only permitted with an authorized guide.

Similarly, the once major trans-Africa travel "pipeline" from Yaoundé in Cameroon to Kampala in Uganda, via CAR and DRC (then Zaire) was effectively blocked up by wars and banditry more than a decade ago. The odd intrepid hobo still braves the route using available transport and lots of foot-slogging, but the days of commercial overland expedition trucks passing every few hours are gone: those trips now fly the distance and use trucks based at each end.

The Atlantic Route: West Africa from Morocco to Cameroon

Travellers' crossroads on the Atlantic Route: Dakhla, Nouadhibou, Nouakchott, Dakar, Banjul, Bamako, Mopti, Bobo-Dioulasso, Accra, Cape Coast, Lomé, Cotonou

Until the late 1980s, the main overland routes to West Africa were across the **Algerian Sahara** to Gao in Mali or to Agadez in Niger. With the collapse of security in Algeria and desert border areas, those routes are effectively off-limits. People still manage to get through the

Wild times

"They're exquisite!", exclaimed by companion. "And I never thought I'd say that about a pig!" Exquisite wasn't the adjective that came to mind when I saw my first red river hogs. I'd had to crawl along the sandy earth for fifteen minutes just to get within 100m of them. As soon as I lifted my body out of the long grass, the heavily whiskered, tassel-eared beasts sensed my presence and stampeded off into the forest.

The same happened with a group of shaggy forest buffalo with the same tasselled ears. And the small family group of elephants that power-walked away from me along the beach. During my first few days in Gabon I'd seen far more animal backsides than faces. The nearest I got to a hippo was seeing some tracks on a gorgeous white-sand beach, while my hoped-for wild gorilla sighting was reduced to a fresh but empty nest, just 100m from our camp.

That's Gabon for you. Frustrating, tantalizing, exasperating. But it is also oh so hauntingly beautiful and magical. Would I go back ... you bet!

Lyn Hughes, founder of *Wanderlust* magazine

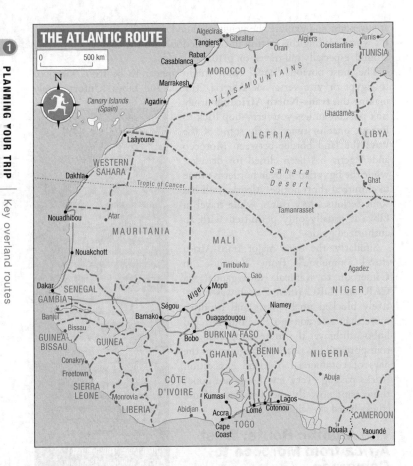

THE ATLANTIC ROUTE

0   500 km

N

Niger-Algeria side, but only by paying for escorts and various other fees – and the area is prone to banditry and kidnappings.

In the 1990s, the **Atlantic route** opened up from **Morocco** via Western Sahara to Mauritania, Senegal and the rest of West Africa. For a decade the Atlantic route became increasingly busy and straightforward, with a minimal bottleneck where an escort was necessary between Western Sahara and Mauritania, and it got even simpler when a new tarmac road across **Mauritania** from Nouadhibou to Nouakchott was opened. Unfortunately in recent years there's been a serious decline in security in Mauritania (see p.25), so that the last remaining overland route to West Africa is now seriously threatened. If you do this trip, allow two to three weeks from Morocco to Dakar – assuming you don't travel flat out and you spend at least a few days in Mauritania en route, perhaps in the Adrar region.

If you're already in West Africa, the major overland route starts in **Senegal**, running from Dakar to Bamako in **Mali** (the train is out of commission at present but the new, mostly tarred road is in reasonable shape). From there, many travellers follow the Niger River through Mali by road to Ségou, Mopti and Djenné, or go along the river itself by ferry or passenger vessels as far as Mopti or Korioumé, the port for Timbuktu (depending on the time of year and the depth of the water). You should allow at least two weeks from Dakar to Timbuktu, and at least three if travelling on the river.

After **Mali**, onward routes tend to go via **Burkina Faso** (Ouagadougou and/or Bobo-Dioulasso) to **Ghana** (Kumasi) and its Atlantic coast (Accra, Cape Coast), or to Lomé in **Togo** and/or Cotonou in **Benin**. For either route, one to two weeks is about the minimum to enjoy the travelling, though you can get from A to B quite fast in this region if you want to (from Ouagadougou to the coast in around 15–20hr).

From these cities the onward choices are flying somewhere or plunging into **Nigeria**, which far more travellers would contemplate were it not for the fearsome, and not entirely justified, reputation of Lagos. There are multiple routes through Nigeria, however, and although you should steer clear of the Niger delta, the rest of the country is straightforward enough – though tourists are always a novelty. You might dodge Lagos by crossing from Benin to Nigeria further north, for example. It's better to cross into **Cameroon** at one of the minor highland border crossings than at Mamfé, which can be a hassle.

Once in Cameroon, which is an absorbing destination in its own right, you can **fly to East Africa** (Kampala, Dar es Salaam or Nairobi), or try to pick your way overland south towards **DRC** and **Angola**. Few travellers currently contemplate heading east towards CAR and northern DRC (see box, p.24).

The Nile Route: Egypt to East Africa

Travellers' crossroads on the Nile Route: Cairo, Khartoum, Addis Ababa, Nairobi, Jinja, Arusha, Mombasa, Zanzibar

The classic African overland route of the 1960s and 1970s – before civil war erupted in Sudan – is once again feasible, and segues directly into the Cape Route from East Africa to Cape Town. As well as allowing you the possibility of starting your trip on a leisurely Nile cruise, it kicks off in a country that has been hosting travellers since the days of Thomas Cook.

Rather than taking the bus south from **Egypt**, a popular choice is the train from Cairo to Aswan, followed by the weekly ferry from Aswan to Wadi Halfa in **Sudan**, then a connecting train service to Khartoum that takes the best part of two days. Alternatively, take the road from Wadi Halfa to Khartoum as it has been surfaced the whole way. Allow at least

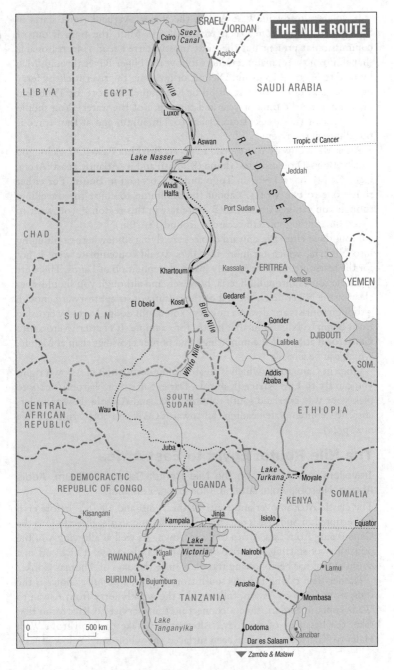

THE NILE ROUTE

ISRAEL JORDAN

Cairo
Suez
Canal
Aqaba

LIBYA   EGYPT   SAUDI ARABIA

Nile

Luxor

Aswan   Tropic of Cancer

Lake Nasser

Jeddah

Wadi
Halfa

Port Sudan

CHAD

Khartoum   Kassala   ERITREA

Gedaref   Asmara   YEMEN

El Obeid   Kosti   Gonder

SUDAN   Blue Nile   Lalibela   DJIBOUTI

White Nile   SOM.

Addis
Ababa

CENTRAL
AFRICAN
REPUBLIC   Wau   SOUTH
SUDAN   ETHIOPIA

Juba

DEMOCRACTIC
REPUBLIC OF CONGO   Lake
Turkana   Moyale

UGANDA   KENYA   SOMALIA

Kisangani   Kampala   Jinja   Isiolo   Equator

Lake
Victoria

RWANDA   Kigali   Nairobi

Lamu

BURUNDI   Bujumbura   Arusha

TANZANIA   Mombasa

0   500 km   Dodoma
Lake
Tanganyika   Zanzibar

Dar es Salaam

▼ Zambia & Malawi

a week for the journey, though the actual travelling time is less than that (Cairo–Aswan is an overnight train journey, but the ferry and Sudanese trains will eat up the hours).

From Khartoum, most travellers head for Addis Ababa in Ethiopia. It's possible to go south via Wau to Juba and **Uganda** (though the bush roads can be very bad in the rains so allow plenty of time).

From **Ethiopia**, the obvious onward route is south to Nairobi, which is fine as far as the **Kenya** border, but from there the rough desert road to Isiolo is prone to banditry and ethnic conflict and you may be delayed or have to join a convoy or wait for an escort. How long you spend in Ethiopia will depend on how much you enjoy it (most people give it a big thumbs-up and plenty of time), but you could get through the country in a matter of days.

Nairobi is one of Africa's major travel crossroads, with excellent surface connections in every direction. As well as enjoying **Kenya's** own, multifarious attractions, and perhaps pausing for a week or two on the coast near Mombasa or Lamu, many travellers head into **Uganda** for white-water rafting at Jinja, and for gorillas further west; others take one of the regular buses to Arusha in **Tanzania** or continue to **Zanzibar**.

The Cape Route: East Africa to Cape Town

Travellers' crossroads on the Cape Route: Nairobi, Arusha, Mombasa, Dar es Salaam, Zanzibar, Mbeya, Nkhata Bay, Chipata, Lusaka, Harare, Bulawayo, Gaborone, Johannesburg, Durban, Cape Town

The overland route from **East Africa to Cape Town** is the most important traveller's artery in Africa. Safe, reasonably predictable and peppered with attractions along the way, from gorillas and game parks in the north, past giant lakes and beaches, further wildlife parks in southern Africa and the cosmopolitan delights of South Africa itself, it's a very popular three-to-six week journey on an overland truck tour and is equally feasible in your own vehicle or travelling by public transport.

The majority of travellers start in **Kenya's** capital, Nairobi, or Arusha on **Tanzania's** northern safari circuit. From here the route goes to Dar es Salaam for the start of the journey to Zambia. Whether you go by road or rail, you'll travel through the heart of southern Tanzania, crossing the Rufiji River and passing Mikumi and Ruaha national parks and the vast Selous Game Reserve. You'll end up in the small junction town of Kapiri Mposhi, where train travellers usually switch to bus travel for the last few hours to Lusaka.

If you have more time, stop before Lusaka at Mbeya and cross to **Malawi** for a stay on the shore of Lake Malawi. It can be hard to tear yourself away from the beach resorts, with their backpacker lodges, dive

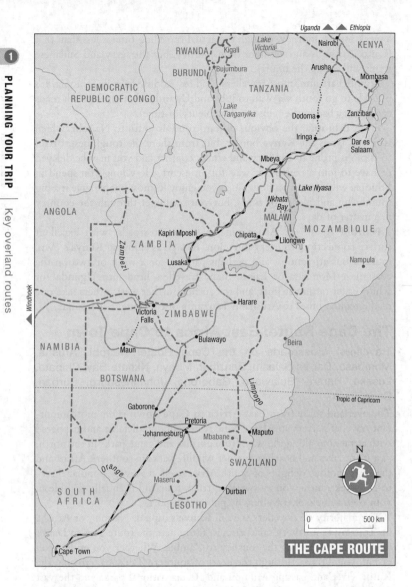

Uganda ▲▲ ▲ Ethiopia

THE CAPE ROUTE

0   500 km

N

centres and campsites, but a good next target is Chipata, on the Zambian side of the border, further south, which makes a good base for visiting South Luangwa National Park.

From Lusaka, there are more choices to make: southeast into **Zimbabwe** or southwest to Victoria Falls, which is also the route to **Botswana**'s Okavango Delta and **Namibia**. Forging on south, the main route goes via

Culture shock

If you fly in to a big city, the desperate **poverty** can come as a shock. Try to give yourself a day or two to start adjusting before plunging into work or travels. If you can make your arrival less of a jolt – by couchsurfing, for example (see p.125) – that's all to the good.

And try not to be disappointed by the tawdriness of the urban landscape: barefoot children in cast-off clothes; roadsides ankle-deep in plastic cold-drinks bags; everything worn out and covered in a grimy paste of dust and diesel fumes.

Of course the cities have compensations for travellers, as you'll soon come to appreciate if you're on the road for some time: lots of restaurants, bars and shops, the best chances to hear local music, and better media and communications. But it takes some time to adjust to the experience of the impoverished city-dwellers that you'll see all around you. For more solutions to culture shock, see p.187.

Bulawayo and then on to Gaborone or into **South Africa** to Johannesburg, which is big and amorphous but has plenty of good backpackers' lodges, especially in the northern suburbs.

From Jo'burg, you're only hours away from the Indian Ocean at Durban or laidback Maputo in **Mozambique**. Jo'burg to Cape Town is a two-day drive or 27-hour train journey on the excellent and affordable Shosholoza Meyl tourist train.

Flights to Africa

Unless you arrive in Africa by ferry from southern Europe, or from the Middle East by land into Egypt, you're almost certain to **fly** into Africa. And you're likely to depart the same way, though you might well want to leave from a different city. For information on flights within Africa, see p.104.

If you're used to the relatively stress-free business of tapping out an online airline booking to exactly the destination you want from wherever you are, you may be somewhat surprised to find a fairly limited range of direct – and particularly non-stop – flights to Africa. The best selections of flights are to be found departing from **London**, **Paris**, **Brussels** and other large European capitals. There's also a good range of flights to North, East and southern Africa departing from the Middle East and South Asia.

Few trans-Atlantic flights make Africa their first port of call, partly because North Atlantic routings around the globe mean Western Europe is actually en route to most of Africa from North America. If you're starting from the USA or Canada, you'll do best to compare the price and convenience of connections through to your desired arrival airport with the combination of a flight to Europe followed by a second, independently purchased flight to Africa.

If you're starting from Australia, New Zealand or the Far East, then a connection through South Asia or the Middle East is likely to be the best route: the only direct flights from Australasia to Africa are the regular Qantas/South African Airways services between Perth and Johannesburg.

Deals and ticket types

Getting the **best deal** – or rather, knowing you've got the best deal – is notoriously difficult, but a combination of online quotes and phoning around is the best plan. Student and under-26 discounts are worth asking for, and if you're in one of those categories you should gravitate to a specialist student/youth travel agent (see p.408).

The European **holiday seasons** (Easter, July and August and December to early January) tend to feature the highest prices but online booking systems such as British Airways' (one of the biggest carriers to Africa) are so nimble that you can get a relative bargain at almost any time, depending on demand in the market: no airline can afford to fly with empty seats.

Round-trip (return) tickets are usually better value than one-way tickets (in fact they can be cheaper). If you want an **"open-jaw"** arrangement – flying out to one city and back from another – this will cost more, but may be more convenient than flying out on a one-way ticket and having to buy your outbound flight later.

On scheduled airlines, expect to pay upwards of US$1200 for a round-trip fare from the USA to North or West Africa, with special deals to Cairo and Casablanca dropping below US$1000. If you're starting from London, typical return fares to many West and East African destinations are in the £500–600 bracket, but you also have the option of short-stay charter flights to Morocco, Tunisia, Egypt, The Gambia and Kenya, which can work out cheaper. In southern Africa, flying to Johannesburg is likely to be the cheapest option.

If you were thinking of making your African travels part of a **Round-the-World ticket**, you'll find the options limited and expensive. Like South America, most RTW deals bypass Africa completely. Some routings includes Cairo, Nairobi or Johannesburg, but you won't be able

Cruises

Relatively few **ocean cruise ships** visit Africa. The Indian Ocean piracy problem is a strong disincentive to combining a cruise with a safari. In North Africa, Morocco, Algeria, Tunisia and Libya can be included in an antiquities and cities cruise. Cape Town is a regular port of call for world cruises and one or two ports on the West African coast, including Dakar and Cotonou, are also occasionally visited by liners. River cruises are restricted to the busy Nile cruise industry (recommended – but choose carefully) and one or two private vessels with occasional passenger groups on the Congo, the Senegal and the Zambezi (mostly short excursion cruises). See p.104 and individual country profiles.

When you need a friend

Tripbod or **couchsurfing** are a good option for solo travellers or anyone who wants to immerse themselves in the place they're travelling to. Tripbod recruits local experts to advise you about a visit to their country or city. You can sign up for a few days of email advice or an extended period of consultation. Couchsurfing is a completely free sofa-networking exchange, which allows you to bunk in someone's apartment in Accra or share a rooftop in Bamako. In theory, you should be in a position to reciprocate, though it may be some years before all these hosts get their visas. Meanwhile, the laudable aims of both organizations, to bring the world together, remain unchanged. See p.125.

to include, for example, West Africa on the same RTW ticket unless you construct the itinerary from a series of individual flights at great expense.

Before you commit to buying tickets, always check the **cancellation charges** (some low-cost fares have cancellation charges of 100 percent, meaning you won't get a refund if you have to cancel), ensure your money is safe with the agent if they or the airline collapses (an **ATOL** licence in the UK and local bonding arrangements in other countries should see to that) and be sure to buy **travel insurance** at the same time (see p.80).

Starting the big adventure

How you travel – alone, with a friend or partner, or in a group, with a tour company or independently – will naturally depend in part on your own tastes and circumstances, but if you have plenty of time, there's no reason not to change the setup en route.

Independent trips

There's nothing to stop you setting off from home and making your way **independently** to the African continent, paying for transport as you go, flying if and when necessary and possibly taking a tent (see p.123). Setting off by land from the UK, you could be in Morocco in a few days and in Senegal in two to three weeks – or if you chose to start with a flight you could be more or less anywhere in Africa.

The **low-budget independent** style of travel gives you the most direct and vivid contact with Africa, and especially with local people, but the physical effort of budget travel can be gruelling and there will be occasions when inevitably you miss attractions, landmark sites and key experiences that are only available if you have complete control over your transport. You can certainly avoid missing out too often by taking time over your trip and breaking your journey frequently to explore and make your own discoveries. An independent trip like this would commonly take at least three months and often six months or more.

Who to go with

Travelling **alone** is really the best way if you want to get to know Africa rather than your travelling companion/s, but it's not for everyone. If you've done it before and enjoyed the experience, then there's no reason not to go solo. This decision is easier for men than women, but there's nothing intrinsically more dangerous about Africa for the single female traveller than anywhere else – in fact quite possibly less (see p.222).

There are some practical advantages to **travelling with someone else**, as your overall costs are likely to be lower – shared rooms, meals and some transport (taxis and car rental for example) will all be cheaper. And with two people, there's more flexibility about getting information, checking out rooms, buying tickets, shopping and even going to the loo, as one person can wait with the bags while the other does the business (there's nothing quite so foul and miserable as dealing with diarrhoea while balancing over a squatter with your backpack on your back).

If two's company, three or more can definitely be a crowd. **Small groups** often don't last long. If you're intending to travel as part of one (self-drive overland trips often involve three or more people, partly because the costs of setting up the vehicle are usually high) then be sure that each participant is honest about their expectations for themselves, and of each other. It's good if each participant has a clear role, but keeping a larger group together without resorting to a leader can be hard. If you can make it work, there are certainly advantages in being able to create smaller sub-groups, and in cutting costs.

Rather than relying on public transport, you could buy a **Land Rover or a similar vehicle** and spend several months and a small fortune kitting it out for a trans-Africa trip. Taking your own world along with you in the form of a vehicle converted for overland travel and living is wonderful when it goes right – although when things go wrong, they tend to go wrong in grand style, leaving you with no wheels, nowhere to store all the equipment and very out of pocket.

Perhaps the biggest consideration if you're planning to take your own vehicle is the "vehicle passport" or *tryptique* commonly known as the Carnet de Passage en Douanes, issued by your national motoring organization. The CPD is a permit to import the vehicle temporarily without paying import duty. It is valid for roughly a third of African countries – Burundi, Cameroon, CAR, Chad, DRC, Djibouti, Egypt, Ethiopia, Ghana, Guinea-Bissau, Kenya, Lesotho, Libya, Nigeria, Rwanda, Senegal, Sudan, Swaziland, Uganda – and it normally costs either a substantial refundable sum (tied up for the duration of your trip) or a smaller insurance indemnity payment. Some countries (Mali is the latest) will insist that you pay a local bond, often of €1000–2000 or more, to obtain a local carnet or *laissez-passer*. The guarantee will be repaid to you on departure. See p.405 for contacts.

If you have the time and stamina for long-distance **cycling**, meanwhile, you'll find it's the best way to absorb your surroundings while also making slow but significant progress (faster than walking, anyway). You get to pass the time of day with village people while having the flexibility to stop wherever you like, explore big towns and do your own thing. Both the author of the first edition of this book and one of the two second-edition authors independently introduced themselves to Africa on a bicycle saddle. For further information, see p.110.

Tours

Most travellers to Africa get online, research some tour operators and choose a **ready-made trip**. Everything from a short package trip to The Gambia to escorted natural history tours of Madagascar or a six-month overland trip is available. These days, there are very few parts of Africa where somebody isn't selling an adventure. If you go on an organized trip, find out at the outset if the company you're dealing with is the operator or just an agent. There are plenty of good agents, but it's as well to know who's running the trip. Recommended operators and agents are listed on pp.401–411.

Overland trips (crossing several countries in a specially converted and durable bus or truck, often camping on the way) mean you get looked after, usually by an experienced trans-Africa driver and leader, you get a lot of experiences in a relatively short period, and you see it all from a wonderful high vantage point that will give you memories to last a lifetime. But if you're not very outgoing and generous-spirited, the joys of bumping through Africa with a bunch of strangers (they soon become friends of course, but...) can swiftly pall.

Be sure to check how many crew will be accompanying the tour (ideally two or more), whether there are any "local payments" on top of the basic price and exactly how many overnight stays and meals, park entry fees and other costs are included in the price. If the tour starts and/or finishes in Africa, connecting flights will not be included, so you need to add those in. Prices vary greatly, so summon your inquisitorial skills when getting quotes. See p.405 for recommended companies.

Cultural and wildlife trips and volunteering

If you don't want a regular, packaged vacation, or view the prospect of gallivanting around such a poor part of the world with a degree of discomfort, there are different ways to experience Africa. You could book a more **educational holiday** to learn about aspects of African culture, such as drumming, dancing, cooking, mythology or heritage. Field courses run by guiding associations (see p.171) take in both practical training and theoretical study – a six-month stint of introductory training would probably take in zoology, botany, geology, tracking, bush lore and weapon-handling, although shorter courses are available. Specialist conservation safaris and natural history expeditions, meanwhile, will prime you on a wide range of issues, from wildlife management to human-predator conflict. You may even be able to work for a week or two as a paying conservation volunteer, helping collar animals or recording their behaviour. Conservation safaris available include big cat projects in Namibia, dolphin research in Mauritius and wildlife veterinary care in South Africa, among others (see p.208).

"Voluntourism", or **charity travel**, ideally tries to match the skills and interests of the traveller with the needs of the community they're visiting. You might help build a school, teach English or clear paths in a national park. While many courses and projects are enjoyable and worthwhile, both for you and for the communities or wilderness areas you visit, they can be pricey (up to £2000 plus flights for a two-week conservation trip, camping in the South African bush) and can be controversial. Some voluntary work travel companies have been accused of profiting from poverty by charging large sums of money to enable tourists to do tasks that local people could be paid a fraction of the price to carry out. The best plan is to seek feedback from past participants (reputable project organizers and agents will happily pass on contacts) and look for a programme which seems responsibly run, and which includes activities you know you'll enjoy. See p.209 for more details. If you're interested in a longer-term professional or voluntary commitment though a development organization, further advice and contacts are given on p.209.

Finally, another way to engage with your surroundings is to sign up for a **sponsored trip** – anything from climbing Kilimanjaro to a Sahara-set distance run. See p.176 for more details and p.409 for a list of companies.

Paid work in Africa

While long-term expatriate **employment opportunities** do come up in certain fields such as teaching and engineering, fixing up a short-term paid job in Africa isn't as straightforward as you might think. Unlike other stops on the global travel circuit – Australia, New Zealand and Thailand, for example – most African countries don't have working-holiday visa systems, so breaking up a long trip (and boosting your finances) with casual language-teaching, crop-picking or bar work isn't really an option. An exception is South Africa – see p.208 for contacts.

When to go

U nder normal circumstances, there's no such thing as a bad time to visit Africa, but you should still choose the **dates of your trip** with care. You will want to embark on your travels in a relaxed frame of mind, knowing that home and work commitments are taken care of for the duration of your trip. For most people, certain times of year are far busier than others: if you can, try to avoid squeezing your African travels into a tight gap in a jam-packed schedule. You should feel confident that you've allowed enough time to complete your itinerary at a pace that suits you, and that you have a little contingency time in case your return should be delayed for any reason.

Other questions to ask include: what kind of weather would you prefer, or prefer to avoid? Do you want to attend any festivals or sporting fixtures? Are you hoping to witness a natural phenomenon that only takes place at certain times? Are you a keen wildlife-watcher or landscape photographer? Are you determined to travel at peak time, even if it costs you an arm and a leg? Or would you rather travel at a less popular time, thus avoiding the crowds and saving money?

Africa's climate

With a total landmass of well over 30 million square kilometres covering around 70 degrees of latitude, and with altitudes which vary from below sea level to just short of 6000m, Africa encompasses a huge range of **climate zones**.

Those who react badly to **heat** can, with a little planning, dodge the most sweltering temperatures. Here, your choice of destination is in fact more important than your choice of season as in most African countries, particularly in the tropics, seasonal fluctuations in daytime temperature tend to be fairly insignificant, at around 6°C. **Rain** should definitely be

THE BIG ADVENTURE

taken into consideration, however, as the volume you can expect varies wildly from place to place and from month to month – we give you the lowdown for each country from p.223 onwards.

Perhaps the best tip is to time your trip, if you can, to coincide with the three or four weeks immediately after any **rainy season**. The tremendous appeal of this window in the calendar is Africa's best-kept secret. Once the big storms are over, but before the crowds return, the days tend to be cool, the air bright and clear and the views sublime.

Can you visit Africa during the rainy season?

The regularity and ferocity of Africa's **seasonal rains** vary hugely from region to region – we discuss some of the most notable variations on pp.55–56 – but in general the answer is yes, it's perfectly OK to visit Africa during the rainy season, as long as you have a certain tolerance for humidity (and getting wet).

African **thunderstorms**, particularly tropical ones, can be spectacular, with flashes of lightning illuminating rolling banks of purple cloud. Once the worst is over, you're rewarded with sparkling sunshine and iridescent rainbows; rejuvenated by a good soaking, plants appear to grow before your eyes and there's a corresponding crescendo in animal and bird activity. The rains can make wildlife-watching tricky – when they have plenty of freshly filled waterholes to choose from, animals scatter into the new, long grass. However, patience may reward you with some spectacular sightings, as for many species, the rainy season is the time for mating and giving birth – sexed-up birds in colourful breeding plumage sing their catchiest numbers and the parks and reserves become playgrounds for zebra foals, impala fawns and improbably tiny warthog piglets. Many African towns and villages benefit from the cleansing effects of a downpour, too (as long as it's not too severe or too prolonged) and tempers are eased by the drop in humidity. Even in the hardest-hit areas, more storms occur by night than by day, so while daytime conditions may be cloudy, a full day's rain is rare.

Some tourism businesses dub the rainy season the **green season** or, even more poetically, the "emerald season", and promote it as a special-interest time to visit. Even if the promise of fresh growth, interesting wildlife and uncrowded reserves isn't enough to convince you, you may be won over by the bargain prices that are usually on offer at this time.

Despite all these advantages, the rainy season does have its drawbacks. It can turn a road journey through remote, rural Africa into a nightmare: some areas, particularly in West and Central Africa, are cut off for weeks on end after heavy rains, their dirt tracks impassable. The only way to tackle **waterlogged roads** is slowly, by sturdy 4WD equipped with sandmats, a jack, a winch and spades for digging. Even in areas with relatively good roads, storms can hamper your progress as flood waters can surge across tarmac. In the semi-desert regions, **flash floods** can surge down channels and gorges, sweeping up anything, including vehicles, in their path. Wherever you are, power cuts tend to be more common at this time, too. It's also important to be aware that for Africans in the poorest rural areas, the rainy season can be a time of sickness and **hunger** – crops are not yet ready to be harvested, last year's supplies are dwindling or gone, and insect-borne infections such as malaria are at their most prevalent. Naturally, you may find this emotionally troubling – and if you're travelling independently at a time when the market stalls are almost bare of fresh produce, your physical stamina is likely to take a pounding, too.

North Africa and the Sahara

The most pleasant times to be in the North are **spring** (March–May) and **autumn** (Sept–Nov), when skies are clear and temperatures moderate. A little rain falls between December and February, but the winter sunseekers heading for Morocco, Tunisia and Egypt's Mediterranean and Red Sea resorts will still find them warmer and sunnier than southern Europe.

The coastal regions are temperate but the Moroccan Atlantic is far breezier than the sultry Mediterranean; Morocco's windsurfing capital, Essaouira, is lashed by chilly winds between June and August. The Red Sea is fed by mild currents all year, even when the surrounding desert is searing, and rarely gets quite as hot as the Caribbean or the waters around Southeast Asia.

Inland, in the lowlands, temperatures during high **summer** (June–Aug) can be uncomfortably high. You should definitely avoid the Sahara between May and September, when it's blighted by blistering heat (temperatures topping 50°C are common enough) and sandstorms. A cool, dust-laden Saharan trade wind, the Harmattan (or *Alizé*), blows all **winter**, peaking between February and April; its effects can be felt throughout North and West Africa. As you'd expect, the Atlas and Rif mountains are cooler than the rest of the region, with snow in winter.

West and Central Africa

In West Africa, the year divides into two seasons – **rainy** and **dry**. The driest months (Nov–May) are the most comfortable time to visit, although the rainy season may have a certain appeal to those who can cope with extreme humidity (see box opposite). The months immediately preceding the rainy season are the hottest, particularly at night.

In the Sahel, the dusty inland semi-desert fringing the Sahara, the rains are meagre, falling in July and August. Along the Atlantic coast, they start earlier – in the easternmost areas, as early as April – and are more prolonged, peaking in July or August and continuing until October or November. Humidity starts to build a month or so before the rains break, particularly in the coastal wetlands.

During the dry season, rain is very rare and the sky can become hazy with dust, especially between February and April, when the Harmattan blows down from the Sahara.

In equatorial Central Africa, you can expect high temperatures, high humidity and sudden downpours at any time of the year. The soakings tend to ease off a little between June and August.

East Africa and the Horn of Africa

Thanks to the Indian Ocean's monsoon winds, **East Africa** has two **rainy seasons** each year. The best time to visit is during the long **dry season**

(June–Nov), which is followed by a short period of rain (Nov–Dec), then a hot, dry season (Dec–March). The long rains (April–June) peak in late April or May, with downpours most afternoons.

In the **Horn of Africa**, the less hot months between November and February are the best; this region is hot and dry all year apart from July and August, when it's rainy and stifling.

Southern Africa

North of the Tropic of Capricorn, the dry **winter season** (April–Oct) is generally the best time to visit. The rains (Nov–March) are most pronounced in the east: the Kalahari, Namib and Karoo semi-deserts rarely receive more than a sprinkling.

The Cape is more temperate, with four seasons: **spring** (Sept–Nov), **summer** (Dec–Feb), **autumn** (March–May) and **winter** (June–Aug). Most safari-goers choose to visit between May and September, when the thinning grass reveals animals that are hard to see at other times and many species congregate around the dwindling waterholes. However, late September brings glorious spring colours to the landscape and the summer months are the sunniest. The mountains of Lesotho can be cold and snowy in winter.

Beating the heat

I'd always been convinced I was more of a jungle person than a desert person, but my first trip to Namibia changed all that. There was something very pure and no-nonsense about the heat. It was so dry that I could barely feel myself sweating.

I asked my guide how anything managed to survive such extreme temperatures. It turned out that ingenious animals were his favourite subject. He told me all about the oryx, a dazed-looking gazelle that can let its body temperature soar to 45°C without any ill effects, and showed me some deep gashes in a dried-up riverbed, the sign that elephants had been prospecting for water there. Another day, he took me out onto the foggy dunes at dawn just to see a beetle doing a headstand. Clever little bug – this trick allows droplets of dew to run down its body and into its mouth.

He was particularly keen on geckos, even though their strategy seemed far more mundane – once the sun was up, they simply tucked themselves away in sandy burrows. They were cute, though. By day, there was no sign of their presence, but at sunset, you could hear them calling – a bright sound, like two stones chinking together – and in the cool of the night you could pick out their beady little eyes with a torch.

John Garry

Public holidays, festivals and celebrations

Make a local celebration the focus of your trip, and you're bound to generate memories to enjoy for years to come. We've described a few of the biggest events below; a good travel guide will fill you in on plenty more.

Traditional African festivals and rituals

For generations, African societies have commemorated historic events, rites of passage and the changing of the seasons with **music**, **drumming** and **sacred rituals**. To summon up ancestral spirits, dancers may don elaborate masquerade costumes: the Nigerian Ijele perform in a brightly coloured lantern-like costume of fabric and flags, the orange-daubed Senegambian Kankurang dance dressed in leaves and bark, and the Gule Wamkule of Malawi, Zambia and Mozambique walk on stilts, clad in rags, skins, shells and a large mask.

Many ancient customs are dying out, or are already extinct, partly because Africans are becoming more and more urbanized, their outlook altered by global concerns. Other rituals are simply evolving. If you spend more than a month or so in a rural community, you're likely to be invited to at least one cultural event such as a naming ceremony; in the more traditional rural areas you may witness more. The following take place each year.

- **January: Vodun festival, Benin** Vodun is the Fon word for voodoo, a belief system shared by many in Benin and Togo; its festive rituals involve making animal sacrifices, drinking herbal remedies and trance dancing, as well as more routine jollity.
- **January: Festival au Désert, Timbuktu, Mali** Once an obscure Saharan gathering of Tuareg camel-drivers, this nomad festival of music, storytelling and socializing has caught the attention of international world music aficionados in recent years, and is enjoying some commercial success.
- **February: Carnaval, Mindelo, Cape Verde** All the island communities of Cape Verde celebrate Mardi Gras, but Mindelo lays on the biggest party. Though ostensibly a Christian festival, the Rio-style parades which flood the city with feathers, sequins and glitz have their roots in pre-Christian traditions.
- **February or March: Kuomboka, western Zambia** Lozi pastoralists celebrate the start of the flood season in the Upper Zambezi with waterborne parades. Teams of paddlers manoeuvre massive canoes to the heavy beat of royal drums.
- **April, May or June: Egungun festival, western Nigeria** Egungun is a Yoruba deity representing the collective spirit of the ancestors, worshipped with acrobatic masquerades, drumming and dance.
- **Late September: Marriage moussem, Imilchil, Morocco** Berbers in ceremonial *djelabas*, their heads wrapped or hooded, travel to Imilchil to take part in massed marriage ceremonies.
- **November: Mukanda, northwest Zambia and Angola** An initiation rite for young boys, this is marked by a Makishi

A year of adventures

Most of Africa's most memorable activities and natural phenomena are seasonal: even those which you can sample at any time of year may be far better in some months than in others. Here are the best times to experience some of the highlights.

	Jan	Feb	Mar
Wildlife-watching in calving season, East and southern Africa	✓	✓	✓
Windsurfing in Cape Verde and Senegal	✓	✓	✓
Skiing in the High Atlas, Morocco		✓	✓
Paragliding in Namibia		✓	✓
Seeing Victoria Falls in full spate, Zambia/Zimbabwe		✓	✓
Surfing in South Africa			✓
Trekking in the Central Highlands of Madagascar			
Gorilla-tracking in Gabon			
Great white shark cage-diving in South Africa			
Diving and snorkelling in Mozambique			
Chimp-tracking in Uganda and Tanzania			
Enjoying Lake Malawi's beaches, Malawi/Mozambique			
Mokoro trips in the Okavango Delta, Botswana			
Chasing the sardine run in KwaZulu Natal, South Africa			
Whale-watching in Gabon			
Gorilla-tracking in Rwanda and Uganda	✓		
Enjoying the Indian Ocean beaches, Kenya/Tanzania		✓	✓
Climbing Mount Kenya, Kenya	✓	✓	
Climbing Kilimanjaro, Tanzania			
Trekking in the High Atlas, Morocco			
Watching birds in breeding plumage in West Africa			
Wildlife-watching at East African waterholes	✓	✓	
Seeing the semi-desert bloom in Namaqualand			
Witnessing the Great Migration, Masai Mara			
Whale-watching in Mozambique			
Wildlife-watching at southern African waterholes			
Travelling on the River Niger by ferry, Mali/Niger			
Whitewater rafting on the Zambezi, Zambia/Zimbabwe	✓	✓	✓
Trekking in the Simien Mountains, Ethiopia			
Scuba diving and snorkelling in Kenya and Tanzania		✓	✓
Whale-watching in South Africa			
Cruising on the Nile, Egypt	✓	✓	✓
Watching migrant birds in sub-Saharan Africa	✓	✓	✓
Crossing the Sahara, North Africa	✓	✓	✓
Trekking in the Rif Mountains, Morocco	✓	✓	✓
Watching birds in breeding plumage in southern Africa	✓	✓	✓
Watching nesting marine turtles in Gabon	✓	✓	✓

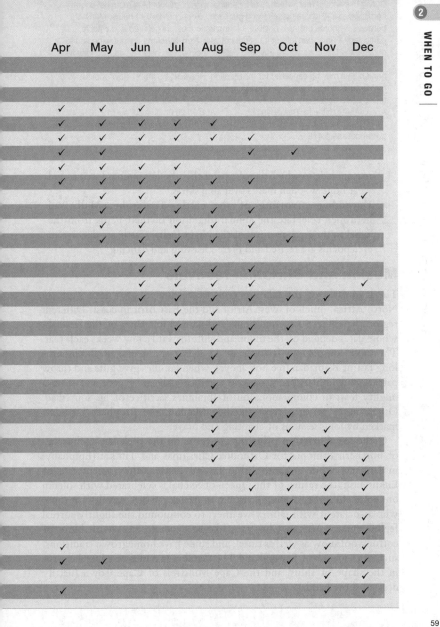

	Apr	May	Jun	Jul	Aug	Sep	Oct	Nov	Dec
	✓	✓	✓						
	✓	✓	✓	✓	✓				
	✓	✓	✓	✓	✓	✓			
	✓	✓				✓	✓		
	✓	✓	✓	✓					
	✓	✓	✓	✓	✓	✓			
		✓	✓	✓				✓	✓
		✓	✓	✓	✓	✓			
		✓	✓	✓	✓	✓			
		✓	✓	✓	✓	✓	✓		
			✓	✓					
		✓	✓	✓	✓	✓			
			✓	✓	✓	✓			✓
		✓	✓	✓	✓	✓	✓	✓	
				✓	✓				
				✓	✓	✓	✓		
				✓	✓	✓	✓		
				✓	✓	✓	✓	✓	
					✓	✓			
					✓	✓	✓		
					✓	✓	✓		
					✓	✓	✓	✓	
					✓	✓	✓	✓	
					✓	✓	✓	✓	✓
						✓	✓	✓	✓
						✓	✓	✓	✓
							✓	✓	
							✓	✓	✓
							✓	✓	✓
	✓						✓	✓	✓
	✓	✓					✓	✓	✓
								✓	✓
	✓							✓	✓

Visiting Muslim areas during Ramadan

During this annual **fast**, which lasts for a lunar month, devout Muslims must abstain from food, drink, cigarettes, chewing gum and sex during daylight hours. Many believers welcome this as a positive, healing period; others get tired and irritable, particularly if Ramadan falls at a hot time of year. **Non-Muslims** are not expected to observe the fast but if you're travelling outside the most-touristed areas, you may find it hard to find anywhere serving food during the day and regular social events such as band nights may be cancelled for the duration. However, no matter how oppressive the daytime atmosphere, it always lifts at sunset. The main upside is having the chance to witness a significant cultural event, whose closing celebrations are truly joyous. Approximate dates for Ramadan are: Aug 1–Aug 30 2011, July 20–Aug 19 2012, July 9–Aug 8 2013, June 28–July 28 2014, June 18–July 17 2015. For further guidance, see p.413.

masquerade in which dancers paint their bodies in broad stripes and wear huge wooden masks over sisal skirts.

- **December: Crossing of the cattle, Diafarabé, Mali** Peul herdsmen celebrate the annual migration of their herds from the Sahel to the fresh pastures of the Niger Delta. Cattle are decorated, epic poems are recited and there's feasting and dancing.

Muslim and Christian festivals

The landmarks of the **Islamic year** are celebrated with great gusto in North Africa, much of West Africa and the East African coast. Different regions have their own traditions (and names) for many of the festivals, whose dates depend on the moon and shift forward a few weeks each year. The most conspicuous festivals are Id al-Fitr at the end of the month-long fast of Ramadan (see box above), when families give gifts and throw parties, and Id al-Adha, a time to sacrifice a sheep or goat and share a mighty feast in commemoration of Ibrahim's sacrifice of his son Ishaq. Other, more private, events include Maulidi, the Prophet's birthday, marked by long sessions of chanting and prayer.

Orthodox **Christian pilgrims** converge on the rock-hewn churches of northern Ethiopia for Orthodox Christmas and Timkat (Epiphany) in January, while in both Ethiopia and Eritrea, the ancient rite of Enkutatash (the return of the Queen of Sheba) is celebrated with solemn but colourful processions. Christmas in Africa can be a novelty for those who associate it with wintry weather: to compound the slightly surreal feeling, many African Christians like to decorate trees with blobs of cottonwool snow as well as tinsel, and some have homegrown traditions, such as the *fanals* of Senegal and The Gambia (parades of paper lanterns in the shape of ships) and the Cape Minstrels of Cape Town (nattily dressed show bands).

Arts festivals

Africa has scores of first-rate music, cinema and arts festivals. The following are particularly worth building into your itinerary.

- **January: Festival au Désert, Timbuktu, Mali** Ⓦwww.festival-au-desert.org. Attracts the leading lights of Mali's music scene, among others.
- **February: Sauti Za Busara, Zanzibar, Tanzania** Ⓦbusaramusic.org. A family-friendly event where the crowd swings to *taarab* and *bongo flava* (funky Swahili hip-hop).
- **February: Festival Panafricain du Cinéma de Ouagadougou (FESPACO)** Ⓦfespaco.bf. The region's biggest film festival; biennial, in odd-numbered years.
- **April: Splashy Fen, Underberg, South Africa** Ⓦwww.splashyfen.co.za. Glastonbury-style frolics in the southern Drakensberg.
- **April: Cape Town International Jazz Festival, South Africa** Ⓦwww.capetownjazzfest.com. A high profile two-day event which mixes edgy *kwaito* with more traditional music from homegrown and international singers, instrumentalists and bands.
- **Late May: Festival International de Jazz de Saint-Louis, Senegal** Ⓦsaintlouisjazz.com. West Africa's biggest jazz fest celebrates the crossover between traditional African music, trad jazz and blues.
- **Late May or June: Festival de Fès des Musiques Sacrés du Monde, Morocco** Ⓦfesfestival.com. Sufi chants in palace courtyards and scented gardens.
- **June: National Arts Festival, Grahamstown, South Africa** Ⓦwww.nafest.co.za. Africa's largest arts festival, a world-class ten-day event featuring classical music, jazz, opera, theatre, poetry, cinema and dance.
- **Late June: Festival Gnaoua et Musiques du Monde, Essaouira, Morocco** Ⓦfestival-gnaoua.net. Hypnotic traditional music sessions featuring lute, percussion, chanting and acrobatic dancing from *gnawa* bands, who share the limelight with big names from the world music scene.
- **October: Lake of Stars, Nkopola, Malawi** Ⓦlakeofstars.co.uk. British and African DJs join forces with traditional bands for a relaxed offering of up-to-the-minute music on the lakeshore.
- **December: Thousand Stars Music Festival, Arba Minch, Ethiopia** Ⓦgughe.org. Traditional music and dance, deep in the remote Rift Valley.
- **December: Mother City Queer Project, Cape Town, South Africa** Ⓦmcqp.co.za. Glamorous LGBT party people strut their stuff.

Times to avoid

Your specific interests and inclinations may rule out certain months as viable travelling times; we've listed some pointers below. Some advice which applies to everyone is to avoid visiting any African country with a recent history of political unrest in the run-up or aftermath of a **general election**. In recent years, election-related violence has flared up in Kenya, Ethiopia, Zimbabwe and South Africa, and there has been considerable tension in Gabon.

Certain local events may disrupt your plans if you're not aware of them in advance. In the days preceding and following **religious festivals**, public transport is packed with people travelling to visit their familes, while on **public holidays**, shops, banks and restaurants may be closed. Keep a watch on local media for announcements concerning the **national clean-up days** held every month or so in a number of countries; travelling is not permitted on these days as all citizens must instead cooperate in efforts to improve their immediate environment.

- **Big Five wildlife-watchers** If you go on safari in Africa's major parks and reserves during or shortly after the rains, grasses will be high and the game scattered, rather than concentrated at waterholes, making conventional wildlife-watching challenging.

- **Budget travellers** Avoid flying in the run-up to Christmas and New Year when all airfares are sky high, or making last-minute plans to visit a major festival (when all but the priciest accommodation will be booked up).

- **Landscape photographers** You may be disappointed by the flat, hazy light typical of the West African dry season, particularly January to May, and the heavy skies which occur during the relatively dry months of July to September in Central Africa. In East and southern Africa, the height of the dry season can be very dusty.

- **Mountaineers** Don't plan an attempt on Kilimanjaro or Mount Kenya during a period of heavy rain; you may not even be allowed into the national parks.

- **Scuba-divers** The waters of the Red Sea are relatively warm all year round so there's no need to subject yourself to the harsh summer sun – go in winter (Nov–Feb) instead. In Kenya, Tanzania and Mozambique, conditions can be choppy, with poor visibility, in January, February and April.

- **Sunseekers** Don't book a southern African holiday during May to July; while you're bound to get at least a day or two of sunshine, these are the cloudiest months. The same applies in East Africa from June to August and in West Africa from June to September.

Public holidays

Few travellers time their trips to coincide with the days on which African nations celebrate their **independence** – see the start of each country profile, from p.223 onwards, for details – but these can be impressive occasions, with colourful assemblies in city arenas. You'll see schoolkids in immaculate uniforms parading alongside flag-carrying marching bands, while rows of dignitaries look on.

Visas

For seasoned and novice travellers alike, the prospect of obtaining all the **visas** you'll need for a trip across Africa can seem daunting. The best way to minimize the worry and aggravation is to plan the process carefully. This is particularly true if your itinerary includes any of the less-visited countries – as a rule of thumb, the further off the beaten track you intend to venture, the more time, money and patience the necessary bureaucracy will demand.

If you're travelling with a tour operator, they may offer to obtain those all-important passport stamps for you. If you're making your own arrangements, you'll need to make sure that you will have time to source all the visas you will require – either before you leave home or en route, at consulates and border posts. Information on the availability of visas and contact details for consulates are given in our individual country profiles, from p.223.

Types of visa

Visa **terms and conditions** vary widely, so always check yours carefully as soon as it's been issued, regardless of how huge a queue of impatient fellow travellers there may be behind you. Also, remember that a visa doesn't guarantee safe passage into a country – you can still be turned away if you're in breach of some other condition of entry.

- **Transit visa** Available on arrival at an airport or land border, usually for free, to travellers who can prove they will be leaving the country within a short period, generally 24 or 48 hours. In some cases, air passengers are not allowed to leave the airport during this time.
- **Single-entry tourist visa** Allows you to enter the country once within the validity period (typically three or six months), and stay for a specified time (typically up to fifteen or thirty days).

- **Multiple-entry tourist visa** Allows you to enter and leave the country several times within the validity period. Typically costs around thirty percent more than a single-entry visa, so represents a saving. Useful if you're using the country as your arrival and departure point, or if you're planning a side trip into another country during your stay. Not available in all countries.
- **Business, volunteer, study, work or residence visa** Allows you to stay for a longer period. Fees may be higher and conditions more stringent. Some countries require travellers on working holidays or "voluntourism" projects (see p.206) to obtain a business or volunteer visa, rather than a tourist visa.
- **Multi-country visa** Unavailable at the time of writing, but may be re-introduced. The Visa Touristique Entente (VTE), valid for two months and allowing one entry to each of five West African countries (Togo, Begin, Niger, Burkina Faso and Côte d'Ivoire), may soon be replaced by a visa which will cover additional Francophone countries. Another scheme, the East African Single Tourist Visa – covering Kenya, Tanzania and Uganda – is still on the drawing board.
- **Non-standard visas** These may be issued on request, so you might want to consider requesting more time than you think you'll need, just in case – though there may be an additional fee.

Extending your visa

To stay longer than your allotted time, you must **renew** your visa before it expires, either by going to the nearest immigration office or, in countries where visas are issued on arrival, by leaving and re-entering. Immigration offices, which are typically located in capital cities, can usually renew visas on the spot on payment of a fee; in larger countries, district police departments may be authorized to do the same. If you overstay the limit of your visa you risk a fine, which in some countries can amount to US$150 per day, and deportation.

When should you apply?

Some visas must be obtained in **advance**, by submitting your passport and application documents to the consulate nearest your home or, if you're overlanding, nearest your entry point. Others can be obtained on **arrival** at a border post, sometimes for considerably lower fees than those charged by the country's consulates abroad; however, you may prefer to buy these in advance, too, to reduce the amount of cash you'll need to carry on your trip, to speed your passage through immigration or just for peace of mind. As a rule, it's harder to get visas at land borders than at airports.

If you have several visas to obtain, you'll need to plan ahead as you will have no access to your passport while each is being processed. Start by adding up every consulate's estimated turnaround and delivery times, then add some extra time for public holidays and contingencies. Typical turnaround times per visa are three or four working days for applications made in person and up to ten working days for applications by post (notable exceptions are Algeria and Angola, which may take much longer). Some consulates offer a rush service for an extra fee.

Once you've worked out a plan, double-check it. If one of your African contacts has given you verbal assurance that you will be able to get a visa for their country at the airport when you arrive, check this with your airline – if the airline's own rules say you must have a visa in advance, check-in staff will examine your passport and if there's no visa in it, you won't be allowed to fly.

To be sure of obtaining pre-departure visas in good time, it's wise to get the ball rolling as soon as you have a clear idea of your arrival and departure dates for each country: you will be required to indicate these on your application forms, and you may also be required to supply a tour company or airline reservation. Beware of applying too far in advance, though, as all visas have a use-by date. Most are valid for entry within three or six months from the date of issue.

Buying visas in advance

- **In person** If you live in or near London, Paris, Ottawa or Washington DC or are starting your African travels in or near Pretoria, it's worth taking your applications to each consulate in person. You won't jump the queue but you'll have the reassurance of a fixed waiting time or collection date. Start by checking when each consulate is open to the public: some limit this to a couple of hours each weekday.
- **By post or courier** Despatch your applications via a delivery service with tracking and insurance, and check each consulate's instructions regarding return delivery.
- **Visa agencies** Private companies which charge a (considerable) service fee on top of standard visa fees to make applications on your behalf won't necessarily get the job done much quicker, but may save you some legwork. Options include Trailfinders in the UK (Ⓦwww.trailfinders.co.uk; service fee from around £30 per visa); VisaHQ in the US (Ⓦwww.visahq.com; from US$70) and Visa Link in Australia (Ⓦwww.visalink.com.au; from A$60).

Buying visas on arrival

You can't assume that credit cards will be accepted at border posts, so bring enough **cash** for the fees. US dollars are accepted everywhere; some countries also accept pounds or euros. Getting through immigration,

Front of the queue

The first time that we flew into Mauritius, Mark and I had no idea what to expect of the immigration officers. It's not a place with a reputation for bureaucratic thuggery – far from it – but the chap in charge of passport control had a very stern appearance, and a huge planeload of arrivals to deal with.

We were in a hurry, so had rushed to get to the front of the queue. The stern-faced official was checking absolutely everything on our immigration forms in painstaking detail. After a while, we politely asked if everything was in order.

"No, I'm afraid it's not", he said. Our hearts sank. What was coming next?

"Just here", he said with a curious look of satisfaction. "You've just put the name of some hotel, but no address."

Damn. We didn't know the address. All we knew was that the hotel's pick-up service was waiting outside to take us there – and we were already late.

When a corrupt official finds a trivial error like this, it makes their day. We wondered, silently, what this character's agenda might be. Would we be shoved to one side and made to stand there, helplessly, as he dealt with everybody else's passports? Would we be made to pay some kind of jumped-up fine?

Tempting though it was to invent an address on the spot, we confessed our ignorance.

"Not a problem!" said our man, with the dazzling smile of somebody who likes nothing better than a nice bit of form-filling. "Just leave it with me. I'll Google it later, and write it in for you."

And with a gracious nod, he gave us our entry stamps, complete with dodo motif, and sent us on our way.

Raffa Spencer

whether at an airport or at a land border, can be painfully slow, but hair-raising encounters with bullying extortionists, while popular as campfire tales, are rare in practice.

What will you need to supply?

Once you've compiled all your documents, make photocopies for your records in case anything goes astray.

- **Application form/s** Many consulates allow you to download forms from their websites, but applications cannot be filed online or sent by email or fax: signed hard copies are required.
- **Passport** Must be valid for at least six months beyond the end of your trip, with at least one blank page per country you intend to visit – some visas are a full-page label.
- **Additional documents** Some consulates require one or more of the following: yellow fever vaccination certificate (see p.67), return plane ticket, tour itinerary, bank statement or proof of employment (such as a letter from your employer), proof of residency (such as a utilities bill or driving licence) and letter of invitation from a local sponsor.
- **Passport photos** For each visa you need a colour, head-and-shoulders, plain-background photo of yourself wearing a neutral expression, trimmed to 45x35mm, with your name written on the back. Some consulates require several copies. If you have a digital camera and

a colour printer, there's no need to use a booth or a professional service; to make things easy, your printer software may have an option for formatting a sheet of pictures to the correct size. It's a good idea to carry some extras on your travels (see p.89).

- **Fee** Visa fees vary according to type, your nationality and where you apply. Each consulate specifies the methods of payment it accepts (typically bank transfer or cash in pounds, euros or US dollars). Fees are non-refundable in the event of cancellation or refusal. A single-entry visa for a thirty-day stay, valid for ninety days, typically costs US\$30–50, but visas for several countries (including Angola, Cameroon, Democratic Republic of Congo, Liberia, Mali, Niger, Nigeria, Sudan) cost considerably more. As a reciprocal measure in response to US immigration policy, US citizens have to pay particularly high fees for these countries and several others (including Benin, Burkina Faso, Burundi and Tanzania).
- **A local address** If you will be touring or have yet to book your accommodation, give the name of a well-known hotel or safari company. However, bear in mind that in some cases you will also be asked for a letter confirming your reservation.
- **Points of arrival and departure**.
- **Personal details** As well as your date of birth and home address, you will be asked your occupation. If you can, it's best to keep things simple; rather than "consumer data research and analysis executive", just call yourself an "analyst". Reporters and photojournalists are unwelcome in some countries, so think of an uncontroversial alternative if you can do so honestly.
- **Reason for visit** If appropriate, a simple answer such as "tourism" is best.
- **Dates of visit**.

Yellow fever

African immigration officials may require you to present a **yellow fever certificate** if you have visited any of the following countries within a week of your arrival:

Angola, Burundi, Benin, Burkina Faso, Cameroon, Central Africa Republic, Chad, Congo Republic, Côte d'Ivoire, DRC, Equatorial Guinea, Ethiopia, Gambia, Gabon, Ghana, Guinea, Guinea-Bissau, Kenya, Liberia, Mali, Niger, Nigeria, Rwanda, São Tomé and Príncipe, Senegal, Sierra Leone, Somalia, Sudan, Tanzania, Togo, Uganda, Bolivia, Brazil, Colombia, Ecuador, French Guyana, Guyana, Panama, Peru, Surinam, Venezuela.

Whether you have visited any of the above countries or not, you will be required to present a certificate on arrival at any of the following African countries:

Benin, Burkina Faso, Burundi, Cameroon, CAR, DRC, Congo Republic, Côte d'Ivoire, Gabon, Ghana, Liberia, Mali, Mauritania, Rwanda, São Tomé and Príncipe, Senegal, Togo.

For further guidance see p.71.

VISAS | What will you need to supply?

Health and insurance

You can't afford to be blasé about your **health** in Africa. The good news, however, is that most travellers remain in excellent shape throughout their trip, bar a few insect bites and the odd bout of gut trouble. The vast majority of the diseases and ailments found in Africa are avoidable through vaccinations, preventative medicines, good hygiene and common sense.

Conditions vary a great deal from one part of the continent to the next. Dangerous diseases are prevalent in some areas and many regions lack sophisticated healthcare facilities, so it's important to be well informed. Even minor complaints, such as those caused by dehydration and unfamiliar food, can take a serious toll on your wellbeing.

The following key points should help you get your plans underway.

- The better shape you're in, the less likely you are to succumb to any illnesses. If you're due for a **dental** or **medical check-up**, book it well in advance of your trip.
- If you haven't travelled to the tropics before, make sure you **budget** for all the vaccinations you will need. It's worth researching your needs carefully: some jabs are expensive, and you don't want your arms perforated with any you don't need. **Travel clinics** charge the most, but they're convenient and efficient, offering advice as well as other services. There's also plenty of free and inexpensive information to be gleaned from specialist **travel health websites** (see p.70), **books** such as *The Rough Guide to Travel Health* and your **family surgery**. While family doctors and practice nurses tend to have less knowledge of tropical diseases than travel clinic staff, they have access

to a database of current advice and can provide many vaccinations and prescriptions at lower prices than commercial outfits. Make an appointment to see your doctor six or seven weeks prior to your trip.

- Allow plenty of **time** for vaccinations. Some are effective immediately; others must be given at least two weeks before you travel, but preferably a month before. Some need to be spaced out over several sessions. If you will be visiting a malarial region, you must begin a course of antimalarials beforehand (see p.71).

- Make sure that all your vaccinations (including any you've had in the past which are still current) are recorded in a **Health Passport**: see p.70. Some immigration officers will demand to see this.

- Your **prescription drugs** may not be available in your destination. So, for peace of mind, carry enough to cover your entire trip plus some extra for contingencies. Take a copy of your prescription, too, in case a local pharmacist or a suspicious immigration officer needs to see it.

- Remember that your loved ones, especially those who won't be travelling with you, may be more worried about you than you think. Make sure you're fully **insured**. Knowing that if the very worst happens you can be airlifted home will take a load off everybody's mind.

- Put together a **first-aid kit** and once you're on the road, keep it accessible. In the tropics, minor cuts and grazes can become infected more quickly than in temperate regions.

Basic medical kit

Essentials you should pack include **sunblock**, **insect repellent**, a **first-aid kit**, **prescription drugs** and, if you'll be visiting a malarial region, **antimalarial pills** (see p.71). If you have a choice, blister packs of pills are better than loose ones that may absorb humidity. If you're travelling independently off the beaten track you will also need a means of **purifying water** such as iodine drops, chlorine tablets or a UV purifier.

Your first-aid kit should contain: anti-diarrhoea tablets, antiseptic liquid, bite relief cream, fungicidal cream, painkillers, plasters (band-aids), oral rehydration salts, sterile emergency pack (dressings, surgical tape, needles and syringes), thermometer and throat lozenges. Other items you may need include: vitamin tablets (no substitute for a balanced diet, but helpful as a supplement, particularly for women prone to cystitis), antihistamine pills or an EpiPen (if you're allergic), hycosine patches (for motion sickness), Diamox (acetazolamide, for mountain sickness, if you will be climbing above 3000m during your trip), eye ointment (for styes), laxative tablets and contact lens solution.

It's generally best to buy all the items you need separately and pack sensible quantities of each: pre-packed medical kits can be pricey and the contents may not suit your needs.

Ask your family doctor for advice about supplementing the basics with prescription drugs such as **antibiotics** to treat bronchial or intestinal infections, and **antimalarial pills** of a different type to the ones you are taking as a prophylactic, to treat malaria.

HEALTH AND INSURANCE

● Some tropical illnesses have a lengthy **incubation period** after which they inflict symptoms which could, at first, be mistaken for flu. If you develop a fever within a few weeks of visiting Africa, seek medical advice immediately, explaining exactly where you have travelled.

Immunization

Checking that your vaccinations are **up to date** should be top of your list of travel preparations. They offer immunity for between one and ten years, after which they can be topped up with boosters. Most injections are extremely quick and practically painless; the worst you can expect is that some jabs, such as typhoid, may leave you with a tender and aching upper arm for a day or so. An oral vaccine (capsules) is also available for typhoid, but it's only effective for one year; the jab lasts you for three years.

Make sure your **Health Passport** is up to date, too – if you don't have one, your family doctor, practice nurse or travel clinic will provide one for free. It's typically a yellow booklet which your doctor or nurse will fill out with batch numbers and expiry dates and will then stamp and sign. They can include details of jabs you've had in the past by checking your records. One section will be given over to an **International Vaccination Certificate** for yellow fever, if you've had that jab.

Which inoculations do you need?

Doctors now agree that everyone who travels to the tropics should be inoculated against **tuberculosis** (most people are immunized against this in childhood), **tetanus**, **diptheria** and **polio** (these are administered together and need to be boosted every ten years), along with **hepatitis A** and **typhoid** (available separately or as a combined vaccine). For UK citizens, these vaccinations are all available on the NHS for free.

Health resources for travellers

The following give specialist advice and provide lists of travel health clinics.
Canadian Society for International Health Ⓦ csih.org.
CDC (Centers for Disease Control and Prevention, USA) Ⓦ cdc.gov.
The Hospital for Tropical Diseases, London Ⓦ thehtd.org.
ISTM (International Society for Travel Medicine, USA) Ⓦ istm.org.
MASTA (Medical Advisory Service for Travellers Abroad, UK) Ⓦ masta.org.
NaTHNac (National Travel Health Network and Centre, UK) Ⓦ nathnac.org.
The Travel Doctor-TMVC (Australia) Ⓦ tmvc.com.au.
Tropical Medical Bureau, Ireland Ⓦ tmb.ie.

If you'll be travelling far off the beaten track, your doctor may also recommend some or all of the following (charges almost always apply):

- **Cholera** Spread through water and food contaminated with bacteria, cholera can be a risk to those who intend to spend time in slum areas, especially during the rainy season. Symptoms include severe vomiting and diarrhoea. Without treatment, it's very dangerous; if antibiotics and a rehydration solution are taken promptly it's fatal in one percent of cases. For UK travellers, an oral vaccine is available free on the NHS.
- **Hepatitis B** You are only at risk of getting hepatitis B if you come into contact with blood or needles or have unprotected sex. A course of three injections gives protection.
- **Meningococcal meningitis** This jab is recommended if you're going to have close, prolonged contact with local populations – for example, if you'll be staying with locals in villages. Meningitis, a nasty infection of the brain, can cause severe fever and septicaemia and is transmitted through coughing or sneezing.
- **Rabies** You can catch rabies by being bitten or licked by an infected animal, such as a dog, bat or monkey. The course (three injections spread out over a month) doesn't give you immunity, but it slows the spread of the infection so you have time to seek treatment, without which rabies is very dangerous. It's recommended for those who are likely to come into close contact with feral animals in remote areas. As a general rule, don't touch any non-domestic animals – even appealing-looking dogs.
- **Yellow fever** Transmitted by Aedes aegypti mosquitoes, yellow fever is fatal in five percent of cases. The injection is more expensive than most but is required if you're visiting any of the places listed on p.67: immigration officers may ask to see your valid International Vaccination Certificate when you arrive in these countries. It's only available from certain surgeries and travel clinics and is valid from ten days after your jab, for ten years.

Malaria

While recent health programmes have made good progress towards eradicating **malaria**, for now it remains a major cause of illness and death among Africans, particularly babies and children from poor communities. North Africa is generally safe, but anopheles mosquitoes carrying the parasites which cause the disease are found in most of sub-Saharan Africa except the far southwest (southern Namibia, southern Botswana and southern South Africa). All visitors to this region are at risk. Malaria is preventable and treatable, but you can't be vaccinated against it. Instead, you need to take active precautions while visiting a malarial area.

Antimalarial drugs do not offer one hundred percent immunity; the main barrier to infection is to avoid being bitten by malarial mosquitoes, which are most active from sunset until dawn. Satisfying though it may be to obliterate the little blighters with a well-aimed swat, they will always have reinforcements waiting in the wings. Instead, spray your skin with strong **repellent** at the end of each day. Deet-based brands work best, but they melt some plastics: take care to clean your fingers before handling your sunglasses or camera. Gentler, more natural repellents are generally less effective and are simply not worth the risk. You should also wear **clothing** which covers you completely, including your arms, legs and feet, and is either loose enough or tough enough for mosquitoes to be prevented from biting you through it. At night, sleep under a **mosquito net**, arranged in such a way that you're unlikely to roll against it in your sleep; to be extra sure, you could also spray your room with **insecticide** (paying particular attention to bathrooms and dark corners) or burn mosquito coils (carefully placed to avoid setting your entire room or tent on fire).

Despite your best efforts, you may still get bitten and it's essential you also protect yourself with antimalarial drugs, most of which require a prescription from a doctor's surgery or travel clinic. It's best to take all the antimalarials you need with you, as fakes occasionally circulate in Africa.

Which antimalarials should you take?

There are several factors to be taken into account when choosing a malaria prophylactic, including the length of your trip and your medical history. Pregnant women have particular concerns, too (see below). In all cases, you must take your pills regularly for a specified period, so a certain amount of self-discipline is required. Most can make you feel nauseous or uncomfortable if taken on an empty stomach or immediately before bed: straight after your main meal of the day is best.

The recommended choice for most short trips (up to three weeks) is currently **Malarone** (atovaquone plus proguanil), which should be started one or two days before you enter a malarial region, taken daily and contin-ued for seven days after you leave. It has relatively few side effects; its main disadvantage is that it's more expensive than other options.

Doxycycline, an antibiotic, is a cheaper alternative that is taken daily, starting two days before your trip and continuing for four weeks after you leave. It can be taken for longer periods than Malarone (you should discuss the details with your doctor) and has the useful side effect of offering some protection against stomach upsets. Its disadvantages are that it may make your skin more prone to sunburn than usual (so you should compensate by always wearing sunblock) and it reduces the effectiveness of the contraceptive pill. It should not be taken by pregnant women.

There are two further options which may be recommended if Malarone or Doxycycline are not suitable. **Lariam** (mefloquine) is taken once a week from three weeks before your trip until four weeks after leaving. Some people who take it report seriously unpleasant side effects including chronic depression, panic attacks and insomnia. A combination of **Avlochlor** (chloroquine, taken once a week) and **Proguanil** (paludrine, taken daily) is cheap and can be bought without a prescription, but is the least effective option available, as many strains of the parasite are resistant to chloroquine. It's only worth considering as a last resort. You need to start the course a week before your trip and continue it for four weeks after you leave.

Heat, sunburn, dehydration and dust

Overexposure to heat and ultraviolet rays can be extremely damaging. If you haven't travelled to tropical or equatorial regions before, you may be surprised at how harsh the African **sun** can be when it's directly overhead.

Even the most dedicated of sun-worshippers will need to

Malaria and me ...

I'm sorry to say that I have only myself to blame for catching cerebral malaria in Africa. The first time was on a one-week trip to Zanzibar. I'd visited Africa many, many times, sometimes staying for months, and I'd never had malaria before so I assumed I was immune – I had that classic "it's never going to happen to me" mentality. I thought about taking antimalarials, but decided not to bother – it was such a short trip, and I'm always careful to cover up and use repellent, mainly to avoid the sheer discomfort of getting bitten.

Back in the UK I went down with a terrible Victorian-old-lady chill – severe aches and exhaustion. I thought it was just post-trip tiredness and I'd soon sleep it off, but I woke up feeling as if all the bone marrow had drained out of my body, sweating like a pig and shaking like a cartoon character. I was hospitalized for a week.

The second time was three years later, in a very sparsely populated area of northern Ghana where I was conducting a wildlife survey. I made the mistake of thinking it was a low-risk region and a low-risk time of year, so I could skip the antimalarials. Back home, the fever struck.

I now realize how important it is to protect yourself. Worryingly, all too many people make wrong assumptions. For example, some people think you're only in danger if you're roughing it. Research has shown that over a quarter of British travellers staying at four-and five-star resorts in malarial areas do not protect themselves. Perhaps they think that in places where there are hot and cold running G&Ts, the staff will have taken care of all the mosquitoes too.

For me, as someone who loves Africa, surviving malaria has been particularly humbling, because I know that the vast majority of Africans who catch malaria every year just can't get the kind of treatment that was available to me. For travellers to ignore the preventative advice that's freely available is nothing short of criminal.

Kate Humble, a campaigner for increased awareness of malaria's dangers adjust their behaviour in Africa, especially if taking antimalarials which increase vulnerability to sunburn. Make it a part of your morning routine to apply high SPF **sunscreen**, even if the weather is grey – clouds do not present much of a barrier to harmful UV. Bare feet, necks, shoulders, noses, ears and balding heads all need particular attention when slapping on the sunblock, as the sun's rays may be uncompromisingly vertical for much of the day. The one exception is if you're going snorkelling over coral reefs – sunscreen in the water can harm coral polyps and a T-shirt or surfer's rash vest worn over shorts offers you much better protection.

Take extra care when spending time in exposed, reflective environments such as rivers, lakes, mountains, deserts or at sea. Remembering the old adage about mad dogs and Englishmen, it's wise to take your lead from the locals: when the sun is hottest, shield your skin from the worst of the rays by covering up in loose clothing and a hat, and ducking into the shade as much as possible. You should also protect your eyes with good quality sunglasses, remembering, for politeness, to take them off when you want to talk to somebody. Heat rashes can flare up in humid conditions; cool clothing and warm showers, to open the pores, can help.

Since everybody's needs are different, guidelines which command you to drink a certain number of litres of **water** a day are not particularly helpful. Pacing yourself is important, though – just as there's little point in pouring a bucket of water over a thirsty plant then neglecting it for days, the best plan is to keep drinking small amounts at a higher and steadier frequency than normal, adjusting as you go. You may need to consume more salt than usual, too.

Learn to recognize the symptoms of **dehydration** in yourself and your companions. If your urine is darker than usual and you're feeling fatigued and grumpy for no apparent reason, you're probably not drinking enough water. In extreme conditions this can turn into full-blown heat exhaustion or even heatstroke, complete with pounding head, dizziness, vomiting and diarrhoea. So head for the shade, drink water and cool down.

The **dust** that's inescapable when travelling in Africa's desert and semi-desert regions can play havoc with your eyes and sinuses. If you have the luxury of a vehicle with air-conditioning, it's best to keep the windows up, tempting though it may be to feel the breeze. If that's not possible, try covering your head, nose and mouth with a scarf, just as the locals do. Contact lens wearers should switch to glasses; eye drops and a nasal decongestant may help too.

How to purify drinking water

Bottled water is available in all but the remotest of regions; it's common for upmarket safari lodges to supply it to their guests as a matter of course.

However, it has several downsides, including its cost and environmental impact. In many parts of Africa, tap water is safe to drink, so always check – but if you're in any doubt, **purify** it. The quickest way to do this is with iodine from a bottle with a dropper (available from pharmacies), adding five drops per litre of water and leaving it to stand for ten minutes. The resulting flavour, though odd, is easy enough to get used to. Though cheap, safe and effective, this use of iodine for water purification has recently been excluded from EU health directives so adventure shops no longer sell it and recommend using chlorine-based tablets or drops instead, which cost more and taste worse.

The old-fashioned way to kill off bugs in contaminated water is to filter and **boil** it; depending on the altitude and ambient temperature, you may need to keep it on the boil for a full half-hour. Far more convenient, though pricey at around £55/US$80, are water purification gadgets such as the SteriPen, a UV radiation torch with a timer that you immerse in water for just under a minute to kill off any bacteria, viruses and protozoa present.

It's important to remember that in areas where it's not safe to drink the water, ice and salad aren't safe either.

The magic of muesli

Simon and I had at last made it all the way from Dakar to Freetown by bush taxi and were feeling frazzled. We booked into the best hotel in town, treated ourselves to a huge meal, and flopped.

In the middle of the night, Simon woke me up in a state. For the first time ever in our long, lazy trip, he was ill. Not just spot-of-tummy-trouble-ill, but gut-wrenchingly, ago-nizingly ill. I'll spare you the details, but moving from the en suite (thank goodness we had one) was just not an option.

After two long days in which all the usual remedies had no effect, I called in a doctor. He was Lebanese, and a paragon of brisk efficiency. He diagnosed amoebic dysentery, and calmly wrote out a prescription.

Three more days passed and Simon still couldn't keep anything down. The doctor came back, turned pale, and took me to one side. "We'd better act fast," he said. "We might lose him." So I cashed in our travel insurance in what must be the fastest time known to man.

Within 24 hours, we'd been repatriated back to the UK, and Simon was eating the food he always misses the most when we're in West Africa – Sainsbury's muesli. There must be something miraculous in the stuff. By the end of that day, he was almost completely better.

Claire Graham

Vomiting and diarrhoea

Being careful about what you eat and drink will help keep your digestive system on an even keel. Traditional **African recipes** in which fresh ingredients are cooked for several hours in a covered pot or given a thorough roasting over a hot barbecue tend to be healthy as well as delicious: the preparation processes eliminate harmful bacteria. Problems can arise, however, when African kitchens attempt **Western-style cuisine** – re-freezing

Sit-downs and long-drops

Toilet facilities in Africa vary from the sublime – some safari lodges take great pride in their "loos with a view" which overlook glorious open bushland – to the grim. Most are perfectly acceptable, but some take a little getting used to.

Wherever you are, toilets in tourist-class hotels and restaurants are of standard, plumbed in, **sit-down** type complete with toilet paper. However, the "continental" style of squatter loo still persists in more basic places, especially across North Africa and the French-speaking countries. In all cases, the plumbing may be somewhat creaky, so if there's a basket by the loo, toss your paper there.

Campsites and village compounds typically have **long-drops** – a fenced-off hole in the ground, often with some kind of seat on top. These can be every bit as comfortable as plumbed-in facilities and, if well-kept, no more smelly, as they're usually open to the sky so that air can circulate. However, some long-drops are pretty ghastly – especially the ones that require you to squat rather than sit. The emanations from these can be overpowering, and the contortions you need to adopt to avoid passing out may require you to partially undress in advance. As you do so, take care not to drop anything into the hole – obvious advice but so easily overlooked. In some areas, Africans resort to using public places, particularly the type of beaches which are mainly used for work (such as fishing) rather than leisure – worth knowing when taking a coastal stroll.

You'll rarely find **paper** in the more basic facilities, particularly in North, West and Central Africa, where the preferred option is to wash yourself with a plastic kettle or dipper of water. For this, it's customary to use the left hand only: hence the convention that you should never give somebody something, money in a shop, for example, with your left hand, and wherever possible you should eat one-handed, using your right hand. This is a hygienic practice, if performed carefully (it's worth carrying your own small bottle of antibacterial handwash to be sure), and worth mastering, as it's far better than using paper, and then having to bury it, if you're caught short out in the wilds.

---

frozen ingredients, perhaps, making creamy sauces, or washing salads in water which isn't 100 percent clean.

Even if you've been careful in your food choices and fastidious about hygiene, changes in climate and diet can land you with a bout of **tummy trouble**. This is rarely cause for serious alarm. Before you reach for a pharmaceutical remedy, try dosing yourself with plenty of bottled or purified water and, if you can manage it, bland, fat-free food such as plain bread or rice – your illness may soon pass. Papaya, pips and all, bananas, low-fat yogurt and flat cola also have a settling effect. If your condition worsens or you need to travel, it's worth taking anti-diarrhoea tablets along with a solution of oral rehydration salts. Make sure, however, that you see a doctor if you develop a fever or your symptoms continue for more than four or five days.

Altitude sickness

Impaired breathing, severe headaches, nausea, dizziness and fatigue can all strike at **altitudes over 3000m** as a result of the decrease in atmospheric pressure, which causes each breath you take to contain fewer molecules of oxygen than you're used to. Altitude sickness affects different people in different ways; you will not avoid the symptoms just by being physically fit. Since all ten of Africa's highest peaks are over 4500m high, a climbing trip requires careful planning. Mount Kenya (5199m) or Kilimanjaro (5895m) should only be attempted at a pace which gives your body time to **acclimatize**. Consuming plenty of **fluids** and **high-calorie food** and taking preventative medicines such as **Diamox** (acetazolamide) can help stave off the worst. However, if you're badly affected, the only safe option is to call it a day and descend to a lower altitude.

Sexually transmitted diseases and infections

Sub-Saharan Africa has by far the world's highest prevalence of **HIV/ AIDS**; this and other sexually transmitted diseases, including **hepatitis B**, pose a considerable threat to African communities. Mosquitoes, for all their crimes, cannot be blamed for passing on any of these infections: unprotected sex or direct contact with infected blood are generally to blame. Using **condoms** will decrease your vulnerability: you should bring your own supply. Inoculation against hepatitis B is available.

Other ailments

- **Dengue fever** Transmitted by Aedes aegypti mosquitoes, which bite during daylight hours (particularly early morning and late afternoon), this viral disease is less of a problem in Africa than in Southeast Asia, but has been recorded in many sub-Saharan countries apart from the far south of the continent. There's no vaccine; the best way to stay safe is to avoid being bitten.
- **Ebola** Though a source of fascination among those who like to relate ghoulish tales of ghastly tropical afflictions, ebola haemorrhagic fever poses very little danger to tourists. It's highly localized; outbreaks are occasionally reported in Democratic Republic of Congo, but burn out quickly as it kills people too quickly to be transmitted widely.
- **Leprosy** Another disease with terrible associations, most of them biblical, leprosy can be cured if treated early. It isn't really a danger to tourists as it's rare and not particularly contagious.
- **Rickettsial disease (tick bite fever) and Rift Valley fever** These relatively rare illnesses are carried by infected ticks (in the case of Rickettsial disease) and mosquitoes (Rift Valley fever). They are treatable with antibiotics such as tetracycline, but prevention is best – use insect repellent to ensure you're not bitten by mosquitoes,

and wear long trousers when walking through grasslands, forests or brush to protect yourself against ticks.

● **Schistosomiasis (bilharzia)** Caused by tiny parasitic worms found in snails in areas of stagnant water at the edges of some rivers and lakes, this illness is not particularly easy to catch but can, if you're unlucky, be picked up by wading, swimming or washing in affected water. Areas affected include parts of Lake Malawi, the oases of southern Morocco and the slower stretches of the Nile. Chlorination kills the parasites, so swimming pools are usually safe. No vaccine exists. The illness can be treated with praziquantel.

● **Trypanosomiasis (sleeping sickness)** Although the full-blown version of this disease, transmitted by tsetse flies, is rare, many people react badly to tsetse fly bites – symptoms include nasty swellings and fatigue. The flies, which are found in humid areas such as rivers and wetlands, will bite through clothing and are attracted to moving objects including boats and vehicles and to black, dark grey and blue; avoiding these colours will help protect you from being bitten.

● **Leeches** Despite their starring role in *The African Queen*, these annoying parasites aren't all that common in Africa. A few might latch on to your lower legs if you find yourself wading through the wetlands of Central Africa – but they'll be small, and easy to yank off.

Staying healthy on the plane

Jet lag shouldn't be a problem on flights from Europe to Africa as the time difference is minimal, but **dehydration** can leave you exhausted, as can **sleeplessness** on an overnight flight.

The following can help:

• Wear **flight socks** which compress your ankles and calves. For the rest of your body, choose **comfortable, layered clothing** which keeps you warm and doesn't restrict your circulation.

• Drink plenty of **water** and limit your intake of coffee, tea, alcohol and salt. Tap water is rarely offered in sufficient quantities, so keep asking for more or, even better, walking down to the galley to get some.

• **Move around** at regular intervals. While seated, perform simple physical exercises such as ankle stretches from time to time.

• On night flights, wrap up in a blanket and wear an eye mask and earplugs or noise-reducing headphones to help you **sleep**.

As well as improving your general wellbeing, the above will help stave off **deep vein thrombosis** (DVT) – blood clots which can form in the veins of the thigh or calf muscles during long periods of inactivity. This condition is not always dangerous, but can be fatal in extreme cases. It's not unique to air travel: it can occur in any cramped situation. Dehydration and immobility increases your vulnerability; smokers, the over-40s, the overweight and women taking the Pill are more at risk than others.

Healthcare in Africa

Pharmacies, the advance guard of Africa's healthcare system, are found in most towns but the volume and breadth of stock they carry varies widely from region to region. Throughout Africa, **public hospitals** face tremendous pressures including overcrowding and shortage of staff, equipment and supplies. If you're in need of medical or dental treatment, it's best to avoid adding to their burden: hunt down a **private clinic** instead. Embassy or high commission staff, foreign volunteers and other expats may be able to offer recommendations. Private treatment is typically of a similar standard to that found in the West, but lower in cost, so on a long trip it's usually far better to get an illness checked out on the spot than to hang on until you get home. Your **insurance** should cover you for all but the most minor of necessary treatments; as a rule, you'll need to pay in cash or by credit card and put in a claim later.

Traditional medicine

Tribal **healers**, some of whom double as spiritual leaders, are highly respected in traditional African society. Their practices are founded on the principle that physical ailments indicate a sickness of the conscience or spirit, so as well as adminstering medicines they also preside over rituals to call up ancestral forces, and make luck-changing **amulets** from fragments of sacred text bound up with animal, vegetable and mineral material. Many Africans wear a small, leather-covered amulet or *grigris* from babyhood. Some markets feature fetish stalls, crammed with a mind-boggling array of roots,

Elvis and high fever

On a sweltering Christmas Day we cooked on a beach just outside Lomé, Togo's dilapidated capital. I remember barbecued suckling pig (gruesomely butchered by Michael the mercenary from Mozambique), fried cassava chips, warm beer, Alpha Blondy on someone's sound system and mosquitoes the size of training shoes.

On New Year's Eve I felt strange, but then we were at the Seamen's Mission with shifty sailors, dodgy hookers, palm gin, and Max Romeo & the Upsetters, so I didn't think too much of it. The next morning I went for a dip and thought I was swimming in cottage cheese. "I'm fine, just a hangover," I said through chattering teeth as I swathed myself in sleeping bags and struggled to count in a game of backgammon that I seemed to be playing with Elvis Presley. "Has anybody got any pear drops?" I asked, before vomiting into my sock.

That night I woke up sweating inside my eyelids and I knew I just had to find the garden hose. But I forgot we were sleeping under the net on the roof of the Land Rover. I fell to the ground and twisted my ankle. As I did so, I shat myself. Right down into my flip-flops.

Fever, hallucinations, vomiting and diarrhoea – I was ticking all the boxes with some intensity. It was malaria. I was lucky, I had some Fansidar tablets, now discontinued, that I'd bought in Tangiers, so I could self-medicate there and then. Others are not so fortunate.

Kate Hawkings

bark, herbs, cowrie shells and dried animal remains, destined to be used in **potions** and **cures**.

Travel insurance

It's essential to equip yourself with a good travel insurance policy which includes comprehensive health insurance, including **24-hour emergency treatment** and, if necessary, **repatriation**, as standard. Your policy should also cover you for certain types of travel cancellation or delay and the **loss** or **theft** of money, valuables and other possessions to a strictly limited maximum value (you may have to rely on specialist or household cover for some items).

Policies vary a great deal in price and value, so you should shop around – price comparison websites are helpful for this – and read the terms carefully. A cheap policy may exclude possessions insurance, or have high excess charges (the fixed fees that your insurer will deduct from any claim you make). Watch out for time limits which might restrict your plans: some annual multi-trip policies, for example, won't cover you for trips lasting more than 31 days, and some single-trip policies have a fixed end date, with no extensions allowed. If you're pregnant, you have a pre-existing medical condition, you're planning to take part in hazardous activities such as mountaineering, whitewater rafting, paragliding or scuba-diving, or you're visiting a region listed as no-go in your nation's foreign office travel advice, you may not be covered by a standard policy and should take specialist advice.

Make sure you keep a copy of your policy, with the policy number and helpline number highlighted, in a safe and accessible place, in case you need it in an emergency. If the worst happens, your insurer will take immediate action. You may be advised to pay for medical treatment locally, then make a claim later, in which case you will need to keep your receipts. Similarly, any **claim** for delays, thefts or losses will need to be backed up with documentary evidence such as an airline or police report (see p.211 for tips on dealing with bureaucracy and the police). It can take time for any money you claim as compensation to reach you, so make sure you always have access to back-up funds; a credit card, stored in a separate place from your other valuables, may come in handy for this.

What to take

The savvy traveller's mantra is: **travel light**. The less you have to carry, the more mobile you will be – a liberating feeling. But inevitably, packing decisions will always involve some element of compromise.

The best way to decide what you do and don't need to take with you to Africa is to analyse the nature and style of your trip. Forget those clichéd notions about making a pile of all the things you'd like to pack, then leaving half of it behind – instead, ask yourself rational questions about each object. Will you really use it? Is there anything smaller, lighter or more versatile which will do the same job better? Do you definitely have to bring it from home, or can you hire or buy it along the way? Is it replaceable, and if not, how will you feel if you lose it?

Choosing your bags

Your **main bag** and your **day bag** are arguably your most important items of kit. Choose unwisely and you could find yourself in a temper each time you're getting ready to travel on to a new destination.

Backpack or suitcase?

Your choice of main bag will depend on where you'll be going and which methods of transport you'll be using. If you're splashing out on the kind of **luxury holiday** on which porters will look after your luggage at every turn, your only concern is likely to be your airline's weight limits; 20–25kg is typical. You can calculate the weight of your bags by holding them as you step on your bathroom scales. Bear in mind that if your itinerary includes internal flights by light aircraft, you may be limited to just one non-rigid bag.

For a short **city** or **resort holiday**, a suitcase with wheels or a trolley is a good choice; cases can be locked securely, cope well with rough treatment and are easier to pack and unpack than backpacks. However, since small wheels struggle on bumpy or sandy surfaces, backpacks are more versatile.

If you're planning any serious **hiking**, a good backpack is essential. They're also very useful if you'll be travelling from place to place via **public transport**. Well-designed packs distribute the weight of your gear in such a way that the strain on your shoulders and spine is minimized and you have maximum freedom of movement. It's crucial to find a strong one which fits comfortably, so before you commit, ask the advice of a specialist supplier and try several options. You should budget at least £100/US$150 for your pack; it's possible to spend more than double this. The best manufacturers have different models for men and women.

Try to be realistic when selecting a size – the smaller your bag, the more convenient it may seem, but the easiest bag to pack and unpack is one that's a few litres larger than you need. A capacity of 55–65 litres works well for most travellers.

Day bags

As you're likely to have your day bag by your side (or strapped onto your body) for most of your waking hours, it's crucial to choose well. It should be large enough to carry everything you're likely to want with you on a day-trip or a flight, including any items you may need in the event of your main bag being lost or delayed. Specialist **hiking bags** with multiple pockets and built-in water supplies aren't for everyone – a simple, light backpack or shoulder bag can serve just as well.

I never travel without ...

For Sir David Attenborough, it's an MP3 player loaded up with classical music, so he can bliss out to Schubert in his safari tent when he has a moment or two to himself while he's on location. What key items do other travellers always pack?

A hip flask and my little beanbag labrador called Holly. *Sue Watt*

My camera. When I am old and my brain is frazzled, I will still have my pictures to remind me of my marvellous travels. *Dale Morris*

An old piece of clothing for our bizarre, but vital, last-night ritual when visiting South Africa. We burn it on our braai then dance round the fire. We're convinced that it ensures us a return trip. *Ann and Steve Toon*

My flip-flops. The lightweight, multipurpose footwear of the nomad. Essential in campsite showers. *Genevieve Swart*

My kikoi. I can use it as a towel in a run-down hotel, a wrap for early morning coffee on a veranda or a scarf for sudden chilly desert nights. *Hamilton Wende*

My diary. It reminds me that adventures are always possible, however small. *Victoria Upton*

A dictionary of the local language. It seems right and respectful to try to master at least a couple of words, if only to give the locals a good laugh at your outrageously bad accent. *Melanie McGrath*

Insect repellent. They love me, I hate them. *Huw Williams*

My LED head torch and, if humanly possible, a cheese and tomato sandwich.

Jane Barsby

The best way to choose a bag is to try it out – so go bag-shopping armed with your travel essentials (a full water bottle, phone, guidebook, sunscreen etc) and see how they all fit, how accessible they are and how comfortable the whole thing feels. Compact **backpacks** are comfortable to wear for long periods, but a **shoulder bag**, worn across the body, teams better with a rucksack.

With the exception of a few well-known blackspots, bag-snatching is no more of a concern in Africa than anywhere else, but women's handbags remain an unsuitable choice for all but the most protected of African adventures as they're just too tempting a target. For similar reasons, you may prefer to carry your camera in an inconspicuous 25-litre backpack rather than a showy camera bag. There may be times when you'll want to take this principle to an extreme by locking your day bag away at your hotel and carrying your water bottle and other essentials in a tatty plastic bag.

Clever packing

With a little foresight and practice, you may find it's possible to strip your kit down to a bare minimum without feeling bereft. You can also do a great deal to protect yourself against accidental loss or theft.

How to travel light

- **Minimize your wardrobe** Choose durable, layerable clothes which go together, are easy to wash and look good without ironing. To stave off the boredom of wearing the same clothes day after day on a long trip, accessorize, or revamp your wardrobe periodically at local shops, markets and tailors.
- **Source multipurpose items** See p.87.
- **Buy travel sizes** Many hotels provide shampoo, soap and other essentials, so you may need less of these items than you think. Extra supplies are easy to obtain.
- **Share with your travel companions** This can apply to many items, from books and clothes to medicines and toiletries.
- **Shed packaging and cut up your guidebooks** Books are surprisingly heavy, so consider chucking away chapters covering places you won't be visiting. You may want to chop out street plans and listings pages at the same time, to carry in a pocket when you're out and about.
- **Limit yourself to a few small reminders of home** Just one or two small items such as a mascot or some family photos can make even the most nondescript hotel room feel welcoming, and help you miss all your other stuff a lot less.
- **Reduce your baggage as you go** Specialist equipment such as scuba, camping or hiking gear which you no longer need can be sold,

bartered or posted home. Books and maps can be exchanged with other travellers. Clothing can be given away and replaced with local finds. You may want to pass some items on to people who need them more – see box, p.85.

How to keep everything safe

- **Copy your documents** Before you leave home, take photocopies of the ID page and relevant visas in your passport, your driving licence, insurance documents, flight tickets and itineraries. Leave one set with a friend or relative and pack another separately from the documents themselves. It's worth uploading scans to an online storage facility, too, for extra peace of mind.

- **Wear a money belt** Your money belt should be invisible under your clothing, and should be used to stash cash, credit cards, your passport and other documents you're unlikely to need while you're out and about – start fishing about in it and you immediately broadcast its location to any nearby thieves. The most comfortable money belts to wear in hot weather are made of plain cotton. To make sure the contents don't dissolve when things get really sweaty, wrap your stuff in the kind of plastic bag issued by forex bureaus. Carry ready cash in a separate wallet, and don't flash this about – see p.211 for further advice on avoiding crime.

- **Dispense with inessential gadgets and luxuries** People had thoroughly enjoyable travel experiences in the days before MP3 players, laptops, electronic games and GPS devices were invented. These, along with conspicuous jewellery and watches, may make you a target for muggers, so think hard before deciding which, if any, are likely to make or break your trip. It's also worth bearing in mind that gadgets can suffer in extreme heat and dust, and that electricity supplies in Africa can be unreliable (see box, p.90). If all you want to do is check your email and social networking accounts every so often, it may be best to leave your laptop at home and make do with internet centres. A GPS device can be a life-saver if you're visiting uninhabited regions – elsewhere, asking directions can work just as well, and may lead to an interesting conversation.

- **Aim to fit everything into one bag** The fewer objects you need to keep track of, the better. Don't encumber yourself with separate camera bags, flight bags and purses if a single day bag, small enough to fit in the top of your main bag, will suffice. Make sure your day bag is big enough to hold a decent-sized water bottle.

- **Use plastic bags and boxes to protect and organize your gear** Invest in some strong, transparent plastic bags and boxes and use them to separate rolled-up clothes, books, gadgets and other items

Lighten your load, help others

A clever website, ⓦstuffyourrucksack.com, acts as a notice board to advise travellers of items which are sorely needed by schools, orphanages and non-profit organizations in Africa and elsewhere, so you can bring them out with you and donate them in person. You can also make room in your pack for some extra souvenirs by, on the last day of your trip, giving away your mosquito net to somebody who needs it more than you do.

within your main bag. Not only will this keep rain and dust at bay, it will also make packing and unpacking a speedy and methodical process. Small zip lock bags provide an efficient, lightweight alternative to wash bags, make-up and medicine bags. If you're travelling to Zanzibar, Rwanda or Eritrea, which have banned plastic bags because of their effect on the environment, choose bags which don't look disposable. If you're planning to go canoeing or sailing, you may want a dry bag to protect any items you'd like to take with you.

● **Hide your most treasured possessions** Any items which might appeal to thieves are best buried in the middle of your suitcase, rucksack or day bag, and never placed in outside pockets.

● **Lock up** A small, light luggage lock won't protect your bag from determined thieves, but it's a useful deterrent. A light, flexible bicycle lock may prove useful too, for attaching a bag to the seat of a minibus, for example.

● **Protect your backpack** If you'll be travelling by public transport in regions where crime is a grave problem, it's worth considering armouring your pack against bag-slashers by lining it with wire mesh.

Clothes and shoes

The **sartorial needs** of a traveller who will be spending a few weeks touring by public transport, climbing Kilimanjaro and serving as a volunteer on a gorilla conservation project will inevitably be very different from those of another who will be exploring Moroccan souks, swanning around luxury safari lodges or just chilling on Indian Ocean beaches.

In deciding what to bring, you'll also need to consider the **season** and the **cultural context** of your trip. Even the most conservative of African communities will make allowances for the dress of foreigners, but nonetheless women will enjoy a more relaxed and respectful reception in Muslim-dominated regions if they wear long skirts or trousers and modest tops, and keep long hair tied back or covered with a hat or scarf (for more guidance, see p.204).

Colour matters

When choosing **clothes** and **luggage**, it's wise to avoid blue or black (which may attract tsetse flies in the tropics) and military camouflage (which may be misinterpreted by obnoxious officials). Khakis (beige cotton safari gear) are not obligatory on safari, but they're sensible, and you'll fit right in. Cool though white clothing may seem, it's useless for wildlife watching – your guide may even ban you from wearing it as it will make you conspicuous, as will clothing with bright patterns and lots of contrast. White is also a terrible choice for any lengthy overland trip as the red dust of Africa has a habit of staining everything permanently – even underwear.

If, while in East Africa, you'd prefer to keep dangerous animals at bay, it might help to wear a scarlet shuka, Maasai-style – generations of bitter experience have taught lions to steer clear of anyone dressed like a spear-carrying warrior.

If you'll be visiting areas plagued by **insects**, you'll feel most comfortable in full-length trousers and tops with long sleeves. These, plus shoes, socks and insect repellent, are essential wear after sunset in malarial regions.

High-tech fabrics designed for hot climates and natural fibres such as cotton and linen are the way to go. Before packing favourite items, it's worth bearing in mind that the combination of sunshine, sweat and local handwashing techniques may soon take their toll, bleaching colours and wearing out all but the toughest fabrics.

- **On the road** Keeping cool and comfortable should be your first priority. Tempting though it may seem to strip off when the sun is hot, it's better to copy the locals and cover up – a loose-fitting hat worn with equally loose cotton clothing, leaving very little skin exposed to the sun's rays, will keep you far cooler than close-fitting vest tops, shorts and a bare head, and will stave off dehydration. Your feet are likely to be happiest in sturdy hiking sandals or light, breathable walking shoes, unless you specifically need the protection of boots, for example when hiking. Keeping your clothes clean may be a concern when roaring along dusty roads with the windows open – but often the best you can do is to choose colours and fabrics which don't show the dirt too much. As for underwear, since smooth tarmac is relatively rare in Africa, you're likely to be very glad of the support that good quality cotton and lycra can provide.
- **On safari** Safari-goers tend to adopt a practical daytime uniform of shirts and trousers or baggy shorts worn with hiking sandals or light walking shoes, with an extra layer for after-dark game drives. The colour of your clothing can be an issue – see above. No matter how swanky the lodge, evening attire is never as formal as it is at luxury city and beach hotels.
- **On the beach** Swimwear and sarongs are fine on beaches and around hotel pools, but elsewhere in coastal regions you should dress more

modestly. Beach sandals or neoprene shoes are recommended for beaches fringed by jagged coral rocks.

- **Mountaineering** Africa's great climbs require sturdy, worn-in footwear with ankle support and lightweight, breathable thermal clothing, from base layers to waterproofs, hats and gloves. All this is best obtained from specialist suppliers in your home country: you can hire gear at the main climbing rendezvous for Mount Kenya and Kilimanjaro, among other likely spots, but this is a pricey and somewhat unreliable option.
- **In the city** Urban Africans are highly style-conscious – if you're planning any business meetings or official transactions, including visa renewals, you'll need at least one reasonably smart outfit (for men, a shirt rather than a T-shirt worn with trousers and possibly a jacket; for women, something stylish and clean that doesn't show any leg above the knees; for all, tidy footwear). When going out after dark, locals don their smartest or glitziest gear.
- **In cold and rainy weather** The winter months in North Africa (Nov–Feb) and southern Africa (May–Aug) bring cold weather. In the desert and highland regions, temperatures tend to plummet by **night**, while the northern and southern parts of Africa's Atlantic coast can be lashed with cold winds at any time of year. Lightweight layers are the best way to cope. If you're likely to encounter seasonal rains, or you're travelling to Central Africa (where downpours can occur at any time) then pack beach sandals or Gore-Tex footwear and a lightweight folding poncho that's big enough to cover you and your day bag.

What to pack – and what to leave at home

There's nothing worse than having your luggage cramp your style, just because it's so heavy and it takes forever to pack and unpack. Knowing what you don't need is every bit as important as knowing what you can't manage without.

Multipurpose essentials

The following miracle items should help lighten your bag.

- **Mobile phone** Can serve as a phone, web browser, FM radio, calculator, notebook, recording device, alarm clock and torch.
- **Multipurpose pocket knife** Preferably with scissors and tweezers as well as blades.
- **Sarong** Can serve as a garment, towel, mat, tablecloth, curtain and bag. Easy to buy or replace in Africa, too.

- **Small bar of soap** Compact, and can double as detergent for washing clothes (a better option than cheap local washing powder, which usually contains bleach).
- **Tissues or wipes** In small packets: useful for those emergencies when there's no paper or water available, these are more practical to carry than loo roll (to which you should try to lose any attachment; see p.76).

Specialist items

- **Bicycle** Cheap mountain bikes imported from China can be bought in most African cities, but if you take your cycling seriously you may prefer to fly your own machine out. Bring your own accessories – helmet, lights, water bottle, repair kit, tools and spares.
- **Binoculars** If you're going on safari, your guide may possibly be able to lend you a spare pair – but if you're a keen birdwatcher you'll want your own to ensure you won't miss a thing.
- **Camping gear** The ability to set up a shelter and cook for yourself in the wilderness can transform your trip, but it's not essential to load yourself up with stuff. In southern Africa, in particular, locals prepare meals over a campfire without complicated cooking equipment and sleep under the stars without a tent as long as it's safe, and warm enough, to do so. On mountaineering trips, however, you shouldn't scrimp on quality tents, sleeping bags and water containers.
- **Diving, snorkelling and surfing gear** Serious divers and surfers will want to carry their own gear with them. However, the gear supplied on loan by most African watersports centres is carefully maintained, and you can inspect it before you commit. Whether you're diving or just snorkelling, a well-fitting mask and fins will improve your experience immeasurably and are worth bringing; if the underwater part of your trip comes near the beginning, consider giving them away or bartering them afterwards.
- **Laptop, camera, video recording gear** A laptop may be worth the weight and the worry if you'll be doing a lot of photography, video or online communication and publishing. For satisfying wildlife close-ups with a digital SLR camera, you'll need a quality zoom with a focal length of at least 400mm; supplement this with at least one more versatile mid-to-wide angle lens. If you prefer compact cameras, invest in the best you can afford. Bring plenty of memory cards, an external hard drive or other back-up device, filters, batteries and chargers, anti-humidity silica gel sachets, dustproofing, waterproofing and cleaning materials, too. Whichever gadgets you choose to take, ensure that your insurance covers you – many standard policies won't.

- **GPS device** Recommended for anyone travelling through uninhabited areas, particularly if you will be hiring a vehicle and driving without a guide.
- **Mosquito net** Most African hotels, however humble, either supply nets or spray rooms thoroughly with insecticide. However, a few don't. The nets sold in Africa, though cheap, are generally bulky, and you're better off with a lightweight one from an adventure shop close to home. If it's a hanging one, make sure you check its size and quality and carry extra string or tape to attach it over your bed. Or opt for a mosquito net zip-up tent that you can use anywhere.
- **Pocket short-wave radio** Allows you to pick up the BBC World Service and other international stations, which can be a lifeline.

Basics to pack

The following are far easier to bring from home than to obtain locally in Africa.

- **Business cards and passport photos** Whether you're travelling on business or just for fun, you're likely to encounter plenty of people who are keen to keep in touch. It's therefore handy to carry a stock of cards with your contact details (perhaps with an email address created specifically for this purpose); they can even be home-made. Small photos of yourself are useful for en-route visa applications (see p.66) and for quick, personal notes.
- **Contraceptives** All over Africa, these are easy to find but of variable quality.

- **Eye mask and earplugs** To help you sleep on the plane, and in cheap hotels. Noise-reducing headphones are worth considering, too, if you feel like splashing out.
- **Gifts from home** A great way to break the ice with strangers or show appreciation to your hosts is to offer a token gift, especially if it's something distinctive from your home. Pencils are always popular with kids, as are pocket dictionaries with students, mini bottles of toiletries or perfume with women and anything to do with football with just about anybody. Just make sure you consider your actions carefully and avoid presenting yourself as a Santa Claus type – in some parts of Africa, kids bunk off school in order to chase after tourists, yelling for sweets and money, thanks to well-meaning but unthinking visitors doling out handouts in the street. For more guidance, see p.202.
- **Guidebooks and maps** Only found in major African cities and tourist centres, where they're often expensive.
- **Head torch** Safer than candles in a power cut or when camping, and more useful than a handheld flashlight. Batteries are easy to find.
- **Insect repellent** Only bring the strong stuff – and plenty of it (see p.72).
- **Medicines and first-aid kit** While basics such as painkillers and some (but not all) antimalarials are cheap and easy to find, others, such as effective relief from insect bites, are not. For more guidance, see p.69.

Plugging in and powering up

Africans are used to **blackouts**. In off-grid wilderness areas and the many towns which are plagued by mains power cuts, you'll find yourself relying on generator power, which may only be available for a few hours a day, or doing without **electricity** altogether. Eco-lodges and community-based power projects have been popping up all over the place in recent years, but, despite this, it's likely to be some time before renewable energy is remotely commonplace.

Still want to bring a fistful of nifty gadgets? As well as your chargers and power supplies, you'll need some **travel adaptors** for mains sockets. The norms in Africa are UK-style three-flat-pin sockets in English-speaking West and East African countries, three-round-pin sockets in southern African countries and European-style, two-round-pin ones everywhere else – but exceptions occur, so it's wise to be prepared with a multi-country adaptor. A multi-plug adaptor can be handy, too, as there may be times when you're forced to make do with a single socket.

If you're travelling by private vehicle, you may be able to charge electrical items while you're on the move by plugging a car charger into the lighter socket – if it actually works. Portable **solar chargers** may seem neat, if pricey, but their efficiency varies a great deal. Since this technology is evolving fast, it's best to study user reviews carefully before investing. As for those times when the skies are black and there's not a single working socket for miles – have some spare batteries and a head torch at the ready.

Keeping a journal of your trip

Whether you create a state-of-the-art multimedia **travel blog** promoted through updates to social media sites or prefer the gentle art of keeping a **hand-written diary**, a journal is an excellent medium for chronicling your experiences and sharing them with family, friends and fellow travellers.

There are no rules. Some of the best journals evolve, to some extent, as a trip progresses – switching, perhaps, from a simple record of notable events and encounters to a full-blown scrapbook, or from a personal blog to a campaign site on behalf of a cause which has caught your attention. A little forward planning is essential if you are to have the right tools to hand, be it a bundle of notebooks (aficionados swear by Moleskine and Muji), pens, pencils and glue, watercolours and paper, or a laptop and all the gadgets you'll need to capture photos, video and sound (for guidance on photographing people in Africa, see p.205).

If you've decided that a website is the way to go, get the design sorted out in advance, and make sure it's easy to update no matter how sluggish the connection – you won't want to be sweating over this in some internet centre deep in rural Africa.

- **Memory cards and sticks** For electronic gadgets. If you don't have enough space for all your photos, texts and data, you will never forgive yourself.
- **Socket adaptors and chargers** See box opposite.
- **Sunglasses** Only very cheap ones and very expensive ones are easy to buy in Africa.
- **Sunscreen** Yours should have a high SPF; brands sold in Africa are of variable quality.
- **Tampons** Far rarer in small towns than pads.
- **Wallet** Large enough to hold a hefty wad of African banknotes. Keep most of your cash in a money belt (see p.84), though.
- **Water bottle** Light aluminium is preferable to disposable plastic.
- **Water purification kit** Boiling water can be inconvenient; iodine or chlorine-based drops or a UV purifier are good alternatives; see p.74.

Basics you can buy in Africa

The following are easy to obtain, so don't pack more than you'll need for the first couple of weeks of a long trip. Nosing around African shops and markets can be fun, and you'll help boost the local economy in the process.

- **Basic medicines, detergents and toiletries** You may like to try local concoctions such as handmade shea butter.
- **Batteries** Standard AAs are sold everywhere, although others can be harder to find.
- **Candles, matches and lighters**.
- **Traditional gifts** Gift-giving is a time-honoured part of social interaction everywhere in Africa. Favourites such as kola nuts and

bags of rice or meal, found in any African market, will always go down well with local hosts.

● **Mobile SIM cards and phonecards** Often much cheaper than your home mobile provider's roaming rates.

● **Mosquito coils and insecticide spray** The place you're staying may provide these; if not, effective ones are cheap and easy to buy, even from village shops.

● **Notebooks, pens and pencils** Every village shop has at least a basic selection.

● **Inexpensive clothes** You need never run out of things to wear. Cheap imports, distinctive regional sarongs and secondhand clothes are sold in every market, tailors will run up garments to order and major cities have boutiques, too.

Getting around

P rivate car ownership isn't common across most of Africa, and most local people rely on walking, cycling or public transport – where there is any. **Road transport** is a good way to get around cheaply and journeys like this, especially shared taxi rides, can be occasions to enjoy, giving you close contact with local people, and some memorable, and often hilarious, encounters. Generally, however, the more you get off the beaten track, the more beat-up are the vehicles, and no matter how rewarding the journeys are in hindsight, the physical stress can really test your patience and endurance.

With a few exceptions where the infrastructure is reasonably good – all of North Africa except the remote rural areas and nearly all of South Africa – it's a mistake to set yourself a rigid **timetable** when planning extensive travels in Africa, since delays on all modes of transport are commonplace. Even flight schedules are rarely guaranteed. At least you have plenty of choice: apart from an organized tour on which someone else makes the travel arrangements, there's car rental (with or without a driver), buses or shared taxis, trains, ferries and river barges, planes (regular intercity airliners or small, propeller planes used in the bush), bicycles and motor-bikes (bought, rented or where you're simply a passenger), pack animals and of course your own two, well-shod feet.

General transport tips:

- **Give yourself time** Transport always takes longer than you anticipate. If you're in a rush, you'll miss the point of the journey, get stressed, and quite possibly lose things along the way.
- **Don't believe a word of it** Double-check everything you're told and, without giving offence, avoid daily disappointment by never assuming you're going anywhere.
- **Make yourself at home** Always be prepared for a twenty-four hour delay. Snacks, drinks, a good book and comforts like a pillow, toilet

paper, wet wipes and hand cleaner will enable you to make the most of your immediate circumstances.

- **Don't pay bribes** It's useful to stand by the principle of never paying bribes to police and other highway obstacles in uniform. Patience and good humour are usually just as effective when travelling by public transport, if any bribe is paid it's the driver or conductor who does so, not you the passenger.
- **Stay cool** Easier said than done when the temperature is nudging 35°C and there's 100 percent humidity, but whatever the situation, don't let it get to you. Even if you think the customs official/ traffic cop/visa officer/bus driver is being obstructive, a smile and a comment of understanding from you may break the logjam and will certainly make you feel better.

Shared taxis

The classic form of African public transport is the **shared taxi** or **bush taxi**. Bush taxis are nearly all licensed passenger vehicles, serving approved routes at fixed rates (very few are completely informal). Many even have notional schedules, though these are never published and rarely adhered to. Note that in more remote areas, where a service has no clear schedule, if a driver tells you he's "going today", it doesn't necessarily mean he expects to arrive today.

The vehicle itself can vary wildly. You might get a reasonably comfortable estate car (station wagon – usually an old **Peugeot**, **Mercedes** or **Toyota Corolla**) seating five or six plus driver (or up to ten in great discomfort), a converted Japanese pick-up with slat-wood benches and a canvas awning jammed with fifteen people or more, or a larger, box van with up to thirty passengers – the latter increasingly replaced by **Japanese** and **Korean minibuses**. Any shared taxi is quite likely to harbour a basket of defeated chickens stuffed somewhere, and maybe a goat or two tied to the roof, as regular fare-paying additions. The Japanese and Korean vans are no less zoo-like, though padded benches or seats help, as does the extra ventilation. Most vehicles have roof-rack luggage carriers and a more expensive seat or two at the front, next to the driver. Cheapest of all are the bum-killingly uncomfortable converted pick-ups (*camions bâchés* in French, after their tarpaulins) which are often the only way to get to more obscure destinations.

Whatever vehicle you choose, you are going to be in very **close proximity** to a number of strangers, often for hours at a time. You may need to get used to hands and limbs draped naturally wherever their owners find most comfortable, which can include your legs or shoulders, and to toddlers being placed on your lap if necessary.

Toyota Corolla and Peugeot taxis will generally collect fares then drive straight from A to B with minimal stops. They often do the trip in half

Room for one more: shared taxi terms

There's a great variety of names for the privately owned, communal vehicles that pass for public transport across much of the continent. In French, **taxi collectif**, **taxi brousse** or **louage** are the main terms. You'll also hear **aluger** (Cape Verde), **candongeiro** (Angola), **chapa** (Mozambique), **dala-dala** (Tanzania), **gelleh-gelleh** (The Gambia), **magbana** (Guinea), **matatu** (Kenya), **tro-tro** (Ghana) **molue** (Nigeria), **matola** (Malawi), **taxi-be** (Madagascar) and **poda-poda** (Sierra Leone).

the time it takes a more beat-up shared taxi, which may drop people off and take fares en route.

Given that it's rare to undertake any journey over 20km without encountering a posse of uniforms at the side of the road, you should pay some attention to the condition of driver and vehicle before giving him your custom. A neatly turned-out car with a well-tied load is likely to pause for a greeting and move on; a battered, tin-box minibus with 26 passengers, no lights and the contents of someone's house on the roof may be detained for some hours.

If the vehicle's condition should give you pause, it's the driver who will be in charge of your life. A bad bush-taxi driver is probably the most danger-ous thing on the road, so don't be afraid to make a very big fuss if yours appears to have lost his coordination or his judgement or has his foot glued to the accelerator. Even if fellow passengers appear unconcerned, be ready to yell at him to slow down (and if necessary to stop and drop you off, with a partial refund), if he seems determined to test his faith in his maker.

Assuming you're reasonably happy to stay in the vehicle, the following tips for better road trips may help to pass the hours more comfortably:

- The ideal time to travel is **early in the morning**. By a couple of hours after sunrise the best vehicles have gone. In many parts there won't be another until the next day.

- The **sliding windows** on some air-conditioned vehicles are fixed shut: if the air-conditioning then doesn't work, you're in for an uncomfortable ride. Check out your vehicle in advance.

- If you're travelling in a van with an **engine** mounted underneath the front cab, be sure not to sit near it. What can seem pleasantly warm in the early morning will soon become burning hot, even through the usual stack of makeshift insulation. You will melt.

- If you've bought some **CDs** on your travels it's worth offering them to play, but be cautious of foisting your tastes on your fellow passengers as they may be too polite to complain.

- In most parts of West Africa, sharing some **kola nuts** goes down well with fellow passengers (see p.192), but smoking, eating and khat-chewing (see p.218) are generally frowned upon. Assess people's mood.

Buses

Bus travel is usually more comfortable and sometimes less expensive than going by shared taxi. Although certain buses are little better than gigantic bush taxis and not always much faster, in the more developed countries you'll find modern fleets with good seats and on-board entertainment. The big advantage of most buses is having an allocated seat and being able to buy tickets in advance, often the day before, for a set departure time. As with shared taxis, there's usually a discussion over the cost of transporting your luggage, but it's rarely a big issue because the locked baggage holds have plenty of room.

The large companies have **ticket offices** near the transport parks where they list their routes and prices. Their parking bays are often unmarked, however, and there are usually no published timetables or departure boards (North African countries are generally exceptions, as is South Africa). The easiest procedure is to mention your destination to a few people at the bus park, and then check out the torrent of offers. Keep asking – it's virtually impossible to get on the wrong bus. Once you've acquired a seat, the wait can be almost a pleasure if you're in no hurry, as you watch the throng outside and field a continuous stream of vendors proffering wares through the window. Alternatively, if you buy a ticket for a fairly imminent departure, you can leave a small item of no value on a seat to reserve it (like a bottle of water) and avoid having to wait inside the vehicle.

Although some bus companies have websites, they're not always very up to date. One that's well worth flagging up, however, is the South African Baz Bus – the country's famous backpacker hop-on-hop-off backpacker service (Ⓦ www.bazbus.com).

Transport parks

Most towns have a **transport park** ("garage", "motor park", "station", "stand" or in French *gare routière* or *autogare*) – the equivalent of a bus station without much of the apparatus – where vehicles assemble. Larger towns may have several, each serving different routes and usually located towards the edge of town on the relevant road out.

The shady side of the bus

When travelling by road, whatever your vehicle, it's really worth considering your general direction through the trip and which side to sit on for the **shadiest ride**. This is especially important on dirt roads, when the combination of a slow, bumpy ride, billowing dust and fierce sun can be truly horrible. If you're travelling on a busy dirt road with lots of other traffic, you don't want to be seated on the **offside** (usually the left) of the vehicle in any case as this is the side that receives oncoming dust in greatest volume.

Practice varies from country to country, but on arrival you'll generally find you're quickly surrounded (and sometimes mobbed) by touts trying to get you into their vehicle. This can be frustrating, and sometimes unnerving. It pays to behave robustly and to know the exact name of your destination – and the names of any towns en route or beyond. It's often the case that your destination is not where all the vehicles are headed, so you may have to change vehicle.

Always choose a **bus** or **shared taxi** that's close to full or you'll have to wait until they're ready to go, sometimes for hours: they don't run on schedules. Beware of being used as **bait** by the driver to encourage passengers to choose his vehicle, and equally of a driver filling his car with young touts pretending to be passengers (spot them by the newspapers and lack of luggage). Competition is intense and people will tell brazen lies to persuade you the vehicle is leaving any minute now. It's true your presence will encourage other passengers to join you – which is why they wanted you there in the first place.

Sometimes it's better to forget overambitious travel plans, especially any time after midday, or to take a shorter journey with a vehicle that really is about to go. Transport parks are full of interest, but a half-day spent acting as passenger bait is a waste of time. (Beware, incidentally, of inadvertently **chartering** a bush taxi – an exclusive trip, "town trip", "drop" or *déplacement* in French – which some drivers will assume you, as a foreign visitor, require. When you charter the vehicle, you pay for all the seats.)

As for **fares**: in order to guarantee you'll stay and attract others, drivers, owners and touts will often attempt to get you to pay up front. Unless actual tickets are being sold (sometimes from a booth, in which case you should be able to see how many places have been sold in your vehicle), try not to hand over any money before you've left town. This isn't a question of being ripped off, but too often the first departure is just a soft launch, cruising around town rounding up more passengers and buying fuel, and then going back to square one to wait some more.

Overcharging passengers is almost unheard of. It's your **luggage** that will cost you if you don't argue fiercely about how small, light and streamlined it is as anything beyond the equivalent of a small carry-on bag is usually charged for and generally has no fixed price. Local fellow passengers are just as likely to suffer from this situation, but are in fact in a worse bargaining position than you. You should compare and contrast, amiably remind people that you're a visitor and tell the crowd how he's trying to kill you with his grasping ways. Make them laugh and make him happy to give you a good price. If you get nowhere, take him to one side and be conspiratorial – this may appeal to the shrewd businessman in him. You shouldn't have to pay more than one third of your fare (and normally much less) for a backpack or large bag. Remember, you can argue forever about what you're going to pay, but once you've paid it, the argument is over.

During **long waits**, keep an eye on your luggage. Anything tied on the roof is safe, but transport parks are notorious haunts for pickpockets, and small bags sometimes get grabbed through open windows. Keep valuables round your neck.

Lorries and trucks

Although it's usually technically against the law, in more remote regions you'll nearly always be able to travel by **truck**. In fact, where there is no regular shared minibus service, hitching a lift on a goods vehicle, for a price, is the usual fallback for local people, though progress is usually slow: you can expect the lorry to stop at every checkpoint to pay bribes. It's easiest to pick up lifts in villages or along the road: because of its illegality, you'll rarely get a truck ride from a large town. You need to know the equivalent bush-taxi or bus fares and distances or you'll find yourself paying over the odds.

There's sometimes a spare seat or two in the cab, but space is more often available in the back with the goods. Travelling in the back of enclosed vehicles is pretty miserable, but older trucks are usually open at the back with wood frame sides. When loaded with suitable cargo, these can be a delight. You get great views and sometimes even a comfortable ride in a semi-recumbent position. Do bear in mind your safety however (when driving through forest or woodland, be very careful about low branches) and avoid getting the driver in trouble with the police by being conspicuous or foolhardy in the way you ride.

Travelling in an **empty goods lorry** on bad roads can be close to intolerable, but because they aren't carrying paying freight, they are often available (driver/owners always want to cover their costs). When empty, they go much faster and you're typically forced to stand in the back and clasp the sides as the vehicle smashes through potholes. Lorries often drive late into the night, so if you're not in the cab, especially in hilly regions, get something warm out of your bag to wear later.

Around town

Only a few years ago, **urban transport** in most countries was based around government-subsidized bus services supplemented by droves of predatory taxis and shared minibuses. Although there are still a few city-run commuter buses, economic "structural adjustment" killed off most subsidized bus services. Defiant commuters, their only other option the daily sardine-can taxi run, began to innovate.

In less than a decade, two-wheel commuter services have become the norm across much of the continent. Jobless young men with **bicycles** or **mopeds** earning a few dollars a day ferrying people across no-mans-land at border crossings soon spread their "boda-boda", or "piki-piki" services to the rest of the country. Welders got to work creating passenger seats and the wheel builders did a roaring trade in spoke replacement. Nowadays, there's hardly a large town on the continent where you can't get a five-minute ride on the back of a bike or moped for around US$0.25. The drivers don't carry helmets, and if you're burdened with luggage you may not be able to use them, but they're a good standby, especially once you've found a base and want to explore town. You'll need a pocketful of change, as they seem never to have any.

Auto-rickshaws, often known by the Asian name **tuk-tuk**, are another new development of the last decade, mostly seen in flatter towns where their underpowered motors can cope. Slow, breezy and a perhaps a third cheaper than the equivalent taxi ride, they're handy when you first arrive in town. Traditional equivalents are the horse or mule drawn (or in Madagascar cattle-drawn) **carts** or **carriages** known as *gari* in Ethiopia, *calèche* in Senegal or *charette* – a generic French term – in most other francophone countries. These are good for moving heavy luggage short distances (railway station to nearby hotel, for example), but you wouldn't choose one to cross the city.

If you want a regular cab, private **taxis** are universally available. You'll need to discuss the fare in advance. They never have **meters**, but there is almost always a notional fare for the journey you propose. Most drivers will want to be earning something like US$5 an hour, so US$2–3 should

Light rail and rapid bus services

They're coming: many big cities in Africa have plans for metro networks and/or bus rapid transport (BRT) services, using physically separated bus lanes to take the pressure off crowded commuter routes. But as yet very few are in operation. **Cairo** has a clean and efficient metro system that opened in 1987; **Johannesburg**'s Gautrain was inaugurated just in time for the 2010 World Cup; and the opening of the **Algiers** metro is imminent. The first part of the new Lagbus BRT system in **Lagos** surprised Nigerians when it opened in 2008, and **Cape Town**'s MyCiTi BRT system and **Johannesburg**'s Rea Vaya BRT opened in 2010.

cover an average journey, but airport-to-town-centre fares can often start at more like US$20 before settling at a reasonable US$10 for an hour or more of traffic and stop-start driving. At most airports there is usually a taxi-regulator's office, or drivers' meeting point of some kind and if you can be bothered to ask around, you will often be able to find out what the agreed fare is for your journey.

Hitchhiking

For the majority of people in rural Africa, **waving down a vehicle** is the routine fallback if there's no available public transport, but they invariably pay for the ride. As a relatively wealthy visitor, you should assume you'll be making a contribution, which will probably be similar to the bus or shared taxi fare.

The major exceptions are South Africa and several of its neighbours, where the volume of private traffic and awareness of hitchhiking makes getting **free lifts** relatively easy, and where a clear sign on a big piece of cardboard can work wonders, and North Africa, where private cars are also relatively common and the sheer hospitality of people can sometimes make hitching very easy. Offering to help pay for the fuel is a good thing to do, though it will often be refused. The main advantage can be speed and flexibility, but you can also find yourself dropped at a junction in the middle of nowhere, possibly with no shade, so you should always carry food and water.

Conventional free hitchhiking in other parts of Africa, is obviously easiest on the **main highways**, and in the vicinity of major attractions, for example around Victoria Falls, or along the Nairobi–Mombasa highway in the area around the Tsavo national parks (although getting lifts into national parks is difficult as vehicles tend to be full and their occupants on an itinerary). In sub-Saharan Africa the best countries for conventional hitching are, in West and Central Africa, Cape Verde, Senegal, Mali, Ghana, Nigeria and Gabon, and in East and southern Africa, Kenya, Zambia, Zimbabwe, Botswana, Namibia and South Africa.

It's often easier to ask motorists directly at police roadblocks and petrol stations. The **drivers** who pick you up are usually expat residents or foreign-educated business types seeking a conversation, and ninety-nine percent of the time you'll have a carefree lift. Again, offering a fuel contribution is only polite, though it will usually be refused. You need to accept, however, that you are making yourself potentially vulnerable: while unpleasant incidents are very rare, getting into a vehicle with a stranger always carries risks and women should be particularly cautious.

In regions where travellers are not often seen, hitching techniques need to be exuberant, partly for the simple reason that it usually won't occur to people that you might want a lift with them. Across most of sub-Saharan Africa, a thumb in the air is more likely to be interpreted as a friendly or possibly rude gesture than as a request. Beckon the driver to stop with your palm. You'll feel like a police officer but that doesn't matter: many drivers will come to a halt right next to you (be sure to choose a safe spot with room to pull over). If you don't want to pay, always explain that first, but don't be surprised if, after some conferring among the occupants, you're left at the side of the road.

If you're lucky, you may get a lift with a private **overland vehicle** (commercial overland tour operators hardly ever give lifts), which can sometimes provide the opportunity to visit parks and other relatively inaccessible attractions. Of course, assuming you all get on, you're soon likely to be contributing to the running costs of the vehicle – in fact doing so is likely to be a prerequisite for being welcome in the vehicle for more than a day.

Trains

Africa's **railway** map has remained largely unchanged since the early twentieth century. In fact, many of the lines that twist into the interior from the coast, only to come to a halt some way before reaching the next country, are barely operational, and a number of those in West and Central Africa haven't felt the clank of wheels on iron for decades. The lines are still there – in cities you see their embankments used as convenient footpaths – and occasionally a plan is put forward to revive a service, but with a few exceptions, mostly in South Africa and the North African region, train travel is in steady decline.

And yet, despite the collapsing infrastructure, it's still possible to travel vast distances by rail, and the allure of African train travel is undeniable. The lines often snake through the bush miles from the nearest road,

The sandal that got away

I once found myself with no option but to travel overnight through an area of Niger renowned for banditry. I was piled into a small minibus with about twenty other people. To improve security (though I'm not sure how), we drove in convoy with three other minibuses, but I sat tensely for many hours, staring into the darkness of the desert on the lookout for suspicious movements. Eventually I fell into an exhausted sleep, only to wake up at the break of dawn as we were pulling into Maradi. With relief I grabbed for my stuff, ready to jump out. But I couldn't find one of my sandals. Much searching ensued, which to my embarrassment involved everybody, all still half-asleep, clambering out of the minibus so we could check under the seats. It was gone. After much head-shaking the hugely apologetic driver and conductor agreed that it must have fallen out during one of our stops. I walked into Maradi as the town was waking up, the European stranger wearing one sandal.

Lone Mouritsen

offering vistas of swamp and jungle, stately baobabs and even herds of plains animals. The **Cairo-to-Cape route** of colonial ambitions, although never completed, remains a viable journey: you just need to be prepared to get on the road again in Sudan or Ethiopia and make your way south (or fly) to rejoin the decrepit railway networks of Kenya and Tanzania and then stay more or less on the rails all the way to Cape Town.

The trains in **Egypt and Morocco** are popular and good value: riding first class from Tangiers to Marrakesh through the North African countryside (US$25; ⓦwww.oncf.ma), or taking the comfortable sleeper from Cairo to Luxor (US$60; ⓦwww.bit.ly/EgyptRail) are experiences to savour. In **South Africa**, there are trains at down-to-earth prices as well as super-luxury services like the Blue Train from Cape Town to Pretoria (*from* US$1300; ⓦwww.bluetrain.co.za).

Across the rest of the continent, taking the train is usually a matter of coinciding with a service (there are often only a few each week), taking an overnight train for convenience, such as Kenya's thrice-weekly **Nairobi–Mombasa–Nairobi** run (ⓦwww.krc.co.ke), or eating up the miles in a slow, but relatively assured fashion, for example on the **Abidjan–Ouagadougou** line in West Africa, or between **Yaoundé and Ngaoundéré** in Cameroon.

Across most of sub-Saharan Africa, train travel is slower than road – the continent still has no high-speed trains – and although you will usually get there in the end, just like road travel, breakdowns are all too common and lengthy delays the rule rather than the exception. Slow progress fortunately means accidents are extremely rare.

There's often some kind of **catering** service on board – in Kenya full meals are served by white-uniformed waiting staff – and you can usually get street food through the windows at stations, which is often the best option. Bottled water is usually sold on board, but you should take enough drinking water to last you.

There are always two **classes of rail travel** (essentially hard and soft) and often three, with third class hideously overcrowded, not so much by passengers (who rarely outnumber seats), but by their mountains of luggage, both inanimate and alive and kicking. If you're on an overnight service, you'll probably opt for first or second class, invariably with shared (usually single-sex) **cabins** allocated and bedding provided. First-class cabins are often just two- or four-berth. Meals are generally extra.

Services usually run full, and whatever you've heard about schedules and organized chaos is generally true. But the bureaucracy that rules each train network continues to grind away in the background, so book early (usually at a main station booking office where you'll probably need to show your passport), and expect to queue.

On some of the continent's old **railway lines** you're travelling on tracks laid more than a century ago and, despite the delays that result, the old lines are highly enjoyable if your itinerary is flexible. If you have the money, try the Rovos experience in South Africa which is a slick and memorable exception.

The Fianarantsoa–Côte Est Railway

One of Africa's most spectacular railways, the French built Madagascar's FCE line (Ⓦmadarail.mg) with forced labour before World War II. At an average speed of 20kph, it takes eight hours to climb the 160km from the coast to the chilly highlands and the old royal city of Fianarantsoa, through wonderful scenery that includes more than a hundred bridges and tunnels. If you're climbing, sit on the right for the best views.

The Imperial Railway Company of Ethiopia

The 780km journey from Addis Ababa to Djibouti is now reduced to a single overnight service every few days, between Djibouti and Dire Dawa, about halfway to Addis. The train is shambolic, overcrowded and stops regularly, but it's a good approach to Ethiopia as long as your itinerary is flexible and you watch your belongings. The company is friendly, partly because everyone chews *chat* (khat), a herbal stimulant.

Kenya's Lunatic Express

The ambitious Victorian-era railway line from Mombasa to Lake Victoria cost the lives of hundreds of Indian labourers (dozens in the jaws of the man-eaters of Tsavo). Nearly 120 years later, the same narrow-gauge tracks support wobbly, thrice-weekly overnight services (Ⓦkrc.co.ke) between Nairobi and Mombasa and Nairobi and Kisumu. Almost routine delays mean extra hours to watch animals on the plains approaching Nairobi and the sultry crawl down to the ocean on the way into Mombasa.

The Marrakesh Express

"Looking at the world through the sunset in your eyes/ Travelling the train through clear Moroccan skies/ Ducks and pigs and chickens call/ Animal carpet wall to wall/ American ladies five-foot tall in blue". While Graham Nash's lyrics (from "Marrakesh Express") were possibly more the product of too much *kif* than close observation, the thrilling essence remains. Just a few hours from the short Mediterranean crossing you're deep in another culture, absorbing an unforgettable introduction to Africa. Ⓦoncf.ma.

Rovos Rail

The South African operator, Rovos Rail (Ⓦrovos.co.za), runs extraordinary rail safaris in its own refurbished trains of wood-panelled coaches, including a two-week trip from Cape Town to Dar es Salaam, with guest lecturers. The train halts periodically, allowing you to disembark from your luxury suite for a game drive, or to do some souvenir hunting or visit Victoria Falls. Don't look for change from US$10,000.

The TAZARA Railway

This Tanzania Zambia Railway Authority's 1870km line (Ⓦazarasite.com) from Dar es Salaam to Zambia was constructed by China in the early 1970s. Exhausting and ramshackle, this is a favourite among rail fans and a key link in many people's East African travel plans, passing between Mikumi National Park and the huge Selous Game Reserve, then over the rugged Southern Highlands.

Boats, barges and ferries

There are hundreds of small hand-hauled or spluttering diesel **ferries** pulling people and vehicles across the rivers of Africa, and a handful of larger vessels running lake and river services as a slower, if sometimes more convenient and often cheaper alternative to going by road. Indeed, the water's lulling motion – especially compared to being thumped about in uncomfortable seats on rough roads – makes taking the ferry anywhere an appealing prospect.

The most interesting **ferry or barge services** run on the Nile in Egypt and Sudan; along the Niger in Mali (generally only Aug–Jan); up and down the Congo between Kisangani and Kinshasa; and across lakes Victoria, Tanganyika and Malawi.

Cruises on the Nile are a special case, where you are ensconced in greater or lesser luxury in a private cabin on a custom-outfitted vessel, with frequent stops to visit antiquities and shop for souvenirs. Many tour operators offer Nile cruises (from around US$100 per person per day), and it's well worth selecting your ship carefully, using search engines and travel forums to check its credentials. You'll need to choose between a more traditional wooden vessel and something more akin to a modern ocean liner, with swimming pools and entertainment. Most offer guest lecturers.

If you have the time, on most rivers and lakes you can usually negotiate a passage in a **plank or dugout canoe** (known as *pirogue* in most franco-phone countries), either chartering the journey for yourself at a price you negotiate with your pilot/poler/oarsman, or sharing a local service and paying the fare. You can do the same thing at any harbour or port with the owner of a motorboat.

It's important to realize that most vessels in Africa don't come anywhere near international standards of **seaworthiness**. Always give yourself time to establish the captain's credentials: it's much better if he comes recommended by someone you trust. Craft of every kind, but especially small boats, capsize and sink all too often and, with life vests rarely stowed, it's every man, woman and child for themselves. If the boat on which you're about to depart fills at the last minute with passengers way beyond your worst expectations, grab your bags and disembark: you can worry about the refund later.

There's virtually no scheduled **sea transport** around Africa's coasts except for the inter-island ferries in Cape Verde, the Comoros, the Seychelles and Zanzibar and Madagascar's coastal cargo boats.

Flights

If you're on a fairly tight budget, you might have assumed your flight into Africa would be the last one you'd take until leaving the continent again.

Flights between countries and short **domestic hops** can be very useful and don't have to break the bank, but be sure your flight makes sense: air travel isn't automatically the quickest option for getting from A to B when you take transfers, security and the usual delays into account.

Not every country has its own **airline**, but those which do exist are generally better than popular legend would suggest. Among the better ones are Royal Air Maroc, Afriqiyah Airways (Libya), EgyptAir, Ethiopian Airlines, Kenya Airways and South African Airways. All these have long-haul services as well as important African networks: to fly from West Africa to East Africa, for example, you're most likely to go on Kenya Airways via Nairobi or Ethiopian via Addis.

Flights in Africa tend to be expensive and there's little fare-discounting. Expect to pay around US$25 per 100km for shorter flights and perhaps US$20 per 100km for longer ones. If you have an ISIC **student card** it's always worth asking for a reduction. **Low-cost airlines** are beginning to emerge, with Morocco's Atlas Blue, Kenya's Fly540 and South Africa's Kulula increasing regional coverage in their neighbourhoods.

Always **reserve a seat** as soon as you can and then rebook if your plans change, rather than wait until you're certain. Bookings don't always require a deposit. This also gives you leverage in terms of personal recognition at the airline office. Be utterly sceptical of a "confirmed seat" until you're sitting in it. Arrive at the airport long before the flight if you've any doubt about the status of your booking, and always reconfirm your seat in person two days before the flight.

Domestic flights of an hour or less are often operated by small propeller planes seating as few as a dozen passengers, tucked behind the pilot, with baggage simply stowed in the tail. A luggage limit of 15kg is common on these flight, but in practice paying for excess baggage is rare. As they fly much lower than international jets, and have unpressurized cabins with ordinary window glass, the **photo opportunities** can be excellent, so have your camera at the ready.

Finally, **chartering a small plane** for trips to safari parks and remote airstrips is an option worth considering if you're cash-rich but time-poor, and especially if you have some cash-rich friends to go with you. Costs for a plane seating two passengers are typically around US$2 per kilometre, with a five-seater more like US$5 per kilometre.

Car rental and driving

Car rental is available in nearly every capital city, many large airports and, in a number of countries, at some provincial towns. Given the freedom of choice it gives you – the chance to follow any side road or attraction that catches your eye – and that all Africa's national parks and reserves are open to private vehicles as well as commercial safari operators, there's a lot to be said for renting a vehicle. Unless you're in a group of three or more, though, it won't save you money over one of the cheaper camping safaris.

Key points to bear in mind:

- **Self-drive car rental** is relatively rare in Africa. Major exceptions are Morocco, South Africa, Mauritius, Namibia and Kenya. Rented cars cannot usually be driven into neighbouring countries. The minimum age to drive a rental vehicle is generally 23, sometimes 25.
- **Driver included** You're often expected, or obliged under the terms of the renter's insurance cover, to take a driver with the car, which doesn't make much difference to the price and can work out brilliantly if he (it's always a he) is a good communicator. Drivers are invariably supplied by the rental company.
- **Get an international driving permit** Whether you're driving or being driven, it's worth having an IDP – usually issued by a country's biggest driving organization – as well as your own national driver's licence.
- **Shop around for the best deals** If you decide to rent, negotiate as you might with any purchase, bearing in mind how long you need and the season. Rates in safari countries like Kenya, Tanzania and Namibia are generally higher at peak season. Some operators include unlimited mileage while others don't – something to add to your bargaining mix, perhaps.
- **Read the small print** Check the insurance details and always pay the daily collision damage waiver as even a small bump could be very costly otherwise. Theft protection waiver might also be worth paying for. You'll still be liable for the "excess", the first part of any costs incurred in an accident or loss, usually US$500–1000. Only the costs above the excess are covered by insurance.
- **Taxi and driver** An alternative to renting from a company is to consider renting a taxi on a daily basis. Pay for the fuel separately and settle every other question – including the driver's expenses – in advance. However good the price, don't take on a vehicle that's unsafe, or a driver you don't like.
- **Buying a secondhand vehicle** is a realistic possibility in a few countries, mostly in East and southern Africa, though prices are high for what you can get. It's worth considering, though, if you're planning wide travels: check the poster boards at any big mall or shopping centre.

Choosing and running a vehicle

If you rent a vehicle and **driver**, and the driver knows the country or region well, he'll save you a lot of time and hassle. Be sure the renter

..

On your motorbike

Motorcycle rental is less common than car rental, but available in some cities. However, if you have some riding experience, it is well worth considering buying a machine in Africa, avoiding the expense and paperwork of riding or shipping a bike all the way from Europe. The popular, kit-form Chinese mopeds flooding into Africa cost about US$400. They're reliable and economical and it shouldn't be too hard to find a buyer for your bike at the end of your trip.

If you're thinking of riding a motorcycle in – or to – Africa, one website is a mine of information and support: ⓦsahara-overland.com.

provides you with a written agreement covering your driver's expenses and hours. Doing the driving yourself will not really save you much money (the driver's daily wage and per diem expenses combined will usually amount to less than US$20) and, in any case, having a driver means no parking or security concerns, no dealing with city traffic and someone else to cope with breakdown problems.

Talking of breakdowns, don't automatically assume that the vehicle is in a good state of **roadworthiness**. Before setting off, have a look at the engine and tyres and don't leave without checking water, battery and spare tyre (preferably two, with the means to change them) and making sure you have a few tools. If you're driving off the main roads, it's important to keep jerry cans of water and spare fuel on board. As for breakdowns, local mechanics are usually excellent and can apply creative ingenuity to the most disastrous situations. But spare parts, tools and proper equipment are rare away from the main highways – and not really common along them.

Four-wheel drive (4WD or 4x4) is necessary in mountainous areas and on some dirt roads during rain, but you can manage without on main highways. Agencies will rarely rent out non-4WD vehicles for use in the parks, and park rangers will sometimes turn away such cars at the gate. Thanks to the dire state of many roads, **high clearance** is essential everywhere.

Land Rovers are common in several countries, but it's Toyota's **RAV4** and various **Land Cruisers** and Mitsubishi's **Pajero** that dominate the field in 4WD vehicles. Each has its fans but Land Rovers probably win out overall in the all-important mud battle (new Land Cruisers are very heavy and sit a bit lower on the road). Four-wheel drive **Suzuki jeeps** are also widely available: ensure you get a long wheelbase model with rear seats. These are more stable than the stumpy short-wheelbase versions. Suzukis are light and dependable, capable of great feats in negotiating rough terrain (though beware of toppling over on steep roadside shoulders), and can nearly always be fixed by a local repair shop.

You (and your driver if you're being driven) are responsible for any **repair** and maintenance work that needs doing while you're renting the vehicle, but the better firms in safari countries will expect you to call them if you have a breakdown, and will even come out to help you. They should always reimburse you for any running repairs, against receipts. When you get a flat tyre, as you will, get it mended straight away: it costs very little (usually around US$1) and can be done almost anywhere. Local mechanics are usually very good and can apply ingenuity to the most disastrous situations. But spare parts, tools and proper equipment are rare off the main routes. Always settle on a price before work begins.

The price of **petrol** (gasoline, always unleaded) ranges from roughly US$1 to US$1.50 per litre or US$4–6 per US gallon) depending on the retailer, the remoteness of the town and the cost of the latest imports. Diesel is usually a little more expensive. When filling, which is always done by an attendant, check that the pump is set to zero. In city petrol stations you can sometimes pay by credit card, but don't count on it as their card reader may be out of action.

Rules of the road

When **driving on the highway**, beware of animals, people, rocks, branches, ditches and potholes – any combination of which may appear at any time. It is accepted practice to honk your horn stridently to warn pedestrians and cyclists as you approach them. Other vehicles are probably the biggest menace, especially close to towns where shared taxis are constantly pulling over to drop and pick up passengers. It's common practice to flash oncoming vehicles, especially if they're leaving you little room to pass.

It is important to recognize the supplementary meanings of **left and right signals** particularly common among truck drivers. In left-hand drive countries, a right signal by the driver ahead of you means "Don't try to pass me", while the left signal which usually follows it means "Feel free to pass me now". The rules are obviously reversed in right-hand drive countries. Don't automatically assume, however, that the driver in front can really see that it is safe for you to pass. In fact, never assume anything about other drivers.

If that all sounds rather intimidating, try absorbing the following tips and rules:

- **Avoid driving at night** Roads away from the big cities are virtually never lit. If you do drive at night, be extra careful when passing heavy vehicles – the diesel fumes can cut off your visibility.

Right or left?

Most of Africa drives on the **right**. The **left-hand driving** exceptions are all neighbours in East and southern Africa: **Kenya, Uganda, Tanzania, Zambia, Malawi, Mozambique, Zimbabwe, Botswana, Namibia, South Africa, Lesotho, Swaziland** and **Mauritius**. In practice, across vast swathes of the continent, vehicles keep to the best part of the road until they have to pass each other.

- **Be cautious of abrupt changes in road surface** On busy roads, "tramlines" often develop, caused by heavy trucks ploughing over hot blacktop. These can be deep and treacherous, making steering difficult.
- **Beware of "speed bumps"** Various inventive traffic-calming measures are often found wherever a busy road goes through a village, and on the way into and out of many towns. White-painted rocks at the roadside may warn you of them, but usually the first you'll know of speed bumps is when your head hits the roof.
- **Take a SatNav** There are very few road signs in most countries, and equally few detailed, accurate road maps. Although there is still not much satellite mapping, a basic GPS unit that draws your route as you drive will enable you to retrace it back to where you came from, meaning you'll never lose your bearings, even in the desert.
- **If you have a breakdown**, the first thing you should do is pile bundles of sticks or foliage 30m or so behind and in front of the vehicle. These are the universally recognized "red warning triangles" of Africa, and their placing is scrupulously observed, as is the wedging of a stone behind at least one wheel to stop the vehicle rolling away.
- **Park carefully** When you finally reach a big town, don't assume the rules of the bush still apply. Parking may look like a free-for-all, but the chances are that, if you pull over in the wrong place, someone will try to fine you. Look out for traffic wardens, often issuing cheap parking tickets to park anywhere in the city limits.
- **Assert yourself in towns** You may need to adopt a robust approach, or risk waiting permanently at the first busy junction you come to. Most drivers only yield when physically blocked by another vehicle or someone in uniform with a weapon.
- **Don't be intimidated** If these rules and strategies sound unnerving, remember that most of the time you'll be driving in very low traffic (it's common to roll along the road for half an hour and not see another vehicle). Cities take some getting used to, but traffic usually moves slowly, and if you're a confident driver at home, you'll be fine.

Off-road driving

You would be well advised not to go far off tarmac in a 2WD vehicle, as a short cloudburst can transform a good dirt road into a quagmire. A covering of vegetation usually means a relatively solid surface that should not trouble a 4WD.

If you have to go through a large **muddy puddle**, first kick off your shoes and wade the entire length to check it out. If it only comes half way up to your knees, and the base is relatively firm, you should be able to drive through. Engage 4WD, slip into first gear, and drive slowly straight across, or, if there's a sufficiently firm area to one side, drive across at speed with one wheel in the water and one out. For smaller puddles, getting up speed on the approach and then charging across in second gear usually works.

Approaching **deep mud**, you should drive in as fast as you dare and pray. On a mushy surface of "black cotton soil" especially during or after rain, you'll need all your wits about you, as even the sturdiest 4WDs have little or no grip on this and some vehicles – heavy Land Cruisers for example – are notoriously hard to control. Stay in second gear as much as possible and try to keep at least one wheel on vegetation-covered ground or in a well-defined rut.

If you do get stuck, stop immediately, as spinning the wheels will only make it worse. Try reversing, just once, by revving the engine as far as you can before engaging reverse gear. If that doesn't work, and you don't have a winch and a nearby tree, you're in for a lot of sweaty work unless another vehicle comes along.

Cycling

In many ways a **bicycle** is the ideal form of transport in Africa – as endorsed by the thousands of locals doing everything by bike, including carrying livestock, their whole family or a new sofa. A bike gives you complete independence, and full scope for exploring off the beaten track and getting round cities. Routes that can't be used by motor vehicles – even motorcycles – because they're too rough, or involve crossing rivers, are all accessible. With a tough **mountain bike**, you can explore off the roads altogether, using bush paths.

Unfettered by the tortures of bush-taxi travel, you can cycle out of any town and **camp** deep in the bush if you want, or take your bike into hotel rooms with you. If you get tired of pedalling, you have the simple option of transporting your bike on top of a bush taxi or bus (reckon on paying about half-fare) or even "cycle-hitching".

As for the **distances** you can cover, depending on your fitness and enthusiasm, expect to cycle around 1000km per month, including at least two days off for every three on the road. During periods when you're basically cycling from A to B (often on a paved road, which is somewhat slow on a mountain bike), you'll find 40 to 50km in the early morning and 20 to 30km more in the afternoon is plenty.

Finding and carrying **water** is a daily chore on a long cycle trip. You'll need at least one five-litre container per person per day, and two such containers if you're camping out and want a quick shower – fill up at the end of the day, before cycling a few kilometres to camp.

If time is limited, you can **fly your bike** to West Africa. To avoid paying excess-baggage charges, contact the airline in advance, pack as many heavy items into your hand luggage as possible and arrive several hours before the flight to get to know the check-in staff. It's rare that you'll be obliged to pay any excess-baggage charge and not all airlines will even insist your bike is boxed or bagged, but it's best to turn the handlebars into the frame and tie them down, invert the pedals and deflate the tyres.

Out on the road, you'll probably want to carry your gear in **panniers**. When not attached to the bike, however, these are fiendishly inconvenient, and you might consider sacrificing ideal load-bearing and streamlining for a backpack you can lash down on the **rear carrier**; you'll probably have to do this anyway if you buy a bike locally. Using the kind of cane used for local cane furniture, plus lashings made from inner-tube rubber strips, you can create your own highly unaerodynamic carrier, with room for a box of food and a gallon of water underneath.

With a bike from home, remember to take a good, **battery lighting system** as it's surprising how often you'll need it – street lighting is scarce. The front light doubles as a torch and getting batteries is no problem. It's worth taking a **U-bolt cycle lock**: in towns, where it's essential you lock the bike, you'll always find something to lock it to; while out in the bush locking up is less important. Alternatively, you can improvise with a padlock and chain inside a piece of soft hosepipe, a lock that you can buy and fix up in any market. One, final essential piece of kit is a **rear-view mirror**: indispensable, both on quiet highways when a vehicle can arrive on your tail unexpectedly, and on busy city roads.

Apart from the commonest parts, **spares** for mountain bikes are rare in Africa. But take only essentials – spare tubes, spare spokes and a good tool kit. If you need to do anything major, you can always borrow tools at any roadside service station. On a long trip, it's worth talking to a reputable dealer before you leave, then, in an emergency, you can email for a part to be sent out by courier.

The Bob Marley border option

The border between Mauritania and Senegal at Rosso is notorious for its con artists. Due to the border times and bus connections, I once had to spend a night there on the Mauritanian side before crossing the following morning. After I had checked into the only reputable hotel in town, a man drove up in a shiny Mercedes to inform me that the border would be closed the next day, but that he knew the guards and could get me a visa and stamp overnight if I handed him my passport and some foreign currency. His refusal to take no for an answer and penchant for spitting every fifteen seconds towards my shoes suggested he might be something of a shyster. I vaguely said I'd think about it, and then got up before dawn and drove the track west for a couple of hours past a lovely, flamingo-filled national park towards the crossing over the dam at Maka-Diama. When I rocked up there, the border guards were listening to Bob Marley, and they wore wide smiles as they let me enter Senegal in peace and quiet – and for free!

Roger Norum
Ⓦ rogernorum.com

You can avoid the hassles and risks of having an expensive bike by buying one **locally**. There are bicycle shops and market areas devoted to cycling in most large towns, with good new or secondhand possibilities from about US$100 for the kind of slow, heavy, hub-gear or gearless Chinese Phoenix or Indian Hero roadsters so beloved of local people for their load-bearing capacities. Alternatively, you should be able to get a new "mountain bike" (sportier frame, derailleur gears, fat tyres, but still fairly heavy) for less than US$200.

Wherever there are bikes you can **rent** one (you can always make informal arrangements to borrow a bike for a few days), and in tourist resorts there are proper rental outlets. But they're not usually well-adapted for touring, although they often have carriers.

Walking and riding

If you're fairly fit and hardy and not tied to any schedule, you can simply **walk**. All over the continent, you'll come across local people walking vast distances because they have no money for transport. Half the West Africans in Johannesburg will have walked at least some of the way, often for months, to get to the city of their dreams. If you're hiking for a few days you can fall in with local travellers (if you can keep up), but their French or English may well be limited.

Using a **beast of burden** for your travels is also an attractive idea for time-rich, cash-poor nomads. Unfortunately a horse in good shape is expensive and horses tend to succumb quickly in the tsetse-fly regions north and south of the equator. If you know what to look for and how to care for a **horse**, the most promising areas are in the West African Sahel, Ethiopia or northern Cameroon. **Mules** are a lot tougher as they're used to long treks, and also cheaper, and they will happily venture closer to the equator in the dry season. For information on riding safaris, see p.169.

Then there are **camels** (dromedaries: *méharis* in Arabic or *chameaux* in French). It's possible to sign up for a few days on a camel-assisted walking safari (see p.169), and not impossible to join an authentic caravan in the desert, though fewer and fewer such journeys are made these days. But buying, equipping and travelling with **your own animals** is not to be undertaken lightly – even by the best qualified and most romantically inclined modern Lawrence of Arabia.

Accommodation

A frica has a huge range of places to lay your head at night. As you might expect, most of the capitals and many other big cities have at least one **international-class hotel**, and often a whole smorgasbord of them, competing for business travellers and tourists. In smaller towns, rural areas, or out in the bush, places at this level are few and far between. But don't assume, just because you've left the tarmac, that there won't be anywhere decent to stay: some of the best accommodation on the continent is out in the middle of nowhere, with brilliant management teams, surprising facilities and attentive staff.

Equally, you should never equate **local construction methods**, or a lack of glass, steel and concrete, with rudimentary amenities. The reverse is often the case. Until you've floated in a solar-powered infinity pool while gazing at elephants in the valley below, or whiled away a hot afternoon in the cool shade of a grass-thatched roof while picking out the sounds of the savanna, you haven't got the full picture of what accommodation in Africa can be.

Of course, you may not be able to afford such places very often, or at all, but there are plenty of less expensive hotels to choose from, and even the smallest town will have some kind of basic guesthouse. If your budget doesn't usually stretch to hotels of any description, and you were thinking more of **hostels** or less formal accommodation, you'll find Hostelling International hostels across North Africa and plenty of dormitory accommodation in South Africa catering for local and overseas **backpackers**.

Camping is always an option and the cheapest solution for time-rich, cash-poor travellers, but combining it with using local transport can be tricky, as sites are often out of town. Finally, opportunities to stay as a **guest** with local people can also emerge, particularly if you're travelling by public transport, and especially in North Africa, where hospitality to strangers sometimes seems to be inscribed in law – and where you may occasionally have to tear yourself away from over-attentive hosts.

Booking tips

Arranging accommodation **in advance** has obvious advantages, and always reduces the stress of arriving in a new location. Here are some simple tips.

- **Think where you want to stay in the city.** How far is your potential overnight base from the airport or your point of arrival? Is the place close to your departure point – airport, railway station or bus station? Would you rather stay in a more salubrious area and if necessary get public transport or a cab across town on your day of departure? And do you want to enter the fray immediately or would you rather ease yourself into the country gently in an expat enclave or surrounded by other travellers?
- **Confirm your reservation.** Don't expect to simply turn up with no reservation and get a room. Make contact by email or phone and keep prodding away until you get a clear confirmation. Some smaller places may rely on the manager's mobile phone, in which case you should send a text message and be sure to get a reply. If you aren't going to show up, remember to cancel.
- **What are the options?** Guidebooks are a great start, but listings become dated, and even long-established hotels eventually close or evolve into something else – often, it seems, just before you arrive. Firm up your ideas on travel forums and by checking the hotel's own website.
- **Learn to be sceptical.** Don't rely on anything being as described or how you expect (and ignore hotel stars). If you're counting on a swimming pool and free wi-fi, then double-check that both are actually available. Fifty percent of the time one of them won't be, but it cushions the blow, and is somehow pleasantly empowering, to have that knowledge in advance.

Hotels

There tends to be a significant gap between the expensive hotels and the dives, and you sometimes need to look hard to find something good at a reasonable price. Beware of local star ratings: when they are used (which is not that often), they are a pretty hopeless indication of value for money. **High-end places** usually have good security, a couple of decent options for a meal and a drink, business and internet facilities, and a useable pool. Most of the hotels in this category are fairly bland and forgettable, but there are welcome shoots of creativity, sometimes springing up out of relationships between travellers who've settled with local partners. A number of striking **designer hotels** have been built over the last decade in places as far apart as Timbuktu and Nairobi.

Mid-range hotels are often well run and can be nice enough places to stay, but if they don't attract enough local travelling business, their income tends to be derived from the bar, meaning overnight guests are thin on the ground and the rooms and furnishings tend to be tired.

Small-town **budget hotels** or lodgings houses – and of course the cheapest joints in the cities – are usually equated with drinking and prostitution, though this varies from country to country, and from region to region, and isn't an issue in North Africa. Very often built around a lock-in courtyard and parking area, such places are generally secure. But rooms in these hotels are often taken for an hour or two only, and there may well be a group of women and their young children permanently in residence – sometimes indistinguishable from the staff. It can all be quite a surprise, to put it mildly, when you first encounter such a hotel. But don't be put off unduly. These can be enjoyable places to stay – and are not necessarily intimidating for female travellers – though you need to use your discretion and pick a room carefully to ensure anything like a quiet night. Male travellers are very likely to be propositioned, but it's quite okay to say no thanks, and obviously risky if you accept (see p.221).

For travellers on modest budgets, there are occasionally alternative types of "hotel" in the rural areas. **Campements**, in French-speaking

A budget hotel checklist

Some tips for choosing a cheap hotel – and worth bearing in mind for more expensive places, too:

Think about noise If a hotel's bar is noisy in the afternoon, it will be cacophonous at night, so ask for a room away from the source of the din.

Check the security Having done this, don't be afraid to turn down a place if you don't like the feel of it. It's generally not a good idea to leave your door key with the management (certainly not if you think the reception will ever be unstaffed). If your door locks by padlock, use your own padlock to double-lock it, and check the fixture on the door and doorframe.

Inspect the plumbing If you don't like the sight, or odour, of your bathroom, ask for another room (non-ensuite rooms are always cheaper and the shared bathrooms may be cleaner). Ensure you have either running water or a guaranteed supply delivered to your room whenever you want. If you're in a highland region or it's the cool season, a bucket of hot water is usually offered to supplement the cold water supply – but you may have to ask.

If there's a fan or air conditioner, check it works Don't pay a supplement if there's no electricity to justify it. If it's only on for half your stay, you should claim a fifty percent discount on the supplement.

Check the electrics Cheap electric showers are often badly wired and can be very dangerous.

In malarial regions, ensure the mosquito nets are secure Avoid rooms with screened windows and no nets: you will be bitten.

countries, have a fairly loose definition. They are certainly not campsites, though you can sometimes camp at them, but represent more the modern equivalent of a colonial *caravanserai* or "encampment" in the bush, often associated with game parks and areas of natural beauty. *Campements* tend to consist of huts, or blocks of rooms constructed of local materials (often mud bricks and thatch), with shared washing and toilet facilities. At the top end, they're effectively motels, and they're likely places for self-drive overlanders and public transport travellers to bump into each other.

In a cheap hotel, when inspecting the room you've been offered, don't be surprised if it looks like a tornado's passed through, especially early in the morning, before it's been cleaned. Always ask for fresh clean sheets, towel and soap if you're not happy with any of them. If you suspect bedbugs may lurk behind the plaster, pull the beds away from the wall.

How much is a hotel room?

It's always worth trying to negotiate a **discount**. Managers of budget hotels and basic lodging houses will often bend over backwards to remind you that their rates can be discussed, and if not, the simplest approach is just to ask "Is that the best price you can offer me?". Deals based on **staying for several nights** are common. In places with a two-tier tariff for **residents and non-residents**, a perfectly acceptable negotiating tactic is to claim to be a resident, though you may have to eat humble pie if they demand to see proof.

Prices can be **seasonal**. Always bargain for the best deal you can negotiate, especially if you're visiting at the time when seasons change. Cheap hotels don't change their rates seasonally, but most resort hotels, safari lodges and tented camps have separate high-, mid- and low-season rates, and there's sometimes a peak season too, covering just the Christmas and New Year break. Low-season rates can be anything from a third to a half of the high-season tariff.

In an **international-class hotel**, expect to pay US$100–300 per night for a single or twin room including a good breakfast buffet. Bargain hard and you may get a twenty or thirty per cent discount. Likewise, the US$40–80 you'll probably pay in a mid-range, more locally patronized hotel (usually including a more limited breakfast), can often be knocked down by a similar proportion. If you need a single room, expect the single-occupancy rate to be around two-thirds of the double or twin rate.

Rooms in basic **lodging houses** are usually available for around US$10–30 per night. If they do breakfast it will usually be extra or, if you want to have breakfast elsewhere, the price will be deducted. Features such as TVs, room safes, fans and air conditioning all put the price up, and may be optional, allowing you to make relatively big savings.

Hostels

Youth hostels affiliated to **Hostelling International** (ⓦ hihostels.com) are only found in North Africa (a handful or more in each of Morocco, Tunisia, Libya, Egypt and Sudan and no less than 64 across Algeria), Kenya (which has one in Nairobi) and South Africa (which counts eighteen). They can be well-run and good places to meet other travellers, but don't count on either: the private competition, especially in South Africa in the shape of the country's ubiquitous **backpacker lodges**, is often miles ahead in terms of service and facilities. These usually offer clean and decent twin and multi-bedded rooms, some en-suite, plus reasonably well-equipped communal kitchen, eating and lounge areas, usually with TV, internet access and cold-drinks machines.

Often better than HI hostels, and certainly worth checking out for long-term stays, are the hostels run by the international **YMCA** (ⓦ ymca .int) and **YWCA** (ⓦ worldywca.org) and their local affiliates. These are found in sub-Saharan Africa, including Ethiopia, The Gambia, Kenya, Liberia, Senegal, Sierra Leone, South Africa and Togo. They tend to be permanently full of students and single professionals but if you can get a room (it's worth booking ahead), they're great places to meet locals. Although generally run by slightly pious types, you don't need to be a Christian, and there are few limiting restrictions on what you do and when – though alcohol isn't allowed on the premises. Both genders of Y accept people of the opposite sex, usually in separate dorms or on different floors, and many hostels also have rooms for married couples.

Bling-chintz in Guinea

I'd just arrived from Dakar, partied out after two weeks of trawling the Senegalese capital's diverse music clubs. But just when I thought African nightlife couldn't get any better, I turned up in Conakry, a city exploding with hedonism. Despite economic turmoil and a series of coups, the Guinean capital simmers like nowhere else. There are scores of drinking and dance joints and each night they put on anything from folksy local sounds to international DJ parties. I prefer African sounds in Africa, so for nine nights in a row my body was irresistibly moved by soft lilting tunes that exploded into gorgeous, grooving dance workouts melding *zouk* and *mbalax*, all infused with the region's trademark trebly electric guitar.

Every night ended near dawn at one of the large disco clubs, where the decor might be described as bling-chintz: matte black walls decorated with tinsel and a shiny disco ball over the dance floor. The dance halls were crowded, sweaty, beautiful places – packed with svelte Guinean twenty-somethings, the occasional foreigner and a coterie of prostitutes checking themselves out in the mirrors.

I'm from New York, I live in London and I regularly visit Berlin, but I've yet to visit anywhere that parties like Conakry.

Roger Norum
ⓦ rogernorum.com

Official resthouses

In some of the English-speaking countries, networks of **government resthouses**, for the use of officials on tour, are theoretically at the disposal of travellers when rooms aren't occupied. Some of the francophone countries have similar networks of government "villas". These places are very often unused for long periods and tend to need a good airing, and the water and electricity are often turned off or disconnected. First, in any case, you have to find the caretaker to open up. Despite the caveats, if you have your own transport, and you're self-catering, official resthouses can be very good value: prices are often as little as US$10 for a room, or even less. The difficulty is in locating them and finding the person with the key.

There are also the resthouses (usually free) associated with **NGOs** –aid, development, voluntary and other non-governmental organizations, including the US Peace Corps (more than 2500 of whose graduate volunteers are on placements in more than 20 African countries at any one time) and **Christian missions** of various stripes. If you're travelling widely, you may find these alternatives helpful and generous. But it tends to depend on the location: some closed their doors to travellers years ago when the traffic became too heavy, while in other cases – a few of the Peace Corps resthouses, for example – there's a special tariff for "outsiders". But in general you'll be staying strictly privately, as an invited guest, using facilities intended for others, so always leave a donation.

Cottages, villas and apartments

Increasingly, it's possible to book self-catering **apartments**, **villas** or **cottages** in various countries – generally the obvious tourist destinations. While Morocco and South Africa are the most likely places to find somewhere, it's also worth looking if you want to stay in Cape Verde, Egypt, Kenya or Senegal: there are even rental properties in Madagascar and Mozambique. Try ⓦholiday-renatals.co.uk, vrbo.com and holiday homeskenya.com.

Although you're "self-catering", this is different from renting a villa in Europe or a cabin in the US: properties are typically rented with one or two staff included, who live locally and come in daily, doing your cleaning and cooking. You're responsible for deciding what to eat, and buying it, and for remembering to tip them properly when you depart – their wages, included as part of your rental payment, are invariably very low.

Homestays, riads and unusual overnights

Bed & breakfasts (B&Bs) are widespread in South Africa, as are **farmstays**, but both are non-existent across the rest of the continent. Local tourist offices in South Africa can provide lists of licensed addresses.

Riads, in Morocco, are traditional family homes in old city medinas (the core of the town) based around a garden courtyard, with a number of garden-facing rooms. These days they have usually been opulently converted to suit cross-cultural tastes, often with pools and beautiful landscaping and architecture. Although effectively boutique hotels, often serving excellent meals, their design and attention to detail distinguish them. You can find them on the web, or through Moroccan tourist offices. The best *riads* tend to get booked up months ahead.

For something unusual, try a **houseboat** on Lake Kariba in Zimbabwe (ⓦkaribahouseboats.com) which gives you gently moving accommodation and plenty of wildlife action – crocs and hippos fore and aft and all the big savanna game on the lake's indented coastline and many islands.

Lastly, many a memorable night spent while travelling in Africa has been spent…travelling in Africa. Overnights on **trains** and **riverboats**,

Accommodation terms

AC Air-conditioned.

AI All-inclusive.

American plan Room only.

askari Guard, nightwatchman (Swahili).

auberge Guesthouse or family-run lodging, usually in simple huts (French).

banda Thatched cottage or chalet, usually rented out on a self-catering basis, but sometimes referring to chalet-style rooms at lodges (Swahili).

BB Bed and breakfast.

boarding & lodging Cheap guesthouse (East Africa).

campement Found in most French-speaking countries, where they are sometimes also called *campings*, these are basically rustic motels, usually in the bush.

case Hut or small house (French).

chambre de passage Lodging house (French), usually rented by the hour.

chambre ventilée A room with a fan (French).

FB Full board, ie lunch, dinner, bed and breakfast.

gardien Security man, nightwatchman (French).

fly camp Mobile camp used on private safaris.

HB Half-board, ie dinner, bed and breakfast.

hoteli Cheap restaurant or café (Swahili), not a hotel.

lodge Safari hotel in the bush.

long-drop Toilet over a cesspit.

mabati Corrugated-iron roof (Swahili).

package Usual obligatory arrangement in high-end safari camps and lodges, in which all meals, drinks and activities are included.

pensão Portuguese word meaning family-run hotel, often with strict rules.

pps Per person sharing.

RO Room only.

rondavel Small, round hut, containing beds but no bathroom (Afrikaans).

SO single occupancy.

safari shower Refillable reservoir of hot water above the shower area.

tôle ondulée Corrugated iron (French).

self-contained Room with en-suite bathroom.

star-bed Four-poster bed mounted on vehicle wheels, pulled onto a deck at night.

tented camp Lodge in the bush, or in a game park, using large, furnished tents with a solid bathroom at the back.

tree-hotel Animal-viewing hotel on stilts, after the style of Kenya's *Treetops*.

and even on one of the more comfortable modern **buses** where the roads are good, allow you to put on the miles while saving money on hotel bills. It can be a great experience, but don't do it too often: you'll see nothing and you may never come that way again.

Safari lodges and tented camps

Early hunting safaris took caravans of porters through the bush, but as visitors began to shoot with cameras rather than guns and stay in one place for a few days or more, the tourist industry started to build hotels to accommodate them.

In the 1950s and 1960s, just having a hotel in the bush was a major achievement, and the oldest **safari lodges** often show their age with unimaginative design and boring little rooms. Today, the best of the big lodges have public areas offering spectacular panoramas and game-viewing decks, while the rooms are usually comfortably furnished chalets or bandas. The most expensive boutique lodges usually incorporate deadwood branches and bare rock, eschewing straight lines wherever possible. Some have just half a dozen "rooms", constructed entirely of local materials, ingeniously open-fronted yet secure, with great views and invigorating open-air bathrooms.

Many travellers on safari like to get even closer to the environment by staying in a tent. You won't have to put up your own: tented camps have large, custom-made, traditionally shaped tents, standing beneath solid thatched roofs and mounted over hard floors. The canvas may flap in the breeze, but the bathroom is a permanent, plumbed-in section at the back, with a regular toilet and shower. All the usual amenities, including electricity and comfortable (not camp) beds are installed, and at night everything is zipped up to keep the insects out.

At the heart of a tented camp are the public areas, where you'll find the dining room and bar, also often under canvas. In the smaller, more boutique camps, these are often combined as one large "mess tent", often with rugs and sofas, where you eat with your hosts and the other guests and share the day's excitements.

Some lodges and camps are surrounded by an **electric fence**, giving you the freedom to wander at will, but detracting from a sense of being in the wild. The majority of properties, which are still unfenced, increasingly ask you to sign a disclaimer to limit their liability in the unlikely event that an animal encounter should bring your safari to an early conclusion. Unfenced camps and lodge employ animal watchmen – in East Africa they're often traditionally dressed, spear-carrying warriors – and after dark, they escort you to and from your room or tent. In practice, although large mammals do wander into camps quite frequently, serious **incidents** are exceptionally rare and at well-managed properties you have nothing to worry about.

Meals in the lodges and camps are prepared in fully equipped kitchens and served by waiters who are often very knowledgeable about local wildlife and customs. Although the food can sometimes be a tad dull, with heavy sauces and overcooked meat and veg, the best places have their own organic vegetable and herb gardens and prepare truly gourmet cuisine in the middle of nowhere.

Lodge and tented camp **prices** tend to be high, with US$300–500 for two, on a full-board basis, not unusual, and some properties reaching US$1000 a night for two people. This, however, will invariably include all meals and local drinks, game drives and, where possible, game walks. For more information on what safaris involve, see Chapter 11.

Eco-lodges

Because tented camps are relatively easy to construct and reconfigure, they're at the vanguard of Africa's nascent **responsible tourism** movement. The most eco-friendly camps and lodges limit their use of electricity to what can be generated by solar panels, provide "safari showers" to order rather than constant hot water, and take care to limit their environmental footprint in other ways, for example by compost-ing all their organic waste and trucking out non-biodegradable trash rather than burning it (scavenging marabou storks at camps and lodges are a sure sign of poor waste management, and a bad advert if you were thinking of staying).

Several countries have some kind of environmental or social respon-sibility rating system, but as yet, as elsewhere worldwide, there are no agreed criteria within countries, let alone across the continent, and much of the pressure comes from the owners of key establishments. Morocco, Egypt, The Gambia, Ghana, Kenya, Uganda, Tanzania, Malawi, Zambia, Mozambique, Mauritius, South Africa, Botswana and Namibia all have a variety of eco-friendly places to stay. But you should always press for further details when considering staying at an "eco-lodge": there's a bit of a tendency to dress up ordinary, pragmatic solutions in green cloth-ing and some well-meaning property owners are a little timid about the preparedness of their clientele to adjust to a genuinely low-footprint, sustainable stay.

While an environmental approach is the mark of any efficient hospital-ity business where there is no properly functioning infrastructure – using local materials because they're cheap and available, solar panels because there's no electricity grid, and composting waste because there's no mains drainage – it's the **community initiatives** in local accommoda-tion that tend to make the most impact, because sheer poverty is still Africa's biggest single problem, rather than wasted resources or excessive carbon dioxide emissions. A typical community-run lodge employs staff only from the local ethnic community, and usually leases the land from them too, if the property is not actually owned by them. The advantage to visitors is a far more integrated experience, where you're hosted and guided by people who were born in this spot. (All too often, when talking to staff about the area, you realize that, since their family home is 500km away and in another tribal district, they're hardly any more familiar with the environs of the lodge than you are.) The biggest benefit of community lodges, however, is that a much larger part of your money goes to the local community: at the luxury *Il Ngwesi Lodge*, in Kenya, for example, all the income from the six rooms goes directly to the 6000-strong local Maasai community, supporting their schools, clinics, veterinary fees and wildlife conservation.

At the other end of the price spectrum, in Senegal, a network of **budget homestays**, known as *campements touristiques rurals integrés* or CTRIs ("rurally integrated tourist camps"), have been built with government loans, in a variety of traditional architectural styles, by local villagers specifically to host independent travellers. Although there are not yet any other examples of similar budget-priced networks, dozens of individual budget lodges, camps and *auberges* across the continent are inspired by the same broadly green ideals: you just have to look for them.

Camping

Proper **campsites or campgrounds** are relatively rare in Africa. The major exceptions are **South Africa** and **Namibia**, which together have a long-established camping and caravanning culture and large numbers of well-equipped campsites. At the other end of the continent, there's a reasonable scattering of tourist campsites in Morocco and Tunisia and a handful of more elementary campsites in the national parks and reserves of Kenya, Uganda and Tanzania.

For the campsites in **East Africa** you need to be fully self-sufficient: they're intended for organized groups, or private individuals with their own vehicles, so if you're relying on public transport, getting to them may be tricky. You often get little more than a place to pitch your tent and park your vehicle. This applies equally to the so-called "special campsites", which are special in location and higher fees only: they are absolutely devoid of facilities, so you have to bring everything with you, including water. Even at the parks' and reserves' "public campsites", showers and toilets are often rudimentary and the other normal features of a campsite, such as a shop or café, are generally non-existent, though occasionally there's an elementary bar with some kind of kitchen attached that will sometimes open if enough people check in.

If you're **taking a tent**, bring the lightest one you can afford and remember that its main purpose in usually very warm conditions is to keep insects out. There are lots of good models around these days with snap-together aluminium frames.

Wild camping

Wild camping doesn't suit everyone and will always carry some inherent risk but, across much of the continent, it is the only option if you want to camp. And it offers big rewards: night-time noises, especially in forest regions, where you'll hear some spectacularly eerie shrieks and calls, merely add to the atmosphere, and in practice wild animals pose little threat (see p.220).

If you have **your own vehicle** it's just a question of finding a good spot for the night. When you're driving in the desert, making camp is the best part of the day. But in more populated areas, don't assume you'll be able to camp clandestinely. A vehicle in the bush is unusual; people are likely to hear it, and will flock to watch you.

Bush camping is easier if you're **cycling or hiking**. For safety's sake, always get right away from the main road to avoid being accidentally run over or exciting the interest of occasional, motorized bandits. You may quite possibly be visited by delegations of machete-wielding villagers – especially if you light a fire – but confirmation that you're harmless is usually their first and only concern, and offering cigarettes, sweets or cookies will soon break the ice. In some countries, especially in North Africa, you may not be *allowed* to sleep out: people will implore you to spend the night as their guest, probably after having fed you an enormous feast of couscous.

If you're **travelling by public transport**, it's a lot harder to camp out effectively night after night. Buses, trains and shared taxis go from town to town and it's rare to be dropped off at just the right spot in between them, ready and supplied for a night under the stars. Walking for miles out of town in search of a place to camp (even in rural areas it can take you an hour or two before you find a place that seems comfortably isolated) is an exercise that soon palls.

The following wild camping tips are all worth noting:

- In more heavily populated or farmed districts, it's best to ask someone before pitching a tent, and never leave it unattended.
- Fill your water bottles before looking for a pitching site.
- During the dry season, you'll rarely have trouble finding wood for a small fire, but use it sparingly and smother it when you go to sleep.
- A portable gas stove isn't essential, though they are cheap and can be very useful – in wet weather, where you can't find firewood or where fires are prohibited. You'll find the gas canisters (Ⓦbit.ly /CampingGaz) for them in most big cities. Alternatively, portable petrol (gasoline) stoves are smaller and more convenient, if pricier.
- If you're hiking, or cycle-camping, a small kerosene lamp can be carried fairly easily. However, be sure to buy kerosene for it (*pétrole* in French), and not petrol/gasoline (*essence*).

- Camping in dry riverbeds, or on trails used by animals going to water, is highly inadvisable (see p.220).

Hosted camping

The alternative to getting away from people to camp is actively to search for safe, **private property** that looks like it could happily stand having a tent on it for the night: mission lawns, school grounds and private gardens are all candidates. So long as the site is fairly secluded, and somebody is more or less watching over you (usually the nightwatch-man), this is often a good solution and you'll usually have access to water. You just have to ask. Leave a donation if you can.

Staying with people

All over Africa, from Morocco to Madagascar and from Cape Verde to Cape Delgado, you'll run into people who want to put you up for the night as an **invited guest**. Such invitations often arise from your attempts to camp nearby, or

Cartoon dialogue

The accommodation, in a dusty village in northern Kenya, was basic, with just enough room for a small bed and for some reason a wooden chair. Why the chair? The notion of having company in the tiny room seemed absurd and entertaining clients a long shot. Maybe it was just for sitting, pondering life's mysteries in the darkness under the corrugated iron roof. The bed sheets, clearly intended to brighten up the place, were a colourful homage to American cartoons.

I slept quite soundly until 7am when there was a banging on my door. Drunk with sleep I pulled myself up and found a stern-faced young woman asking me for "chweets". At first I had no idea what she meant. It took me a groggy minute or two to realize she must be asking for sweets, like the hordes of pestering kids the day before had chanted at us, desperate for candy.

I told her I didn't have any, closed the door and went back to bed. An hour later when I left my room, I found the girl in the courtyard, bent over a bucket, washing the sheets of every room except mine. The wet faces of SpongeBob SquarePants and Snow White mocked me from the washing line.

Brook Driver

while you're waiting for transport at a quiet crossroads. A fairly warm if sometimes rather dutiful hospitality often characterizes these contacts and it can be difficult to know how to repay such kindness, particularly since it often seems so disruptive of family life, with you set up in the master bedroom and the junior wives, cousins and children sent running for special things for the guests. While it's impossible to generalize, for female guests a trip to the market with the women of the household is an opportunity to pay for everything. Male travellers can't do this, but buying a sack of rice or sugar, a big bundle of yams, a crate of beer or something similar makes a good gift. You'll probably have to ask a member of the household to get it for you, giving them the money. Everyone will be delighted.

The alternative to staying with people by chance, is doing so deliberately: **couchsurfing**. The non-profit ⓦcouchsurfing.com has 30,000 members across Africa, including couchsurfer-hosts in every country on the continent, who offer a free "couch" to passing travellers. You'll meet locals, especially outgoing student types, but older people too, as well as expat workers and NGOs. Membership and accommodation are free, and you don't have to host someone first in order to participate, but you should plan well ahead. In a very similar vein for **cyclists**, there's the much smaller ⓦwarmshowers.org.

Food and drink

Compared to Asia or Europe, gourmets don't pay Africa much attention. Perhaps it's because so many Africans are forced to subsist on stodgy poverty rations – cheap staples such as *fufu*, *sadza* and ugali, for example, are almost unbearably bland, no matter how delicious a sauce is spooned on top. Or perhaps it's because restaurants don't really feature in traditional African culture – the focus is firmly on simple home cooking, shared with family.

Despite this, the best **African cuisine** is so memorable, both for its flavours and for its customs, that culinary discoveries could become a focus of your trip. As you'd expect in a continent where a curvaceous figure is considered beautiful, good food in copious quantities is a key element in every African celebration and social gathering. Classic African dishes make excellent use of fresh local ingredients such as juicy tropical fruit, fish, meat and game, flavoured with rich palm oil, peanuts, coconut, chilli and earthy local spices. Some are truly imaginative, such as the one-pot stews and campfire cakes prepared in the bush by safari chefs, and many are designed to be enjoyed communally.

In the **restaurants** found in tourist resorts, traditional African cuisine of the home-cooked type is rare – instead you'll find an abundance of Western standards prepared from African ingredients, such as steak and chips, seafood pasta or grilled tuna with rice. Most resorts, towns and cities have a scattering of foreign restaurants and cafés: you'll find Portuguese cafés in Mozambique, Angola and São Tomé, French-style bistros in the former French colonies of North and West Africa, German beer-and-wurst places in Namibia, and Lebanese restaurants all the way along the West African coast. Italian, Indian and even American-style eateries crop up all over the place and China's influence is growing exponentially.

Naturally enough, the top culinary talent is found in the most **upmarket hotels** and **safari lodges**. South Africa and the holiday islands of

Mauritius, the Seychelles and the Quirimbas in Mozambique have an excellent reputation for fine dining, as do the exclusive bush camps dotted over East and southern Africa. Here, you will be treated to beautifully presented luxury cuisine including international-style dishes with an African twist, such as roast springbok with rosemary and red wine jus, or grilled tilapia with steamed green beans and spicy potatoes.

Regional specialities

The classic **African meal** consists of a starchy staple such as bread, rice, pounded cassava, mashed plantain or maize porridge, garnished with stewed or grilled meat or fish and vegetables such as bitter tomatoes, onions and squashes, flavoured with garlic, herbs and spices. Within this simple format, there are countless variations. A typical African breakfast usually features some sturdy carbs, too, in the form of porridge or bread made from the favourite local grain, washed down with a hot drink.

Traditional African fare is eaten out of a shared bowl, or set of bowls, usually with the right hand. For further guidance on being invited to eat with an African family, and information on food culture in Muslim communities during Ramadan, see p.191, p.60 & p.204.

North Africa

Many **North African** dishes are familiar to Western diners. Typical starters (called *kemia* or mezze) include *harira* (thick, spicy bean and pasta bean soup) or a salad of tomatoes, aubergines, peppers and garlic with bread and *harissa* (chilli oil). These are usually followed by meatballs, kebabs or some kind of spicy stew with flatbread or couscous. Spices are universal: visit any North African market and you will see stalls displaying cinnamon, cumin, turmeric, ginger, pepper, paprika and saffron in strikingly colourful conical piles.

Morocco is rightly famous for its tajines, stews of meat (usually beef or lamb), vegetables, fruit and spices cooked in a heavy clay pot and served with couscous. A conical or dome-shaped lid helps steam the contents, keeping them tender as they simmer gently in a low oven. Tunisians are fond of couscous dishes, too, particularly hot ones, such as *chakchouka* (with chickpeas) and *koucha* (with lamb and potatoes). They don't call these tajines, though – they reserve this word for a dish resembling a frittata or tortilla. In Egypt, the classic meal is *kofta* (spicy meatballs) with dips such as hummus (made from chickpeas), *babaghanoush* (sesame and aubergine) and *fuul* (mashed broad beans).

West Africa

In **West Africa**, you will almost certainly encounter flavours and textures you have never experienced elsewhere. Particularly distinctive are dishes such as Ghanaian *fufu* (or foofoo) with palm oil, dried fish and chilli sauce – you make a ball of the *fufu*, a gooey stodge made from pounded cassava (also called manioc), dip it in the fiery sauce and pop it in your mouth – and Nigerian *obe ata* (pepper soup).

As in North Africa, slow-cooked one-pot stews are very popular, but here the favourite sauce ingredients are peanuts, onions, cassava leaves, Maggi stock cubes, bitter tomatoes and chillies. Classic recipes include peanut and meat stew (called *domodah* in The Gambia and *maafé* in Senegal and Nigeria); fish and tomato risotto (called *benachin*, *jollof* rice or *thiéboudienne*, a speciality of The Gambia and Senegal); grilled fish stuffed with spices; chicken with garlic, onions and lemon (*poulet yassa*, again Senegalese); and finely chopped greens cooked in palm oil (called *plasas* or *palava* sauce, respectively, in Guinea and Sierra Leone).

East Africa

The **Swahili Coast** – particularly Lamu, Zanzibar and Mombasa – specializes in wonderful seafood dishes and mild curries prepared with coconut and exotic spices, originally planted here by Arab traders. Kenya and Tanzania are excellent for meat, including *nyama choma* (roasted or barbecued beef, goat or mutton) popular either as a snack (see box, p.130) or as an all-out blowout.

Ethiopian cuisine is still relatively little known in the West, and is something of an acquired taste. One of its signature dishes is *injera*, a large, nutty-tasting sourdough pancake served with *wat*, a variety of stews, some mild, some searingly spicy; you scoop these up with torn-off bits of *injera*.

Southern Africa

In **the south**, you're well-placed to sample game such as giraffe, zebra, impala, guinea fowl, ostrich and crocodile. Wild and exotic as these may

Oddities to sample (and a couple to avoid)

Africa has no end of strange offerings to tempt the culinary curious – at least two of which are definitely best avoided. **Kalia**, fermented mutton preserved in its own fat, is enjoyed with eggs for breakfast in remote parts of southern Morocco. The effect is, quite literally, putrid. **Bushmeat** is a blanket term encompassing wild monkeys, reptiles, antelopes and rodents, some of which may be responsibly hunted and hygienically prepared, but much of which is neither. As a rule, you should consider all primate meat potentially dangerous, and steer clear.

The following are all worth a try, however.

Amarula Elephants are so partial to the fermented windfalls of the marula tree that they will gorge themselves until intoxicated. Amarula, a famous liqueur made from marula fruit, has an elephant on the label; it looks and tastes much like Baileys and is a favourite after-dinner tipple in southern African safari lodges.

Bunny chow A South African takeaway which has nothing to do with Easter, or Bugs: it's a dollop of curried beans or chicken served in a hollowed-out half-loaf of bread or a *roti* (chapati).

Brains, tongues and eyes The juicier parts of the heads of cows and sheep are considered a delicacy in North Africa and may crop up in Nigerian dishes, too. In Tanzania, tongue, heart, liver and lungs are the main ingredients of a stew called *supu* that's served up for breakfast in some rural communities.

Camel meat The Ethiopian answer to steak tartare is *tire siga*, chunks of freshly butchered raw camel steak eaten with lemon juice and *berbere* sauce made from chilli, garlic, ginger, onions and spices.

Clay In Uganda, people chew on chunks of the stuff; it's considered a good natural source of iron and minerals.

Giant snails Archeological evidence suggests that North and West Africans were eating snails long before their European colonizers, the French, caught on. Today, while Moroccans content themselves with small snails as snacks or in soup, the Ghanaians and Togolese tuck into tiger snails, the world's largest land snail, whose stripey shells can grow to 30cm long.

Grasshoppers, locusts and termites Insects deep-fried in oil and served with a dash of chilli sauce are a popular snack in rural Kenya, Uganda, Malawi and several West African countries including Cameroon. They taste much like seafood; the main problem is that the legs and wings can get stuck between your teeth.

Killer bee honey A favourite of the Ju/'hoansi San of the Kalahari, one of Botswana's hunter-gatherer tribes.

Monkeygland sauce Happily, no monkeys are harmed in the making of this condiment, a piquant blend of fruit and spices that's dolloped onto steaks, ribs and chicken at South African *braais*, or into burgers at fast-food joints.

Mopane worms Africa's answer to Australia's witchetty grub, the mopane (pronounced "moparney") worm is the protein-packed caterpillar of the mopane emperor moth. Boiled, sundried and then deep-fried or roasted, they're considered a delicacy by rural southern Africans, who harvest them in their millions by shaking them down from mopane trees. Other tasty larvae eaten in Africa include those of the rhinoceros beetle.

Pee Cola Unique to Ghana and sadly rather hard to find these days, this strong-tasting would-be rival to Coke and Pepsi is named after its creator – Pee being a common enough surname.

sound, they're sourced from game ranches, kudu and eland are among the tastiest. *Biltong* (spiced cured meat, made from any kind of game) is a favourite snack. In Mozambique, the seafood is superb too, particularly when served with hot *peri-peri* sauce.

South Africa's signature dishes are Afrikaner or Cape Malay in origin. They include *potjiekos* (pronounced "poikiekos") – a delicious one-pot stew, carefully assembled in layers and baked in a three-legged cast-iron pot, and *bobotie*, a minced beef curry baked with a thick egg sauce on top. But by far the favourite culinary event down here is the *braai* (pronounced "bry"), an abbreviation of the Afrikaans for barbecue, which has been adopted with gusto all over southern Africa and is as important a part of local social life as barbies are to the Aussies – with macho blokes doing all the cooking. At a bring-and-*braai*, huge steaks, ribs and boerewors sausages (pronounced "booravorce") are grilled over wood or charcoal and served with mealie *pap* (maize porridge, pronounced "pup") and *chakalaka*, a spicy vegetable relish, along with plenty of beer.

Eating out in Africa

For Africans, **eating out** is traditionally a matter of necessity rather than choice – something to be endured when travelling, for example, or working away from home. Africa's major cities have a growing foodie scene but elsewhere, restaurant culture is not nearly as developed as it is in Europe, North America or Australasia. Resort areas have plenty of places to eat which stay open all day, but many target tourists by offering long, crowd-pleasing menus of Western standards such as chicken, pizza, burgers and chips – off-putting to those in search of something more authentic. For the real thing, head to a market or transport stop in the early morning or at lunchtime and tuck into some of the everyday food eaten by local workers and travellers.

Cafés, bistros and restaurants

In African countries with a strong French or Portuguese influence – Morocco, Senegal and Cape Verde, for example – you'll find a scattering of **European-style cafés and bistros** with pavement tables and cool interiors, serving tasty *plats du jour* or *pratos do dia*. The Alliances Françaises (French cultural centres) found in many African cities are also good places to find excellent, simple lunches of steak and salad. North and West African cities also have plenty of **eastern Mediterranean** places including rotisseries and sharwarma bars, while **Chinese restaurants** are found all over the continent.

East and southern Africa is the place to be for a **meat** feast, with steaks, ribs and chops from a considerable array of animal species receiving star billing on the most popular restaurant menus. Almost every urban restaurant which is reasonably close to the ocean, a river or a lake – which means most of them – also serves grilled, baked or stewed fish or seafood, often with delicious spicy sauces.

Simple restaurants often have a policy of having just a few dishes prepared in advance (in Nigeria these are called, plainly enough, **food-is-ready**); anything else on the menu must be prepared to order, which in some cases includes buying the ingredients – a process which naturally takes time. Ordering in advance is a good plan. The commercial districts of many African towns have informal restaurants catering for local workers: in Ghana and Nigeria these are called **chop bars**, elsewhere they're just called **local restaurants**. They're usually basic shacks with a communal table, benches and an open kitchen where the cook dishes up cheap, tasty portions of rice, *fufu* or *sadza* with spicy sauce.

Breakfasts

Wherever you are, hotel and guesthouse breakfasts consist at least of bread, butter, jam and tea or coffee; the swankier the accommodation, the more elaborate the buffet which might accompany this. On a southern safari, the traditional way to wake yourself up for a game drive is with a hot drink and a rusk (a bafflingly hard cookie); later in the morning, once you've worked up an appetite, there'll be a full spread back at your lodge or camp. In the simpler cafés of French-speaking Africa, you may be offered a breakfast of baguette with sweet tea or coffee, and perhaps an omelette; in basic East African eateries, you could try savoury broth or *maandazi* (sweet little doughnuts); while in the south, maize pap, tomato relish and boerewors may be on the menu – a lifesaver after a night on the tiles.

Desserts and fruit

Desserts are not common in Africa but yogurt, pastries and sugary fritters are available in many countries. **Fruit** is abundant just about everywhere, from cascades of oasis and orchard fruit such as figs, dates, raisins, oranges and apricots in North Africa to superb tropical papayas, pineapples, passion fruits, coconuts and many varieties of melon, mango and banana.

Street food

Barbecued skewered meat with French-style bread is a favourite snack to be grabbed on the run – you'll spot stalls at just about any transport stop and market on the continent. Most countries have their own version – examples include *afra* in The Gambia, *brochettes* in francophone North and West Africa, peanut-coated *suya* in Nigeria, *nyama choma* in Kenya and *coupé-coupé* in Central Africa. You order by weight. **Fried snacks** are also immensely popular; these can be dollops of batter in a spicy sauce, or sweet little nuggets of dough (called *beignets* or *panketos* in West Africa and *maandazi* in East Africa).

Meat and vegetable **pies** are found in several countries. In Morocco (particularly Fes) and Algeria, they take the form of *pastillas*, crunchy, sweet and savoury parcels of poultry (traditionally young pigeon meat, but now usually chicken) mixed with ground almonds, cinnamon and beaten egg. Tunisians love *briks à l'oeuf*, fried tuna and runny egg pastries; Indian-style samosas are popular in East Africa and Nigerians make brilliant meat pies.

Other quick snacks include freshly made **sandwiches** (called *bocadillos* in Morocco, sandwiches just about everywhere else) of bread spread with butter and jam or stuffed with boiled egg, spicy meatballs or fish. If you're prepared to sit down with a bowl of something, you can fill up on **pasta** or **rice** with the sauce of the day from any number of street-side sellers. Street food **breakfasts** include porridge, omelettes in bread or offal soup with hot, sweet tea, coffee or a malt drink (any of which may be referred to as tea).

Itinerant vendors peddle **peanuts** or **cashews** wrapped in twists of paper, **biscuits**, **cakes** and whatever **fruit** happens to be in season – if you're on public transport you'll be offered these at every stop.

What if you're vegetarian?

The blunt truth is that in many parts of Africa, you may find the options rather monotonous. Most Africans who can afford it eat meat with every meal. Even in poorer communities, where meat is a delicacy that's not available every day, strictly **vegetarian** dishes are uncommon: chicken leftovers or cheap cuts of beef, goat or mutton are often used to make the stock for soups and stews made from beans, tomatoes, cassava leaves or

---

Mmm, delicious ...

"I was once offered a pig penis by a proud local dignitary in Ghana. The choice was to feign spontaneous death or to eat. It looked like a huge, curly earthworm and, mercifully, it tasted like a huge, curly earthworm." Melanie McGrath

Just in case you find yourself in such a predicament, equip yourself with a few of these phrases, all of which mean "How delicious!"

Afrikaans (southern Africa) *Lekker!*
Amharic (Ethiopia) *Betam konjo no!*
Arabic (Sudan) *Lazeez!*
Madi (Uganda) *Limi da ko!*
Moore (Burkina Faso) *Riba ya soma!*
Shona (Zimbabwe) *Chinonaka!*
SiSwati (Swaziland) *Kumnadzi!*
Swahili (Kenya) *Chakula ni tama sana!*
Twi (Ghana) *Boroboro, eyeh de!*
Zulu (South Africa) *Mnandi!*

other vegetables. You may find yourself eating a lot of omelettes, peanuts and margherita pizzas. Those who eat **fish and seafood** will have an easier time of it, though, as the choices on offer tend to be superb.

You'll also be fine in resorts and lodges catering specifically for Western tourists, which always have at least one or two vegetarian choices on the menu. Restaurants in **North Africa** serve vegetarians pretty well – fresh cheese, olives, salads and dishes based on fava beans, lentils or chickpeas are popular and tasty – while **Indian restaurants** are great for veggie food.

If you're in a position to prepare your own meals rather than relying on restaurant meals, you'll be spoilt for choice, as seasonal vegetables, nuts, eggs and local spices are generally easy to obtain; these can be supplemented with canned vegetables and local or imported cheese.

Buying your own food

If you decide to spend some time **camping** or staying in **self-catering accommodation** – a common enough option in Morocco, South African national parks and the East African coast, among other places – then you'll have the pleasure of browsing local markets, supermarkets, delis and village shops for ingredients. Large towns offer plenty of choice, their food shops stuffed not only with local items but also fresh and frozen imports from all over the continent and beyond. Picking your way through the apparent chaos of a hectic city market and bargaining with spirited vendors for handfuls of vegetables and pinches of spices counts among Africa's quintessential travel experiences. Village supplies tend to be more variable, depending heavily on the time of year and how good the most recent harvests have been.

Local drinks

Green tea in North and West Africa and local **lager** in the east and south are drunk with great gusto to lubricate acquaintances and cement friendships, while in South Africa, **wine** appreciation is taken extremely seriously. Africans like to drink at home or in open-air meeting places; while **bars** (including South African and Zimbabwean township shebeens) can be great places to catch sporting fixtures on TV or hear live music, many have a rather macho atmosphere, and any local woman who makes an appearance is presumed to be on the game.

Tea and coffee

The brewing of strong, sweet **green tea** – a pick-me-up with a powerful kick – is one of Africa's quintessential social rituals. Popular all over the Maghreb, the Sahara and much of West Africa, the brew is poured repeatedly between a pair of small glass tumblers, with great flourish, to make it froth. It's then sipped, noisily and enthusiastically. Two more rounds may be produced from the same pot, with the tea getting sweeter and milder each time. South Africans love **rooibos** or redbush tea, a herbal infusion made from the leaves of a fynbos plant which is only found in a small part of Western Cape Province. East Africa's favourite morning brew is **chai**, a legacy of English and Indian influences, tea with plenty of sugar and milk. Ethiopians like tea perfumed with cinnamon, cardamom or cloves.

Coffee-drinking is a national pastime in North African countries but elsewhere, good, strong coffee is rather uncommon; notable exceptions include Cape Verde, Angola, Mozambique and São Tomé & Príncipe, where *bicas* (espressos) and *galãos* (lattes) are served Portuguese-style, and Ethiopia, where for the sake of authenticity you should try it black with a spoonful of butter. In other countries, instant is the norm – often simply called Nescafé. In West African chop shops and roadside stalls, this is served with sweet condensed milk.

Sodas, juices and water

The **tap water** in many African countries is safe to drink, but if you're in doubt you should purify it (see p.74) or stick to **bottled water**, which is widely sold, though pricey. The range of non-alcoholic drinks sold by most African bars is, disappointingly, limited to locally bottled **sodas**: Coke, Fanta, Sprite, bitter lemon and tonic, with low-sugar versions a rarity. In markets and cafés, however, you may find vendors making fruit juices and smoothies, which can be spectacular, though you may need to ask them to go easy on the sugar and water (and if you're not yet accustomed to local tap water, you should steer clear altogether). In West Africa, street vendors sell little bags of frozen infusions of *gingembre* (ginger, brown), *bouyi* (baobab, white) or *wonjo* or *bissap* (hibiscus, red) – home-made and delicious. Hibiscus is also popular in Egypt, where it's called *karkaday*.

Alcoholic drinks

Most African countries have a favourite local **bottled beer**, typically a lager, which is sold everywhere, no matter how remote. On a lengthy African tour, you'll get a chance to compare a series of national brews and log some of their names – Stella in Egypt, Gazelle in Senegal, Julbrew in The Gambia, Star in Ghana, La Béninoise in Benin, Tusker in Kenya, Kilimanjaro in Tanzania, Windhoek in Namibia, Mosi in Zambia, 2M, pronounced "dosh-em", in Mozambique, Castle in South Africa, and so on. They're as integral a part of national identity as Guinness is in Ireland (although, surprisingly perhaps, Africa also has several Guinness breweries: the black stuff sells fairly well in The Gambia, Nigeria, Kenya, Namibia and South Africa).

Many African communities also make **home brew** from local ingredients. In rural Mali and Ghana, for example, the favourite is millet beer, typically served in a half-calabash, often with a couple of insects doing butterfly in the top. Rwandans make *urwagwa* from fermented banana juice and sorghum flour; Ethiopians make *tej* from honey; and Chibuku Shake Shake, a cheap, yeasty sorghum and maize beer that's as rough as home brew, is marketed commercially throughout southern Africa.

Wine is a less popular tipple, on the whole, because it usually has to be imported (no matter how long they've been independent, French-speaking countries still tend to prefer French wines, while lusophone Africa favours Portuguese). South Africa is the main exception: its world-class wines can be sampled at the wineries of Western Cape Province or at quality restaurants throughout southern Africa and the Indian Ocean islands. For something truly distinctive, try **pinotage**. Ethiopia has some vineyards, too, a legacy of its Italian occupation; Morocco also makes wine, but it's not the best.

The spirits you'll find in African bars tend to be expensive imports, but informal setups sell local firewater, sometimes illicitly: sample these with supreme caution only. West Africans have a tradition of making **palm wine** from fresh or fermented palm sap, while on the islands of Cape Verde and Mauritius, where sugar cane is grown, hard-hitting **rum** (known simply as *grogue* in Cape Verde) is more popular than beer. Kenyans make rum, too, and muddle it with vodka, honey and lime to make *dawa*, a lethal **cocktail** which translates as "medicine".

Money and costs

t's perhaps surprising to find that Africa is, in general, an **expensive** part of the world. Mere survival can be dirt cheap, but anything like a Western lifestyle tends to cost as much, if not more, than in Europe or North America. Less surprisingly, safaris, mountain treks and anything involving renting vehicles can quickly see your costs skyrocket. It's wise to take more than you plan to spend and never a good idea to set off on a longer trip than you can really afford.

That said, if you are travelling on a **tight budget**, you can keep to it by using public transport, eating market food and staying in cheap hotels – with perhaps an occasional free night camping in the bush. Travelling like this, it's possible to get by in many countries on around US$30 per day, say US$1000 a month, though twice as much split between two of you tends to get you more for your money as you can share rooms and meals. It's always much harder to keep costs down in the big cities, where a panoply of tempting comforts and consumables is available and where it's hard to avoid staying in more expensive hotels – likely to be your biggest regular outlay. If you're on a really tight budget, you will probably not be able to do some of the things that you can only do in Africa – such as going on safari – so do try to avoid scrimping. You don't want to deny yourself once-in-a-lifetime experiences, while denying the local economy your hard-earned cash.

Whatever budget you're on, bear the following points in mind:

● Before you leave, **notify your bank** and credit card company about your travels. If you don't, you may find your cards have been blocked when the bank notices unusual transactions, requiring you to call them to explain and clear their use.

- Africa is largely a **cash-based economy**. The infrastructure for card payments is still in its infancy in many regions, and almost non-existent in some countries. Be patient with banking systems, which struggle with poor communications and power cuts.

- If you're **changing hard currency** (euros, UK pounds or US dollars), it's always a good idea to check out the local foreign exchange (forex) bureaux, which are invariably more efficient than the banks, and usually offer a better rate.

- Most countries have done away with currency controls, liberalizing the circulation of foreign currency, meaning that local people can buy US dollars or euros. There is consequently little in the way of a parallel "**black market**" and rarely any reason to buy local currency on the street except for the sake of convenience.

- Try to avoid accepting **large denomination local banknotes**, as anything worth more than about US$20 is likely to be hard to change, especially if you're buying fruit in a market, or paying for a moped ride.

- **Be safe and be insured**. Carry your money and other valuables securely (see p.84) and avoid online banking from internet cafés (see p.149). Check your insurance cover will last the whole trip and, if you're going to be making any claims, be sure to get a police report or clearly itemized receipts.

Costs

Unless you're going to Africa by surface travel from Europe, your single biggest expense is likely to be a **flight** (see p.47). If you're on a big overland trip, organized and pre-booked or travelling independently, another major cost will be **visas** (see p.63). If you allow US$50 per country, that should cover it, although you may not have much change. Another likely significant expense on a long trip is **medication**, both pre-departure jabs, and ongoing malaria protection (see p.71). Give yourself time to get the best deal possible as health and medication providers vary widely in how much they charge.

Once you're on the road, as a very general guide, a twin or double room in a very cheap, basic **hotel** can usually be had for less than US$20, but

Student cards

An **International Student Identity Card** (ISIC; ⓦisic.org) is no guarantee of cheap deals, but is worth waving for many payments (airlines, railways, museum entrance fees) you may make. If you're a student, it's also useful to have a rubber-stamped letter confirming the fact.

only very rarely for less than US$10, while in some cities you could be looking at US$40 or more. The cheaper places are likely to be open to a little gentle bargaining, especially if you plan to stay for several nights. Also be aware that accommodation prices tend to shoot up during the high tourist season (where there is one) and during local holiday and festival periods. Long-distance **road transport** works out at about US$5 per 100km, as a rough average, although of course it varies from country to country, and with the quality and speed of the vehicle. **Train travel,** where it is an option, tends to be somewhat cheaper and **river travel** more expensive. As for **food**, you can usually fill yourself for under US$2 if you eat street food or go to a cheap restaurant in a market or transport park, while a bottle of cold beer from a streetside fridge – the promise of which keeps many overlanders' spirits up – is usually around US$1–2.

At the other end of the spectrum, **tourist-class** or international-standard hotels are predictably expensive in most cities (reckon at least US$100 for a twin or double, and not much less for single-person occupancy). **Car rental** rates are some of the highest in the world: in many countries, US$100 per day for a compact is normal (see p.105), though Morocco, Tunisia, Egypt and South Africa are cheaper. A local guide will cost around US$10 per day in most countries, though if s/he is qualified and also works as your driver, the rate is more likely to be US$20 or more, and can easily skyrocket if you employ a well-known individual. Eating at an international-style, full-service **restaurant**, you should be thinking in terms of US$15–20 for a meal, while air-conditioned **bars and clubs** will generally charge you US$2–5 for a drink.

Entrance fees to the more expensive **national parks** can often be US$40 or more, and the norm is to charge per 24-hour period, which means that low-budget, off-the-shelf, camping safaris priced at less than US$100 per day per person are rare across the continent, while something more comfortable in an exclusive small group of your own is likely to start from around US$200 per day per person. For more on safaris, see p.165.

Although you should be on the lookout for "**tourist prices**", and prepared for people to try to charge you over the going rate (see p.142), the costs of most basic services, including public transport, meals and cheap hotels, are the same for locals and visitors. Where prices are marked, and receipts or tickets issued, they are generally fixed. One important area of difference is in park and museum **entrance fees** and **luxury hotels**, where there are usually two tiers – international visitors and local residents. A distinction is also sometimes made between temporary residents and citizens.

It's difficult to generalize, but the countries of North Africa, especially Morocco and Egypt, are generally somewhat cheaper than most countries

Minimum costs and sample budgets

Each country chapter in the book starts with a box of essential facts and advice, including **minimum costs** (beginning on p.225). The figure given is an estimate of how much it will cost per person per day, *on average*, based on **two economical travellers** spending a month in that country. A figure of US$50 means the two of you would spend US$3000 for the month.

The minimum budget does include **public transport** averaging about 1500km over the month, **simple accommodation** (not necessarily with an en-suite bathroom), **meals** eaten in basic roadside restaurants or at market stalls, a couple of **drinks** in a bar every other day and a more expensive evening once a week. To make the month's minimum budget work, it's assumed you are prepared to take advantage of the occasional offer of **free accommodation** and maybe to sleep on overnight transport once or twice. And although it doesn't assume you'll be **camping**, if you do have your own equipment that obviously makes it easier to manage.

As it's an average, the estimated daily minimum also includes sufficient funds to spend at least a few days doing some of the country's **highlighted activities**, based on the cheapest available options. In Kenya, for example, where the estimated daily minimum is US$50, that might include a short, budget safari, several days car rental and an internal flight. A budget **organized trip** put together by a specialist holiday company covering a similar itinerary might not be much more expensive, although prices vary hugely according to the level of luxury provided, the activities on offer and when you book.

The following possible budgets are per-person costs based on two people travelling together.

Two months through West Africa

Travelling from Dakar to Nigeria or Cameroon by public transport on a low budget is likely to cost you an average of at least US$40 per day, so for a two-month trip you'd be likely to spend around US$2500. The advantage of this region for people with low budgets is that there are relatively few expensive attractions, though if you were hoping to visit any of the national parks, renting a car and perhaps staying in a game lodge would put up your costs considerably.

Two months from Cairo to Nairobi

Although you might start by taking a pleasant train journey up the Nile through inexpensive Egypt, much of this is tough travelling, with parts of Sudan and northern Kenya rugged and rather insecure. You're likely to spend at least half your time in Ethiopia, which has a wealth of things to do and isn't particularly expensive (allow a minimum of US$30 per day for basic costs). So long as you leave major safari plans for a later part of your trip or a return visit, you could do this route for around US$1500.

One month from Kenya to South Africa

Going on safari or tracking gorillas are the big costs in the safari heartlands. If you simply avoid the expensive parks and leave the gorillas for a future return visit, you could get by on US$40 per day, allowing you to do this trip for around US$1200. But if you include a week on a budget camping safari and the US$500 gorilla-tracking permit, you'd be looking at more like US$3000.

in sub-Saharan Africa, while at the other end of the continent, South Africa is also very good value. Your actual costs will always depend on your style of travel, of course.

Currencies

The 55 countries and territories covered in this guide use forty different **currencies**. The currency of the majority of the francophone countries is the **CFA franc**. There are in fact two types of CFA (pronounced "seffa" or "siffa", and standing for Communauté Financière de l'Afrique). All the West African francophone states, with the exceptions of Mauritania and Guinea, are members of the Union Monètaire Ouest Africaine, and these countries, along with Guinea-Bissau, use the West African CFA franc. The francophone countries of Central Africa (with the exceptions of Democratic Republic of Congo, Burundi and Rwanda) also use CFA francs, but of a different regional grouping, the Communauté Économique et Monétaire Financiére de l'Afrique Centrale.

CFA francs are guaranteed by the French treasury and have a fixed value of CFA656 to €1. CFA francs come in coins of 1, 5, 10, 25, 50, 100 and 250 francs, and notes of 500, 1000, 2500, 5000 and 10,000 francs, making this easily the most convenient African currency, in a continent where fistfuls of filthy, low-value notes is the norm.

Although of equal value, the two types of CFA can't be spent outside their own region, and cannot be exchanged in any bank in the region either. Because of French backing, the CFA is a relatively hard currency – major banks in Europe will sometimes exchange CFA francs at their euro equivalent – and currency laws in the countries which use it are generally relaxed. In theory there are limits to the value of CFA you can export, even from one CFA state to another, but in practice these are very rarely enforced and wouldn't inconvenience ordinary travellers.

The countries outside the CFA Franc zone have their own, usually weaker "**soft**" **currencies**, although some are pegged to the euro or US dollar. Most of them are unique, often related to the former colonial power. The currencies of Sierra Leone, Nigeria, Malawi and Zambia, for example, all replaced the British pound, and were originally pegged at 2:1, while Kenya, Uganda and Tanzania inherited shillings, also on par with old, pre-decimalization, British shillings.

Rates of **inflation** in recent years have generally been manageable, except in the case of Zimbabwe. Here, after successive devaluations that saw the government printing banknotes of US$100 trillion Zimbabwe dollars and annual inflation passing 200 million percent, the government gave up the pretence and liberalized foreign currency transactions in 2009. Since then, Zimbabwe's de facto currency has been the US dollar.

Bargaining

General stores, groceries and supermarkets invariably have **fixed prices**. Transport costs are usually subject to state or syndicate control and almost always fixed, but baggage can be haggled over. Pretty well every other service (including budget hotel rooms in most countries) can and should be bargained over.

Some travellers find the whole question of **haggling**, sometimes over the equivalent of a few cents, demeaning to the seller, who is almost certainly poorer than the buyer. In fact it's quite the reverse: you may be taken for a mug if you pay more than the item is worth, while local people will tend to be priced out of that particular market, which leads to resentment of those traders who have access to tourists and their foreign currency. If you want to splash your money around, buy more, and pay a fair price for your purchases, rather than paying over the odds. For advice about giving back and donating, see p.202.

Before starting a bargaining session, try to assess the range of **prices** for what you're interested in by visiting reputable shops and hotel boutiques. It's often possible to get a sense of the real price by chatting to managers and sales staff in these places in a way that's not possible in a market or crafts stall. And when you're in bargaining mode try to avoid looking too much like a tourist – leave the camera in the hotel and wear the sort of clothes a resident expat might dress in.

Bargaining itself is often just a case of showing reluctance to pay what you're told is the going rate, and in turn getting some sort of "discount". There's enormous flexibility around a few immutable rules. The most important is never to engage in bargaining if you've no intention of buying the service or item at any price. To offer what you thought was a silly price and then refuse to pay it can cause grave offence.

When negotiating, don't automatically assume you're in the clutches of a rip-off merchant. Concepts of honour are very important, and stalls are often minded by the owners' friends and relatives with whom you can sometimes strike real bargains. Most importantly, men should make physical contact – hand-clasping (a prolonged handshake) is usually enough to emphasize a point. Be as jocular as possible and don't be shy of making a big scene – the bluffing and mock outrage on both sides are part of the fun. Women can't pursue these negotiating tactics in quite the same way, except when buying from women – invariably much tougher anyway.

If you're very keen on a **particular item**, it obviously doesn't serve your cause to display massive enthusiasm. Feigning disinterest, and maybe including it as part of a bigger deal on a selection of things, is a much better tactic. As usual, wearing sunglasses is always helpful in disguising your feelings, if possibly a little rude in this context. Removing them at just the right moment to emphasize a point can sometimes work wonders, however.

> ## Received with thanks
>
> Petty bureaucracy is deeply engrained in Africa and you will often be given a handwritten, carbon-copied and sometimes even rubber-stamped **receipt** after making the most elementary payment. If you doubt whether the sum you're being asked to pay is officially sanctioned, however – for example, an obscure entrance fee, a fee for a guide, or on occasions when police try to impose an on-the-spot fine – just asking for a receipt will often clarify matters.

Getting down to figures, try to delay the moment when you have to name **your price**: you want the seller to pitch first. You can often avoid silly first prices by having a chat and establishing your streetwise credentials. When you hear "One hundred, how much you pay?", say nothing. It's amazing how often the seller's price drops way below your expectation before you've made any offer, so forget the standard "offer-a-third-come-up-to-a-half" formulas, and if the seller is happy to make two or three successively lower bids for every one of yours, you should be happy. If you seem to have reached a stalemate, a bored companion tugging your sleeve can often help to move the price that final notch. But if you do arrive at an unbridgeable gap you can always drop the matter and come by later – though that will indicate your preparedness to pay more.

Debit and credit cards

The simplest way to get local cash is to make withdrawals using your current account (checking account) **debit card** from an **ATM**. Cards with either a Visa or Mastercard/Maestro/Cirrus symbol (nearly all cards) work in most ATMs: the ideal would be to have one of each. ATMs are steadily springing up in towns and even more rural areas in many countries and the flat transaction fee is usually fairly small – though all those small charges do eventually add up. Be security-conscious when using an ATM; many are physically protected by a cabin, but you should also check that the slot hasn't been tampered with, as card-reading scams are an ongoing problem in countries where an ATM network is being rapidly rolled out.

Credit cards are very useful for large payments and can sometimes be used to obtain a cash advance, either at an ATM or over a bank counter. Cash advances are generally possible in the more developed countries and in the CFA zone, though you will always have to track down the right bank. Remember a credit-card cash advance is a loan, with interest accruing daily from the date of withdrawal. Visa and MasterCard are the widely recognized cards (with Visa enjoying a definite advantage and other cards having next to no recognition) and can increasingly be used for payment

ATM coverage

Coverage varies across the continent, from one **ATM** in the capital to thousands spread throughout the country. In some countries, such as Gabon, Guinea, Madagascar and Rwanda, ATM reliability is an issue and machines don't always function properly. In most countries, however, coverage is improving rapidly – to check ATM locations, visit ⓦbit.ly /ATMs-Mastercard or ⓦbit.ly/VisaATMs.

	Visa	Mastercard/ Maestro/ Cirrus		Visa	Mastercard/ Maestro/ Cirrus
Algeria	✓	-	Libya	✓	✓
Angola	✓	✓	Madagascar	✓	-
Benin	✓	-	Malawi	-	✓
Botswana	✓	✓	Mali	✓	-
Burkina Faso	✓	-	Mauritania	✓	-
Burundi	-	-	Mauritius	✓	✓
Cameroon	✓	-	Mayotte	✓	-
Cape Verde	✓	-	Morocco	✓	✓
CAR	-	-	Mozambique	✓	✓
Chad	✓	-	Namibia	✓	✓
Comoros	-	-	Niger	-	-
Congo Republic	-	-	Nigeria	✓	✓
DRC	✓	✓	Réunion	✓	✓
Côte d'Ivoire	✓	-	Rwanda	✓	-
Djibouti	✓	✓	São Tomé & Príncipe	-	-
Egypt	✓	✓	Senegal	✓	✓
Equatorial Guinea	-	-	Seychelles	-	✓
Eritrea	-	-	Sierra Leone	✓	-
Ethiopia	✓	-	South Africa	✓	✓
Gabon	✓	-	Sudan	-	-
The Gambia	✓	-	Swaziland	-	✓
Ghana	✓	✓	Tanzania	✓	✓
Guinea	✓	-	Togo	✓	-
Guinea-Bissau	-	-	Tunisia	✓	✓
Kenya	✓	✓	Uganda	✓	✓
Lesotho	✓	✓	Zambia	✓	✓
Liberia	-	-	Zimbabwe	✓	✓

at high-end hotels, top restaurants and other large businesses. You will usually have to sign; PIN-based automatic payment is still a rarity.

Travellers' cheques

Travellers' cheques have never been an easy solution to carrying money in Africa, and now that ATMs and credit card payment services are emerging, their days are numbered. As well as inspecting your passport, banks often require to see the receipt for the original purchase of the cheques. But the real problem is that many bank staff are no longer familiar with them, and the process can take hours. Make sure you keep a safe record of the serial numbers separately from the cheques themselves. In the event your cheques are lost or stolen, the issuing company will expect you to report the loss immediately before reissuing them.

Cash and the "black market"

Having some cash in a **hard currency** (probably US dollars, UK pounds or euros) is always convenient, for when the ATMs don't exist, aren't working or have run out of local currency. But it's also risky, so US$250–500 is probably the most you would want to carry around. US dollars are widely accepted as payment for more expensive goods and services, as are euros, especially in the CFA Franc countries. CFA prices converted to euros tend to work out a little under the official fixed rate of CFA656 to €1 (a commission for the work of exchanging the money, you'll be told), so expect to pay €1 for CFA640 or CFA650 at the most.

The denominations of euros, UK pounds or US dollars that you carry should be as small as you can manage, bearing in mind the issue of counterfeit high denominations of US dollars "(see box below)", and also bearing in mind the likelihood that once you've changed your greenbacks or other hard currency the local banknotes you get in return may often be in the form of very big, and often rather soggy and ragged bundles, each unhygienic note worth just a few cents.

When you reach a border town with **surplus local currency**, you may not always be able to change it back easily at banks or forex bureaux (and when it is possible to do so you'll get a lower rate than you paid for it), but it can generally be exchanged with ease in the street or at a shop on the parallel market – the so-called **black market** – no longer considered illegal in the liberalized economies of most African countries. Border-town moneychangers often carry the currencies of several neighbouring countries and, as long as you know the exchange rate, using them is convenient and usually straightforward.

Africa and the US dollar

People are widely suspicious of US$100 bills, which have acquired some notoriety as popular subjects for **counterfeiting**, and businesses will often refuse them, especially if they are more than five years old. The details of the practice vary from country to country. However, small denomination notes are often unacceptable, too, as the rates for exchanging them back into local currency can be poor. Notes of US$20 and US$50 are a good compromise. Similar issues may arise around large denomination euro and UK pound notes, and even high-denomination local-currency notes can arouse suspicion, especially when newly issued.

If you do use the parallel market, either at a border town, or when you arrive somewhere out of hours and can't find a working ATM, you should avoid literally standing in the street for the transaction. Either use a shop-based currency trader (just ask around), or adjourn to a shop or somewhere similar with the dealer and count everything before handing over your cash. Always be sure you know the approximate rate of exchange, use a calculator if you need to, and, if possible, be accompanied: two pairs of eyes and ears are better than one.

Wiring money

Having money **wired** from home is easy, but because of the cost – typically 2.5 to 6 percent as a flat transaction charge (the more you send the smaller the percentage) and a 3 to 5 percent commission on the conversion rate – it's probably still a last resort. Money is usually only paid out in the local currency. Using the companies' websites, you can wire money to yourself (beware of doing this from an internet café), paying on your credit card and picking it up at your nominated local agent.

● **MoneyGram** ⓦ **moneygram.com.**
● **Western Union** ⓦ **westernunion .com.**

Tipping

Tipping is an area of much discussion for travellers in Africa. Many local people are so poor that they won't hesitate to hold a hand out to request a gift for the slightest service, or even just because you can afford to give one. But you'll also meet professional people on very low salaries who wouldn't dream of asking for money, and who will take pride in helping you out and having a conversation.

Staff at **cheap hotels**, roadside **restaurants**, **bars** and **cafés** don't expect tips, though leaving some

Lost in conversion

The first two weeks of travel in Mauritania with my girlfriend Ania had gone swimmingly. But things got way out of hand one afternoon when an older couple who drove us all the way from Chinguetti to Nouakchott demanded 20,000 Ougiya (around US$70) for the ride once we had arrived – having quoted us only 5000 Ougiya at the start. When I refused to pay up, the husband became extremely angry and almost instantaneously several dozen men arrived from nowhere and surrounded us in the street. I yelled at the man in Arabic that I would call the police. Maybe the Arabic was a bad idea – perhaps I should have acted baffled? He responded "Fine, let's go to the police" and his wife pushed Ania against the van. At that point, for better or worse, my adrenaline kicked in. I reached into my pocket for my wad of small bills, totalling maybe US$30, threw them into the air at the crowd, and we both ran for it. I never found out what had gone wrong, but something was definitely lost in translation. It's often wise to get the price in writing.

Roger Norum
ⓦ rogernorum.com

small change or the equivalent of a dollar is always welcome. You never tip on **public transport**, whether it's a train or bus, or a more chaotic shared taxi-minibus. Similarly, nobody ever tips **taxi drivers**, since they rarely have working meters (or any meter at all), and tend to work for themselves and hustle for the best fare they can get from you, even when they are supposed to be sticking to approved prices.

If you're staying at a full-service, tourist or **international-class hotel**, with porters and room staff, then roughly US\$1 to carry your bags on arrival is about right (these jobs are much sought after for exactly that reason). Although the room-introduction ritual is tiresome the world over, there shouldn't be any need to tip staff again during your stay, though you might want to leave a collective tip for all the staff on your departure, in the staff tip box which many hotels have in the lobby, which should ensure that all the backroom, kitchen and maintenance staff share it. If you do that, then US\$10–20 per room per day would be generous. In the more expensive city and resort **restaurants**, ten percent tip for the waiting staff is the norm. You wouldn't normally tip in cheaper, family-run restaurants or local eating spots.

Safari guides are a special case. Good guides are far more than animal spotters: they are often gifted linguists, practical in every way, and excellent bush companions. Many will have trained for years and passed national exams in their profession (see p.170). In turn, some visitors become close friends of their guides and are drawn back to the same company to renew the friendship. Guides usually earn reasonable salaries by local standards, but clients' tips still make up a large proportion of their income, accounting sometimes for more than half their earnings.

Tipping can often cause misunderstandings between clients, who are usually expected to organize themselves to give **collective gratuities** on the last day of the safari. Good companies make suggestions in their briefing packs, but you should budget for between US\$5–10 per member of staff per day from each client – perhaps slightly more for a small, upmarket group and less for a large group or a **budget** camping trip. For great service, where you've relied on just one guide, you might show your appreciation with even more. If these figures sound like a lot in local terms – and they are – bear in mind that people employed in the tourist industry may spend many weeks each year not working and not earning a cent.

Staying in touch

Gone are the days when you could disappear in Africa for weeks at a time, emerging sporadically to contact family and friends by reverse-charge phone call, or to pick up precious airmail letters from a remote post office. With the ubiquity of mobile phones and the internet, the humble letter is less significant in twenty-first century travel, but there are still occasions when you may need to receive something in the post or even post something yourself.

It's easier to get the basics of communications sorted in advance of travelling, so don't leave things until you actually need them late at night in an unfamiliar city. Check that your cellphone is unlocked (see opposite) and that your provider has enabled roaming, ensure your webmail, Facebook, Twitter and Skype accounts are operative, and copy any software or files you want onto a memory stick or a CD.

Phones and cellphones

The **landline telephone** systems in most countries (the North African region and South Africa excepted) are poorly maintained and in many cases all but defunct. If you have access to a landline phone, or you can find a working payphone (some large post offices have working boxes), then you should be able to call internationally. Some countries also offer prepaid calling cards. Reverse charge or collect calls ("PCV" in French) are possible from most countries.

Mobile phone technology has transformed communications: most adults have access to a basic model and few people rely on the old telephone systems. In fact there are mobile masts in many areas where

IDD codes

To make an **international call**, dial the international access code, which is usually 00 (or +), followed by the country code, then the number you want, omitting any initial zero. **Country codes** for each African country are given in the fact file at the start of each country profile, from p.223.

wired telephone networks have never been installed. Unless your mobile is very old, it is almost certain to work in Africa, but very high charges make using it on roaming unattractive for anything but emergencies. Instead, it's often better to buy a local **pay-as-you-go SIM card** (usually costing the equivalent of US$2–3) to temporarily replace your home SIM. Check with your service provider before you travel that your phone is not locked to their network (unlocking, if necessary, can be done anywhere, but it's one more hassle), and remember to store your numbers on your phone's memory rather than the original SIM, otherwise they won't be available when you change it. Once you have inserted a local SIM, you can buy airtime vouchers in many outlets. Of course, your usual number will be unavailable, so your first calls or texts will simply be to notify people of your temporary in-country number.

Internet access

Internet cafés are increasingly widespread, with most cities offering hundreds of outlets, but they can still be thin on the ground in rural areas, where they may consist of little more than a PC in a store that also offers stationery and photocopying. **Connections** can be painfully slow and **power cuts** are a frequent hassle – warn your contacts, and be diligent about saving and backing up. **Wi-fi** hot spots are still relatively rare, but some hotels and coffee chains offer them, usually for a small charge. Browsing charges are generally the equivalent of one or two US cents per minute. The alternative, using a hotel "business centre", can cost up to US$1 per minute. Don't expect all internet café PCs to be equipped with **USB ports** or CD burners and prepare for some frustrations as you adjust to unfamiliar keyboard layouts. **Skype** is usually installed at internet café terminals.

Of course using a public computer to access secure data carries with it inherent **risks** and it's wise to avoid doing any internet banking or using important passwords. You could install antivirus and anti-spyware, if the business allows you to do so (the free Hotspot Shield – ⓦhotspotshield .com – is highly rated), but then they could themselves be your security risk, so always erase your tracks by deleting your history, passwords and downloads. For a list of useful news sites, discussion boards and other **online resources**, see p.418.

Laptops and netbooks

With a 3G **mobile phone**, you can get online in most countries, either roaming with your home service provider or using a local SIM card. Data costs can mount up terrifyingly fast, however, so for most people this is only an emergency option. Alternatively, if you take a **laptop or netbook**, you can in many countries buy a local ISP's modem and SIM card (a "dongle") to give you mobile broadband access. The hardware and pay-as-you-go rates are dropping all the time across the continent and connectivity and speeds are improving, but be prepared for some frustration if you're aiming to do more than send emails and browse. And whatever you select, ensure everything is working before you leave the shop.

Taking a laptop or netbook raises its own set of problems of **weight and security** (see p.84), so get the lightest machine that does what you need it to do, and ensure you back up regularly to a virtual storage facility of some kind, such as Apple's iDisk. Most machines are too expensive to be covered by ordinary travel insurance, so if you lose it, it's gone. If you can accept that, there's no question that being able to access the internet when you need to (more or less: there are still huge gaps in coverage, and many towns where data connections are few and far between) can be extremely convenient, while having a place to download and sort **photos** is worth the hassle on its own to some travellers.

Keeping it zipped

In The Gambia, why would it not be a good idea to ask if you can take a Mandinka-speaker's *photo*? In Arabic, why is it important to roll the "r" when asking for a chair? And why should you refer to a zip fastener as a *slide* fastener when explaining it to a class of tittering English students in an Arabic-speaking country?

The answer, as I found out to my cost and their amusement, is sex. Because in each case you sound as if you're referring to genitalia. In Arabic, *kurrsi* is a chair, but *kusi* is a vagina, while *zip* means penis – as does *foto* in Mandinka.

And while I remember, there's a reason why my friend Nicholas doesn't shorten his name to Nick in Arabic-speaking countries: *nik* means "fuck". Take care now!

Peter Verney
Ⓦ sudanupdate.org

Mail and addresses

There is a main **post office** with a poste restante service in every country's capital city and usually several larger towns, holding mail for collection (though provincial deliveries can easily take a week longer or more). In English-speaking countries, you should look for the general post office, or GPO, in francophone countries the Hôtel des Postes or PTT (Postes, Télécommunications et Télédiffusion) and in Portuguese-speaking countries the Correio or CTT. There are often separate counters (*guichets* in French) for different services, so make sure you're in the right queue. From Europe, allow two to three weeks for post to be received. Tell your senders to address envelopes clearly to your surname, in upper case letters, followed by your first name, then "Poste Restante" and the name of the city and country. If anyone sends you a package, there's a high risk of not receiving it. Assuming it does arrive and there's a note in poste restante advising you of the fact, it may be opened and inspected in front of you, and you may have to pay import duty on the contents. Ask the sender to ensure they indicate that it's a gift of little value.

If you have urgent **mail to send**, the best place is usually not the main post office but the airport, from where mail is often sent on the next flight out. For parcels, it's best to use a courier service such as DHL, which is widely represented, rather than risking your items vanishing in the sorting office.

The postman rarely comes in Africa. **Mail** is usually sorted into post office boxes, or PO boxes (BP in French, CP in Portuguese) or sometimes into Private Mail Bags (PMB) and recipients have to visit their boxes with their key and collect their mail. Usually, the lower the number, the older the address (the French Embassy in Senegal, for example, is BP 2, Dakar), which can sometimes be a useful indication of long-established credentials when making bookings or enquiries. For more on city addresses, see the box on p.98.

Newspapers, radio and TV

Of the **foreign press**, weekly editions of British, French and American newspapers reach areas with substantial expat populations, and in the main tourist areas of Morocco, Tunisia, The Gambia, Egypt, Kenya, Tanzania and South Africa you can find a fair number of yesterday's papers in the busier resorts in high season. You'll find some of them, along with *Time*, *The Economist* and *Jeune Afrique* available in hotel lobbies and, a few days later, from street vendors.

Newspapers

There was a rebirth of the **local press** across much of Africa with the movement towards multi-party democracy in the early 1990s. Countries that formerly had almost no newspapers often now have a thriving press, and reading local papers can give you a true insight into what makes a country tick – letters pages can be fascinating.

Critical and independent editors, however, can still find themselves in serious trouble with governments – or government figures – who are uncomfortable with scrutiny of their policies or personal behaviour. **Reporters Without Borders** (Ⓦen.rsf.org) publish an annual Press Freedom Index gauging **censorship** and journalistic rights: in 2010,

Namibia was Africa's best performer, while truly out-worsting the competition was Eritrea in bottom place. Equatorial Guinea, Tunisia, Sudan and, perhaps surprisingly, Rwanda, also performed very poorly, while Benin, Togo, Liberia, Burkina Faso and Cape Verde were more respectable. By comparison, the UK was at 19, the USA at 20, Spain at 39, France at 44 and Singapore at 136.

Radio and TV

Along with the print media, national and local **radio stations** have blossomed in recent years. It's now common to have dozens of national and local stations, although, like the press, they're frequently subject to all sorts of harassment. **National TV** stations usually combine an uninspired mix of deeds and words from government ministers with imported movies, "Nollywood" soaps and dramas (from Nigeria) and Egyptian or Latin American soaps. Most hotel TVs these days receive satellite channels, so you'll be able to watch BBC World News and CNN if you are so inclined.

Long pre-dating these services, **BBC World Service radio** is a real institution across the continent (you'll soon start hearing

Press Freedom Index 2010: Africa table

Namibia	21	Gabon	107
Cape Verde	26=	Burundi	108
Ghana	26=	Djibouti	110
Mali	26=	Chad	112
South Africa	38	Guinea	113
Tanzania	41	Congo Republic	114
Burkina Faso	49	Madagascar	116
Togo	60	Côte d'Ivoire	118
Botswana	62	Zimbabwe	123
Mauritius	65=	The Gambia	125
Seychelles	65=	Egypt	127
Guinea-Bissau	67	Cameroon	129
Central African Republic	69	Algeria	133
Benin	70=	Morocco	135
Comoros	70=	Ethiopia	139
Kenya	70=	Nigeria	145
Malawi	79	DRC	148
Zambia	82	Swaziland	155
Liberia	84	Libya	160
Lesotho	90	Somalia	161
Sierra Leone	91	Tunisia	164
Senegal	93	Equatorial Guinea	167
Mauritania	95	Rwanda	169
Uganda	96	Sudan	172
Angola	104=	Eritrea	178
Niger	104=		

that distinctive signature tune, "Lilliburlero", in the most remote corners of the continent). They produce several excellent Africa Service programmes, including the morning magazine *Network Africa* and the vital news analysis programme, *Focus on Africa*, broadcast in the afternoon and evening Monday to Friday. If you're travelling for any length of time, it's a good idea to invest in a pocket-sized radio that includes short wave, though the World Service can also be heard on FM in many cities. For details of current schedules and frequencies, check Ⓦbbc.co.uk /worldservice.

With a short-wave radio you can also pick up the Voice of America (Ⓦvoa.gov) and other international broadcasters. The **internet** is also increasingly important for national broadcasters, but local radio stations have been first off the ground with live feeds, providing an invaluable way to get in the mood before you arrive in Africa. There's a selection from most countries at Ⓦlive-radio.net/africa.shtml.

Wildlife and safaris

Africa's **wildlife** has been hit heavily by human population growth and the spread of agriculture and industry, but there is still plenty to see, and many first-time visitors to the national parks are bowled over to see giraffes, antelopes and zebras grazing as casually as sheep and cows back home. From the ubiquitous lizards and monkeys to hundreds of varieties of birds and most of the earth's remaining megafauna – giant mammals like rhinos, elephants and giraffes – Africa's animal spectacle is still intact, just. Vast areas remain if not untouched then still little disturbed, either too remote to be easily exploited, or accessible enough but adequately protected.

The continent puts on a spectacular display of **trees and plants**, too, encompassing everything from South Africa's unique karoo vegetation (a riot of colour when it bursts into flower in the southern spring) to the unmistakeable shapes of baobabs silhouetted on the horizon. If you're a big fan of flora, then Africa will knock you out, and the best safari guides know their plants and trees almost as well as their animals.

The most animal-rich countries stretch from Kenya to South Africa and include hundreds of parks, reserves and sanctuaries, all of which can be visited independently or, more often, as part of an organized tour – a **safari**. For a first-time experience of game-watching, it's best to focus on an area with good facilities where the wildlife is abundant and easy to see. Kenya, Uganda, Tanzania, Zambia, Botswana, Namibia and South Africa meet those criteria: all of them have safari-friendly parks and reserves that are excellent for zebra, buffalo and giraffe, a wide variety of antelope species, the three big cats (leopard, cheetah and lion), elephants and hippos. Rhinos are also present in certain parks in these countries.

Away from the safari heartlands, the rest of the continent doesn't have the same wildlife concentrations, although there are many major national parks that are worth taking in if you're an enthusiastic naturalist. It's worth remembering that some of the best offshore **whale-watching** in the world can be done in South Africa, while Madagascar offers a wildlife experience that can only be compared with the Galapagos islands for its unique and astonishing diversity.

Going **on safari** can be expensive, with park entry fees ranging from a few dollars to more than US$100 a day. But don't be too despondent if you're on a strict budget: outside the parks, it's possible to see a good variety of Africa's birds and mammals just by travelling through their habitats. Roads across the continent pass through desert and savanna, dry woodland, lowland rainforest, and cooler, moor-covered uplands above the tree line. If you're travelling by public transport, it pays to spend a little more on a seat at the front, giving you the best chance of seeing wildlife.

Where to see wildlife

Most countries in Africa have some sort of **national park** network. Entrance fees, facilities and access (some parks are closed during the rainy season) vary considerably. Some of the smaller parks and reserves are low-key enough – and certain enough of not harbouring dangerous predators – to permit entrance on foot. Whichever parks you visit, a pair of good, lightweight binoculars is essential for game-spotting and birdwatching.

In **East** and **southern Africa**, Kenya, Uganda, Tanzania, Zambia, Botswana, Namibia and South Africa have the greatest number of parks and reserves. **Central Africa** has some magnificent if remote parks, several incorporating large regions of virtually unexplored rainforest, but for now, the lack of infrastructure, and the security problems in the region, threaten the viability of many of them. **West Africa**'s main parks are vulnerable to the spread of farming and herding, but the best of them – in Benin, Ghana, Senegal and Nigeria – are comparable with those of East and southern Africa. **North Africa** has just a few national parks and there's little large wildlife, though there are isolated populations of leopards and cheetahs in one or two areas in the Sahara.

Watching wildlife is more than a question of getting yourself to the nearest national park or patch of forest or savanna. While some locations boast an extraordinary density of species, in many parts of the continent you're likely to gravitate to specific areas to see particular animals.

Primates

In sub-Saharan Africa, the animals you'll see most often out by the road are **monkeys**, of which Africa has more than fifty species. You should be

Gorillas

I felt closer to death than at any other point in my life. When they say "don't look a silverback in the eye", they mean it. I kept my camera glued to my face and stood my ground. I half saw, half felt this massive boulder of muscle and raw power thundering towards me. Then he stopped a few metres away, turned, sneered over his shoulder with a look that said "you're not worth the effort" and lumbered back to his tree-top nest.

It had taken us six hours to machete our way through the choking lantanas and jungle of DRC's Virunga National Park, firstly to find where the group had been the previous day, then to track them to last night's nesting place and finally to follow that trail to today's location, all in the cloying humidity. Once we'd arrived, though, it was beyond worth it for the precious sixty minutes spent in the presence of these extraordinary creatures. Maintaining the minimum distance of five metres is so difficult, not least because cheeky and daring youngsters will approach and even touch you if you are as fortunate as I was. To me, the most overwhelming realization was that ultimately the only real differences are their thick black fur and our power of speech. Truly humbling, and one of the best experiences of my life.

Fiona McDuie

cautious of close encounters with the fairly large, dog-like baboons which, from The Gambia to Cape Town's Table Mountain, can be a serious menace as they have grown accustomed to feeding on scraps. Male baboons, in particular, can be intimidating and dangerous. Other monkeys, for example populations of vervet and Sykes' monkeys on the coast of Kenya, have also become habituated to humans and frequently grab food or anything else that takes their fancy.

The monkeys' large cousins, the **great apes** – gorillas, chimpanzees and pygmy chimps or bonobos – are infinitely rarer and more localized and you're very unlikely to chance upon them in the forest: sightings have to be organized and usually involve expensive treks to visit habituated groups. West Africa has small and isolated populations of chimpanzees between Senegal and Ghana. Guinea's Monts Nimba Reserve is the most likely place to track them in West Africa. The best places to see chimps, however, are further east, in Uganda's Kibale Forest and at Tanzania's Mahale Mountains National Park and Gombe Stream – the latter made famous by researcher Jane Goodall.

From eastern Nigeria eastwards, the great ape habitats are slightly more numerous – all the Central African countries have chimpanzees, and lowland gorillas are found in suitable rainforest habitats. The fascinatingly promiscuous bonobo is restricted to one country – the Democratic Republic of the Congo (DRC), south of the River Congo itself – while the highly endangered mountain gorilla is only found in the highlands of eastern DRC, Uganda and Rwanda. Tracking gorillas is a highlight of many people's trips, with a handful of habituated groups of mountain gorillas the usual subjects. To the west, you can also track lowland gorillas in Central African Republic (CAR), Cameroon, Congo Republic and

Gorilla tracking

Wildlife-tracking excursions raise funds for research and conservation programmes, and offer a glimpse of wildlife management in action. You may set off by vehicle or on foot, with guides either using traditional tracking methods (looking for fresh tracks, dung, calls and other signs, keeping quiet and staying downwind), or carrying an antenna whose signal changes as you approach a radio-collared animal.

You can track a number of species, including big cats, wild dogs and chimps in Tanzania and Uganda, but the endangered **mountain gorillas** of Uganda, Rwanda and DRC are the best-known subjects. Entrance is only by special permit, which tend to be very limited in number, often booked up months and even years in advance, and extremely pricey (one-day gorilla-tracking permits in Uganda cost US$500). You will be following animals that are wild but have been habituated to the presence of humans by conservationists. Months of patient work have reassured them that they don't need to resort to aggression or escape when their main predator – man – comes into close range.

The surge of adrenaline and emotion that comes with your first glimpse of your subjects is ample reward for the long slog along steep, humid forest paths walled in with green. Sightings are never guaranteed, but the experience of tracking animals through an unspoilt landscape is tremendously enjoyable in itself.

Gabon. Wherever you plan to track gorillas, set aside several days for the experience and reserve a place as far ahead as you can (see box above).

Madagascar is the only place in the world where you'll see **lemurs** in the wild – the primates evolved on the island in a completely separate line from mainland monkeys and apes. There are more than 100 species here, ranging from the **mouse lemurs** to the baboon-sized **indri**, and including the spectacular **ring-tailed lemur** and the grotesque, gremlin-like **aye-aye**. Many species are relatively easy to see once you've reached their parks and reserves.

Antelopes and other grazing animals

Gazelles and other small **antelope** are quite common across much of the continent, especially in the scrubby bush of West Africa south of the Sahel, and in the east and southern African savanna regions. Other, mostly larger species, including bushbuck, kob, waterbuck, hartebeest and eland are also found across the savanna from West Africa to Kenya. In Central, East and southern Africa they join more than a dozen other species, including greater and lesser kudu, bongo, sitatunga, impala, and sable antelope.

Fairly common and widespread throughout sub-Saharan Africa is the **buffalo** or Cape buffalo (not the same animal as the domesticated Asian water buffalo, which can be seen working the fields in Egypt). They're sometimes encountered in huge herds of hundreds of animals, which are not usually threatening, but beware of solitary bulls, which can be dangerous.

Don't confuse the buffalo with the **wildebeest**, which is more of a goat than a cow. One of Africa's archetypal scenes is the Serengeti-Mara ecosystem's annual wildebeest migration, in which as many as a million white-bearded wildebeest move across the savanna in search of fresh pasture, pursued by local predators in a vast feeding frenzy. Elsewhere in East and southern Africa, wildebeest tend to be less nomadic.

There are three species of **zebra**: the localized mountain zebra in South Africa and Namibia; the finely striped, big-eared Grevy's zebra in northern Kenya and Ethiopia; and the much more prolific common or Burchell's zebra across the east and southern African savanna arc, from Ethiopia to Angola. They're often seen mingling with wildebeest herds and other plains game, using other species as decoys in the event of an attack by hyenas or lions.

Throughout North Africa, and in most of the more arid parts of West and East Africa, you're likely to see **camels**. These are the single-humped Arabian camel, or dromedary, and all of them are domestic animals. When not working, they're usually tethered or hobbled to keep them from straying. They can be a problem on the roads in North Africa, especially at night, when they often cause accidents.

You may be surprised how often you see wild pigs – usually **warthogs**. From Senegal to Sudan and from Ethiopia to South Africa, even in very arid areas, you can see warthog families scurrying across the plain, tails pointing up in alarm, raising dust like a wagon train. Much rarer are three long-haired, nocturnal relatives: the **bushpig**, its close relation the **red river hog** and their distant cousin the even more hirsute – and slightly terrifying – **giant forest hog**.

Hippos, though more familiar, have a deservedly dangerous reputation, especially when accidentally trapped on dry land or panicked in the water (see p.220). They are nocturnal, dozing in the water by day, and emerging at dusk to spend the night grazing. You're quite likely to see them from a boat on any lake or large river between Timbuktu and the Limpopo, with huge pods sometimes seen in Liwonde National Park in Malawi and Katavi in western Tanzania. The hippo's miniature cousin, the **pygmy hippo**, found only in Sierra Leone, Liberia and Côte d'Ivoire, is extremely rare, and you're very unlikely to see one unless you spend night after night patiently waiting for one to cross your path at Tiwai Island sanctuary in Sierra Leone.

Elephants

Elephants survive in dwindling numbers in a surprising number of countries – across most of sub-Saharan Africa in fact – but most populations are in a dire predicament, isolated and threatened by poaching. By contrast, in countries where hunting is banned and poaching largely under control, such as Kenya, the elephant population in some areas exceeds the capacity of the ecosystem to sustain it, and herds then threaten neighbouring farms and plantations. Migration corridors are kept open, where possible, to allow elephants to migrate in search of food and water.

Watching elephants is always a joy, particularly because their behaviour and social life often seem to have uncanny parallels with human society: tumbling toddlers, stroppy teenagers and wise old aunts spring to mind frequently. The best places to see large herds are the parks of Kenya and Tanzania (particularly Amboseli and Tarangire), Kruger in South Africa, Okavango in Botswana, and South Luangwa in Zambia. For dramatic encounters, you could do worse than the desert elephants of Etosha in Namibia and Gourma in Mali, though to see the latter you'll need to get your seasonal timing right and be very lucky.

Rhinos

Africa's two species of rhino are very different beasts, but both bear the highly valuable horns composed of dense hair-like keratin that are used in traditional Chinese medicine. The larger, slightly hump-backed **white rhino** is a placid grazer whose population in managed environments has recovered from fifty in South Africa at the beginning of the twentieth century to more than 15,000 in southern Africa and Kenya today. Hluhluwe-Imfolozi Game Reserve in South Africa was the focus of this programme and still has more than 1500 white rhinos.

The more aggressive, solitary, bush-browsing **black rhino** (individuals of neither species have any notable colour beyond the tone of the mud they last rolled in) faces severe challenges to its continued survival, as it needs a securely fenced habitat or round-the-clock armed protection from poachers. Scattered populations are confined to eastern and southern African sanctuaries and amount to fewer than 3000 individuals. Lewa and Ol Pejeta in Kenya, Ngorongoro in Tanzania and northern Damaraland in Namibia, which has the biggest population, are the best places to see them.

Giraffes

Giraffes, which browse on trees rather than graze, are found in open, wooded country across much of Africa from Ethiopia to South Africa and Angola, with small, scattered populations further west in CAR,

Meeting in the bush

I had spent a full day on a game walk, stomping around Mole National Park in northern Ghana looking for elephants with an armed guide. I had cut my hands on sharp reeds and destroyed my shoes in sucking mud. "Stick close", the guide kept hissing. "They can be very dangerous, especially the solitary ones." But there was nothing to be seen but a troop of warthogs and a few antelope. It was the rainy season, and they told us that was normal.

Back at the lodge, I opted to rent one of their old bikes to cycle to the nearest village. The sun was starting to set, forcing me to turn back again, when suddenly, fifty metres ahead of me, an enormous bull elephant emerged from the trees. I screeched to a halt on rusty brakes. This was him, the lethal lone elephant! He was beautiful, his massive ears gleaming blue against the crimson sky. Our eyes met for a moment as he flapped them and considered me. And then he carried on, vanishing completely into the bush.

Hilary Heuler
@hilaryheuler.wordpress.com

Chad, Cameroon, Niger, Benin and Burkina Faso. Although there is only one species, the markings vary distinctively between different subspecies and races. In East Africa, giraffes are not uncommon in some areas, even outside the parks, and can be seen strolling across the countryside even in relatively disturbed habitats.

The giraffe's reclusive cousin the **okapi** is a handsome, horse-sized, stripe-legged, forest-dwelling relative, found only in a small area of central DRC.

Predators

You're extremely unlikely to see any large predators outside the parks. And while there are places in the obvious safari destinations where visitors can become blasé about predator sightings, seeing lions, and especially a cheetah or leopard, in most parts of sub-Saharan Africa is cause for celebration. Smaller and even less often seen are the pretty, striped and spotted **serval cat**, and the tuft-eared **caracal**.

Leopards are very widespread across the continent (including possibly still in very small numbers in Morocco's Atlas mountains), and can be found in almost every habitat, from desert to rainforest, but the solitary habits of these expert tree and rock climbers make them hard to see, even if you're woken in the dead of night by a leopard's unmistakeable rasping cough. At some lodges they are baited with meat in trees for the benefit of tourists' cameras, a practice that is censured by conservationists for interfering with the balance of nature.

Lions are largely confined to protected areas in the great arc of savanna and open bush country that curls around the Congo Basin from northern Central African Republic (CAR) to southern Ethiopia and down through the countries of the Rift Valley to South Africa. Although they are endangered, largely through inevitable confrontations with people and their livestock, there are private hunting concessions in South Africa where their numbers are anything but declining.

Cheetahs inhabit similar environments to lions, although they need more open country to thrive. North of the equator, apart from in East Africa, they are rare. Namibia, Botswana, Kenya and Tanzania are your best bets.

Packs of the rare and nomadic **wild dog** or **hunting dog** are found in the same savanna arc, but sightings are invariably fleeting encounters. You're most likely to come across them in Botswana's Okavango Delta or Moremi Game Reserve or, increasingly, in Kenya's Maasai Mara, Tsavo and Laikipia regions and Tanzania's Mikumi, Selous and Ruaha national parks. Wherever they're seen, they're likely to be 100km distant within days.

The much-maligned **spotted hyena** is a more sedentary creature with a fascinating social life that figures prominently in local myths. You can see them (and often hear their unearthly whoops) in all the parks and reserves of East and southern Africa, and, with a bit more luck, in suitable parks and other habitats in the Sahel and savanna zones of Central and West Africa. Unlike spotted hyenas, the slighter **striped hyena** of north and East Africa is usually solitary, as is southern Africa's **brown hyena**.

If you spend any time in the savanna parks, you'll soon become familiar with the three species of fearless, roving **jackals** – black-backed, golden or side-striped – often seen in pairs. They rarely sit still for long. Other canids include delightful **bat-eared foxes** (East Africa and southwest Africa) and the tiny **fennec fox**, found only in the Sahara. The most localized member of the dog family in Africa is the magnificent **Ethiopian wolf**, a long-legged russet and cream highland hunter, sadly now very rare.

Smaller predators include the various species of often colony-dwelling **mongooses** (of which southern Africa's suricate or **meerkat** is the best known and most entertaining), the slender, arboreal, cat-like **genets** (which easily become habituated to humans), the chunkier **civets** and the indomitable, badger-like **ratel**.

Two animals that you almost certainly won't see are also nocturnal: the scaly-backed ant- and termite-eating **pangolins** (four species, mostly found in forests) and that unmistakeable dictionary-leader, the **aardvark**, another termite-feeder, which looks like the unintended result of a genetic experiment, part pig, part kangaroo.

Whales and dolphins

South Africa is one of the very few countries in the world where it's easy to watch migrating **whales** from the shore. Between June and November, southern right whales (so-called because they were the right species for whalers to target) swim from the cold waters of the Antarctic to the warmer seas of the southern Atlantic and Indian

The circle of life

Male lions have the ability to identify their own offspring by smell. The situation in my pride became tense one morning when Nura (we name the lions we're observing) carefully carried her young cubs away from Caesar – one of the most impressive male lions I have seen – when the cubs wobbled too close. Caesar was making his move to take over the pride. In a takeover, females have to be in oestrus – in other words, not suckling cubs – so the male can mate.

I was parked off to the side when a flurry of movement and a barrage of snarls, growls and hisses grabbed my attention. I could see Nura fighting tooth and claw with Caesar for the survival of her cubs. Having seen the powerful lioness bring down a wildebeest bull single-pawed, I thought she might fend him off. Sadly, she wasn't up to it. Caesar is some 100kg heavier than her, and I watched gloomily as he purposefully dispatched each cub with a bite. My heart was in my mouth – it was terrifying, exciting and emotional.

Yet two days later, Nura was mating with Caesar, which was the purpose of his infanticide. Her determination and ultimate failure to protect her cubs was followed immediately by her equal willingness to accept the new male and another opportunity to raise a litter. Hormones rule: it's not *The Lion King*, that's for sure.

Sara Blackburn
Ⓦ LivingWithLions.org/Mara

oceans where they breed, passing very close to the coast as they cruise past the Cape.

Humpback whales, meanwhile, follow similar routes, typically breeding further north. The Atlantic near Gabon and São Tomé and Príncipe (from June/July to Sept) or the northern Mozambican Indian Ocean (Aug to Oct) are good places to see them.

Dolphins are permanent residents of Africa's coasts, with some pods limiting their movements to a fairly small home range, making spotting them pretty straightforward. Dolphin-watching boat trips pull in the crowds in Egypt, The Gambia, Kenya, Mauritius, Zanzibar and South Africa, but some captains are guilty of harassing the animals by approaching too closely, so it's worth doing a little research before booking.

Birds

Africa's birdlife, ranging from the diminutive pygmy woodpecker to the ostrich, is breathtakingly diverse. Its more than 2300 species, of which more than 1750 are found only in Africa, represent nearly a quarter of the world's species. Characteristic sights are the urbanite pied crows of the Sahel and electric-blue Abyssinian rollers, perched on telephone wires in the grasslands. Even more memorable is the marvellous, lurching flight of hornbills swooping across the road in forest and wooded savanna areas. Showy birds like the **lilac-breasted roller** or weird-looking species like

Africa's best birding

If you're serious about **birding**, you may want to join a specialist trip led by an expert guide. Ghana, The Gambia, Kenya, Tanzania, Uganda, Rwanda and Zambia are all popular destinations. If you'd rather go it alone, then the following are well worth building into your itinerary and easy to visit independently.

- **Parc National des Oiseaux de Djoudj, Senegal** In this showcase reserve, thousands of flamingos and white pelicans – among the largest concentrations in the world – can be seen all year round. Between October and April, they're joined by Palearctic migrants.
- **Bao Bolon Wetland Reserve, The Gambia** In a country that offers outstanding birding thanks to the great variety of different habitats it packs into a small area, this is a superb place to watch water birds by boat.
- **Murchison Falls National Park, Uganda** Famous for its population of shoebills, large, lugubrious-looking birds with massive beaks.
- **Rift Valley Lakes, East Africa** The extreme, caustic conditions of Lake Natron in Tanzania and lakes Nakuru and Bogoria in Kenya seem to suit greater and lesser flamingos, which mass on these lakes in gigantic flocks, tingeing the landscape pink.
- **Caprivi Strip, Namibia** Generous rains make this by far the lushest part of Namibia, its waterways, papyrus reed beds and wetland forests teeming with an enormous variety of birds.
- **Kruger National Park, South Africa** This vast but accessible park has good visitor facilities and more than five hundred bird species, more than a fifth of the total number found in Africa.

the **ground hornbill** never fail to impress and quirky adaptations such as the nest-building skills of **sociable weavers**, the canny hunting tricks of **black egrets** and the sheer cheek of **oxpeckers**, which harvest ticks from the noses and backs of buffalos and zebras, are just as compelling. If you're into birds, wherever you go in Africa will be a delight.

If you're serious about your birdwatching, you will probably be a member of a local club, but the **African Bird Club**, with its excellent website and publications, should be your first port of call when planning a trip (ⓦafricanbirdclub.org). The website includes a superb collection of **birdsong** recordings. If possible, time a visit for the European winter, when the bird numbers are swelled by Palearctic migrants.

In terms of bird lists, **Kenya**, **Uganda** and **Tanzania** are probably the continent's top birding countries, each with more than 1000 species and a huge diversity of habitats within their borders. DRC has an even bigger bird list (1139 species), but for practical and security reasons holds less appeal. Top sites include Uganda's Rwenzori Mountains National Park, Kenya's Lakes Naivasha, Nakuru and Baringo, Kruger National Park in South Africa and Lochinvar National Park in Zambia, each of which has a list of more than 400 species. **Madagascar** has Africa's biggest endemic country list, with more than 100 species of birds found nowhere else.

Reptiles and amphibians

Nile crocodiles (the commonest of Africa's three species and the largest at three metres or more) are hard to spot, and widely hunted where they live because they do grab people at the water's edge. Read any newspaper from Nigeria to Zambia and you'll come across reports of croc attacks, and you should always be cautious by rivers and lakes and never swim in inland waters unless you are categorically assured it is safe to do so and you see others swimming. In many parts of West Africa, village ponds contain semi-domesticated Nile crocodiles. These reptiles are the object of veneration and fed meat scraps, sometimes paid for by tourists' contributions.

Lizards are common everywhere, and south of the Sahara you'll soon become familiar with the vigorous push-ups of the red-headed, male **rock agama**. Some towns seem to be positively swarming with them. In some areas, at night, **house geckos** come out like translucent little aliens to scuttle across the ceiling and walls in their useful pursuit of moths and mosquitoes. Brilliant green **day geckos** and camouflaged **leaf-tailed geckos** are found in Madagascar. Larger lizards (all species are harmless) include the monitors, of which the grey-and-yellow **Nile monitor** grows to an impressive two metres and can sometimes be seen dashing across the road. **Chameleons** are also often seen, making slower progress, or squashed flat on the tarmac. Madagascar, again, has a wonderful array of chameleon species.

There are plenty of **snakes** around, but it's hard to see them (see p.220) and you can spend months travelling in Africa and only ever see them in

Forget the Big Five

Don't get hung up on ticking off animals, especially if you're missing one of the **Big Five** – elephant, black rhino, lion, leopard and buffalo. These were traditionally the hunter's most-prized trophies, not the photographer's, and seeing all of them doesn't have to be your sole aim. A half-hour watching hyena pups playing near their burrows on a golden dawn morning, a magnificent fish eagle devouring breakfast, or even the antics of lizards or mongooses around the lodge, can be just as rewarding. Many first-time safari-travellers do see extraordinary sights – a kill, lions fighting, elephants mating – but invariably when they and their guide were least expecting it, and often en route to see something completely different. Keep your eyes peeled, scan left and right, and relax. Fun though it is to be the one to spot a rare beast, the enjoyment and privilege of being where you are can be at least as rewarding.

boxes in so-called "snake parks". The most impressive species is the very widespread **rock python**, which can reach five metres in length, and the super-fast, arboreal and highly venomous **green mamba**. The snake that causes most deaths among local people (tourists are almost never bitten) is the **puff adder**, a very widespread, prettily marked and rather sluggish serpent. You almost certainly won't see one, partly because they are so well camouflaged, but do keep an eye out, and your shoes on.

Spotting a tortoise or turtle is a good deal more likely than seeing a snake. **Sea turtles** come ashore to lay their eggs all around the continent (Boa Vista island in Cape Verde, the Bazaruto islands in Mozambique and Watamu in Kenya are good sites for a nocturnal vigil at the right time of year), and you can see them when snorkelling, too. Good-sized **leopard tortoises** can often be seen in the parks and any lake or pond at a low or moderate altitude will have a population of **pond turtles** or **soft-shelled turtles**.

Ponds, streams and marshes are the main habitat for Africa's **frogs and toads**, though they tend to make themselves most noticeable by their nocturnal choruses. Toads often wait for insects near light sources after rain, so if you're interested, have a look around the base of garden lights at your lodge or hotel.

Fish

You're more likely to see examples of Africa's **fish** on your plate than in the water, but Africa's lakes and rivers, as well as its seas, have an astonishing variety, from the catfish that supply so much protein along the banks of the Niger to the giant Nile perch, found all over the continent, and the tilapia that ends up as fillets in the freezer section of every African supermarket. The Indian Ocean's **coral reefs**, stretching from Egypt's Red Sea to the border of South Africa provide a rich habitat – and one you can easily enter by diving or snorkelling – and beyond the reef there are sharks, huge billfish and whale sharks. You might also like to dive in the crystal-clear waters of Lakes Malawi and Tanganyika, which contain hundreds of species of colourful cichlids – including many that are popular aquarium species – or head down to South Africa's lively scene, where you can share the water with vast sardine shoals or get up close to a great white shark. See p.178 for more on diving.

Invertebrates

Spiders, **scorpions** and various other multi-legged invertebrates are less often encountered than you might expect, or fear. There are some huge, armoured **beetles** to be seen in the Central African forest regions, and East Africa is well known for its harmless giant millipedes, 20cm vegetation-processers often seen trundling across the road after rain. The **butterflies** are extensive and colourful, especially in the lowland forests. Africa has a total of more than 2400 different varieties, of which as many as a thousand species are found in some districts.

Safaris

Going **on safari** – the classic journey into the bush (from Swahili kusafiri: to travel) in search of wild animals – is often the highlight of travels in Africa. Safari styles vary from country to country, and equally within each country, depending on the variety of national parks and other protected areas – and also on more subtle variables. Botswana, for example, has always marketed itself to an upmarket clientele, while Kenya includes a lot of relatively low-priced options. That in turn means that at one extreme safaris can be relatively mass-market, with clients travelling by minibus and staying in large, package-style lodges, while at the other end of the spectrum, clients are privately guided and stay in immaculate, exclusive camps deep in the bush. For more on accommodation types, see p.121. Whatever you decide, avoid going on safari for less than two nights, which barely gives you time to adjust and start absorbing your environment.

Don't assume the national parks or national reserves are invariably the best game-watching and photo-hunting grounds. Community-owned **conservancies** (see p.201) and mixed use **game-sanctuaries/ranches** often have just as many wild animals, and while they are perhaps more managed than the national parks, their more flexible approach is often more sustainable and also more closely resembles the ecosystems of the past, before the Europeans arrived, when the pastoralists and farmers had to live with the constant danger of lions, leopards, buffalos and elephants. If you're staying on community land, rather than in a lodge owned by an international chain, there's a good chance that more of your money will end up in the hands of the community. Some camps and lodges are built on this principle, and are sometimes entirely run by members of the local tribe, with every cent of the profits staying in the area. For further guidance on **responsible safaris**, see box, p.200.

Increasingly, in managed areas, some animals may be tagged with radio collars for research and monitoring. You may have the opportunity to track **tagged animals** by taking a radio antenna on your game drive – an idea that, if it first feels unsettling, does allow you to participate a little in conservation activities (see box, p.157).

Assuming you're not up for do-it-yourself safari, in which case the decisions are all about choosing a vehicle (see p.105), you're likely to be considering where to spend your money on an **organized safari**. Before anything else, bear in mind that the professionalism and experience of your guide can transform any trip. Some countries have established qualification schemes (see p.170), and you should always enquire about the experience of your guide. Then think about whether you want comfort or a grittier experience, and whether you want the convenience of having it pre-booked as part of a package holiday, or the independence of picking and choosing online, or once you're on the ground in Africa.

Types of safari

Air safaris, also known as fly-in safaris, use internal flights to get you around, but vehicles on the ground for game drives. They usually add significantly to the cost and comfort of your trip and give you spectacular views, but offer a much less intimate contact with the country below. A week-long air safari will typically work out in the range of US$3000–5000 per person, but the price will depend on the quality of accommodation, the size of your party and whether you're using a local scheduled airline or chartering flights for your tour. Your **game drives**, or sometimes game walks (the two-to-three hour excursions you take at dawn and before sundown), will be organized by the host lodge or camp and included in the price (camp-based drives are invariably operated in sturdy 4WD vehicles), along with all your meals and usually some drinks.

On a **road safari**, you'll be driven between camps or lodges by minibus or 4WD in a group of anything from two to nine clients. The long bumpy drives to meet the demands of the itinerary can be exhausting, as hours of your time are eaten away in a cloud of dust. Moreover, opportunities to see much of the landscape or have any kind of engagement with the communities through which you're passing can be somewhat limited, though this depends on the route you take, the quality of your vehicle and the level of interest of your guide. The best road safaris follow realistic itineraries, including plenty of down time, in comfortable vehicles with plenty of space and excellent viewing facilities. On this kind of trip, the travel is part of the experience, with your guide giving you a fascinating commentary on everything from roadside produce to traditional marriage, and from pesticides to Chinese road-building companies.

Game drives

Heading out into the bush in a rugged vehicle with an expert guide, in radio contact with other guides, and often with an assistant to act as spotter, is the classic way to watch African wildlife. In many national parks and reserves, **game drives** are the only way to watch wildlife, as you're not allowed to step outside your vehicle beyond the boundaries of your camp (for some exceptions, see p.169).

Most top-end lodges and camps in Africa's safari heartlands offer small-group game drives in open-sided **Land Rovers** or other 4WD vehicles as a standard excursion, included in the price of your stay. You'll generally go out early in the morning, returning for breakfast, and again late in the afternoon (corresponding to the times of the day when diurnal animals are most active), often rounding off the experience with sundowners at a gloriously scenic vantage point.

Mid-range and budget camps don't usually have their own vehicles and your game drives are likely to be taken in the minibus or 4WD that you're travelling with. The views won't be as good while you're in motion, but there will always be a roof hatch for game-viewing while you're stationary.

In most wildlife areas you can also **drive around yourself**, having rented a suitable vehicle if you don't have your own. To maximize your sightings, you might want to hire a freelance field guide to accompany you (for contacts, see p.170).

On an organized trip, you don't have to take a passive attitude to game drives. If you want to go on an early drive, or spend the whole morning out looking for leopards, don't be afraid to suggest to the tour leader that you skip breakfast, or take sandwiches. Too often, each day's **itinerary** is a product of what tour operators think customers want (passed from management to drivers and cooks) constrained by the driver's fuel allowance. Game drives that try to please too many people may land you in a convoy of vehicles, all tearing across the bush from place to place on the whim of every radio rumour – a good way to observe human behaviour, but a lousy way to watch animals.

As a general rule, your best chance of a quality wildlife experience – one in which you can relax and observe animals or birds quietly and in detail, rather than just catching a fleeting glimpse in passing, or seeing a flurry of rear ends disappearing into the dust – is to head for a place where they drink or feed, and stake it out for a while. For this reason, small groups with similar wildlife interests are likely to enjoy their game drive far more than a large, mismatched group of strangers.

In certain wildlife-watching areas you can take night drives, using a powerful spotlight to pick out animal activity. It's an absorbing, though often chilly, variation that's not allowed in all national parks and reserves and is already restricted in some permitted areas to avoid subjecting the wildlife to a 24/7 bombardment of vehicle-borne visitors.

In East and southern Africa, most road safaris take you from one safari lodge or camp to another, typically staying two or three nights at each, usually using minibuses with pop-top roofs for photography. Make sure you have a window seat. On pricier road safaris, you travel in a more rugged vehicle that's higher off the ground – a 4WD Land Rover or Land Cruiser or even an open-sided lorry – giving more flexibility over the route. A week's safari by road, staying at lodges or tented camps, will cost in the range of US$1200–3000 per person, again depending on numbers and where you stay. The cheapest safaris have regular departures based on minimum number of clients and, unless your party is fairly large, you are likely to have to share the vehicle for game drives and when transferring to the next camp. Your accommodation is private, however, and you normally eat at your own table, exactly as in a hotel in other words – except in boutique tented camps where guests often eat together with the host-manger, and perhaps a senior guide, and you get a great chance to swap tales.

The alternative to a standard lodge or tented camp safari is a true **camping safari**, on which the crew (or you, if it's a budget trip) pitch your tents each day in a "fly camp" – a temporary campsite. With this kind of trip you have to be prepared for a degree of discomfort along with the self-sufficiency: insects can occasionally be a menace; you may not get a shower every night; the food won't be so lavish; and the beer not so cold (and you'll probably have to pay for drinks separately). The price here should be in the range of US$120–200 per day per person, depending on the itinerary. Budget camping trips are often off-the-shelf deals, but if you're in a group of four or more, it's worth pushing for the greater flexibility of exclusive arrangements for your party. For budget safaris, park entrance fees can be a major part of the cost, too, so do ensure they are included.

Whether you're transported by road or air, **high-end camping safaris** come very expensive indeed: you can easily expect to pay US$600–1000 per day per person. But you'll be guided by expert guides and usually looked after superbly, with top-quality tents ready for your arrival at your fly-camp every evening, good meals, cold beer and good wine included in the price, and lots of animated, campfire conversation in which your guide will play an active role.

Booking safaris direct

If you want the flexibility of booking your own safari, rather than having a travel agent or operator at home organize the whole trip for you, then you will be dealing with **local agents or operators**. They tend to be based in whichever large town offers the most straightforward access to the largest number of parks in the country – Nairobi or the Mombasa North Coast in Kenya, Arusha in Tanzania, Livingstone or Lusaka in Zambia, Maun in Botswana – and they all have websites.

Most first-time safari-goers enjoy their safaris and even inexperienced operators are mostly resourceful and hardworking. But it's always much better to spend more on a safari from a company with a blue-chip reputation – at any level of budget – than to cast caution to the winds and follow a beach boy to a booking hut with a phone and a promise of a pick-up on Saturday morning.

Many safari companies, especially in the busy safari markets of Kenya and Tanzania, present the trips they sell as if they were the operator. You can, however, be sure that a website that doesn't include photos of their vehicles emblazoned with the name of the company isn't an operator's

Game walks, rides and boat trips

As a first-time safari-goer, you might be disappointed to discover you'll be confined in a **vehicle** for most of your wildlife-watching time. One answer is to opt for a vehicle-free safari, on which game walks, riding or boating take the place of game drives (and in some cases also provides your transport between overnight stops). Not only is this eco-friendly, it's also highly enjoyable. You'll need to base yourself in a wildlife-watching region in which such activities are permitted and ensure you have an expert guide and armed protection on hand to avert any hazardous situations.

Wildlife-watching on foot is very different from a game drive: you're physically engaged, your senses are attuned to the sounds and smells of the bush and you'll have the chance to observe intimate details such as ant-lion traps, ripening fruit, the swivelling eyes of chameleons and the acrobatic feats of mating insects. While skittish antelopes and will usually disappear before you get close, and seeing signature species such as lions and leopards is less common than from a vehicle – and down to the skill of your tracker – you will certainly see their spoor in the dust and the sense of freedom and adventure is intoxicating.

Zambia's South Luangwa National Park is the classic walking safari destination, its excellent reputation partly due to the fact that its guides undergo stringent training and walking groups are limited to a maximum of seven, plus the guide and an armed scout. Other good options include Hobatere and Ongava in Namibia's Etosha region, some of the conservancies in northwest Botswana and northern Kenya, and parts of South Africa's Greater Kruger.

Horseback safaris are exhilarating if you're a confident rider, and you can get surprisingly close to the wildlife, none of which seems to recognize mounted humans as much of a threat. A number of ranches across Africa's safari countries offer horseback safaris – though like wildlife-watching on foot, you can't enter every wildlife area on horseback.

Elephant and **camel safaris** are an easy, though somewhat gimmicky, group ramble through the bush on the back of a placid pachyderm or ungulate, piloted by an experienced handler. African elephants are much harder to domesticate than the Asian species, and elephant-back safaris are the preserve of just a few specialist outfits in Botswana, South Africa and Zimbabwe, while wildlife-watching by camel is offered in northwest Tanzania and parts of central and northern Kenya. You can ride camels in North Africa as well, of course, but these trips tend to be more about experiencing the landscape than watching wildlife. Any camel trip longer than a few hours tends to mean walking with camels rather than riding them, as most travellers find the experience highly uncomfortable.

Depending on the region, the deck of a **cruiser** or the seat of a **canoe** offers a great vantage point from which to observe water-loving mammals or watch birds, with several of Africa's biodiverse rivers and wetland areas accessible by powered or paddled craft. Bear in mind, however, that hippos and crocodiles can inflict serious damage and it's crucial that you're led by a guide who knows the locality well.

Waterborne wildlife-watching opportunities include watching egrets and herons from a Nile felucca in Egypt, idling along the glassy, lily-strewn waters of Botswana's Okavango Delta in a *mokoro*, relaxing on a houseboat in Namibia's Caprivi Strip, cruising past elephants as they ford the Rufiji River in Tanzania, dodging hippos while canoeing the Zambezi below Victoria Falls or exploring The Gambia's bird-rich mangrove creeks by traditional pirogue.

website at all, but that of an **agent** who has some contacts and is earning a sales commission.

Good agents explain their business clearly and of course offer a wider choice than a single operator. There are also some operators who, while personally experienced and trustworthy, don't own enough vehicles and other equipment to operate all the trips for which they manage to sell seats. Consequently, the **sub-contracting** of services, and sometimes sub-sub-contracting, is endemic, especially in high season. If you opt for a cheap safari from an inexperienced operator, you're more likely to get in difficulties: being stuck in a broken-down vehicle, out of mobile phone signal range and with no replacement vehicle available is no fun for anyone.

Before making a **down payment**, as most companies will expect, ensure the company you're booking with is a member of the national tour operators' association (see p.171) and has been recommended, either personally, in a reputable travel guide, or by independent users of a travel forum – but beware of companies posing as their own clients.

Guides

The one aspect of your safari that is out of your hands once you've booked is the calibre of your **guide**: always ask in advance. A few countries are addressing the question of qualifications, with the Field Guides Association of South Africa (Ⓦ fgasa.co.za) setting the benchmarks. Since the late 1990s, the Kenya Professional Safari Guides Association (Ⓦ safariguides.org) has taken the lead in Kenya, holding monthly bronze exams and periodic exams for the silver qualification, which requires three years of study and guiding.

Highly qualified guides can offer memorable insights into animal behaviour and can be remarkably adept at tracking animals and interpreting their observations: a good guide will know, for example, why two male lions are being chased by a lioness, and what you might expect to find if you discreetly follow the lioness later.

Hunting

Unpalatable as it may seem to those with an interest in peaceful wildlife-watching, **trophy hunting** (by vehicle, from a blind or hide, on foot, or a combination) is legal and fairly common in parts of Africa's safari heartland – notably in dedicated concessions in Tanzania, Zambia, Namibia, Botswana, Zimbabwe and South Africa (it's illegal throughout Kenya). It also takes place in a number of other countries, including CAR, Cameroon and Benin. When planning a wildlife-watching safari, it's worth checking whether there's a hunting concession nearby, or whether hunting has taken place in the recent past, as this can have a profound effect on wildlife behaviour. Hunting is controversial, but hunting-trip operators and several governments claim that it plays a positive role in conservation by generating revenues which are re-invested in wildlife management.

Travelling with a good guide will also make your trip safer. Accidents can and do happen when visitors venture within close range of wild animals, but a conscientious and well-trained guide should spot the first signs of danger, and take decisive action.

To locate a qualified freelance field guide contact: the FGASA or the KPSGA (above); one of the following organizations; or the national parks and wildlife authority of the country that interests you. Guides can also sometimes be hired at the offices at national park gates.

- **Cape Tourist Guides Association** ⓦctga.org.za
- **Gauteng Guides Association** ⓦguidessa.org
- **Namibian Academy for Tourism & Hospitality** ⓦnathnamibia.org
- **Tourist Guide Association of Namibia** ⓦnatron.net/tan
- **Zimbabwe Professional Hunters & Guides Association** ⓦzphga .com

If the safari goes wrong

Unlicensed or unscrupulous **camping operators**, mostly in the biggest safari destinations, Kenya and Tanzania, sell safaris at the very bottom of the market in a price war that undercuts the legitimate firms. You can be sure that any safari which is offered at less than US$100 per day is going to be cutting corners one way or another, often by not paying park entry fees, either by dodging the gates or bribing rangers. Some companies also make a habit of failing to deliver on their promises, knowing that a combination of clients' goodwill and inadequate legal recourse will allow them to get away with it.

At the budget end, it's difficult to find a company that's absolutely consistent, but the local grapevine and online forums are probably your best guide. If the company is a member of the **national tour operators' association**, such as KATO, TATO, AUTO, TOAZ, SATOA, TASA or HATAB (respectively the tour operators associations of Kenya, Tanzania, Uganda, Zambia, South Africa, Namibia and Botswana), that is a good sign, but don't take it as a guarantee – most of them are loathe to turn away new members.

Unpredictable factors such as weather, illness, visibility of animals and group relations among the passengers can all contribute to the degree of success of the trip. More controllable factors, however, like breakdowns, food, equipment and the competence of the drivers and guides, are what really determine reputations. If anything goes wrong, reputable companies will do their best to compensate on the spot (a partial refund, an extra day if you broke down, a night in a lodge if you didn't make it to a campsite). If your grievance is unresolved, you might want to contact the relevant national association, which will sometimes intercede with their members on clients' behalf.

Activities

A frica's deserts, mountains, forests, beaches and oceans offer a wealth of tempting challenges. Many visitors make wildlife-watching activities the focus of their trip (see Chapter 11) but there's plenty to do besides. Those keen to stretch their legs can opt for something as relaxed as a **lakeside stroll**, as engrossing as an **orchid-spotting walk** or as demanding as an **expedition** to the top of the continent's highest mountain, Kilimanjaro. You can test your mettle on the water, surfing, windsurfing or sailing, or under it, exploring the continent's many intricate reefs and wrecks; and for something truly spine-tingling, you can soar over the bush in a microlight, or fling yourself into the great unknown on the end of a bungee rope.

Some of Africa's **archeological remains** and museums are truly remarkable, and lend themselves to history tours, either guided or of your own devising. While Africa's oral tradition has preserved some strands of history more robustly than others, there's much to be gleaned from other sources, too: palaeontologists who have pored over Africa's richly significant fossil record consider the continent to be the birthplace of modern man, and the ruins and monuments of North Africa, the palaces and mosques of the West and the once-grand trading posts of the East are poignant reminders of ancient civilizations.

Contemporary Africa can be every bit as intriguing. Cultural tourism programmes open a window on everyday life, while attending festivals of music and dance, or sacred rituals held to mark rites of passage and the changing seasons, will immerse you in ancient traditions at their most exuberant and expressive. Those who would like to tap into the spirit of modern, urban Africa will want a few days spent touring its most happening **cities**, but those seeking something more sedate and serene are well served, too, by an abundance of gorgeous **beaches** and peaceful, health-enhancing **retreats**.

Making it happen

Africa may be impoverished but certain aspects of its tourist industry are highly developed, with first-rate adventure and culture **tour companies**, **operators** and **guides** scattered all over the continent. Safety and quality standards and ethics do vary, however, so research the options carefully before making your choice. You should also check whether your preferred activities are seasonal; for some pointers, see the box on p.58.

The best way to ensure the safest and most enjoyable experience is to book an **activity-based trip**, or one which offers activities as an option, through a reputable operator (for contacts, see pp.401–411). Look up professional reviews in guidebooks, newspapers, magazines and websites, scan through some customer feedback and check what exactly is included in the price; for some activities, equipment hire, luxury trips and meals or special tuition may cost extra.

Where activities are integral to the itinerary, you'll want to make sure that they're **well run** by asking questions specific to your interests. For safaris, you should ask questions to help you assess the experience and attitude of your guide, tour company and camp or lodge staff as well as checking basics such as location and group size – for more details, see Chapter 11. If booking a history tour, you should ask about your guide's academic credentials; if considering a walking holiday, you'll want to be sure it includes a well-thought-out series of guided hikes that suit your level of fitness; a diving holiday should offer professionally run, accredited training sessions, boat trips or shore dives, using well-maintained equipment. You'll want to ask similar questions about any activities you book ad hoc as part of a leisure or sightseeing trip: **package holidays** based in beach resorts or city hotels may throw in a few activities for free (in all-inclusive resorts, the selection may be extensive) and on-site holiday reps will suggest others which you can book with them on the spot.

If you're **travelling independently**, your options are wide open, so careful research is even more important. For straightforward activities such as walking, cycling or snorkelling, you don't necessarily need to find yourself a guide, let alone an activity company, though both can add enormously to your experience. For others, such as white-water rafting, microlighting or township tours, you'll almost certainly need the services of a specialist: whether you secure your slot by booking in advance or wait till you're on the ground and can chat face-to-face is entirely up to you. In all cases, guidebooks, tourist offices, national parks and wildlife management agencies, and feedback from other travellers, can help you track down good destinations, routes and contacts.

Tracks and trails

Setting off on **foot** or by **bicycle** for the simple pleasure of it is a great way to bond with the "real" Africa of wide-open spaces and scattered villages. If you decide to pedal, potter or stride through populated rural areas, the friendly interest of locals is likely to add colour to your trip. For many Africans, walking and cycling are nothing more than a means of getting from A to B – a necessary chore in the absence of speedier and easier alternative modes of transport – so some find the concept of doing either just for fun baffling and, frankly, hilarious.

It's also possible to explore Africa's beaches and bush trails on **horse-back** (Kenya, Botswana, Lesotho and South Africa are all good places for this), or to head off on an excursion by **elephant** or **camel** (for details, see p.169). To step your physical exertions up a notch, you could have a bash at **mountaineering**: Africa's highest peaks offer a temptingly feasible challenge to the eager and fit.

Walking, hiking and cycling

Africa has some superb terrain for **walking**, **hiking**, **cycle touring** and **mountain biking**. Even though great swathes of the continent are effectively off-limits due to everything from national park regulations and private ownership to extreme desert conditions, dangerous animals, banditry and minefields, there are enough peaceful and seductive spots to last you a lifetime.

One of the most pleasant and exciting ways to experience the African wilderness on foot is to join a **walking safari** (a tour which focuses on wildlife-watching bushwalks); for details, see p.169. Africa also has numerous regions which, though less rich in wildlife, are blessed with beautiful scenery. The following represent just a glimpse of the most accessible highlights which you could explore independently, with a local guide or as part of an organized tour. On long trips, you'll need to be resourceful and self-sufficient: for general advice on exploring Africa on two feet or two wheels, see pp.110–112.

- **Atlas Mountains, Morocco** The Berber homelands offer clear mountain air, snowy peaks and far-flung villages with tiny mosques, connected only by mule trails.
- **Fogo, Brava, Santiago, São Nicolau and Santo Antão, Cape Verde** The craggier of the Cape Verde Islands are gaining a big following among hiking fanatics for their gasp-inducing ridges, vertiginous pinnacles and stunning slopes, reminiscent of the mountains of Peru. On Fogo, you can climb the cone of an active volcano which last erupted in 1995.
- **The Gambia** Friendly and more or less flat, with plenty of hospitable villages connected by pleasant coastal and riverine bush, this is a great country for easy-going cycling or walking.
- **Fouta Djalon, Guinea** This beautiful, verdant plateau is one of West Africa's best regions for walking or cycling, following footpaths from village to village and enjoying rolling views of well-watered plantations and jungle-filled valleys.
- **Simien Mountains, Ethiopia** Home to large groups of Gelada baboons, this largely roadless region of highland moors and valleys is a wonderfully green Afro-Alpine wilderness.
- **Crater Highlands, Tanzania** Trekking through Maasai lands, with their sacred mountain, Ol Doinyo Lengai, brooding over the scene, you can make your way from Empakaai Crater to Lake Natron to be greeted by flocks of flamingos.

- **Nyika Plateau and Nyika National Park, Zambia/Malawi** Zebras, eland and roan antelope graze peacefully in this highland region, its grasslands sprinkled with wildflowers after the rains; its tracks can be explored by mountain bike or on foot.
- **Central Highlands, Madagascar** Scattered over the Hauts Plateaux are endless hiking routes with views of paddy fields, granite peaks and rainforest-draped slopes, and sightings of lemurs.
- **Fish River Canyon, Namibia** This multi-day, 80km endurance test is one of southern Africa's classic outdoor experiences, taking you through an imposing landscape of sand and rock; to participate, you need to join an organized trek.
- **Lesotho** The tiny nation's expanses of unfenced wilderness make it a brilliant option for accessible but unspoilt highland trekking.
- **The Garden Route, South Africa** In Western Cape Province, walkers and bikers are served by an excellent network of well-marked and maintained trails, with accommodation en route. Options include the Otter Trail, a coastal walk that requires a permit; it's so popular you have to book months in advance.

Mountaineering

Africa's **highest peaks** can be climbed without special skills or training, but it's important not to skimp on the preparation – as well as the right boots and clothes you may need camping gear (your own or hired), a guide and a support team. You'll also have to work out a system to keep hydrated and energized, and set aside enough time to take things easy so that you don't succumb to altitude sickness – a glitch which prevents many from completing their final ascent. Finally, since the fees really add up, you'll need to prepare yourself for a hefty bill, especially if your goal is the top of Kilimanjaro in Tanzania (around US$2000 per person).

Kili (5893m) is of course one that everyone wants to conquer, but Mount Kenya (5200m) comes a close second. Other satisfying climbs include Tanzania's second highest mountain, Mount Meru (4566m), Jebel Toubkal in Morocco (4167m) and Mount Cameroon (4070m). All are enjoyable not only for the physical challenge of the climb but also for their fine scenery, clear air and, in some cases, distinctive vegetation: the giant lobelias and groundsels which thrive halfway up East Africa's mighty peaks are particularly bizarre.

Adventure activities and watersports

Africa has plenty of options for thrill seekers, with the main **adventure-sport** centres set in the east and south, particularly the Zambia-Zimbabwe border and South Africa. The twin centres of Victoria Falls town and

Fit for a purpose

Completing one of Africa's **extreme challenges** can do wonders for your physical fitness and self-esteem, but for the ultimate sense of achievement, you could raise some sponsorship and leave the planet in better shape, too. One approach is to devise your own **sponsored challenge**, be it climbing Kilimanjaro or Jebel Toubkal, hiking across the Sahara or completing a long-distance bike ride. Websites that can help you evaluate suitable charities include Charity Facts (Wcharityfacts.org) and Intelligent Giving (Wintelligentgiving.com).

An alternative is to sign up for a **group event** or trip through a charity or specialist agent (for contacts, see p.409). These companies generally offer two options – they can offer you an adventure trip for a standard price, with no charitable donation included, or they can assist you in turning your adventure into a fundraising event. If you're up for the latter, they will set a minimum price for the trip (a hefty £3750 for a ten-day climb-Kilimanjaro trip, including flights from the UK, is typical). It's then up to you to decide how much of this total to raise in sponsorship; they will offer tips and practical support. You should always quiz them about how much of the total will reach your chosen charity and how much will simply be covering the costs and fees associated with your trip: you can then share this information with your sponsors. It's also best to be very clear with your sponsors about how much you're contributing yourself – you wouldn't want them to feel they're just paying for you to go on holiday.

Kiliman Adventure Challenge, Tanzania Wkilimanjaro-man.com, Feb. A hardcore Ironman-style competitive event whereby, having climbed Kilimanjaro, you battle through a 246-km cycle race and a 42.2-km run in rapid succession.

Marathon des Sables, Morocco Wdarbaroud.com, April. Running doesn't get much harder than this seven-day, 240-km race across the desert. The heat is intense, the terrain unforgiving, and you have to carry all your stuff in a pack on your back. The ultimate endorphin high, or extreme torture, depending on how much sand manages to work its way into your trainers each day. Amazingly, a third of all competitors come back for more another year.

Lewa Marathon, Kenya Wlewa.org, June. Pound along the dirt tracks of the Lewa Wildlife Conservancy, home to big game, to support wildlife conservation and community projects which improve local healthcare and school facilities.

Big Five Marathon, South Africa Wbig-five-marathon.com, June. Run 88km along sandy tracks through the Entabeni Game Reserve – prime safari country – with rangers on hand to ensure that dangerous animals don't get too close.

Great Ethiopian Run, Ethiopia Wethiopianrun.org, Nov. A high-altitude 10km run at high temperatures, held in Addis Ababa. Attracting 35,000 amateurs and pros, it's the biggest race on the continent.

Livingstone have long been magnets for enthusiasts, with masses of activities on offer – there's something about all that water plummeting over the Falls that really gets the heart pumping. Jinja in Uganda and Swakopmund in Namibia also act as hubs. Meanwhile, South Africans seem to think up new ways to scare themselves stupid all the time – there are activities aplenty around Cape Town, on the Garden Route and in KwaZulu-Natal.

For a gentler adventure, you could snorkel through coral gardens, cruise a placid river or kayak along a lakeshore; these and many other activities are possible at idyllic spots all over the continent.

Rafts, boats and boards

Adrenaline junkies claim that you have to try white-water rafting at least once in your life, and the continent's creeks, rivers, lakes and oceans offer masses of other opportunities on boat or board.

- **White-water rafting** Negotiating the turbulent Zambezi, just downstream from mighty Victoria Falls and accessible from either Vic Falls town or Livingstone, is one of the most exciting river trips in the world. Conditions in the Ugandan section of the Nile near Jinja and the Orange River on the Namibian and South African border can be stimulating, too, while there are more manageable rapids to shoot in the relatively little-visited rivers of the High and Middle Atlas in Morocco.

- **Kayaking and canoeing** Africa has far more good stretches of ocean, river and lake with paddling potential than rental outfits, so if you're serious you might want to bring your own kayak or canoe with you. However, the busiest waterfront resorts will often have a few to borrow or hire: excellent spots include southeast Mauritius, Bom Bom Island Resort on Príncipe and the rafting locations mentioned above. Lake Malawi offers thoroughly memorable kayaking on water that's often so calm and transparent that you can see the fish dancing beneath your paddle.

- **Surfing, windsurfing and kitesurfing** Africa's small but serious scene is mainly concentrated in Atlantic hotspots including Morocco, Senegal (near Dakar), Cape Verde (particularly Sal and Boa Vista) and Liberia (particularly Robertsport), plus a few parts of South Africa, notably near Cape Town, Jeffreys Bay and Durban. Cape Verde and South Africa are both good places to take lessons: beginners can learn the ropes on calmer days, while in peak season conditions are truly impressive. You can also windsurf and kitesurf in the Red Sea off Egypt, from Dahab and Hurghada, both of which have training centres for all levels.

- **Sailing, boating and river cruising** Chartering a yacht or a dhow is a fine way to explore the stunningly beautiful Indian Ocean islands of Mauritius, Madagascar, Zanzibar, Mozambique or the Seychelles, as long as you're careful not to leave their safe waters. Some of the more developed beach resorts of North, East, southern Africa and the Indian Ocean islands offer power-boating and jet-ski hire, but before signing up you should consider the possible impact on marine wildlife. For something more laidback, you could enjoy the classic adventure of cruising for a day or more on Africa's peaceful inland waterways: taking a pirogue through the bird-rich maze of mangrove creeks leading off the River Gambia, meandering through Botswana's idyllic Okavango Delta by *mokoro*, sipping a cool beer at sunset on an Upper Zambezi cruise in Zambia or drifting along to the sound of the muezzin aboard a Nile felucca in Egypt.

● **Sport fishing** Heading out by boat to go angling for marlin and other big game species is popular in The Gambia (both in the Gambia estuary and the open Atlantic), the Pemba Channel in Kenya, and the coasts of South Africa and Mozambique. Lake Kariba in Zimbabwe and the section of the Zambezi upstream from Victoria Falls (reached from Zambia, Zimbabwe, Botswana or Namibia's Caprivi Strip) are renowned for their fearsome tigerfish.

Diving and snorkelling

Africa's **scuba-diving** and **snorkelling** takes in some of the world's best sites. Egypt's **Red Sea** is truly superb: its coral reefs and wrecks harbour outstanding biodiversity and its comfortable, well-established beach resorts offer excellent facilities and a good social scene. Sudan and Djibouti are far less developed but offer sightings of whale sharks, hammerheads and other shark species.

In the **Indian Ocean**, the coast of Mozambique is a clear winner for its pristine sites. This is Africa's most promising emerging destination: the gardens around its islands shimmer with tropical fish, with nudibranchs, gastropods which look like tiny squeezes of brightly coloured paint, adding extra interest. Mozambique is also good for large species including whale sharks, manta rays and turtles. Laidback Tofo or the distinctly upmarket Bazaruto Archipelago or Quirimbas Archipelago are the places to go. Elsewhere on the eastern side of the continent, dynamite fishing has taken its toll on many reefs, but there's plenty to be seen in marine parks such as Mafia Island Marine Park in Tanzania, Watamu Marine National Park in Kenya and iSimangaliso (Greater St Lucia) Wetland Park in KwaZulu-Natal, South Africa.

There's not as much diving to be done in the **Atlantic**, but its volcanic islands are surrounded by underwater pinnacles, caves and wrecks which are worth a look. There are scuba centres in both São Tomé and Príncipe and Cape Verde; the latter has a marine archeology museum stuffed with finds hauled up from sunken galleons.

● **PADI try-dives and training courses** To get a taste of scuba-diving before committing to a course, you can join a carefully escorted trial session which will take you deep enough to examine the coral in close-up, while fish flit by. An open water qualification (attainable after four days' training, the classroom part of which can be completed in your home country before you set off) will enable you to dive deeper and for longer. There are plenty of more advanced options to consider once you have that under your belt. Egypt, Kenya, Tanzania and South Africa have numerous PADI centres; there are a few in other countries too.

- **Day-trips and liveaboards** Most divers and snorkellers base themselves at a coastal resort, swimming straight out from shore or heading out by boat for anything from an hour to a full day. For the chance to reach a wider range of far-off sites, you could join a liveaboard boat which stays out at sea for a number of days; common in the Red Sea and growing in popularity in Tanzania and Mozambique, trips can be booked in advance through diving holiday companies, or fixed up on the ground.

- **Marine conservation experiences** To add an extra dimension to your diving, you could join a survey or conservation training programme in Kenya, Mozambique, Madagascar, Mauritius or the Red Sea – your project could involve counting coral species or observing the behaviour of turtles or dolphins. Specialist scuba holiday and voluntourism companies can help fix you up.

- **Extreme diving** South Africa's lively scene includes speciality experiences such as KwaZulu-Natal's extraordinary annual sardine run, an encounter with frenzied sharks and dolphins that's strictly for the proficient. Baited observation cages offer close encounters with great white sharks but are controversial – some experts believe they could lead to aggression, while others argue that few ill effects have been observed and that by raising awareness of sharks, the practice helps conserve them. To find out first-hand, head for Hermanus or Gansbaai.

- **Freshwater diving and snorkelling** The best place for this is Lake Malawi, home to a huge array of colourful cichlid fish species. Get local advice about bilharzia before plunging in.

Downhill adventures

As well as good spots for leaping down gorges or tearing down slopes, Africa has some great terrain for downhill biking (see pp.174–175).

Into the blue

It was such a joy to fly straight from the UK to the Red Sea and climb aboard a boat the very first day. All we had to do was relax on the gently undulating deck, the clear air sharpening our slim view of the desert.

We arrived at our dive site and it was time to suit up. Immediately, my heart began pounding with multiple anxieties. It was to be my first "proper" dive.

The dive master ran through the safety procedures and told us what to look out for. The list seemed endless. By now I was even more anxious, convinced I'd never remember.

At last we were ready, checks done, sitting on the edge of the boat, our backs to the water.

"Clear behind!"

I rolled in. A huge splash and I was surrounded by foaming, cooling sea water. Down I went, into the quietness and wonder of a limitless aquarium. The water was as clear as the air above. The fish and the coral were every conceivable colour.

My breathing calmed and a deep sense of peace spread through me. This was where I was meant to be …

Nathan Pope

- **Sandboarding** Much like snowboarding, but on sand dunes. Swakopmund in Namibia is a popular place to try this.
- **Skiing** Yes, really – you can hit the snowy slopes in Africa, notably at Oukaïmeden (Ouka) in Morocco, where there's fairly reliable (and affordable) downhill and cross-country skiing from February to April. You can also ski in Lesotho (June to Aug), although conditions here can be very icy.
- **Zorbing** Ever wondered what it might feel like to roll down a hill inside a giant plastic ball? You can find out in South Africa.
- **Kloofing** South Africa's answer to canyoning – you hike to a deep ravine then scramble, abseil or fling yourself down it, typically landing in a pool at the bottom. Popular spots include the none-too-cheerfully named Suicide Gorge near Cape Town.

Airborne adventures

Take to the skies and you'll gain an astonishing new perspective on the landscape and its wildlife, as well as a natural high.

- **Microlighting and paragliding** A magical way to view the Victoria Falls is from the back seat of a microlight, smelling the musky dampness as you circle and dip into the spray. In South Africa's adventure heartlands (KwaZulu-Natal and the Garden Route), you can take to the air for a spot of paragliding.
- **Skydiving** Adventure-mad South Africans will gladly take you up in a plane – and then invite you to throw yourself out of it.
- **Hot air ballooning** For a surprisingly manageable sum (from around €100), you can take a flight from Luxor over some of Egypt's magnificent ancient sites, wafting over temples and villages so close that you can smell the cooking fires and hear conversations below. Equally enthralling, though much pricier, is a game-viewing balloon trip over the Serengeti in Tanzania, Masai Mara in Kenya, Namib Desert in Namibia or Busanga Plains in Zambia. Once it's all over, you're brought down to earth with a pop as the pilot cracks open the champagne.

Ropes and wires

Strictly for the daring, the following count among Africa's most popular adrenaline experiences.

- **Bungee jumping** If the idea of flying though thin air on the end of a rope appeals, you can sample this one-of-a-kind sensation at the Bloukrans Bridge (216m) near Plettenberg Bay, South Africa; the Victoria Falls Bridge (111m) over the Zambezi, reachable from both Zimbabwe and Zambia; and the Nile High Bungee (44m) over the Nile near the Bujagali Falls, Jinja, Uganda.

- **Ziplining** Having bungeed off the Bloukrans Bridge, you can try a flying fox run near the bridge, or whizz through the forest canopy at nearby Tsitsikamma. There are ziplining and gorge-swinging rigs near Victoria Falls, too.
- **Abseiling and rock climbing** Head for the mountains of Morocco, South Africa or Lesotho, the gorges near Victoria Falls or the strikingly beautiful Main de Fatima near Hombori in Mali.

Cultural experiences, events and tours

Little by little, the African tourism industry has been cottoning on to the fact that many visitors would like more from their African adventure than a close brush with wildlife in a glorious landscape – they're also extremely interested in, and concerned about, the history, traditions and daily lives of **African people**. One way to get into traditional and contemporary African culture is through visiting towns, museums and historic sites, dropping in on festivals or just striking up friendships and seeing where they take you. It's also well worth trying some of the organized cultural activities which are aimed at those who'd like something a little more structured.

Cultural tourism

Tribal immersion programmes, village visits, township tours, learning experiences, music and dance shows and community-run outdoor activities are beginning to pop up all over Africa. These can either be booked as add-ons to a holiday itinerary, or fixed up with the organizers ad hoc. While some offerings can feel forced or under-rehearsed it's more common for travellers to rate **cultural experiences** as the highlight of their trip.

Morocco offers numerous guided tours which explore rural areas in depth, introducing you to Berber culture and lifestyles. In northeast Namibia, you can spend time with San Bushmen, walking and camping in the wilds, learning how to interpret the landscape, gather honey and trap small animals. In Ethiopia, a rural homestay programme allows

Having a ball

Team sports contribute greatly to African social life. **Football** is the big one: just about every city, town or village community has a cheerful kick-about at weekends on the nearest pitch, which may just be a scrap of beach. In some parts of the continent – particularly South Africa – **rugby** and **cricket** are massively popular, too. For visitors, a trip to a local league match, an international fixture or a traditional sporting event (see p.195) can be quite a buzz, while joining or organizing an informal game can be a fine way to engage with local people.

hikers to enjoy a hands-on taste of village life. Tanzania has an extensive community-run cultural tourism programme which offers the chance to go bushwalking with Maasai tribesmen or to learn about local mythology, among many other options. Township tours in urban South Africa and organized visits to villages, farms and schools in rural communities all over the continent can offer a fascinating insight into ordinary people's lives, and lead to interesting exchanges if your guide is a good communicator.

In Central African Republic and Cameroon, it's possible to spend time in the rainforest with Ba'Aka or Baka tribespeople, joining them on a hunting expedition and finding out about natural remedies and other traditions. West African countries, particularly The Gambia, Senegal, Mali and Ghana, are good places to study traditional drumming and dance, or a more complex musical instrument such as the kora. Other skills you can try to pick up on any African trip include greeting people in their local language and cooking regional specialities; in the absence of a formal course, hotel and safari camp staff may be delighted to help.

Music, celebrations and festivals

If you'd simply like to appreciate **music**, rather than learn how to play it, Africa is your oyster – wherever you go, you'll find gloriously infectious and atmospheric melodies and rhythms seeping out of car radios, shop windows, mosques, churches, bars and clubs. Live music and dancing is the entertainment of choice all over the continent.

The best thing to do is simply dive in; most towns and many villages host regular concerts, club nights and other events, particularly in the most music-mad countries. Classic styles to listen out for include Moroccan *rai*, Cape Verdan *morna*, Senegalese *mbalax*, *kora* music from The Gambia, Mali and Guinea, Malian desert blues, Congolese *soukous* and South African *kwaito*. While resorts and towns have their share of tacky tourist places and sleazy clubs, there are plenty of fun, progressive nightspots too. To seek out one of these, or a place playing authentic traditional music, your best bet is to hook up with a knowledgeable local.

If you're lucky enough to be invited to a family or community **celebration**, grab the opportunity – great music will almost certainly feature.

Ideally, try to time your visit to coincide with one of Africa's many supremely exuberant festivals; for some ideas, see pp.56–62.

History tours

Africa's secrets and mysteries include monumental **ruins** which have confounded Western analysts, eleventh-century **churches** thought to have been carved by angels, and human-like **fossils** which pre-date modern man. Though widely scattered, many historic sites are accessible to independent travellers, and some can be strung together to make a tour.

- **Prehistory** You can piece together fragments of Africa's past by poring over hominid remains at the National Museum of Ethiopia in Addis Ababa, the National Museum of Tanzania in Dar es Salaam or the Cradle of Humankind museum in Maropeng, South Africa, or visiting some of Africa's many ancient hunter-gatherer rock art sites.
- **North African civilizations** The influence of the Pharaohs, Phoenicians and Romans can still be felt in the archeological splendours of Tunisia, Libya, Egypt and Sudan, most notably Leptis Magna in Libya and Egypt's pyramids and temples.
- **Great Zimbabwe** These substantial stone walls are the remains of a city which served as the capital of an international gold and ivory trading network between the eleventh and fifteen centuries.
- **Oriental Orthodox Ethiopia** Among many visitable treasures are the monolithic rock-hewn churches of Lalibela, which were created out of the rock on which they still stand, in the twelfth and thirteenth centuries.
- **West African empires and kingdoms** Mali's gorgeously curvy thirteenth-century Soudanic mosques, such as the Grande Mosquée in Djenné and those in Timbuktu, are the most conspicuous reminders of the powerful empires of Ghana, Mali and Songhaï, while there are fine examples of traditional nineteenth-century Ashanti architecture near Kumasi in Ghana.
- **Transatlantic slave trade** Visitors can meditate on the legacy of the trade at ruined fortresses such as those on James Island in The Gambia and at Cape Coast in Ghana.
- **Swahili stone towns** You can marvel at intricately carved doors and the remains of sumptuous palaces on the islands of Lamu in Kenya, Zanzibar in Tanzania, and Ibo and Moçambique in Mozambique.
- **Twentieth-century colonial history** There's beautiful, though rather forlorn, colonial architecture in Saint-Louis (Senegal), Asmara (Eritrea), and on the island of São Tomé, formerly French, Italian and Portuguese respectively. South Africa has numerous poignant heritage sites including Boer War battlefields and apartheid museums.

Urban adventures

Think Africa and a **city break** doesn't spring readily to mind. However, a handful of African cities have so much to offer that you could easily while away a week or two in exploring them.

The Maghrebian cities of Marrakesh, Fes and Tunis wear their many layers of history gracefully, their medinas an absorbing blend of mystery and ostentatious colour and noise. Cape Town is Africa's darling, with a stunning setting and a sophisticated atmosphere. Johannesburg, despite its reputation for crime, is an irrepressibly upbeat and vibrant city that's stuffed with things to do and see, including some of the best museums in Africa.

Other, smaller towns which are simply pleasant or atmospheric places to spend a few days include Essaouira in Morocco, Saint-Louis in Senegal, Asmara in Eritrea, Stone Town on Zanzibar, Port Louis on Mauritius, Victoria in the Seychelles, Maputo in Mozambique and São Filipe on the Cape Verdean island of Fogo.

Relaxation

Whether you're craving an antidote to the demands of a busy life or just a break from routine, a few days enjoying Africa's **beaches**, **spas** and **wide open spaces** can be just the job.

Myths and mortality

By the time I hit the seven-week mark of my time in Uganda, my Lusoga was coming on quite well and we were learning more about the culture. We kept being told the tale of the night dancers. You utter the word in Lusoga and it makes hundreds of kids fall silent. They are people who come out at night and walk on their hands. They have very wide eyes and they are thought to eat the bodies of recently buried people, so, after every burial, someone guards the grave for three days ...

Alex Pearman

Africa's best beaches

Since you're taking the time to read this book, it's unlikely that you're planning to travel all the way to Africa just to flop on a beach and do nothing, but some of the continent's **coastal regions** are so beautiful and enticing that there's no shame in choosing to do exactly that for at least a day or two. Tunisia, Egypt, The Gambia, Kenya, Tanzania, Mauritius, the Seychelles and South Africa all have well-established beach-holiday industries catering for large numbers of English-speaking tourists, while other countries including Senegal, Cape Verde, Mozambique, Ghana, Madagascar, Comoros, Mayotte and São Tomé and Príncipe have specialist appeal.

Which **location** to choose is a matter of taste, but you can't go wrong with the very pretty beaches on the Indian Ocean islands of Zanzibar, the Seychelles, Madagascar and Mozambique and the little-visited Gulf of

Guinea island of Príncipe. On the mainland, the Indian Ocean beaches are generally more appealing than the Mediterranean, Red Sea and Atlantic ones; although the latter often have fine sweeps of pale sand, they can sometimes be windy or just bleak, with dangerous currents. Inland, much of Lake Malawi's shoreline is truly lovely.

Compared to the mega-resorts found in parts of Europe and the Caribbean, African **beach resorts** tend to be fairly small and tasteful, with clutches of informal bars and restaurants among well-spaced, low-rise hotels, often sympathetically designed using wood and thatch. With the exception of private islands and the carefully guarded beaches fringing exclusive hotels, resort beaches are rarely quiet and you may have to think up a strategy to deal with irritating trinket-sellers and hustlers. However, travel beyond the resorts and you may find wilder beaches where crabs scuttle along the shore and, in season, turtles haul themselves up the sand to nest.

Some of the most interesting beaches to visit, though by no means the cleanest, are **working beaches** which serve as boat yards, fish markets, smokeries, running tracks and football pitches for the locals; the buzz of activity morphs into a family-holiday atmosphere at weekends.

One thing to bear in mind is that, contrary to popular imaginings, the sun doesn't always shine in Africa – pick the wrong **season** and you may find your chosen spot lashed by tropical storms (common on the Indian Ocean during the rainy season) or simply drizzly and grey (a real possibility on the Mediterranean in winter). At other times, the sun's rays may be so merciless you'll want to cower in the shade (see pp.53–56).

Wild swimming

Anywhere that's good for snorkelling (see p.178) is also good for **swimming**; other places for a delicious dip include Morocco's Cascades d'Ouzoud, Ghana's Wli Falls, Togo's Kpimé Falls, Nigeria's Wikki Warm Springs and the many other enticing waterfalls and natural pools scattered all over the continent. The Devil's Pool, a natural, rock-walled infinity pool right at the lip of Victoria Falls, on the Zambian side, is the classic spot to recline in the waters of the Zambezi in the dry season (see p.393).

Yoga, wellness and spas

These days, practically every luxury lodge or hotel in Africa has some kind of **wellness centre**. Many also offer yoga classes, massage and spa treatments using local oils, salts and minerals, sometimes adapting recipes and techniques derived from tribal traditions. A n hour or so of this is a great way to unwind after a few days scuba-diving or bumping around in a safari vehicle. Mauritius, the Seychelles and South Africa have some particularly gorgeous places to chill out and there are inspiring yoga and meditation holidays available in Morocco, Egypt, The Gambia and Kenya.

African culture

I f your first taste of Africa is a visit to one of its more Western-feeling cities – Cape Town or Windhoek, for example – it may take a little while for the essence of the continent to seep in. But dig deeper and a more distinctive side of Africa, complex and somewhat chaotic, is likely to leave an indelible impression.

People sometimes talk about the "**real**" **Africa**, by which they usually mean Africa at its most earthy and beguiling – a kaleidoscope of colours, sounds and customs that is quite different from anything found anywhere else. Some visitors are knocked sideways by the continent's rich-poor divide; others are swept off their feet by the sheer energy of it's villages, towns and cities – the jumble of new and crumblingly old, the cacophony and the commercial vigour. You may be delighted by Africans' warmth, friendliness and decency; you may also find yourself bemused by their unsentimental attitudes to animals and relaxed sense of time.

Africans are inured to non-Africans thinking of Africa as a single, troubled country. While this kind of gaffe may spark anything from wry amusement to resentment and frustration, many have long shared a conviction that the most effective way to elevate their continent's status in the global arena is not only through good governance, but also through political and economic unification. Heartfelt feelings of **pan-African solidarity** really took flight during the 2010 World Cup Finals in South Africa. However, such sentiments are all too often contradicted by fierce **ethnic rivalries**. For these and countless other reasons, Africa can be bewildering, particularly if you start out with minimal grounding in what makes the place tick.

Some tourists fly out, spend a fortnight in gorgeous, remote safari lodges and then fly home again without making any meaningful contact with the "real" Africa at all. While there's nothing wrong with this, a much richer and more rounded experience can had by taking time to get to know people and make a few personal discoveries about life in this much-misunderstood continent.

Building an understanding

If, like many outsiders, your knowledge of Africa is based on a hotchpotch of wildlife documentaries and news reports, you'll probably want to do some homework. Reading African **newspapers** and **magazines** online, sifting through **guidebooks** and dipping into **novels**, **history and art books** can fill in some gaps, while the **blogs** of volunteers and travellers can offer an extremely useful insight into what it feels like as a foreigner to experience Africa first-hand.

Once you arrive, try not to insulate yourself. Instead, get **involved**: travelling by public transport, exploring on foot, breaking away from your travel companions and striking up conversations with people in everyday situations can all be great ways to make worthwhile discoveries.

Coping with culture shock

Even those who have travelled in the developing world before can sometimes find themselves floored by the blunt realities of life in Africa. The **stark contrasts** between African living conditions and those that you're used to can seem overwhelming, and unfamiliar social norms may leave you embarrassed and confused. It's perfectly normal for travellers to experience a rush of conflicting responses. You'll be particularly vulnerable to this if you're suffering from fatigue and the type of "climate shock" which can hit you like a punch if, for example, you've come straight from a crisp North American winter into steamy equatorial Africa.

When it comes to tackling culture shock, **knowledge** is power – the more you can learn and understand about your surroundings, the steadier you will feel on your feet. You may not necessarily like all you discover, but you will feel more confident in your assessments and better equipped to seek out positive experiences. You'll be less likely to jump to wrong conclusions, too – the gulf between rich and poor in Africa and the contrast between the developed and developing worlds may seem shocking, but the situation is more complex and nuanced than at first it may appear.

If you're feeling at sea, take your time and try to adopt a positive, open-minded attitude. Making **friends**, whether they're locals, fellow travellers or both, will help soothe your feelings of disorientation and alienation: being able to laugh and chat with somebody will ground and relax you, and lend a sense of belonging. When you're ready, get out and **explore**, aiming to demystify your surroundings little by little. If you're lucky enough to be the optimistic type who delights in everything new and so escapes the worst of first-impression culture shock, watch out for a post-honeymoon stage when harsh truths and homesickness begin to wear you down.

Whatever your strategy for dealing with culture shock, you should make sure you remain true to who you are – total immersion can have serious destabilizing effects in the long term. So **stay in touch** with

⑬

Love in a hot climate

What could be better than deepening your knowledge, understanding and love of Africa by spending a little quality time with somebody new? Those who decide to embark on a **holiday romance** during their stay in Africa won't need convincing of the advantages, so here, for the sake of balance, are a few of the drawbacks.

- **They may not be all that into you** Especially in resort towns, certain young locals – both male and female – make their living by striking up relationships in the hope of being treated to cash, gifts and invitations to the tourist's homeland. In such affairs, any rewards which pass from one to the other are considered payment, but are not necessarily referred to as such. Nor do the individuals concerned label themselves prostitutes: unlike the latter, who quickly let potential clients know the score (see p.221), romancers don't necessarily make upfront requests, relying instead on gentle persuasion and hopeful hints. In some cases, such relationships are happy arrangements in which both parties understand exactly what the other expects. Sometimes, though, one half of a couple (whether tourist or local) is simply exploited. It may be some time before they realize this – many con artists are highly plausible and masters of the long game. You don't want to be the victim, obviously, and nor do you want people to think of you as a chancer.

- **It's all too easy to lose your head** And, for the unwary and supremely unlucky, it's easy to lose your money, your valuables and your dream trip, too. Taking care of your possessions does not mean you don't trust your new partner – it's just common sense. Spending time with the object of your affections might seem more important than anything else right now but before you jettison your travel plans (let alone your return journey), try to think forward to the point at which it will all come to an end. Will you be plagued with regrets over all those travel experiences you missed?

- **You don't know the rules** If things do turn sour for any reason, you may find yourself totally out of your depth. Your partner's friends and family may be extremely protective and you can't assume they'll be willing to listen to your side of the story.

- **Your health is at stake** HIV/AIDS and other sexually transmitted diseases are no joke; see p.77.

people and events back home and try keeping some kind of **journal** to help organize your thoughts. Meanwhile, if you feel like dosing up on familiar, non-African food and online TV from time to time, go for it.

Once your trip comes to an end, it's time to prepare for **reverse culture shock**. This can strike particularly hard after a lengthy stay in which you've bonded deeply with a particular region or community. Keeping in touch with African friends, reading African news, taking an active role in supporting relevant causes and seeking out people who share your interests and experience will help soothe the pangs.

Toubab! Mzungu!

As a non-African in Africa, it's hard not to feel **conspicuous** – partly because people will keep reminding you of your otherness. Africans will automatically categorize you as a foreigner first and a student, a lawyer, a friend or whatever else you might be second, and will treat you accordingly, right down to the way in which they greet you.

This affects all travellers, regardless of their ethnic origin, but if you happen to be white, you may feel it particularly acutely. It's common-place in Africa for whites to be referred to (both to their face, and in general discussion) by the local slang for "white person". In several West African countries, the label used is *toubab*, although nobody really knows why – some say the name is a corruption of a word meaning doctor. The origins of its East African equivalent, *mzungu*, are clearer – it's the Swahili for "person who wanders around", and was first applied to European explorers, much to their chagrin, no doubt. Other parts of Africa have their own terms, such as the straightforward *branco* (white) you'll hear in the ex-Portuguese colonies. Most of the time there's no insult intended – it's just a convention to apply these terms indiscrimi-nately to any non-black.

African **children** can get over-excited when they spot a white visitor, particularly in rural areas, where they may run full tilt towards tourist vehicles, regardless of the danger, screeching "*Toubab!*" or "*Mzungu!*" at the tops of their voices. You'll quickly discover that behind all the smiles and rapt attention, these kids can be shame-less beggars, chanting out requests for pens, sweets or, more aggressively, money. Try to resist: if you'd like to give gifts to kids, it's far better to trust them to a parent or teacher who will share them out fairly at an appropriate time.

Some children (and adults) have less mercenary intentions, however: often the greeting *Toubab!* or *Mzungu!* may simply be an invitation to **chat**. Time after time you will be bombarded with the same rather mundane questions: "Hello! What is your name? Where is your husband/wife? From which country? From which hotel? Where are you going?" and so on. Try not to get irritated. You don't need to be too specific in your replies: these are stand-ard **forms of address** similar to those which Africans use on each other as a greeting or a preamble to a conversa-tion. If there's sufficient enthusiasm, and language skills, on both sides, you can then move on to more interesting topics.

Toubab, give me!

Thirsty after a walk around Janjanbureh, I was heading back to camp to refill my water bottles.

An enterprising little lad spotted me from a distance and yelled out one of the shoutier children's favourite demands: "Toubab! Give me your big bottle!"

Scampering over, he reached up to give the larger of my two bottles an emphatic tap. I had no idea whether he was hoping to sell it, or just play with it. Either way, a gentle word seemed in order.

"Look, mate", I said, calmly, with a smile. "It's a bit rude to yell 'Toubab, give me your big bottle' like that. Didn't your parents teach you to respect your elders?"

Something seemed to have hit home, as the lad looked thoughtful and contrite. He pondered the matter for a few paces, until eventually he had decided on the correct apology.

"Sorry! Toubab, give me your *small* bottle!"

Nathan Pope

Daily life

Spend a little time in any African village – or just hang out with the staff of your hotel or lodge for a few hours – and you'll pick up on certain elements of African culture right from the start. Other aspects are more subtle and may only be unearthed, let alone understood, through patient enquiry. You may decide that you'd like to adjust your behaviour out of respect for certain norms and expectations: for guidance, see Chapter 14.

Greetings and debates

In many parts of Africa, the fastest way to grab a random stranger's attention is with a hiss – abrupt though this may seem to foreign ears, it's not considered impolite. Between friends, acquaintances and business partners, however, every encounter begins with a **greeting** along with (for men) a handshake, a hand-hold or a respectful hand-on-heart gesture – if you're travelling widely, you'll soon catch on to the regional variations. Blanking an acquaintance in the street or launching into a conversation or transaction without at least a courteous "Hello, how are you?" is considered the height of rudeness, and may prompt a frosty, uncooperative response; by contrast, a friendly greeting is likely to elicit broad smiles. Old friends, associates or close relatives may engage in a lengthy series of ritualized enquiries and responses which, to outsiders, may seem maddeningly long-winded, but which help cement personal relationships and pass news around. On road journeys through remote regions, your driver may stop for a long chat with every other driver he passes, enquiring after their health, their family, their livestock, their business and so on.

Just as important as the habit of greeting and sharing pleasantries and news is the custom of gathering to **discuss** topics and issues of current interest. Here, there tends to be a strong gender divide – in traditional societies, women will hold informal debates at home or on the way to work or to collect water, while men will head out to a specific meeting place. In the simplest rural villages, this may be a platform or shelter set up under a venerable old shade tree; in towns and cities it is, as you might expect, the social club, pub, bar, café or shebeen.

The extended family

Solitude, let alone loneliness, are unthinkable concepts for most Africans, many of whom grow up in close-knit communities consisting of large family groups. While Western-style houses and apartments are becoming more and more common in many parts of Africa, in the less-developed regions the family home may be a **compound** or yard containing a hand-built house or two with shared sleeping quarters, perhaps separated up with curtains.

While some might consider such a way of life claustrophobic, some choose to appreciate it as a social support mechanism. Respect for the elderly is key among those who live together in a compound and, for women at least, domestic duties such as cooking, cleaning and caring for the young are shared.

Family ties are so strong, and the obligations which go with them so powerful, that wage-earners often feel obliged to distribute their entire income among relatives who are either too old or too young to work themselves, even if their numbers run into dozens. Those who aren't earning are expected to pull their weight, too, by mucking in with the daily chores, which can be extremely labour-intensive, particularly if the home lacks reliable power and mains water.

Within the extended family and beyond, males and females typically assume different roles. Despite women being responsible for more than their fair share of productive labour and holding high-level positions in some governments, much of Africa remains powerfully male-dominated. Campaigners are trying to redress the balance by stirring up debate on labour rights, unequal working conditions and certain ethnically specific cultural practices, such as female circumcision.

Hospitality and gift-giving

The giving and receiving of **gifts** is stitched firmly into the fabric of African society, as are gestures of **hospitality**, from offering a new friend a glass or two of sweet green tea brewed by the roadside to inviting them for an extended stay.

The cheerful belief that those whom God has smiled upon should be glad to share their good fortune with others can manifest itself in a level of **expectation** that some find hard to take. Many a modestly successful African feels a certain amount of trepidation about going home to visit their extended family, knowing that they will be expected to bring presents and money for all. But when an African asks somebody who they assume is better off than themselves for a gift, they do not always expect to be taken seriously, and they certainly don't mean to cause offence; such requests are simply considered logical.

Given that asking for gifts is socially acceptable, it's hardly surprising that **corruption** manages to worm its way into many layers of African life – there's a fine line, after all, between a gift or a tip and an outright bribe. See p.215.

Shared meals

In traditional societies all over the continent, groups of people with a common bond – relatives, those who share a compound or co-workers, for example – usually eat the main meal of the day together, often from a large, round, **communal bowl**, or a set of **shared dishes**. It's commonplace, particularly in North Africa, for men to be served separately from

Kola nuts

In West Africa, the giving and receiving of **kola nuts** – the pink and white chestnut-sized fruits of the kola tree – is a traditional expression of friendship, trust and respect, or of hope that good fortune is on the way. As such, they're more highly prized and graciously received than money. Kola nuts also have a crucial ritual function as a symbolic gift in social and business transactions such as marriages and the purchase of land.

The inside of the kola nut has its own cryptic meaning. It divides into segments, with six being the luckiest number – the African answer to a four-leaf clover. When chewed for their bitter juice, the nuts act as an appetite depressant and a mild stimulant: before the arrival of tobacco, cannabis, tea and coffee, kola was the main non-alcoholic drug of the region. They are often shared on long journeys and make an excellent present to offer a village chief on first meeting.

women and children. Typically, the dish will consist of the local staple – rice, couscous, ugali or some other starchy food – with a central pile of spicy stew (usually called sauce in West Africa and relish in southern Africa) including chunks of meat, fish or vegetables.

Communal eating is a supremely companionable way to dine, though it takes a little mastering. First, everyone cleans up; somebody may offer to pour water straight onto other people's hands for this purpose. Next, having taken their places in the circle, each reaches forward with their right hand only (never the left, which is considered unclean in North, West and Central Africa – see p.76) to make a ball of the starchy stuff in the fingers, dipping it in the sauce and (of course) complimenting the cook. It's important not to stretch right across the bowl or to help oneself to the tastier morsels; the polite thing to do is to wait for the host to nudge pieces over. If spoons are used instead of fingers, they should never be left in the bowl while others are eating.

Religious and spiritual traditions

The Western trend towards secularism is not echoed in Africa, where religious traditions have a tangible influence over many facets of everyday life, from eating, drinking and washing habits to names, greetings, marital practices and manner of dress.

Islam and **Christianity** dominate the continent, with most Africans adhering to one or the other for life; agnosticism, let alone atheism, is given little credence. However, the crusaders and missionaries of centuries past did not manage to extinguish African's traditional beliefs altogether and today, many still consider it acceptable and logical to lace their Muslim or Christian devotion with a lasting faith in ancestral spirits and the power of the forces of nature.

Taking the continent as a whole, Christians outnumber Muslims; there are literally thousands of different denominations including Roman Catholic, Pentecostal and Baptist sects, with evangelical movements particularly strong, especially in the south. Southern Africa's Zion Christian Church, a branch created by black South Africans in the early twentieth century, has almost twenty million members. As elsewhere in the Christian world, biblical and saints' names are common. Church attendance is enthusiastic, with well-dressed believers piling into their place of worship each Sunday. The most distinctive Christian traditions in Africa are those of the ancient **Oriental Orthodox Church of Ethiopia**, famous for its rich heritage of icons and devotional murals, and for the monolithic churches of Lalibela. The holiest object in any Ethiopian church is a tabot, a replica of the tablets on which the Ten Commandments were inscribed; wrapped in coloured cloths, it takes pride of place in the solemn processions held to mark important festivals such as Timkat (Epiphany), accompanied by drums, the beating of prayer sticks and the shaking of sistrums, a type of rattle.

In Muslim communities – particularly common in North and West Africa and the East African coast – the **mosque** is a focal point of towns and villages and the call to prayer, which in some districts can be an ear-shattering chant broadcast through crackly speakers and in others the most beautiful ethereal music, is heard in every neighbourhood. The prescribed routines of the faithful punctuate the days, with five prayer times daily; the weeks, with everyone dressed in their finest for Friday prayers at the mosque; and the years, with the observance of festivals and the holy month of Ramadan.

Many African Muslims have traditional Koranic names, often an Africanization of the Arabic, and greet each other with the universal blessing, *Salaam aleikum* ("Peace be upon you"), and response, *Aleikum salaam* ("And upon you"). Other Arabic phrases that crop up in everyday speech include *Insh'Allah* ("God willing") and *Alhamdulilla* ("Thanks be to God"). African Muslims are very proud of the sense of morality, discipline and cleanliness engendered by their faith, and some (though not all) view the Islamic sanctioning of polygamy as a great privilege – many men aspire to having more than one wife. The Muslim practice of abstention from alcohol is commonly but not always strictly followed.

A large proportion of African tribes and individuals, particularly in the remoter areas of the continent, adhere in some way to **traditional beliefs**, while some consider themselves wholly **animist**. Animism – a blanket term for a panoply of spiritual allegiances – is based around the conviction that natural phenomena, such as trees and animals, plus specially created objects such as idols, masks and fetishes, have spiritual power. Every ethnic group has their own distinctive traditions which rely on the existence of non-abstract supernatural forces, some harmful and some beneficial, controlled by witch doctors, herbalists, diviners and marabouts. These spiritual guides also act as mediators between the living and the dead, enabling people to communicate with their ancestors. They have the power to create amulets, sometimes called *jujus* or *grisgris*, which

Wandering through Stone Town

Zanzibar. Spice island. Tropical island of dreams. The narrow street in the old quarter of the capital is clean in that grubby sort of way you come to know and love when travelling. Well-swept, but with a ground-in layer of grime that has been there for generations, that will remain for generations.

It's hot in the sun, but that barely reaches down here. Tall, ancient buildings form the valley walls of our route. In centuries past, these were the homes of wealthy Arab merchants who came to this hub of civilization to trade in spices and exotic woods, silks and humans. The cooling gusts smell of a thousand crossing paths, creating a kaleidoscope of imagined stories.

While the buildings are suffering the usual tropical decay, their glorious teak-and-iron doors defy the ravages of time. And what did the worthies of their day decorate them with? Brass studs and iron spikes, in wonderful patterns. Why? To deter the elephants, of course. No, there aren't any elephants on Zanzibar, and probably never have been. These beautiful, heavy doors were carried here from India, to become as much a part of the rich tapestry of Zanzibar as spices and dhows.

Nathan Pope

can bring good luck or influence the course of events.

Rites of passage

In traditional African society, a person's passage through life is marked by a series of cornerstone **rituals** that bestow blessings and confirm the individual's position and role in their family, clan or extended family, and in society at large. These rites of passage, and the social structures that underpin them, are mutating and, in some cases, becoming extinct as Africa becomes more outward-looking, but many Africans remain extremely proud of their cultural heritage and are reluctant to give up the ways of the past.

Death, marriage, the initiation of children at puberty and the naming of a newborn are all observed in a formal manner, with the details of proceedings varying from region to region and tribe to tribe. Common ingredients tend to be feasting, music and dance. For some rituals, the timing is rather precise – naming ceremonies typically take place a certain number of days after the birth – while others may be less predictable. Initiation ceremonies, for example, may be so lengthy, elaborate and costly for the participating families that they can only be held once every three years or so. Visitors who spend an extended period in a rural community may be invited to witness proceedings first-hand.

Music, dance, visual arts and sport

Rhythm and melody add texture and colour to just about every aspect of life in Africa, from journeying by public transport or strolling through town to family celebrations, festivals and major civic events. The study of African **music** and **dance** and their rich cultural context could easily become a lifetime's work, but much is extremely accessible through tourist-friendly recordings, concerts and shows. Africa's **visual arts** tradition focuses on two main strands – textiles and woodcarving – but in recent decades Africans have also begun to make an impact in architecture, painting and cinema. For details of cultural tourism programmes, festivals and events which are accessible to visitors, see pp.56–62 and pp.181–183.

Football is a great leveller: thanks to bars and "video clubs" showing satellite TV broadcasts of British, European and international matches, everyone keeps up with the game and has their favourite celebrity players, while groups of friends of all ages love nothing better than a kick-about.

Many countries have homegrown sports, too, though an increasing number are endangered. Typically these are ritualized activities in which tough young men compete to win honour for their family or region and impress eligible young women. Traditional West African wrestling (*lutte traditionnelle* in francophone countries) is an impressive show of machismo, with pairs of burly opponents grappling in a dusty arena. Several cultures practice martial arts: examples include Tahtib stick-fencing, performed at festivals and weddings in Egypt, and the more violent Donga stick-fights of the Suri, Ethiopia.

Contemporary issues

It's perfectly possible to enjoy Africa at face value, but if you take an interest in a few of the underlying issues that the continent faces, your understanding and appreciation will increase a notch a two. Key concerns, from poverty to conservation, are summed up below.

The poverty gap

Groaning under intolerably large burdens of debt and saddled with corrupt governments, a harsh climate, recurring famine and widespread disease, it's hardly surprising that some African countries have found it impossibly difficult to shake off the curse of **poverty**. Other factors are also at play, such as the bitter legacy of colonial regimes which stirred up tribal divisions and failed to invest in education, leaving populations fractured and ill-equipped to manage their own affairs. Even in nations which are at peace, entrepreneurship – an African speciality – may be stifled by insufficient access to business loans.

For outsiders, the thing which may be hardest to comprehend in this, the continent with the lowest per capita income, is the poverty gap. Evidence of the gulf between rich and poor is everywhere, striking hardest when worlds collide: when a massive 4WD vehicle cruises past a rickety bush taxi or an amputee begs outside an ATM. The apparent injustice is toughest of all in those countries which are rich in oil or mineral resources, such as Nigeria, Guinea and Angola.

There are some reasons for optimism, however. South Africa and the North African states are far more developed than the bulk of sub-Saharan countries, and even in the poorest regions, the advent of **modern technology**, including affordable mobile phones and internet access, have become key factors in the empowerment of ordinary Africans. Those who previously struggled to gain access to financial institutions are now beginning to benefit from electronic banking services including money transfers, loans, insurance and interest-earning accounts – all crucial steps on the road towards greater prosperity.

Urban drift and globalization

Africa has tremendous **agricultural potential** but, according to the United Nations Environment Programme, in many countries less than a quarter of the cultivable land is in use. Agricultural output per capita is low, with most farmers relying on subsistence crops, grown with little or no mechanization. One crippling season may be enough to prompt a farmer to seek alternative ways of earning a living; the result is urban drift. Greater Cairo houses more than seventeen million people and is the eleventh largest metropolitan area in the world. Lagos has a population of more than eleven million; by 2015, it is predicted to be over eleven times larger than it was in 1970.

Many of the new arrivals end up eking out an existence on the city fringes, setting up home in shanties perched on beaches, rubbish dumps or reclaimed wetlands. The authorities' response can be brutal: a programme of slum clearance is underway in Lagos and other overgrown cities such as Nairobi. While migration to the cities is eroding some tribal customs, community spirit and family loyalty tend to be resilient, with newcomers adapting to their new environment with entrepreneurial flair.

An advantage of urban living, for some, is access to **international business connections**. Accelerated by new technology, global tastes and opportunities are influencing African lives more and more. However, the route to international success has its own problems; the African business community has to find a way of dealing with those who exploit vulner-abilities – using child labour, for example – if it is to win its battle against unfair trade. For some Africans, the urge to improve their prospects is so desperate that they will risk their lives on an intercontinental **migration** attempt – crossing the Atlantic from West Africa to the Canary Islands, or travelling by trans-Saharan lorry via Libya to Italy or via Morocco to Spain – all highly hazardous journeys which regularly fail.

Health issues

Africa is more seriously affected by treatable diseases such as **malaria** and **HIV/AIDS** than any other continent. Around 90 percent of all deaths from malaria occur in Africa, with babies and children particularly vulnerable, HIV/AIDS is a forceful obstacle to development as it attacks otherwise healthy adults: the section of the population which should normally be the most economically productive. Until very recently, there was a chronic delay in providing sufferers with drugs thanks largely to the non-cooperation of government officials with deep-seated cultural objections and a stitch-up of the supply chain by large pharmaceutical companies. Only now has this begun to turn around, partly thanks to international pressure fuelled by awareness campaigns.

Tribal division

Civil war in Nigeria during the Biafra conflict, intercommunal strife in South Africa in the years leading up to democracy, the Rwandan genocide and the complicated war in Darfur; all have made headlines in recent decades. Bitter rivalry over land and political power lie at the root of most **conflicts** in Africa, with the former colonial governments often deeply implicated. The principle of divide and rule often applied in British regions, while the French adopted a more paternalistic approach that gifted elite minorities French citizenship. Politics are messy and corrupt across the continent as a result, and for many citizens loyalty to **clan** or **tribe** is still more powerful than patriotic fervour, even in the era of democracy.

The formidable African talent for **languages** is, paradoxically, a major obstacle to ethnic harmony: as long as multilingualism is commonplace and formal education is inadequately funded, it's likely to remain the case that in most African countries no single language is spoken fluently by the majority of the people. Africa accommodates so many linguistic groups that communication difficulties and the perpetuation of tribal divisions are inevitable; in Nigeria alone, there are more than 500 spoken languages.

Overseas aid, development and investment

High profile **campaigns** such as those calling for aid to Ethiopia in the mid-1980s and the cancellation of unsustainable foreign debt in the early 2000s, along with long-running movements in favour of poverty reduction, fair trade and HIV/AIDS awareness, have kept the issues surrounding aid to Africa in the public eye in recent decades. They continue to spark emotive debate. Concerns typically centre on the extent to which funds, supplies, skills and information actually benefit the recipients, with aid schemes regularly coming under scrutiny for corruption, waste and misdirected effort. Meanwhile, stringent **conditions** imposed on African governments by the IMF and the World Bank, intended to boost economic growth, have arguably contributed to the continent's woes.

Overseas powers have taken turns at investing in (and exploiting) Africa. The latest big player is **China**, which has been heavily involved in almost every African country in recent decades. China's policy regarding

Africa appears to be evolving, with other nations looking on suspiciously, fearing a negative net effect on human rights and the natural environment.

Population pressures and the environment

Africa's **population** has now topped one billion and is growing at a rate of about 24 million per year. Despite a deceleration of the birth rate in large parts of North Africa, current predictions estimate that there could be more than two billion people living in Africa by 2050. Only 28 percent of married African women of child-bearing age use contraception – less than half the global average – and sub-Saharan Africa has by far the most youthful population on the planet; in 2050 almost a third of the world's young people will be African.

In a continent that's already troubled by deforestation, drought and regional shortages of natural resources, the future holds many challenges. Conservation experts worry that human pressures on the **environment** are so great that time is running out for Africa's network of protected areas and wildlife corridors.

Some of the **solutions** which have already been suggested or trialled are highly controversial – the displacement of peoples from their ancestral homelands to make way for mining concessions, for example, or the planting of genetically modified crops to increase agricultural yield.

Less controversial, and arguably more successful, are the type of holistic solutions which empower groups which have previously been at loggerheads, such as farmers and conservationists. In East and southern Africa, several schemes exist whereby a community-led approach to land management allows rural people to co-exist with, and profit from, wild animals. Little by little, considerable human and financial resources are being devoted to agro-forestry: recent projects in Ethiopia, Madagascar and Sudan, for example, have successfully replanted denuded orchards, wetlands and hillsides, providing gainful employment for locals in the process.

14
Responsible travel

Being a **responsible traveller** is much like being a good house guest: a little politeness, consideration, humility and common sense will go a long way towards making your stay a happy one for all concerned. And the more you know and understand about conservation, local culture and the environment, the more meaningful your trip is likely to be.

By choosing Africa as a destination, you are helping transfer wealth from the developed to the developing world – but that's just the beginning. You may also be keen to know whether your trip will help conserve the best of Africa's natural and cultural heritage, encourage ethical entrepreneurship and create worthwhile jobs – making your destination a better place both to visit and to live in. Responsible travel can do all of these things, while bringing people together in a way that fosters communication and understanding.

So much for the theory. In practice, it would be madness to get so obsessed with environmental awareness and political correctness that you forget to **enjoy your travels**. Instead, you could concentrate on a few top priorities – if you get this right, then even a short, fun trip should have an overwhelmingly positive impact. If, however, you're ready for a bigger commitment, you could consider a longer stay, possibly with some worthwhile **voluntary work** built in.

How to be a responsible traveller

As a visitor from the developed world, one of the greatest contributions you can make is simply to think carefully about how to spend your

Is your trip as green as it seems?

An unfortunate by-product of our growing appetite for holidays which "give something back" has been the advent of **greenwashing**. Some hotels, tour operators, voluntourism companies and agents can't seem to resist exaggerating their sustainable, ethical, eco-friendly and carbon-neutral credentials.

There have been cases, for example, of companies bending the truth by promoting holidays on certain private reserves as **conservation safaris**, without mentioning that pastoralists have been forcibly evicted to make way for the game. The terms **eco-tourism** and **eco-lodge** are particularly open to abuse: they have no internationally recognized definition and can be used to describe any offering which provides some contact with nature, whether ecologically sound or not.

If you're thinking of booking a package, don't be afraid to put the company concerned on the spot by asking to see their **sustainable tourism policy** or **ethical code**, regardless of whether they're a large tour operator or a small independent outfit.

A few searching **questions about your trip** itself may help clarify things, too.

- How does it benefit the local community? For example, is it partly or wholly owned and run by locals? Does it fund a profit-share or welfare system?
- How does it contribute to the conservation of local wildlife, habitats and traditional culture?
- To what extent does it rely on ethical building, recycling, energy-generation, food sourcing and transport policies?
- Does it have a related carbon-offset scheme, such as a development or reforestation programme?

relative **wealth** – no matter how much or how little it may amount to in real terms. You should also be clued-up about environmental and cultural issues. You don't need to be an expert, but it pays to be receptive and open-minded about ideas which are foreign or new to you. Organizations exploring the impact of tourism – and the businesses that rely on it – are listed on p.411.

Spending your money wisely

Key decisions such as when you travel, where you stay and where you shop can have a significant bearing on your impact.

- **Consider visiting in the low season** Not only will this save you money, you'll also be contributing directly to the local economy at a time when cashflow is slow. For further guidance, see pp.53–62.
- **Think about opting for flight-only rather than a package** Choosing your accommodation, eating and touring options independently gives you freedom of movement and maximizes the proportion of your money going to local businesses. Package-tour companies buy the components of their holidays from local suppliers at a huge discount, little of which is passed on to their customers: it's the multinationals who benefit.

- **Choose locally owned accommodation** Independent places to stay tend to contribute more to their community than those belonging to large chains or foreign investors. The most enlightened examples, though relatively rare, are professionally run community or conservancy lodges sited on the ancestral land of settled farmers or nomads, who take care to look after the surrounding environment in order to maximize their share of the profits. By contrast, large resort hotels often put pressure on the environment, and may source supplies and staff from outside the local area in the name of efficiency.

- **Shop locally** If you're staying in a resort, don't spend all your money there – share the benefit of your hard-earned cash and support the erosion of them-and-us culture by checking out the shops, bars, restaurants and markets where the locals go. You'll get to sample genuine regional produce and your experience is likely to be all the richer for it.

- **Travel off the beaten track** In many countries, the tourist industry is highly localized, with other regions receiving little financial benefit and possibly even suffering, perhaps through a generation of young locals opting out of farmwork and migrating to the resorts. To help restore some balance, try to make a few visits to far-flung villages, community tourism projects and bush camps.

- **Hire local guides** The arrangement can be casual – asking a child to show you the way in exchange for a coin or two – or formal, whereby you hire somebody to guide you on a professional basis. Either way you stand to benefit from their insight. Some countries have training and qualification schemes and codes of practice for guides (see p.170): great news for those requiring a birdwatching specialist. However, in certain circumstances – a trip to the local market, say – an unqualified guide may be just what you need. It's crucial that you and your guide have a good understanding, so have a good chat about their experience and your expectations before striking a deal. In touristed areas where visitors are hassled by would-be guides, hiring one will stave off unwanted attention from the rest.

- **Avoid false economies** Even if you're feeling cash-strapped, keep a sense of proportion. By all means haggle, but do so good-humouredly, and don't scrimp on tips. Try not to lapse into scruffiness, either, even if you're in modest surroundings, as Africans may find this disrespectful. Finally, staying in dodgy accommodation, walking when it would be safer to take a taxi or skipping essential health precautions (such as antimalarials or sunblock) just to save money are all risks that simply aren't worth taking: if the worst happens, others will have to pick up the pieces.

- **Make your donations count** The most straightforward way to donate money or items for which you know there is a need is through a registered charity or a trusted local authority such as a school teacher. During your trip, you may encounter beggars with distressing disabilities: Africans who can afford it tend to give alms without a second thought and you may to want to follow suit. Other pleas may cause you to struggle with your conscience, so it pays to have a policy and stick to it. Occasionally, people may approach you out of the blue, claiming to be in desperate need; there's no obligation to take them seriously, especially if you suspect a scam (see p.217). You may also be driven to distraction by the yells and demands of hyperactive African kids. Don't submit to outright begging for sweets and money – visitors who hand out goodies like Santa Claus set a dangerous precedent, encouraging kids to bunk off school and chase after tourists. Have a friendly chat instead – kids love to practise their English – perhaps entrusting a few gifts to a parent or teacher who knows which kids need them most. Lasting items such as pencils, books and footballs are well worth considering.

Holidaying in another world

I think I am a little different to the others here. As much as I have gathered from conversations between mouthfuls at dinner, everyone else is involved in some type of conservation work, or is spending months travelling. Not me! I'm a so-called IT professional, was owed some holiday and couldn't stand the idea of sitting on a beach reading and sunning myself ... so I packed my bags and headed to Kenya for a couple of weeks on a dolphin research project. That was two weeks ago, and I am wondering how I can wangle more time off work so I can come back.

To say conditions here are rustic is an understatement; the only fresh water is collected when it rains, the shower is a bucket and jug and the toilet is, literally, a hole in the floor. And with all this comes probably the greatest sense of community and togetherness I have ever experienced. You are never alone here. If you're feeling under the weather, everyone does whatever they can to help; if you're feeling down, they will cheer you up and if you do want some time to yourself, they will leave you to it.

Working in marine conservation is quite simply amazing. Were it possible, I would stay out here longer. Unfortunately, the "modern world" beckons. I've been two weeks without television, internet, cars, running water, a microwave and have only sent and received ten texts in total, which for an IT professional borders on heresy ... and I've loved every minute of it.

Tom Odell (GVI volunteer)

Being environmentally aware

In Africa, the health of the **natural environment** and the welfare of human communities are intricately linked. Africa's expanding population cannot afford to be profligate with natural resources such as the water on which its farmers depend and the wildlife and wilderness regions which are the mainstays of the tourist industry: as Nelson Mandela once said, a devastated geography makes for a devastated people. As a guest in Africa, you're likely to want your impact on this delicate balance to be a positive one.

- **Minimize your carbon footprint** One long stay is much more carbon-efficient than several short trips. From time to time, try travelling by bike or on foot rather than by vehicle – you'll meet people and see things from a fresh angle.
- **Consume water, fuel and power sparingly** If your room has air conditioning, heating, TV, a shower and electric lighting, think before you turn them on (or up). Insist to your room staff that you will re-use your towels and bed linen just as you would at home. And don't automatically reach for a bottle of water in a region where the tap water is safe to drink.
- **Dispose of waste thoughtfully** If you generate waste such as batteries, packaging, plastic bags and bottles, find out whether there's a community recycling project nearby.
- **Leave natural products and living things alone** Don't buy or collect coral, ivory, skins or rare wood, or anything made from these. Be careful to stick to footpaths and roads, watch animals and birds from a discreet distance and avoid stepping on or touching live coral when snorkelling or diving.
- **Consider the impact of adventure activities** Complain to your guide or rep if you feel that wildlife or habitats are disturbed during excursions. Culprits include those who drive off-road through virgin bush or along beaches used by crabs, turtles and seabirds, and safari groups that crowd around predators.

Respecting local customs and sensibilities

You don't need to pretend to be somebody you're not to fit in while in Africa – you just need to respect other people's right to be who they are, and abide by certain **courtesies**.

Most Africans won't expect you to be fully familiar with local norms, but will appreciate any efforts you make. In general, you should try to be alert to messages, spoken and unspoken. You may feel shy at first – unsure, perhaps, of how to make yourself understood, overwhelmed by an acute sense of cultural difference or simply at a loss as to how to break the ice. Of course, these feelings may be mutual! You could try practising an opening gambit, such as offering a polite greeting then asking to take photos and sharing the results.

No matter how solicitous you may be, sensitive situations may arise. Some communities are more conservative than others, particularly with regards to **gender dynamics**. In traditional North African communities, for example, any suggestion which would require women to behave unconventionally – such as an invitation to join a group of men for a meal – may cause severe embarrassment. Women tourists may be treated as honorary men in many situations, but if you're in any doubt, ask your hosts for guidance.

Religious tolerance is the norm in Africa but it's useful to be aware of certain customs. In all Muslim communities, you should make special allowances during Ramadan (see p.60). If you're a non-believer, you won't be expected to fast, but your respect will be appreciated: the best plan is to avoid being blatant or insensitive about eating, drinking or smoking in front of Muslims during daylight hours and remember that, come the late afternoon, they will be in a hurry to get home for *iftar* (the first meal after sunset).

The chapter beginning on p.186 introduces some other important aspects of African culture. It's wise to try to keep an open mind if, during your trip, you find yourself confronted by attitudes which don't match your own: these could concern anything from litter to women's rights. You'll deal with such situations best if you're feeling relaxed and healthy, so look after your general wellbeing: don't exhaust yourself by trying to travel vast distances in a short time, or cramming in too many new experiences.

When it comes to making everyday decisions about how to behave, the following tips may help:

- **Always, always greet people** Africans are masters of the elaborate, lengthy greeting. While you don't need to go quite as far as they do, the very least you should attempt when encountering someone you know or opening a transaction is a courteous "Hello, how are you?" If you make the effort to greet people in their own language, you'll be a hit. You should be particularly respectful to the elderly, just as Africans are. Those in positions of authority, real or imagined, usually expect courteous treatment, too, and it's best to humour them.

- **Be discreet** Swimwear may be fine on the beach or by the pool, but elsewhere the very minimum you should wear is shorts or a skirt and a T-shirt, while in formal or conservative company, it's best to make an effort (see pp.85–87). Feelings about public nudity vary a great deal; if in any doubt, cover up. Africans tend to reserve intimacy for private moments, so to avoid embarrassment, you should avoid public displays of affection.

- **Observe the right hand rule** In North, West and Central Africa, the right hand is the only one you should ever use to shake hands, handle food and offer money or other objects (see p.76).

- **Be tactful and respect people's boundaries** All over Africa, much of everyday life, from working, eating and socializing to nursing babies, takes place outdoors, in the public eye and in some situations – on public transport, for example – personal space may be non-existent. Nonetheless, you should try not to intrude; it is sometimes considered rude to march up to somebody uninvited. Certain sacred sites are off-limits to non-believers, or to those dressed inappropriately; if in doubt, ask first. Common sense should tell you when it's best not to flaunt your relative wealth; you should also tread carefully during discussions relating to politics.

- **Be prepared to offer gifts** If you're invited to an African friend's home for a meal or a celebration – a real privilege which you should grab if you can – it's polite to bring a present. While some families will be delighted with a bottle of something, others may prefer a bag of kola nuts, rice or cornmeal, or its cash equivalent. As a rule of thumb, you should assume that a gift whose value exceeds the cost of anything you're likely to consume yourself is expected – your hosts will peg this on an assumption of what you can afford. You may later be asked for more, but if your hosts are genuine, they won't necessarily expect you to comply. Remember to keep any promises you make, though, in this or any other situation: if you take a photo of somebody and say you'll email it to them, don't forget; if you say you're going to raise funds for a village school when you get home, be sure to follow through.
- **Don't assume you can just help yourself** If you'd like to camp or just draw water from a village well, seek out the chief or local governor first. Similarly, there will be times when the locals need shared services more than you; if all the buses are jammed with

---

Is it OK to take photos of people?

The simple answer is: only when they say so. Attitudes to **photography** vary widely across the continent; many adults and most kids love it (aim your camera at one child and a grinning mob will rush in to join them) but some people take grave offence. Rural North Africans, the women who work in West African markets and officials of all varieties tend to be particularly strident in their objections. It's not always practical to ask permission when you're shooting crowd scenes or candid portraits however; in these circumstances, you should be ready with smiles and polite apologies, perhaps showing any disgruntled parties the screen of your camera so that they have the chance to veto the pictures you've just taken.

Inevitably, you will occasionally receive requests or even demands for **money** in exchange for photos. This can present a real dilemma. Every time a tourist pays over the odds for a minor service, they are contributing, in a small way, to the phenomenon whereby kids drop out of school and adults abandon traditional jobs in order to try their luck at wangling a living in tourist areas. Some Africans go around in tribal costume in the hope that someone will pay for photos of them; tourists who do so may think they are helping keep traditional culture alive, but in fact they are in danger of trivializing it.

Rather than refusing all requests for payment or doling out money like confetti, you could try, every so often, picking just one or two people or families that you'd really like to photograph, spending some quality time with them and offering them a small gift at the end of it.

people rushing home to their families for a festival, for example, think about paying for a taxi instead.

● **Be prepared to adjust your timetable** People and events are often late in Africa. Outside the urban areas, notions of time and duration can be pretty hazy, with dusk and dawn the only significant markers. That said, if you try to anticipate delays, you may be caught out. Scheduled transport leaves on time at least some of the time.

Getting stuck in

Many first-time visitors to Africa are perfectly content for their holiday or journey to revolve around conventional tourist activities such as splurging in a souk, wildlife-watching from a minibus or blissing out on a beach, all of which can, with a little thought, bring positive benefits to local people and places. However if you'd prefer to get more involved in African life, it's well worth considering a **voluntourism** (volunteer-tourism) experience or **conservation expedition**.

Working on teaching, welfare, development or conservation projects as a volunteer has rocketed in popularity in recent years, with entire books now devoted to the subject. The term voluntourism was coined to distinguish paid-for working-holiday experiences which are open to anyone, skilled or unskilled, from conventional, vocational volunteer placements which normally have specific selection criteria. Setting aside at least part of your time in Africa for this kind of activity can help add shape and purpose to your travels, and offer the immense satisfaction of "giving something back". If you'd just like a taster, you could book a two-week sightseeing and adventure holiday which has a couple of days' work built into the itinerary. Africa also has a great many dedicated voluntourism programmes, lasting anything from a week to a couple of years; some of these are specifically geared towards students and under-25s on a **gap year**, or to those planning a **career break** or **sabbatical**.

The easiest way to find something suitable is through an **intermediary**, usually a specialist travel agent or project coordinator, although a few projects are set up for direct bookings; see pp.408–411 for contacts. As well as offering your time, energy and commitment, you have to pay a sum to cover your expenses and the administration fees, just as you would if you were booking any other holiday or activity. In some cases, the money you pay may have a greater positive impact than any of the tasks you'll undertake – but that shouldn't necessarily put you off. The best programmes can also be positive in other ways, greatly increasing your understanding of Africa and enhancing your sense of connection with local people and your natural surroundings.

The following pointers may help you choose between the vast array of options:

- **What's included?** Just like any other holiday, you should check the itinerary, exclusions and refund policy of the programmes which interest you. Confusingly, some companies describe their paid-for programmes simply as volunteer placements rather than voluntourism holidays. Others are clear about charging fees, but vague about what they cover: you may have to ask for a breakdown. Some options are complete packages with international flights, board and lodging included; others may provide a roof but leave the rest up to you. A donation to charity may be included, but this isn't always the case. Your lodgings may be simple (camping, perhaps, or a room in a village compound), which tends to keep costs down, but some companies (such as ⓦhandsupholidays.com) also cater for people who'd rather not rough it. For the most desirable but logistically complex conservation projects, prices can be very high.

- **What prior experience will you need?** Age limits aside, many voluntourism programmes have no entry criteria: you're expected to decide for yourself whether you have the experience, skills and personality to cope well with the tasks. Think carefully, as you may be thrown in at the deep end, with minimal training.

- **What will be expected of you?** You'll need to be happy to put the needs of others before your own – these are team-based working holidays, after all – but the actual duties vary a great deal. Some projects are flexible, letting you choose from a range of tasks or think up your own, while others are more structured, with a heavy focus on supervised group activities. There may be time for organized tours, fun activities, barbecues and days off – but, again, this varies, so check in advance.

- **Who will benefit most: the local community or environment, the organizers, the agent, or you?** Ideally, all four will have a decent share. However, some voluntourism companies exploit tourists' goodwill by charging over the odds, or making disingenuous claims: exaggerating the conservation value of a wildlife project, for example, or promoting a school-building or language-teaching project as something that will enrich the lives of rural children, without mentioning that skilled local people may lose out on paid work in the process. It's therefore a good idea to do your own research into the needs of the local area and consider whether the project will have lasting value. You could start by seeking feedback from past participants: good project organizers and agents will happily pass on some contacts.

- **What about red tape?** In most cases, voluntourism participants just have to remember to mark "tourism" rather than "work" on their immigration forms, but in a few countries, tourists are not allowed to accept work of any kind, even if it's unpaid. In South Africa, you can currently work for no pay for the duration of your tourist visa; Australian and Canadian students and recent graduates can extend this to a year (and land certain types of paid work, too) by applying for a working holiday visa. The Australian scheme is run by IEP Work South Africa (@iep.org.au); the registration fee of A$1930 covers the visa and a starter pack of goodies including internet access and a few nights' accommodation. An equivalent scheme for Canadians is run by SWAP (@swap.ca, registration fee CA$1080).

Conservation safaris and expeditions

Africa's most popular responsible tourism experiences focus on wildlife and nature. While most organized wildlife-watching trips have some educational element, specialist **conservation safaris** and **eco-tourism trips** go further by focusing on sustainability, showing you examples of conservation in action and priming you in a wide range of issues such as wildlife management, environmental pressures, human-predator conflict and the preservation of endangered species. Generally these trips are led by top-quality guides, sometimes in conjuction with full-time conservationists who have been specially invited to take part; for this reason, you can expect to pay considerably more than you would for a standard safari.

Wildlife or conservation **voluntourism experiences** and **expeditions** offer a taste of life as a full-time researcher for a wildlife or conservation NGO. As well as taking part in fieldwork, you may receive formal or informal instruction in zoology, botany and other relevant subjects. Typical opportunities include projects concerned with rehabilitating orphaned animals, monitoring populations, carrying out coral reef surveys, observing animal behaviour or mapping rare and endangered

---

Learning the art of field guiding

If you're intrigued by everything from kopjes and kori bustards to rhinos and rhino beetles, and would like to take things a stage further, you may enjoy a **field guide course** or a **nature reserve internship** in Africa's safari heartland. You'll learn about habitats, flora and fauna and be instructed in practical skills by professional field guides who are highly respected, some for their quiet wisdom, others for their action-hero antics and hilarious campfire tales. Prior experience isn't necessary, but you'll need to be physically fit.

It takes years to get as good as the top guides, but a six-month stint of introductory training will set you on the right road. The guiding associations on pp.170–171 can put you in touch with training centres in Kenya, Zimbabwe, Namibia, Botswana and South Africa. Shorter options are available through some of the voluntourism companies listed on pp.408–411: for example, you could spend two weeks in the Tuli Block, southern Botswana, learning the basics of bush survival and big-game tracking.

plants. You might end up collecting information on wild dolphin groups and clearing nearby beaches in Mauritius, helping to dart lions in Kenya or setting camera traps for leopards and taking casts of their spoor in Namibia. Some have a special focus on the balance between the needs of wildlife and those of local people. Well-established projects are currently running in Kenya, Mauritius, Madagascar, Namibia and the Seychelles. South Africa has the widest range of opportunities, including some with a vocational element, such as wildlife veterinary placements.

Community voluntourism and internships

Voluntourism experiences which focus on **education** or **welfare** can be a great way of getting involved with African communities in a positive and meaningful way, and learning about local issues at a grass-roots level.

These projects attract a little more **controversy** than conservation projects. There's an argument that handing development roles over to unqualified Westerners is inefficient, and even unpalatable; some feel that participants would do more good if, instead of investing in this kind of trip, they simply gave the money directly to a well-run charity. Nonetheless, many community voluntourism projects do have tangible benefits, not least in fostering understanding between people from different cultures: the people who take part often strike up lifelong friendships and connections with their host communities. Obviously, the more you have to offer, the better for all concerned: if you have much-needed medical, counselling, care-giving, teaching or technical skills then a short voluntourism placement may be a very good use of your time.

Some projects demand great emotional maturity – you could teach English to kids in deprived urban areas in Kenya, help run an emergency medical service in remote, rural Namibia or work as an assistant caregiver to people with HIV/AIDS in South Africa. Others are more physical: you could offer your skills as a sports coach or help restore a historic building, fix a well or build a rural school or clinic.

As an alternative to development work, you could opt for a short **internship** or **work exchange** at, say, a radio station, newspaper, clinic, or community lodge; some voluntourism companies organize these, while others are advertised by word-of-mouth. You'll be expected to check visa regulations, cover all your expenses and pay some kind of participation fee, just like any other voluntourism experience.

Working as a paid volunteer

If you believe you have more to offer and are prepared to take on a lengthy commitment, you may want to consider working as a **paid volunteer** for an Africa-based charity or non-governmental organization,

Baboons and humans

When I first started working with baboons in Kenya, every day brought fresh insights. The juveniles in the troop, always the most curious, would be the first to "geck". Gecking – the perfect word when you hear this particular vocalization – is a sign of distress and sometimes suggests ambivalence between two strong emotions, often fear and attraction. On this one occasion, the numerous gecks brought more baboons to investigate. I was on foot and approached cautiously, expecting to see something dangerous. I had to laugh: the focus of their interest was an old tennis shoe or trainer, carried there by something (a hyena perhaps?) or someone from a distant Maasai encampment. Ten years later I recalled the trainer incident in a scene that was almost identical – except this time it was taking place at the entrance to a small cave. And the baboons now had reason to be both curious and fearful, because inside, cornered by the baboons, was a leopard cub.

Shirley Strum, Ⓦ baboonsRUs.com

perhaps via a dedicated international volunteer programme such as VSO (Ⓦ vsointernational.org), the Peace Corps (Ⓦ peacecorps.gov) or their equivalents (see p.411). The payment you'll receive for taking part will normally be just enough to cover your basic expenses, in cash or in kind.

The role of volunteer organizations in Africa is complex and delicate – the best ones play a supremely **positive** role in development, by sharing skills which help empower communities, or offering useful guidance on conservation matters; others stand accused of **neo-colonialism** or futile goals. If you're happy to pick your way through this minefield, then programme recruitment departments and handbooks on the topic can help you find a placement.

Unlike voluntourism experiences and internships in which you pay to take part, paid volunteer placements are not usually open to unskilled applicants, no matter how enthusiastic they may be. A notable exception is the Peace Corps, which kicks off every placement with a few weeks of rigorous (and often excellent) training.

Paid voluntary service tends to be much **longer** than most voluntourism experiences – a stint of eight weeks to two years is typical. While voluntourism projects tend to be designed for instant appeal – dealing with charismatic wild animals, for example – vocational projects focus on the most pressing needs and may therefore seem somewhat **unglamorous**. You may be working as an IT trainer, education officer or agro-forestry advisor in a disadvantaged district or town that's far from any tourist attractions. However, you'll have plenty of scope for making plans and putting them into practice; in fact, the more initiative you show, the more constructive and successful your posting is likely to be. You'll also have time to learn **languages** and other skills, and build lasting relationships, all of which can produce a very satisfying feeling of progress and purpose.

Crime and safety

t's easy to exaggerate Africa's potential for mishap and disaster. True, there's a scattering of large towns and cities where snatch robberies and muggings are fairly common – and a few countries have areas that are effectively no-go zones (see pp.24–25) – but the main problems for travellers are minor **theft** and **corruption**. By taking care of your belongings, the first can be largely avoided, while your dealings with people in uniforms can become a game, once you know the rules. While it's important to remember that Africa's fifty-plus nations are not uniform in respect of personal security – with North Africa having a somewhat different set of issues and South Africa being a unique case – the vast majority of visitors to the developing countries of sub-Saharan Africa have no problems at all.

For impoverished **local people**, of course, without the safety nets of insurance, credit cards and diplomatic representatives, life can be perilous, whether in the cities or in the rural areas. Africa's environment poses some inherent risks, and if you're heading to a remote area, on a hiking trip for example, it's worth leaving details with your country's embassy, high commission or honorary consul. And even when you feel perfectly safe, it's wise to be aware that your hotel might have dodgy wiring, or your bus might be leaking brake fluid: the chances are nobody will ever inspect either.

When first arriving in any **big city**, it's certainly wise to be very cautious for the first day or two. There's always a lot happening on the street and it's important to get used to the harmless, robust interaction that you will usually encounter on public transport and in markets. Try not to be daunted by this, and don't confuse upfront friendliness and curiosity with threats to you or your belongings. Don't forget to buy **travel insurance** before you set off (see p.80).

Thieves

If you flaunt the trappings of wealth where there's urban poverty, you can be sure that somebody will want to remove them from you. There's less risk in leaving your valuables in a securely locked hotel room. If you clearly have nothing on you (no jewellery, no day bag), you're unlikely to feel, or be, threatened. Above all, don't feel victimized: every rural migrant coming to the city for the first time goes through exactly the same process, and most will be considerably less streetwise than you. And don't forget that fellow travellers are as likely – or as unlikely – to steal from you as anyone else.

Border saviours

Crossing the border between Niger and Nigeria at the eastern border post near Lake Chad is supposed to be easy. I arrived in a packed minibus and was immediately called into a shack where a drunk, red-eyed border guard was leaning back in his chair expecting a good *dash* (kickback) from this single white female. Feeling an immense dislike for this overblown grub, I sat down with my book and started reading, leaving the guard to examine my perfectly valid visa.

Much was my shock when he suddenly pulled out his gun and started shouting that my passport was fake and that I was going to be arrested. I started explaining that it looked different because it was Danish (this was before the purple EU passports) and that I had travelled into Nigeria many times before with this passport – showing him the old visas. He then decided I was a spy.

I was beginning to lose my patience. Thankfully, so were my fellow passengers – they stormed the shack and started shouting at the border guard telling him enough was enough. Remarkably this seemed to do the trick: he stamped my passport and let me go. Continuing on our journey there was much merriment in the minibus, and a palpable sense of empowerment. Bloody border guards.

Lone Mouritsen

Pickpocketing can happen anywhere: it's usually the work of pocket-high thieves, hanging around in markets or other crowded places. Carry out with you only what you need, and make sure your valuables are secure (see p.84). More serious **muggings**, in which something is grabbed from you by an assailant who dashes off at high speed, usually take place in specific areas of the city where visitors like yourself are most likely to be found, for example in crowded, downtown shopping streets, city-centre parks and central markets. Don't feel unduly intimidated at bus stations and taxi parks as they are always full of tough young men working as drivers or ticket sellers, who tend to be on the lookout for threats to their passengers. Lower-income suburbs away from the city centre also tend to be safer, as people just aren't used to seeing travellers, and you're unlikely to be targeted. Slum ghettos are a different matter, especially where they are located in close proximity to affluent districts. Visiting such areas is usually best done with a guide from a local tour company.

Avoiding theft from **hotel rooms** or **public transport** is largely in your hands. Basic precautions include choosing a reputable hotel (those where thefts seem to be inside jobs quickly become hot topics on the traveller's grapevine) and keeping the key when you go out, rather than leaving it at reception. Use the room safe if there is one, get into the habit of tucking valuables out of sight and be sure to close windows when you leave the room. When you're actually on the move, keep a close eye on your belongings at all times. On buses you will typically find your main luggage is stowed separately, either in the hold beneath, or tied down on the top rack. Luggage on the rack is invariably safe, but if it's in the hold make sure the guys in charge are good at their job. It's not a bad idea to get out at each stop to stretch your legs and ensure your bag doesn't leave the bus before you do. Probably the commonest way to lose valuables on a bus is by falling asleep with your precious items strewn around you. Keep your belongings safely tucked away at all times and out of reach of fellow passengers.

If you're **driving**, there is a low but real risk of highway banditry in parts of some countries. This is often flagged up on government travel advisories, and police roadblocks will often advise as to the danger and – in some cases – insist on vehicles travelling in convoy with an escort.

Avoiding city dangers

Most **robberies** take place in cities, and if you're on foot, it's always a good idea to have a clear route in mind. Try to avoid shaking the hands of strangers who may try to offer you something, fall into step with you or otherwise waylay you. These are usually innocent enough interactions in rural areas, but in the city can often presage a more aggressive encounter.

Avoiding **looking like a tourist** can be hard, but nevertheless it's worth trying to dress like a local expat, for example in a short-sleeved, collared shirt and slacks or skirt. For the same reason, it's never a good idea to start a trip in brand-new shoes that mark you out as just arrived. Sunglasses will make you feel more confident and your inexperience less easy to read (don't forget to take them off when you want to talk to someone).

If you're unlucky enough to be mugged, it will be over in seconds and you're unlikely to be hurt. But the headaches that quickly accumulate as soon as you try to do something about it (see p.214) make it doubly imperative not to let it happen in the first place. Street thieves who get caught are often dealt with summarily by the crowd, and may be badly beaten or even killed, so if you shout "thief" you should be very sure how much you value the item and be quick to intercede once you've retrieved it. If you want to make a claim on your travel insurance, you'll need to get a police report.

Police

Most **police forces** constitute a separate entity from the rest of the people: they have their own compounds and staff villages and receive – or procure – subsidized rations and services. While it's usually wise to avoid them as far as possible you are bound to come into contact with the police occasionally, as the notion of "control" remains highly developed in the majority of African countries, even where you're no longer obliged to check in at the local police station on arrival in every town. Checks on people's movements, and on goods by customs officers, take place at junctions and along highways in most countries and many capital cities have major checkpoints on their access roads.

If you are the victim of crime, usually the first reaction is to go to the police. Unless you've lost irreplaceable property or important documents, however, think twice about doing this. They rarely do something for nothing – even stamping an insurance form may cost you – and you should consider the ramifications if you and they set off to try to catch the culprits. If you're not certain of their identities, pointing the finger of suspicion at people is the worst possible thing to do. If they're arrested, as they probably will be, a night in the cells usually means a beating and confiscation of their possessions.

In **smaller towns**, or where you have some contacts, a workable alternative to police involvement is to offer a reward or enlist traditional help in searching for your stolen belongings. Various diviners and traditional doctors operate nearly everywhere and if the culprits get to hear of what you're doing you may get some of your stuff back. Local people will often go out of their way to help.

If you have **official business** with the police, smiles and handshakes always help, as do terms of address like "sir" or "officer". In unofficial dealings, especially in remote outposts, the police can sometimes go out of their way to assist you with transport, accommodation and food. Try to reciprocate. Police salaries are always low and often months overdue, and they rely on unofficial income to get by.

Accidentally breaking the law

There are several ways you can inadvertently get into trouble by infringing local laws with which you may not be familiar. Firstly, never go out and about without identification: failure to carry a **photo ID** (*carte d'identité*, *papiers* or *pièces* in French) is usually against the law, and ignorance is no excuse. You don't have to carry your passport at all times, but a photocopy of the page showing your personal details in a plastic wallet is very useful and you can hand it over without worrying about having your passport mysteriously confiscated while you think about paying an instant fine.

Failure to observe the following points of public etiquette can get you arrested or force you to pay a bribe.

- Stand still on any occasion when the country's national anthem is played or its flag being raised or lowered.

- If you're driving, pull off the road completely if a caravan of motorcycle outriders and cars appears. If you're on foot, stand still. It usually means the president is coming by.
- Destroying banknotes – even if they are worthless.

Bribery and corruption

Bribery is indeed a way of life, but probably not yours. Increasingly, people in Africa believe they shouldn't have to live with corruption either, and it's beginning to lose its grip as democracy and accountability make inroads across the continent. Nevertheless, for most African citizens, it is remarkable how much petty corruption percolates every aspect of their transactions with officials, who demand a *cadeau* (francophone countries), a *dash* (anglophone West Africa) or just *kitu kidogo* or "something small" in Swahili-speaking regions. Whether sitting an exam, passing a driving test, retrieving a parcel from the post office or applying for a job, money will very often change hands, beyond any official fees. The expectation is so deep-rooted that people on the public payroll are often prepared to put up with low salaries because of the financial opportunities they are guaranteed. The problem finds its most gratuitous expression in dealings with the **police**, who usually strike fear and contempt in the people they are supposed to be protecting. Where loathing isn't the response, a weary humour takes over: local people often accept the need to pay what is effectively protection money, and grumble about excessive demands, rather than protesting at the principle itself.

Whatever locals do, if you as a traveller find yourself confronting an implacable person in uniform, you do *not* have to give in to tacit demands for money. If you can't, or won't, give gifts to officials, give words: the golden rule is to keep talking. Most laws are there to be discussed rather than enforced, including imaginary ones about the importation of backpacks, the writing of diaries or the possession of two cameras; politeness and good humour usually help move matters along.

If you're undertaking extensive African travels, you have literally hundreds of police, army, customs, immigration and security **checkpoints** to cross. With the right attitude, you'll sail through ninety percent of them, and with patience and good humour the other ten percent can be negotiated relatively painlessly. When you and the policeman both know that the "infraction" he claims you have committed is bogus, or when the immigration officer pauses before stamping your passport and asks what you brought him from your country, just keep talking, keep smiling and hang on. If necessary, be very humble and plead your case in hushed and reverend tones.

Travelling by **bus, lorry** or **bush taxi**, note that it's the driver who pays. If you're singled out for any reason, remind them it should be the driver who pays. And always avoid any show of temper – aggressive travellers

215

Soap for the soldiers

Northern Uganda has always been a hazardous area to travel due to the prevalence of armed insurgents such as the Lord's Resistance Army. However it was even more difficult in the 1980s, when it was hard to distinguish between various rebel factions, undisciplined government troops and remnants of Idi Amin's recently-defeated army.

The first time I travelled there I thus sought advice from those familiar with the area, and was told to "take soap for the soldiers". I dutifully purchased a couple of bars of local laundry soap before setting off. After a somewhat hair-raising journey across southern Sudan, which entailed a four-hour truck chase after escaping from an ambush by armed robbers, I finally reached the comparative safety of the Ugandan border.

The first border guard I encountered regarded me with great interest, and slowly and ostentatiously cocked his assault rifle, before shoving its barrel into my nose. "And what have you got for me, mzungu?", he enquired menacingly. Without missing a beat I replied, "For you my friend, I have a bar of soap". I was relieved when he appeared entirely satisfied to have extorted such a luxurious item.

Exactly the same routine continued at the next three roadblocks over the next 10km, leaving my supply of soap greatly depleted. As we approached yet another roadblock I was wondering what I could sacrifice next. But this one was different: instead of a horde of soldiers barking orders, there was simply a small hand-painted sign, saying "Stop, Tsetse Control Picket". Eventually, an old man dressed in rags appeared out of the jungle with an ancient hand pump, and wordlessly began spraying the truck.

Despite the total chaos all around, and the pull-out of aid workers from the area, this old gent was determined to continue his part in the otherwise abandoned tsetse fly control programme, intended to eradicate sleeping sickness in the region.

Peter Moszynski

always have the worst police stories.

There are occasions when you will be asked for money and you'll be hard pressed to know whether you're being hit on for a little present, or being charged a genuine fee. Border crossings with bridges or odd bits of no-man's-land sometimes spawn a thriving fee culture. Asking for a **receipt** is always a good way of finding out if it's legitimate: the handwritten, carbon-copied, thumpingly stamped receipt, torn from a dog-eared booklet, is a cherished icon of every official financial transaction. Even the most corrupt petty official wouldn't issue a receipt for a bribe.

On the road

If you're **driving**, your obvious relative wealth makes it harder to avoid shelling out, especially at border crossings, and you may occasionally be forced to pay sweeteners to speed your exit from one country and entry to the next. If you haven't got all day, a "small present" – couched in exactly those terms – is all it usually takes to resolve matters, though you should haggle over it as you would any payment. The equivalent of a few dollars is often enough to oil the wheels.

For travellers in their own vehicles, being stopped by the police is a common experience on virtually any road. **Checkpoints** are generally marked by a rope across the road, sometimes stretched between concrete-filled oil drums, or by strips of spikes, with just enough room to slalom through. Always stop completely, greet the nearest officer and wait to be waved through. If you're accused of breaking any law, then politely accept what you are told and be prepared to call their bluff. Agree that this is all unfortunate but you need to be sure it's being dealt with in the proper way, and if they would just explain the procedure to you, you will be happy to oblige. Of course, court appearances and official channels are rarely on their radar. Refusing to play the game, unless you've brushed up against a very stubborn, greedy or drunken individual, will only cost you a short delay until he gives up on you to try another potential source of income.

If you're driving, it's never a good idea to leave your **vehicle** unguarded if it has anything whatever of value in it, even if it's locked. Remember, it has plenty of value *on* it, such as the wheels. In towns, there will usually be someone who will volunteer to guard it for you for a tip (half up front, half when you return). Most hotels and other lodgings will provide a secure, guarded parking area, within their compound.

Scams

The kind of **scams** that occasionally sting unwary travellers in Africa invariably take place in towns and are usually quite transparent attempts to persuade you to a) stop and interact and b) part with some cash. Changing money on the **black market** (see p.145) is an obvious risk, so choose your location and moneychanger carefully, know the rate and what the notes should look like, and always have a companion with you.

There are many scams that are used to lure you (and not just you, but local people too) into a decision to part with some cash voluntarily. The classic one is the student subversive/terrorist suspect routine in which you are approached by a genial young person who engages you in conversation and then makes a **request for money** for school fees, to repay a loan or medical bills or something similar. Eventually you either give him a little money or simply exchange contact details. As soon as he's gone and you're possibly breathing a sigh of relief that you weren't conned, a group of more threatening heavies turn up. They claim to be undercover police officers and accuse you of assisting a suspect to engage in seditious/criminal/terrorist activities, for which you could be fined or arrested. When they suggest that you simply pay a fine now, you should offer instead to go to the nearest police station, but only with someone in uniform. At the same time, make very loud protestations of innocence and be sure people in the vicinity can see and hear what's been going on. The gang will melt away.

Another popular ruse that plays on liberal sensibilities is performed by a stranger who approaches you asking whether you **recognize them**, "from the hotel", "from the restaurant", "from the other day" or just "because I think you know me". Trust your instincts: you don't know this person, and you're not about to lend them money, pay for their urgent medicine, or help them out with the school fees that will help lead them to an unblemished life in the service of the Lord.

On public transport, **doping** scams have occasionally been a problem, with individuals managing to drug tourists and relieve them of their belongings. Even at the risk of causing offence it's best not to accept gifts of food or drink on public transport.

Approaches in the street from "schoolboys" with sponsorship forms and from "refugees" with long stories are not uncommon and probably best shrugged off, even though some, unfortunately, may be genuine. These scams are sometimes played out quietly on public transport, allowing you to brood over your possible meanness and the comparatively low cost of salving your conscience – even though you know you have nothing to be ashamed of.

If you're **driving**, you may experience the "something wrong with your car" scam as several people at the side of the road (always more than one, to provide credibility) seem independently to be pointing out dripping oil, a flat tyre or something amiss with your vehicle as you drive by. This is inherently implausible (there's so much wrong with ninety-nine percent of vehicles on the roads that you'd have to be driving with no tyres for anyone to notice) and on no account should you stop.

Drugs

Cannabis is the biggest illegal drug in Africa, widely, if clandestinely cultivated. You will see rastas in many parts of the continent, though in some countries their openly rebellious lifestyle is barely tolerated. Many social problems are routinely attributed to smoking the "grass that kills" and it's widely believed to cause insanity. In practice, if you indulge discreetly, it's not likely to get you into trouble, but if you are caught and convicted, you're not likely to escape without a severe penalty – usually a fine and deportation, but sometimes a prison sentence. The mild stimulant bush **qat** or **khat** is legal in some countries, including Kenya, but illegal in Tanzania and many other countries. It is particularly popular in the Somali community.

In recent years, **cocaine** has increasingly been shipped from South America to West Africa and then smuggled north to Europe. After years of use as a Colombian trans-shipment zone, Guinea-Bissau is now virtually a narco-state. Some of the consignments get on to the streets of West Africa's big cities, together with the associated tensions and paranoia. Stay well clear: very long prison sentences and the death penalty are not unknown for those convicted of involvement in the trade.

Hustlers and phoney guides

In most parts of Africa where tourism is a source of income, a sub-culture of **would-be guides**, hangers-on, hustlers and beach boys exists on the fringes. Occasionally, these usually young men know their area and are ready and willing to show you around for a negotiated hourly or daily fee. In some places they are organized, with an office and approved membership.

But all too often the guys who will find you (rather than the other way round) are chancers, out to make a quick buck from your gullibility, or the commission on any business they can introduce you to. The easy ones to get rid of are the obnoxious characters with phoney accents who you don't mind telling to get lost. The clever hustlers are more subtle and persuasive and can be extremely clingy. Even against your own better judgement, it's easy to allow yourself to fall prey to misunderstandings in your dealings with anyone who comes across as honest and good-natured.

You should never assume anything is being done out of simple kindness. It may be, but if it isn't you must expect to **pay** something and if you have any suspicion, it's best to deal with the matter head-on at an early stage and either agree a price or apologize for the offence caused. What you must never do, as when bargaining, is enter into an unspoken contract and then break it by refusing to pay for the service. That can be something as simple as being shown the way for a couple of blocks (people rarely explain directions, they go with you). If you're being bugged by someone whose help you don't need, let them know you can't pay anything for their trouble. It may not make you a friend, but it always works and it's better than a row and recriminations.

Natural dangers

Tectonically, Africa is stable throughout most of the continent: only in the far north, notably Algeria, is there any **earthquake** danger, though minor earthquakes also happen along the Rift Valley system between Eritrea and Malawi. Volcanoes in the Rwenzori range can pose a threat, but after the last great spewing of lava across the town of Goma from Mount Nyiragongo in 2002, local people are acutely aware of the potential for a repeat. You should be aware that nearby Lake Kivu, which is saturated with carbon dioxide from volcanic activity, is also potentially life-threatening: Lake Nyos in Cameroon, a similar gas-saturated crater lake, erupted in 1986, silently emitting a cloud of undetectable carbon dioxide that suffocated 1700 villagers while they slept. Fortunately, such incidents are exceedingly rare (Nyos was the first case ever to have come under scientific scrutiny) and Africa has few other natural threats on this scale.

Heavy rain in dry regions often results in **flash floods**: never camp in a dry riverbed, especially not while purple clouds are massing over the nearby hills. In Kenya, in 2010, the Ewaso Nyiro River flooded on an unprecedented scale, destroying safari camps and lodges in Samburu National Reserve. While Africa's floods can be as severe as its droughts, the continent does not specialize in tropical storms. Africa's **coasts** can be dangerous, though: East Africa and the Mediterranean have few strong currents, but the south-facing portion of the West African coast is prone to local currents that quite often sweep people out to sea.

Although **snakes** are fairly common, they will invariably detect your footsteps and flee before you see them. However, you should never go barefoot except on the beach. Poisonous **insects**, spiders and scorpions are similarly unlikely to pose any threat, assuming you are not deliberately poking around looking for them. The biggest threats are posed by **crocodiles** and **hippos**, and throughout sub-Saharan Africa (and indeed in lakes and rivers on the fringes of the Sahara itself) you should be on the lookout for both. Crocs are most dangerous to swimmers and to local people collecting water from the bank. Swimming in inland waters is always very unwise, and can also carry a risk of bilharzia (see p.78). Hippos, which spend their days in the water sleeping and keeping cool, and their nights grazing on land, pose a threat to small boats, so take care if you're kayaking or rafting. If you camp near a river or lake, be sure not to block their route to the water.

Other dangerous animals, such as **elephants**, **rhinos** and **buffalos**, and predators such as **lions** and **leopards** are largely, if not exclusively, confined to the protected areas of national parks and reserves which, while mostly unfenced, have strict rules for human visitors, meaning you'll normally be inside a vehicle, or in the safe compound of a lodge or camp. Of these animals, it's elephants that are responsible for most accidents, as they are relatively fearless and can be very aggressive when protecting calves. Lastly, beware of **monkeys** – especially male baboons, which can be intimidatingly large – as they can carry rabies and have a reputation for biting when they become dependent on discarded food.

Terrorism

Although easily overstated, the issue of Islamic fundamentalist terrorism, as outlined on p.24, will exercise governments across Africa for years to come. **Al-Qaeda** truck bombs at the American embassies in Nairobi and Dar-es-Salaam killed hundreds in 1998. Other attacks have taken place in Egypt, Morocco, Algeria, Tunisia, Mali, Mauritania, Niger, Kenya and Uganda, but the number of victims over more than a decade represents an insignificant risk when set against the tens of millions of tourists who have travelled all over Africa in the same period.

The emergence of a group called **Al-Qaeda in the Maghreb**, largely made up of Algerian former anti-government rebels, has been the subject of much speculation. In turn, the US has quietly opened up a West African front in its "War on Terror", recruiting Algeria, Mali, Niger and Mauritania to its campaign. The results of this escalation for tourists have included closed routes across the Sahara, threats to music festivals in Mali and a very uncertain future for the nascent tourist industry in Mauritania.

Sexual attitudes

While it's a sweeping statement, the **sexual attitudes** of sub-Saharan Africa are broadly liberal. Although you'll rarely see open displays of affection between men and women, expressive sexuality is a very obvious part of the social fabric in most communities, and even in Muslim areas Islamic moral strictures tend to be generously interpreted – though across the Maghreb some communities are deeply conservative and patriarchal. South of the Sahara, all adults are regarded as naturally sexually active, and sex is often openly discussed – though not in the presence of children. If you travel with an opposite-sex **partner**, you'll find the relationship tends to insulate you somewhat from locals of the opposite sex.

Advice for gay travellers

Attitudes to **gay people** are mixed and often reactionary. People from traditional backgrounds will commonly deny the existence of homosexuality, or claim that it's a Western fashion or at best a harmless peculiarity. As for the legality of gay sex, most countries still adhere to the fossilized laws of their colonial rulers. While prosecutions are rare, recent years have seen a growing polarization of opinions in several countries, as human rights advocacy groups struggle to be heard while traditionalists have responded with a media backlash. The notable exception is **South Africa**, where the constitution embeds some of the most progressive sexual and gender rights legislation in the world, gay marriage and adoption are fully sanctioned, and there's a flourishing LGBT scene.

For gay male visitors, outside of South Africa the only parts of the continent where you'll find like-minded company are very occasional and discreet bars or clubs in the more cosmopolitan capital cities and tourist resort areas. Equally, except in South Africa, gay women can't hope to find any sign of an uncloseted lesbian community anywhere.

Advice for men

Female **prostitution** thrives throughout sub-Saharan Africa, with many cheaper hotels doubling as informal brothels (by contrast, prostitution in North Africa is completely hidden). There is rarely any sign of an organized sex trade: prostitution seems to merge seamlessly into casual promiscuity. You're likely to find flirtatious and sometimes physical pestering a fairly constant part of the scene, especially if you visit bars and stay in cheap lodgings. With HIV infection rates very high, however, even protected sex is extremely inadvisable.

Advice for women

Female travellers will be glad to find that male egos in Africa are generally softened by reserves of humour. You can travel widely on your own or with a female travelling companion without the major problems sometimes experienced in parts of Europe, Asia and Latin America. All the same, you can expect plenty of male attention, especially if you visit bars and stay in cheaper hotels. You can help to keep this in check by modifying your appearance and dress (see p.204). Whether you're travelling alone or with another woman, you may be targeted by the occasional persistent hassler, but seldom much worse, except in North Africa where the attention can sometimes reach intolerable levels. Universal rules apply: if you suspect ulterior motives, stonily refuse to converse and you will, usually, be left alone eventually. If you're losing patience, don't be afraid to lose your temper publicly: that's what a local woman would do.

When **travelling alone**, you will usually be made to feel welcome. On public transport a single woman tourist causes quite a stir and fellow passengers don't want to see you treated badly. If you're staying in cheaper and therefore less reputable hotels, there will often be female company – employees, family, bar-girls – to look after you.

In sub-Saharan Africa, **flirting** is universal and almost impossible to avoid. If a man asks you to "come and see where I live", he probably means you should come and see where he and you are going to sleep together. You'll have no shortage of offers and they're usually easy to turn down if you refuse as frankly as you're asked: unwanted physical advances are extremely rare. But it always helps to avoid offence if you make your intentions (or lack of them) clear from the outset. If you're not already accompanied by a man, a fictitious husband in the background, much as you might prefer to avoid the ploy, is always useful. All this can be fun: there's really no reason you shouldn't spend an evening dancing and chatting and still go back to your bed alone and unharassed.

Tips for female travellers

- Carry pictures of your family to demonstrate your unavailability.
- Beware of big men in small towns. Don't accept an invitation to the disco from the local police commandant unless you're on very firm ground.
- Never meet someone as arranged if you're uncomfortable about it.
- Always lock your door at night.
- Take a supply of condoms. Don't tell yourself it will never happen and be prepared.

First-Time Africa

Where to go

Algeria

Area 2,382,000 square kilometres
Capital Algiers
Population 35 million
Language Arabic (official); French, Kabyle, Tamashek and several others
Religion Muslim; tiny Christian and Jewish minorities
Government Presidential democracy, supported by the military

Independence July 5, 1962 (from France)
Best time to go Oct–April (north, winter/spring); Nov–March (south, cool season)
Country code +213
Currency Algerian dinar (DZD); US$1: DA74
Minimum daily budget US$50

Poor Algeria. The second biggest country in Africa, after Sudan, was a much-abused French colony for 132 years, the last eight of which were taken up by a bloody war for independence. Then, after almost three decades of socialist rule from Algiers, the first democratic elections, in 1991, gave a popular mandate to the Islamic Salvation Front (FIS), a fundamentalist party intent on establishing sharia law. The government annulled the elections and banned the FIS, and eleven years of civil war and terrorist massacres ensued, with the identity of the perpetrators frequently unclear (government or even foreign *agents provocateurs* were sometimes suspected, and the army often did little to defend threatened villages). By 2002, the violence had diminished and since then, most attacks have been isolated incidents in northeast Algeria. However, kidnappings, murders and banditry have spread into the Sahara, making the whole country's security status at best murky and at worst dangerous.

Geographically, Algeria ranges from a picturesque, hilly and mountainous region bordering the Mediterranean to a much drier and less populated scene just 150km south, which in turn gives way to the vast barren landscapes and striking dune systems of the Sahara. Despite its repressive government, from the late 1960s to the late 1980s

Mean temperatures and rainfall

	Jan	Feb	Mar	Apr	May	Jun	Jul	Aug	Sep	Oct	Nov	Dec
Algiers												
max °C	15	16	18	20	23	26	29	29	27	23	19	16
min °C	9	10	11	13	15	18	21	22	20	17	13	10
rainfall mm	112	84	74	41	46	15	0	5	41	27	130	137
Tamanrasset												
max °C	19	22	26	30	33	35	35	34	33	30	25	21
min °C	5	7	11	15	19	23	22	22	21	16	10	7
rainfall mm	1	1	3	2	6	4	5	6	8	3	2	2

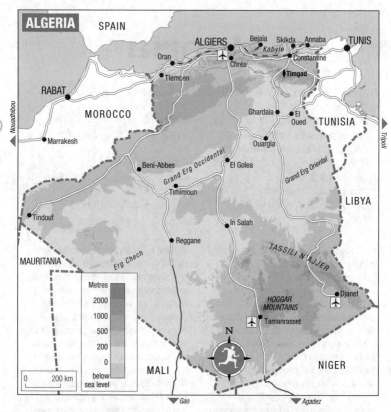

ALGERIA

SPAIN

ALGIERS Bejaïa Skikda Annaba TUNIS
Kabyle
Oran   Constantine
Chréa
Tlemcen   Timgad

RABAT

MOROCCO   Ghardaia   El
                                   Oued   TUNISIA

Marrakesh   Ouargla

Beni-Abbes   El Golea
            Grand Erg Occidental   Grand Erg Oriental
        Timimoun   LIBYA

Tindouf   In Salah

MAURITANIA   Erg Chech   TASSILI N'AJJER

            Reggane

Metres
2000   Djanet
1000
500   HOGGAR
200   MOUNTAINS
0   Tamanrasset
below
sea level   N
0   200 km

MALI   NIGER

Gao   Agadez

it was a wonderful country for offbeat, independent travellers; though always much tougher for women.

Today, Algeria remains appealing – the country's people are lavishly hospitable, and the combination of historical sites, old city kasbahs, desert oases and mountain scenery is comparable only with Morocco, but on an even grander scale. But, sadly, as much as the country has to offer, it's hard to recommend it unreservedly, and you should do your research very carefully before going.

Main attractions

● **Algiers** One of North Africa's great metropolises, Algiers is a stately bowl of a city, swooping from suburban and residential heights, through steep, upmarket hillsides down to the kasbah and the Western-style central business district. Museums (including the superb Bardo), the Palais de Raïs (an Ottoman mansion), the fishing port and the UNESCO-protected, warren-like kasbah, the old Turkish quarter, are all very much worth visiting. Seek local advice before going sightseeing, though.

● **Beni-Abbes** Take a detour from the trans-Saharan highway to visit this wonderful oasis, rambling along the Oued Saoura, wedged between a plateau and the magnificent dunes of the Gran Erg Occidental. In the town, founded in the eleventh century,

ALGERIA

Nouadhibou

Tripoli

mud-brick houses and thousands of date palms give the place a Mesopotamian feel. You can camp in the palm groves and watch local children tobogganing down the sand dunes.

● **Djanet and the Tassili N'Ajjer National Park** Once busy with tourists, thanks to regular charter flights from France, the people of pretty Djanet in this mountainous region deep in the Sahara are these days likely to welcome you with open arms. The exuberant scenery takes in cliffs, pinnacles, arches and overhangs – like sketches for an experimental planet – and prehistoric rock art shows hunters and beasts. Tours have always been expensive, but getting up close to the vivid evidence of the Sahara's once-green landscapes is unforgettable.

● **Constantine** Algeria's third city perches on a rocky plateau in the northeast, its neighbourhoods connected by six dramatic bridges across the Oued Rhumel canyon. You'll get great photos from all of them, but Pont Sidi Msid, a narrow suspension bridge hanging 150m above the river, is the standout. The city centre – a 600m by 500m oblong – is ideal for exploring on foot: don't miss the sumptuous Ahmed Bey Palace, the city's old embroidery shops and the soaring Monument aux Martyrs viewpoint.

● **Timgad** Algeria's pre-eminent Roman site was founded in 100 AD by the Emperor Trajan and built to a strict town plan in what was then a relatively fertile area. It was abandoned in the seventh century and smothered under drifting Saharan sand for 1400 years. Trajan's majestic arch, still standing, dominates the ruins, and every July there's a music festival in the amphitheatre.

● **Skiing at Chréa** Algeria's only ski resort (Jan–Feb) is located inside the Chréa National Park, a mountainous and wooded area less than 60km south of Algiers. The park is also home to Barbary macaques, the only monkey that lives in North Africa.

Routes in and out

Algiers has the country's only big international airport, with reasonable worldwide connections. French charter flights are sometimes available to Tamanrasset and Djanet. There are ferries from France and Spain to Algiers, Annaba, Bejaïa, Oran and Skikda. Overland, options are limited. Algeria's borders with Morocco and Mauritania are closed. Most of the Tunisian border crossings are open but the border crossings with Libya are sometimes closed. Crossing the Sahara from north to south is still just about feasible on the Route du Hoggar, via Tamanrasset to Agadez, though you'll need a guide-escort and will be at serious risk from banditry and kidnapping. The other trans-Saharan route, the Tanezrouft from Adrar to Gao, isn't currently being used except by military forces: stay well clear.

Red tape

Visas Required by UK, Ire, US, Can, Aus, NZ and SA nationals. Must be obtained in advance. A letter of invitation from a local organization or individual is required. You may not enter if you have an Israeli stamp in your passport.

Nearest consulates Agadez. The consulates in Niamey, Rabat, Tripoli and Tunis do not normally issue visas to foreigners.

Other consulates Canberra (Ⓦalgeriaemb.org.au); London (Ⓦwww .algerian-consulate.org.uk); Ottawa (Ⓦambalgott.com); Pretoria (Ⓣ+27 12 342 5074, Ⓔembalgpta@intekom.co.za); Washington, DC (Ⓦalgeria-us.org).

Angola

Area 1,246,700 square kilometres	**Independence** 11 Nov, 1975 (from Portugal)
Capital Luanda	
Population 18.5 million	**Best time to go** May–Oct (dry season) in the north; Dec–Feb (dry season) in the south
Language Portuguese (official); Kikongo, Kimbundu, Umbundu and many other ethnic languages	
	Country code +244
Religion Traditional, Christian	**Currency** Kwanza (AOA); US$1: Kw94
Government Presidential republic; in practice authoritarian	
	Minimum daily budget US$40

Angola has masses going for it – pristine Atlantic beaches, steamy tropical forests, roaring waterfalls, sensuous music and intriguing cultural connections with both Portugal and Brazil – but this is a destination for the truly adventurous. A hard-hearted colonial regime, a bloody struggle for independence and an even bloodier civil war have left the country in tatters. Angola has been at peace since 2002 but during the forty years that war raged, roads and bridges were wrecked and towns and villages ringed with landmines. It will take decades to pick up all the pieces.

The Angolan population is thinly spread and more urbanized than its immediate neighbours; much of the nation is uninhabited rainforest and savanna. The government has been quick to launch regeneration programmes in both urban and rural areas, with income from its abundant oil and mineral reserves boosted by investment from China. However, for now, few benefits are trickling down to ordinary Angolans – and life expectancy (less than 40 years) is so poor that few have any memory of the pre-war years. Nonetheless, the atmosphere is optimistic, particularly among the new middle class, who frequent the shopping malls and nightclubs which are beginning to pop up in Luanda.

Black rhino, big cats and rare antelopes once patrolled Angola's game parks, but these were poached bare during the war years. In the meantime, Angola's wild coastline, mountains, gorges and rivers are the key attractions. In rural villages, where Soviet tanks still lie in the undergrowth, quietly rusting away, you'll be welcomed as a novelty.

To explore, you're best off joining an organized trip with one of the few tour

Mean temperatures and rainfall

Luanda	Jan	Feb	Mar	Apr	May	Jun	Jul	Aug	Sep	Oct	Nov	Dec
max °C	28	29	30	29	28	25	23	23	24	26	28	28
min °C	23	24	24	24	23	20	18	18	19	22	23	23
rainfall mm	25	36	76	117	13	0	0	0	3	5	28	20

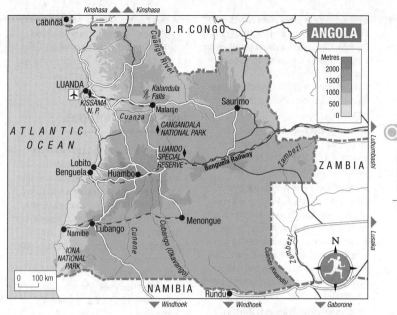

companies that operate here. The road network is rudimentary and public transport and accommodation scarce, so a camping safari by 4WD or, if funds allow, light aircraft, is the obvious option.

Main attractions

● **Luanda** Set on an attractive bay, its waters cooled by the Benguela Current, Angola's capital was once an elegant colonial town of shady squares around a twin-towered cathedral; less appealingly, it was also a notorious slave trading hub defended by the vast Fortaleza de São Miguel, which now houses a military museum. The chaos of the war years, when the poor crammed into shell-damaged tower blocks, has yet to recede and crime is still a problem, but today the city has a swagger in its step. The seafront (Marginal), dominated by the palatial national bank, is embellished with a marina and the

horizon is punctuated by skyscrapers and oil platforms. There are beaches to enjoy, museums of anthropology, natural history and slavery to nose around, and throbbing nightlife to explore.

● **Kissama National Park (Parque Nacional do Quiçama)** This vast expanse of coastal floodplains, grasslands and wooded savanna dotted with ancient baobabs has recovered from the war years better than any other Angolan national park. Situated around three hours' drive south of Luanda, its lions, elephants, rhinos and dwarf forest buffaloes are making a tentative comeback, aided by the translocation of game from Namibia and Botswana. If you're lucky you may catch a glimpse of one of Angola's endemic and critically endangered giant sable antelopes.

● **Kalandula Falls (Quedas de Calandula)** Also known as the Duque de Braganza Falls, these are reachable on a two-day trip from Luanda, staying

229

overnight in the provincial town of Malanje then continuing into the Luando Reserve. The journey takes you through rugged bushland marked by large rock formations. The sight of the Lucala River tumbling over a cliff is majestic all year round, with pools where, with care, you can take a dip.

● **Benguela** Angola's second city has a more relaxed atmosphere than the capital, its fine sandy beaches performing the role of public parks.

● **Benguela Railway** In the age of steam, the Benguela Railway was one of southern Africa's most ambitious and profitable lines, carrying copper from Democratic Republic of Congo and Zambia to the Atlantic Coast. Civil war brought services to a halt, but a restoration programme is underway and the entire line may re-open in 2012.

● **Cangandala National Park** This small park was originally created to protect several herds of giant sable antelope; a captive breeding programme is now underway to replenish the population. Situated east of Luanda in Malanje province, it encompasses papyrus swamps, miombo woodland and grasslands and offers some rewarding birdwatching.

● **Iona National Park** In Angola's arid southwest, separated from Namibia by the raging Kunene River, this park's most notable feature is the Epupa Falls, which can also be approached from the Namibian side.

● **Lubango** An appealing inland town in the southwest, Lubango was little-affected by the civil war and now has an embryonic tourist industry. Nearby, there are waterfalls, mountains and rock formations to visit.

● **Ceremonies and festivals** Visit the southeast during November and you may see Chokwe boys with stripes painted on their bodies wearing masks and sisal skirts in preparation for Mukanda, their tribal initiation. In Luanda, carnival time in February is wild, with glitzy parades and long nights of drumming and semba dancing.

Routes in and out

At the time of writing, Luanda's international airport is being replaced by a new airport at Viana, 40km outside the city. There are also numerous airstrips. The easiest and safest road route into the country is from Namibia; travellers heading to or from Zambia or DRC have to deal with bone-shattering roads and enervating bureaucracy. In the north, Cabinda and Lunda Provinces are currently unsafe. There's a risk of landmines close to the border with Zambia.

Red tape

Visas Required by UK, Ire, US, Can, Aus, NZ and SA nationals. Must be obtained in advance, and take 15–30 days to process. Apply in your home country rather than at one of Angola's African consulates, where availability and processing times can be unpredictable. You must provide a letter of invitation from a local organization or individual, an itinerary and proof that you have US$100 per day to support yourself.

Nearest consulates Brazzaville; Kinshasa; Oshakati.

Other consulates Johannesburg (☎+27 11 622 6025; ✉comu @consuladoferalangola.co.za); London (⊛angola.org.uk); Ottawa (⊛embangola -can.org); Singapore (⊛angolaembassy singapore.com); Washington, DC (⊛angola.org).

Benin

Area 113,000 square kilometres	**Independence** Aug 1, 1960
Capital Porto Novo	(from France)
Population 9 million	**Best time to go** Dec–March
Language French (official); Fon,	(dry season); Aug–Sept (dry season,
Yoruba, more than 50 others	south only)
Religion Christian, Muslim, Vodun	**Country code** +229
(voodoo)	**Currency** West African CFA franc
Government Presidential	(XOF); US$1: CFA506
democracy	**Minimum daily budget** US$40

Although Benin (see map, p.288) is now a relatively popular and straightforward place to travel, the world's lack of awareness of the country is perhaps not surprising. After independence, when it was known as Dahomey, it had two reclusive decades under one of West Africa's least successful and most repressive regimes, re-naming itself the People's Republic of Benin in 1975 – a move that confused it with the historical kingdom of Benin in neighbouring Nigeria.

Benin's years of isolation have left it an intriguing country, much more open and friendly than you might expect, with a steadily improving tourist infrastructure and some unique features. One of Africa's most sophisticated indigenous states developed here at Abomey – the capital of the kingdom of Dan-Homey, in the heart of the southern savanna. From the sixteenth to the nineteenth centuries Dan-Homey was one of Africa's biggest slaving centres, and the trade only ended in 1885 when the last Portuguese slaver steamed out of Ouidah, bound for Brazil.

Benin is mostly thinly wooded savanna, part of the open country known as the "Dahomey Gap" that penetrates south to the coast between the rainforests of eastern Nigeria and western Ghana. The open landscape partly accounts for the region's pre-colonial history, dominated by international trade and military conquests.

On the coast, the flat sandy plain is broken up by a string of picturesque lakes and lagoons. Although the Atlantic beaches are pretty, the sea has terrifying currents, so swimming is unwise. But the old towns – including Porto Novo and the voodoo centre of Ouidah – have a certain flaked-out appeal, and contain fascinating museums and markets.

Inland, a gentle plateau rises gradually north to spread over the entire centre

Mean temperatures and rainfall

	Jan	Feb	Mar	Apr	May	Jun	Jul	Aug	Sep	Oct	Nov	Dec
max °C	27	28	28	28	27	26	26	25	26	27	28	27
min °C	23	25	26	26	24	23	23	23	23	24	24	24
rainfall mm	33	33	117	125	254	366	89	38	66	135	58	13

of the country in a rich patchwork of agriculture. In the northwest, the sheer cliffs and abundant greenery of the Atakora Mountains rear up in a long, dramatic ridge, announcing the highland region of the long-isolated Somba tribe.

Main attractions

● **Ouidah** The old Brazilian quarters of this slave town and voodoo centre are hauntingly quiet after centuries of violent history. Retrace the Route des Esclaves, leading down to the beach and the Door of No Return. There are voodoo temples everywhere (the python temple is, admittedly, rather touristy) and the Kpasse Sacred Forest is a good excuse for a walk through some pretty woods.

● **Grand Popo** Once a major slaving port to rival Ouidah and Porto Novo, Grand Popo's economic decline has been compounded by severe coastal erosion so that today it looks as basic and ephemeral as most coastal villages. It has a pretty setting, though, and is an ideal spot for relaxing on the sands, with several good resort hotels nearby.

● **Abomey** The old history of Dan-Homey is easy to explore through the palaces of Abomey, a warren of buildings now partially restored as a UNESCO World Heritage Site that vividly evokes the kingdom's past grandeur and extraordinary cruelty. Look out for the throne built on top of four human skulls, symbolizing the king's dominion over weaker peoples.

● **Parc National Pendjari** On the border with Burkina Faso, this is one of West Africa's best national parks, with straightforward access and some budget accommodation options (including camping) as well as a lodge with a swimming pool. You may spot

elephants, buffalos, hippos and crocs, and this is one area outside East and southern Africa where you've a good chance of seeing lions.

● **Tatas-Somba** The Somba, one of West Africa's most interesting and inaccessible cultures, lived in these impressive mountains in relative isolation until the 1970s. Their fascinating, fortress-like homes (*tatas*, built as defence from slave raiders – you'll find a concentration near the remote village of Boukoumbé) draw visitors up from the main highway.

● **Ganvié** This stilt village – said to be the largest of its kind in Africa – is a compelling attraction. Home to more than 20,000 fishing people, it's said to have developed (like the Tatas-Somba) in response to slave raiding, as the Dan-Homey did not attack across water. Such niceties don't worry Cotonou's tour operators, who regularly mount photographic raiding parties of tourists. The locals, who have the deal largely sewn up, seem alternately impervious and disgruntled, depending on their stake in the proceeds.

Also recommended

● **Porto Novo** The narrow streets of Benin's crumbling capital are full of interest. When you're done just wandering, check out the superb ethnography museum, which has an excellent range of regional items including voodoo masks and musical instruments, and the Da Silva museum, which is evocative of the "Viceroy of Ouidah" epoch (see p.427).

● **Parc National du "W" du Niger** Pronounced *double-vé* in French, the "W" refers to the double U-bend in the Niger River, though the most accessible area is along the banks of a tributary, the

Mékrou. Plentiful hippos and antelopes and the chance to see some of Benin's remaining elephants make it well worth the visit, though you'll need a 4WD. Alternatively you could make for the Alfa Kouara waterhole and viewing deck, close to the road.

● **Cotonou** Grimy, post-revolutionary Cotonou, the country's largest city, makes a poor first impression, but there's an unmistakeable intellectual vibrancy in the air and the vast markets and pumping nightlife are genuine attractions. Look out for the excellent handicrafts at the Centre de Promotion de l'Artisanat and the macabre animal body parts in the voodoo, fetish and medicinal section at Dantokpa market.

Routes in and out

International flights all operate to Cotonou and, apart from Paris and Brussels, come mostly from West African capitals. The busiest overland point of entry is the Badagri coastal road from Lagos to Kraké. From Niger and Burkina Faso, the roads are tarred or at least in reasonable shape, with decent long-distance bus services linking Cotonou with Niamey and Ouagadougou. Along the coast, taxis speed down the highway between Lomé and Cotonou. In the north, there are some recommended scenic routes between Benin and Togo.

Red tape

Visas Required by UK, Ire, US, Can, Aus, NZ and SA nationals. If arriving by air, visas must be obtained in advance. If you arrive by land, you can obtain a single-entry visa at the border, but you may have to renew it (or leave the country) within two days.

Nearest consulates Abuja; Accra; Agadez; Lagos; Niamey. No consulate in Burkina Faso.

Other consulates London (☎020 8830 8612; ✉l.landau@btinternet .com); Ottawa (🌐benin.ca); Paris (☎+33 1 45 00 98 82); Pretoria (☎+27 12 342 6978; ✉embbenin@yebo.co.za); Tokyo (+81 3 3556 2562; ✉abenintyo @mist.ocn.ne.jp); Washington, DC (🌐beninembassy.us).

Botswana

Area 600,370 square kilometres
Capital Gaborone
Population 2 million
Language English (official); Tswana (more commonly spoken) and other tribal languages
Religion Christian; traditional minority
Government Parliamentary republic

Independence 30 Sept, 1966 (from UK)
Best time to go July–Oct (dry season) for most wildlife, though prices are high; Dec–March (rainy season) for Nxai Pan and Central Kalahari
Country code +267
Currency Pula (BWP); US$1: 7 pula
Minimum daily budget US$60

Botswana is the quintessential safari destination. No other African country has such a rich mosaic of pristine habitats, from russet-coloured dunes to glittering seasonal wetlands. Much is desert – the semi-arid Kalahari covers over eighty percent of the country. But when distant rainfall floods the sandy basins and salt pans, enormous numbers of animals arrive, including the iconic Big Five – lions, leopards, elephants, buffalos and rhinos – and rarities such as red lechwes, pukus, sitatungas and wild dogs.

Urban development is concentrated around the capital, Gaborone, near the South African border; much of the remaining land, an area slightly larger than France, is protected by parks and reserves. The north receives far more water than the south: in the northeast,

the Chobe River flows out to join the Zambezi, and in the northwest, the Okavango River flows in from Angola and Namibia, creating the country's most remarkable natural feature, the Okavango Delta.

Blessed with substantial mineral wealth, Botswana has prospered under more than four decades of stable democratic government. The downside of its reliance on diamond-mining as a source of revenue is the effect this industry has had on the indigenous San (Bushman) communities of the Central Kalahari Game Reserve; some have been forcibly evicted from their diamond-rich homelands, desert regions where their ancestors have lived as hunter-gatherers for centuries.

While it's perfectly possible to explore Botswana's landscapes, towns and

Mean temperatures and rainfall

Gaborone	Jan	Feb	Mar	Apr	May	Jun	Jul	Aug	Sep	Oct	Nov	Dec
max °C	30	30	28	25	24	20	20	24	27	28	30	30
min °C	22	21	18	16	10	7	7	10	15	18	20	21
rainfall mm	98	84	71	41	13	6	3	6	16	43	67	90

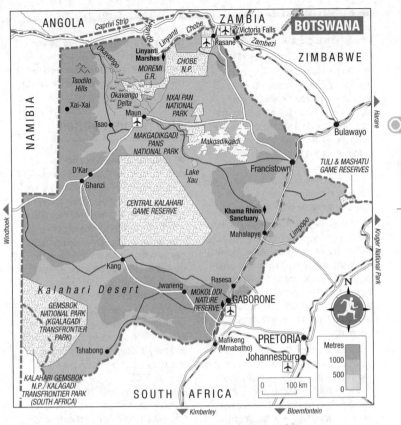

ANGOLA — Caprivi Strip — ZAMBIA — **BOTSWANA**

Victoria Falls

Kasane — Zambezi — ZIMBABWE

Linyanti Marshes — CHOBE N.P.

MOREMI G.R.

Tsodilo Hills

Okavango Delta

Xai-Xai

NXAI PAN NATIONAL PARK

Tsao — Maun

MAKGADIKGADI PANS NATIONAL PARK — Makgadikgadi

Bulawayo

D'Kar

Ghanzi

Lake Xau — Francistown

TULI & MASHATU GAME RESERVES

CENTRAL KALAHARI GAME RESERVE

Khama Rhino Sanctuary

Mahalapye — Limpopo

Kang

Kalahari Desert

Jwaneng — Rasesa

MOKOLODI NATURE RESERVE — **GABORONE**

GEMSBOK NATIONAL PARK (KGALAGADI TRANSFRONTIER PARK)

Tshabong

Mafikeng (Mmabatho) — **PRETORIA**

Johannesburg

KALAHARI GEMSBOK N.P./ KALAGADI TRANSFRONTIER PARK (SOUTH AFRICA)

SOUTH AFRICA

Kimberley — Bloemfontein

Metres
1000
500
0
0   100 km

N

NAMIBIA

Windhoek

Harare

Kruger National Park

villages independently, most visitors opt for a wildlife-watching safari. A national policy which favours high-spending, low-impact tourism over mass-market alternatives means that just about every kind of safari is available here – camping, walking, self-driving, horseriding, elephant-back – but prices are universally high. Happily, you get what you pay for: nothing can beat the thrill of a light aircraft flight to one of Botswana's remote safari lodges, which are among Africa's finest. From simple seasonal camps to sumptuous boutique lodges, most are decorated in unpretentious good taste and staffed by excellent cooks and expert guides.

Main attractions

● **Okavango Delta** One of Africa's most beautiful wilderness destinations, this huge, seasonal expanse of sparkling streams, lakes and islands is breathtaking. Torrential rain on the mountains of Angola causes the waters of the Okavango River to surge southwards, but they never make it as far as the ocean – instead, in July and August, they fan out over the northern Kalahari and are gradually sucked dry. Settle into a *mokoro* – the Batswana answer to an Oxbridge punt – and you'll get low-level views of the elephants, hippos, crocodiles and birds found among the delicate reeds and waterlilies. When the flood waters recede, game drives take over from *mokoro* trips.

● **Chobe National Park** A game drive through Chobe in northern Botswana is another of Africa's classic safari experiences. Huge herds of elephants, up to four-hundred strong, congregate along the Chobe River, lions are plentiful at the park's waterholes and, after the summer rains, rare antelopes such as lechwe and sitatunga can be seen in the freshwater swamps. Boat trips on the river offer fantastic birdwatching.

● **Makgadikgadi Pans National Park** Here, the stark, salt-encrusted bed of an ancient sea offers surreal vistas. Sowa Pan in the east is the breeding ground for greater and lesser flamingos, while the western reaches become grassy after the rains, attracting wildebeest, zebras and lions between February and April.

● **Moremi Game Reserve** On the edge of the Okavango Delta, this reserve offers rewarding wildlife-watching from April to October – before, during and after the flood season. All the Big Five are here, including the elusive leopard. There's a wider choice of safari lodges than in the Delta itself, from delightful boutique lodges to rustic tented camps.

● **Nxai Pan National Park** The area north of Makgadikgadi is another seasonal grassland; when the foliage is abundant, impalas, springboks, zebras, giraffes, blue wildebeest and red hartebeest graze here. It's also an excellent place to see bat-eared foxes, jackals and brown hyenas.

● **Tsodilo Hills** Chosen, perhaps, because of the way they stand out so conspicuously from the surrounding sea of sand dunes, this quartet of 800-million-year-old hills is sacred to the Ju/'hoansi San of the Kalahari. Local guides will show you some of the hundreds of rock paintings of human and animal figures and explain their mythological significance. Laurens van der Post famously called this remarkable site a "Louvre in the desert".

Also recommended

● **Gaborone** Like Windhoek in neighbouring Namibia, Gabs is more of a small town than a city, and that's key to its appeal. It's the obvious entry point for those travelling overland from South Africa, with a wide choice of places to stay, eat and shop. Overlooking the city from the west, with fine views, is Kgale Hill. On Independence Avenue in the city centre, the displays on indigenous traditions at the National Museum are worth a browse; to continue your researches, head out to the Phuthadikobo Museum in Mochudi and the Matsieng Footprints rock art site, whose San Bushman petroglyphs are over 3000 years old. Also within easy reach of the city, Mokolodi Nature Reserve offers white rhino tracking and features elephants, cheetahs, giraffes and warthogs so habituated you can literally walk among them.

● **Kuru Museum and Cultural Centre** The village of D'Kar near Ghanzi, in a remote region west of the Central Kalahari Game Reserve, hosts a project focusing on San culture, with a heritage museum, a gallery of contemporary art and an annual dance festival, held in August.

● **Kgalagadi Transfrontier National Park** Straddling the boundary with South Africa and co-managed by the two countries, this park includes beautiful stretches of semi-arid duneland in the classic Kalahari palette of deep red and ochre. Oryx, elands, blue wildebeest and black-maned lions are found here, and birds flock in when the rain transforms the salt pans into lakes.

● **Khama Rhino Sanctuary** This community-run conservation project near Serowe was set up in the early 1990s. In the previous decade, the rhinos of the Botswanan and Namibian Kalahari had been poached to near-extinction. Both black and white rhinos share the reserve with other desert-adapted species including antelopes, hyenas, ostriches and bat-eared foxes. You can join game drives and stay overnight in chalets.

● **Kwando River, Linyanti Marshes and Savuti Channel** Large herds of buffalo, giraffes, hippos, antelopes and crocodiles abound in this magnificent wetland region on the west side of Chobe.

● **Tuli Block and the Mashutu Game Reserve** Near the Limpopo River, the lovely lodges in Botswana's eastern spur offer horseback tours through a dramatic, deeply eroded sandstone landscape that's home to elephants, giraffes, antelopes and big cats.

● **Xai-/Xai** Around six hours' drive from Maun, near the Namibian border, this community-run tourism project offers visitors the chance to spend some meaningful time in the desert with San hunter-gatherers and Herero herders, hunting with bows and arrows, gathering veld foods and taking part in traditional dancing, singing and storytelling sessions.

Routes in and out

International flights land at Sir Seretse Khama International Airport in Gaborone, Maun (for the Okavango Delta and the northwest) and Kasane (for Chobe and the northeast). Many safari lodges can only be reached by light aircraft. There are several road routes to and from Namibia, South Africa and Zimbabwe. Gaborone is under 300km from Johannesburg in South Africa; intercity buses connect the two cities. From Windhoek in Namibia, intercity buses run north to the Caprivi Strip and Victoria Falls on the Zimbabwe/Zambia border, for access to northern Botswana. The Kazengula ferry crossing over the Zambezi River links northern Botswana and southern Zambia.

Red tape

Visas Not required by UK, Ire, US, Can, Aus, NZ or SA nationals staying ninety days or less: free entry stamp issued at Botswana's airports and land borders.

Nearest consulates Harare; Johannesburg (☎+27 11 403 3748); Lusaka; Pretoria (☎+27 12 430 9640); Windhoek.

Other consulates Canberra (Ⓦbotswanahighcom.org.au); London (☎020 7499 0031, Ⓔbohico@govbw .com); Washington, DC (Ⓦbotswana embassy.org).

Burkina Faso

Area 275,000 square kilometres	**Independence** Aug 5, 1960
Capital Ouagadougou	(from France)
Population 14 million	**Best time to go** Nov–May
Language French (official), More,	(dry season)
Fula, Dioula, more than sixty others	**Country code** +226
Religion Muslim; Christian and	**Currency** CFA franc (XOF);
traditional minorities	US$1: CFA506
Government Presidential	**Minimum daily budget** US$30
democracy, tending towards	
authoritarianism	

Although desperately poor, and with an almost total lack of raw materials or natural resources, landlocked Burkina Faso ("Land of the Honourable") is a country that most visitors really enjoy. The poverty is no more apparent than in neighbouring countries, the military checkpoints that once littered the country are much less evident than they once were, and the soldiers and customs officers who you do meet treat you with respect, venturing a "Bonne arrivée, ça va?" while verifying your passport. Indeed, the friendliness of the Burkinabè is something all visitors remark upon.

With some sixty different language groups, Burkina has the usual ethno-linguistic mosaic. But it's quite unusual in having an overwhelming majority of a single people, the More-speaking Mossi, who live in the central plains around Ouagadougou ("Ouaga"), and make up more than half the population. Other tribes include the Fula (who are also called Peul or Fulani), the Hausa, the Senoufo and the Gourounsi, while the Lobi, towards the border with Ghana, remain one of the most isolated peoples in the country. Burkina is also unusual in having a good range of cultural

festivals, supported as much by locals as by foreign visitors (see p.412).

Burkina is largely flat, and most of the country is swathed in semi-arid grasslands. Only in the southern regions of Banfora and the Lobi country will you find much greenery. The further north you go, the drier things become, until you arrive at the denuded landscapes of the extreme north. Although three big rivers, the Volta Blanche, Volta Rouge and Volta Noire all rise in Burkina Faso, only the Volta Noire flows all year round.

Outside of busy Ouagadougou, specific targets include Burkina's second city, Bobo-Dioulasso ("Bobo"), one of the most attractive cities in West Africa; the hilly and prettily wooded Banfora region in the southwest; the mysterious stone ruins of the remote and fascinating Lobi country in the south; and the lively market at Gorom-Gorom in the northern Sahel region.

Main attractions

● **FESPACO** Ouaga comes alive during its internationally renowned

Mean temperatures and rainfall												
	Jan	Feb	Mar	Apr	May	Jun	Jul	Aug	Sep	Oct	Nov	Dec
Ouagadougou												
min °C	16	20	23	26	26	24	23	22	23	23	22	17
max °C	33	37	40	39	38	36	33	31	32	35	36	35
rainfall mm	0	3	13	15	84	122	203	277	145	33	0	0

Festival Panafricain du Cinéma, held in February and March in odd-numbered years (🌐fespaco.bf). Attracting tens of thousands of visitors, this is one of Africa's most star-studded events.

● **Bobo-Dioulasso** Burkina's second city is rare in being a large African town that is thoroughly likeable, with some fine examples of *style-soudanais* colonial architecture and a pleasant, shady environment thanks to its thousands of mango trees. Visit the *grand marché* and the mosque, and maybe treat yourself to a night in a Bobo institution, *L'Auberge*, with its fantastic pool.

● **Balafons** The addictive rhythmic sounds of these West African xylophones, often accompanied by calabash drums, are a fine and affordable entertainment. Any millet beer bar in the Bolomakoté quarter of Bobo-Dioulasso is worth a visit to see if anyone is playing.

● **The Nabayius Gou** Strange name for a strange custom, the weekly (Fri, 7am) re-enactment at the palace of the traditional king of Ouagadougou of the personal sacrifice made by his eighteenth-century ancestor. The king acts out his predecessor's jealousy and anger at his favourite wife's failure to

return from visiting her relatives and then his decision not to risk war but to stay at home and take care of his people. It's a tradition rather than a tourist event; you have to visit respectfully, and photos aren't allowed.

● **Gorom-Gorom** This dynamic and colourful market on the edge of the Sahara takes place every Thursday, when robed merchants ride in from the desert on camels, Fula herders sell livestock and Songhai leather-workers and jewellers show their wares. The "guides" and their camel treks can be fun, but bargain hard.

● **Lobi country** Quench your thirst with a calabash or two of *chapalo* (millet beer) in one of the numerous *cabarets* (tiny drinking dens), and absorb the unique customs and traditions of the Lobi. Outside the village of Loropeni, enigmatic stone ruins rise through the bush.

● **Parc National de Deux Balés** West of Ouaga, the flat plains are relieved by the crocodile pool at Sabou (a tourist trap, so skip it) and then the more wooded conservation area between the Petit Balé and Grand Balé rivers, where you can often see elephants, especially in the dry season.

● **SIAO** Taking place in even-numbered years in October, the Salon International de l'Artisanat de Ouagadougou (Ⓦsiao .bf) is the largest crafts festival in Africa, with the entire city centre filled with exhibitors' booths and stalls – plus music, food, fashion shows, and dance and theatre happening on every street corner.

● **Tiébélé** Deep in Gourounsi country south of Ouaga, the town of Tiébélé boasts wonderful architecture and intricately painted houses. You'll be met on arrival by waiting guides who, for a small fee, will show you round the chief's palace.

Routes in and out

Ouagadougou has the country's only international airport, with flights to neighbouring countries and a few services to Europe, although there are better connections via Abidjan in Côte d'Ivoire. Reasonably busy roads connect Burkina Faso with all its neighbours. The 500km road to Niamey in Niger is one of the most important, though there have been bandit attacks on the Nigérien portion of the route and you may have to go by convoy. There are several routes to Mali, with direct buses between Ouaga and Bamako and rougher roads to Mali's Dogon country. Public transport links with Benin, Togo, Ghana and Côte d'Ivoire are good, and Côte d'Ivoire and Burkina are connected via the forty-hour Gazelle train service.

Red tape

Visas Required by UK, Ire, US, Can, Aus, NZ and SA nationals. Available on arrival by air at Ouagadougou airport. If you arrive by land without a visa, you can obtain a single-entry visa at the border, but you may have to renew it at Immigration (or leave the country) within seven days.

Nearest consulates Abidjan; Accra; Bamako. Visas also issued by French consulates in Cotonou, Lomé and Niamey.

Other consulates Dorking, UK (Ⓦcolinseelig.co.uk/consul); Ottawa (Ⓦburkinafaso.ca); Paris (Ⓦambaburkina-fr.org); Pretoria (☏+27 12 342 2246); Sydney (via French Consulate-General, Ⓦambafrance-au.org); Washington, DC (☏+1 202 332 5577).

Burundi

Area 27,800 square kilometres
Capital Bujumbura
Population 9 million
Languages French and Rundi (both official); Swahili
Religion Christian; Muslim and traditional minorities
Government Dictatorship, with trappings of democracy

Independence July 1, 1962 (from Belgium)
Best time to go June–Sept, Dec–Feb (dry seasons)
Country code +257
Currency Burundi franc (BIF); US$1: BFr1220
Minimum daily budget US$30

Most of Burundi (bigger than Wales, but smaller than Belgium – see map, p.350) is a fertile, undulating plateau, ridged into hills and countless homesteads and smallholdings. The landscapes here are gentle scenes of rural farms and pasture, although the mountains running down to the lake through the west of the country are soaring and impressive. Densely populated, but with only one large town, Burundi is an intriguing country that gets few tourists.

Like its similarly small and mountainous neighbour Rwanda (see p.349), Burundi has a complex history of kings, landlords and serfs. In fact, until the late nineteenth century the two "countries" shared the same history. A German protectorate was accepted by the king of Urundi in 1904, but the kingdom passed into Belgium's care after 1916. Although under UN mandate, in practice the Belgians' 46-year occupation treated Burundi as a classic, divide-and-rule colony, investing Tutsis with power and privilege and treating Hutus (and Twa, the "Pygmy" people of the forests) with contempt. Ten years after independence, the last king was assassinated and a mass-extermination of Hutus followed in revenge, in which at least 150,000

people were massacred. For the next two decades the country was run with abject brutality. Hopes for a change after the first multi-party elections in 1993 were dashed when the moderate Hutu president was assassinated and the country was plunged into twelve years of civil war. UN peacekeepers have been in the country since 2004 and disarmament in 2009 looked promising.

But the peace may not last. In the presidential elections of 2010, all the opposition candidates pulled out in protest at flagrant rigging by the Hutu frontrunner. Much of Burundi is probably safe, but you wouldn't know that from reading the warnings about rebels and banditry on various government travel advisories. Before visiting, do your research carefully, as the situation changes fast here, and the infrastructure is limited.

Main attractions

● **Bujumbura** Little "Buj" tends to be the safest place in the country. Tucked between the green walls of the western branch of the Great Rift Valley, this manageable capital has a good

Mean temperatures and rainfall

Bujumbura	Jan	Feb	Mar	Apr	May	Jun	Jul	Aug	Sep	Oct	Nov	Dec
max °C	29	29	29	29	29	29	29	31	32	30	29	28
min °C	20	20	19	20	18	17	17	18	19	19	19	19
rainfall mm	94	109	121	125	57	11	5	11	37	64	100	114

market, excellent views from the hillside university and a scattering of Art Deco Belgian colonial buildings. Head down to the old Cercle Nautique watersports club for a drink at sunset.

● **Lake Tanganyika's beaches** The world's longest and second-deepest freshwater lake washes Burundi's 150km coast. The beautiful beach at Saga Rasha, an hour south of Bujumbura, is the best in the country, but for a quick getaway from the city, the Plage des Cocotiers ("Coconut Beach") – deserted in the early morning and lively at weekends, when the bars and grilled meat stands open – is a fifteen-minute taxi ride west of downtown.

● **Parc National de la Rusizi** West of the capital, beyond the beach and just before the Democratic Republic of Congo border, the road crosses the Rusizi River and you can organize a short dugout ride into the lush reed beds of the park. It's only 3km to the river mouth, but you'll see crocs and lizards and plenty of birdlife – red-breasted sunbird and chirping cisticola are two of the local specialities – on the way. Hippos and sitatunga antelope are harder to spot.

● **The Royal Drummers of Burundi** Based in Muramvya province, east of Bujumbura, this drumming troupe were the inspiration for the first WOMAD festival, in 1982. Outstanding on their own, their thunderous, unforgettable rhythms have also backed artists from Joni Mitchell to The Clash. If they're in the country, make every effort to watch them perform.

Routes in and out

Burundi's airport at Bujumbura handles a few flights from East and Central Africa and fewer still from Europe. Overland, the main links are north to Rwanda via Kayanza and south and east to Tanzania. The roads are straightforward enough, assuming security in Burundi's provinces is adequate. Crossing into DRC is another matter: although the border crossing west of Bujumbura into the town of Uvira is open, check carefully in Bujumbura beforehand as security in this part of DRC is very poor.

Red tape

Visas Required by UK, Ire, US, Can, Aus, NZ and SA nationals. Must be obtained in advance.

Nearest consulates Dar es Salaam; Kampala; Kigali; Kigoma.

Other consulates Brussels (Ⓦambassade-burundi.be); Pretoria (☎+27 12 342 4881, Ⓔambabusa @mweb.co.za); Washington, DC (☎+1 202 342 2574). Aus/NZ citizens should apply for visas via the consulate in Washington, DC.

Cameroon

Area 475,000 square kilometres **Capital** Yaoundé **Population** 19 million **Languages** French and English (both official); Fula, Duala, Bassa, more than 250 others **Religion** Christian, traditional, Muslim **Government** Presidential democracy	**Independence** Jan 1, 1960 (from France and UK) **Best time to go** Nov–Feb (southern dry season); Nov–April (northern dry season) **Country code** +237 **Currency** Central African CFA franc (XOF); US$1: CFA506 **Minimum daily budget** US$40

From the fringes of the Sahara to the borders of the Congo basin, Cameroon takes in every African variation: equatorial rainforest, tree-scattered savanna, gaunt volcanic ranges and the highest mountain in West and Central Africa. Poised on the threshold of West, Central and North Africa, its landscapes are some of the most dramatic and diverse on the continent.

The population is highly diverse, too, with the strongly Arabized Muslim sultanates of the north alongside the non-Muslims of the neighbouring Mandara mountain, while in the southern forests the region's original "Pygmy" inhabitants live the hunter-gather lifestyle. In the Grassfields – the hilly pastures of northwest Cameroon – a remarkable complex of kingdoms has emerged over the last four centuries, with their own very distinctive culture and palace architecture. Coupled with its natural diversity, this is a country that can justifiably claim to embody elements of the entire continent – "African in miniature" as it's often touted.

Cameroon's French-English bilingualism is unique in Africa (though each province uses mostly one language or the other in official use) and the country has a fine array of old traditions.

But it's also becoming more cosmopolitan and outward looking. The police controls that used to dog visitors from the moment they arrived are no longer so aggressive, though there are still numerous roadblocks – corrupt little havens where police and customs officials extract "dash money" or bribes (Cameroon is often cited as one of the most corrupt countries in the world).

Something worth bearing in mind: the timing of your visit can have a major impact on your trip. The region around Mount Cameroon is one of the wettest places on earth, and roads around the scenic Grassfields region are often un-motorable during the rains. A long wait for transport here might mean waiting until the end of the rainy season itself.

Main attractions

● **Climbing Mount Cameroon**
The trek up this active volcano is a challenging but perfectly feasible ascent. West Africa's highest mountain (at 4095m, on a par with peaks in the Alps), offers a range of landscapes and views en route, with high winds, occasional freezing rain and snow at the summit.

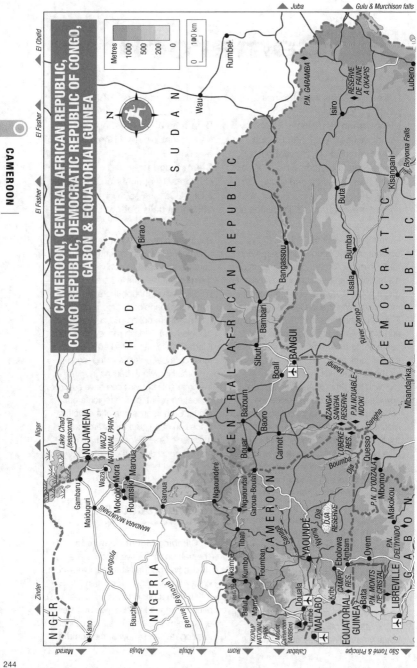

CAMEROON

CAMEROON, CENTRAL AFRICAN REPUBLIC,
CONGO REPUBLIC, DEMOCRATIC REPUBLIC OF CONGO,
GABON & EQUATORIAL GUINEA

FIRST-TIME AFRICA

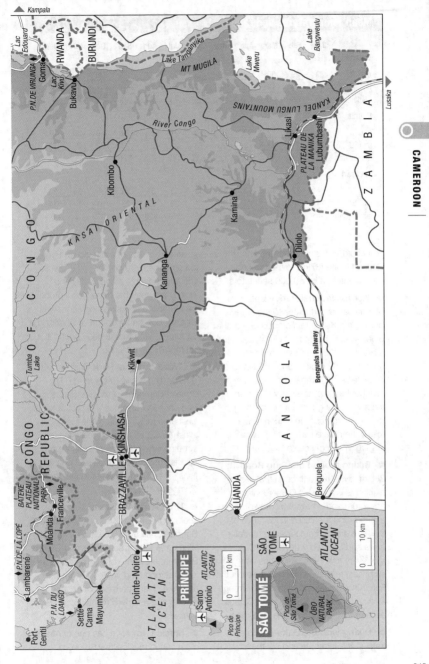

Kampala

Lac Edouard
RWANDA
BURUNDI
Lac Kivu
P.N. DE VIRUNGA
Goma
Bukavu
Lake Tanganyika
MT MUGILA
Lake Mweru
Lake Bangweulu

River Congo
KANDEL LUNGU MOUNTAINS
Likasi
Lubumbashi
PLATEAU DE LA MANIKA

Kibombo
KASAI ORIENTAL
Kamina

D E M O C R A T I C   R E P U B L I C   O F   C O N G O

ZAMBIA

Lusaka

Kananga

Dilolo

Kikwit

Tumba Lake

CONGO REPUBLIC

BATEKE PLATEAU NATIONAL PARK

Franceville
Moanda

P.N. DE LA LOPÉ

Lambarené

P.N. DU LOANGO
Sette Cama
Mayumba

Port-Gentil

KINSHASA
BRAZZAVILLE

Pointe-Noire

ATLANTIC OCEAN

LUANDA

A N G O L A

Benguela Railway

Benguela

PRÍNCIPE
Santo António
ATLANTIC OCEAN
Pico de Príncipe
0   10 km

SÃO TOMÉ
SÃO TOMÉ
ATLANTIC OCEAN
Pico de São Tomé
ÔBO NATURAL PARK
0   10 km

Mean temperatures and rainfall

	Jan	Feb	Mar	Apr	May	Jun	Jul	Aug	Sep	Oct	Nov	Dec
Yaoundé												
max °C	29	29	30	29	28	28	26	26	27	28	28	29
min °C	19	19	19	19	19	19	19	18	19	18	19	19
rainfall mm	23	66	147	170	196	152	74	79	213	295	117	23
Douala												
max°C	31	32	32	32	31	29	27	27	29	30	30	31
min °C	23	23	23	23	23	23	22	22	23	22	23	23
rainfall mm	46	94	203	231	300	539	742	693	531	429	155	64
Kousséri												
max °C	34	37	40	42	40	38	33	31	33	36	36	33
min °C	14	16	21	23	25	24	22	22	22	21	17	14
rainfall mm	0	0	0	3	31	66	170	320	119	36	0	0

You could also sign up for the annual Race of Hope (37km to the top and back), watched by 50,000 spectators.

● **Korup National Park** Inland from Mount Cameroon, close to the Nigerian border, the Korup rainforest is one of the oldest and richest forests in Africa, with more than 400 species of birds, 101 mammals, 82 reptiles and 950 species of butterflies. Chimpanzees, the very rare drill monkey and a recently discovered freshwater flying fish are outstanding denizens. You can do a short visit and follow the nature trail, or hike for days, staying in one of several camps.

● **Biking around the Ring Road** This 360km cycle route through the western highlands is a classic Cameroonian adventure and an excellent way of experiencing the varied landscapes of the Grassfields, from savanna to crater lakes and forested valley sides. Culturally, too, every town and village has new surprises, from the palace complex of the Fon (King) of Bafut (call ahead to arrange a tour) to the mixed Islamic and Catholic aspects of the Fon's palace in Kumbo.

● **Hiking with the Baka** Rainforest treks in the far south and southeast, with guides from one of the region's "Pygmy" communities, are not for softies: while the forest people move swiftly and quietly between the trees, you'll probably be stumbling and sweating some way behind. But the sensation of inhabiting a separate – and threatened – world is a memorable experience.

● **Waza National Park** Cameroon's outstanding wildlife reserve –1700 square kilometres of flat grasslands and seasonal swamps – is probably the best area for savanna game-viewing in West Africa, offering a good chance of spotting giraffe and elephants, several species of large antelope and possibly lions. There's an excellent lodge, the *Campement de Waza*.

● **Kribi** White sand beaches and seafood feasts are Kribi's selling points. But don't halt at the town itself. A few kilometres further south, beyond Grand Batanga, are some of the finest beaches in Cameroon, and you can camp out (with the chief's permission) or stay in rooms at a superb restaurant, the *Mimado*.

● **Music** Cameroon has one of Africa's most varied musical feasts – from sexy urban *makossa* (the mainstream pop of the country for the last fifty years) and insanely revved-up *bikutsi* (especially popular in Yaoundé) to the haunting vocals and various traditional instruments of the forest-dwelling Baka.

● **Tracking gorillas** The domain of lowland gorillas – quite prolific in certain areas – is the far south and southeast, where the rainforest reserves of Campo Ma'an, Dja and Lake Lobéké are gradually becoming more accessible and equipped. With a Baka tracker, you walk to a forest clearing, or *bai*, and set up camp at a watchtower (booked in advance). Unlike East Africa, there's no certainty of an encounter, but patience and a flexible itinerary make seeing gorillas fairly likely.

Also recommended

● **Foumban** This old sultanate in the Bamoun district, with its palace, museum and crafts workshops, is a thriving and colourful destination. You're unlikely to be the only tourists in town, but the slightly hustly atmosphere shouldn't put you off. Be sure to visit the real Village des Artisans, outside town, not just the souvenir shops in the square.

● **Hiking in the Mandara Mountains** Exploring the otherworldly, volcanic landscapes of these peaks in the far north is relatively easy – the lads who hit on every visitor on arrival will guide you – but really getting to know the staunchly independent Kirdi ("pagan") culture of the region, rather than just the youthful guides, is a lot harder. Give yourself at least a week in the area.

● **Limbé** An hour's drive from Douala, Cameroon's second city, the black-sand beaches of Limbé, in South West Province, are a good, quick getaway from the exhausting city, and the town has pleasant resort hotels and guesthouses.

Routes in and out

Douala is the main airport (though a few international flights go to Yaoundé and Garoua). Overland links are more tenuous. The two main routes from Nigeria head for Mamfé in the west and the even more remote village of Mora in the north. In the far north, there's a bridge between Kousséri and Ndjamena, the capital of Chad. Links with the Central African Republic are fragile: western CAR is lawless, and the border area has become very unsafe in recent years. From Equatorial Guinea, the main road from Bata heads far inland to Ebebiyin, at the meeting point of Gabon, Cameroon and Equatorial Guinea, though you can also travel directly north on the dirt road to the border town of Yengue on the Ntem River, where you can pick up pirogues to Campo in Cameroon. If you're travelling from Gabon, you'll use the Ebebiyin route. The border between Cameroon and Congo Republic is currently closed.

Red tape

Visas Required by UK, Ire, US, Can, Aus, NZ and SA nationals. Must be obtained in advance.

Nearest consulates Bangui; Brazzaville; Lagos; Libreville; Malabo; Ndjamena.

Other consulates London (Ⓦcameroonhighcommission.co.uk); Ottawa (Ⓦhc-cameroon-ottawa.org); Pretoria (Ⓦcamhicom.co.za); Sydney (Ⓦcameroonconsul.com); Washington, DC (Ⓦambacam-usa.org).

Cape Verde

Area 4033 square kilometres
Capital Praia
Population 500,000
Language Portuguese (official);
Creole (Kriolu and Kriole) are more
commonly spoken
Religion Roman Catholic (majority)
Government Parliamentary republic
Independence July 5, 1975

(from Portugal)
Best time to go April–July (dry
season) for walking and sunbathing;
Jan–March for windsurfing
Currency Escudo (CVE);
US$1: CV$81.2
Minimum daily budget US$85
(including internal flights)
Country code +238

Named after the nearest section of mainland, Cap Vert in Senegal, 600km away, the Cape Verde archipelago (Cabo Verde in Portuguese) is Africa's westernmost territory. Conditions around these nine ruggedly volcanic Atlantic islands and their nearby islets out here are stormy, to say the least, to the extent that the three oldest islands – Sal, Boa Vista and Maio – have weathered down to flat expanses of barren desert dotted with isolated peaks and calderas. The youngest, the near-perfectly conical Fogo, is an active volcano which last erupted in 1995, and the remainder of the group is a varied collection of mountainous islands, each with its own distinctive character.

Quite unlike anywhere else in Africa in location, topography and culture, Cape Verde has one of the world's most egalitarian and peaceful mixed-race societies. Caboverdeans set great store

by two abstract concepts – *sodade*, a melancholic, nostalgic love for their homeland which is expressed through their superb, gypsy-like music, and *morabeza*, which roughly translates as warm hospitality, a quality which you will not fail to experience if you venture away from the newly developed resort areas to seek out the islands' local hangouts. Some towns, notably Mindelo on São Vicente, São Filipe on Fogo, Sal Rei on Boa Vista, Ribeira Brava on São Nicolau and the central Platô district of Praia on Santiago, retain a strong colonial feel in their beautiful Portuguese architecture and cobbled streets.

In recent years, the islands of Sal and Boa Vista have been discovered by windsurfing enthusiasts and sun-and-sand tourists, drawn by the promise of warm sunshine and breezy but pristine beaches. The mountainous islands of

Mean temperatures and rainfall

	Jan	Feb	Mar	Apr	May	Jun	Jul	Aug	Sep	Oct	Nov	Dec
Praia												
max °C	25	25	26	26	27	27	28	29	29	29	28	26
min °C	20	19	20	21	21	22	24	24	25	24	23	22
rainfall mm	3	0	0	0	0	0	5	97	114	31	8	3

Santiago, Santo Antão, São Nicolau, Fogo and Brava are laced with appealing hiking trails, while São Vicente has the islands' most seductive town, Mindelo, birthplace of the celebrated singer Cesária Évora.

Main attractions

● **Mindelo, São Vicente** Cape Verde's cultural capital, which has retained much of its colonial architecture, is a pleasant place to spend a few days, strolling along the colourful seafront, relaxing in shady squares and rubbing shoulders with the locals in lively cafés and clubs. In February, Shrove Tuesday carnival celebrations fill the city with colour and noise as revellers of all ages decked out in satin, feathers and sequins take to the streets for several days.

● **Parque Natural do Fogo,** Evidence of Fogo's recent eruptions abound – its steep sides are streaked with dark lava flows and parts of its coastline are honeycombed with basalt hollows and caves. Drive up into its massive crater and you immerse yourself in an otherworldly landscape of particularly fresh-looking

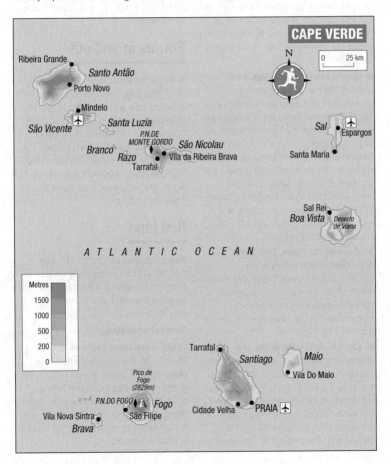

lava. It's possible to climb the cone on foot, a strenuous ascent made uncomfortable by the loose gravel and ash underfoot, but worth it for its dramatic views of the charred landscape.

● **Santo Antão** Like a scrap of South America transported to the West African Atlantic, the north side of the island of Santo Antão is remote, mountainous and green, with terraces of banana and maize plants carved out of the perilously steep slopes. A network of hiking trails, some of them extremely demanding, lead to charming cliffside villages such as Fontainhas and lush enclaves such as the Vale do Paúl. In contrast, the south side is arid and barren, while the central peaks are covered in cool, cloud-draped pine forests.

● **Santa Maria beach, Sal** Santa Maria is the hub of Cape Verde's growing sun-and-sand tourist industry. Much of Sal and Santa Maria village itself is forgettable, but the beach is a glorious strip of long, pale sand. It's too windy to sunbathe in comfort for much of the winter, but it's great for strolling and windsurfing. Locals surge down here every weekend to play football and dive off the pier; laidback beach cafés and restaurants make it a fun place to hang out at any time of year.

● **Deserto de Viana, Boa Vista** Accumulated over millennia, the dazzling, bone-white dunes of this inland desert region have a calm beauty that contrasts intriguingly with the rock-strewn desert found elsewhere on the island of Boa Vista.

● **Cidade Velha, Santiago** The present-day village of Cidade Velha on the south coast of the island of Santiago occupies the site of Cape Verde's earliest settlement, once a stopover for pirates and slave traders. Archeological digs and restoration and research work is underway at the sites of the settlement's several ecclesiastical buildings, and there are ancient cottages, a stony beach and a fort to explore. Treasures hauled up from the bay are on display at the Museu de Arqueologia in the capital, Praia.

● **Brava** One of Cape Verde's smallest and prettiest islands, Brava receives few visitors as there's no airport and the ferry crossing from Fogo is stormy and unreliable. Its capital, Vila Nova Sintra, has a lost-in-time charm and its hillsides offer rewarding hiking. The coastal village of Fajã d'Água is particularly scenic, set on a stunning, rocky bay, fringed by palms and cradled by mountains.

Routes in and out

International flights land on the islands of Sal, Santiago and Boa Vista; São Vicente's new airport may receive international flights in due course. The other islands are reached by internal flights, which take between 15 and 50 minutes each, or by inter-island ferry. From mainland West Africa, there are flights, but no ferries, from Dakar to Praia on Santiago.

Red tape

Visas Required by UK, Ire, US, Can, Aus, NZ and SA nationals. Must be obtained in advance, or arranged in advance through a tour operator and paid for on arrival.

Nearest consulates Dakar.

Other consulates Brussels (☎+32 2643 6270, ✉emb.caboverde @skynet.be); Luanda (☎+244 232 1765, ✉embaicv.ang@snct.co.ao); Toronto (☎+1 416 252 9881); Washington, DC (🌐virtualcapeverde.net). Aus/NZ citizens should apply for visas via the consulate in Washington, DC.

Central African Republic

Area 623,000 square kilometres
Capital Bangui
Population 4.5 million
Languages French and Sango (official)
Religion Christian, Islam, traditional
Government Presidential democracy, with military support

Independence Aug 30, 1960 (from France)
Best time to go Nov–March (dry season)
Country code +236
Currency Central African CFA franc (XAF); US$1: CFA506
Minimum daily budget US$50

The Central African Republic or CAR (Centrafrique or RCA in French; see map, p.244) is a product of the nineteenth century colonial carve-up of Africa that has never fully established itself as a viable nation. Landlocked and overlooked – except by French big game hunters and mineral prospecting companies – its borders are porous, its infrastructure negligible and conditions for its population, especially beyond Bangui's city limits, very harsh. In the 1970s it was ruled, with French backing, by notorious self-proclaimed "Emperor" Jean-Bedel Bokassa. Since the current president took power in a coup in 2003 (making himself more comfortable after winning elections in 2005) CAR has been beset by conflict in rural areas as

rebel groups and disaffected government troops fight the security forces and each other for control of trade routes and forest resources. Following the code of "Françafrique", the French government and French corporations still underwrite the CAR government, and locally based French troops ensure their chosen man stays in power.

Geographically, CAR is a rolling plateau, cut by streams and rivers flowing south into the great Oubangui River, itself a tributary of the Congo. Grasslands and wooded water courses feature throughout much of the country, which is drier towards the northeast and more fertile and forested in the south, an area which is still the home of indigenous hunter-gatherers – the

Mean temperatures and rainfall

Bangui	Jan	Feb	Mar	Apr	May	Jun	Jul	Aug	Sep	Oct	Nov	Dec
max °C	33	34	33	33	32	31	30	29	31	31	32	32
min °C	19	20	21	21	21	21	20	20	20	20	20	19
rainfall mm	26	42	130	133	186	109	225	210	148	208	124	7

so-called "Pygmies" (see p.37). The country has some fine scenery and interesting cultural attractions, as well as a major rainforest national park, but only the capital is realistically feasible to visit without making special plans.

If you do plan to visit CAR, you'd be wise to seek expert advice in advance from CAR contacts or locally based expats. Keep your ear to the ground and read all the travel advisories. If you can stay safe, which recent reports suggest you often can, then try at least to visit the rainforest: you'll have an utterly unforgettable adventure.

Main attractions

● **Dzanga-Sangha Reserve** Top billing goes to this celebrated national park, one of Central Africa's pre-eminent wilderness areas. It forms the core of a 28,000-square-kilometre transnational protected rainforest region tucked between the borders of Cameroon and the Congo Republic, astride the Sangha river. Two semi-habituated groups of lowland gorillas can be tracked here by groups of a maximum of three people. Forest elephants, bongo antelopes, chimpanzees and a host of birdlife and other fauna can also be seen.

● **Bangui markets** As the one place in CAR with a degree of reliable security, Bangui also sees most of the country's trade. The Marché Centrale, between the Place de l'Indépendance and the river, is the easiest target, with some wood carvings available. Marché Km-5 (at the 5km checkpoint) is the biggest market, but this whole newcomer's district has a notorious reputation for muggings.

● **Musée Ethnographique Barthélémy Boganda** The country's national museum, named after the pan-Africanist who led the country to independence, is surprisingly good, and includes a good range of local musical instruments, weapons, tools and displays about traditional architecture and religion.

● **Rainforest communities** The southwest corner of the country is heavily forested and the home of indigenous "Pygmy" communities who still live by hunting and gathering. By paying to participate in (or at least watch and follow) community activities you channel much-needed cash to families. Leaf-house building, net hunting, plant-gathering and music-making are all on the menu.

Also recommended

● **Centre Artisanal** While masks, batiks and jewellery are fairly widespread, Bangui's local speciality, very much on show in the capital's crafts centre, is butterfly wing pictures, created from the wings of fallen *papillons* at the end of the rainy season.

● **Bambari rock art** Scattered across CAR is the rock-engraved evidence of an ancient civilization pre-dating the country's modern peoples. Bambari, 380km from Bangui, has some of the finest examples, with drawings depicting antelopes and big cats.

● **Bouar megaliths** Near the town of Bouar, along the watershed of the Congo River and Lake Chad, close to the Cameroon border, large numbers of Stonehenge-like megaliths stand in concentric circles. Still barely studied, they are further fascinating evidence of CAR's ancient cultures.

● **Chutes de Boali** This pretty stack of seasonal waterfalls, tumbling through jungle-shrouded rocks and clefts, 85km northwest of Bangui, form the city's most popular excursion. There's even an under-used hotel here.

Routes in and out

CAR's only international airport is at Bangui, with scheduled flights from a handful of African cities and a weekly flight from Paris. Surface connections with neighbouring countries are tenuous at best. The most significant overland route links Bangui with Yaoundé in Cameroon, but the highway is in poor condition and prone to banditry, with little if any regular public transport. The roads to Ndjamena in Chad, Nyala in Sudan's Darfur region and Juba in South Sudan are all highly insecure, with the latter following the border of DRC for more than 500km – a remote area that has been invaded by the extremely violent Lord's Resistance Army. Southwards, the ferry crossing at Bangui to Zongo in the DRC is not always open to foreigners and this part of DRC itself is not recommended owing to the security situation. Likewise, river links downstream to DRC or the Congo Republic are sporadic and potentially unsafe.

Red tape

Visas Required by UK, Ire, US, Can, Aus, NZ and SA nationals. Available on arrival at Bangui airport and at CAR's land borders with Cameroon and DRC; availability at other borders is not guaranteed.

Nearest consulates Khartoum; Kinshasa; Ndjamena; Yaoundé.

Other consulates Paris (☎+33 1 42 24 42 56); Washington, DC (☎+1 202 483 7800). Visas can also be obtained from the following French consulates: Johannesburg (⊛consulfrance-jhb.org); London (⊛ambafrance-uk.org); Sydney (⊛ambafrance-au.org).

Chad

Area 1,284,000 square kilometres	**Independence** Aug 11, 1960
Capital Ndjamena	(from France)
Population 10.5 million	**Best time to go** Nov–April
Languages French and Arabic	(dry season)
(official); Sara, Kanuri, Zaghawa,	**Country code** +235
more than 100 others	**Currency** Central African CFA franc
Religion Muslim; Christian and	(XAF); US$1: CFA506
traditional minorities	**Minimum daily budget** US$60
Government Presidential	
democracy, supported by the army	

A great slab of Central Africa – the continent's biggest landlocked country and one of its least densely populated – Chad (see map, p.372) has never been on the overland and tourist routes and is a real unknown outside the French-speaking world, where it is spelled Tchad. The flat, more heavily populated southern savanna region, prone to seasonal flooding, gives way to drier grassland and bush to the north and ultimately to the sandy deserts and dramatic, rocky massifs of the Sahara's Tibesti plateau close to the Libyan border.

Chad's long-running civil war peaked in 2008, when fighting erupted in Ndjamena. The UN peace keeping presence was wound up in 2010, but French military support is ubiquitous. Despite its new-found oil wealth (a pipeline runs to Cameroon), Chad still has an ongoing rebellion in the east, and is also coping with refugees from the fighting in Darfur and northern Central African Republic.

The two big blocks on travel are travel permits (required to go almost anywhere and hard to obtain for the far north) and getting around the rest of the country once the rains have started (the roads, which are nearly all earth, are mostly in poor condition). There's no question that Chad has great appeal for adventurous travellers but, needless to say, if you choose to visit, do your security research thoroughly. Landmines are a real menace in many parts of the country.

Main attractions

● **Faya (Faya-Largeau)** The biggest town in the north and one of the biggest

Mean temperatures and rainfall

Ndjamena	Jan	Feb	Mar	Apr	May	Jun	Jul	Aug	Sep	Oct	Nov	Dec
max °C	34	36	39	41	40	39	34	32	31	36	37	34
min °C	14	16	21	23	24	24	23	22	22	21	13	15
rainfall mm	0	0	0	5	34	66	168	322	125	37	0	0

oases in the Sahara, with vast groves of date palms supported by plentiful underground water, Faya makes a highly worthwhile target – if you can get the travel permit. There are superb rock paintings and wind-sculpted rock formations in the vicinity.

● **Lake Chad** Vast but shallow (for the most part only a couple of metres deep), this former inland sea is shrinking. With myriad marshes, sandy islands and channels, its shape changes with every wet season. Bol is the main Chadian "port" for the lake, where you can hire a pirogue and a man to pole it and go birdwatching and, if you're lucky, hippo-spotting.

● **Ndjamena** The capital and Chad's only large city – a low-rise sprawl of sandy streets and mud buildings – lies low on the banks of the Chari River. Here, the once tree-shaded streets of the old European quarter (most were felled during the 2008 rebel incursion) radiate out from place de l'Etoile, while the poorer quarters spread east across the plain. Sightseeing is limited to the National Museum and the lively central market. It's worth going to the ancient potters' village of Gaoui, 10km northeast of the city, for a visit to its beautiful museum of Sao culture, in a mud-brick former sultan's palace.

● **Parc National de Zakouma** Chad's one significant conservation area, supported by the EU, is located deep in the seasonally flooded plains in the south of the country. Elephant, giraffe, buffalo, greater kudu and roan antelope are easily seen, with all the cats (lion, leopard, cheetah, caracal, serval) present, but shy. There's a good lodge, *Tinga*.

● **Sarh** On the banks of the Chari River, with a good hotel, great hippo-watching and even a decent museum, Sarh is well worth a visit, but do assess the region's CAR refugee situation before going.

Routes in and out

Chad's only international airport is at Ndjamena. The northern border with Libya is closed. The two border crossings with Sudan are in Darfur so not to be recommended, while the border with CAR is equally ill-advised as the area is over-run with rebels fighting the government in Bangui. The bridge across the Chari river from Ndjamena to Kousséri in Cameroon is usually open – in fact at times thousands of Chadian refugees have streamed across it to a less insecure life in Cameroon or Nigeria – and most of the other crossing points to Cameroon are open. The short border with Nigeria runs through the middle of Lake Chad (see p.346), and is not a regular crossing point for travellers. The long desert border with Niger is normally open, though not always safe (see p.342).

Red tape

Visas Required by UK, Ire, US, Can, Aus, NZ and SA nationals. Must be obtained in advance. Within 72 hours of your arrival, your passport must be registered with the police.

Nearby consulates Abuja; Bangui; Niamey; Yaoundé. The consulate in Tripoli does not normally issue visas to foreigners.

Other consulates Brussels (☎+32 2 215 1975, ✉ambassade.tchad@chello .be); Paris (☎+33 1 45 53 36 75); Pretoria (☎+27 12 460 1596, ✉chadembassy@telkomsa.net); Washington, DC (☎+1 202 462 4009). Aus/NZ citizens should apply for visas via Washington, DC.

Comoros and Mayotte

Area 2235 square km (Comoros); 374 square km (Mayotte)
Capitals Moroni (Co); Mamoudzo (Ma)
Population 750,000 (Co); 190,000 (Ma)
Language French (official), Arabic (official in Co); Shikomor/Comorian, Malagasy (Ma)
Religion Sunni Muslim
Government Federal republic, in practice authoritarian (Co); overseas département of France (Ma)
Independence July 6, 1975 (Co only, from France)
Country code +269 (C); +262 (Ma)
Best time to go June–Oct (driest weather); March–May & Oct–Nov (best scuba visibility).
Currency Comorian franc (KMF); US$1: Fr387 (Co); Euro (EUR); US$1: €0.79 (Ma)
Minimum daily budget US$40 (Co); US$60 (Ma)

Situated south of the Seychelles, Comoros and Mayotte (see map, p.310) are little-known islands with lush vegetation and rich marine life. Though remote and somewhat ramshackle, they have the kind of faraway atmosphere that might appeal to independent-minded tourists with reasonable French and an interest in nature.

There are four main islands in this spice-scented Islamic archipelago: Mayotte, which is French, and Grande Comore, Mohéli and Anjouan, which together comprise the republic of the Union of Comoros (Union des Comores). The islands' position, between northwest Madagascar and northeast Mozambique, made them attractive to the merchants from Persia and Yemen who set up trading stations along the spice route between India and Africa in the fifteenth and sixteenth centuries, laying the foundations of Swahili culture in this part of the Indian Ocean. Like the other islands in the region, the archipelago still has a few once-grand Swahili mansions, plus plantation houses and mosques. Other attractions include beaches, coral reefs, volcanic scenery and, on the less densely populated islands, native forest harbouring endemic owls, bats, lemurs and other rare species.

Since breaking free from France, Comoros has been hampered by instability and poverty. French tourists used to visit the islands in considerable numbers, but in recent years hotels have fallen into disrepair for lack of government support. These days, you're best off exploring independently, seeking out locally owned *pensions* and homestays. Mayotte has fared better: in 2009, the islanders voted to become an overseas *département* of France, giving them access to grants to help develop their tourism industry.

Mean temperatures and rainfall

Moroni	Jan	Feb	Mar	Apr	May	Jun	Jul	Aug	Sep	Oct	Nov	Dec
max °C	30	30	31	30	29	28	28	27	28	29	31	31
min °C	23	23	23	23	21	20	19	18	19	20	22	23
rainfall mm	345	311	300	296	233	215	194	118	117	91	102	220

Main attractions

● **Moroni, Grande Comore** Backed by sloping plantations of palm trees, the waterfront town of Moroni is a charming, ramshackle capital. A grand mosque overlooks the timber fishing boats in the harbour while, in the market, vendors chat beside enamel bowls of fruit or baskets of charcoal.

● **Touring Grand Comore** On a trip around the largest of the Comoros, there are fine tropical beaches, ylang-ylang, jasmine and cinnamon plantations and a crater lagoon to explore. The island's highest point is an active volcano, Mount Karthala (2361m), whose forested slopes can be climbed in one long day; you can camp near its kilometre-wide crater.

● **Mohéli** Relatively sparsely populated, this island has attractive beaches and great opportunities for hiking, cycling, snorkelling and boat trips by dhow. Giant flying foxes with wingspans over a metre flap through the island's lush tropical rainforest and over its waterfalls, while turtles nest on Otsamia beach.

● **Mayotte** The southernmost island in the archipelago is a relatively short hop from Madagascar and feels more African than the others. Its most remarkable natural feature is a vast coral-fringed lagoon: paddling about in its calm waters feels like exploring a giant aquarium. A 100km hiking trail offers glimpses of maki lemurs, roussette flying foxes and magnificent wild orchids.

● **Mutsamudu, Anjouan** Farming has caused extensive deforestation on this poor and densely populated island, but its historic sites are worth a visit. The ancient Swahili-style city of Mutsamudu is a maze of medieval alleyways, reminiscent of Stone Town on Zanzibar but unrestored, overlooked by the ruins of a citadel.

Routes in and out

International flights land at Dzaoudzi Pamandzi Airport on Mayotte and at Moroni's Prince Said Airport on Grande Comore. There are flights to Mayotte from Paris via Réunion and from Nairobi, plus flights to Grande Comore from Madagascar, Tanzania and Mozambique.

Red tape

To visit Mayotte, South Africans must obtain a visa in advance from a French consulate (such as Nairobi or Jo'burg). UK, Ire, US, Can, Aus and NZ nationals don't require a visa. To visit the Comoros:

Visas Required by UK, Ire, US, Can, Aus, NZ and SA nationals. If you arrive without one, you can obtain a single-entry visa on arrival, but may have to renew it within 24 hours.

Consulates Antananarivo; Bujumbura; New York (@un.int/wcm/content/site /Comoros); Paris (☎+33 1 40 67 90 54); Pretoria (@embacom.co.za). Aus/NZ citizens should apply via Washington, DC.

Congo Republic

Area 342,000 square kilometres
Capital Brazzaville
Population 3.7 million
Language French (official); Lingala,
Kituba, Kikongo
Religion Christian, traditional
Government Presidential republic;
in practice authoritarian

Independence Aug 15, 1960
(from France)
Best time to go June–Sept
(drier months)
Country code +242
Currency Central African CFA franc
(XAF); US$1: CFA540
Minimum daily budget US$60

As one of the last remaining places where ancient customs survive intact among tribes who share their rainforest home with chimpanzees and lowland gorillas, the Congo Republic (see map, p.244) could have been made for adventure travel. However, as elsewhere in Central Africa, there's trouble in this paradise. In 2007, rebel forces wound up ten years of civil war and insurgencies by committing to peace, but the security situation remains uncertain. Meanwhile, Congo-Brazzaville (as the smaller of the two Congos is also known) remains, like its large, unruly neighbour the Democratic Republic of Congo, crippled by corruption in everything from election-rigging, embezzlement and blood-diamond trading to the everyday cajolings of petty officials. Visitors should proceed with caution and expect their progress to be slow.

Despite these failings, the Congolese are warm and spirited, with great musical flair and a flamboyant sense of style. Ever since the 1970s when, in neighbouring Zaïre, President Mobutu advocated utilitarian attire as part of his oppressive *Authenticité* campaign, the people of Congo-Brazzaville have been eager to set themselves apart by dressing as beautifully as their limited funds will allow. Today, Brazzaville's *sapeurs* (dandies) keep up the tradition by strutting about in sharp suits with immaculate Gucci loafers.

Away from the capital, Congo is rich in wild scenery. As well as its impressive rainforests, natural attractions include an Atlantic coastline washed by brisk surf where hardcore longboarders and bodyboarders test their mettle. Upcountry Congo is considered safer to explore than the wilds of Cameroon, Central African Rebulic or DRC, so this is a good place to get a taste of rural life in the Congo Basin – sampling roasted

Mean temperatures and rainfall

	Jan	Feb	Mar	Apr	May	Jun	Jul	Aug	Sep	Oct	Nov	Dec
Brazzaville												
max °C	31	32	33	33	32	29	28	29	31	32	31	31
min °C	21	21	21	22	21	18	17	18	20	21	21	21
rainfall mm	160	125	188	178	109	15	0	0	56	137	292	213

caterpillars or river fish baked in cassava leaves, perhaps, or challenging the locals to a game of *babyfoot* on a rickety table under a mango tree.

Main attractions

● **Brazzaville** Built in elegant French colonial style but since battered by civil war, Brazzaville – once dubbed the Paris of Africa – is considerably easier on the nerves than its raffish neighbour Kinshasa, capital of DRC, which faces it across the mighty Congo river. Affluent oil-industry types hang out at formal French-style restaurants and patisseries behind the riverfront, while beyond there are superbly colourful African markets to explore. The nightlife pales in comparison to Kinshasa's, but there are a few backstreet bars and nightclubs where you can dose up on the region's infectious rhythms.

● **Pointe-Noire** Apart from Brazzaville, this is the only town that really matters in Congo; it's the well-groomed, well-to-do hub of the nation's oil industry, with a lively expat scene. It's also the nearest thing to an Atlantic beach resort, with plenty of chic hotels, seafood restaurants and surf. The contrast with upcountry Congo couldn't be more extreme.

● **Parc National de Nouabalé-Ndoki** Rich in primary mahogany forest, this park is adjacent to the equally spectacular Dzanga-Sangha Special Reserve in CAR; together they comprise one of Central Africa's most interesting protected areas. Thanks to initiatives driven by the World Conservation Society, the park is managed by locally trained eco-guards who receive support in kind from the park's population of Ba'Aka "Pygmies" and Bantu villagers. An airstrip and a camp with viewing platforms makes Nouabalé-Ndoki relatively accessible; visitors can be guided around by pirogue to look for

rare species including primates, forest elephants, forest buffalo and bongo antelopes.

● **Parc National d'Odzala** Less than 500km north of Brazzaville, near the Gabonese border, but very hard to reach – there's no nearby airport and, by road, the journey may take several days – this is a dense, verdant chunk of rainforest and grassy clearings populated by western lowland gorillas and other primates, plus forest elephants. The park is occasionally hit by Ebola outbreaks, so check the current situation.

Routes in and out

International flights land at Brazzaville's Maya-Maya Airport and at Pointe-Noire. A river Congo vehicle and passenger ferry connects Brazzaville with Kinshasa. It's also possible to enter Congo overland from Angola and Gabon; many roads are in poor condition but Chinese-funded improvements are underway. However, foreign offices currently advise against travelling in the far northeast of Congo, bordering DRC (where there's a refugee crisis), or the Pool region surrounding Brazzaville (where there's a risk of rebel activity). The borders with Cameroon and CAR are closed.

Red tape

Visas Required by UK, Ire, US, Can, Aus, NZ and SA nationals. Must be obtained in advance.

Nearest consulates Bangui; Kinshasa; Libreville; Luanda; Yaoundé.

Other consulates Paris (☎+33 1 45 00 60 57); Pretoria (☎+27 12 342 5508; congo@starpost.com); Washington, DC (☎+1 202 726 5500). Aus/NZ citizens should apply for visas via the consulate in Washington, DC.

Côte d'Ivoire

Area 322,000 square kilometres
Capitals Yamoussoukro, Abidjan
Population 21 million
Language French (official); Akan languages, Bamana, Mandinka, Dan, more than fifty others
Religion Muslim, Christian and traditional
Government On-off government of national unity

Independence Aug 7, 1960 (from France)
Best time to go Dec–April & Aug–Sept (dry seasons, south); Nov–May (dry season, north)
Country code +225
Currency West African CFA franc (XOF) US$1: CFA506
Minimum daily costs US$40

Once considered an "African miracle" and a "model of stability", a place where Western economic principles got along famously with African values, Côte d'Ivoire ran into the buffers in 1993 when its long-term dictator died. The deeply Francophile President Félix Houphouët-Boigny had been stumbling towards democracy, but his death seemed to paralyze the country, which imploded as decades of suppressed ethnic tension boiled over. Northerners, and the country's 25 percent foreign population (mostly migrant workers from Burkina Faso) were the targets in an escalating, decade-long crisis. In 2002, civil war broke out between northern rebels and government forces based in Abidjan. Fighting continued sporadically for nearly five years, only ending with the appointment of the Force Nouvelles rebel leader as Prime Minister.

Since 2007, Côte d'Ivoire has tried to present an impression of business as usual, but if the country is no longer at war, the physical north–south divide is a fact on the ground, with opposed political groups running different parts of the country and mounting hundreds of lucrative checkpoints, monitored by UN and French peacekeepers. While it's no longer dangerous to travel around Côte d'Ivoire, the once relatively dynamic tourist industry has far from recovered and the presence in the west of rebel and bandit forces outside the political process makes the picture even more complicated. Most official travel advisories, including the British FCO and the US State Department, strongly advise against travel beyond Abidjan, and especially in the north and west.

Mean temperatures and rainfall

	Jan	Feb	Mar	Apr	May	Jun	Jul	Aug	Sep	Oct	Nov	Dec
Abidjan												
max °C	30	31	31	32	31	29	28	27	28	29	31	31
min °C	23	23	24	25	24	23	23	21	22	23	24	24
rainfall mm	41	53	99	125	361	495	213	53	71	168	201	79

All of this is a great pity, as Côte d'Ivoire undoubtedly has some of the most vibrant culture, most verdant landscapes and most exploration-worthy natural areas in West Africa, and while the infrastructure is tatty, it's still largely there. Travellers are using the Abidjan–Ouagadougou train and reporting essentially no trouble, but for now the country can really only be recommended for adventurous souls. Watch this space.

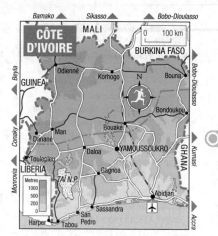

Main attractions

- **Abidjan** One of Africa's mega-cities, the country's economic capital at first appears to be all glass and concrete, and the big shock on arrival is how familiar it all seems. The snaking fingers of the Ebrié lagoon wind through the heart of the city, separating a Manhattan-like urban landscape into manageable districts linked by road bridges. Limited sightseeing includes the impressive, saint-shaped Cathédrale St-Paul with its glorious stained-glass tableaux and the crafts collections of the national museum. For restaurants and nightlife, explore Zone 04, on the way to the airport. Yopougon, a sprawling mainland suburb west of the centre, also has great nightlife, but it's not for the faint-hearted.

- **Man** Even in normal times, you wouldn't visit Man for Man itself: the ugly town is the capital of the beautiful Dix-Huit Montagnes region. For now, with Man just over the northern side of the country's civil divide, you need to think about security: Man is full of peacekeepers and safe enough, but take care in the districts north and (especially) south. The hilly and forested region has ample rewards, including the Dan tribe's stilt dances, waterfalls and hanging bridges, and Mont Tonkoui, the highest

peak in the country (1189m), with a hiking trail to the summit and glorious views.

- **Yamoussoukro** Home village of the former president, this burgeoning city is the country's official capital, though it has still to take over many administrative and diplomatic functions. The one and only – and staggering – sight is the colossal Basilique de Notre Dame de la Paix, Houphouët-Boigny's vainglorious "gift" to his people. Taller than St Peter's in Rome, it took four years to complete, using a labour force of 1500 working in shifts for 19 hours a day, and incorporates the equivalent of a whole year's output of French white cement. The cathedral is burdened with hundreds of similar statistics of which you'll get a good sample on the very worthwhile guided tour.

- **Eating in a maquis** Côte d'Ivoire's culinary institution is the open-air, thatch-shaded *maquis*, serving a wide variety of dishes – notably spicy chicken and excellent fish – to accompany starch such as *atieké* (steamed, grated cassava) *aloko* (deep-fried plantain) or rice. Wash it all down with a Drogba – a litre of cold Solibra

CÔTE D'IVOIRE

261

Rock beer, nicknamed after the Ivoirian footballer.

● **Parc National de Taï** Côte d'Ivoire's forests, which fifty years ago covered most of the southern half of the country, are now hugely reduced. If you're looking for adventure, however, the far southwest still contains large stretches of rainforest, of which the biggest is Taï National Park, a UNESCO world heritage site and home of the monkey-eating chimps of TV fame.

● **Poli-Plage** For the best beaches, make for the southwest coast, where some of Africa's most idyllic palm-rustled strands and coves are still almost untouched. Sassandra isn't too far from Abidjan and makes a good base. Hire a cab to take you to Poli-Plage and pick you up again later. But take care in the sea: strong currents and tidal races claim many lives.

Routes in and out

Abidjan, as one of Africa's most important cities, with Côte d'Ivoire's only international airport, is well connected to Europe and the rest of Africa. Overland routes are reasonable from Ghana, Mali and Burkina Faso (with the option of the train service from Ouagadougou to Abidjan), but you should bear in mind Côte d'Ivoire's fragile political state when choosing a route. Coming overland from Guinea, conditions are rougher (the road from Kankan to Côte d'Ivoire is in a terrible state), while if you're travelling by land from Liberia, you should go via Harper and Tabou – the crossings into Côte d'Ivoire at Toulepleu and Danané are in an insecure region.

Red tape

Visas Required by UK, Ire, US, Can, Aus, NZ and SA nationals (US citizens are no longer exempt). Must be obtained in advance.

Nearest consulates Accra; Bamako; Conakry; Monrovia; Ouagadougou; visas also issued by French consulates in Cotonou, Lomé and Niamey.

Other consulates London (☎020 7235 6991, ✉info@ambaci-uk.org); Ottawa (🌐canada.diplomatie.gouv.ci); Pretoria (☎+27 12 342 6913); Washington, DC (☎+1 202 797 0300). In Sydney, visas can be obtained from the French Consulate-General (🌐ambafrance -au.org).

Democratic Republic of Congo

Area 2,344,858 square kilometres	**Independence** June 13, 1960
Capital Kinshasa	(from Belgium)
Population 66 million	**Best time to go** Nov–March
Language French (official); Lingala,	(northern dry season), April–Oct
Kituba, Kikongo, Swahili, Tshiluba	(southern dry season)
Religion Majority Christian; also	**Country code** +243
Muslim, traditional	**Currency** Congolese franc (CDF);
Government Presidential republic;	US$1: Fr875
in practice authoritarian	**Minimum daily budget** US$90

With a vast land mass, rich mineral reserves and a rainforest ecosystem that's as crucial to Africa as the Amazon basin is to South America, the Democratic Republic of Congo (see map, p.244) should be a jewel at the heart of the continent. However, corruption and civil war have impoverished the people of DRC (RDC in French, it's also known as Congo-Kinshasa) and diminished their natural resources. Peace agreements have been in place since 2003 and the country's first-ever democratic elections were held in 2006, but neither have halted fighting in the east of the country. While in theory it's possible for travellers to spend time in and around Kinshasa, the capital, and explore, with extreme caution, the gorilla-tracking trails near Goma, it's inadvisable to plan a trip without making careful enquiries about the latest situation.

Some argue that DRC is still struggling to break a cycle of violence engendered by colonial atrocities. This, after all, is the territory depicted in Joseph Conrad's classic novella *Heart of Darkness*, a tale inspired by a six-month journey up the Congo river which the author shared with ivory hunters, rubber traders and cannibals in 1890. In the early decades of independence, the bitter legacy of Belgian rule was compounded by one of Africa's most notorious dictators, Mobutu Sésé Seko, who controlled what was then Zaïre for 32 years up to 1997. Soon after Mobutu's demise, the nation collapsed into conflict.

Mean temperatures and rainfall

	Jan	Feb	Mar	Apr	May	Jun	Jul	Aug	Sep	Oct	Nov	Dec
Kisangani (for Kinshasa, see Brazzaville, p.258)												
max °C	31	31	31	31	31	30	29	28	29	30	29	30
min °C	21	21	21	21	21	21	19	20	20	20	20	20
rainfall mm	53	84	178	158	137	114	132	165	183	218	198	84

DRC has been more or less off the map for travellers since the mid-1990s, but in slightly happier times the lakeside town of Goma was a busy hub for mountain gorilla tracking trips into the volcanic jungle of the Parc National de Virunga on the Rwandan border. Hardy travellers could recreate the era of adventure and exploration by taking a Congo steamer from Kinshasa to Kisangani, or hiking through virgin wilderness and swimming under waterfalls. If, but only if, lasting peace returns, DRC could become one of Africa's most exciting adventure destinations once again.

Main attractions

● **Kinshasa** Built by the Belgians in grand colonial style but since ripped apart at the seams, the capital sprawls like a vast market-cum-shanty-town beside the Congo. Bilingual in French and Lingala, it's close enough to Brazzaville, capital of Congo Republic, on the opposite bank of the river for the two to be considered a single conurbation; of the two, Kinshasa is considerably more hectic and crime-ridden.

● **Music scene, Kinshasa** Aficionados from all over Africa, and beyond, have been swaying to Congolese *soukous* for decades. For all their troubles, the Congolese certainly know how to party: to see the locals at their upbeat best, hang out in one of Kinshasa's ramshackle bars, soaking up the high-energy music that's the country's trademark.

● **Lola ya Bonobo Sanctuary** At this sanctuary just outside Kinshasa, near the Chutes de Lukia (Lukaya Falls), you can bounce around with bonobos. Orphaned by bushmeat hunters and raised by humans, the bonobos are used to close contact and seem to enjoy larking about with visitors. See ⓦfriendsofbonobos.org.

● **Parc National de Virunga** Close to Goma, but best visited on a pre-booked trip starting in Rwanda, this spectacular, densely forested park is home to chimps, lowland gorillas and around eighty mountain gorillas. Places on treks, run by the park rangers, tend to be easier and cheaper to secure than their equivalent in Rwanda and Uganda, since so few tourists are prepared to venture into DRC. You'll struggle through rugged, humid jungle for anything up to five hours in order to find the gorillas – your reward is usually an unforgettable hour in close proximity with a family group.

Routes in and out

International flights land at N'djili Airport, Kinshasa, and a Congo vehicle and passenger ferry connects Kinshasa with Brazzaville. Foreign offices currently advise against all but essential travel in DRC, particularly the east, northeast and northwest. It's possible, but inadvisable, to enter DRC overland from Rwanda, Burundi or Uganda in the east, or from Angola in the southwest; onward travel within the country can be dangerous, with rebels, bandits and atrocious roads to contend with. There's a risk of landmines close to the border with Zambia. The borders with Tanzania, Sudan and Central African Republic are closed.

Red tape

Visas Required by UK, Ire, US, Can, Aus, NZ and SA nationals. These must be obtained in advance.

Nearest consulates Bangui; Brazzaville; Bujumbura; Dar es Salaam; Khartoum; Kigali; Kigoma; Luanda; Lusaka.

Other consulates London (☎020 7278 9825); Pretoria (☎+27 12 344 6475; ⓔrdcongo@lantic.net); Washington, DC (ⓦambardcusa.org). Aus/NZ citizens should apply for visas via Washington, DC.

Djibouti

Area 22,980 square kilometres
Capital Djibouti
Population 740,000
Languages French and Arabic (both official); Somali, Afar
Religion Muslim, minority Christian
Government Presidential republic
Independence June 27, 1977

(from France)
Best time to go Oct–April (cooler conditions); March–Sept (scuba visibility)
Country code +253
Currency Djiboutian franc (DJF); US$1: Fr180
Minimum daily budget US$40

Perched at the point where the Red Sea and the Gulf of Aden meet, Djibouti (see map, p.279) is one of Africa's smallest countries, with an area not much larger than Wales. It's also one of the hottest: in the coastal capital, the temperature regularly soars to over 30ºC, while the inland regions bake at well over 50ºC in June, July and August.

Outside the capital, there's little coastal development; the crystal clear sea laps straight onto sand, salt flats and solid lava, and most of the provincial population ekes out a living inland. This rugged terrain attracts geologists and vulcanologists: situated at the northern limit of Africa's Great Rift Valley, where three tectonic plates meet, its mountains and deserts have been carved by volcanic activity. A new cone, Ardoukoba, emerged in 1978, creating dramatic, ash-strewn hiking country.

Like much of the Horn of Africa, Djibouti is woefully poor, with rudimentary infrastructure. A large portion of the population are desert nomads; you may see Afar herders leading hardy sheep or camels across the close-bitten plains, seemingly a long way from anywhere. For most visitors, the main attractions are underwater – this is a superb, little-explored diving destination where you can wonder at schools of barracuda, shimmering reef fish and those rare giants of the deep, whale sharks.

Main attractions

● **Djibouti** The capital lies right on the Gulf of Aden, with many of its dusty streets laid out on reclaimed land. But while the port is prosperous and the seafood excellent, there's not much of a seaside feel to the city, which has a rather derelict atmosphere, its blend of

Mean temperatures and rainfall

Djibouti city	Jan	Feb	Mar	Apr	May	Jun	Jul	Aug	Sep	Oct	Nov	Dec
max °C	29	29	31	32	34	37	41	39	36	33	31	29
max °C	23	24	25	26	28	30	31	29	29	27	25	23
rainfall mm	10	13	25	13	5	0	3	8	8	10	23	13

Moorish and French colonial architecture falling apart at the seams. The delivery of Ethiopian *qat* chewing leaves, which account for a large proportion of household expenditure, is the highlight of each afternoon.

● **Lac Assal** Just over 100km west of the capital, this salt lake is part of the Danakil Depression which, at 155m below sea level, is Africa's lowest region. Beautiful but bleak, it's set among volcanoes and ringed with blindingly white gypsum and halite deposits; these cake any objects, such as wood or animal bones, which drop here.

● **Moucha and Maskali Islands** Just offshore from the capital, these islands can be reached in twenty minutes by motorboat, but are little visited. There are pale sandy beaches to lounge on and clear waters containing rare corals and wrecks for snorkellers and divers to explore.

● **Gulf of Tadjourah** Djibouti city lies at the mouth of a wide bay, the Gulf of Tadjourah, where young male whale sharks stop to feed on a plankton bloom during their annual migration (Nov–Jan) – a superb opportunity for divers and snorkellers. The gulf ends in Ghoubet al Kharab (Lake Ghoubet), containing a low volcanic cone, Guinni Koma (Devil's Island), which is enshrouded in local myth.

● **Gulf of Aden** Extensive reefs cover much of Djibouti's coastline; go scuba-diving here (ideally by liveaboard) and you may see grey sharks, nurse sharks and large schools of barracudas and jacks. Les Sept Frères archipelago in the Bab al-Mandab Strait, between the Gulf of Aden and the Red Sea, is a key site for experienced divers: sharks and dolphins are frequently seen here, and it's a good spot for deep dives.

● **Lake Abhe** Lying southwest of the capital on the Ethiopian border, this eerie and remote alkaline lake is framed by tufa columns and mounds formed by sulphurous fumaroles, natural geothermal chimneys which look like the backdrop to a sci-fi set. When there's water, it's dotted with flamingos, ibis and pelicans.

● **Monts Goda and Forêt du Day** The uplands northwest of the Gulf of Tadjourah are blanketed with green, especially after rain – a rare occurrence, but more common than elsewhere in this drought-scorched nation. The region includes the Forêt du Day, Djibouti's only national park, with a good scattering of hiking camps nearby and cool, misty tracks to explore, looking out for monkeys, leopard tracks and rare birds.

Routes in and out

International flights land at Djibouti-Ambouli Airport. Battered buses and 4WDs connect Djibouti with Ethiopia and Somaliland; there's also a dilapidated railway service between Djibouti and Addis Ababa. The border between Eritrea and Djibouti is effectively closed, and the northern border region is out of bounds to tourists, with a risk of fighting between Eritrean and Djiboutian forces. Dhows sail from the port of Djibouti to Mokha in Yemen on demand.

Red tape

Visas Required by UK, Ire, US, Can, Aus, NZ and SA nationals. Available in advance or on arrival at Djibouti airport and other points of entry.

Nearest consulates Addis Ababa (if applying for a visa here you'll need a letter of introduction from your embassy); Asmara; Cairo.

Other consulates Washington, DC (☎+1 202 331 0270). Visas can also be obtained from the following French consulates: London (🌐ambafrance-uk .org); Johannesburg (🌐consulfrance-jhb .org); Sydney (🌐ambafrance-au.org).

Egypt

Area 1,001,450 square kilometres
Capital Cairo
Population 78.6 million
Language Arabic (official); English, French (among the educated)
Religion Muslim; Coptic Christian minority
Government Presidential republic
Independence Feb 28, 1922 (from UK); the national day (July 23) celebrates the 1952 revolution
Best time to go April–Oct on the Med; March–April & Oct–Nov (fresher months) in Cairo; Dec–Feb (cooler months) in Luxor; Oct–April (moderate temperatures) on the Red Sea
Country code +20
Currency Egyptian pound (EGP); US$1: E£5.70
Minimum daily budget US$30

Invaders, raiders, adventurers, historians and tourists have been converging on Egypt's astounding array of historic temples, tombs and treasures for over four millennia. Impressions of ancient Egypt – its pyramids, mummies, hieroglyphics, jewel-encrusted decorative objects and enigmatic dynasties – are stitched firmly into the fabric of global culture, having inspired writers and cinematographers such as William Shakespeare, Agatha Christie, Cecil B. DeMille, Steven Spielberg and, from the 1920s, a whole generation of architects and designers.

For large numbers of visitors, Egypt's natural wonders are an even stronger lure. As well as being blessed with a sunny southern Mediterranean coast, Egypt boasts the sandy beaches and teeming coral gardens of the Red Sea, offering easily the best diving and snorkelling within six hours' flight time of Western Europe. The charismatic Nile can be experienced by traditional or modern cruise boat, and the wind-hewn desert's verdant oases are explorable by jeep, 4WD, quad bike or camel.

Many peoples have inhabited the Nile's fertile valley and delta before, during and since the long rule of the Pharaohs, and contemporary Egypt incorporates numerous cultures including the Berbers of Siwa, the Bedouin Arabs of the Sinai Peninsula and the Nubians of the Nile valley, south of Aswan. Nowhere is the cultural fusion more apparent than in Cairo, which rivals Lagos as Africa's biggest city. Here, Europeans live alongside Arabs and

Mean temperatures and rainfall

	Jan	Feb	Mar	Apr	May	Jun	Jul	Aug	Sep	Oct	Nov	Dec
Cairo												
max °C	18	21	24	28	33	35	36	35	32	30	26	20
min °C	8	9	11	14	17	20	21	22	20	18	14	10
rainfall mm	5	5	5	3	3	0	0	0	0	0	3	5

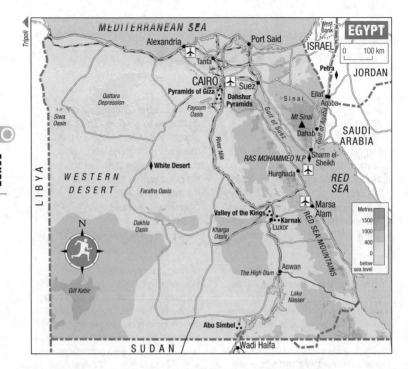

the trappings of modern life are layered upon an ancient, conservative settlement of souks, mosques and Coptic churches.

Egypt's embarrassment of riches is such that it's an immensely popular destination, with no end of travel options and a tourist industry that's been little dented by the isolated terrorist attacks of the 2000s. Visitors are therefore faced with two significant challenges: deciding which of the many superlative attractions to opt for, and working out how to avoid – or tolerate – the worst of the crowds. If you'll be visiting with a tour company (the most common choice) be extra sure it's a good one. The finest trips not only show you the sights in their best light, but also make imaginative use of Egypt's many transport options: Luxor, for example is a long slog from Cairo

by road, but an enjoyable adventure by overnight train, internal flight or Nile cruise.

Main attractions

● **The Great Pyramid, Giza** Just southwest of Cairo lie Egypt's most breathtaking monuments, including a true blockbuster, The Great Pyramid of Khufu. This massive mausoleum is the last of the Seven Wonders of the World as defined by the ancient Greeks, who called it the Pyramid of Cheops. It took around twenty years to build, from 2580 BC to 2560 BC; thus when Herodotus visited in 450 BC, it was more ancient to him than the time of Christ is to us. Its original height made it the world's tallest building for almost four

EGYPT

thousand years when, in 1311, it was topped by Lincoln Cathedral's original 160m spire. Also at Giza is another potent symbol of ancient Egypt – the Sphinx, the world's largest and oldest monolith sculpture. The earlier you visit, the better your chances of avoiding the tour buses – try approaching by camel at dawn.

● **Cairo** The capital's fifteen-million-strong population share a noisy, congested, chaotic metropolis built upon centuries of Islamic and Coptic history. One of its highlights is the Egyptian Museum, which has fascinating and beautiful displays of jewellery, decorated thrones, busts and papyruses, including the famed treasures of Tutankhamun's tomb. Islamic Cairo, the city's medieval heart, is a maze of alleyways, domes, minarets and souks including the Khan el-Khalili bazaar – a good area to find traditional restaurants where you can sample *fuul* (cooked beans), kebabs with *tahina* (sesame sauce) or delicious mezze dishes, and draw on a sheesha.

● **Red Sea Riviera** Sandwiched between the barren deserts of eastern Egypt and the life-rich waters of the Red Sea are beach resorts catering for different tastes and budgets and offering world-class diving and snorkelling (see p.178). On the Sinai peninsula, Sharm el-Sheikh and Na'ama Bay provide an upmarket selection of hotels, restaurants and scuba facilities, while Dahab, though developing fast, remains more budget-orientated, with an alternative vibe and good opportunities for windsurfing and other watersports. Hurghada on the east coast is a fun resort that's hugely popular for mid-range package holidays; its drawbacks are that it lacks authentic character and over-exploitation has damaged some of its coral reefs. Further south, Marsa Alam offers a mix

of remote luxury hotels and seashore camps with easy access to stunning dive sites.

● **Red Sea diving and snorkelling** A very popular target is Ras Mohammed National Park at the Sinai peninsula's southern tip, where the convergence of the Gulf of Suez and the Gulf of Aqaba supports an extraordinary range of marine life including reef fish, turtles and rays. Nearby is one of the Red Sea's most celebrated wrecks, the *Thistlegorm*; despite disintegrating considerably since it sank in 1941, the remains of its cargo of trucks, motorbikes and aircraft wings are still visible. In the waters closer to Sudan, where heavy tourist traffic has yet to take its toll, the diving is superb: at Marsa Alam, you can dive straight off the beach into spectacular coral gardens, caves and tunnels, while on a liveaboard trip, you can visit sites which are even more distant and beautiful.

● **Luxor, the Valley of the Kings and Karnak** Sometimes considered the greatest outdoor museum in the world, Luxor and the ancient temple complexes around it are Egypt's grandest and most visited sites after Giza. The town of Luxor was built among the ruins of Thebes, capital of the New Kingdom, whose tombs and mortuary temples remain on the opposite bank of the Nile, stripped of their treasures but still embellished with hieroglyphs. The Theban Necropolis includes the Valley of the Kings, home to Tutankhamun's famous tomb, which lay undisturbed for 3274 years before being opened in 1922. Its mummy and innermost solid gold coffin remain *in situ*, surrounded by colourful murals. On the east bank is Karnak's massive Precinct of Amun, large enough to accommodate ten cathedrals, along with an avenue of sphinxes.

● **Aswan and Abu Simbel** Aswan is best known for its dams, which created Lake Nasser, and for being a gateway to a region rich in monuments, including Philae and Abu Simbel. It's the most attractive city on the Nile, with appealing bazaars, feluccas (lateen-rigged yachts) flitting by and palm trees softening the scene. The culture here is largely Nubian, its residents descended from a five-thousand-year-old Sudanese-Egyptian civilization. Philae and its Temple of Isis contain superb carved reliefs, while the Sun Temple of Abu Simbel, 280km south of Aswan by road (and also reachable by internal flight), is guarded by stupendous stone images of Ramses II, which are strikingly lit by a nightly son et lumière show.

● **The Nile** Egypt's great vein takes on a new beauty and significance when seen from the decks of a slow-moving cruiser, felucca or *dahabiya* (luxury house boat). The classic Nile cruise takes you from Aswan to Luxor or vice versa, and possibly back again; four to seven days gives you plenty of time to adjust to the languid rhythm of the river on this meander through history, visiting sites such as the Temple of Horus at Edfu, the largest and most complete of the Pharaonic temples. The main downside is that you'll have to conform to a timetable which may mean that you'll be seeing temples at times when the light is flat and the crowds at their worst. Standards of comfort and catering vary a great deal, too, so make careful enquiries. Those with less time or money can opt for a dinner cruise.

Also recommended

● **Alexandria** The hassle-free atmosphere and faded elegance of Egypt's second city, once a focus of the Hellenistic and Roman worlds, makes it an appealing place to hang out, while the inspiring modern architecture of its Bibliotecha Alexandrina, the modern incarnation of a legendary library, brings it right up to date. Reposing gracefully on the Mediterranean, its cafés and breezy waterfront fish restaurants give it a more European flavour than Cairo. All sorts of archeological litter lies submerged in its bay, making this an intriguing place to dive; some found objects are displayed in its National Museum.

● **Mount Sinai** The rugged 2285m peak where, according to the Bible, Moses received the Ten Commandments, can be climbed on an excursion from the Sinai Red Sea resorts. The trek begins with a two-and-a-half-hour slog up an uneven ascent to Elijah's Basin, 300m below the summit, and finishes with a flight of 700 steps. If you make the climb in the small hours of the morning, you're rewarded with a rosy view of the dawn. Pilgrims flock here for Christian festivals; it's also sacred to Jews and Muslims.

● **Siwa** This isolated western desert oasis, close to the Libyan border, is home to a Berber community whose mud-brick homes nestle, intriguingly, among the crumbling remains of older buildings, fringed by date palms and olive groves. The most notable of its historic ruins is the Temple of the Oracle of Amun, consulted by Alexander the Great in the fourth century BC for reassurance of his claim to the title of Pharaoah of Egypt. To get to Siwa by bus, it's an arduous nine hours from Cairo or a slightly more comfortable eight hours from Alexandria.

● **The White Desert** In the bone-dry desert southwest of Cairo, wind erosion has sculpted white limestone outcrops into bizarre shapes resembling icebergs on a snowy sea. You can explore this region of big skies and wide horizons by jeep or camel safari, starting out from Farafra oasis and camping under the stars.

● **Dakhla** The simple, mud-built villages of this oasis offer a vivid impression of life deep in the western desert, surrounded by pink-dusted mountains and sweeping dunes. There are many hot springs here, and atmospheric, sandy streets to wander including those of Al-Qasr, dominated by its twelfth-century minaret.

● **Gilf Kebir** Close to the Libyan border in the remote southwest, south of the Great Sand Sea, is this plateau, notable for its petroglyphs featuring long-absent game including giraffes and ostrich, and ice age people swimming. To visit the region, you must obtain the permission of the Egyptian Ministry of the Interior.

● **Dahshur Pyramids** Around 25km south of Giza is an isolated collection of pyramids that's comparatively little known, allowing you to visit with something of the sense of wonder that must have possessed the earliest adventurers. They include the strangely comical-looking Bent Pyramid, whose angles alter halfway up, perhaps to correct a design error or simply as a cost-cutting measure.

● **Moulids** Egypt's many *moulids* (pilgim festivals honouring religious figures) are ardent occasions, with traditional music and good food accompanying the ceremonies. One of the biggest and most impressive, marking the birthdate of the thirteenth-century Sufi saint Sayyid Ahmad al-Badawi Tanta in October, attracts more than a million worshippers from Egypt, Sudan and the Middle East.

Routes in and out

The main international airport is Cairo in Heliopolis, 22km northeast of the city. There are also international flights to Borg el Arab Airport and Alexandria, and direct access to the Red Sea resorts via Sharm El Sheikh International at Ras Nasrani, Hurghada or Marsa Alam. Buses run between Cairo, Alexandria and Tripoli, while ferries connect Nuweiba in Sinai with Aqaba in Jordan and Suez, east of Cairo, with Jeddah, near Mecca in Saudi Arabia. Southwest Egypt, near the borders with Sudan and Libya, can be dangerous; to travel in this region, you must apply for a travel permit from the Egyptian Ministry of the Interior. The northeastern region, close to the border with Gaza, can also be dangerous. The borders with Sudan and with Gaza are not open to tourists.

Red tape

Visas Citizens from the EU and USA visiting Sharm El Sheikh, Dahab, Nuweiba or Taba resorts for fourteen days or less (and not travelling beyond the Sinai region) do not need a visa: you will receive a free entry stamp on arrival. Visas are required by all other UK, Ire, US, Can, Aus, NZ and SA nationals and are available on arrival at Egyptian airports; if arriving by land, they must be obtained in advance.

Nearest consulates Benghazi; Khartoum; Tripoli.

Other consulates Dublin (Ⓦembegyptireland.ie); London (Ⓦegyptianconsulate.co.uk); Pretoria (Ⓣ+27 12 343 1590, Ⓔegyptemb @global.co.za); Sydney (Ⓦegypt.org.au; Washington, DC (Ⓦegyptembassy.net).

Equatorial Guinea

Area 28,051 square kilometres
Capital Malabo
Population 660,000
Languages Spanish, French and
Portuguese (all official); Fang, Bubi
Religion Christian; traditional
minority
Government Presidential republic;
in practice authoritarian

Independence Oct 12, 1968
(from Spain)
Best time to go Oct–May in Bioko;
June–Aug & Dec–March in Río Muni
(drier months)
Country code +240
Currency Central African CFA franc
(XAF); US$1: CFA540
Minimum daily budget US$70

Equatorial Guinea (see map, p.244) is
an unlikely, scattered nation, its colonial
ties – uniquely for sub-Saharan Africa
– reaching to Spain. Its main parts are
Bioko, a small island just off the coast
of Cameroon, and Río Muni, a patch of
mainland 200km to the southeast; it also
incorporates a few tiny islands including
Annobón to the southwest, beyond
São Tomé and Príncipe. Between the
fifteenth and eighteenth centuries, the
entire region was Portuguese, but in
1778 Spain bought a swathe of it,
offering a part of Brazil in return. The
Spanish did little to defend their acquisi-
tion, losing most of it to other colonizers,
but hung on to present-day Equatorial
Guinea until Independence.

If it weren't for its lucrative oil reserves,
Equatorial Guinea would probably
languish in obscurity, but as things stand
it has one of the world's fastest growing
economies. Unfortunately, the benefits

of the oil industry are very thinly spread.
This is a nation blighted by a rich-poor
divide that's shocking even by African
standards: while the elite flash their cash
in the expensive, international-style bars,
restaurants and casinos of its capital,
Malabo, fewer than half the rural population have access to clean drinking water.

With all that black gold under the
ocean, tourism is not top of the list
of Equatorial Guinea's priorities. The
processes of obtaining a visa is notoriously fraught – US citizens are among
the few nationalities to be spared this
ordeal – and, to travel around, you have
to grit your teeth and smile your way
through one checkpoint after another.
Consequently, the few visitors who
make it here tend to have the wildlife-
rich forests and palm-fringed tropical
beaches all to themselves.

Equatorial Guinea has two lively
coastal cities: Malabo dominates the

Mean temperatures and rainfall

	Jan	Feb	Mar	Apr	May	Jun	Jul	Aug	Sep	Oct	Nov	Dec
Malabo												
max °C	31	32	31	32	31	29	29	29	30	30	30	31
min °C	19	21	21	21	22	21	21	21	21	21	22	21
rainfall mm	5	31	193	163	262	302	160	114	201	231	117	20

strikingly mountainous island of Bioko, while Bata lies on Río Muni's Atlantic shore. While relatively few locals speak Spanish as a first language these days, most have a Spanish first name, and on streets called *calles*, *carreteras* and *avenidas* you'll see a few remnants of colonial architecture along with restaurants and shops selling Spanish-style food and wine. Upcountry Equatorial Guinea is also interesting to visit, despite the hardships suffered by its villagers. Here, the lush hiking terrain is populated by chimpanzees, lowland gorillas, reptiles and a breathtaking variety of birds.

Main attractions

● **Malabo** This small but cosmopolitan city has a large enough population of affluent expats to engender the kind of white-male-dominated, cash-fuelled nightlife that's rare in Central Africa. Despite Malabo's flashy modern architecture and imposing Spanish colonial cathedral, it also has a ramshackle side, leaving you in no doubt that this is an African capital.

● **Bioko** Outside the capital, the island of Bioko has a trio of volcanic peaks, wild cocoa trees (the remnants of century-old Spanish plantations) and stands of sugar cane (the raw ingredient for *malamba*, the local firewater). Along the rugged coast are dark-sand beaches where marine turtles dig their nests, and one beach with golden sand, Arena Blanca, an hour south of Malabo.

● **Bata** The port of Bata is the principal settlement on the mainland; though smaller than Malabo, a steady influx of oil money has fuelled its rapid development. Now an up-and-coming city with tidy central avenues and a smart, modern seafront promenade overlooked by new apartment blocks,

it also retains some pleasant colonial buildings and hectic traditional markets.

● **Monte Alen National Park** Protected from logging, this lush inland rainforest harbours chimpanzees, gorillas, mandrills, crocodiles and birds. Local guides trained by Ecofac (Ⓦecofac.org /Ecotourisme/) run wildlife-watching hikes.

● **Annobón and Corisco** The tiny volcanic island of Annobón (also called Pagalu), 600km to the southwest of Bata is breathtakingly remote (you may be able to bag a passage on the weekly cargo ship from Bata), with deserted beaches. An easier target, reachable by motorized pirogue from Cogo in the southwest, is Isla Corisco, off the coast of Gabon; here, there's a tiny, traditional community, the ruins of churches built by the Portuguese and little to do beyond flopping on the white sand.

Routes in and out

International flights land at Malabo Airport; the national airline operates connecting services to Bata. Río Muni can also be entered overland from Gabon (via tarmac roads) and Cameroon (via dirt tracks).

Red tape

Visas Required by UK, Ire, Can, Aus, NZ and SA nationals. Must be obtained in advance; a letter of invitation may be requested. US citizens do not require a visa for a stay of ninety days or less.

Nearest consulates Bangui; Brazzaville; Lagos; Libreville; Yaoundé.

Other consulates London (Ⓦembarege-londres.org); Pretoria (☎+27 12 342 9945); Washington, DC (☎+1 202 518 5700). Aus/NZ citizens should use Washington, DC.

Eritrea

Area 124,320 square kilometres
Capital Asmara
Population 5.6 million
Languages Arabic and Tigrinya
(both official); English, Italian
Religion Muslim, Christian
Government Single-party
presidential republic

Independence May 24, 1993
(from Ethiopia)
Best time to go Oct–April
(dry season, cooler)
Country code +291
Currency Nakfa (ERN);
US$1: Nfk15
Minimum daily budget US$30

Corralled within Africa's most troubled region, Eritrea (see map, p.279) receives precious little of the attention it deserves. It has much to offer travellers, not least a fascinating capital, striking semi-desert highlands and excellent Red Sea diving, but few venture here. And with long-running tensions with neighbouring Ethiopia and Djibouti bubbling under the surface, tourism is not a priority.

Eritrea broke free from Ethiopia in 1993 after a bitter thirty-year struggle for independence. Before that, the strongest outside influence came from the Italians, who were here for around 150 years, including a golden age of industrial development and architectural blossoming under Mussolini in the 1930s. Il Duce had a vision of Eritrea becoming the jewel of an empire to rival ancient Rome, and he gave architects free rein to express the spirit of the age through *architettura razionale*, the fascist response to Art Deco. Miraculously,

most of the best buildings in the capital city of Asmara survived the war against Ethiopia and remain gleamingly intact.

Though impoverished and stifled by an intransigent, repressive government, Eritrea is a buoyant and vigorous country which is committed to regeneration projects such as road building, tree planting and healthcare. Everywhere is spotless, and there's a well-mannered atmosphere to the nation which is highly seductive.

Main attractions

● **Asmara** This petite highland city is orderly, hassle-free and a pleasure to visit. At around 2400m, it rivals Addis Ababa as the highest capital in Africa, with a wonderfully clear, bright climate. Exploring on foot is easy and is the best way to appreciate the superb 1930s architecture. The strong Italian atmosphere is infused with heady

Mean temperatures and rainfall

Asmara	Jan	Feb	Mar	Apr	May	Jun	Jul	Aug	Sep	Oct	Nov	Dec
max °C	22	23	24	25	26	25	23	23	22	22	22	22
min °C	4	5	8	9	11	11	10	10	9	8	7	5
rainfall mm	0	0	15	30	34	48	190	162	28	26	29	5

memories of *la dolce vita* – elderly locals in suits and trilbies greet each other over nerve-jangling espressos with a *"buon giorno"* in the old-fashioned cafés, the pastries and pizza are as superb as the *injera* (doughy pancakes served with spicy stews), and the late afternoon *passeggiata* is a much-loved ritual.

● **Art Deco cinemas and the Fiat Tagliero building** Asmara's picture palaces are temples to 1930s style. The facade of the 1937 Cinema Impero on Harnett (Liberation Avenue), the main street, is dotted with porthole lamps like giant radio knobs; Cinema Roma is decked out in marble and dark wood; and Cinema Odeon has an authentic interior for Art Deco fans to swoon over. Asmara also boasts what could well be the world's most glamorous petrol station, the 1938 Fiat Tagliero building, a stunning futuristic concoction resembling an aeroplane.

● **Massawa** The road from Asmara in the highlands down to Massawa (Mitsiwa) on the Red Sea coastal plain (a two-hour drive by car, or four by bus) winds its way, via whirling hairpin bends, through striking semi-desert scenery dotted with cacti and succulents. Steam trains ply a restored, Italian-built railway line which traces a similar route. The historic but war-scarred port town of Massawa is liveliest on market day, Friday, when it's packed with vendors and well-dressed women in dark velvet or vividly coloured robes and large gold nose rings.

● **Dahlak Archipelago** Less than two hours by boat from Massawa, this collection of around two hundred Red Sea islands is largely undeveloped and somewhat bleak on the surface. Underwater, it's a different story: with plenty of manta rays, sharks and colourful reef fish patrolling the waters, the diving and snorkelling is excellent, though expensive (pricey package trips are the only option).

● **Keren** Eritrea's second city, 90km northwest of Asmara, has some beautiful Art Deco buildings, several impressive mosques and Catholic churches and a nineteenth-century fortress. There are fine silversmiths' workshops and an enjoyable Monday market where camels and other livestock change hands.

● **Qohaito and Metera** The pillars and caves scattered over Eritrea's southern deserts will appeal to archeology enthusiasts. A permit from the National Museum in Asmara is required to visit.

● **Barentu** The staunchly Muslim western lowlands have a very different atmosphere from the more Christian highlands. The town of Barentu, four hours southwest of Keren, is a good target, particularly on market days (Thurs & Sat).

Routes in and out

International flights land at Yohannes IV Airport, Asmara. Land borders with Ethiopia, Sudan and Djibouti are either closed, unsafe (with a risk of military incursions) or both. It's inadvisable to travel in the far north or within 25km of the border between Eritrea and Djibouti in the far southeast.

Red tape

Visas Required by UK, Ire, US, Can, Aus, NZ and SA nationals. Must be obtained in advance. To travel beyond Asmara, you must obtain a permit from the Ministry of Tourism in Asmara.
Nearest consulates Cairo; Djibouti; Khartoum; Nairobi.
Other consulates London (☎020 7713 0096; ✉eriemba@eriembauk.com); Maribyrnong, Melbourne (🌐ericon.org .au); Pretoria (🌐eritreaembassy.co.za); Washington, DC (☎+1 202 319 1991).

Ethiopia

Area 1,104,000 square kilometres
Capital Addis Ababa
Population 88 million
Language Amharic (official); Oromo,
Tigrinya and more than sixty others
Religion Christian, Muslim;
traditional minority
Government One-party state with
democratic trappings

Independence Always been
independent
Best time to go Oct–March
(dry season)
Country code +251
Currency Ethiopian Birr (ETB)
US$1: Br13.6
Minimum daily budget US$30

The only country in Africa never to have been a colony, Ethiopia, with its hallmark moor-covered mountain landscapes, history and rich culture, is different in so many ways from everywhere else on the continent that it stands as an utterly distinct destination.

A profoundly Christian nation, with its own indigenous Ethiopian Orthodox Church founded in the fourth century, Ethiopia also has a huge Muslim population and a tribal region in the Omo valley of the far southwest where some of the most independent, little-contacted

peoples in the world still live beyond the influence of the country's national infrastructure.

The last emperor, Haile Selassie, ruled from 1917 to 1974, with a five-year interruption when Italy occupied the country from 1936 to 1941. After the emperor was deposed in a coup in 1974, the country was pulverized by seventeen years of brutal military rule followed by more than a decade of internal conflict, culminating in bloody and futile trench warfare with its neighbour, Eritrea, which had split from Ethiopia in 1991.

Mean temperatures and rainfall

	Jan	Feb	Mar	Apr	May	Jun	Jul	Aug	Sep	Oct	Nov	Dec
Addis Ababa												
max °C	26	27	27	28	28	25	25	24	24	26	25	25
min °C	4	6	7	7	7	8	8	8	7	5	4	4
rainfall mm	16	37	72	88	86	141	278	306	184	19	17	6
Harar												
max °C	26	26	26	26	25	24	23	23	24	26	26	23
min °C	13	14	15	15	15	14	14	14	14	14	13	13
rainfall mm	10	31	75	117	130	88	132	157	94	38	14	12
Moyale												
max °C	33	33	33	31	27	27	26	27	29	29	29	31
min °C	15	17	17	16	16	14	14	14	14	15	16	16
rainfall mm	20	19	56	197	129	17	18	20	22	140	103	42

Massacres, famines and forced migrations characterized nearly all of the first three decades of the post-Imperial era.

Today, the second most populous country in Africa remains exceptionally poor, with daunting social and economic challenges. Despite other uncomfortable truths – the government has veered way off the democratic course and invaded Somalia in 2006 with US backing – it remains a safe, stunningly beautiful and intensely rewarding place to travel.

Main attractions

● **Addis Ababa** One of Africa's biggest capitals (and its highest, alongside Asmara in Eritrea, at 2400m), with a population of more than four million, Addis is a sprawling, rough-edged city with a fine climate, a strong sense of identity and serious global credentials as a UN centre and headquarters of the African Union. Great restaurants, running the global gamut, are here in abundance, and the market – still called the Mercato seventy years after the brief Italian occupation – is the biggest on the continent and worth an extended browse. Don't miss the wonderful Ethnological and National museums and the massive granite tomb of Haile Selassie at the Holy Trinity Cathedral. If you're into Ethiopia's fabulous, soulful, pentatonic pop, check out the CD shops at the Mercato and ask people who's playing tonight in the city's *azmaribets*, or music bars.

● **Lalibela** In a land of must-see sights, Lalibela, a UNESCO World Heritage Site named after the twelfth-century king of this region, is the jewel in Ethiopia's crown. Off the main road network, in a landscape of towering, misty mountains, its remote community – just a few thousand strong – survive largely on income from pilgrims and tourists. The extraordinary subterranean churches hewn from the red volcanic tufa rock of the area are not the only such churches in Ethiopia but they're by far the most impressive. Many incorporate tunnels and passages, niches, hermits' and monks' cells and tombs, and the breathtaking architecture includes the largest freestanding, rock-hewn church in the world, Bet Medhane Alem – the oldest at Lalibela.

● **Simien National Park** The great massif of the Simien range (Ras Dashen, at 4620m, is Ethiopia's highest peak) is broken into towering plateaus and peaks by a slew of rivers and waterfalls. The park itself is a spellbinding wilderness of fertile valleys and grassy moors – a largely roadless region, traced by footpaths and scattered with Amhara villages (the mountains were also the home of Ethiopia's Jews before they emigrated to Israel). Three large mammals live in these highlands: the impressively horned and vulnerable Walia ibex; the critically rare, red-coated Simien wolf; and the remarkable, grass-eating Gelada baboon, which you often see grazing on the steep meadows, sometimes in troops of hundreds. Walking with mules is the usual transport, against a backdrop of vertiginous gorges, giant Afro-Alpine vegetation and birdlife that includes soaring lammergeyer vultures.

● **Aksum** Devout Ethiopian Christians credit Aksum, in the far north, with being the site of the Ark of the Covenant, a rarely seen vessel kept there in the Church of Our Lady Mary of Zion – and (one of several "arks" around the world). The Dongar ruins are said to be the Palace of the Queen of Sheba, and innumerable, mysterious stelae – inscribed columns, some more than 20m high – rise up around the town. Whatever its endlessly debatable biblical connections, this UNESCO World Heritage Site was certainly the capital of the kingdom of Aksum (or Axum), which reached its apogee some 1800 years ago. If the town itself is underwhelming, the sense of archeological discovery is addictive – especially if you spend some time in the excellent museum.

● **Harar Jugol** This magical walled city occupies the eastern side of the modern town of Harar and is instantly reminiscent of similar cities in North Africa. Harar Jugol's countless alleys and corners invite exploration in the comfort of knowing the place is completely safe and you can't get lost – though it's worth taking a guide to avoid being pestered by every other guide in town. Despite Harar's eighty-something mosques, it has no shortage of drinking places and chewing the mild stimulant *chat* (khat) seems to be the town's main occupation – joining in makes for a convivial atmosphere in the evening. Suitably refreshed, you might want to go outside the walls to see the touristy nightly spectacle of one of Harar's "hyena men" feeding these feral predators.

● **Lake Tana and the Blue Nile Falls** Ethiopia's contribution to the world's longest river starts in the greeny-brown waters of the country's biggest lake, a huge, shallow pool, set at an altitude of 1830m. Flowing south out of Lake Tana, past the pretty resort town of Bahir Dar, the river tumbles over a scarp at the famous Blue Nile Falls – now much reduced thanks to a recent hydro-electric dam. Intriguingly, you can visit (but in most cases only if you're male) the two-dozen monasteries and churches scattered on Lake Tana's tiny islands and around its shores, some dating from the fourteenth century. Several have superb frescoes and ancient libraries. You can also take the weekly ferry around the west side of the lake, rent boats and seek out the local pelicans and hippos.

● **Bale Mountains National Park** Highly endangered Ethiopian wolves and mountain nyala antelope are the outstanding denizens of this high-altitude park south of Addis. The area was only properly explored by European scientists in the 1950s and soon came to be recognized as a unique habitat. Although broadly similar Afro-Alpine ecosystems exist elsewhere, there's nowhere that compares with Bale's scale: the Sanetti plateau, for example, is Africa's biggest Afro-Alpine moor, a huge area of glaciated heathland, with stunning wild flowers after the rains. The best plan is to give yourself plenty of time and hire a guide and a pony to explore the park.

● **Gondar** Just north of Lake Tana, hilly Gondar was the capital of Ethiopia from the middle of the seventeenth century to the end of the nineteenth. It has some of the most magnificent Christian art in the country at the Debre Birhan Selassie church, isolated on a hilltop on the east side of town. In the town itself, behind the massive walls of the central Royal Enclosure – 400m from north to south and 200m across – stand no fewer than six castle-palaces, in various degrees of ruin, all dating from Gondar's golden age in the seventeenth and eighteenth centuries. The centrepiece, restored by UNESCO, is the palace of the founder of Gondar, Fasilidas, with its rooftop views across the city and out to Lake Tana.

● **South Omo valley** The nascent tourism in this extremely remote district is now at least partly organized by local people (choose your company carefully), allowing you to witness the Mursi's dramatic stick fights and lip disks and the Kara's intricate, personalized body art in a manner that's welcome rather than intrusive. In the case of the Hamar's bull-jumping ceremony, it's the casual

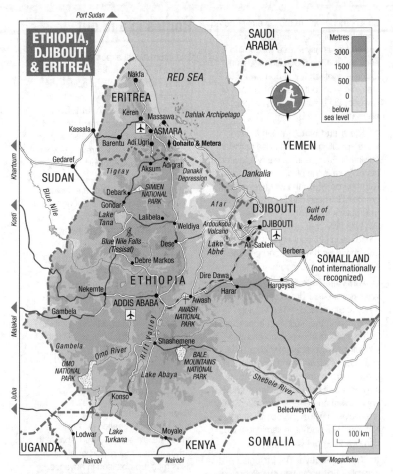

violence of the girl-whippers, rather than the slightly comic jumping itself that stays with you. Laughing, flirting and competing for scars, girls approach their feather-headdressed male peers for a swipe with a cane, borne without flinching, to show their devotion to their brothers. The ceremony climaxes with a group of steers being dragged into a row, side by side. Out of the crowd dashes a naked youth, who must complete four runs across the bulls' backs without tripping to pass into adulthood.

Also recommended

● **Ethiopia's Rastas** Ethiopia may have been the home of Tafari Mekonnen (dubbed "Ras" or prince and later "Haile Selassie" when he became emperor in 1930), but his dreadlocked followers are thin on the ground. Indeed, most of the country's Rastas are recent immigrants from Jamaica, where the religion that reveres Haile Selassie was founded in the 1930s. The majority live in the unprepossessing Rift Valley town of

Shashemene, where the several hundred inhabitants of the Rasta neighbourhood known as "Jamaica", are welcoming enough. Visit the Black Lion Museum to make contact. If you don't want to stay, carry on to the lakeshore town of Awassa, 25km further south, a popular alternative rest stop.

● **Njera and wat** Although it often looks appalling, the distinctive national cuisine of Ethiopia is an easily acquired taste. *Njera* is the pleasantly sour, moist flatbread on which the *wat* (stews) are presented. These can be anything from mild pulses to chicken, goat, beef and fish with fiery chilli. Tear off a corner of bread using just your right hand, use it to scoop up the stew, and pop the whole thing in your mouth.

● **Rift Valley lakes** A chain of eight lakes run like tear drops along the Rift Valley south of Addis, their varying salinity giving them different ecosystems. Some are popular weekend escapes for well-off city-dwellers: Lake Ziway has spectacular birdwatching (and hippos), Lake Langano has good places to stay on its western shore, and shallow Lake Abiata and deep crater lake Shala are enclosed within the Abiata-Shala National Park and have flamingos and European migrant wading birds.

● **Timket Festival** The Ethiopian festival of Epiphany, usually celebrated around January 19, and particularly important at Lalibela and other Christian centres in the highlands, is the most important date of the Julian calendar (see p.413) and marked by mass baptisms and the downing of huge volumes of *tej* – mead. Timket is the culmination of a three-day party, with processions of *tabots* – replicas of the tablets from the Ark of the Covenant – led by flamboyantly dressed priests.

Routes in and out

The international airport, home of reputable Ethiopian Airlines, is at Addis Ababa, with connections across the continent and to Europe, the Middle East, Asia and the USA. Ethiopia's land borders are less straightforward. Overland travel between Khartoum and Addis is feasible, while travel between South Sudan and Ethiopia is disrupted by very bad earth roads. Looking south, the route between Addis and Nairobi would be straightforward enough were it not for the poor security and brain-rattling "roads" of northern Kenya. Seek local advice before setting out in either direction as your vehicle may need an escort. Ethiopia's borders with Somalia and Eritrea are closed, but the border with Djibouti is open. You can also travel overland between Dire Dawa and Hargeisa and Berbera in the independent breakaway state of Somaliland.

Red tape

Visas Required by UK, Ire, US, Can, Aus, NZ and SA nationals. Available on arrival at Bole airport, Addis Ababa. If arriving at another airport or by land, visas must be obtained in advance.

Nearest consulates Cairo; Djibouti; Kampala; Khartoum; Nairobi (consulate issues visas for entry by air only).

Other consulates Dublin (Ⓦethiopianembassy.ie); Fitzroy, Victoria (Ⓦconsul.com.au); London (Ⓦethioembassy.org.uk); Ottawa (Ⓦembassyofethiopia.net); Pretoria (☎+27 12 346 3542); Washington, DC (Ⓦethiopianembassy.org).

Gabon

Area 267,667 square kilometres
Capital Libreville
Population 1.5 million
Language French (official); Fang
Religion Christian; traditional minority
Government Presidential republic; in practice authoritarian
Independence Aug 17, 1960 (from France)

Best time to go April–May (rainy season) for wildlife; June–Aug (relatively cool with less rain) for hiking
Country code +241
Currency Central African CFA franc (XAF); US$1: CFA540
Minimum daily budget US$80

GABON

In the early 2000s, Gabon (see map, p.244), the most accessible country in the little-visited Congo Basin, leaped to world attention as Africa's most promising new wildlife-watching destination. The president, Omar Bongo, aware that his nation's lucrative oil reserves would dwindle in time, had been casting around for alternative revenue streams. Convinced of the potential of upmarket, low-impact conservation tourism, he created thirteen new national parks, protecting vast swathes of primary equatorial rainforest, pristine wetlands and unblemished Atlantic coast from loggers, developers and industrialists. Since the country's 2009 change in government, there's been some doubt about the future direction of conservation in this treasure box of a country – its leading conservation tourism operator and charter aviation company have

recently pulled out – but with so much potential revenue at stake, it's hoped that it will soon take a positive turn once more.

As an eco-tourism destination, Gabon's greatest advantage over the other equatorial African nations is that its population is small, localized and peaceful. Its natural habitats are fertile, well-watered and stunningly varied – there's pretty much everything here except desert. Among the abundance of large mammals, butterflies, birds and marine fauna are rarities such as lowland gorillas, mandrills and forest elephants.

Yet while most travellers come here for the flora and fauna, Gabon also has cultural riches to explore: the forests are home to Ba'Aka, Bibayak, Babongo and Mitsogo tribes, many of whom practice Bwiti. This is a form of ancestor worship whose ritual dances are fuelled

Mean temperatures and rainfall

	Jan	Feb	Mar	Apr	May	Jun	Jul	Aug	Sep	Oct	Nov	Dec
Libreville												
max °C	31	31	32	32	31	29	28	29	29	30	30	31
min °C	23	22	23	23	22	21	20	21	22	22	22	22
rainfall mm	249	236	335	340	244	13	3	18	104	345	373	249

by *iboga*, a natural narcotic to which Gabon's forest elephants are also rather partial.

For visitors, the main downsides are that tourism is still so new that the options, particularly for independent travel, are limited – it's tricky to get around under your own steam and the safari infrastructure is minimal.

Main attractions

● **Libreville** This swanky, modern capital is a costly but energizing city to visit. You can splurge on imported goods in its air-conditioned shopping malls, dine out on Vietnamese specialities or gourmet burgers in its restaurants, or sample everything from palm wine to the finest French champagne in the bars and clubs of the Quartier Louis. High-rise hotels line the oceanside boulevards, the nearby beaches at Pointe-Dénis are good for watersports, and there's seaside seclusion at Cocobeach and Cap Estérias.

● **Fernan-Vaz Gorilla Project** On Evengué Island near Loango, this primate research and rehabilitation centre cares for western lowland gorillas that have been orphaned by the bushmeat trade. There's a charming waterfront lodge, from which it's a short walk to the pleasant viewing area.

● **Parc National de l'Ivindo** In the heart of this remote inland park near Makokou, around 550km east of Libreville, is Langoué Bai, a large natural forest clearing rich in salt deposits and surrounded by dense vegetation. It's a magnet for elusive wildlife such as forest elephants, lowland gorillas, forest buffaloes, duikers and sitatungas. The clearing, which is a long, sweaty trek from camp, has viewing platforms from which to enjoy the cavalcade.

● **Parc National de la Lopé** This patchwork of forest and savanna was Gabon's first protected area and is well set up for excursions. As well as being home to extraordinarily large troops of mandrills, mangabeys and baboons, it's notable for its many ancient, geometric petroglyphs, thought to have been engraved with iron tools around two thousand years ago. At the Mikongo Conservation Centre, run by the Zoological Society of London, you can join forest treks and find out about gorilla habituation.

● **Birdwatching** With more than 700 resident and migrant species, Gabon is prime twitching territory. As well as forest birds, there's also an abundance of coastal, river and wetland species. More than 350 have been recorded in Lopé National Park alone, and Lambaréné (where Albert Schweitzer founded his hospital) is also an excellent target. Here, Gabon's major waterway, the Ogooué River, spreads into one of Africa's largest deltas, its waters alive with herons, pelicans, spoonbills and egrets.

● **Whales and turtles** Humpback whales breed near the coast of Gabon between mid-July and mid-September and can be seen on whale-watching boat trips. Gabon's Atlantic beaches are also one of the world's most significant nesting sites for leatherback turtles (Sept–Dec); Mayumba National Park in the far south is a good place to see them.

● **Parc National du Loango** Loango was until recently Gabon's most visited wilderness area, with a well-established lodge and satellite camps. At the time of writing these are closed, but it's hoped that they may re-open again in the future. The park incorporates a fascinating variety of forest, river and coastal habitats and is famous for the forest elephants and hippos which sometimes stroll along the Atlantic beach (Nov–April), even sampling the surf. As you coast down the rivers, you may see tree-climbing dwarf crocodiles and wading elephants. The grasslands are home to forest buffalos and red river hogs, whose tufty ears give them a comical, gremlin look.

Also recommended

● **Setté Cama** Close to the Nodogo lagoon and the southern entrance to Loango National Park, this village makes a good alternative base to the camps within the park, with wilderness to explore on its doorstep.

● **Port-Gentil** Gabon's second city is prosperous, thanks to the oil industry, but more easy-going than Libreville. From here, you can travel by boat into the region's coastal lagoons and wetlands, possibly visiting Eglise Sainte-Anne, a lagoonside mission church designed by Gustav Eiffel.

● **Parc National des Monts de Cristal** The ancient, misty forests of this mountain park are dotted with delicate orchids and giant begonias.

Routes in and out

International flights land at Libreville, with direct links both to Europe and to Africa's main hubs. Local airlines and charter services also fly to the basic airport at Port-Gentil and the airstrips elsewhere in the country. Overland travel from Equatorial Guinea, Cameroon or Congo is possible, but slow.

Entry requirements

Visas Required by UK, Ire, US, Can, Aus, NZ and SA nationals. Must be obtained in advance. Letter of invitation from a local organization (such as a travel company) or individual required.

Nearest consulates Brazzaville; Luanda; Malabo; São Tomé; Yaoundé.

Other consulates Fairlight, New South Wales (☎+61 2 9907 8707); London (☎020 7823 9986); Ottawa (☎+1 613 232 5301); Pretoria (Ⓦgabonembassy.org.za); Washington, DC (Ⓦgabonembassy.net).

The Gambia

Area 11,295 square kilometres
Capital Banjul
Population 1.7 million
Language English (official);
Mandinka, Wolof, Fula
Religion Muslim majority
Government Presidential republic
with elements of authoritarianism
Independence Feb 18, 1965
Best time to go Nov–April (dry
season); birdwatching year-round
Country code +220
Currency Dalasi (GMD); US$1: D30
Minimum daily budget US$50

English-speaking, peaceful and friendly,
The Gambia is an excellent starting
point for a trip through West Africa. Its
beach resorts offer the chance to acclimatize in comfort before easing yourself
on to more demanding regions. With
a well-established sun-and-fun tourist
industry, flights are relatively cheap and
easy to obtain and there's a great variety
of places to stay, from rustic huts to
air-conditioned hotels.

The key features in this eccentrically
shaped country are its Atlantic coast
and its river. Offering access to valuable
resources such as timber, skins, ivory
and slaves plus (for a while) the hope of a
link to the River Niger, the River Gambia
was fought over by European explorers
and traders until, in the late nineteenth
century, control of the river and its
Atlantic port was transferred to a relatively
benign British colonial government.

Under the current, somewhat ruthless
regime, development has been patchy:
while foreign donations have funded
much-needed public construction and
engineering projects, some roads and
services worsened, particularly in rural
areas. If, despite this, you make the
effort to explore the upcountry wilderness, you'll find much to enjoy including
bird-rich wetlands and undeveloped

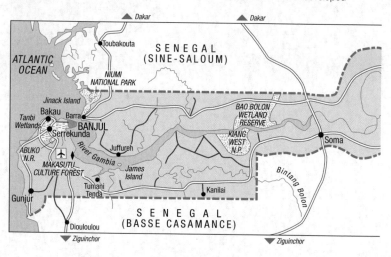

Mean temperatures and rainfall

	Jan	Feb	Mar	Apr	May	Jun	Jul	Aug	Sep	Oct	Nov	Dec
Banjul												
max °C	31	32	34	33	32	32	30	29	31	32	32	31
min °C	15	16	17	18	19	23	23	23	23	22	22	16
rainfall mm	3	3	0	0	10	58	282	500	310	109	18	3

beaches. Meanwhile, in the villages, life follows traditional, tranquil patterns: men chat in the shade of mango trees and children play imaginative games while their mothers tend vegetable patches or pound grain in wooden mortars.

Main attractions

● **Bakau and Fajara** Clustered on the Atlantic coast near Banjul and Serrekunda are four neighbouring beach resorts, Kololi, Kotu, Fajara and Bakau, which form the main focus of The Gambia's holiday industry. While Kololi and Kotu are unashamedly touristy, adjacent Fajara and Bakau have a far more authentic feel. There's an interesting mix of accommodation scattered between the shanty-like dwellings of fishermen and the smart dwellings of well-to-do expats, plus a bustling local market and a great selection of places to eat.

● **Southwest coast** The further you travel down the Atlantic coast from the main beach resorts, the wilder the landscape becomes, with palm-fringed beaches where crab and cattle tracks crisscross the sand and brightly coloured fishing pirogues ply the waters. Tucked away in the coastal forest are a handful of basic but charming lodges.

● **Makasutu Culture Forest** Founded by two British enthusiasts, this eco-attraction offers visitors an introduction to forest flora and fauna and tribal lore while promoting the preservation of The Gambia's long-dwindling woodland and wetland regions. Most visitors tour the forest trails with a guide, followed by lunch and entertainment from a local

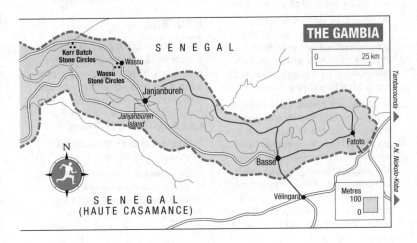

dance troupe. Those who'd like more than a day-trip can stay in a beautifully designed riverside eco-lodge.

● **Birdwatching** After its beaches, The Gambia's varied and abundant birdlife is its greatest selling point. Many prime habitats are crammed into its small area, allowing a wide range of species to thrive here all year round – the count swells to more than 560 during the European winter as migrants arrive from chillier climes. Local and visiting guides run specialist birding trips, taking in the Atlantic coast, the wetlands adjoining the River Gambia and the protected woodlands and open savannas upcountry. The Tanbi Wetlands is a maze of mangrove creeks a short hop from The Gambia's main beach resorts; the Bao Bolon Wetland Reserve is less accessible but even more enjoyable, home to an astonishing variety of species including jewel-like kingfishers and stately herons.

● **Abuko Nature Reserve** This pocket of forest is close to the main urban areas, but has been protected for long enough to ensure a healthy population of birds, monkeys and reptiles. All are used to visitors; if you visit early in the morning, before the tour groups arrive, you can be certain of close-up sightings.

● **River Gambia** Chilling out on a slow boat up the river, you can spot parrots, monkeys and even hippos as the landscape changes from the thick mangroves of the lower stretches to the lush tropical forest further inland.

● **Music and festivals** Live music is key to Gambian social life and many hotels and restaurants invite Wolof singers and drummers and Mandinka *kora* players to entertain their guests. The village of Kartong stages a music and culture festival every February and Gambians really let their hair down at the celebrations of traditional Jola music, culture and wrestling held each year at the President's home village of Kanilai, usually in June.

● **Banjul** The Gambian capital is small and manageable, with a bustling port, remnants of colonial architecture and a superb show of produce at the Albert market.

● **Serrekunda** By far The Gambia's largest urban area and trading centre, Serrekunda is always on the go. For visitors who don't mind heat and crowds, the main attractions are the sprawling traditional market and its nearby curio shops, and Jokor, the locals' favourite nightspot.

● **Basse** This upcountry market town serves as a crossroads for travellers and traders from all over the region. Set right on the riverbank, it's a great place to get a feel for life in the provinces.

Routes in and out

International flights land at Yundum Airport near Banjul, Serrekunda and the main Atlantic beach resorts. There are several hassle-free overland routes to northern Senegal. Seek local advice before planning an overland trip to southern Senegal: the Casamance region of Senegal is prone to unrest and banditry.

Red tape

Visas UK, Ire, Can, Aus and NZ nationals don't require a visa for a stay of ninety days or less. US and SA nationals require a visa: if you arrive without, you will usually be issued with an entry pass, but you'll have to obtain a visa at Immigration (or leave the country) within 48 hours.

Nearest consulates Bissau; Dakar; Freetown; Lagos; Rabat.

Other consulates London (☎020 7937 6316, ©gambiahighcomuk@btconnect .com); Johannesburg (☎+27 11 430 7640); Taipei (☎+86 2875 3711); Washington, DC (®gambiaembassy.us).

Ghana

Area 239,000 square kilometres
Capital Accra
Population 24 million
Language English (official), Akan-Twi (Asante/Fante), Ewe, more than seventy others
Religion Christian; Muslim and traditional minorities
Government Presidential democracy

Independence March 6, 1957 (from UK)
Best time to go Nov–Feb & July–Aug (dry seasons, south); Nov–April (dry season, north)
Country code +233
Currency Cedi (GHS); US$1: GH¢1.43
Minimum daily budget US$30

Ghana ticks more travellers' boxes than any other West African nation. It really has the lot: excellent transport and accommodation, a rewarding cultural mix (and tribal traditions that for once really are colourful), fascinating historical sites along the coast, where European slaving forts still stand, and superb beaches. Ghanaians themselves might complain about inefficiency, but since the near-collapse of the economy in 1979, conditions have improved out of all recognition.

Ghana, formerly the Gold Coast, was the first modern African country to retrieve its independence. In the early 1960s it was one of the richest nations on the continent – the world's leading cocoa exporter and producer of a tenth of the world's gold. After the optimistic start made by independence leader Kwame Nkrumah, it suffered a two-decade descent into violence and repression, but the country is viewed today as a shining example of an African democracy. Moreover, the people of Ghana are hospitable and generous to a fault, and there's more warmth to be experienced here than in either of its coastal neighbours.

Of the myriad ethnic groups who people Ghana, the Akan – including the Fante and Asante (also spelled Ashanti) – predominate. The Asante occupy the central forest, and in pre-colonial days their empire stretched much further west and east, into the regions of present-day

Mean temperatures and rainfall

	Jan	Feb	Mar	Apr	May	Jun	Jul	Aug	Sep	Oct	Nov	Dec
Accra												
max °C	31	31	31	31	31	29	27	27	27	29	31	31
min °C	23	24	24	24	23	23	23	22	23	23	24	24
rainfall mm	15	33	56	81	142	178	46	15	36	64	36	23
Tamale												
max °C	36	37	37	36	33	31	29	29	30	32	34	35
min °C	21	23	24	24	24	22	22	22	22	22	22	20
rainfall mm	3	3	53	69	104	142	135	196	226	99	10	5

Côte d'Ivoire and Togo. Education, now going back five generations or more, has had a major impact, and you'll notice the inventiveness with language straight away – especially in the slogans emblazoned on shared minibus-taxis – and signs of a budding digital economy.

You're bound to pass through the capital, Accra. After decades of neglect, it once again looks the part, with decent roads and thriving businesses. The rest of the country has so much to offer that you'll perhaps want to spend only a few days here before getting out along the coast or into the interior (unless you're into the music, and your visit coincides with some weekend live shows), but you'll find Accra friendly and manageable enough while you're here.

The second city, Kumasi, in the centre of the country, has a strong sense of Asante identity. The district to the south is the heart of Ghana's goldfields, and around them the rolling green landscapes of farms and cocoa plantations give way to sizeable districts of dense rainforest with giant hardwoods and palms vying for space.

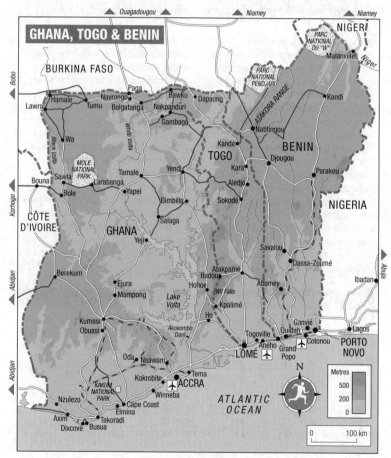

The north, with its arid landscapes and More-speaking people, has more in common with Burkina Faso, but has a pleasant climate, the major attraction of Mole National Park and a fascinating ethnic history.

In the eastern Volta region, between Lake Volta and the Togolese border, the hills of the Akwapim range create verdant green valleys and gentle peaks. And then there's Lake Volta, the vast artificial lake that was flooded into the wooded savanna in 1966, to supply the Akosombo dam with a source of hydro-electricity. The lake has totally changed the anatomy of the country – not to mention the lives of the thousands of rural dwellers its waters displaced.

Main attractions

● **Cape Coast Castle** Started by Swedish traders in 1653, and later adapted by the British for use as a slaving base, this UNESCO World Heritage Site is one of the most moving vestiges of the slave trade in West Africa. For more than 200 years, anything from 2000 to 10,000 slaves were shipped across the Atlantic from this and other castles on the Gold Coast. The castle has been sensitively restored (the dungeons and Door of No Return are particularly evocative) and houses informative displays on the slave trade.

● **Mole National Park** The best safari opportunity in the country, and indeed across several countries, as it's relatively easy to get to, and you can do so by public transport, right to the lodge in the park. It's a great spot to relax and unwind, spotting elephants from the poolside, or go out actively looking for wildlife every day at dawn and late afternoon. Guided walking safaris and rides on bicycles informally rented from the rangers are good alternatives to driving around.

● **Old Accra** If you don't go beyond Accra's central business district, you won't get under the skin of what was, just a few generations ago, a fishing village of the Ga people. You can take a walking tour of Old Accra, the atmospheric warren of sandy lanes and tin-roofed houses ruled by King Tackie Tawiah III, the paramount chief of the Ga people.

● **Beach lodges around Busua** The best-known of Ghana's coastal resorts is a wonderful place to chill, with a great beach and good restaurants. If it's too crowded (as can be the case at weekends in the high season), check out *Hideout Lodge*, tucked into the shore at Butre, 3km east of Busua, or the delightful *Green Turtle* at Akwidaa, 10km further east. Alternatively, go west from Busua, past Cape Three Points to the magical *Lou Moon* at Axim, towards the border of Côte d'Ivoire, where the beaches face the setting sun.

● **Fante tribal culture** Wherever you go on the coast, you'll see the Fante tribe's weird and often beautifully executed *posuban* – richly symbolic roadside shrines of pastel-coloured cement, incorporating religious and cultural figures from wild animals to statues of biblical characters – built by local Asafo companies. The Asafo were the traditional military units of the Fante, but with the onset of colonialism were reinvented as competitive social and welfare clubs. Each town has at least two clubs, and some have as many as twenty or more. Each company also has its own brilliantly coloured appliqué-work flag, of which you can sometimes buy small copies.

● **Kumasi** The sprawling, hectic, Asante capital has a powerful cultural and historical identity. In the nineteenth century, Asante was one of the most powerful African nations and it's still at the heart of everything that matters in Ghana. Take a morning or afternoon to roam through Kejetia market (the largest in West Africa), bargaining for dazzling *kente* cloth (the distinctive Asante fabric) and using your diplomatic and negotiating skills to take photos of the market mamas.

● **Coffins** The tendency of the Ga to send their deceased relatives to the afterlife in flamboyantly appropriate coffins (a huge fish for a fishing captain, a plane for a pilot) has spawned a unique cottage industry in Accra, and a flourishing trade in replica souvenirs for tourists. The mobile phone is a particularly popular model. The main coffin-makers' workshops are along the coast road east of the city centre.

● **Kakum National Park** Just a short journey inland from Cape Coast, this 600-square-kilometre rainforest sanctuary shelters a diverse fauna and flora, including antelopes, leopards and even forest elephants. But you're most likely to see birds and monkeys from the famous 300m canopy walk, an aerial walkway through the rainforest canopy. Giant, buttress-rooted trees tower all around, survivors of a century of logging that is finally slowing down.

Also recommended

● **The Oguaa Fetu harvest festival** One of Ghana's biggest festivals takes place on the first Saturday in September, when district chiefs, bedecked with gold crowns and medallions, parade in sumptuous *kente*-cloth togas or are carried in canoe-like stretchers balanced on the heads of servants. They're accompanied by the queen mothers, wearing even more jewellery, including gold ornaments in their beehive coiffures. Fetish priests dance through the procession and the palm wine flows freely. The party continues through the night with brass bands, music and dancing. Book a hotel in advance – most are crammed solid.

● **Adae festival, Kumasi** If you're lucky, your visit to Kumasi may coincide with an Adae festival (held roughly once every six weeks on a Sunday: you can check with the tourist office in Kumasi's National Cultural Centre), when the Asantehene, or King of Asante, receives the public. You can join in with the crowds, in their best *kente* cloth, the chiefs shaded by umbrella-toting retainers.

● **Pleasure cruises on Lake Volta** For a enjoyable take on Lake Volta, take the noisy weekend pleasure cruise on the Dodi Princess out to the lake's Dodi Island. On-board entertainments include a plunge pool for children and occasional live music – it can sometimes be a bit of a non-stop party, depending on the other passengers.

● **Wli Falls** A high waterfall in the hilly Volta Region, reached by an hour-long path traced through the jungle over eleven log bridges. The cascade itself, set in a cool and sheltered combe where thousands of bats nest, plunges 30m into a pool just deep enough for swimming. With your own gear you can camp by the falls, where the tranquility is disturbed only by kids shooting the bats with home-made flintlocks (they'll happily sell and cook you a sample).

● **Bolgatanga** An important crossroads town in northern Ghana, Bolga's pride is the modern central market, where all manner of traditional crafts are sold, including leather items, superb basketwork and clothes, all still made by hand. Look out for the beautiful examples of handmade fugu tunics (like a huge T-shirt), sewn from locally woven material and worn by men throughout the region.

● **Nzulezo** A glorious canoe trip, nosing through lush creek jungle, takes you to this community of stilt-house-dwellers on the Amansuri lagoon, close to the border with Côte d'Ivoire. The Ghana Wildlife Society visitor centre in the nearby village of Beyin can arrange your visit, and the chance to stay overnight.

Routes in and out

All international flights arrive into Accra and there are good links with cities across Africa, as well as Europe. From Burkina Faso, you can either take a bush taxi or bus to the border at Paga, or get transport through to Navrongo, Bolgatanga or Accra. Other crossings include Léo–Tumu and a crossing at Hamale. The fast route to Accra goes via Tamale, Kintampo and Kumasi; the more easterly route, involving a Lake Volta ferry or canoe crossing between Makongo and Yeji, is rougher and slower. Between Ghana and Togo, the border at Aflao–Lomé is open.

The various other possible Togo–Ghana crossing points involve rough travel and delays due to a lack of transport, which is much easier to find on relevant market days. Overland from Côte d'Ivoire, the stretch of coastal road between Abidjan and Accra is in good condition, and inter-city buses and bush taxis connect the two capitals in around fourteen hours. There's also a fast route linking Abidjan with Kumasi via Abengourou.

Red tape

Visas Required by UK, Ire, US, Can Aus, NZ and SA nationals. Should be obtained in advance but can sometimes, by prior arrangement, be collected on arrival at Kotaka airport, Accra.

Nearest consulates Abidjan; Bamako; Cotonou; Lagos; Lomé; Ouagadougou.

Other consulates Canberra (Ⓦghanahighcom.org.au); London (Ⓦghanahighcommissionuk.com); Ottawa (Ⓦghc-ca.com); Pretoria (Ⓣ+27 12 342 5847; Ⓔghcom27@icon.co.za); Sydney (wghanacg.com.au); Washington, DC (Ⓦghanaembassy.org).

Guinea

Area 246,000 square kilometres	democratic transition
Capital Conakry	**Independence** Oct 2, 1958
Population 10 million	(from France)
Language French (official); Fula (Peulh), Malinké, Susu, more than thirty others	**Best time to go** Nov–March (dry season)
	Country code +224
Religion Islam; small Christian and traditional minorities	**Currency** Guinean Franc (GNF); US$1: GNF5030
Government Military junta, in	**Minimum daily budget** US$25

Guinea has enormous appeal as a place to travel, sprawling in a great arc of mountains and plains from the creeks, mud banks and mangroves of the coast to the hilly forests on the border with Côte d'Ivoire. The great rivers of West Africa – the Gambia, Senegal and Niger – all rise in Guinea, and the country is full of scenic routes. On the plains of Haute Guinée, towards the Malian border, you feel the cultural echoes of the Niger valley's old kingdoms – this was the heartland of the Mali Empire – and the Niger and its tributaries the Tinkisso and the Milo meander across rolling savannas traditionally rich in big game. Although much of the wildlife has disappeared, the region's mango-shaded old towns – Dinguiraye, Kankan,

Kouroussa and Siguiri – still hold plenty of allure and the cultural heritage is strong.

In central Guinea lie the Fouta Djalon highlands, a plateau dramatically cut into countless hills, valleys and waterfalls like a rock garden. The Fula inhabitants of the eighteenth and nineteenth centuries lived under a local Muslim theocracy, whose influence spread far and wide in West Africa – a history that makes the region very distinctive to this day.

But despite these natural and cultural riches Guinea is one of Africa's poorest countries. Although it holds the world's third-largest reserves of bauxite (aluminium ore) and is potentially rich in agriculture and fisheries, its lack of infrastructure and ever-present corruption

Mean temperatures and rainfall

	Jan	Feb	Mar	Apr	May	Jun	Jul	Aug	Sep	Oct	Nov	Dec
Conakry												
max °C	31	31	32	32	32	30	28	28	29	31	31	31
min °C	22	23	23	23	24	23	22	22	23	23	24	23
rainfall mm	3	3	10	23	158	559	1298	1054	683	371	122	1
Labé												
max °C	32	33	34	34	34	31	28	28	28	29	31	31
min °C	6	5	5	12	15	15	15	16	15	13	8	6
rainfall mm	2	4	9	35	140	235	315	342	288	140	35	2

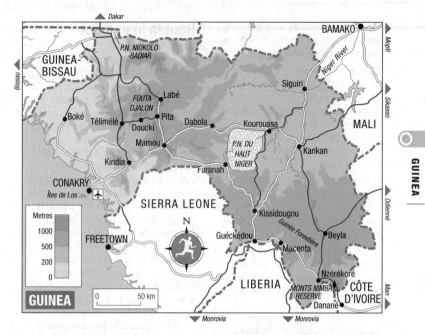

mean the wealth doesn't trickle down very far. For visitors, there is no semblance of a functioning tourist industry, and travel around the country is as rough as it is exciting. At least it is currently also very cheap, partly because the Guinean Franc is steadily losing value, and partly because there is nothing much to spend your money on – certainly no organized safaris or expensive activities.

Between 1958, when it reclaimed its independence and effectively cut itself off from France, and the death of the first dictator, Sekou Touré, in 1984, Guinea (sometimes known as Guinea-Conakry to distinguish it from the world's three other Guineas) was an isolated and secretive country. In the 1980s it finally began to open its borders to visitors. At the time of writing, however, the country is in a state of suspense. Although the conflicts in its neighbours have abated, Guinea's political climate is far from

sunny and there are still fears that it will plunge into turmoil. You should check the security situation as carefully as you can before visiting.

Main attractions

● **Conakry nightlife** With its predatory cops and tense atmosphere, Conakry is not the easiest city to like. The city's nightlife is its saving grace: the astonishingly good club scene is dominated by hip-hop and Euro-pop, but there's also a handful of live music spots where you can see some of Guinea's best musicians and commune with the wellsprings of one of Africa's most influential musical cultures.

● **The Îles de Los** A short boat ride off the coast from Conakry, this attractive cluster of erstwhile pirate/treasure islands offers some of Guinea's best and most accessible beach destinations.

The secluded beaches along the west shore of Kassa are the nicest. There are various hotels and restaurants, too.

● **Tracking chimps at Monts Nimba Reserve** Rising from the lush forests of the south, Guinea's tallest peak offers opportunities to track wild chimpanzees. Unusually, they're tool-users; they've been studied by a team of Guinean and Japanese primatologists for more than three decades.

● **Doucki** A tiny village perched on the edge of one of the Fouta Djalon's most spectacular drop-offs, Doucki offers views and hiking to rival anything else west of Cameroon.

● **Kankan Market** The vast *marché central* in this historic Haute Guinée university town is one of the country's best. One area specializes in old bits of carving, gris-gris and amulets. If you're interested in receiving some supernatural assistance, then Kankan is the place to ask: marabouts here are considered some of the most powerful in Africa and potions can be obtained easily.

● **La Voile de la Mariée** Named for their resemblance to a bridal veil, these spectacular waterfalls drop for 60m over a cliff amidst a pretty green landscape near Kindia, on the western fringes of the Fouta Djalon highlands.

● **Parc National Niokolo-Badiar** An exciting new park on the Senegalese border, and home to a wide variety of mammals, including antelopes, monkeys and, it's claimed, lions.

● **Pita to Télimélé** One of the finest 4WD, trail bike, mountain bike and hiking trails in the country, this route offers a great range of magnificent scenery and warm encounters with local people.

Routes in and out

Guinea's only international airport is Conakry, which has a few flights to Europe and reasonable West African connections. That's just as well, because the only straightforward overland route is the good paved road from Bamako in Mali to Kankan. Overland from Guinea-Bissau, the usual route is inland via Gabú, Pitche, Buruntuma/Kandika, Koundara and eventually back onto a paved road at Labé. From The Gambia and Senegal the easiest route goes from Basse in The Gambia or Diaobé in Senegal via the border posts at Dialadiang (Senegal) and Missira (Guinea). If you're coming from Sierra Leone, there's a paved main route from Freetown via Kambia and Pamelap to Conakry, though once again not much public transport on it. As for Liberia, there's a range of border crossings along the watershed frontier, but these borders can be troublesome to negotiate. Finally, travelling overland from Côte d'Ivoire involves transiting through "rebel" (Forces Nouvelle) territory in Côte d'Ivoire. You're probably better off flying.

Entry requirements

Visas Required by UK, Ire, US, Can, Aus, NZ and SA nationals. Must be obtained in advance.

Nearest consulates Abidjan; Bamako; Banjul; Bissau; Dakar; Freetown; Monrovia.

Other consulates London (☎020 7316 1861, ✉ambaguineeuk@yahoo.co.uk); Ottawa (☎+1 613 789 8444); Pretoria (☎+27 12 342 7348, ✉mbaguinea@l .africa.com); Tokyo (☎+81 3 3770 4640); Washington, DC (☎+1 202 986 4300).

Guinea-Bissau

Area 36,000 square kilometres	**Independence** Sept 24, 1973
Capital Bissau	(from Portugal)
Population 1.6 million	**Best time to go** Dec–Feb
Language Portuguese (official);	(dry season)
Kriolu, Fula, Bijagó, eighteen others	**Country code** +245
Religion Traditional, Muslim, Christian	**Currency** CFA Franc (XOF)
Government Presidential	US$1: CFA506
democracy, run by the military	**Minimum daily budget** US$40

Although it's well off the tourist trail, and little-known even among its neighbours – let alone beyond Africa – pint-sized Guinea-Bissau offers real opportunities for adventure and discovery. The Bijagós islands, which scatter into the Atlantic off the compact mainland, have preserved a unique culture, and have escaped most of the unrest that has troubled the country in recent years. Before visiting, however, check the latest news and visit the travel advisory sites, as this is one of Africa's least stable nations. And in practical terms, ensure the public ferries you travel in are seaworthy.

The country covers an area barely half the size of Scotland or Maine and is ruled by a fragile, nominally democratic government. But the army pulls the strings here, and is also involved in the country's sinister new status as a narco-state: Guinea-Bissau's myriad creeks and islands are used for the transhipment of cocaine from Latin America.

The rest of the country's economy, largely dependent on cashew nuts, is struggling, and after a civil war in the late 1990s, followed by fragile peace and inertia, the infrastructure is in tatters. Mains electricity is rare, which means most hotels, restaurants, ministries and embassies use their own generators. However, generators get rarer and nights darker the further you venture from the capital.

A significant and influential proportion of Guinea-Bissauans are mixed-race Kriolu-speakers, the majority of whom are Cape Verdean by descent. Despite their circumstances, the Guinea-Bissauans are renowned for being very laidback company, and the country is refreshingly free of hassle – though it's important to be aware of how unpredictable it has become.

Mean temperatures and rainfall

Bissau	Jan	Feb	Mar	Apr	May	Jun	Jul	Aug	Sep	Oct	Nov	Dec
max °C	32	33	34	34	33	31	30	29	30	31	32	30
min °C	18	19	20	21	22	23	23	23	23	23	22	19
rainfall mm	2	2	8	1	45	202	851	906	389	180	39	5

Main attractions

● **Carnival in Bissau** Most visitors merely pass through Bissau on the way to the islands, though it's a good place to be during *carnaval* – February or March – when, on Shrove Tuesday (Mardi Gras), an endless stream of floats and elaborate papier-mâché masks is paraded through the streets.

● **Bolama town** Decaying colonial buildings, crumbling monuments and leafy scenery all make this a fascinating offshore destination.

● **Orango** This island not only features pristine tropical beaches but is home to unusual wildlife too – a population of saltwater-dwelling hippos.

● **Praia da Bruce** On the island of Bubaque, this is a postcard-pretty beach with hardly a soul in sight. Rent a bike in Bubaque town and cycle on the empty road through the jungle to get there.

● **Varela** A beach to rival Senegal's Cap Skiring coast just across the border – superb swimming, pine trees and low cliffs.

● **Bafatá** Nestling in the forests of the interior, a small, pretty town with a languid river and a complement of red-roofed, Portuguese-style houses.

Routes in and out

The only international airport is Bissau, which has few flights to neighbouring capitals, and even fewer to Europe. Overland, the route from Dakar is reasonably straightforward, though you will have to change vehicles and spend the night in Ziguinchor or Kolda en route. Driving from Guinea, you have a choice between two main routes, both with patchy public transport: the tarmac road to Labé, then north to Koundara crossing the border at Kandika, and following the difficult bush track to Gabú, followed by tarmac all the way to Bissau; or from Conakry north to Boké, through Koumbia and Foula-Mori, rejoining the main road to Bissau at Pitche. The third route, via Boké and Buba, is an arduous trek on rough tracks.

Red tape

Visas Required by UK, Ire, US, Can, Aus, NZ and SA nationals. Available on arrival at Bissau airport. If arriving by land, visas must be obtained in advance.

Nearest consulates Banjul; Conakry; Dakar; Ziguinchor.

Other consulates Lisbon (☎+21 303 0440); Johannesburg (☎+27 11 622 3688); Rockville, Maryland (☎+1 301 947 3958); Tunbridge Wells, UK (☎01892 530478). Aus/NZ nationals should apply for visas via the consulate in Lisbon.

Kenya

Area 580,400 square kilometres **Capital** Nairobi **Population** 32 million **Language** English and Swahili (official); more than 40 tribal languages **Government** Presidential democracy **Independence** Dec 12, 1963 (from UK)	**Religion** Majority Christian; also Muslim, traditional **Best time to go** Dec–Feb (dry season); July–Aug for the wildebeest migration **Country code** +254 **Currency** Kenya shilling (KES); US$1: Ksh78 **Minimum daily budget** US$50

With the Indian Ocean lapping its coral-fringed coast and Mount Kenya rising from the middle of its extraordinarily beautiful natural environment, Kenya is one of Africa's most rewarding countries to explore. Its diverse scenery, rich variety of wildlife and stimulating social tapestry – from traditionally dressed Maasai herders to sarong-wrapped Swahili fishermen – can keep travellers enthralled for months. The safari was invented here, and the infrastructure makes travel much easier than in most parts of the continent. Kenya is not all postcard-perfect – get into conversation and you'll soon get a handle on its deep economic and social tensions, as exemplified by the violent ethnic clashes after the 2007 elections – but it takes some beating as a country to thrill and impress a first-time visitor to Africa.

Kenya's much-vaunted game parks and Indian Ocean beaches and coral reefs are the most popular areas to visit. The wildlife spectacle remains a compelling experience despite the impact of human population pressures – both from locals grazing their livestock and from the tourists in their minibuses and Land

Mean temperatures and rainfall

	Jan	Feb	Mar	Apr	May	Jun	Jul	Aug	Sep	Oct	Nov	Dec
Nairobi												
max °C	25	26	25	24	22	21	21	21	24	24	23	23
min °C	2	13	14	14	13	12	11	11	11	13	13	13
rainfall mm	38	64	125	211	158	46	15	23	31	53	109	86
Mombasa												
max °C	31	31	31	30	28	28	27	27	28	29	29	30
min °C	24	24	25	24	24	23	22	22	22	23	24	24
rainfall mm	25	18	64	196	320	119	89	66	63	86	97	61
Kisumu												
max °C	29	29	28	28	27	27	27	27	28	29	29	29
min °C	18	19	19	18	18	17	17	17	17	18	18	18
rainfall mm	48	81	140	191	155	84	58	76	64	56	86	102

Rovers hoping to see "unspoiled Africa". Huge herds of elephants, lions lazing around a kill and the natural phenomenon of the Mara River's mass wildebeest crossings are sights that any visitor can witness. And it's not difficult to avoid being part of the tourist crowd – either by deliberately going off the beaten track in your self-drive car or by public transport, or just by asking your safari driver not to follow the other vehicles. On the coast

you can either opt for all-inclusive resort comforts or something less packagey – self-catering for example, or staying in budget guesthouses.

Most of Kenya's popular wildlife parks are located in the savanna districts that fringe the hillier areas where the majority of the population live as subsistence farmers. The great rent of the Rift Valley runs through the heart of these highlands, bisecting the country from north to south,

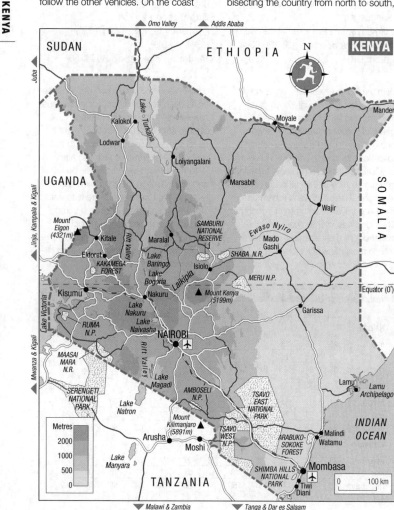

splashed by lakes – including the famous flamingo home of Lake Nakuru – and studded by volcanoes. At the highlands' southern edge stands the booming sprawl of Nairobi, a city you're likely to pass through more than once. It has its fair share of hustle and threat, but most people enjoy it for its full-on range of diversions – including excellent restaurants and nightlife and some worthwhile museums and wildlife activities.

Northeast Kenya, towards the Somalian border, is unsafe for travel, but the routes to wild and remote Lake Turkana in the northwest are open and offer access to one of the most spectacular and memorable of all African regions, where the giant lake shimmers almost unnaturally blue in the arid wilderness, sheltering thousands of crocodiles and providing fishing for traditional Turkana communities around the shore.

On the coast you could be in a different country – with mosques and coconut palms the standout features, and jungle-shrouded ruins marking the region's ancient and still-living Swahili civilization. The beaches – palm-shaded white sand dipping into clear, warm lagoons – are the stuff of tropical paradise fantasy. If they're occasionally marred by over-attentive hawkers and beach boys, you only have to strike out a little further to find your seaside idyll.

Main attractions

● **Maasai Mara** World-famous for its annual wildebeest migration, and home of the BBC's long-running *Big Cat Diary*, the Mara is the quintessential East African safari destination, where a glance across the savanna from your vehicle can reveal a scene like a children's animal wall frieze, as a dozen or more species of big game amble about on the short grass plains. If you visit between July and October, you may be lucky enough to see the wildebeest herds surging over the flood-swollen Mara River at one of the crocodile-infested crossing points. There are few places on earth where nature is quite so dramatic – it's like being in the New York of the natural world – but choose your safari operator and camp carefully to avoid a processed experience.

● **Mount Kenya** Africa's second highest peak, glacier-topped Mount Kenya is an extinct volcano straddling the equator. You can hike the lower slopes at will, but if you attempt the 5199m summit you need to go slowly enough to acclimatize to the altitude. Allow at least five days, with four of them to get to Point Lenana at dawn (at 4985m the highest summit attainable by casual hikers) and one to get down again. You can buy or rent clothes and camping equipment locally and it's best to take on a guide-porter to accompany you.

● **Laikipia** This rolling, 8000-square-kilometre plateau of valleys and crags between the foothills of Mount Kenya and the arid deserts of the north is a district of ranch lands, cut through by the Ewaso Nyiro River and its tributaries. Most of the region has been converted to wildlife conservancies run by partnerships of private landowners and local communities. Some of the country's most innovative conservation projects are based here, along with most of the country's black rhinos and a slew of superb, boutique camps and lodges, several of them espousing eco-tourism principles – running on solar energy, delivering income directly into the hands of the local staff who run them and the local community who lease the land to them, and offering guided walks and rides as well as game drives.

● **Lamu** A compelling, history-soaked city-state and UNESCO World Heritage

Site, with no roads or vehicles, the island of Lamu also has one of Kenya's very best beaches, still blessedly devoid of any commercial exploitation. Lamu town itself is a warren of narrow lanes and high, whitewashed houses, among which you'll find 23 mosques and some of Kenya's best value backpacker lodgings and boutique hotels. Stay in town for cultural immersion and atmosphere, or fifteen minutes away by boat near the beach in the village of Shela, which is gradually succumbing to villa conversions and property development.

● **Tsavo West** One half of a mega-park the size of Wales, split by the Nairobi–Mombasa highway, Tsavo West National Park incorporates rolling vistas of hills and bush, stark, volcanic outpourings honeycombed with tunnels, the Tsavo river itself and the Eden-like pools of crystal-clear water overhung by palms and fig trees known as Mzima Springs. Here you can get out of your vehicle and follow a nature trail to an underwater viewing chamber at the end of a short pier, through the windows of which you will, with patience, get the sight of four metres of sinuous crocodile or a gracefully tiptoeing hippo.

● **Amboseli** With its emerald swamps and huge herds of elephants, Amboseli feels like an oasis in Kenya's dusty, southern savanna. Its great selling point is the vast backdrop of Mount Kilimanjaro, across the border in Tanzania. Kili's majestic sweep up through the clouds is memorable and with giraffe or elephant in the foreground it's hugely photogenic on a clear day, although perhaps fifty percent of the time it's just not visible. The wildlife concentrations make up for it, though choose where you stay carefully as some lodges and camps are poor value for money and out of the way.

● **Watamu** The stunning bays, islets and casuarina-shaded beaches of this small resort between Mombasa and Malindi are matched by glorious coral gardens and good diving opportunities. When you add the impressive, thirteenth-century ruins of Gedi and the natural attractions of Mida Creek and the Arabuko-Sokoke forest, it's surprising more people don't make a beeline for it.

Also recommended

● **Lake Turkana** Shimmering in the northern deserts lies Kenya's biggest lake, a briny sickle-shaped expanse containing Africa's largest population of Nile crocodiles. Tiny Central Island National Park, an extinct volcanic cone poking up in the middle, contains three miniature lakes which are a crocodile breeding ground. Visit in April or May when the rains break to see crocs hatching. Loiyangalani, on the eastern shore, is the main town, with basic places to stay and resident Turkana and El-Molo people who will readily host and entertain you.

● **Lake Victoria** Barack Obama's family background shone a spotlight on this part of western Kenya, but his father's resting place, the village of Kogelo, has not been transformed into a tourism magnet, and the region's real attractions remain the remote islands of Rusinga and Mfangano, with their hominid fossil finds and luxury fishing lodges, the pretty Ruma National Park with its Rothschild's giraffes and roan antelope, and the magnificent lakeshore scenery.

● **Kakamega Forest** An isolated patch of the equatorial forest that once girdled the breadth of Africa, Kakamega is a haven for hundreds of species of birds, reptiles and mammals that exist nowhere else in Kenya. There are no fancy lodges here – just a couple of basic little dorm-style places and a rather pukka converted tea-planter's residence – and no shortages of forest paths to explore. Elephants, buffalo and large predators are all absent, making it safe to camp and explore on foot or bicycle.

● **Lakes Baringo and Bogoria** The Great Rift Valley is dotted with jewel-like lakes. These two, just a thirty-minute drive apart, are two of the smallest and most distinctive. Baringo is a freshwater lake, with extraordinary birdlife and excellent accommodation, while Bogoria is a soda lake, fringed with bubbling geysers, where flocks of flamingo regularly settle. There are some lovely, wild campsites here.

● **Meru National Park** This spellbindingly beautiful grassland park on the well-watered east side of Mount Kenya is where George and Joy Adamson released the lioness Elsa. Recently the focus of a complete rehabilitation, it's now the Kenya Wildlife Service's model park, and has superb facilities for visitors on a budget as well as a unique and splendid safari lodge, *Elsa's Kopje*, complete with rock-hewn swimming pool and private terraces hidden among the rocks and trees.

● **Mombasa** Despite its infrastructure challenges, Kenya's second city, occupying an island of the same name, is a likeable town, with a historic atmosphere and a much less intimidating reputation than Nairobi. The much fought-over Fort Jesus (first built in the sixteenth century by the Portuguese and now a well-maintained museum overlooking the harbour) is a fine target for a city visit, and the old town, souvenir shops and good places to stop for a meal are all within easy walking distance.

● **Tiwi Beach** Diani Beach is the famous south coast resort area, and wonderful in many ways, but Tiwi, just to the north, is far less developed and equally beautiful. Places to stay here are much more low-key (there's only one international-style hotel) and several of them cater for backpackers and locals on modest budgets.

Routes in and out

The main airport for international connections is Jomo Kenyatta in Nairobi, with Moi International in Mombasa getting charter flights from Europe. There are direct buses between Nairobi and Kampala, Nairobi and Arusha and Mombasa and Dar es Salaam, and the border crossings are straightforward. Land connections with South Sudan and Ethiopia are more tenuous (allow plenty of time). International ferry routes on Kenya's portion of Lake Victoria are suspended, as are cross-border rail links. Note that there is no official border crossing between Kenya's Maasai Mara and Tanzania's Serengeti.

Red tape

Visas Required by UK, Ire, US, Can, Aus, NZ and SA nationals. Available on arrival at airports or at land borders with Uganda and Tanzania. Availability at the borders with Sudan and Ethiopia is not guaranteed.

Nearest consulates Addis Ababa; Dar es Salaam; Kampala; Khartoum; Kigali.

Other consulates Canberra (Ⓦkenya .asn.au); Dublin (Ⓦkenyaembassyireland .net); London (Ⓦkenyahighcommission .net); Ottawa (Ⓦkenyahighcommission .ca); Pretoria (Ⓦkenya.org.za); Washington, DC (Ⓦkenyaembassy.com).

Lesotho

Area 30,355 square kilometres
Capital Maseru
Population 2 million
Language English (official); Sotho
Religion Christian; traditional minority
Government Constitutional monarchy, governed by parliament
Independence Oct 4, 1966

(from UK)
Best time to go Aug–Oct & Feb–April (spring and autumn) for hiking
Country code +266
Currency Loti (LSL, plural maloti, equivalent to SA rand, which is also accepted); US$1: M7.7
Minimum daily budget US$40

Surrounded by a powerful neighbour which upstages it in almost every way, Lesotho (see map, p.366; pronounced "Leezutu") is overlooked by all too many visitors. Far poorer than South Africa, with HIV/AIDS at crisis levels and water its sole natural resource of commercial value, Lesotho nonetheless has much to inspire visitors, including lofty basalt mountains and an ancient and distinctive cultural heritage.

The Basotho are descended from a nineteenth-century community which survived the onslaughts of Shaka Zulu thanks to the leadership of their legendary ruler, King Moshoeshoe the Great, whose lineage continues today. Many are forced to migrate to South Africa in search of work; those that stay behind tend to live as farmers and herders in scattered villages of thatched rondavels. Much of the terrain is inaccessible by vehicle, so people rely on horseback as their prime means of transport. The entire country lies above 1000m in altitude, earning it the name Kingdom in the Sky; temperatures can plummet at any time of year and, during the bitterly cold winters, everyone wraps themselves in woollen blankets.

Lesotho's peaceful isolation makes it an intriguing place to explore, particularly for those who enjoy pony trekking, hiking and skiing far off the beaten track. Making your way across the rugged landscape, you're likely to discover rushing streams, waterfalls and countless examples of San rock art.

Main attractions

● **Malealea** At this appealing village you can saddle up a Basotho pony and head for the hills. A cross between European and Javanese stock, Basotho ponies are highly prized, tough-spirited beasts of burden, perfectly suited to

Mean temperatures and rainfall

	Jan	Feb	Mar	Apr	May	Jun	Jul	Aug	Sep	Oct	Nov	Dec
Maseru												
max °C	30	28	26	23	19	17	16	19	23	26	27	29
min °C	16	15	13	8	4	1	1	3	6	10	12	14
rainfall mm	91	79	76	56	25	8	10	20	20	51	66	61

stomping over steep and rugged terrain. Villagers can provide ponies and guides, and may introduce you to *sangomas* (traditional healers) or invite you to sample some millet home-brew.

● **Semonkong** This village is another good base from which to begin a pony-trekking trip. Nearby destinations include the Maletsunyane (or Semonkong) Falls, where water plummets over a sheer cliff face, and the smaller Ketane Falls in the beautiful, wild Thaba Putsoa mountains. You can ride from Semonkong to Malealea in around five days, bedding down in stone rondavels overnight.

● **Ts'ehlanyane National Park and Bokong Nature Reserve** Best visited with an experienced bush-hiking guide, these protected areas are home to Lesotho's only surviving patch of indigenous alpine forest, with stunning valley views, abundant birdlife and ancient rock art to admire.

● **Thabana-Ntlenyana** At 3482m, this is one of Africa's highest peaks. The ascent to the top is fairly straightforward as long as you have a local guide to show the way.

● **Sehlabathebe National Park** Protected since 1970, this is not a wildlife-watching destination, but it can be good for birding and also attracts hikers, horseback-trekkers and anglers. The terrain is superbly rugged, with splendid waterfalls and the remains of early settlements, including stone dwellings and petroglyphs.

Also recommended

● **Maseru** The capital, Lesotho's commercial and transport hub, is a modestly sized sprawl with a temperate climate. Apart from its Catholic cathedral, the city has few sights, but is good for places to eat and drink including several Asian restaurants and down-to-earth bars. While robbery can happen here, particularly after dark, the dangers are minimal compared to nearby Jo'burg. Popular out-of-town excursions include Teyateyaneng, where you can find out about village arts and crafts, and Thaba-Bosiu, King Moshoeshoe's original mountain stronghold.

● **Morija** This small southern town is home to a museum of Lesotho's history and culture, open daily, with examples of dinosaur fossils, San rock art, Boer War memorabilia and traditional Sotho artefacts such as pipes and quivers.

● **Skiing** In mid-winter (June–Aug), you can ski the (often very icy) 2km slope at Mahlesela Hill near Oxbow in the northwest. The lodge at Oxbow offers equipment hire.

Routes in and out

International flights land at Moshoeshoe Airport, 20km south of Maseru, which lies on the northwest border with South Africa. Most overland routes from South Africa are straightforward, though the dramatic Sani Pass requires 4WD.

Red tape

Visas Not required by UK, Ire, US, Can, Aus, NZ and SA nationals: a free fourteen-day entry stamp is issued on arrival, and can be extended on request.

Nearest consulates Johannesburg (☏ +27 11 339 3653); Pretoria (☏ +27 12 460 7642, ⊛ lesothoh@global.co.za).

Other consulates Dublin (ⓦ lesothoembassy.ie); Kuala Lumpur (☏ +60 3 4253 2162); London (ⓦ lesotholondon.org.uk); Ottawa (ⓦ lesothocanada.gov.ls); Washington, DC (ⓦ lesothoemb-usa.gov.ls).

Liberia

Area 111,000 square kilometres	**Independence** July 26, 1847
Capital Monrovia	(from the USA)
Population 4 million	**Best time to go** Dec–March (dry
Language English (official); Kpelle,	season); March–Oct (surfing)
Bassa, Kru, more than twenty others	**Dialling code** +231
Religion Christian, Muslim, traditional	**Currency** Liberian dollar (LRD)
Government Presidential	US$1: L$71
democracy	**Minimum daily budget** US$50

The first independent country in Africa was established as a freed slave colony in the 1820s and settled with former slaves. Modelling their country on a US state, with fifteen counties, the settlers established an economic, legal and social structure that separated ruling class "Americans" from inferior natives or "country people". It's surprising that it took more than 150 years for civil war to erupt, a brutal fourteen-year quagmire that was finally resolved in 2003. Since then, the country has begun, shakily, to reinvent itself, with UN troops providing security on the ground, electing Africa's first female head of state, Ellen Johnson-Sirleaf, in 2005. Even the US Peace Corps have returned. Timber, rubber and iron ore exports have resumed and Monrovia's markets and restaurants are thriving.

The capital, the former headquarters of American interests in Africa, still has something of the Burger-King-and-Coke culture you might anticipate, but it's chiefly remarkable for being the world's wettest capital city, deluged by a magnificent five metres of rain every year – between four and ten times as much as the average British or American city. The other coastal towns are gone-to-seed backwaters, sleepily reminiscent of their African-American roots. Perched on rocky promontories on a coast of creeks and mangroves, they're redeemed by some beautiful beaches and don't get as much rain as Monrovia.

Upcountry Liberia is very different. Beyond the maze of tidal creeks, the land rises into rolling, forested hills, peaking above 1000m. Nearly a fifth of the country has a dense covering of rainforest – the biggest tracts anywhere in West Africa – and the population density remains low.

Mean temperatures and rainfall

	Jan	Feb	Mar	Apr	May	Jun	Jul	Aug	Sep	Oct	Nov	Dec
Monrovia												
max °C	30	29	31	31	30	27	27	27	27	28	29	30
min °C	23	23	23	23	22	23	22	23	22	22	23	23
rainfall mm	31	56	97	216	516	973	996	373	744	772	236	130

Main attractions

● **Monrovia** You don't choose Monrovia for a vacation, but the capital is better than its reputation would suggest, with good international links, decent services and several dozen Asian and Middle Eastern restaurants alongside local "cook shops". The somewhat makeshift National Museum and the hulk of the Masonic Temple are the sightseeing standouts.

● **Surfing at Robertsport** Liberia's coolest location is this Monrovia weekend getaway and nascent surfing resort, a couple of hours' drive up the coast from Monrovia. There are one or two low-key places to stay, and good surf at Sembehun beach, where most keen surfers simply camp.

● **Sapo National Park** With its rainforest and rare species, Liberia's only park, in the remote southeast of the country inland from Greenville, used to be a major attraction for hardy travellers, with canoe trips organized on the Sinoe River every year. The park is still home to pygmy hippos and, possibly, forest elephants. The problem is getting here and the need to be fully self-sufficient.

● **Crafts markets** Monrovia's Waterside Market is the first place to head for crafts: look out for secret society masks, drums and other musical instruments and indigo-dyed fabric. If you can't find what you want, street vendors near the Mamba Point Hotel will get it for you – but be prepared to haggle like crazy.

Routes in and out

The only international airport is 60km from the centre of Monrovia. There

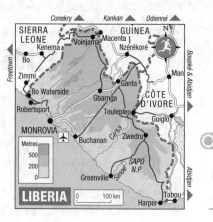

are limited connections with a number of African cities, notably Accra, and very limited links with Europe and the USA. Overland, there's regular public transport between Bo (Sierra Leone) and Monrovia, and more sporadic and hassle-strewn crossings between southeast Guinea and the highlands of northeast Liberia. The most straightforward crossing with Côte d'Ivoire is the Harper–Tabou border, near the coast.

Red tape

Visas Required by UK, Ire, US, Can, Aus, NZ and SA nationals. Must be obtained in advance.

Nearest consulates Abidjan; Conakry; Freetown.

Other consulates London (Ⓦembassyofliberia.org.uk); Montreal (☎+1 514 871 4741); Pretoria (☎+27 12 342 2734); libempta@pta.lia.net); Washington, DC (Ⓦliberianembassyus.org).

Libya

Area 1,775,500 square kilometres
Capital Tripoli
Population 6.4 million
Language Arabic (official); English, Italian (widely understood)
Religion Sunni Muslim
Government Authoritarian state
Independence Dec 24, 1951 (from UK & France; previously from Italy)
Best time to go Feb–April & Oct–Nov (the north); Nov–Feb (the south)
Country code +218
Currency Libyan dinar (LYD); US$1: LYD1.3
Minimum daily budget US$60

Ever since the mid-2000s, when Colonel Gaddafi's Libya took responsibility for the 1988 Pan Am plane bombing over Lockerbie, stepped out of the nuclear and chemical arms race and was dropped from the US government's list of states which sponsor terrorism, this desert nation has been tiptoeing its way back into the fold of tourist-friendly countries.

It has much to offer. Studded with enough heritage sites from Greek, Roman and Byzantine times to make it a thoroughly absorbing extension to a tour of historic Tunisia or Egypt, those with an interest in Saharan life and landscapes might consider it a worthwhile destination in its own right. Around ninety percent of Libya's landmass is desert, and south of the Mediterranean coastline a barren wasteland of scrub and dunes quickly encroaches. Amid the vast seas of sand, alluring oasis towns such as Ghadames and Ghat are surprisingly accessible.

It's likely to be some time before tourism in Libya becomes mainstream. For now, border crossings can be fraught and the process of obtaining a visa requires an unusual amount of hoop-jumping. Once you've made it into the country, you can only travel with an official tour guide. And while Libyans consider themselves cosmopolitan and worldly, you'll receive a much more relaxed reception if you're mindful of conservative Muslim sensibilities.

Main attractions

● **Tripoli** Like the other great North African Mediterranean cities, the Libyan capital is a layer-cake of history. Founded by the Phoenicians around 2500 years ago, it's now a bustling port where market stalls and flashy boutiques sit side by side and modern towers loom

Mean temperatures and rainfall

Tripoli	Jan	Feb	Mar	Apr	May	Jun	Jul	Aug	Sep	Oct	Nov	Dec
max °C	16	17	19	22	24	27	29	30	29	27	23	18
min °C	8	9	11	14	16	19	22	22	22	18	14	9
rainfall mm	81	46	28	10	5	3	0	0	10	41	66	94

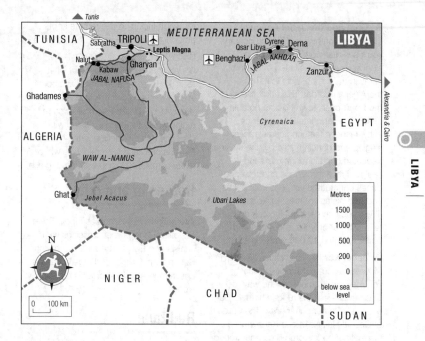

Alexandria & Cairo

over Ottoman mosques and Italian colonial buildings. In the whitewashed medina, tourists are a relative novelty; as a result, the souks, which are stuffed with chandeliers, period furniture, carpets and silver teapots, are more relaxed than in other North African countries. Within the medina is the Al-Saraya Al-Hamra (Red Castle), which houses the Jamahiriya Museum, a superb collection of archeological artefacts.

● **Leptis Magna** Immaculately preserved by the arid desert climate, Libya's coastal ruins are global treasures. The best archeological site is Leptis Magna which, like Tripoli, around 120km to the west, was founded by the Phoenicians. It was under the Romans that the settlement really shone: they made it their largest North African settlement after Carthage and Alexandria. At its peak, Leptis Magna channelled the sumptuous fruits of

a fertile colony – grain, fruit, olive oil and exotic animals for the Colosseum in Rome – across the Mediterranean. Visible highlights include the public baths, a magnificent arch dedicted to Septimus Severus.

● **Ghadames** The epitome of an ancient oasis town, the World-Heritage-listed Ghadames medina is a picturesque maze of ochre and whitewashed passageways and shady courtyards, edged with palm groves. The architecture may be sober on the outside, but the locals have a real eye for colour – traditional interiors are decorated in bright colours, and shoemakers and carpet weavers create dazzling designs. Your guide may arrange for you to visit a local family for buckwheat pancakes and a shared bowl of spicy sauce. In October, the whole town erupts with music and dancing during the annual Ghadames Festival.

● **Ghat and the Jebel Acacus**
Libya's far southwest is Tuareg country;
you'll see many desert nomads in
all-enveloping robes in the old camel-
caravan trading post of Ghat, on
the Algerian border. This attractive
mud-built oasis town hosts a notable
desert festival in late December or
early January, featuring camel races,
singing and dancing. Nearby, the striking
Acacus mountain range has sand-
sculpted rock formations and towering
dunes punctuated with oases of palms
and wild pistachio trees. Exploring by
4WD, you can seek out its rock art sites,
featuring petroglyphs of hunters and
buffalo painted 12,000 years ago.

● **Jebel Nafusa** The Nafusa (Western)
Mountains south of Tripoli – which
you may pass through on the way to
Ghadames – are the rugged homelands
of Libya's Berber community. The villages
of Qasr al-Haj, Nalut and Kabaw have
fascinating, honeycomb-like underground
houses and fortified mud-built granaries.

● **Sabratha** Another ancient
Phoenician settlement that was later
grabbed by other civilizations including
the Greeks and the Romans, Sabratha
is 80km west of Tripoli and easy to visit
on a day-trip. Among its golden stones
are slender columns, altars, beautiful
mosaics and a breathtaking Roman
theatre, the largest in Africa, with some
immaculately preserved carvings.

● **Cyrene** The graceful temple pillars of
the Ancient Greek city of Cyrene entrance
archeology enthusiasts and the setting,
separated from the Mediterranean by hills
carpeted with greenery and wild flowers
in spring, is lovely. There are more ruins,
mostly Byzantine, down on the coast at
Apollonia, Cyrene's port.

● **Ubari Lakes** For the uniquely
peaceful experience of swimming in
a Saharan salt lake surrounded by
golden dunes and fringed with palms,

it's worth including this remote spot,
around 450km due south of Tripoli, in an
overland itinerary.

● **Waw al-Namus** To find out what it
feels like to be far away from just about
everywhere, you can trek through the
desert by 4WD to this remote volcanic
region where the sand is dusted with
dark powdered lava. Beside the eroded
remains of a cone is a crater lake whose
water sometimes looks eerily red or green.

Routes in and out

International flights land at Tripoli. There
are official land border crossings with
Tunisia and Egypt. The areas bordering
Sudan, Chad, Niger and Algeria can be
unsafe; the Algerian border is completely
closed.

Red tape

Visas Required by UK, Ire, US, Can,
Aus, NZ and SA nationals. Acquiring a
visa must be done in advance through
a Libyan consulate or via a Libyan travel
agent. Regulations may change at short
notice. You'll need a letter of invitation,
proof that you have insurance and access
to at least US$1000 and an official,
stamped Arabic transcript of the ID page
of your passport. You may not enter if you
have an Israeli stamp in your passport;
if affected, get a replacement. Within a
week of your arrival, your passport must
be registered with the police.

Nearest consulates Neighbouring
consulates do not normally issue visas to
foreigners.

Consulates in Europe Canberra
(☎61 2 6290 7900); London (☎020
7589 6120); Ottawa (🌐libyanembassy
.ca); Pretoria (☎27 12 342 3902; libyasa
@telkomsa.net); Washington, DC
(🌐libyanbureaudc.org).

Madagascar

Area 587,040 square kilometres
Capital Antananarivo
Population 19.6 million
Languages French and English
(both official); Malagasy (national)
Religion Traditional, Christian;
Muslim minority
Government Federal presidential
republic

Independence June 26, 1960
(from France)
Best time to go April–Oct (dry
season); April–May & Sept–Oct for
highland trekking
Country code +261
Currency Ariary (MGA);
US$1: Ar2175
Minimum daily budget US$30

Those who head for Madagascar in search of the unusual and exotic are rarely disappointed. This giant, verdant laboratory of evolutionary theory has been separated from mainland Africa for long enough to have given rise to an astonishing array of endemic flora and fauna. Many of its native species are frankly bizarre, from immaculately camouflaged geckos to luridly coloured chameleons and frogs. Stars of this show, and the creatures that everyone wants to see, are the beady-eyed, cuddly-looking, acrobatic lemurs. Even the landscapes are somewhat weird – travel widely, and you'll marvel at Madagascar's strange, jagged pinnacles, lumpy hills and bulbous-trunked baobabs.

Malagasy culture is highly distinctive, too. Many of the linguistic and ritual customs of the first islanders, who were Malay-Polynesian, remain today. Visitors will often hear talk of *fady*, meaning

taboo – actions which should be avoided for fear of offending the ancestors and throwing the natural world out of balance. Pointing at sacred objects or bathing in certain rivers, for example, are *fady*. Being mindful of such conventions will earn you respect and is crucial if you're invited to a traditional ritual such as Famadihana, the Turning of the Bones. At these ceremonies, common between June and September, Central Highlanders venerate their dead relatives by exhuming them for a celebratory dance, fuelled by home-made rum. You may also witness a Hira Gasy, a competitive face-off between folkloric troupes.

For adventurous travellers with at least a smattering of French, Madagascar offers a realm of opportunities for hiking, diving, snorkelling and wildlife-watching, with plenty of perfect tropical beaches on which to recover. The violent unrest which hit the capital in 2009 and early

Mean temperatures and rainfall

Antananarivo	Jan	Feb	Mar	Apr	May	Jun	Jul	Aug	Sep	Oct	Nov	Dec
max °C	26	26	26	24	23	21	20	21	23	27	27	267
min °C	16	16	16	14	12	10	9	9	11	12	14	16
rainfall mm	300	279	178	53	18	8	8	10	18	61	135	287

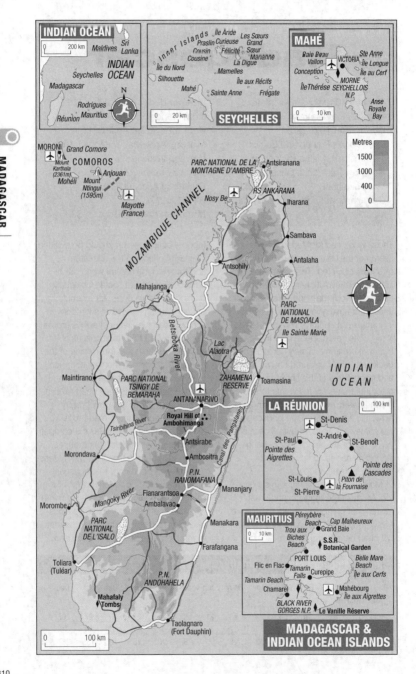

INDIAN OCEAN

0   200 km

Maldives   Sri Lanka

INDIAN OCEAN

Seychelles

Madagascar

Rodrigues

Réunion   Mauritius

N

SEYCHELLES

Inner Islands

Île Aride   Les Sœurs

Praslin   Curieuse   Grand Sœur

Cousin   Félicité   Marianne

Cousine   La Digue

Île du Nord   Mamelles

Silhouette   Île aux Récifs

Mahé   Sainte Anne   Frégate

0   20 km

MAHÉ

Baie Beau   Ste Anne

Vallon   VICTORIA   Île Longue

Conception   Île au Cerf

Île Thérése   MORNE SEYCHELLOIS N.P.

Anse Royale Bay

0   10 km

Metres
1500
1000
400
0

MORONI   Grand Comore

Mount Karthala (2361m)   COMOROS

Mohéli   Anjouan

Mount Ntingui (1595m)

Mayotte (France)

PARC NATIONAL DE LA MONTAGNE D'AMBRE   Antsiranana

RS ANKARANA

Nosy Be   Iharana

Sambava

Antalaha

Antsohily

Mahajanga

PARC NATIONAL DE MASOALA

Île Sainte Marie

Betsiboka River

Lac Alaotra

Maintirano

PARC NATIONAL TSINGY DE BEMARAHA

ZAHAMENA RESERVE   Toamasina

INDIAN OCEAN

ANTANANARIVO

Tsiribihina River

Royal Hill of Ambohimanga

Antsirabe

LA RÉUNION

0   100 km

St-Denis

St-Paul   St-André   St-Benoît

Pointe des Aigrettes

Pointe des Cascades

St-Louis   Piton de la Fournaise

St-Pierre

Morondava

Ambositra

P.N. RANOMAFANA

Mananjary

Mangoky River   Fianarantsoa

Ambalavao

Morombe

PARC NATIONAL DE L'ISALO

Manakara

Farafangana

MAURITIUS

0   10 km

Péreybère Beach   Cap Malheureux

Trou aux Biches Beach   Grand Baie

S.S.R Botanical Garden

PORT LOUIS

Belle Mare Beach

Flic en Flac   Tamarin Falls   Curepipe   Île aux Cerfs

Tamarin Beach

Chamarel

Mahébourg   Île aux Aigrettes

BLACK RIVER GORGES N.P.   Le Vanille Réserve

Toliara (Tuléar)

P.N. ANDOHAHELA

Mahafaly Tombs

Taolagnaro (Fort Dauphin)

0   100 km

N

MOZAMBIQUE CHANNEL

Canal des Pangalanes

MADAGASCAR & INDIAN OCEAN ISLANDS

2010 did not target tourists, and the island remains popular with French and Italian travellers. Flights may be pricey, distances long and roads bumpy, but independent travel by *taxi-brousse* is inexpensive and can be enormous fun.

Main attractions

● **Antananarivo** Known as Tana, the capital of this island nation is not a port but a city in the Hauts-Plateaux, or Central Highlands. First settled around 400 years ago, today most of its buildings are twentieth-century, in European style, scattered attractively over hilly terrain with winding streets and ancient stone steps. For many travellers, it's just a springboard, but its temperate climate, flowering trees and well-stocked patisseries have obvious appeal. Within easy reach are the serene Lac Itasy, the old royal capital of Ambohimanga and Parc National d'Andasibe-Mantadia (Périnet Reserve), home to one of Madagascar's signature species, the indri, a large, fuzzy, black and white lemur with a very loud call.

● **Nosy Be and Antsiranana** The most popular spots for sun-and-sand holiday-makers are in the northwest. Nosy Be (Big Island) offers romantic resorts on tropical beaches, the loveliest of which is at Andilana. Here, you can idle away the days by snorkelling in turquoise water or dining out on fresh fish. The main village has an eccentric name (Hell-Ville) and a laidback African vibe. For a true castaway experience, you can stay on Nosy Be's paradise-island neighbours, tiny Nosy Iranja and Nosy Komba. Back on the mainland, there are gorgeous beaches and relaxed lodges near the colourful town of Antsiranana (Diego Suarez) in the far north.

● **Ile Sainte Marie** This long, skinny island, a one-time pirates' lair northeast of Tana, is another target for beach-lovers.

Though poetically named the Vanilla Coast, this side of the island lies in the cyclone belt and so is not as developed as Nosy Be. Its low-key luxury hotels stand on gasp-inducingly white beaches lapped by gin-clear water, where you can snorkel, dive, watch humpback whales (June–Sept) or just chill out.

● **Parc National de Ranomafana** A key destination for hikers and lemur-watchers, around ten hours south of Tana by road, this is a beautiful park of rolling, rainforest-shrouded hills, dotted with orchids and tree-ferns. A small section is accessible to visitors; the rest is dedicated to the preservation of key species including the rare golden bamboo lemur and the cat-like fossa, immortalized as a baddie in the *Madagascar* films. The climate is fresh, cool and misty.

● **Parc National des Tsingy de Bemaraha** This World Heritage Site west of Tana features surreal-looking seas of *tsingy*, jagged limestone pinnacles, some of them connected by rope bridges. Madagascar's first inhabitants used the caves among the *tsingy* for burials and other sacred rituals. The park is large, with numerous lemur and bird species.

● **Parc National de l'Isalo** Beautiful for hiking, this southern park has wide, dry grasslands dominated by dramatic sandstone ridges and boulders dating back to the Jurassic era. Although popular with visitors, it is large enough to find solitude. You may also see brown, ring-tailed and sifaka lemurs here, particularly around the Canyon des Makis.

● **Avenue des Baobabs** Around 15km outside the town of Morondava on the west coast, this sandy road is guarded by thousand-year-old baobab trees: much photographed, they have unusually straight, lofty trunks and all the presence of elderly statesmen.

● **Southern beaches** The well-surfaced Route du Sud (RN7 highway), which leads southwest from Tana, meets the Indian Ocean at the busy little town of Toliara (also known by its French name Tuléar). From here, you can explore this beautiful coast, its white sands dotted with the brightly painted pirogues of traditional fishing communities. North of Toliara is Ifaty, with access to some memorable dive sites where you're likely to see sharks. To the south is a string of Vezo villages; at Anakao, you can head out across the perfect blue sea to explore the dive sites around the islet of Nosy Ve.

Also recommended

● **Antsirabe and Ambositra** Just down the RN7 from Tana is the genteel Central Highlands spa town of Antsirabe, its wide colonial streets buzzing with colourful *pousse-pousses* (rickshaws) but its thermal baths sadly neglected. This is a good place to ask about any upcoming Famadihana ceremonies, or to plan a trip to the Tsingy de Bemaraha or the Tsiribihina River. Ambositra, further south, is excellent for local crafts such as woodcarving, marquetry and raffia weaving.

● **Fianarantsoa, Manakara and Ambalavao** The large university town of Fianarantsoa, south of Tana, is set among vineyards and tea plantations; from here, you can take a train through lush scenery to the pretty seaside town of Manakara. South of Fianarantsoa is Ambalavao, a peaceful highland town with distinctive medieval-looking buildings.

● **Tsiribihina River** With several days to spare, you can take a leisurely pirogue trip along a remote, 150km stretch of this peaceful waterway, southwest of Tana, to camp in a region that's inaccessible by road. You'll have time to enjoy the sounds of the river, while lemurs stare from the trees.

● **Parc National d'Andohahela** Protecting a swathe of rainforest and

spiny forest in the far south, this park has minimal facilities but is excellent for birds and lemurs.

● **Parc National de Masaola** The large peninsula north of Ile Sainte Marie is a protected region of tropical forest, surrounded by white-sand beaches and coral reefs which are also protected. For the adventurous, this is a superb place to go sea kayaking, snorkelling and forest trekking.

● **Réserve Speciale de l'Ankàrana** Like the Parc National des Tsingy de Bemaraha, this is a place of geological wonders and ancient burial grounds, its limestone pinnacles rising around caves, crevices and canyons which harbour lemurs, bats and crocodiles.

Routes in and out

International flights land at Ivato Airport, 17km north of Antananarivo. The main direct routes are from Paris, Johannesburg, Nairobi and Mauritius. There are also holiday flights to Nosy Be and Ile Sainte Marie, and internal connections to the many airstrips dotted around the country. Cargo ships cross to and from South Africa, Mauritius, Mayotte, Comoros and Mombasa on an irregular basis.

Red tape

Visas Required by UK, Ire, US, Can, Aus, NZ and SA nationals. Available on arrival at Ivato airport, Antananarivo. Free for stays of thirty days or less.

Nearest consulates Nairobi.

Other consulates Cape Town and Pretoria (Ⓦmadagascarconsulate.org .za); London (Ⓦembassy-madagascar -uk.com); Ottawa (Ⓦmadagascar -embassy.ca); Sydney (☎+61 2 9299 2290); Washington, DC (Ⓦmadagascar -embassy.org).

Malawi

Area 118,480 square kilometres
Capital Lilongwe
Population 15.3 million
Language English (official);
Chichewa (national)
Religion Christian; Muslim and
traditional minorities
Government Presidential republic

Independence July 6, 1964
(from UK)
Best time to go May–Sept (dry
season) for beaches and hiking
Country code +265
Currency Malawian kwacha (MWK);
US$1: MK150
Minimum daily budget US$30

Malawi is strangely underrated as a travel destination, its image dominated by a single physical feature – Lake Malawi – only part of which lies within its borders. While the west side of this Rift Valley lake is Malawian, most of the long, crooked eastern shore belongs to Tanzania and Mozambique, both of which still call it Nyasa, thanks to David Livingstone, who mistakenly believed this to be its local name. In fact, *nyasa* is simply the Malawian Yao word for "large body of water" and Maravi, later adapted to Malawi, is its true name. It's the third largest lake in Africa after Victoria and Tanganyika, and it stands out like a gash on satellite images of the continent.

Supremely peaceful and serene, the lake has a soothing effect on the weariest of travellers, particularly at the beginning and end of the day when the horizon melts into the sky. For Malawians, it provides fish as well

as water for drinking, washing and irrigation; to visitors, it offers enticing sandy beaches, laidback lodges and unmissable opportunities for freshwater snorkelling, diving (best between Aug–Dec) and canoeing. Malaria and bilharzia (schistosomiasis) can both be caught here, but with careful precautions your visit should be trouble-free.

One reason for Malawi's low profile among travellers is that it's not highly rated as a wildlife-watching destination, but it does have several enjoyable parks and reserves encompassing mountains, wetlands and grasslands, with decent populations of elephants, hippos, antelopes and monkeys, plus a great many bird species. Wildlife-watching conditions are best in the late dry season (Sept–Nov). Most winningly of all, its colonial-style towns and rustic villages are home to some of the friendliest people in East and southern Africa.

Mean temperatures and rainfall

Lilongwe	Jan	Feb	Mar	Apr	May	Jun	Jul	Aug	Sep	Oct	Nov	Dec
max °C	27	27	27	27	25	23	23	25	27	30	29	28
min °C	17	17	16	14	11	8	7	8	12	15	17	18
rainfall mm	208	218	125	43	3	0	0	0	0	0	53	125

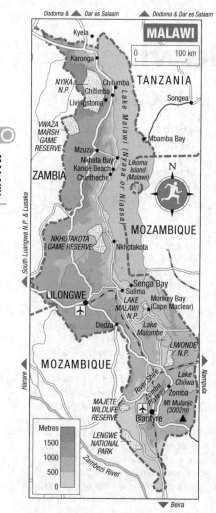

Map labels:
Dodoma & Dar es Salaam   Dodoma & Dar es Salaam
Kyela
MALAWI
0   100 km
Karonga
NYIKA N.P.
Chilumba
Chitimba
TANZANIA
Livingstonia
Songea
VWAZA MARSH GAME RESERVE
Lake Malawi (Nyasa or Niassa)
Mbamba Bay
Mzuzu
Nkhata Bay
Likoma Island (Malawi)
Kande Beach
Chintheche
N
ZAMBIA
South Luangwa N.P. & Lusaka
MOZAMBIQUE
NKHOTAKOTA GAME RESERVE
Nkhotakota
Senga Bay
Salima
LILONGWE
LAKE MALAWI N.P.
Monkey Bay (Cape Maclear)
Harare
Dedza
Lake Malombe
LIWONDE N.P.
Nampula
MOZAMBIQUE
River Shire
Zomba Plateau
Lake Chilwa
Zomba
MAJETE WILDLIFE RESERVE
Blantyre
Mt Mulanje (3002m)
Metres
1500
1000
500
0
LENGWE NATIONAL PARK
Zambezi River
Beira

Main attractions

● **Lake Malawi** Around 600km in length, Malawi's famous lake has plenty of places to stay along its shores, from backpacker hangouts to gorgeous colonial-style lodges, but overall it remains surprisingly wild and undeveloped. Most visitors head for one of its main resort areas: Senga Bay, close to Lilongwe;

Nkhata Bay and Chintheche further north, or Cape Maclear in the south, all of which have some great lodges, campsites and cheap scuba-diving centres. Lake Malawi National Park covers one small and highly scenic southern portion of the lake, including the Nankumba Peninsula and Mumbo Island: on Mumbo and the mainland, a couple of beautiful rustic-luxury camps nestle among the foliage.

● **Mount Mulanje** At 3002m, Malawi's highest peak is a substantial granite massif which towers over the low-lying tea estates and forests which surround it. Serious hikers can make the steep ascent to the large plateau near the summit in a day; here you can rest up at a mountain hut before attempting one or more of its numerous peaks. There are also enjoyable hiking trails along the lower slopes.

● **Liwonde National Park** Just south of the lake, this is Malawi's finest wildlife-watching area, with classic landscapes of river, woodland and scrub. Cruising along the Shire River by small boat, you'll see hippos bobbing around in the water and may have close-up views of crocodiles sunning themselves on the shore or elephants munching on the grassy banks. The focus of the park is Mvuu Lodge (Ⓦwww.mvuulodge.com), a tented camp in a great area for birdwatching.

● **Nyika National Park** Though not quite as rewarding as Liwonde for big game, Nyika is popular because it's so large, with spectacular scenery of rugged, grassy peaks and gorges where more than 200 orchid species bloom shyly in January and February. You can explore its mountainous terrain by 4WD, on foot or on horseback, looking out for Burchell's zebras, elephants and elands.

● **Likoma and Chizumulu islands** Though practically in Mozambique, these inhabited islands belong to Malawi. Grassy and peaceful, they're great places to chill out, with little to do beyond strolling or relaxing beside the turquoise water. You can get here by taking the venerable and comfortable, if mildly chaotic, Malawian lake steamer, *MV Ilala*, named after the palms which shade the shore. Every week, the ferry runs from Monkey Bay (near the southern end of the lake) to Chilumba (near the northern end) and back, via the islands and Nkhata Bay; taking at least two and a half days each way; if you're just going to the islands, you'll probably have one night on board.

● **Freshwater scuba-diving and snorkelling** To evolutionary biologists, Lake Malawi is fascinating, as it contains many hundreds of endemic fish species, including colourful cichlids, familiar to tropical aquarium keepers; take the plunge from Nkhata Bay or Mumbo Island and you can see them in close-up.

Also recommended

● **Lilongwe** The spacious capital has a market stuffed with colourful produce and an imaginative animal sanctuary, Lilongwe Wildlife Centre, which works closely with local communities through environmental and conservation education projects.

● **Lake of Stars Festival** Every October, one of several lakeside locations hosts this enjoyably relaxed Anglo-Malawian music festival (Ⓦlakeofstars .org), featuring DJs and bands from the UK, Malawi and elsewhere in Africa.

● **Vwaza Marsh Game Reserve** Close enough to Nyika to be worth a detour, this well-watered reserve is a great place to see elephants, buffalo and hippos; if you're lucky, you may also catch a glimpse of wild dogs.

● **Chongoni** Close to the pretty highland town of Dedza, this region includes a forest reserve and more than two hundred rock art sites.

● **Zomba Plateau** South of Liwonde and close to Zomba, the old colonial capital, this grassy plateau with patches of pine trees and indigenous forest is a cool, fresh place to go walking or birdwatching; plenty of monkeys can also be seen here.

● **Majete Wildlife Reserve** In recent years, this private reserve has been stocked with several species that Malawi had effectively lost, including black rhino and the rare Liechtenstein's hartebeest.

● **Livingstonia** This highland village, reached by a twisting road, has fine views down over the Rift Valley. Named after its Scottish Presbyterian mission, it still has a faintly Scottish atmosphere, with an imposing, redbrick church. Nearby is Manchewe Falls, an impressive waterfall with a 125m drop over a forested escarpment.

Routes in and out

International flights land at Kumuzu Airport, Lilongwe and Chileka Airport, Blantyre. The land border crossings with Tanzania, Zambia and Mozambique are straightforward, but the Mozambican roads immediately east of Malawi can be tough-going.

Red tape

Visas Not required by UK, Ire, US, Can, Aus, NZ and SA nationals for a stay of thirty days or less.

Nearest consulates Dar es Salaam; Harare; Lusaka; Maputo.

Other consulates Johannesburg (☎+27 11 339 1569); London (Ⓦmalawihighcommission.co.uk); Ottawa (☎+1 613 236 8931); Pretoria (☎+27 12 342 0146); Tokyo (Ⓦmalawiembassy.org); Washington, DC (☎+1 202 797 1007).

Mali

Area 1,240,000 square kilometres	**Government** Democracy
Capital Bamako	**Independence** Sept 22, 1960
Population 15 million	(from France)
Language French (official); Bamana, Fula, Tamashek (Tuareg), Songhai, Dogon, fifty others	**Best time to go** Oct–Feb (dry season), Aug–Dec (Niger navigable)
	Dialling code +223
Religion Muslim; Christian and traditional minorities	**Currency** CFA (XOF) US$1: CFA506
	Minimum daily budget US$40

Geographically and historically, Mali is West Africa's centrepiece: home of one of the continent's most venerable music traditions; site of some of its oldest indigenous states; location of the giant inland delta of the Niger; site of the dramatic Bandiagara escarpment; location of innumerable, adobe-style mosques; home of camel caravans and desert elephants. And those are just for starters: in short, from the traveller's point of view it's a showstopper, and there are more good reasons to visit it than any other country in West Africa. It makes a wonderful country to build a trip around, especially if you're interested in African culture.

Long a bridge between the north and the south – the Sahara and the forest

– the largely flat region outlined by the butterfly shape of the modern country formed the meat of three great empires, the oldest of which was ancient Ghana, which flourished as early as the third century AD. The region's location on the main caravan routes and the banks of the Niger later fuelled the rise of the powerful Mali and Songhai states, which lasted until the sixteenth-century invasion by Morocco. As well as resounding with historical reminders, Mali is home to the Dogon, the largely non-Islamic farmers whose villages cling to the vertiginous Bandiagara escarpment in the centre of the country.

The once-intimidating police state of the early decades of independence was dissolved in the 1990s, making Mali one

Mean temperatures and rainfall

	Jan	Feb	Mar	Apr	May	Jun	Jul	Aug	Sep	Oct	Nov	Dec
Bamako												
max °C	33	36	39	39	39	34	31	30	32	34	34	33
min °C	16	19	22	24	24	23	22	22	22	22	18	17
rainfall mm	0	0	3	15	74	137	279	348	206	43	15	0
Timbuktu												
max °C	31	34	38	42	43	43	39	36	39	40	37	42
min °C	13	14	19	22	26	27	25	24	24	23	18	13
rainfall mm	0	0	3	0	5	23	79	81	38	3	0	0

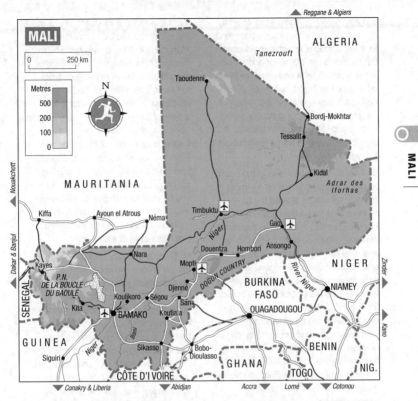

of West Africa's most relaxed countries, and its reputation and prospects for development have been boosted by the establishment of democracy and the hosting of the African Cup of Nations in 2002, which brought thousands of football fans to the country and saw roads and hotels upgraded.

Main attractions

● **Mysterious Timbuktu** The one place in Mali that needs no PR campaign can't live up to its myth-laden status. For centuries a byword for exotic isolation and hidden treasures, the sandy streets and mud-brick houses of today are more likely to remind you of Mali's poverty than of any proud history. Yet this UNESCO World Heritage Site does have libraries of old manuscripts, venerable mosques, plaque-designated explorer's houses and a decent museum, and it retains its allure. Unless you fly, it's very hard to get to, with no easy road access (when you arrive, there's an office where they'll bang that essential stamp into your passport) and if you weren't impressed by Timbuktu's isolation during your stay, you will be when you try to leave again.

● **Bamako's music scene** Mali's capital is one of Africa's best cities for music, and concentrates on its home-grown *jali* tradition (the *jalis* are the caste of musicians born to sing and play *kora* and *ngoni*, the local stringed instruments) and guitar bands. Stars like singer Salif Keita

317

and *kora* maestro Toumani Diabaté may not always feature themselves (they tend to move abroad after achieving success), but the city is still reliable for good sounds at weekends. The famous, original *Buffet de la Gare* has faded, but check out *Le Diplomate*, *Privilège* or *Bla Bla*, where you may see knockout guitarists, sweet singers and virtuoso instrumentalists that the rest of the world will be raving about in two years time.

● **Mopti** The biggest port in the country teems with vibrant commerce – most of the action focusing around the town's *raison d'être*, its harbour, built by the French a century ago. Large, traditional *pinasses*, kitted out with canvas awnings and colourful flags, tie up regularly to unload cargo and passengers, while smaller pirogues taxi people back and forth from different points on the islands that make up the town, and Moorish traders mill around their stacks of marble-like salt slabs, brought by camel caravan from the desert to Timbuktu and then transported by boat to Mopti. Sit in the pink, prominent *Bar Bozo*, above the riverside, and soak it all in.

● **Djenné's Grande Mosquée** Djenné's masterpiece Friday mosque, the biggest example of mud architecture in the world, can hold five thousand worshippers. It dominates the town for miles around and is itself dominated by its ostrich-egg-topped towers and characteristic protruding beams. Every year, the rains wash away the mosque's smooth outer layer and the townspeople climb up the beams to restore it. Try to visit Djenné on a Monday, when traders from across the delta make a commercial pilgrimage to the town. There are few markets anywhere in Africa as animated, colourful and rich – those colossal swaying earrings are solid gold.

● **The Niger** Stories about the Niger long fascinated Europeans, but it took them more than a thousand years and the exploits of the Scottish explorer Mungo Park, among many others, to discover its source and mouth. Today, more than 1000km of the river, from Koulikoro in the west to Gao in the northeast, is still navigable for a few weeks of the year after the rainy season. Take your place on a large *pinasse* trading boat or one of the passenger ferries in Ségou or Mopti and expect to spend up to a week drifting, punting, paddling (and occasionally pushing when you beach) downstream to Korioumé, the port for Timbuktu, passing remote riverbank villages and countless examples of mud architecture.

● **Dogon country** Hiking on the Bandiagara escarpment is an opportunity to see unique, vernacular architecture, witness traditional working culture, and meet the Dogon themselves – sharing their food, sleeping on their roofs and using the same bush pathways and tricky cliff-side alleys that they have navigated for centuries. You have to pay, of course (the costs are modest) but even if some routes are getting well-trodden by tourists, you can still get off the beaten track with patience and flexibility. The best time for actual walking (usually 5–10km between villages) is early morning, when the landscape is bathed in golden light and the sandstone cliffs echo with birdsong, the crowing of cockerels, and the long exchanges of locals greeting each other on the footpaths.

● **Hombori – Mali's Monument Valley** Between Dogon country and the Niger, Mali's highest district consists of sheer mesas and fairy-tale-like rock pinnacles looming up from the plain. Buses stop in the newer part of Hombori town, but Old Hombori is much more interesting: most of the houses here are built of rock, with narrow alleys burrowing between them. The peaks themselves, with the sheer faces rising anything up to 600m above the plain, form one of Africa's premier technical rock-climbing areas, but you'll need to bring your own gear as local kit isn't up to much.

● **Sikasso** Mali's southernmost town is an evergreen place, with a humid climate and flourishing agriculture. The market, impressive on any day of the week, is enormous on Sundays, and outstanding for fruit and vegetables. Within a short drive of Sikasso, there are waterfalls, a natural swimming pool and the ritual sacrifice site of the Grottes de Missirikoro, in a limestone outcrop jutting from the plain. Alongside colonies of bats and a few latter-day cave-dwellers, it's believed to be inhabited by guardian spirits and is still used as a place of worship and sacrificial offering by animists, Muslims and Christians alike. You can scramble up the outcrop for 360-degree views. Take kola nuts as a present for the inhabitants.

● **The train through the Manding Highlands** West of Bamako, the Manding Highlands provide a rare hilly spectacle as they rise to heights of 500–1000m above sea level. This beautiful landscape of dramatic rock formations is best enjoyed at dawn. Take the overnight sleeper from Bamako, which should get you into Kayes, Mali's westernmost town, the following afternoon. If you're stuck here for a few days, the fort in Médine, built by the French in 1855s and 12km southeast of Kayes on the Senegal River, is easily reached by pirogue and is a peaceful picnic and camping spot.

● **Sand, sand, sand – the Festival au Désert** The Sahara's biggest Tuareg music festival, the Festival in the Desert has taken place early each January since 2001. Originally at Essakane, a remote oasis northwest of Timbuktu, it moved to the outskirts of the town itself in 2010 for security reasons – the move also makes access simpler and allows the people of Timbuktu greater participation. This celebration of Tuareg and West African music regularly showcases bands such as Tinariwen and Tamikrest, musicians like Vieux Farka Touré from Mali and Tiken Jah Fakoly from Côte d'Ivoire and Western artists such as Robert Plant and Justin Adams.

Also recommended

● **Catholic Mass in Ségou** Attending the bilingual Bamana-French mass at Ségou's Église de Notre Dame de l'Immaculée Conception is highly recommended, regardless of your faith, or lack of: the combination of drumming and choir is unforgettable. Dress conservatively and be aware of the gender divide, with women and men sitting separately.

● **Le Festival sur le Niger** Ségou's Festival on the River takes place annually on the first weekend of February. While part of its purpose is to focus on environmental threats to the Niger, the festival has a lively programme of concerts by Mali's top musicians as well as films, theatre and dance performances. Check out those life-size crocodile puppets in the river for the marionette shows.

● **Bamako's National Museum** One of Africa's better museums, inspired by the Djenné's mud architecture, houses a well-displayed collection, including some masterpieces of African art and artistry. There's a particularly strong section devoted to cloth-weaving and dyeing and another area has religious objects from Mali's peoples, including antique Dogon sculptures and masks.

● **Kita** Roughly two-thirds of the way from Kayes to Bamako, Kita is one of the former capitals of Sundiata Keita's medieval Mali empire, and if you're into Malian music it's a good place to stop over a night or two, as many traditional *griots* or *jali* hail from around here. Mont Kita Kourou, with caves decorated with rock paintings, rises impressively to the west of the town.

● **Boucle du Baoulé National Park** The buckle-shaped course of the Baoulé River forms the northern border of this 3300-square-kilometre national park of wooded savanna and forest. There's not a great deal of wildlife, but the park is still worth visiting (assuming you have a 4WD vehicle) for the more than two hundred rock art sites, ancient tombs and burial grounds.

● **The elephants of Gourma** A herd of more than three hundred elephants migrates each year from northern Burkina through Mali's Réserve du Gourma, and can quite often be seen at waterholes north of the road between Hombori and Gossi, especially near the Mare de Gossi itself, a small lake. In February or March they begin to trek west through the Réserve de Douentza and then south again, usually crossing the road to the west of Hombori.

Routes in and out

Most flights to Mali use Bamako Airport, but there are also occasional charter flights from France to Mopti and Gao. The once relatively busy overland route from Algeria – the Tanezrouft – has been largely deserted because of insecurity (see p.227). The Gao route to Niger is also largely avoided at present, most people travelling via Burkina Faso (see p.240). Between Mali and Mauritania (see p.323), there is currently no safe direct route. If you have to drive your own vehicle, then doing so via the largely paved road from Dakar to Bamako is the safest option; sadly, the train service between the two cities (see p.358) was suspended indefinitely in 2010. Overland from Côte d'Ivoire, the main point of entry is along the road from Ferkessédougou to Sikasso, linked by daily buses. Overland from Guinea, there are direct bush taxi services between Bamako and Siguiri or Kankan (see p.294).

Red tape

Visas Required by UK, Ire, US, Can, Aus, NZ and SA nationals. Available on arrival.

Nearest consulates Abidjan; Algiers; Conakry; Dakar; Niamey; Nouakchott; Ouagadougou; Tamanrasset. The embassy in Banjul does not issue visas.

Other consulates Brussels (+☎32 2 345 7432); Melbourne (🌐mali.org .au); Paris (+☎33 1 48 07 85 85); Pretoria (☎+27 12 342 7464); Ottawa (🌐ambamalicanada.org); Washington, DC (🌐maliembassy.us).

Mauritania

Area 1,031,000 square kilometres
Capital Nouakchott
Population 3.3 million
Language Arabic (official); French,
Fula (Pulaar), Soninké, Wolof
Religion Muslim
Government Military-backed,
elected dictatorship

Independence Nov 28, 1960
(from France)
Best time to go Nov–March
(cooler season)
Dialling code +222
Currency Ouguiya (MRO)
US$1: Oug274
Minimum daily budget US$40

Mauritania, once well off the map for most travellers to Africa, and still rarely covered by the media, can come as a surprising discovery. The last decade has seen a steady expansion of tourism, encouraged by the country having the only useable trans-Saharan driving route, a physically comfortable, dry climate, the wide-open landscapes of the Sahara and the pleasantly laidback Mauritanians themselves. The majority of visitors who have taken time to get to know it so far have been French or Spanish; if you follow their example, you'll discover a country with dramatic scenery, especially the Adrar landscape of the northeast – *ergs* (dunes) and *regs* (rocky plains) – and a complex history and culture that takes in rock paintings,

medieval mosques, alluring ancient *caravanserai* oases and a deep-rooted class structure. The new Nouadhibou-Nouakchott highway has also made the migrant bird breeding sanctuary of the Banc d'Arguin National Park more accessible. Other attractions, such as Tichit and Oualata in the far south-east, are hard to reach and subject to increasing security threats (see p.25).

Bordered by Senegal, Mali, Morocco and Algeria, Mauritania was referred to by French colonialists as Le Grande Vide ("The Great Void"), but the country's modern name comes from its dominant ethnic group, the Moors, who speak the Hassaniya dialect of Arabic. The Moors are broadly divided into so-called "white" Bidan, who claim

Mean temperatures and rainfall

	Jan	Feb	Mar	Apr	May	Jun	Jul	Aug	Sep	Oct	Nov	Dec
Nouakchott												
max °C	29	31	32	32	34	33	32	32	34	33	32	28
min °C	14	15	17	18	21	23	23	24	24	22	18	13
rainfall mm	0	3	0	0	0	3	13	104	23	10	3	0
Atar												
max °C	31	33	34	39	40	42	43	42	42	38	33	29
min °C	12	13	17	19	22	27	25	26	26	23	17	13
rainfall mm	3	0	0	0	0	3	8	30	28	3	3	0

Before visiting, check the travel advisories and travel forums, and on arrival keep your ear close to the ground.

Main attractions

● **The iron ore trains** Forming some of the longest trains in the world (as many as two hundred wagons), the ore trains are a popular means of transport between Nouadhibou and the Adrar. You can buy a seat or sit on top of the dusty ore wagons for free.

● **Chinguetti and Ouadane** Atmospheric ruins and old libraries distinguish these ancient centres of learning on the Adrar plateau. Both are UNESCO sites; Chinguetti is one of Islam's seven holy cities, a trans-Saharan trading post that had a Portuguese community in the fifteenth century, while 800-year-old, stone-built, pink-hued Ouadane can seem like the Sahara's most spectacular town when the setting sun bathes it in warm light.

● **Terjit** Near Atar, the Adrar region's only large town, the green oasis of Terjit, tucked between cliffs, has a couple of good places to stay and some excellent natural bathing pools, where waterfalls tumble from cliffs draped with brilliant green maidenhair ferns.

● **Oualata** Worth the long trek for its extraordinary bas-relief-decorated houses, the ancient caravan and Koranic scholarship town of Oualata, at the end of southern Mauritania's Route de l'Espoir (Road of Hope), dates back to the eleventh century and once rivalled Timbuktu. Take careful local soundings on the security situation before coming here.

● **Tichit** Dramatically sited at the foot of an escarpment, and featuring regional architecture using distinctive red, green and white stone, remote and inaccessible Tichit also preserves the

Arab and Berber ancestors from North Africa and Arabia, and "black" Haratin, whose physical ancestry lies in Saharan and sub-Saharan Africa and who were subjugated and "Arabized" by the Bidan. Traditionally, the Haratin were vassals to the noble classes, but some Haratin elevated themselves into an independent caste that owed no tribute. The formal abolition of slavery in 1980 decreed that all "ex-slaves" (formerly called Abid) were henceforth to be known as "Haratin" – a source of offence to "real" Haratin and of confusion to outsiders. In addition to the Moors, around forty percent of the population are southerners, most of whom work as farmers and herders near the Senegalese and Malian borders.

While class and race are complicated issues in Mauritania, the role of women is less circumscribed than you might assume in a conservative, Islamic nation. All Mauritanians are, however, reappraising their lives in the light of attacks on a number of "Western" targets in recent years, including drive-by shootings of local expatriates and several kidnappings of tourists and NGO workers, which have been blamed on local supporters of Al-Qaeda (see p.25).

remnants of a complex ethnic division, epitomizing Mauritanian society, in its town plan. Assess security carefully before visiting.

● **The Parc National du Banc d'Arguin** One of the world's great bird-breeding sites and a refuge for European migrants, this vast zone is one of Africa's richest coastal and marine ecosystems, sheltering jackals, striped hyenas, gazelles and fennec foxes, as well as seals, turtles, dolphins and huge shoals of fish that spawn in the cold current.

Routes in and out

Most international flights arrive in the capital, Nouakchott, though Nouadhibou also has a few, including to the Canary Islands. The southbound route from Morocco, via Moroccan-occupied Western Sahara, is currently the only viable way of entering West Africa overland from North Africa, tarred almost the entire way, though distances between fuel supplies are huge. The overland routes between Mauritania and Mali are too unsafe to recommend and it's much better to cross the hustly but routine border with Senegal, and then make your way east to Mali. Mauritania's borders with Algeria and with Western Sahara (except the coast route described on pp.41–43) are closed.

Red tape

Visas Required by UK, Ire, US, Can, Aus, NZ and SA nationals. Must be obtained in advance.

Nearest consulates Algiers; Bamako; Banjul; Dakar; Rabat.

Other consulates Ottawa (Ⓦmauritania-canada.ca); Paris (☎+33 1 45 48 23 88); Pretoria (☎+27 12 362 3578, Ⓔrimanbapretoria @webmail.co.za); Washington, DC (Ⓦmauritaniaembassy.us). Visas can also be obtained from French consulates in London (Ⓦambafrance-uk.org) and Sydney (Ⓦambafrance-au.org).

Mauritius

Area 2040 square kilometres	(from UK)
Capital Port Louis	**Best time to go** July–Sept (dry and
Population 1.3 million	relatively cool); Dec–March (best
Language English (official); French	diving, though cyclones are a risk)
Religion Hindu, Christian; Muslim	**Country code** +230
minority	**Currency** Mauritian rupee (MUR);
Government Parliamentary republic	US$1: Rp32
Independence March 12, 1968	**Minimum daily budget** US$50

At almost 900km beyond Madagascar in the Indian Ocean, Mauritius (see map, p.310) is far enough east to get omitted from most maps of Africa. It's sometimes excluded from accounts of the continent, too, perhaps because its atmosphere, architecture and outlook are so distinct from the mainland. With a proudly multicultural population descended from French, British and Indian settlers as well as Africans, it feels part-European, part-Asian and part-international. In the towns and resorts, tutti-frutti coloured Tamil temples sit jauntily alongside the kind of modern developments that are common to tropical playgrounds such as Queensland and the Caribbean.

Luxury beach and golf resorts are Mauritius' main selling points. If you're the kind of person who likes your sand manicured, your golf clubs polished, your jacuzzi sprinkled with petals and your towels sculpted into swans, you'll fit right in. But while many of the resorts

are exclusive places with world-class restaurants and sky-high prices, there are a few mid-range hotels too, plus a handful of boutique hotels and budget guesthouses. And while some hotels treat the beaches on their doorsteps as private property, there are also plenty of lovely public beaches where local families gather under the casuarina trees for picnics and paddling at weekends, and stalls sell tasty snacks.

Mauritius is quiet, peaceful and wealthy, by African standards, its coffers boosted by foreign investment in its thriving business scene and its luxury housing projects. The roads are in good enough condition to make touring a pleasure and while very little of the landscape remains untouched by farming, logging and hunting, a few beautiful wilderness regions remain, with little-used hiking trails. Dolphins are often spotted in the waters to the west and there are some decent dive sites in the south and east.

Mean temperatures and rainfall

	Jan	Feb	Mar	Apr	May	Jun	Jul	Aug	Sep	Oct	Nov	Dec
Port Louis												
max °C	30	29	29	28	26	24	24	24	25	27	28	29
min °C	23	23	22	21	19	17	17	17	17	18	19	22
rainfall mm	216	198	221	127	97	66	58	64	36	41	46	117

Main attractions

● **Port Louis** The capital is an enjoyably animated little town, with an attractive jumble of French and British colonial architecture, a brilliant market (plump tropical fruit downstairs, spices, throws and dodo-patterned cushions upstairs) and a fascinating local history museum, The Blue Penny, named after the island's notable philatelic treasure, one of the rarest stamps in the world.

● **Sir Seewoosagur Ramgoolam Botanical Garden** Near Pamplemousses in the north, this cool, pleasant public park is a stately expanse of lawns, orchards, spice bushes and lotus pools with many unusual specimens including some eighty species of palm tree. Taking pride of place is an ornamental pond full of enormous water lilies, with moorhens stepping daintily from pad to pad.

● **Watersports** The calm, turquoise waters of Grand Baie in the north are perfect for pottering about in a dinghy or kayak, and those looking for a leisurely sailing experience can cruise the west coast aboard a large catamaran with an on-board barbecue. The breezier coast around Le Morne in the far southwest attracts hardcore windsurfers and kitesurfers. Underwater, around the offshore islands, scuba-divers and snorkellers can explore sunken lava caves and wrecks.

● **Adventure activities** Sugar cane plantation owners have opened their estates to tourists, laying on fun activities such as quad-biking, zip-lining, mountain-biking and horseriding.

● **Black River Gorges** This, the island's prime hiking region, is lush and green, with several waterfalls and trails from which you can spot monkeys, birds and even wild boar.

● **Rodrigues** This picturesque, thinly populated island is Africa's easternmost territory. It's a real gem, largely undiscovered, with great coral reefs, sandy coves and a far-off feel, plus good opportunities for windsurfing, snorkelling, mountain biking and watching seabirds.

● **La Vanille Réserve des Mascareignes** The pathways through this small reserve lead you to an insectarium and enclosures for giant tortoises and crocodiles, via a fragment of native rainforest.

● **Ile aux Aigrettes** This islet is a conservation zone for native flora and the pink pigeon, a rather slow and dumpy bird that's in danger of going the same way as the dodo. You can visit by ferry or kayak.

Routes in and out

International flights land at Sir Seewoosagur Ramgoolam Airport at Plaisance on Mauritius, from which there are daily connections to Rodrigues Island.

Red tape

Visas UK, Ire, US, Can, Aus, NZ and SA nationals do not need a visa for a stay of up to three months. A free two-week (renewable) entry stamp is issued on arrival.

Nearest consulates Antananarivo; Maputo; Pretoria (☎+27 12 342 1283, ✉mhcpta@mweb.co.za).

Other consulates Canberra (☎+61 2 6281 1203, ✉mhccan@cyberone .com.au); London (☎020 7581 0294, ✉londonhc@btinternet.com); Washington, DC (☎+1 202 244 1491, ✉mauritiusembassy@verizon.net).

Morocco and Western Sahara

Area Morocco: 447,000 square kilometres; Western Sahara: 266,000 square kilometres
Capital Morocco: Rabat; Western Sahara: Laayoune
Population Morocco: 32 million; Western Sahara: 500,000
Language Moroccan Arabic (official); French, Berber languages, Hassaniya Arabic in Western Sahara
Religion Muslim; tiny Christian and Jewish minorities

Government Democratic monarchy
Independence March 2, 1956 (from France) and April 7, 1956 (from Spain)
Best time to go May–Oct (summer, for beaches and mountains); Nov–April (winter, Sahara)
Dialling code +212
Currency Moroccan Dirham (MAD) US$1: Dh8.8dh
Minimum daily budget US$30

For sheer immersion in an exotic world, there are few countries in Africa as compellingly alien and alluring as the Kingdom of Morocco. Just an hour's ferry crossing from the familiarity of Europe, you're plunged into an utterly different culture – indigenous Moroccan Berber, overlaid by thirteen centuries of Arab influence and intermarriage – that has been in some ways more resistant to change than many countries further south. Nevertheless, since the young King Mohamed VI took the throne in 1999, Morocco has begun to liberalize. The media is much freer, Berber culture and languages are in resurgence and many parts of the cities look increasingly European.

The old, walled medinas of the four Imperial cities – Fes, Meknes, Marrakesh and the otherwise modern capital Rabat – grab visitors' attention

Mean temperatures and rainfall

	Jan	Feb	Mar	Apr	May	Jun	Jul	Aug	Sep	Oct	Nov	Dec
Tangiers												
max °C	15	16	17	19	21	24	26	27	25	22	19	16
min °C	10	10	11	12	14	17	19	19	18	16	13	10
rainfall mm	104	99	72	62	37	14	2	3	15	65	135	130
Marrakesh												
max °C	18	20	23	26	29	33	38	38	33	28	23	18
min °C	5	7	9	11	14	17	20	20	18	14	10	6
rainfall mm	32	38	38	39	24	5	1	3	6	24	41	31

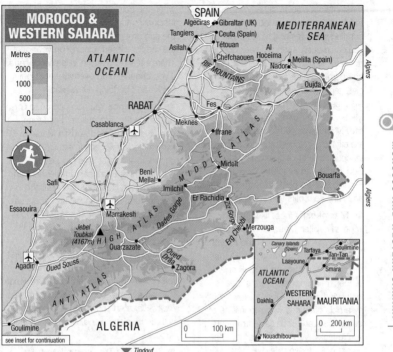

forcefully with their medieval street plans and teeming souks. But there's more here than carpets and kasbahs, as evidenced by Morocco's sweeping beaches, the three ranges of the Atlas mountains and the vast landscapes of the Sahara. The whole country is a delight for culture and history enthusiasts, naturalists, hikers and adventurers.

Western Sahara, the huge tract of mineral-rich desert formerly ruled by Spain and occupied by Morocco when Spain withdrew in 1975, is open to visitors along its seemingly endless Atlantic highway, but most travellers coming down here are only doing so en route to Mauritania and West Africa. A large part of the Sahrawi population fled the country during the war with Morocco that followed its invasion, and have spent the last thirty years living in

refugee camps in Algeria and waiting for UN action.

At the other end of Morocco, Ceuta and Melilla are Spanish enclaves on the Mediterranean coast – historical anomalies with military garrisons and big people- and drug-smuggling problems. Regular ferry links with mainland Spain make the pair an alternative to arriving in Tangiers. Melilla, further from Europe and less hustly, is by far the friendlier of the two.

Main attractions

● **Fes** Morocco's oldest imperial city is a seductively otherworldly urban landscape that has no equal in the country. The old medina quarter, Fes el Bali, is more than a thousand years old and remains the

327

most intact medieval city anywhere in the Arabic-speaking world. Fes el Bali is bursting with sites and monuments and you could easily spend a week dodging donkeys, exploring the alleys and souks and bargaining for crafts, especially the city's famous blue and white pottery. Must-sees include the thirteenth-century Merenid tombs (or at least their hillside site, which gives you a fantastic view of the city), the colourful and odoriferous tanneries and the extraordinary Medersa Bou Inania – an exquisitely beautiful, Koranic student hall, filled with light, colour and intricate motifs and inscriptions.

● **Marrakesh** Once, like Fes, an imperial capital, Marrakesh may not have the same wealth of monuments, but it's almost as unmissable. By day, the city's souks are an assault on the senses, mingling fresh goats' heads with dried medicinal lizards, towering pyramids of spices with mountains of leatherwork and musical instruments. If you're lucky, you'll find a carpet-shop owner who doesn't believe in hard sell, or be treated to a succession of fragrant demonstrations of cedar wood and argane oil at a cosmetics stall. At dusk in the Djemaa el Fna, the famous central square, dozens of lantern-lit food stalls open up and you sit on benches and order what you want – kebabs, aubergines, succulent fish, olives and aromatic bread – washed down with shots of tea. Moving through the crowd, pause by the circles of local onlookers to watch musicians, palm-readers and snake charmers.

● **All aboard the train** The train from Tangiers to Marrakesh is a model of calm efficiency. If you've opted for first class (only a small premium over second), you're escorted to your seat, where the air conditioning is unobtrusive. The passing scenery and village life (including the odd hitchhiker grabbing a ride when the train slows down) makes for a fascinating trip. By late afternoon, with the sun dropping, you're rocking through the reddish desert, closing on your goal. There's a snacks and drinks service, and, if you choose to go overnight, fold-out bunks and bedding are available.

● **Casablanca** You don't come to Casa to sample timeless culture. Less than a century old and modelled on Marseille (which it now exceeds in size), Morocco's commercial capital is its biggest city, with the most European atmosphere and some fine Art Nouveau and Art Deco architecture. Broad shopping streets are home to the classiest stores in Morocco and some very good restaurants, while the colossal Hassan II mosque – the tallest in the world with its 200-m minaret – is open to all. There's nothing much reminiscent of the Bogart-Bacall movie of the same name, but the inevitable replica *Rick's Café*, American-run and complete with centrepiece piano, is an established success.

● **Essaouira** The most relaxed of Morocco's Atlantic resorts is an attractive combination of eighteenth-century walled city, fishing port, rolling sand dunes and watersports centre. To add further appeal, there's a clutch of rocky islands just offshore, the Parc National des Îles d'Essaouira, which are the summer breeding site of the magnificent Eleonora's falcon. The most characterful hotels and *riads* are inside the old city, with some looking out to the ocean across the ramparts. While Essaouira is a good base for exploring southern Morocco, it's very easy to spend time in and around town, enjoying its art galleries, superb woodcarving workshops, wind- and kitesurfing and wonderful open-air fish grills.

● **High Atlas mountains** Jebel Toubkal, Africa's highest peak north of the Sahara (4167m), is the most obvious destination in this soaring, snow-covered range. Whether you're up for some serious trekking or just want a day out from Marrakesh, follow the Ourika valley south of the city for an hour by public transport or cab. The pretty, winding route heads to the village of Setti Fatmi, from where a footpath leads up into a landscape of awe-inspiring peaks and valleys. Further on, you reach pools and waterfalls, passing Berber women, bent over with head-loads of animal forage, on the narrow trail. Alternatively, follow the Ourika further west and you reach Imlil (a day's hike) and the start of the ascent of Toubkal peak.

● **Merzouga** Sand, sand, sand: these orange *erg* (dunes) deep in the Sahara near the Algerian border are the highlight of the region, some of them reaching 150m in height. Getting here is an adventure in itself, the vastness of the horizon by day and the silence and starriness of the nights deeply satisfying and humbling. The road is good, but the area's guides can be a pain, so book a room in advance. For dune-viewing, your best bet is an overnight camel trek, allowing you to watch the sunset and dawn in the heart of the dunes, staying at a Berber camp.

● **Tangiers** Although it has shed its reputation as a den of thieves and international vice, Tangiers' intoxicating vibe is still very much alive. Five minutes after getting off the ferry from Tarifa you enter the medina, where stubble-chinned gentlemen in *djellabas* brood over steaming glasses of mint tea, young dudes take turns to puff on honey-flavoured tobacco from hookah pipes, mountains of olives and dates cascade from shop fronts and CD vendors demonstrate their wares on deafening sound systems. Tangiers has one or two sites – an excellent crafts and antiquities museum in the kasbah and the fascinating American Legation Museum – but just hanging out in one of the cafés on the Petit Socco square (as generations of romantics, beats and hippies have done before you) is always a pleasure.

● **Staying in a riad** Often more expensive than staying in a hotel, a room in a *riad* is also usually more interesting and relaxing. These traditional townhouses, built around a garden-courtyard, are entered through a doorway from the street or alley. Guest rooms can look over the garden, or if higher up also across town. Many *riads* have roof terraces and some now incorporate a swimming pool or plunge pool in the garden. Most serve excellent meals to guests and, in the best *riads*, every little detail, from plant pots to lampshades, has been carefully considered.

● **Ziz Gorge** Traversing the High Atlas, you leave northern Morocco behind and enter the south and the true desert. Nowhere is the transformation more striking than on the road from Midelt to Er Rachidia when you pass through the chasm of the Ziz Gorge, carved by the Ziz ("Gazelle") River, fed by snowmelt from the peaks of the Atlas. The route is magnificent: dramatic mountains on either side, the silver sliver of the river, and ancient *ksour* (fortified, mud-brick villages) interspersed with green, irrigated gardens. Every so often, you see a Foreign Legion fort, still standing from France's "pacification" of the tribes of this region in the 1930s. Out of the gorge beyond Er Rachidia the valley opens up and the landscape is graced by vast groves of swaying date palms – perfect shade – and cool swimming spots.

Also recommended

● **Agadir** If you fly in on a cheap ticket or buy a package, the busy holiday resort of Agadir is an easy introduction to Morocco – and Africa – but you'll want to do some day-trips away from the huge beach. The gorge of Paradise Valley and the striking desert town of Taroudannt are easily accessible by renting a car.

● **Chefchaouen** At the western end of the Rif mountains, but not overwhelmed by the cannabis business like the villages further east, Chefchaouen is a friendly, pretty, highland town, with notes of Andalucia in its blue-painted architecture and small, Spanish-speaking community. Take a picnic on the banks of the Oued el Kebir river.

● **Festival of World Sacred Music, Fes** Now in its seventeenth year, this appealing festival (Ⓦfesfestival.com) runs for a week in June in some of the city's most beautiful spaces, and showcases local as well as international sacred and world music talent, from oud-player Driss el Maloumi to the Blind Boys of Alabama.

● **Gnaoua and World Music Festival, Essaouira** Although it started as a *moussem* religious festival in honour of local saints in 1998, this three-day event, held every June (Ⓦfestival-gnaoua .net), soon became a major fixture in the Essaouira calendar, featuring Gnawa (Sufi brotherhood) musicians and world music stars from abroad, and climaxing in a wonderful, sprawling jam session.

Routes in and out

Morocco is very well connected: the main airports are at Casablanca and Marrakesh, while international airports at Agadir, Al Hoceima, Essaouira, Fes, Ifrane, Nador, Oujda, Ouarzazate, Rabat, Tangiers and Tétouan offer more limited flights, mostly holiday and business links with Europe. Overland routes from Morocco to other parts of North Africa are limited: the border with Algeria is closed and there's just one route south along the coast of Western Sahara to Nouadhibou in Mauritania. Ferry connections to Europe are excellent, with frequent links to several ports in Spain (Tarifa, Algeciras, Almería and Barcelona) from Tangiers, Nador and the Spanish enclaves of Ceuta and Melilla. There are also less frequent crossings from Sète in France and Genoa in Italy to Nador and Tangiers.

Red tape

Visas Required by SA nationals. Available on arrival. Not required by UK, Ire, US, Can, Aus or NZ nationals staying ninety days or less.

Nearest consulates Algiers; Nouakchott.

Other consulates Canberra (Ⓦmoroccoembassy.org.au); Dublin (☎+353 1 660 9449, Ⓔsifamdub@indigo.ie); London (Ⓦmoroccanembassylondon.org.uk); Ottawa (Ⓦambamaroc.ca); Pretoria (☎+27 12 343 0230, Ⓔsifmapre @telkomsa.net); Washington, DC (☎+1 202 462 7979).

Mozambique

Area 801,590 square kilometres
Capital Maputo
Population 21.4 million
Language Portuguese (official);
Emakhuwa, Xichangana
Religion Christian, traditional;
Muslim minority
Government Presidential republic

Independence June 25; 1975
(from Portugal)
Country code +259
Best time to go May–Oct (dry
season); Nov–Dec & May–July
(best diving)
Currency Metical (MZN);
US$1: MT34
Minimum daily budget US$50

With a stunning Indian Ocean coastline and an untamed interior, much of it practically roadless, Mozambique is one of Africa's most intriguing countries. After three long decades of bitter struggle, first for independence and then for unity, it finally achieved peace in 1992. Since then, it has been steadily rebuilding its tourist industry and, to the great credit of those who believed in its potential, is already beginning to blossom as a cutting-edge eco-tourism destination.

If you're keen on marine wildlife and environmental concerns, you may want to make Mozambique the primary focus of your trip. Lodges which deftly mix rustic luxury, sustainability and community responsibility are popping up in Mozambique's remote coastal regions and marine national parks, notably the stunningly beautiful Bazaruto and Quirimbas islands. Here, the diving and snorkelling is remarkable, with immaculate coral reefs patrolled by turtles, manta rays, dolphins and myriad reef fish, while humpback whales and whale sharks ply the open waters.

Wildlife-watching inland is more challenging, as getting around can be arduous and many of Mozambique's once rich national parks were wrecked by poachers during the war years. However, they suit those who like exploring well off the standard tourist trail. Slightly more accessible, but still appealingly offbeat, are the country's heritage sites: the atmospheric remains of once prosperous coastal trading posts such as Ilha de Moçambique and Ilha do Ibo.

Mozambique has a party side too. South Africans, who used to love holidaying here in the pre-war years, are now back in droves to enjoy the sassy, multicultural flavour of Maputo, an easy

Mean temperatures and rainfall

	Jan	Feb	Mar	Apr	May	Jun	Jul	Aug	Sep	Oct	Nov	Dec
Maputo												
max °C	30	31	29	28	27	25	24	26	27	28	28	29
min °C	22	22	21	19	16	13	13	14	16	18	19	21
rainfall mm	130	125	125	53	28	20	13	13	28	48	81	97

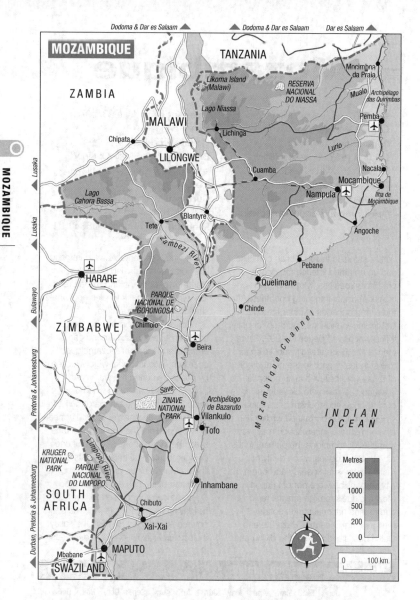

MOZAMBIQUE

TANZANIA

ZAMBIA

Likoma Island
(Malawi)

RESERVA
NACIONAL
DO NIASSA

Mocimboa
da Praia

MALAWI

Lago Niassa

Mualo

Archipélago
das Quirimbas

Chipata

Lichinga

Pemba ✈

LILONGWE

Cuamba

Lurio

Nacala

Lago
Cahora Bassa

Blantyre

Nampula ✈

Mocambique

Ilha de
Moçambique

Tete

Zambezi River

Angoche

HARARE ✈

Pebane

PARQUE
NACIONAL DE
GORONGOSA

Quelimane

ZIMBABWE

Chimoio

Chinde

Beira ✈

Mozambique Channel

Save

ZINAVE
NATIONAL
PARK

Archipélago
de Bazaruto

Vilankulo ✈

INDIAN
OCEAN

Tofo

KRUGER
NATIONAL
PARK

PARQUE
NACIONAL
DO LIMPOPO

Limpopo River

Inhambane

SOUTH
AFRICA

Chibuto

Xai-Xai

Metres	
2000	
1000	
500	
200	
0	

Mbabane

MAPUTO

N

SWAZILAND

0   100 km

MOZAMBIQUE

Lusaka ◄

Lusaka ◄

Bulawayo ◄

Pretoria & Johannesburg ◄

Durban, Pretoria & Johannesburg ◄

hop from Jo'burg or Durban, or to go
fishing or beach-lounging further north.

For travellers who plan to pound the
safari trails of South Africa, Tanzania,
Malawi or Zimbabwe and are looking

for somewhere to chill out afterwards,
gorgeous beaches such as Praia do
Tofo are a great choice – no matter how
tough the journey, the thought of kicking
off your boots and sinking your toes into

the sumptuous, white-gold sand with a well-earned caipirinha in hand is bound to spur you on.

Main attractions

● **Maputo** One of Mozambique's success stories, Maputo has picked itself up after the rigours of war, ditched the worst of its tawdry excesses and re-invented itself as a vibrant capital. It remains, for now, well off the radar for most travellers apart from South Africans, but it's thoroughly pleasant to visit: there's an upbeat atmosphere, with Afro-Latin music bouncing out of cool cafés and jazz clubs, and a thriving art scene. While it's not all pretty, it has buildings designed by Gustave Eiffel and some fine Portuguese colonial houses set on jacaranda-shaded avenues. In the Mercado Central, stalls are heaped with fresh fish and seafood: huge prawns are a local favourite, served grilled with piri-piri sauce.

● **Inhambane, Tofo and the southern coast** The quiet, pretty and leafy bayside town of Inhambane is a jumble of colonial and modern; its eighteenth-century cathedral is a legacy from its days as a hub for Portuguese ivory traders. While the dhows pulling into the harbour add romance, most people come here for the deliciously attractive beaches nearby: Tofo and Barra, to the east, are both superb places to scuba-dive with whale sharks and manta rays. Praia do Tofo is a key stop on the southern African backpacker trail.

● **Vilankulo and the Archipélago de Bazaruto** Snoozing in the Indian Ocean just offshore from the pleasant resort town of Vilankulo, another favourite for backpackers and overlanders, are the Bazarutos. Well-protected within a large marine park, the coral here is in beautiful condition, with hosts of irridescent fish fluttering about; dugongs and turtles are

found here, too. The region has been clobbered by cyclones in recent years (avoid Jan–April), but has recovered well. Vilankulo has some great, laidback lodges, from which it's easy to hop into the park by dhow to go snorkelling and diving – indeed, the archipelago as a whole has some gorgeous (and expensive) lodges.

● **Ilha de Moçambique** Small enough to be easy to explore on foot, this beautiful fortified island is Mozambique's finest heritage site. The first significant African settlement to be built by Europeans, its Stone Town was once the capital of lusophone Africa, with streets and wharves abuzz with gold, ivory and slave traders. Now, after five centuries caught in a time warp, many of its fine buildings are languishing in elegant decay, but investors are slowly beginning to breathe new life into its *praças* by restoring salvageable mansions and opening guesthouses and cafés.

● **Archipélago das Quirimbas** Romantic and remote, the Quirimbas Archipelago is an eco-luxury destination with real cachet. Sprinkled off the northern coast just south of the border with Tanzania, the islands are close to some of the best coral reefs in the Indian Ocean, with superb snorkelling and diving. There are half a dozen lodges, each with a different character; all are the stuff of honeymooners' dreams – and expensive. Just flying in by private charter is a special treat, watching dhows flit over the turquoise water below. Ilha do Ibo has a Stone Town which is fascinating to wander through, its approaches guarded by forts and its once grand merchants' houses, abandoned for decades, visibly crumbling.

● **Pemba and the northern coast** If you'd like to experience the wonderful, pristine beaches and reefs of the north, but your budget won't stretch to a trip out to the Quirimbas, you could console yourself with a stay on the mainland. Pemba (not to be confused with the Tanzanian island of the same name) is a laidback little holiday town on the lip of a huge bay, with some decent, affordable places to stay and access to a swathe of remote coastal wilderness. The villages scattered between Pemba and the border feel half-Tanzanian and half-Mozambican, with Swahili widely spoken and women going about their daily business in the distinctive white face packs that are the northern Mozambicans' favourite beauty treatment.

● **Lago Niassa** The Mozambican shore of this mighty Rift Valley lake, better known outside Mozambique as Lake Malawi, is far less developed than its Malawian counterpart: it's much easier to reach by lake ferry (see p.315) than by road. Right on the shore near Likoma Island is a superb luxury eco-lodge, Nkwichi (⑩mandawilderness.com), that's worth a special trip.

Also recommended

● **Parque Nacional de Gorongosa** Around four hours inland of the grubby town of Beira, this park was once one of Africa's best. During the civil war, poaching obliterated most of the wildlife, but a recovery programme is now in place, the park's small camp has re-opened and an eco-tourism venture is running fly camping trips. There are grasslands and acacia woodlands to explore, and nearby, the waterfall-draped Mount Gorongosa (1863m) to climb.

● **Reserva Nacional do Niassa** This vast reserve lies along the Tanzanian border, adjacent to the remotest part of the Selous. Because it's so isolated, with minimal infrastructure, it's little visited, so if you make it here you can consider yourself a pioneer.

● **Parque Nacional do Limpopo** Though ravaged by poachers during the war years, this southwestern park has a hopeful future: together with Kruger and Gonarezhou national parks, it forms part of the fledgling, 35,000-square-kilometre Great Limpopo Transfrontier Park, shared with South Africa and Zimbabwe.

Routes in and out

The main international airports are at Maputo, Nampula, Beira, Pemba and Vilanculos near Vilankulo. The south is served by flights from Johannesburg; the north from Dar es Salaam and Nairobi. The most used overland routes are from Johannesburg and Lilongwe; crossing to or from Zimbabwe is also straightforward. The land border between Mozambique and Tanzania is remote, with minimal traffic. There's a risk of landmines close to the border with Zambia, so you're best off crossing via Malawi.

Red tape

Visas Required by UK, Ire, US, Can, Aus and NZ nationals. Available on arrival at airports and at the land borders with Malawi, South Africa, Swaziland, Zambia and Zimbabwe (single-entry only). Not available at the land border with Tanzania. If travelling overland by public transport, you must obtain a visa in advance. SA citizens: visa not required.

Nearest consulates Dar es Salaam; Harare; Lilongwe; Lusaka; Mbabane; Nelspruit.

Other consulates London (⑩mozambiquehighcommission.org .uk); Fairlight, NSW (☎+61 2 9907 8890, ⓔjlsibraa@ozemail.com.au); Pretoria (⑩embamoc.co.za); Washington, DC (⑩embamoc-usa.org). Fees charged by the consulate in South Africa are higher than other sources.

Namibia

Area 825,418 square kilometres
Capital Windhoek
Population 2.2 million
Language English (official);
Afrikaans, German, Oshiwambo
Religion Christian (mostly Lutheran);
traditional minority
Government Presidential republic
Independence March 21, 1990
(from South Africa; previously
from Germany)
Best time to go All year; especially
July–Oct for wildlife (driest months,
relatively cool)
Country code +264
Currency Namibian dollar
(NAD, equivalent to South African
rand, which is also accepted);
US$1: $7.7
Minimum daily budget US$50

It's rare for travellers to return from Namibia with anything other than glowing praise – this striking, sparsely populated country has such charisma that it's regularly voted one of the top adventure destinations in the world.

Key to its appeal is the spacious drama of its desert landscapes, where oryx, the kind of antelope Picasso might have dreamed up, pick their way over towering, apricot-coloured dunes, ostriches dash through the shimmering haze and elephants lumber along richly textured gorges. At dusk, Namibia's huge skies mould themselves into a dizzying dome of stars. Best of all, these splendours are accessible – while you might feel apprehensive about venturing into the trackless Sahara, Namibia's great desert regions are loosely criss-crossed with decent gravel roads.

With enough mineral wealth to make it one of Africa's more prosperous countries, Namibia, though somewhat troubled by land reform issues, is largely a model of peace, stability and inter-ethnic respect. It's also a leader in community-based conservation: rural Namibia is dotted with conservancies, wilderness regions whose residents have been granted the right to profit from sustainable tourism and are therefore motivated to care for their environment and its flora and fauna.

Unlike many of Africa's parks, Namibia's best wilderness regions are surprisingly straightforward to navigate independently, as long as you're well-prepared for the rigours of long gravel roads and harsh desert conditions. You can rent a 4WD in Windhoek with optional extras such as rooftop tent,

Mean temperatures and rainfall

Windhoek	Jan	Feb	Mar	Apr	May	Jun	Jul	Aug	Sep	Oct	Nov	Dec
max °C	29	28	27	25	22	20	20	23	25	29	29	30
min °C	17	16	15	13	9	7	6	8	12	15	15	17
rainfall mm	76	74	79	41	8	0	0	0	3	10	23	48

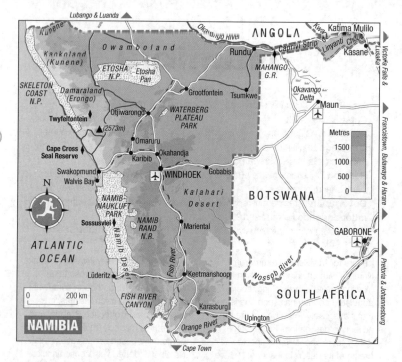

Lubango & Luanda

ANGOLA

Kunene

Owamboland

Kaokoland (Kunene)

ETOSHA N.P. Etosha Pan

SKELETON COAST N.P.

Damaraland (Erongo)

Twyfelfontein

Cape Cross Seal Reserve

Otjiwarongo

▲(2573m)

Omaruru

Okahandja

Karibib

Swakopmund

Walvis Bay

NAMIB-NAUKLUFT PARK

Sossusvlei

NAMIB RAND N.R.

ATLANTIC OCEAN

Lüderitz

FISH RIVER CANYON

NAMIBIA

Rundu

Okavango River

Caprivi Strip

Linyanti Chobe

Katima Mulilo

Kwando

Kasane

MAHANGO G.R.

Okavango Delta

Maun

Grootfontein Tsumkwe

WATERBERG PLATEAU PARK

WINDHOEK Gobabis

Kalahari Desert

BOTSWANA

Mariental

Namib Desert

Fish River

Keetmanshoop

Nossob River

GABORONE

SOUTH AFRICA

Karasburg

Upington

Orange River

Metres
1500
1000
500
0

N

0   200 km

Cape Town

Victoria Falls & Lusaka

Francistown, Bulawayo & Harare

Pretoria & Johannesburg

cooking equipment, spare fuel tanks and child seats, and scoot around the key sights – Sossusvlei, Swakopmund, Damaraland and Etosha – within a fortnight, or enjoy stretching the experience out over several weeks, staying at simple campsites or fabulously designed bush lodges as you go. At the latter, you may be treated to mouth-watering *braais* (barbecues) of local game such as springbok or kudu.

Organized adventures are available, too, and feature some of Africa's rarer experiences, such as spending time with Ju/'hoansi Bushmen, whose ancestors marked rock faces in the northern semi-desert with engravings of giraffes and antelopes, possibly as a wildlife primer for youngsters. You can also explore one of Africa's loneliest coasts, track black rhinos through the semi-desert on foot, or get close to big cats in rescue centres.

For more animal action and superb birdwatching, the busy waterholes of Etosha National Park and the riverine wilderness of the Caprivi Strip, Namibia's green lung, will definitely deliver.

Main attractions

● **Etosha National Park** Though easily one of the finest places in the world to watch wildlife, particularly in the driest months (July–Oct), Etosha remains the preserve of reasonably adventurous safari-goers. The park's signature feature is the 120-km wide Etosha Pan, a blinding expanse of sunbaked salt fringed by grasslands and bush, largely free of human influence. Elephants, giraffes, springbok and ostriches, plus hyenas and big cats, pick their way through the heat haze to drink at the waterholes, many of which are easy to reach by self-drive vehicle or tour. Okaukuejo in the southwest is one of the best to aim for, as it often attracts black rhino and is floodlit after dark. There's comfortable accommodation inside the park at state-owned camps, and a scattering of luxury lodges just outside.

● **Sossusvlei, Namib-Naukluft and the NamibRand** The huge sweep of protected Namib desert southwest of Windhoek is quintessentially Namibian: its mighty shifting dunes are so iconic they're a travel-brochure cliché. At Sossusvlei, it's possible to climb some of the biggest dunes – harder than you might think, thanks to the softness of the sand – for wraparound views of the many-hued landscape. You can then have the fun of bounding down the steepest incline, whooping your head off. An added delight of this region are the skeleton trees adrift in salt pans, and the fairy circles – rings of tufty grasses with a bare patch in the middle that science can't explain. There's a good campsite, several sublime desert lodges and opportunities to go hot air ballooning.

● **Swakopmund** Due west of Windhoek along a tarmac road, the Atlantic resort town of Swakopmund offers a vivid reminder of Namibia's colonial past: the older architecture is Germanic in style, German is widely spoken and the restaurants delight in serving bratwurst. There's even an annual Oktoberfest, a jolly knees-up featuring locally brewed lager and Bavarian-style bands in lederhosen. Like Windhoek, Swakopmund is a safari and backpacker hub with some great shops selling souvenirs including beautiful, locally made jewellery, crafts and curios. This is also Namibia's extreme sports capital, with several operators offering quad-biking, dune buggy racing and sandboarding.

● **Erongo and Kunene regions** Also called Damaraland and Kaokoland, Namibia's wild northwest is a stunning and rugged region of gravel plains and rocky, terracotta-coloured semi-desert. Some parts are scored with river channels that are totally dry for most of the year, but surge with flood water during the rains. Rare desert-adapted elephants can sometimes be seen browsing the mopane trees in the dry beds of the Ugab and Huab rivers, or digging for water with their tusks. Several pioneering, community-owned or conservation-oriented lodges and safari companies operate in this region; potential adventures include joining expert trackers on their daily expeditions to monitor desert-adapted black rhinos, whose population has been brought back from the brink, or looking for desert-adapted lions, currently the subject of detailed research.

● **Skeleton Coast** The forbidding but austerely beautiful coast of northern Erongo and Kunene is carefully protected to preserve its delicate ecosystem. You can drive along the southern section, nearest Swakopmund, by following a road that parallels the foggy Atlantic shore, but the north, which stretches up to the Kunene River, is only accessible by fly-in safari. On nature trails across the sands and gravel plains, you can observe ancient desert-adapted plant species such as welwitschia (an endemic, trunkless tree which sags raggedly on the ground and can live for over 2500 years), lithops and delicate lichens.

● **Herero, Himba and San culture** Maherero Day in August, when Hereros gather in the arty little town of Okahandja, north of Windhoek, to honour their ancestors with parades and celebrations, is one of Namibia's liveliest ethnic festivals. Herero women are instantly recognizable for their traditional dress: voluminous cotton frocks with elaborate cotton headdresses shaped like horns. The semi-nomadic pastoralists of remotest Kunene are just as distinctive, wearing goatskins, heavy jewellery and ochre-daubed hair; by seeking out a *kraal* (homestead) that's set up for visits, you can learn about tribal customs. San Bushman culture is fascinating, too: in the remote village of Tjokwe in northeast Namibia, members of the Ju/'hoansi tribe invite visitors to mug up on desert survival skills such as animal-tracking, digging for water-rich roots and identifying medicinal plants.

● **Caprivi Strip** This narrow strip of territory juts between Zambia and Botswana and touches fingertips with Zimbabwe, giving Namibia access to the Zambezi. As green as the rest of Namibia is arid, it's dotted with villages, fruit trees and vegetable plots. It's also one of Africa's top birding destinations, with a good mixture of basic camps and blissfully comfortable river lodges. From Rundu at the west end, you can head east along the banks of the Okavango to Popa Falls and the Mahango Game Reserve, a birding hotspot that's also the haunt of water-loving lechwe and elephants. Among the swamps and flood plains right at the eastern tip, bordered by the Kwando, Linyanti, Chobe and Zambezi rivers, several lodges offer boating, fishing, hiking and game-viewing, particularly in the Mudumu and Mamili National Parks. Houseboat trips are a highlight.

● **AfriCat Foundation** This predator conservation centre (Ⓦafricat.org) near Otjiwarongo, north of Windhoek, cares for cheetahs, leopards and lions, and addresses the problems which arise when their natural territories overlap with farmers' ranches. Visiting for the day or overnight (there's a superb luxury bush lodge on site) allows you to see rescued animals in close-up by tracking them in their enclosures using radio telemetry.

● **Hiking the Fish River Canyon** You need to apply in advance for a permit to hike this classic 80km trail through a monumental landscape of sand and sheer rock. Starting from Hobas campsite and finishing at Ai-Ais several days later, the demanding trail is only open from May to mid-September, but even then it's hot. Further information is available online (Ⓦwww.nwr.com .na). Those who choose not to test themselves on the hike can admire the canyon from its rim and enjoy the sculptural shapes of the quiver trees in the nearby Kokerboom Forest.

Also recommended

● **Windhoek** Some safari-goers simply breeze through on their way to the wilds, but the capital is hassle-free and pleasant to visit, with an orderly, small-town atmosphere: the population is a mere 300,000. Its handful of modest landmarks includes Christuskirche, a large church with gingerbread-house facades, and the Alte Feste, a fortress housing part of the National Museum. German-trained jewellers sell pieces featuring Namibian diamonds, and the Namibia Craft Centre and Craft Café on the south side of town stocks a beautiful selection of locally made goodies including Herero walking sticks and hand-painted ostrich eggs.

● **Cape Cross** A huge, malodorous colony of Cape fur seals can be seen lolling, barking and gallumphing about on this isolated stretch of rocky shore, with young pups bleating beside their mothers around November.

● **Waterberg Plateau Park** Namibia's only highland national park has great views over broad expanses of woodland savanna. Eagles and vultures soar over the striking red sandstone formations of the plateau, which also harbour rare roan and sable antelopes. There are signposted hiking trails to follow.

● **Twyfelfontein** The intriguing petroglyph sites of the Brandberg and Twyfelfontein area stand amid plains strewn with enormous boulders and rock formations, some of which are the fossilized remains of trees thought to be over 250 million years old. A couple of Namibia's most imaginative wilderness lodges (try Ⓦmowani.com) are nearby.

Routes in and out

International flights (principally from Johannesburg, Cape Town and Frankfurt) land at Windhoek's Hosea Kutako Airport, 42km east of the city, with remoter regions served by airstrips. It's easy enough to travel by land to and from Angola, Botswana and South Africa. There's a direct road between the Caprivi Strip and Zambia, but to travel to or from Zimbabwe, you need to dip into Botswana's Chobe National Park and out again. The 1300km Cape–Namibia route between Cape Town and Windhoek traverses some spectacular regions.

Red tape

Visas UK, Ire, US, Can, Aus, NZ and SA nationals do not need a visa for a stay of up to ninety days (free entry stamp issued on arrival).

Nearest consulates Gaborone; Harare; Luanda; Lusaka; Pretoria.

Other consulates London (Ⓦnamibiahc.org.uk; US/Can citizens should use this consulate); Pretoria (Ⓣ+27 12 481 9100, Ⓔsecretary @namibia.org.za); Sydney (Ⓣ+61 2 9818 8544, Ⓔantonio @namibianconsulaustralia.com.au).

Niger

Area 1,267,000 square kilometres	**Independence** Aug 3, 1960
Capital Niamey	(from France)
Population 16 million	**Best time to go** Nov–March
Language French (official); Hausa,	(dry, and cooler, season)
Fula, Djerma/Songhai, Tamashek,	**Dialling code** +227
eight others	**Currency** West African CFA Franc
Religion Muslim; minority Christian	(XOF) US$1: CFA506
and animist	**Minimum daily budget** US$40
Government Military-backed junta	

Deep in the heart of West Africa, with the north of the country covered by the Sahara and the southern regions consisting of a plain of often drought-stricken savanna and bush, Niger is well off the map for most travellers in Africa. The only areas of significant population are concentrated along the southern border with Nigeria and along a ribbon of farmland in the southwest of the country near the Niger River – which flooded in 2010 with disastrous results.

Niger regularly ranks as the poorest country on earth in the United Nations' human development index. If that isn't a big enough burden, the simmering conflict between the nomadic Tuareg people of the desert and the administration in

Niamey was never resolved as in neighbouring Mali. This rebellion is mostly about uranium in the Aïr mountains, mined by the French and profiting the Niamey elite but bringing no benefits to local Tuareg communities. Although the uprising has nothing to do with the aims of the local Al-Qaeda franchise it is inevitably being dragged into the "War on Terror". To add to the country's troubles, a military coup in 2010 overthrew the ostensibly democratically elected president, who was mired in corruption and inertia.

If the conflict continues, much of Niger will remain effectively off-limits, but, assuming tensions drop once again, there's plenty to come here for. The mountainous desert landscapes of the

Mean temperatures and rainfall

	Jan	Feb	Mar	Apr	May	Jun	Jul	Aug	Sep	Oct	Nov	Dec
Niamey												
max °C	34	37	41	42	41	38	34	32	34	38	38	34
min °C	14	18	22	26	27	25	24	22	23	23	19	15
rainfall mm	0	0	5	8	33	81	132	188	94	13	0	0
Agadez												
max °C	29	33	38	40	43	44	42	40	41	39	33	28
min °C	10	13	17	21	25	24	24	23	23	20	15	12
rainfall mm	0	0	0	2	6	10	35	50	8	0	0	0

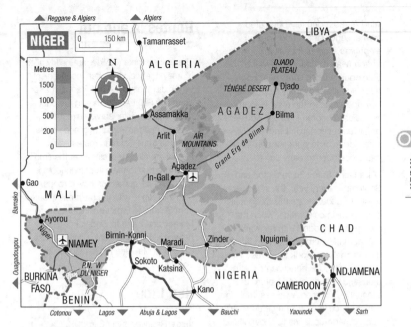

north are compelling, while the old buildings and mosques of Agadez rival those of Timbuktu. Niamey is an easier city to adapt to than many, and the pretty districts around the river in the southwest of the country are relatively secure and full of birds and other wildlife – the country's best national park is here.

Main attractions

● **Agadez, the Aïr and the Ténéré** An ancient desert metropolis and the seat of a powerful sultanate, Agadez is one of the most important centres in the southern Sahara, the minaret of its Grande Mosquée towering over the town's low roofs. The silversmiths here fashion innovative jewellery, most famously the renowned "Croix d'Agadez". For determined travellers, Agadez (in peaceful times) is the starting point for visits to isolated oases in the Ténéré and Bilma regions and to the

historic villages of the less remote Aïr mountains, such as Timia, Iferouâne and Assodé. Be prepared for serious desert travel (and for coughing up some serious money for the experience).

● **The River** The Niger River, flowing for 500km through the southwest, is one of the country's few bodies of water – an attraction in itself. At Ayorou, a riverside town near the Malian border with a fantastic animal market every Sunday, you can rent a pirogue to visit Ayorou Goungou island. Your chances of seeing hippos along this stretch of the river are good, and exotic birds are common, especially near the island of Firgoun, 12km north of town. Or take a pirogue from Ayorou to Tillabéri after the market closes – a one-day voyage, setting off on Sunday evening or Monday morning.

● **Parc National du "W" du Niger** Learn game-watching in French: the park named after the double-bend of the Niger River is one of West

Africa's most densely populated animal sanctuaries. Look out for *éléphants*, *buffles* (buffalo), *cobs de buffon* (waterbuck), *hippotrague* (roan antelope), *phacochères* (warthogs), *babouins* (baboons) and, of course, *hippopotames* in the river. Reports occasionally come in of the odd *léon* or *guépard* (leopard), but they stay very well hidden. The park is open from mid-December to early June.

● **La Cure Salée** Towards the end of September every year, the In-Gall area west of Agadez hosts this traditional homecoming celebration, when the salt flats are flooded with rainwater and nomadic herders return to fatten their animals and look for wives. The most spectacular participants are the thousands of unmarried Bororo or Wodaabé Fula men, who assemble in a performance known as a *gerewol*, with heavily made-up faces to show off the ideal of Fula male beauty to the women – big kohl-lined eyes, white teeth and an aquiline nose – and hopefully pair up with someone.

● **Musée National, Niamey** Opened in 1959, the national museum is the capital's outstanding bit of sightseeing, and far outclasses most African museums. As well as the internal exhibits, which include dinosaur fossils from the country's rich deposits at Gadoufaoua (including monster crocodiles), the extensive grounds include a working crafts centre and examples of traditional architecture.

Routes in and out

The limited flights to Niger are nearly all to Niamey (the majority, often inconveniently, via Abidjan), although the French charter company Point Afrique has in the past run a regular winter service direct from Paris to Agadez. As for overland routes, both the trans-Saharan routes from Algeria are effectively closed at the time of writing due to the risk of kidnapping. From Nigeria, numerous paved roads feed into Niger, with the main entry routes from Sokoto to Birnin-Konni, Katsina to Maradi, and Kano to Zinder. For travel between Niger and Benin, Burkina Faso, Chad and Mali, see those respective chapters.

Red tape

Visas Required by UK, Ire, US, Can, Aus, NZ and SA nationals. Must be obtained in advance. Proof of return travel and access to at least US$500 is required. Those who have never visited Niger before must attend an interview at the consulate.
Nearest consulates Abuja; Algiers; Cotonou; Ndjaména. The consulates in Tripoli and Bamako do not issue visas to foreigners. No consulate in Burkina Faso.
Other consulates Rochford, Essex (Ⓦniger-embassyuk.org); Paris (Ⓣ+33 1 45 04 80 60); Ottawa (Ⓦambanigeracanada.ca); Washington, DC (Ⓦnigerembassyusa.org).

Nigeria

Area 924,000 square kilometres
Capital Abuja
Population 156 million
Language English (official); Yoruba,
Hausa, Igbo, more than 400 others
Religion Muslim and Christian;
minority traditional
Government Presidential, federal
democracy
Independence Oct 1, 1960
(from UK)
Best time to go Nov–Feb
(dry season)
Country code +234
Currency Naira (NGN) US$1: ₦151
Minimum daily budget US$50

Nigeria ought to be Africa's largest economy. It's the most populous country on the continent, bursting with entrepreneurial energy, yet it trails behind smaller countries like Egypt and South Africa. Its tattered infrastructure and terrible leadership (even considering the size of the job), force most Nigerians into permanent survival mode, endured with great good humour. After fifty years of independence, a civil war and only a decade's worth of democracy, the oil-producing Niger delta is still embroiled in a conflict between security forces and armed gangs fighting for regional autonomy and a share of oil wealth, in which hundreds of expat oil workers have been abducted and ransomed.

So, if you don't have to go, why not just avoid Nigeria? The fact is the country contains a cultural and scenic diversity that is the equal of any other nation in Africa. From the mega-cities of the southwest to the rainforests of the southeast corner, the mountains of the far east to the arid savanna of the north with its Muslim walled cities, Nigeria makes a big impression. The dismal reputation for crime and corruption is only a fraction of the truth, for this is also the land that has

Mean temperatures and rainfall

	Jan	Feb	Mar	Apr	May	Jun	Jul	Aug	Sep	Oct	Nov	Dec
Lagos												
max °C	31	32	32	32	32	29	28	28	28	29	31	31
min °C	23	25	26	25	245	23	23	23	23	23	24	24
rainfall mm	28	46	102	150	269	460	279	64	140	206	60	25
Kano												
max °C	30	33	37	38	37	34	31	29	31	34	33	31
min °C	13	15	19	24	24	23	22	21	21	19	16	13
rainfall mm	0	0	3	10	69	117	206	310	142	13	0	0
Calabar												
max °C	30	32	32	31	30	30	28	28	29	29	30	30
min °C	23	23	23	23	23	22	22	22	22	22	23	23
rainfall mm	43	76	153	213	312	406	450	405	427	310	191	43

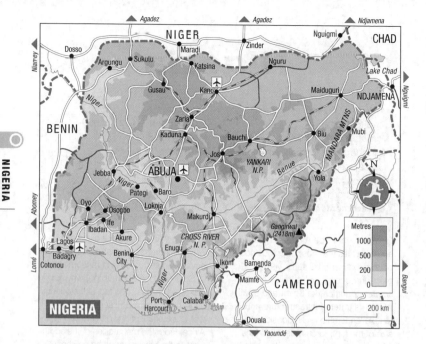

produced inspirational visionaries such as Nobel literature laureate Wole Soyinka and Afrobeat legend Fela Kuti. Put simply, Nigeria is worth it. If you avoid the obvious trouble spots, you shouldn't have any problems beyond the usual setbacks and frustration. Arrive with an open mind and remember – even more than in most of Africa – that this chapter only scratches the surface of a hugely rewarding country.

Main attractions

● **Abuja** The new capital was only started in 1981, but one of the world's biggest construction sites is finally becoming a real city. Though things don't work much better here than anywhere else, the setting is beautiful, beneath a backdrop of giant inselbergs and with plenty of green spaces, and it's certainly Nigeria's most liveable conurbation. The two big landmarks are the golden-domed

Central Mosque and its neighbour, the Ecumenical Cathedral, while the Transcorp Hilton is West Africa's biggest hotel and always fun for a drink.

● **Calabar** Far in distance and atmosphere from the towers of Abuja, the old port of Calabar is Nigeria's most picturesque and easy-going city. This engaging and venerable trading base perches above the river of the same name and, unlike the capital, nearly all the inhabitants are real locals – mostly Efik people whose ancestors first started trading with the Europeans more than 500 years ago. As well as colonial architecture, Calabar features excellent local cuisine and two very worthwhile primate conservation centres, the Drill Monkey Rehab Centre and Cercopan.

● **Yankari National Park** A wildlife park to rival many in East Africa, with a fraction of the visitors, Yankari has various species of antelope, buffalo and elephant, which are all fairly easy to spot, and predators including lions, which are much harder. There are decent places to stay and the park rangers can direct you to other sites, such as prehistoric cave dwellings and the Borkono Falls. They'll also organize transport for game drives if you don't have your own. The Wikki Warm Springs, just down from the main lodge, are an exceptional African highlight. Crystal-clear waters bubble over silver sand from a cleft in the rocks to create an idyllic bathing pool with perfect depth and temperature.

● **Cross River National Park** It was long thought that gorillas had disappeared from Nigeria, but the Worldwide Fund for Nature has located at least four separate populations in Cross River National Park. A trek along its trails will see you crawling through thickets, fording streams and grabbing at branches as you slip on mossy boulders. Expect to come out bruised, battered and blistered – and to have a brilliant time. There are no habituated gorilla groups as yet, but the splendid rainforest scenery compensates for the rarity of sightings.

● **Kano's Old City** The great metropolis of northern Nigeria is a major destination in its own right. Although little remains of the original city walls of this thousand-year-old city, the indigo dye pits near Kofar Mata gate, the Central Mosque a bit further into the old city and the Emir's Palace all build a sense of place. After you've had a look round the Gidan Makama museum and spent some time in the tight maze of Kurmi market (good deals on carved calabashes, beads, pottery, leather, textiles, brass, silver and ironwork), head up Dala Hill for a fabulous rooftop view across the narrow alleyways and old houses. It's worth being here at the end of Ramadan: the spectacular four-day Kano *durbar* feels like a cross between a carnival and a medieval tournament.

● **The Mountain of Death** Nigeria's eastern highlands, close to Cameroon's much better known Rhumsiki region, are some of the most beautiful and unexplored mountains in Africa. The highest peak in Nigeria, its summit on the border itself, is Gangirwal (2418m) – whose dramatic moniker means "Mountain of Death". The six-day trek to the summit and back, through the Gashaka Gumpti National Park, takes you past waterfalls and dramatic rock formations. And keep your eyes open for chimpanzees – as many as two thousand live on the mountain.

● **Osogbo Sacred Forest** In the heart of Yorubaland in southwest Nigeria, this tranquil grove of shrines to the Yoruba water goddess Osun is perhaps the most spectacular traditional religious site anywhere in Africa. On the outskirts of the busy town of Osogbo, a whole forest has been set aside as a reserve for worshippers. The weather-beaten shrines here are almost organic in their inspiration, incorporating humans and animals, moulded in cement and built on steel and wood frames. Worshippers are only too eager to show you around.

● **Lagos** Africa's biggest city is undoubtedly a tough place for its poorer residents, but a visit to this dynamic, noisy, media-saturated and surprisingly friendly city can be a revelation. There are teeming markets and brilliant nightlife (don't leave without experiencing Sunny Ade's *Ariya*, Lágbájá's *Motherlan'* or Femi Kuti's *New Afrika Shrine*), while bonuses like beautiful Badagry beach (west of the city), the old Brazilian architecture on Lagos island and plenty of generator-powered air-conditioned restaurants and bars make the go-slows (traffic jams), power cuts and general mess bearable.

● **Ife National Museum** The magnificent brass and bronze heads in the National Museum in Ife, 200km northeast of Lagos, are among Nigeria's most cherished cultural artefacts. Representing the *oni* or king of Ife and other senior royal figures, and made using the lost-wax method, they date from as far back as the fourteenth century. The sculptors were technical virtuosos, producing heads of rare grace, scored with the fine lines of scarification indicating royal rank.

Also recommended

● **Street food** Suya, the fast food of Nigeria – tiny, spicy kebabs of beef or goat, sold for a few cents each and usually served in French-style bread with a searing sauce – are available everywhere and nearly always delicious. For a more substantial meal at a roadside restaurant, order *eba* (a moist cassava-flour dumpling sitting in a puddle of hot pepper soup) or *fufu* (fermented *eba*). Other favourites include *dodo* (fried plantains), *moin-moin* (beancakes) and *eja gbigbe* (smoked catfish on a stick).

● **Sukur mountain kingdom** Follow the Cameroonian frontier on a map north to Mubi and the next 100km of mountains to the north encompasses the seat of a once powerful kingdom, and now UNESCO World Heritage Site, Sukur. Few travellers make it this far and local people are welcoming. The journey ends with a walk up an extraordinary stone causeway, an ancient civil engineering project that takes you to the village of Sukur itself, where you will greet the *heedi*, or king. He's remarkably hospitable, and will recount the history of Sukur, from the early slave raids to the period when this village was part of Cameroon.

● **Zaria** The old town of Zaria – one of the seven Hausa states – has withstood the tests of time better than most of the other northern emirates. The ancient wall, built by Queen Amina more than 900 years ago, has largely crumbled away, but some of the old gates have been restored and the Emir's Palace is a dazzlingly multicoloured example of traditional architecture, although a modern construction. Almost all the homes in old Zaria are built in the traditional style, and many display the detailed exterior decoration the town is famous for.

Routes in and out

Air connections have been steadily improving in the past few years, most airlines still flying into Lagos rather than Abuja. Overland routes to Niger and Benin are relatively straightforward. The 100km-long border with Chad runs through the seasonally flooded plain that used to be Lake Chad itself, and most people going to or coming from Chad's capital, Ndjamena, travel via the northern extremity of Cameroon. Nigeria's main border crossing point with Cameroon is Mamfé to Ikom, over the Cross River bridge, in the southeast corner of the country. Further north, in the Bamenda Highlands, you can cross on foot from Dumbo in Cameroon to Bissaula in Nigeria – an arduous but rewarding hike – and there are minor crossings all the way along the mountainous border.

Red tape

Visas Required by UK, Ire, US, Can, Aus, NZ and SA nationals. Must be obtained in advance. Download a form from ⓦportal.immigration.gov.ng.

Nearest consulates Accra; Bamako; Bangui; Cotonou; Ndjaména; Niamey; Ouagadougou; Yaoundé.

Other consulates Canberra (ⓦwww .nigeria-can.org.au); Dublin (ⓦnigerianembassy.ie); Johannesburg (ⓦnigeria.co.za); London (ⓦnhcuk .org); Ottawa (ⓦnigeriahcottawa.com); Washington, DC (ⓦnigeriaembassyusa.org).

La Réunion

Area 2512 square kilometres
Capital Saint-Dénis
Population 800,000
Language French (official); Créole
Religion Catholicism
Government Overseas
département of France

Best time to go May–Nov
(dry season)
Country code +262
Currency Euro (EUR) US$1: €0.79
Minimum daily budget US$110
(for one week including a gorilla-trek)

The coconut-shaped island of Réunion (see map, p.310) is an Indian Ocean oddity. Although it lies between Mauritius and Madagascar, it's actually a French overseas *département*, and a euro-spending, boules-playing part of the European Union. Despite their baguette-buying habits, the Réunionais, whose ancestors come from France, Africa and India, are not in any way tropical Parisians. They're a fishing and farming people who speak Créole (based on French, which all Créole-speakers understand), and are usually genial hosts to their visitors, most of whom come from France.

The island offers a compact diversity – all the beaches, reefs and palm trees you'd expect, plus dramatic volcanic scenery, complete with waterfalls and superb hiking trails – but on the downside, the prices are French. Most people are not particularly well off, and street demonstrations, usually focused around prices and unemployment,

occasionally flare up. There's not much appetite, however, for the independence you might expect islanders to be demanding: people recognize the limitations of their location and the benefits of French subsidies and tourism.

Inland from the coast, the three giant calderas of Réunion's ancient volcanic heart have eroded to form a highland region consisting of innumerable valleys and peaks, set around three huge natural depressions, or cirques. At the southern end of the island stands a far-from-dormant volcano, Piton de la Fournaise, which erupted in 2007.

Also in the south is Cap Méchant – the "wicked cape" buffeted by icy rollers from the Southern Ocean, and long feared by seafarers. The island, although you can drive right round it in half a day, has huge variations of climate, with heavy rain on the windward, eastern coast and a much drier climate on the western slopes.

Mean temperatures and rainfall

Saint-Dénis	Jan	Feb	Mar	Apr	May	Jun	Jul	Aug	Sep	Oct	Nov	Dec
max °C	30	30	30	29	27	26	25	25	25	27	28	29
min °C	23	23	23	22	20	18	18	17	18	19	20	22
rainfall mm	304	251	260	173	101	75	76	53	18	44	83	155

Main attractions

● **Saint-Dénis** Réunion's lively capital, on the north coast, is where you'll arrive. It's an easy place to like, with a good-natured, small-town feel and a few things to do: take a look in the pretty cathedral, dating from 1832; visit the botanical gardens at the top of historic Rue de Paris, and look around the excellent collections at the natural history museum, which focus on the fauna and flora of the Indian Ocean.

● **Volcanic scenery** Réunion may be 10,000km from Europe, but a climb up the fertile volcanic slopes brings you to more temperate vegetation zones, as primeval-looking tree ferns, reminiscent of New Zealand, and stands of giant bamboo that could be in the Himalayas finally give out to high-altitude moorland, which actually does start to look like France, with fat cattle – source of the excellent local dairy products – grazing on swathes of lush pasture.

● **Hiking** As in France, GR footpaths – the well-marked *Grande Randonnée* trails – snake through the mountains, and you can either set aside several days for a long hike, stopping at villages or mountain huts en route, or arrange with a taxi driver to take you up for a day out, collecting you a few hours later from an agreed point along the trail.

● **Sugar cane and vanilla** As you travel round the island (by rented car is easy, but there are buses) you'll still see large areas devoted to sugar cane, which tumbles over the road in rural districts. Try to sniff out the local vanilla pods, too. "Bourbon vanilla" as it's called, is the real thing, intensely musky and aromatic and a far cry from the artificial taste you might normally associate with vanilla.

● **Music** Like the island's food, Réunion's music is a sign of cultural mixing. Listen out for local singers and musicians – by turns soulful and rumbustious – with reminders of French folk and sugar plantation slavery underpinned by accordions and hip-shaking rhythms. The two main styles are the bluesy *maloya* and *sega* dance music. The August music festival, Sakifo, should be on your itinerary if you're visiting then.

● **Food and drink** Réunion is the natural home of fusion food, with spicy Creole flavours infusing the excellent fish and pork. Wash your meals down with the island's lager, Bourbon, which you'll see advertised all over Réunion.

Routes in and out

The main airport is Aéroport Roland-Garros, a few minutes from the centre of Saint-Dénis. Most flights land here, including all those from France, the island's main air link beyond the Indian Ocean. There's also a small airport at Saint-Pierre in the southwest which has frequent flights to Mauritius. There are no ferry services to other parts of the Indian Ocean.

Red tape

Visas Required by SA nationals. Must be obtained in advance. Not required by UK, Ire, US, Can, Aus and NZ nationals.

Nearest consulates Johannesburg; Nairobi.

Other consulates Visas are issued by the following French consulates: Johannesburg (Ⓦconsulfrance-jhb .org); London (Ⓦambafrance-uk .org); Sydney (Ⓦambafrance-au.org); Washington, DC (Ⓦconsulfrance -washington.org).

Rwanda

Area 26,000 square kilometres
Capital Kigali
Population 11 million
Languages Kinyarwanda, French and English (all official); Swahili
Religion Christian; small minority Muslim
Government Presidential democracy

Independence July 1, 1962 (from Belgium)
Best time to go Jan–Feb & June–Sept (dry seasons)
Country code +250
Currency Rwandan Franc (RWF) US$1: RFr587
Minimum daily budget US$110 (for one week including a gorilla-trek)

Slightly smaller than its neighbour Burundi – with which it shares a language and cultural history – Rwanda is a country of farms and banana groves, red dirt roads and forested slopes. This quilt-like "land of a thousand hills" is Africa's most densely populated country, with almost every one of its ridges occupied by farming and herding communities of Tutsis and Hutus. In the east lies the more open, rolling savanna of Akagera National Park, and in the west, where the hills become more mountainous and patches of rainforest survive, live the remaining communities of the country's earliest people, the hunting and gathering Twa "Pygmies", who are these days celebrated for their skill as potters.

In Rwanda, one of Africa's greatest experiences – the chance of a close encounter with the rare mountain gorillas of the Virungas – is tempered by the terrible 1994 genocide in which some 800,000 Tutsis and moderate Hutus were murdered by government-sponsored paramilitary gangs. And yet so successful has the new, reforming government been at reconciliation – by their account there are no more Tutsis and Hutus here, just Rwandans – and at attracting foreign aid and invest-ment, that even the genocide has been co-opted into the tourist industry in the shape of memorials and museums.

The history of Rwanda and Burundi is long and opaque. Far from being the tribes of popular opinion, Hutu and Tutsi speak the same language, Kinyarwanda (known in Burundi as Rundi, or Kirundi) and have always intermarried, worked together, lived on the same hillsides, paid tribute to the same king and worshipped the same god. Clans, often incorpo-rating both Tutsi and Hutu, were more

Mean temperatures and rainfall

	Jan	Feb	Mar	Apr	May	Jun	Jul	Aug	Sep	Oct	Nov	Dec
Kigali												
max °C	27	28	27	26	26	27	27	28	28	27	26	27
min °C	16	16	16	16	16	16	15	16	16	16	16	16
rainfall mm	70	102	104	183	92	21	10	34	87	105	132	99

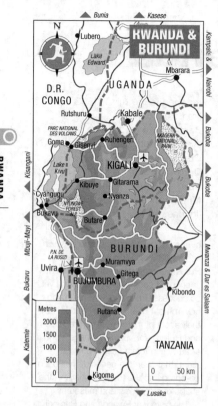

Map labels:
N
Bunia ▲ Kasese ▲

RWANDA & BURUNDI

Lubero
Lake Edward
Mbarara
UGANDA
D.R. CONGO
Rutshuru
Kabale
PARC NATIONAL DES VOLCANS
Goma ● Gisenyi ● Ruhengeri
AKAGERA NATIONAL PARK
Lake Kivu
KIGALI ✈
Kibuye ● Gitarama
Cyangugu ● Nyanza
NYUNGWE FOREST N.P.
Bukavu ● Butare
BURUNDI
P.N. DE LA RUSIZI
Uvira ● Muramvya
BUJUMBURA ● Gitega
Kibondo

Metres
2000
1500
1000
500
0

Rutana
TANZANIA
0   50 km
Kigoma
↓ Lusaka

Side labels: Kampala & Nairobi, Bukoba, Bukoba, Mwanza & Dar es Salaam, Kisangani, Mbuji-Mayi, Bukavu, Kalemie

be taller and lankier and Hutus shorter and stouter. The Belgians, when they couldn't make a physical determination of "ethnic group" for issuing ID cards, assigned a Tutsi identity to people owning ten cows or more and a Hutu one to the rest. Up until Belgian rule, many Rwandans had never given the idea of "ethnic group" much thought.

The myths of origin that seem to explain so plausibly why Rwandan society is the way it is – the Twa "Pygmies" were the original hunter-gatherers who lived in the forests; the Hutu arrived and cultivated the hills; then the Tutsis came from the north with their cattle and took the place over – now tend to be viewed in Rwanda as justifications for injustice, and myths pure and simple, rather than history.

Following the genocide, the Rwandan government's pragmatic, energetic style was refreshing, but its zeal is a cause for increasing concern – 2010 saw opposition politicians threatened and killed, and attempts to prosecute lawyers defending genocide suspects. While Rwanda is in many ways a model of nation-building in the aftermath of war and disaster, the story is not over yet, and there could still be a difficult road ahead. This is a truly remarkable country, with a growing reputation for eco-tourism, and well worth spending time in (and, if you want to track gorillas, a lot of your funds on). However, do read up in advance and watch the news.

Main attractions

● **Gorilla tracking in the Parc National des Volcans** Not just Rwanda's but one of Africa's outstanding highlights, "tracking gorillas" fails to convey the intensity of a close encounter with one of our nearest relatives, in its forest home, on its own terms. Set aside the necessary US$500, plan several

meaningful to most people (because they determined marriage partners, intra-clan marriage being forbidden) than the so-called ethnic distinctions that became so significant later. It is economics that holds the key, however: the Tutsis tended to own cattle, the cash of the pre-colonial economy, while the Hutus tended to be subsistence farmers or worked for Tutsis. Put another way, cattle-owners tended to be considered Tutsi.

Physical differences emerged too, over the course of many centuries of inherited wealth and intermarriage between families of similar economic standing. Although the differences are not as pronounced as popular imagination would suggest, Tutsis do tend to

RWANDA

months ahead (the small group visits are strictly limited) and prepare to be blown away – and in some cases exhausted. You can also track the rare golden monkey, and climb to the summits of the Karisimbi and Visoke volcanoes.

● **Akagera National Park** Covering a great swathe of Rwanda's northeast border area facing Tanzania, this is the country's biggest park, a savanna sanctuary for plains game, bisected by the swampy, meandering Akagera River. You're not going to encounter vast herds here, but head to the less bushy district in the far north and you should see topi and eland, while throughout the park there are buffalo, giraffe, elephant and some predators. Birders won't need reminding that the remarkable shoebill stork can be seen in the swamps, which also have plenty of crocs and hippos.

● **Gisenyi and Lake Kivu** The Belgians, delighting in the combination of equatorial climate and 1500m altitude, created a mini-Riviera at Gisenyi, complete with spa hotels and avenues lined with palms and eucalyptus trees. These days it's mostly busy at weekends, when Kigali's moneyed crowd arrive for waterskiing and windsurfing, as the Nyiragongo volcano, across the border in Democratic Republic of Congo, steams ominously above the lake. It's a perfect spot for relaxing – swim, canoe, bird-watch – with good hotels.

● **Kigali Genocide Memorial** The country's biggest memorial is also the last resting place for nearly a quarter of a million victims. Most memorable are the poignant display of photos, donated by their families, the inexpressibly sad and beautiful sculptures by Laurent Hategekimana and the memorial to the children who died, focusing on individual lives, favourite meals, and on how they were killed. Set in the context of humanity's

history of genocide, it's an emotionally draining but very worthwhile visit.

● **Nyungwe Forest National Park** With thirteen different species of primate (including chimpanzees, one group of which you can easily track), fabulous bird and insect life to be seen from the new canopy walkway and a host of other species, including the rare Johnston's three-horned chameleon and the Rwenzori otter shrew, this imposing mountain rainforest park is one of Rwanda's gems, and one of the biggest areas of intact montane forest in Africa.

Also recommended

● **Dance shows** Traditional Intore dance shows – Tutsi tributes by the kings' warriors – are most impressive when performed by Rwanda's National Ballet, though dancing displays are often on show at the major hotels. You may get a chance to see dance performances by Twa ("Pygmy") as well, which are much less stylized.

● **National Museum** Butare, in southern Rwanda, was an example of nation-building before the genocide, an intellectual centre where Hutus and Tutsis were more mixed than elsewhere. In the event, it suffered as badly, if not worse, than anywhere else and its reconstruction has been even more passionate as a result. The National Museum here is a much respected national institution, with superb interpretive displays of geography, culture, history and crafts.

● **Royal museums** Nyanza was the permanent residence of the *mwami* (king) from 1899 to the abolition of the monarchy in 1961. The Rwakali Palace Museum is a reconstruction of the traditional royal palace, and brings to life the kingdom at its peak at the end of the nineteenth century. The nearby Rwasero Palace museum is an interesting gallery of contemporary art.

Routes in and out

The only international airport is Kigali, which has increasingly good connections within Africa, and reasonable links with Europe. Overland routes are most significant to Uganda (open and always busy) and Tanzania (open, but with poorer roads). The border with Burundi is usually open, but you need to assess security in Burundi before crossing. The same applies to Rwanda's northwest border with DRC, which runs through the lakeside conurbation of Gisenyi (Rwanda) and Goma (DRC): seek clear advice in advance. The other border

crossing with DRC, in the south at Cyangugu/Bukavu, is much less secure.

Red tape

Visas Required by Ire, Aus and NZ nationals. Available on arrival if you apply online at Ⓦmigration.gov.rw at least two weeks in advance. UK, US, Can, and SA nationals don't need a visa for a stay of up to ninety days.

Nearest consulates Bujumbura; Dar es Salaam; Kampala.

Other consulates London (Ⓦambarwanda.org.uk); Melbourne (Ⓦrwandacg.org.au – advice only); Ottawa (Ⓦambarwaottawa.ca); Pretoria (Ⓦrwandaembassy.co.za); Tokyo (Ⓦrwandaembassy-japan.org); Washington, DC (Ⓦrwandaembassy.org).

São Tomé and Príncipe

Area 1001 square kilometres
Capital São Tomé
Population 176,000
Language Portuguese (official);
Forro, Angolar, Lingwa-uyé,
Príncipense
Religion Christian (mostly Catholic);
minority traditional
Government Presidential republic

Independence July 12, 1975
(from Portugal)
Best time to go Jan–Feb &
June–Sept (dry seasons);
Dec–March (best diving visibility)
Country code +239
Currency Dobra (STD);
US$1: Db20,500
Minimum daily budget US$60

Bursting with tropical luxuriance, their mountainsides dotted with wild orchids and their clear waters visited by turtles, the peaceful islands of São Tomé and Príncipe (see map, p.244) have enormous potential as an eco-tourism destination. Flights and visas are pricey, however, and while a handful of pleasant hotels exist, facilities and services remain limited, leaving this remote nation in rather appealing obscurity.

Set apart from the mainland, São Tomé and Príncipe lie south of Nigeria and west of Gabon in the Gulf of Guinea. They're volcanic islands, thick with rainforest, breadfruit trees and giant ferns. Rainy and fertile enough to yield huge crops of sugar, cocoa and coffee, but far too steep for mechanized agriculture, they once generated considerable wealth for Portugal at the expense of a workforce of slaves and indentured labourers from Cape Verde, Angola and the Congos.

Since the departure of the Portuguese in the mid-1970s, the islands have been treading water, their grand colonial buildings crumbling and development more or less halted. Most families live in simple timber shacks on stilts, scraping a living from subsistence farming and fishing. The prospect of future oil wealth may turn their fortunes around, but for now the atmosphere is relaxed to a fault: the people may be poor, but fruit and fish are so plentiful that they need never go hungry. The favourite local sayings – *léve-léve* on São Tomé, *móli-móli* on Príncipe – sum it up: they translate roughly as "take it easy".

Mean temperatures and rainfall

	Jan	Feb	Mar	Apr	May	Jun	Jul	Aug	Sep	Oct	Nov	Dec
São Tomé												
max °C	30	30	31	30	29	28	28	28	29	29	29	29
min °C	23	23	23	23	23	22	21	21	21	22	22	22
rainfall mm	81	107	150	127	135	28	0	0	23	109	117	89

Main attractions

● **São Tomé** With relatively few vehicles in private ownership, the nation's only substantial town – São Tomé Capital, as the locals call it – is spared the fume-belching traffic jams typical of African cities: instead, it has a seafront avenue lined with huge almond trees, squadrons of battered yellow taxis and gung-ho gangs of *motoqueiros* (motorbike taxi drivers). Traders make their way into the market with giant marlin on their heads and women offer ripe tropical fruit from shady stalls, while such expats and tourists as find their way here sip locally grown coffee in Portuguese-style cafés. The Fortaleza de São Sebastião houses the Museu Nacional, with an excellent display of historical artefacts. The town also a stunning avant-garde art gallery.

● **Roças (plantation houses)** Once the grand homes of wealthy plantation owners, most of the islands' many *roças* became state property after independence. Many have since fallen into a state of melancholy decay, but a few have been renovated as simple country hotels with masses of atmosphere.

● **Turtle-watching** Between October and February, marine turtles haul themselves up the sand on several of São Tomé's beaches to lay their eggs. Conservationists do their best to protect as many nests as possible from predators and poachers, moving some of the eggs off to hatcheries so that the young can later be released in safety. It's possible to watch a release, which always takes place at sunset on the beach where the nest concerned was found.

● **Parque Natural Ôbo** Almost a third of the island of São Tomé is protected by this ambitious park, which includes mountains, mangroves, a crater lake and rainforest rich in birds, butterflies, orchids and giant begonias. The park rangers organize guided hikes, birdwatching walks through the forest and trips through the mangrove creeks by dugout canoe.

● **Pico de São Tomé** At 2024m, this is the highest peak in the former Portuguese empire. Starting from the botanical garden at Bom Sucesso, the strenuous hike to the summit and back down to Neves in the north of the island takes two days, with inspiring forest scenery on the way.

● **Jardím Botánico Bom Sucesso** On the edge of Parque Natural Ôbo, the small but well-kept botanical garden offers a good primer to some of the most interesting of the floral species to be found in the park, including delicate orchids and jaunty bico de papagaiao (parrot-beak heliconia) flowers.

● **Príncipe** This beautiful, lush, craggy island is even more laidback than its larger neighbour, with sleepy villages and bumpy roads. On a spotless arc of palm-fringed sand in the north, there's a well-run, English-speaking lodge with a small, friendly diving and snorkelling centre.

Routes in and out

Both São Tomé and Príncipe have basic international airports; the national airline and cargo ships connect the two islands.

Red tape

Visas Required by UK, Ire, US, Can, Aus, NZ and SA nationals. Must be obtained in advance, or arranged in advance through a tour operator and paid for on arrival.

Nearby consulates Libreville; Luanda.

Other consulates Brussels (☎+32 2 734 8966, ✉ambassade @saotomeeprincipe.be); Franschhoek (☎+27 21 876 2494, ✉office @chamonix.co.za); New York (☎+1 212 317 0533).

Senegal

Area 197,000 square kilometres
Capital Dakar
Population 14 million
Language French (official); Wolof, Fula (Peulh), Serer, Jola (Diola), thirty others
Religion Muslim; small minority Catholic, traditional
Government Presidential democracy

Independence April 4, 1960 (from France)
Best time to go Oct–May (dry season)
Country code +221
Currency West Africa CFA Franc (XOF) US$1: CFA506
Minimum daily budget US$30

Senegal is the biggest holiday destination in West Africa, with dozens of beach hotels, mostly catering to French visitors, to the north and south of the relatively handsome capital, Dakar. Head north towards the Mauritanian border, and you reach France's first trading post in the country, the time-warped colonial capital of St-Louis. Turn south and the beaches splinter into sandbars and creeks in the delta of the Saloum River, a fine birdwatching area. Inland, much of the country is flat, baobab-specked savanna and peanut fields, but there are interesting areas, culturally, in the far southeast, where you also find one of West Africa's best national parks, Niokolo-Koba, with significant big game.

Senegal has a close and enduring relationship with France, and you could visit for a week or two and not notice anything very distinctive about the country. But as soon as you start scraping away the French skin, a fascinating nation is revealed: Senegal is a highly stratified society based on class and caste differences and dominated by its biggest tribe, the Wolof. They figure prominently in government and business and their kingdoms used to cover the heart of the country – an area now largely under fields of all-important peanuts. The Wolof control the Mouride Islamic Sufi brotherhood (you'll see its dreadlocked, colourfully robed Baye Fall disciples all over central and northern

Mean temperatures and rainfall

	Jan	Feb	Mar	Apr	May	Jun	Jul	Aug	Sep	Oct	Nov	Dec
Dakar												
max °C	26	27	27	27	29	31	31	31	32	32	30	27
min °C	18	17	18	18	20	23	24	24	24	24	23	19
rainfall mm	0	0	0	0	0	18	89	254	132	38	3	8
Ziguinchor												
max °C	33	34	35	35	35	33	31	30	31	31	32	31
min °C	17	17	19	20	22	24	23	23	23	23	21	18
rainfall mm	0	3	0	0	12	142	406	559	338	160	8	0

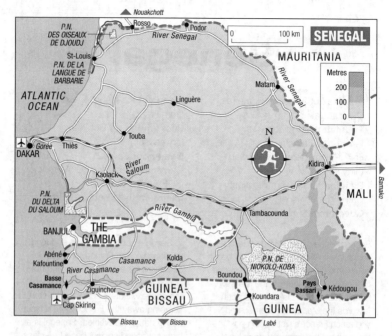

Senegal), while Muslim marabouts – holy men and religious teachers – wield exceptional power across the country, commanding bloc votes at elections and even shaping the course of the economy with their injunctions to followers.

French style and Islamic convictions coexist with great success, though both elements are introductions of the last century and a half. In the far south of Senegal, on the other side of The Gambia, a completely different tribal and social structure prevails in the forests and creeks. However, the conflict between Casamance separatists and the government means that some parts of the region are occasionally off-limits, and you should keep abreast of the situation if you intend to travel there.

Main attractions

● **Basse Casamance** Despite the secessionist rebellion that rumbles on (seek advice before visiting), this southern region is easily the most seductive part of the country, with flooded rice fields, dense forests, wonderful beaches and mellow local people, the Jola. Charter flights bring French tourists straight to all-inclusive hotels at Cap Skiring, but the low-cost village *campements* (see p.123), built in local style are much more memorable places to stay, and the money goes straight into the community. Activities include guided walks through the villages, birdwatching, canoe trips through the mangrove creeks and bike rides. Kafountine, one of the largest villages, has a music festival in February.

● **St-Louis** The fascinating old colonial capital of Senegal – a French city for more than three centuries, centred on an island at the mouth of the Senegal River – offers heaps of faded elegance, some great beaches, easy access to two national parks and an internationally renowned jazz festival. Don't come here expecting a chi-chi resort, though: much of the city is literally falling down and St-Louis is in serious need of care and investment. In an hour or two you can walk right round the island, which is linked to the mainland by the iconic spans of the Pont Faidherbe. Another bridge links the island with the most animated part of St-Louis, on the Langue de Barbarie, the spit of land with its markets and fishing boats that stretches far to the south.

● **Dakar** At once hustly, crime-ridden, slick and sophisticated, Dakar's great restaurants, outstanding music scene and alluring beaches give other African capitals a real run for their money. The architecture and leafy boulevards of the downtown "Plateau" area – a peninsula poking south into the Atlantic – are more evocative of southern France than Africa: to be reminded where you are, visit the IFAN museum, with its large collections of crafts and ritual objects, or any of Dakar's lively markets. Kermel has souvenirs, fish, flowers and fruit, Sandaga offers household goods, CDs and attaché cases made of beer cans, and the Cour des Orfèvres has Moorish silverware.

● **Live music** Youssou N'Dour's home town of Dakar has been a musical hotbed ever since his career took off in the 1980s, with artists from the region flocking to the city's clubs and studios. N'Dour's *Club Thiossane* and *Just 4 U* are two of the best-known venues to hear local *mbalax*, pop and hip-hop. Dress up, and don't arrive before 11pm.

● **Île de Gorée** A twenty-minute voyage in a small ferry from frenetic Dakar brings you to this UNESCO-protected island, sheltered from the Atlantic by the Dakar peninsula. Gorée's notorious history as a slave depot and its sleepy, slightly scholarly present-day incarnation – pastel-coloured mansions and a clutch of museums above the shore – make it an excellent and instructive escape from the city. The Maison des Esclaves (House of Slaves) was used to store "pieces of ebony" before they were shipped to the Americas, and the IFAN Historical Museum, housed in the Fort d'Estrées, takes you through the history of Dakar.

● **Niokolo-Koba National Park** One of the best wildlife reserves in West Africa, tucked far away in the southeast of the country, Niokolo-Koba's river courses, forest, bamboo and savanna are home to numerous antelope species, hippos and crocs, and small numbers of elephants, big cats and chimpanzees.

● **Touba** The burial place of the founder of the Mouride brotherhood, Cheikh Amadou Bamba Mbacke (1850–1927), is home to an 87m high mosque, one of Africa's biggest and finest. Once a year, half a million pilgrims pour into the city for the festival of Magal – an extraordinary experience for which it's best to have a guide.

Also recommended

● **Saloum delta** Equally accessible from Dakar or The Gambia, this maze of creeks and low islands is a fine area for birdwatchers: meander through the mangroves in a pirogue or simply enjoy the quiet life on one of the islands. There are quite a few boutique lodges and fishing camps and the Parc National du Delta du Saloum has good birdlife and turtles.

● **Thiès tapestry workshops** The *Manufactures Sénégalaises des Arts Décoratifs*, in the old railway town east of Dakar, is a world-renowned centre for tapestry weaving, and its output can be seen in public buildings around the world. The centre has a major influence on Senegalese painters, whose works are often selected to be redrawn and crafted in wool.

● **Bou El Mogdad** Take a river cruise up the Senegal River, from St-Louis to Podor, on the fully refitted, colonial-era Bou El Mogdad.

● **Parc National des Oiseaux de Djoudj** This is Senegal's ornithological showcase (open Nov–April), with 100,000 flamingos, thousands of white pelicans and a huge overwintering site for European migrants. Take a pirogue ride through the marshes to get the best access – and photos.

● **Pays Bassari** This little-visited part of southeastern Senegal – more like Mali in many respects – has low hills and traditional Bassari villages, making for great hiking and biking country if you're adventurous. The matrilineal, non-Muslim Bassari have major initiation ceremonies every year and a festival at the end of the dry season in April or May.

● **Surfing** The beaches on the northern outskirts of Dakar at Almadies, N'gor, Ouakam, Virage and Yoff are popular with surfers for their good breaks and there's a small scene, focused around *Malika Surf Camp*. You can also surf at Cap Skiring in Basse Casamance.

Routes in and out

Dakar's airport is a hub for the region, with flights from Europe, North America, North Africa and the rest of the continent. The city is also a crossroads for overlanders using the Atlantic route across Mauritania. The border with Mauritania is the Senegal River crossing at Rosso, but the Diama dam road bridge, near St-Louis, is less hassle. Travelling overland to or from Mali, the Océan–Niger train between Dakar and Bamako used to be the best link, but it's currently out of service and the road is good.

The main route from Guinea-Bissau crosses into Senegal at São Domingos, just south of Ziguinchor. If you're travelling between Senegal and Guinea, Koundara to Tambacounda is the usual route. The Gambia, surrounded by Senegal, ought to be easy to access, but road links are still not very good and there's still no bridge over the river on the trans-Gambienne route. Travelling between Banjul and Dakar involves a car-ferry ride to Barra on the north bank of the Gambia River. Between Banjul and Ziguinchor, the border crossing is at Séléti.

Red tape

Visas Required by Aus and NZ nationals. Available on arrival. UK, Ire, US, Can and SA nationals do not need a visa for stays of up to ninety days but if travelling to Senegal by air, your airline may require you to buy a return ticket.

Nearest consulates Bamako; Banjul; Bissau; Conakry; Nouakchott.

Other consulates Kuala Lumpur (☎+603 4256 7343, ✉senamb_mal @yahoo.fr); London (🌐senegalembassy .com); Ottawa (☎+1 613 238 6392); Pretoria (☎+27 12 460 5263); Washington, DC (☎+1 202 234 0540).

Seychelles

Area 451 square kilometres
Capital Victoria
Population 84,000
Languages English, French,
Seychellois Creole (official)
Religion Majority Christian (mostly
Roman Catholic)
Government Presidential republic

Independence June 29, 1976
(from UK)
Best time to go Year-round (peak
times correspond to European
holidays)
Country code +248
Currency Seychellois rupee (SCR);
US$1: Rp12
Minimum daily budget US$60

Basking in pleasant temperatures all
year round, the shapely granite islands
and coral atolls which make up the
Seychelles (see map, p.310) could have
been custom-made for holiday-making.
This faraway tropical paradise, way out
in the Indian Ocean around 1600km east
of the Tanzanian coast, is best known for
its achingly beautiful beaches – regularly
voted best in the world, and adored by
photographers. It's also good for diving
and snorkelling (March–May & Sept–Nov
have the best visibility) and hiking (best
May–Sept) and it has a commendable
conservation record, making it superb
for eco-tourism.

The population of the Seychelles is
Africa's second smallest, after St Helena,
but the combined area of the nation's
115 landforms is so tiny that its population density is among Africa's highest.
The vast majority of Seychellois – around
ninety percent – live on the island of

Mahé. A mixed-race people whose
language of choice is Creole, they tend to
lead a relaxed, westernized life, but there
are reminders of their mainland African
ancestry in their interest in supernatural
forces and traditional medicine, and their
stirring *séga* and *moutia* dances.

With its eyes set firmly on honeymooners and trip-of-a-lifetime
vacationers, the Seychelles is not a
cheap place to visit (note that hotels
require payment in pounds, euros or
US dollars), but if you're in the market
for a little luxury, you'll find plenty of
delightful cabins, guesthouses and hotels
to choose from, along with superb fish
restaurants. A good network of inter-
island connections makes island-hopping
straightforward, so you could start with
a few days on Mahé and then cruise (or
heli-hop) over to Praslin, La Digue and
perhaps some of the tiny outlying atolls
for a taste of outpost escapism.

Mean temperatures and rainfall

	Jan	Feb	Mar	Apr	May	Jun	Jul	Aug	Sep	Oct	Nov	Dec
Port Victoria												
max °C	28	29	29	30	29	28	27	27	28	28	29	28
min °C	24	25	25	25	25	25	24	24	24	24	24	24
rainfall mm	386	267	234	183	170	102	84	69	130	155	231	340

Main attractions

● **Beaches, Praslin and La Digue**
Stunningly good-looking, with topaz-blue
water, icing-sugar sand and curvaceous
rocks against a backdrop of vivid tropical
woodland, Anse Lazio on Praslin and
Anse Source d'Argent on La Digue are
world famous.

● **Scuba-diving and snorkelling,
Mahé** The reefs and rocks surrounding
all the islands harbour a rainbow of
fish. Beau Vallon in northwest Mahé is
close to some excellent sites, including
Shark Bank, where reef sharks are
common and whale sharks often show
up between February and November.
At Ilot, turtles, clownfish and moray
eels crowd a channel between granite
boulders, while Brissare Rocks is busy
with parrotfish, groupers and snappers.

● **Sailing** The inner islands of Mahé,
Praslin and La Digue offer safe moorings
in pretty coves and easy sailing along
gorgeously scenic coastlines, making
this a very popular place to charter a
catamaran or yacht, with or without
skipper and crew.

● **Birds and giant tortoises** The
smaller islands contain some wonderful
wildlife. Tiny Bird Island is named after the
enormous flocks of terns, shearwaters,
tropicbirds and noddies which nest
here between May and October, and
has a well-run eco-lodge and a famous
permanent resident, Esmeralda, an
ancient giant Aldabra tortoise. The
species' ancestral home, Aldabra,
supports a population of more than
100,000 tortoises and can be visited
with permission (see ⓦsif.sc). Curieuse is
home to a giant Aldabra tortoise breeding
centre that's open to the public.

● **Victoria, Mahé** The majority of
Seychellois live in or around their
capital, which has a splendidly British
atmosphere, a market selling fish and fruit
and a pleasant botanical garden shaded
by potently un-British coco de mer palms.

● **Morne Seychellois National Park,
Mahé** Hiking trails lead through this
park, which protects around a fifth of
Mahé's jungle-clad, mountainous interior
including the highest peak, Morne
Seychellois (905m).

● **Sainte Anne Marine National
Park, Mahé** Glass-bottomed boat trips
from Victoria take tourists around the
six islands east of town for snorkelling
and diving in coral gardens. Some of the
islands have luxury resorts.

● **Vallée de Mai, Praslin** This primeval
forest is home to the endangered black
parrot and all six of the Seychelles'
endemic palm species, but it's the
several thousand coco de mer palms
that everyone wants to see – their large,
buttock-shaped coconuts are a symbol
of the islands. An easy-going hiking
route allows you to circuit the park in
under four hours.

Routes in and out

International flights land on Mahé.
Outside the safe waters of the archipelago, yachts are vulnerable to attack
from Somali pirates.

Red tape

Visas UK, Ire, US, Can, Aus, NZ and SA
nationals don't require a visa for a stay
of up to thirty days (free entry stamp
issued on arrival).

Nearest consulates Dar es Salaam;
Nairobi; Port Louis.

Other consulates London (18 Hanover
Street, W1S 1YN); New York (☎+1 212
972 1785); Narre Warren North VIC
(☎+61 3 9796 9412, ⓔgb@bei.com
.au); Pretoria (☎+27 12 348 0270,
ⓔeconomist.embassy@ymail.com).

Sierra Leone

Area 72,000 square kilometres	**Independence** April 27, 1961 (from UK)
Capital Freetown	**Best time to go** Mid-Nov to April (dry season)
Population 6 million	
Language English (official); Krio, Mende, Temne, Limba and thirteen others	**Country code** +232
Religion Muslim, Christian, traditional	**Currency** Leone (SLL) US$1: Le3900
Government Presidential democracy	**Minimum daily budget** US$40

After a brutal civil war that devastated the country from 1991 to 2001 and saw a third of its population flee into exile, Sierra Leone (or "Salone", as everyone calls their country) is now enjoying peace and stability. With foreign investment piling in and the country's infrastructure being rebuilt, Sierra Leone is reclaiming its pre-war reputation as one of West Africa's most attractive destinations.

Yet, despite its long, sandy, palm-shaded beaches, lush forests and significant nature reserves, tourists are still few and far between. Most people that do come focus on the almost-Caribbean shores of the Freetown Peninsula, but it's really worth getting out into the provinces, towards the borders with Guinea and Liberia. Tiwai Island Nature Reserve and the Gola Forest in the south, the hills and mountains of the east, and Outamba-Kilimi National Park in the north are all very worthwhile targets.

The dramatic transformation in Sierra Leone's fortunes owes a lot to the resilience of a war-weary population. Apart from an interesting mix of indigenous tribes, many with strong connections to their ancestral roots and traditions, one of the most striking aspects of the social mix is the influence of the Krios – ex-slaves of diverse origins who were settled here in the early nineteenth century. The Krio language, partly derived from archaic English, has made a lasting imprint on Sierra Leonean society (and makes conversation a bottomless source of humour and

Mean temperatures and rainfall

	Jan	Feb	Mar	Apr	May	Jun	Jul	Aug	Sep	Oct	Nov	Dec
Freetown												
max °C	29	30	30	31	30	30	32	31	32	29	29	29
min °C	24	24	25	25	25	24	23	23	23	23	24	24
rainfall mm	13	3	13	56	160	302	894	902	610	310	132	41
Koidu-Sefadu												
max °C	32	34	35	34	33	31	29	29	31	32	31	31
min °C	14	17	19	20	21	20	20	20	20	20	19	17
rainfall mm	10	20	96	160	228	282	269	411	401	292	145	41

Map labels: Conakry, Labé, Mamou, Faranah, Bamako & N'zérékoré, Metres 1500 1000 500 200 0, GUINEA, Kabala, OUTAMBA-KILIMI N.R., 0 25 km, Mt Bintumani (1945m), Makeni, Koidu-Sefadu, Lungi, Bunce Is., FREETOWN, Tacugama, Voinjama, Bo, Kenema, LIBERIA, Turtle Islands, Tiwai Island, N, Zimmi, Bo Waterside, Robertsport, SIERRA LEONE, Monrovia

discovery for native English-speakers). Similarly, Krio religious beliefs have given a broadly Christian coloration to the whole country, especially in and around Freetown, although you'll see the mosques of the Muslim majority in the north and east. Indigenous religions are deep-rooted and widely practised, with feared and respected secret societies playing a major role in sustaining them.

Main attractions

● **River No. 2 Beach** Most of Sierra Leone's coast consists of a mixture of low sand dunes and mangrove swamps, backed by tidal creeks that penetrate far inland. The steep shores of the Freetown Peninsula offer a different scene, with one irresistible beach after another. River No. 2 beach, named after the mountain stream that tumbles down to snake its way across the beach, is one of the country's finest and most famous, generally quiet during the week, but busy-to-festive at weekends.

● **Tiwai Island Nature Reserve** Sierra Leone's most celebrated wildlife sanctuary, this small island in the Moa River is blanketed in thick rainforest. Day and night it rings with the calls of birds, insects and other forest animals, and is home to large numbers of chimpanzees, other primates and very rare pygmy hippos – which you're only likely to see if you go jungle-walking at night.

● **The Turtle Islands** These eight, postcard-perfect islands – an archipelago of white sand blobs, ringed with coconut trees and anchored in aquamarine waters – are home to fishing communities but remain totally undeveloped. There are one or two simple places to stay – ideal bases for fishing, snorkelling and letting the world turn without you.

● **Bunce Island** Squatting in the warm, briny waters of the Sierra Leone River estuary, tiny Bunce Island is the site of one of the country's most important historical relics – the ruins of an ancient slave fort, built by the British in 1670. For more than a century, thousands of slaves from the interior were shipped from here each year. With its overgrown walls and scattered antique cannon, it's an eerie place to explore.

● **Mount Bintumani** The highest peak in the Loma mountains, and the highest peak (1945m) in West Africa this side of Mount Cameroon, Bintumani is a superb target for an adventurous trek. The mountains offer spectacular forest scenery and excellent wildlife-spotting opportunities. Whichever route you choose, the climb is steep, wet and ultimately rocky: you'll need good boots, waterproofs, a sleeping bag and a tent.

● **Outamba-Kilimi National Park** The uninhabited savanna and jungle of "OKNP" is a paradise for ornithologists, though you're bound to see some of the park's twelve species of monkeys and various antelopes too. Chimpanzees are harder to spot, although their survival seems fairly assured: the park's forest elephants, by contrast, are seriously threatened by poachers.

● **Tacugama Chimpanzee Reserve** Beyond the old Krio villages of Gloucester and Bathurst, in the heart of the forested Freetown Peninsula, this internationally recognized rescue and rehabilitation centre offers protection to more than eighty chimps, which you can watch at play.

Routes in and out

Sierra Leone is quite isolated, with just two neighbours, Guinea and Liberia, neither of which are well connected themselves. Nearly all visitors arrive by air at Lungi Airport, the only international terminal, inconveniently located across the estuary from Freetown itself. If you're travelling overland between Sierra Leone and Liberia, you'll find regular public transport between the two countries and likewise from Conakry in Guinea. There is also plenty of passenger traffic on large, motorized canoes, known as *pampas*, between Guinea and Sierra Leone.

Red tape

Visas Required by UK, Ire, US, Can, Aus, NZ and SA nationals. Must be obtained in advance.

Nearest consulates Addis Ababa; Conakry; Monrovia.

Other consulates Beijing (☎+86 10 6532 1222); London (⊛slhc-uk.org.uk); Washington, DC (☎+1 202 939 9261).

South Africa

Area 1,221,037 square kilometres
Capital Pretoria
Population 49.3 million
Languages Zulu, Xhosa, English,
Afrikaans and seven others (all official)
Religion Christian, minority
traditional
Government Federal parliamentary
republic

Independence May 31, 1961
(from UK)
Best time to go Nov–April in the
west; May–Oct in the east;
May–Sept (dry season) for wildlife
Country code +27
Currency Rand (ZAR);
US$1: R7.7
Minimum daily budget US$55

South Africa is the continent's trump card. Energetic and brimming with self-confidence, no other country can match it for sheer variety. It holds some of Africa's very best attractions, neatly linked by an efficient, visitor-friendly infrastructure with good onward connections to other countries, making this an ideal place to start or finish a trip.

You could, of course, make this one country your sole focus. If your idea of the perfect African adventure boils down to a spot of Big Five game-watching, a few days on a glorious beach and a quick taste of history and heritage, then South Africa will fit the bill nicely. However, you'd be doing the place an injustice if you left it at that. Make

time during your travels to stride along some of its many stunning hiking trails, sip pinotage on its Cape Dutch wine estates, cruise its happening nightclubs or track down rare creatures such as great white sharks, southern right whales and African penguins, and you have the makings of a truly memorable trip.

Culturally, it's complex and fragmented. A favourite wry quip is that while apartheid may be history, it's not yet in the past. The collective healing process that began after Nelson Mandela led the African National Congress to political victory in 1994 has broken down enough barriers to engender some social mobility, but large-scale progress remains slow.

Mean temperatures and rainfall

	Jan	Feb	Mar	Apr	May	Jun	Jul	Aug	Sep	Oct	Nov	Dec
Cape Town												
max °C	26	26	25	22	19	18	17	18	18	21	23	24
min °C	16	16	14	12	9	8	7	8	9	11	13	14
rainfall mm	15	8	18	48	79	84	89	66	43	31	18	10
Durban												
max °C	27	27	27	26	24	23	22	22	23	24	25	26
min °C	21	21	20	18	14	12	11	13	15	17	18	19
rainfall mm	109	122	130	76	51	33	28	38	71	109	122	119

Many sections of black South African society, including significant numbers of immigrants, are linguistically isolated, economically disadvantaged and politically marginalized; in the run-up to the 2010 World Cup, plans to raze squatter camps and make other brutally cosmetic "improvements" to poor communities were greeted with outrage.

A conventional holiday will generally cocoon you from these concerns. Many visitors stick to the most popular areas – Cape Town, the Garden Route and the wildlife-watching belt of the northeast – and are shown around by safari and tour companies which are typically owned by whites, though they're likely to be staffed by educated and motivated individuals from a healthy mix of ethnic backgrounds. To dig a little deeper into the realities of present-day segregation and survival in the Rainbow Nation – and hear some inspiring solutions to complicated problems – you could take in a cultural visit to a rural district, or spend a day in a township with a local guide.

South Africa's transport options include everything from vintage steam trains to snazzy, air-conditioned intercity buses. To access the wilderness, you'll need to rent a vehicle or join an organized safari, both of which are straightforward to arrange. The well-maintained highway network makes road trips a breeze: crime against drivers does happen, but it's less common than rumours imply, with tourists rarely a target. Best of all, South Africa's range of places to stay is second to none, with a particularly good scattering of backpacker lodges, camps and B&Bs all over the country, and some gorgeous luxury bush retreats in the main safari belt, the northeast.

With several weeks to play with, you could loop around the entire country, enjoying the ever-changing scenery as you hop between lively cities, tidy towns and remote mountains, desert, wetlands or bush. But if your time is more limited then the best plan is to relax, whittle down your options, and save the rest for another time: this may be your first visit, but it's unlikely to be your last.

Main attractions

● **Cape Town** The locals say that Cape Town's good looks beat any harbour city in the world. It may be an ambitious claim, but the place certainly has glamour: its marinas and plush residential enclaves ooze cosmopolitan style and its backdrop, Table Mountain, is stunning. It also has a smattering of fine colonial architecture including Cape Dutch municipal buildings and jaunty, gentrified Bo-Kaap houses. Every year is a social whirl: highlights include a major jazz festival and Africa's most out-there alternative events. Add in the city's trendy shops, restaurants, beaches and comedy clubs, and boredom just isn't an option. There's also a large disadvantaged community, however; you can learn something of its story on a tour of the sprawling townships and squatter camps and a visit to the District Six Museum.

● **Kruger National Park** The star attraction of South Africa's safari belt is this gigantic, 414km long wilderness. If the main things you want from a game park are accessibility, a good choice of accommodation (of all types), escorted game walks, vast herds of grazing animals, and close-up sightings of Big Five animals from your own vehicle, then you're likely to consider it Africa's best. Because so many agree, it can feel crowded, particularly during South African holiday periods. Fringing the park are some highly attractive, more exclusive lodges on small private concessions.

● **Table Mountain** Cape Town's emblematic landmark is a 3km wide massif surrounded by steep cliffs and

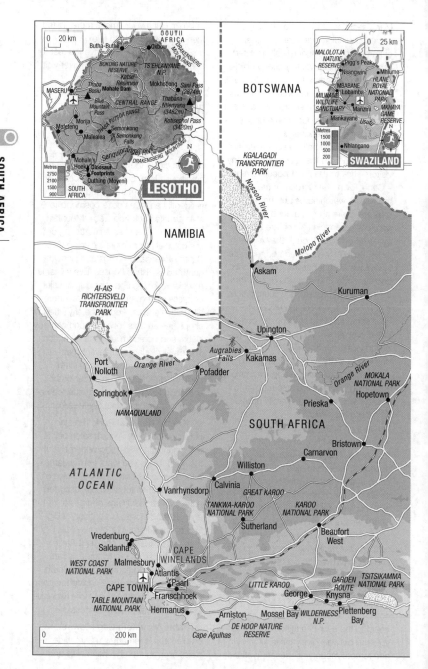

LESOTHO

SWAZILAND

BOTSWANA

NAMIBIA

SOUTH AFRICA

ATLANTIC OCEAN

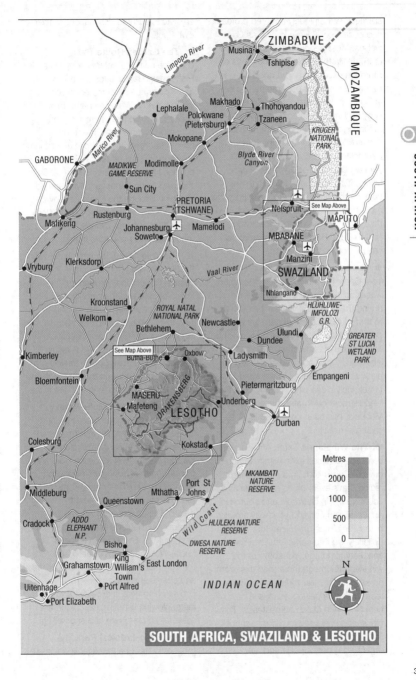

ZIMBABWE

MOZAMBIQUE

Limpopo River

Musina
Tshipise

Makhado
Lephalale
Thohoyandou
Polokwane
(Pietersburg)
Tzaneen
Mokopane

KRUGER
NATIONAL
PARK

Marico River

GABORONE

Blyde River
Canyon

MADIKWE
GAME RESERVE
Modimolle

Sun City

PRETORIA
(TSHWANE)

Nelspruit

See Map Above

MAPUTO

Rustenburg

MBABANE

Mafikeng
Johannesburg
Mamelodi
Soweto

Manzini

SWAZILAND

Klerksdorp

Vaal River

Vryburg

Nhlangano

HLUHLUWE-
IMFOLOZI
G.R.

Kroonstand

ROYAL NATAL
NATIONAL PARK

Newcastle

GREATER
ST LUCIA
WETLAND
PARK

Welkom

Bethlehem

Ulundi
Dundee

Kimberley

See Map Above
Butha-Buthe
Oxbow

Ladysmith

Bloemfontein

MASERU
Mafeteng

DRAKENSBERG

LESOTHO

Pietermaritzburg

Underberg

Empangeni

Durban

Colesburg

Kokstad

Metres

2000

Middleburg

Queenstown

Mthatha

Port St
Johns

MKAMBATI
NATURE
RESERVE

1000

500

Cradock

ADDO
ELEPHANT
N.P.

Wild Coast

HLULEKA NATURE
RESERVE

0

Bisho
Grahamstown
Uitenhage
King
William's
Town
Port Alfred
East London

DWESA NATURE
RESERVE

Port Elizabeth

INDIAN OCEAN

N

SOUTH AFRICA, SWAZILAND & LESOTHO

sprinkled with uniquely adapted proteas and ericas, collectively known as Cape fynbos. Most people reach the summit (1087m) via the cableway: the views en route are excellent, and a good prelude to the breathtaking panoramas you can enjoy from the plateau itself. Sunshine is by no means guaranteed – the mountain's famous tablecloth of cloud is often draped over the top – but you'll definitely see dassies, the mountain's endearingly fluffy rock hyraxes. For hikers, it's a strenuous two- to three-hour climb from the city to the top by the most direct paths, or a highly scenic five-day, 97km trek along the Hoerikwaggo Trail to Cape Point, overnighting at self-catering camps.

● **Robben Island** A half-hour ferry trip from Cape Town takes you to the island where political prisoners were jailed during the apartheid years. There's not all that much to see in what's left of the prison, but it's deeply moving to imagine how the inmates must have felt as they laboured in the courtyards or stared back across Table Bay to the sparkling, tantalizingly close city. The tiny cell of the island's most celebrated prisoner, Nelson Mandela, has been preserved in all its chilling simplicity.

● **The Winelands** South Africa's most venerable wineries all lie within an hour's drive of Cape Town, in a picturesque region that's every bit as enjoyable as its counterparts in California and southeast Australia. You can find your way around by car, or join an organized tour. You'll definitely want to sample the regional speciality, pinotage, but some of the wineries offer much more than this, from horseriding to cellar tours and gourmet food-and-wine pairing lessons in beautiful Cape Dutch homesteads. The pleasant colonial towns of Franschhoek, Paarl and Stellenbosch all have well-organized winery circuits and are

enjoyable, cultured destinations in their own right.

● **The Garden Route** The lush coastline near Mossel Bay, Knysna and Plettenberg Bay is, after Cape Town and Kruger, the most visited region in the country. While the name may conjure up thoughts of croquet and cucumber sandwiches, the region's main attractions are all about adrenaline – hurling yourself off Africa's highest bungee jump (Bloukrans Bridge, 216m); zooming along the nearby flying fox ride; zip-lining through the forest canopy at Tsitsikamma; or hiking the 42km Otter Trail. Other activities include abseiling, mountain biking and horseriding.

● **The Wild Coast** The stretch between East London and Port Edward in the Eastern Cape is the homeland of the Xhosa people, and the birthplace of Nelson Mandela and Thabo Mbeki. True to its name, there's a wildness to its gushing waterfalls, sandy beaches and broad estuaries, but this is also a peaceful, pastoral region, where you can stay in a simple community eco-lodge and go horseriding or canoeing with the locals.

● **Durban and KwaZulu-Natal** With its vibrant Indian community and laidback surf scene, Durban makes an appealing springboard for exploring KwaZulu-Natal. History and culture are popular themes: tours will introduce you to Zulu traditions or show you the monuments marking nineteenth-century battlefields. Of the many wilderness attractions, Hluhluwe-Imfolozi Park is the best, but the iSimangaliso (Greater St Lucia) Wetland Park is superb, too – it's the only place where hippos, crocodiles and sharks share a lagoon. The birdwatching here is excellent and the reefs, glowing with tropical colour, are great for scuba-diving and snorkelling.

● **Hluhluwe-Imfolozi Park** The tongue-twister of a name (shla-shloo-we oom-fer-lo-zi) is well worth mastering, because this an excellent park for wildlife-watching. Despite its small size it's a worthy rival to the Kruger, but with an untamed feel, and the highest concentration of rhinos anywhere; its simpler camps are unfenced, allowing animals to roam through freely. You could spend your days tracking the Big Five or exploring the superb network of walking trails, and your evenings heading out on night drives.

● **The Drakensberg** So daunting that the Afrikaners named them the Dragon Mountains and the Zulu called them the Barrier of Spears (uKhahlamba), this is the highest range in southern Africa. The loftiest peak, Thabana Ntlenyana (3482m) is in Lesotho, but the cloud-lapped crags and escarpments of the South African section offer more than enough drama to tempt hikers and climbers. You could try tackling the Amphitheatre – a long but not-too-challenging climb, with raptors riding on the thermals overhead – and gaze in amazement at the Tugela Falls, the world's second highest waterfall, which tumbles down a sheer cliff face in five stages.

● **Johannesburg, Soweto and Maropeng** Jo'burg has yet to cast off its terrible reputation for crime but, approached with caution, this fast-paced, flashy African metropolis is hugely enjoyable and a must for anyone interested in the history and social fabric of southern Africa. It's primarily a business centre, but culturally, it's hard to beat: catchy jazz and *kwaito* (township house) pound out of its clubs, and its arts scene is world class. Some of the most vibrant projects originate in Soweto: a variety of township tours and activities will take you there. The best of its many excellent museums, the Apartheid Museum, presents a thought-provoking analysis of pre-1994

South Africa, while 50km out of town at Maropeng there's a superb attraction devoted to prehistory, the Cradle of Mankind.

● **Music and arts festivals** South Africa's packed cultural calendar includes a wealth of concerts, parades and events, the largest and most varied being the ten-day National Arts Festival (🆆nafest.co.za; June/July) in Grahamstown. Alternative highlights include the Splashy Fen rock festival (🆆spashyfen.co.za; April) and Cape Town's oh-so-fabulous Mother City Queer Project (🆆mcqp.co.za; Dec).

Also recommended

● **Kirstenbosch National Botanical Garden** On the lower slopes of Table Mountain, this public park is beautifully landscaped and positively stuffed with rare fynbos specimens. In summer, the locals arrive laden with picnics, ready to enjoy open-air concerts.

● **Boulders Beach** Immediately beyond Cape Town's city limits, there's beautiful coastal scenery to explore, including Boulders Beach, home to a cheerful colony of African penguins – you can even join them in the water for a dip.

● **Namaqualand** In August or September, the thirsty plains of the Northern Cape, just south of the Orange River, are transformed by the winter rains, bursting into a mass of wild flowers in vivid, paintbox hues. Some displays only last a few days; you have to rely on local information to get the timing right.

● **The Richtersveld** This transfrontier park, which overlaps the Namibian border just south of Fish River Canyon, is a striking region of shimmering desert, dotted with sculptural succulents.

● **Augrabies Falls** When the Orange River meets the lip of a steep granite escarpment near Upington in the Northern Cape, it becomes a roaring cascade which is at its most dramatic from March to May.

● **Kgalagadi Transfrontier Park** On the border between the Northern Cape and Botswana, this park offers a taste of the austere beauty of the Kalahari; with a vehicle, you can see desert-adapted species such as Kalahari lions and oryx; leopards and cheetahs are found here, too.

● **Madikwe Game Reserve** Well worth the effort to get here, this is a great place to see elephants, lions and, with luck, wild dogs. As it's relatively little visited, it has an appealing, frontier feel, with several community-run lodges.

● **Blyde River Canyon** With half a day to spare you can drive along the lip of this canyon to the north of the Drakensberg, for awe-inspiring views of mountains covered in subtropical foliage.

● **Whale-watching** Between June and November, southern right whales cruise so close to the shore of the southern Cape Coast that you can easily watch them from dry land. Devotion to the mighty marine mammals reaches frenzied heights in Hermanus, which hosts a quirky whale-watching festival every September.

● **Extreme scuba-diving** The variety and sheer drama of South Africa's terrestrial landscapes is echoed underwater. Among the many adventures on offer are a few classics requiring nerves of steel. You can eyeball a great white shark from inside a cage suspended in the cool waters off the Western Cape, a controversial practice that is nonetheless hotly defended by some experts. Or you can get friendly

with gentler blacktips and dusky sharks near Durban in KwaZulu-Natal. The small town of Umkomaas, 50km south of Durban, gives access to Aliwal Shoal – a superb site for sharks. This stretch of coast is the launch point for trips into the annual sardine run, a melee of migrating fish and predatory tuna, dolphins, sharks and gannets that's strictly for experienced divers.

● **Baz Bus** South Africa's legendary hop-on-hop-off backpacker bus service (Ⓦbazbus.com) is a sociable way to tour on a budget, stopping at hostels en route.

Routes in and out

Johannesburg is the transport hub of southern Africa. International flights land at Oliver Reginald Tambo Airport, Johannesburg, Cape Town International Airport and Durban's new King Shaka International Airport at La Mercy. Road connections with Lesotho, Swaziland, Namibia, Botswana, Zimbabwe and Mozambique are straightforward, with intercity buses connecting major cities.

Red tape

Visas UK, Ire, US, Can, Aus and NZ nationals don't require a visa for a stay of up to ninety days (free entry stamp issued on arrival).

Nearest consulates Antananarivo; Gaborone; Harare; Maputo; Maseru; Mbabane; Windhoek.

Other consulates Canberra (Ⓦsahc .org.au); Dublin (☎+353 1 661 5553, Ⓔredmondh@foreign.gov.za); London (Ⓦsouthafricahouse.com); Ottawa (Ⓦsouthafrica-canada.ca); Washington, DC (Ⓦsaembassy.org).

Sudan

Area 2,506,000 square kilometres
Capital Khartoum
Population 42 million
Language Arabic (official); English, Fur, Dinka, over a hundred others
Religion Muslim; Christian and traditional minorities
Government Presidential dictatorship

Independence Jan 1, 1956 (from UK and Egypt)
Best time to go Oct–June (dry season, north), Dec–March (dry season, south)
Country code +249
Currency Sudanese new pound (SDG) US$1: SDG2.37
Minimum daily budget US$30

As the largest country in Africa emerges from fifty years of civil war, the southern third of Sudan was due to hold a referendum in early 2011 (as we went to press) on independence from Khartoum's Islamist government. Assuming the separation happens, Khartoum will be looking down the Nile to its North African neighbours, while the southern city of Juba will become the capital of a new, largely Christian and animist East African nation, with the mineral, agricultural and human potential to be a major player in the region.

In its unified form, Sudan is the most frustrating, beguiling country in Africa. Visitors will encounter monumental volumes of bureaucracy and procrastination, and permit and transport delays can upset the best-laid plans. Just as you finalize some arrangement, you hear that a bridge is down, a ferry out of action or a road waist-deep in mud. Don't worry, you'll be told, you'll soon be on your way, *insh'Allah* – if God wills it.

When you can travel, the deal usually seems worth it. In the dusty north, the ancient civilization of Meroe has left extraordinary pyramids in the desert and a host of archeological sites. Khartoum is an African metropolis unsurpassed in its physical setting, while the Red Sea coast has fine beaches and some of the best

Mean temperatures and rainfall

	Jan	Feb	Mar	Apr	May	Jun	Jul	Aug	Sep	Oct	Nov	Dec
Khartoum												
max °C	31	33	37	40	42	41	38	37	39	39	35	32
min °C	16	17	21	24	27	27	26	25	26	26	21	17
rainfall mm	0	0	0	1	4	5	47	74	25	5	1	0
Juba												
max °C	37	38	37	35	34	32	31	31	33	34	35	36
min °C	20	22	23	23	22	22	21	21	21	21	21	20
rainfall mm	5	12	45	92	149	121	135	144	116	102	45	7

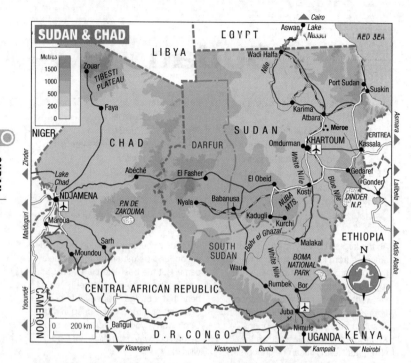

coral reefs in the world; both feel a world away from the fertile Nuba mountains and the forests of the south. Meandering the length of the country, from Nimule on the Ugandan border to Wadi Halfa on the Egyptian, the Nile is the longest river in Africa and the country's source of life, means of transport and cultural focus. And everywhere you go, the Sudanese are extraordinarily welcoming.

Obviously, you need to be aware of the recent war in Darfur, of the north-south religious divide (nuanced and ambiguous as it is) and of the country's potential for security meltdown – in the early 1990s, Osama bin Laden and other Al-Qaeda leaders were based here. Do some background reading, and pay attention to travel advisories, but make up your own mind: Sudan has a lot to offer the adventurous.

Main attractions

● **Khartoum** The biggest city in North Africa after Cairo – and reckoned one of the safest on the continent – Khartoum lies at the confluence of the Blue and White Niles and consists of the twentieth-century city, the expanding industrial suburb of Bahari and the old capital of Omdurman, with its enormous, noisy souk. Every Friday, Sufi dervishes perform their dances in the cemetery of Omdurman's Hamed Al-Nil Mosque and you'll always have the company of a few other visitors witnessing the frenzy. In Khartoum itself, the National Museum contains one of the best collections in Africa. Give yourself time to visit the Nile confluence, and perhaps walk across from the hyper-modern Al Fatih Tower over the bridge to Tuti island's fields and village houses – a quick immersion in rural Sudan.

● **Juba** The main town of southern Sudan sprawls from the left bank of the Nile towards Jebel Kujor – a craggy ridge of hills that makes a good weekend hike. Since the end of the civil war in 2005, the city has absorbed huge numbers of NGO workers and tens of thousands of rural Sudanese: all across the city the grass-thatched huts of the Dinka, Nuer and Bari compete for space with the old Greek trading houses and the tented hotels and guarded compounds of foreigners. Juba is evolving away from Khartoum every month, its markets bursting with energy. In a country that is officially dry, there's even a new brewery with a new beer – White Bull.

● **The pyramids of Meroe** An easy drive north of Khartoum brings you to the biggest tourist attraction in Sudan – an ancient site that is often almost deserted. The Royal Cemetery here contains nearly a hundred steep-sided pyramids – or their remains – marking the burial places of kings, queens and nobles from the third century BC to the third century AD.

● **The Red Sea** The marine life off the country's 800km coastline is just waiting to be explored: it offers some of the clearest seas and biggest shoals of fish, including huge schools of hammerheads, in the world. There are no established resorts: Port Sudan is the base for liveaboard dive operators, who usually include the pristine Suakin archipelago in their cruises.

● **Boma National Park** Remote Boma lies northeast of Bor, 150km from Ethiopia's Gambela National Park. It's part of the vast, seasonally flooded Sudd ecosystem, and shelters hundreds of thousands of animals, including plains antelope, large predators and elephants.

● **Dinder National Park** Hard up against the Ethiopian border, Dinder requires an organized trip from the capital or more likely your own well-equipped 4WD. Despite decades of neglect there's still plenty of wildlife here, including lions.

● **Nuba markets** Any market in the Nuba mountains is good, but Kurchi's, under its famous big tree, is particularly memorable. Come here at harvest season, or *sibir*, and you'll see young men using market day to look for partners by dressing themselves up outlandishly and competing in wrestling bouts.

Routes in and out

The main international airport at Khartoum has reasonable international connections, while the airport at Juba has flights to Kenya and Uganda. Overland routes are less certain. A ferry links Aswan in Egypt with Wadi Halfa (road routes between the two countries are closed). The normal route between Sudan and Ethiopia, via Gedaref to Addis, is open, as is, usually, the crossing between Kassala and Eritrea. In South Sudan, rough routes link Juba with Uganda (usually straightforward) and Kenya (open, but a tougher journey). Routes into Libya, Chad, Central African Republic and Democratic Republic of Congo are either closed or too risky to be worth considering.

Red tape

Visas Must be obtained in advance.

Nearby consulates Addis Ababa; Asmara; Bangui; Cairo; Ndjamena.

Other consulates Jakarta (☎+62 21 51 2099, ✉sudanind@cbn.net.id); London (⊛sudan-embassy.co.uk); Ottawa (⊛sudanembassy.ca); Pretoria (⊛sudani.co.za); Washington, DC (⊛sudanembassy.org).

373

Swaziland

So small that you can drive from border to border in under three hours, Swaziland (see map, p.366) is one of several African nations which describes itself as a continent in miniature. Its scenery is certainly highly varied, with mountains, gorges and waterfalls in the west, excellent for horseriding and hiking, and floodplains and savanna in the east, ideal for game drives and bush walks. Its treescape takes in conifers, umbrella thorns and sausage trees and its reserves are home to lions, elephants, rhinos and zebras.

But what really sets Swaziland apart is its monarchy, regarded as an anach-ronism by many African nations and with distaste elsewhere, but defended by Swazis with tremendous pride. King Mswati is famous for presiding over elaborate ceremonies where dignitaries draped in leopard skins and lourie feathers are entertained by ranks of bare-breasted dancing girls wearing cowrie-shell anklets and colourful pompoms. He's equally famous for lavishing profligate sums on palaces, cars, helicopters and Dubai shopping trips for his thirteen wives – habits that are hard to swallow given that most Swazis are trapped in chronic poverty. Swaziland also has horrific levels of HIV/AIDS infection, thanks at least partly to its cultural acceptance of polygamy and inter-generational sex.

Early attempts at tourism played on South Africa's (now defunct) ban on gambling, with the sleazy casinos and strip clubs of Ezulwini Valley (Valley of Heaven) tempting South Africans across the border. The focus has now shifted to golfing holidays and cultural entertain-ment, while the organizers of traditional festivals such as Incwala and Umhlanga pile on the pomp as part of a heritage tourism drive.

Mean temperatures and rainfall

Mbabane	Jan	Feb	Mar	Apr	May	Jun	Jul	Aug	Sep	Oct	Nov	Dec
max °C	25	25	24	23	21	19	19	21	23	24	24	25
min °C	15	15	14	12	8	6	6	7	9	12	13	14
rainfall mm	254	213	193	71	33	20	23	28	61	127	170	208

SWAZILAND

Main attractions

● **Ezulwini and Malkerns Valleys**
This pretty region is the homeland of the Swazi monarchy. The Royal Kraal, site of famous festivals, is at Lobamba, together with the National Museum and Mantenga Cultural Village, which showcase ethnic traditions; you can tuck into traditional food, watch dances staged by locals and peer inside a beehive hut. Nearby are the lovely Mantenga Falls.

● **Mkhaya Game Reserve** This, the most interesting of Swaziland's five private reserves, particularly for walking safaris, is better value than South Africa's pricey reserves near Kruger Park. Mostly grasslands dotted with acacias and knobthorn trees, it was created to preserve long-horned Nguni cattle, but is now also key to southern Africa's rhino conservation programme: both white and black are found here.

● **Arts and crafts** The quality and creativity of Swazi crafts makes this a good place to shop. Tempting souvenirs include handmade baskets, carvings and candles, or gorgeous glass animals and tableware made from recycled soda bottles.

● **Great Usutu River** On Swaziland's largest river, thrill-seekers in two-man inflatable rafts tumble down rapids (best Nov–May) ranging from Grade 2 to 5. Near the Mkhaya Game Reserve, the river runs through an attractive gorge – not that you'll be gazing at the scenery. There are crocodiles, but they haven't eaten anyone recently.

● **Umhlanga** Held in August or September, the Reed Dance draws thousands of *tingabisa*, unmarried young women, to the Royal Kraal, to dance for the king and present the Queen Mother (known affectionately as The Great She Elephant) with bundles of reeds as a token of loyalty. Incwala (Dec/Jan), an all-male harvest festival, is almost as spectacular.

● **Mbabane** The Swazi capital is a pleasant, hilly town which is far less crime-ridden than the cities in nearby South Africa.

● **Mlilwane Wildlife Sanctuary** As it's in the Ezulwini Valley and easy to get to, this is Swaziland's most visited park. The southern section is good for walks, game drives, horseriding and mountain biking across open grassland while, in the northern section, you can go on guided mountain hikes.

● **Hlane Royal National Park** Once a royal hunting ground, this stretch of lowland bushveld is a good place to track rhinos on foot. There are also lions, elephants and zebras, and breeding white-backed vultures and marabou storks. A variety of raptors perch in the ancient hardwood trees.

Routes in and out

At the time of writing, Matsapha Airport near Manzini was being replaced by the new Sikhuphe International Airport, 60km east of Mbabane. Overland travel from South Africa and Mozambique is straightforward.

Red tape

Visas UK, Ire, US, Can, Aus, NZ and SA nationals don't require a visa for a stay of up to sixty days (free entry stamp issued on arrival).

Nearest consulates Johannesburg; Pretoria (Ⓦswazihighcom.co.za).

Other consulates Kuala Lumpur (☏+60 3 2163 2511, ⒺEswazi@tm.net .my); London (☏020 7630 6611, ⒺEenquiries@swaziland.org.uk); Ottawa (☏+1 613 567 1480, ⒺEshc@direct -internet.net); Washington, DC (☏+1 202 234 5002).

Tanzania

Area 945,000 square kilometres	**Independence** Dec 9, 1961 (from UK)
Capital Dodoma	
Population 43.7 million	**Best time to go** June–Sept (dry season)
Languages Swahili and English (official); various tribal languages	**Country code** +255
Religion Muslim, Christian, traditional	**Currency** Tanzanian shilling (TZS); US$1: Sh1450
Government Presidential republic	**Minimum daily budget** US$40

Think safari, and chances are you'll picture Land Rovers, campfires and sundowners, open grasslands teeming with game and rustic lodges shaded by ancient acacia trees. All can be found in abundance in Tanzania. With over a third of its total area protected, this magnificent East African nation delivers all the classic sights, from wildebeest thundering across the plains and elephants framed by the snow-topped bulk of a dormant volcano to hot air balloons floating serenely through the morning mist.

Superlatives come thick and fast when describing this large and spectacularly diverse country. It includes two of Africa's most celebrated wildlife areas, the subject of countless wildlife documentaries: the Serengeti, home to the highest density of plains game in Africa, and the majestic Ngorongoro, the world's largest single intact volcanic crater. It also contains the world's longest freshwater lake, Tanganyika; Africa's largest reserve, the Selous; and its loftiest and most challenging mountain, Kilimanjaro. It has the largest concentration of mammals on the continent, and one of the largest populations of birds, comparable to Kenya's and second only to the Democratic Republic of Congo in variety. Furthermore, it's the best country in the world for seeing native chimpanzees in the wild.

Most visitors target the perennially popular Northern Safari Circuit where, if superb Big Five game-viewing or a full-on mountaineering expedition are

Mean temperatures and rainfall

	Jan	Feb	Mar	Apr	May	Jun	Jul	Aug	Sep	Oct	Nov	Dec
Dar es Salaam												
max °C	31	31	31	30	29	29	28	28	28	29	30	31
min °C	25	25	24	23	22	20	19	19	19	21	22	24
rainfall mm	66	66	130	290	188	33	31	25	31	41	74	91
Kigoma												
max °C	27	27	27	27	28	28	28	29	29	29	27	26
min °C	19	20	20	19	19	18	17	18	19	21	20	19
rainfall mm	122	127	150	130	43	5	3	5	18	48	142	135

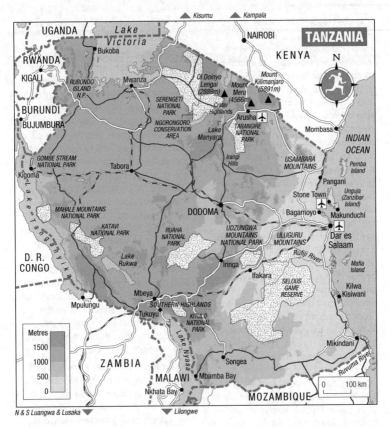

not quite enough, you can also opt for hiking through volcanic landscapes or flamingo-watching beside immense salt lakes. The south and west are less visited but there's plenty to discover here, too, including rainforests, scenic highlands and Rift Valley lakes.

A welcoming atmosphere complements the natural attractions. Tanzania is culturally diverse, with well over a hundred resident tribes, but peaceful and largely free of the ethnic rivalries which hamper other nations. The biggest challenge successive governments have had to face has been to tackle poverty and create jobs in a nation with sparse natural resources. Most Tanzanians

aspire to a modern, westernized way of life but core traditions remain, notably among the cattle-herding Maasai and the devoutly Muslim residents of the alluringly exotic island of Zanzibar.

Main attractions

● **Serengeti** Tanzania's signature park is an Africa icon for good reason: vast and beautiful, its rolling grasslands attract enormous herds of herbivores and predators. Together with Ngorongoro and Kenya's Masai Mara, it hosts one of the world's greatest wildlife spectacles, the Great Migration (May–Nov); during this time, more than

2.5 million wildebeest, zebras, antelopes and other grazers pour northward in search of fresh pasture, crossing the Mara River in Aug–Sept and returning later in the year to breed. The Serengeti and the smaller reserves surrounding it offer a variety of safari accommodation, from luxurious stone-and-thatch lodges to simple fly camps. The only disappointment is that the most popular areas can get crowded with visitors.

● **Ngorongoro Crater** This flat, open plain within the immense caldera of an extinct volcano is one of Africa's greatest conservation areas. Containing just the right cocktail of minerals to produce highly nutritious grass, it's a magnet for plains game. Big cats, buffalo and black rhinos jostle for position among the giraffes, zebras, warthogs and antelopes, and the drama of predator-versus-prey is acted out on a daily basis. Lions are so used to the comings and goings of safari vehicles that they use them for shade or as cover while hunting. The main wildlife-watching areas can get very busy, to the consternation of conservationists. However, accommodation is scarcer than in the Serengeti, with just a handful of lodges and mobile tented camps perched around the rim.

● **Mount Kilimanjaro** Its snowy cap may have receded somewhat in recent decades, but this grand old triple-coned volcano is still a striking sight, looming over the wooded savanna between Kenya and Tanzania. Whichever of the half dozen routes you choose, the five-to-seven day hike to Uhuru Peak (5893m), Africa's highest point, is a genuine challenge and somewhat pricey in park entrance, camping, guiding, portering and transport fees. Only two thirds of hikers complete the ascent; at high altitude, conditions can be uncomfortable, even if you're careful not to hurry. Those you don't make it still have plenty to enjoy in the mid-level forests and moorlands,

which feature giant lobelias and endemic giant groundsels.

● **Zanzibar** One of those magical places whose very name seems soaked in exoticism and romance, Zanzibar offers far more than just spice plantations and icing-sugar beaches. Many assume that it's an island, but in fact it's an archipelago of more than fifty islands and islets. Stone Town, the historic heart of the capital on Unjuga Island, is a treasure box of sultan's palaces and merchant's mansions set on atmospheric alleyways, their riches hidden behind beautifully carved hardwood doors; music fans will want to be here in February, for the Sauti Za Busara festival. The Forodhani market is always lively and Jozani forest, in the lush interior, is home to endearingly bold colobus monkeys. Accommodation options include historic house hotels and package-holiday resorts. The smaller island of Pemba has a simpler, more undiscovered feel, and some of the islets feature gorgeous retreats.

● **Tarangire National Park** This park is all about elephants, which gather in large numbers around its swamps and rivers, particularly when the grasslands are a dessicated golden-brown. Lions, wildebeest, zebras, giraffes, elands, kudus and many bird species make regular appearances, and thousand-year-old baobabs and classic, flat-topped acacia trees add drama to the landscape. Tarangire tends to be far less congested than the larger Northern Circuit parks, Serengeti and Ngorongoro.

● **Selous Game Reserve** The size of a small country – in fact both Rwanda and Burundi could be squeezed within its boundaries – this beautiful reserve is Africa's most extensive protected area. The focus of most visits is the inland delta of the Rufiji River in the north, where hippos, elephants and birds hang out. This region, which can be reached by train as well as by road or light aircraft, has well-spaced camps, so it's rare to see another safari vehicle when you're out wildlife-watching. As a bonus, you can take guided tours by boat or on foot, notably from Sand Rivers or Rufiji River camps. Elsewhere, the infrastructure is minimal; in vast tracts of the park, the wildlife are completely undisturbed.

● **Chimpanzees** Two primate research centres lie on the east bank of Lake Tanganyika, at Gombe Stream and Mahale Mountains National Park; at both, you can enjoy the rare thrill of tracking habituated wild chimpanzees. Visitor numbers are restricted, and neither are straightforward to reach – Gombe requires a three-hour flight or slow train from Dar to Kigoma then a two-hour trip by boat, while Mahale is five hours from Dar or Arusha by light aircraft. Gombe is more famous, thanks to the high profile of its founder, Jane Goodall, but *Greystoke Camp* at Mahale is more visitor-friendly, with expert guides and scouts. Other primates which make their home in the lakeside rainforest include baboons, colubus and vervet monkeys.

● **Scuba-diving** While its reefs can't compare with Mozambique's for sheer vibrancy, Tanzania is still a good spot for underwater adventures. There are impressive sites to explore off Zanzibar, which has a few high-end PADI centres, and Mafia, where everything's a little more informal. As well as the usual crowds of tropical fish and colourful oddities such as nudibranchs, you're likely to see turtles cruising by, although conservationists have to struggle to safeguard them from poachers.

● **Birdwatching** The concentration and variety of birds to be found in Tanzania's grasslands, wetlands, lakes and forests is such that anybody with a pair of binoculars and a bird book can expect to clock up well over three hundred species

in a ten-day trip around the Northern Safari Circuit. An excellent spot for fish eagles, herons and kingfishers is little-known Rubondo Island National Park on Lake Victoria in the northwest.

● **Cultural Tourism** Tanzania was one of the first African countries to create a framework to enable visitors to take part in authentic cultural experiences, or simply chat with locals about their daily lives. Through the Tanzania Cultural Tourism Programme (ⓦtanzaniaculturaltourism .com) you can join enjoyable and eye-opening community-run activities such as guided walks around coffee plantations or banana beer breweries, visits to local schools, cooking lessons, trips to hidden waterfalls and sessions of traditional music and dance.

Also recommended

● **Dar es Salaam** With attractive architecture and a lively music scene, Tanzania's largest urban centre is more comfortable to visit than most East African cities, and a more useful springboard than Dodoma, the administrative capital. In the pleasant German colonial Botanical Gardens, peacocks pose among the palms and ferns. The National Museum contains famous fossil finds including Leakey's Nutcracker Man, key to the story of human evolution. Down on the waterfront, traditional dhows and modern hydrofoils ply their trade, while inland at Kariakoo, the city's main market is a blaze of colour. For lovers of African art, Dar is also a good place to track down vibrant Tingatinga paintings.

● **Lake Tanganyika** Crossing a Rift Valley lake by steamer feels like a journey back in time. To act out your *African Queen* fantasies, you can take a trip down Lake Tanganyika on the vintage MV *Liemba*, a former German battleship that's said to have been the inspiration for the enemy gunboat in C.S. Forester's 1935 novel. When in good repair, it travels from Kigoma to Mpulungu and back once a week, stopping at villages en route.

● **Kondoa Irangi rock paintings** The Irangi Hills, in the semi-desert of central Tanzania, are dotted with rock shelters with petroglyphs of human figures, giraffes, elands and elephants, considered the northernmost examples of prehistoric San art.

● **Kilwa Kisiwani** Between the twelfth and fifteenth centuries, this Swahili island was a rich and powerful city state, controlling the regional trade in gold, ivory and slaves. The remains of its fortress, mosque and palace are still standing, though badly eroded.

● **Ol Doinyo Lengai** From Ngorongoro, you can hike through the austerely scenic Crater Highlands to Ol Doinyo Lengai ("Mountain of God" in Maasai), Tanzania's only active volcano, with wisps of smoke drifting out of its top. Nearby is Lake Natron, which provides an otherworldly haven for flamingos – they're far more tolerant of its caustic conditions than any of their predators.

● **Eastern Arc mountains** The Usambara, Uluguru and Udzungwa ranges in the inland region between Dar and Dodoma, reaching north towards Kenya, offer great hiking through ancient rainforests stuffed with rare flora, primates and birds.

● **Lake Manyara** Superb for birdwatching, this saline lake is a breeding site for lesser flamingos, pelicans and yellow-billed storks, all of which are present in large flocks.

● **Ruaha National Park** Far enough from Dar es Salaam to be relatively little visited, Ruaha is a good option for those looking for a low-key, low-cost safari experience with plenty of antelopes, lions, hyenas and birds to watch; with luck, you may see wild dogs too.

● **Mount Meru** At 4566m, a climb up Meru's dormant cone is a manageable alternative to the slog up Kilimanjaro. The lower slopes are pleasantly forested; higher up, there are fine views of the Roof of Africa in the distance.

Routes in and out

Tanzania's main international airports are at Dar es Salaam, Zanzibar and Kilimanjaro; regional airports include Arusha, Kigoma and Pemba. The slow and unreliable Tazara train service (see p.103) runs from Dar es Salaam to Kapiri Mposhi in Zambia via Mbeya. The overland routes from Kenya, Mozambique, Malawi, Zambia and Rwanda are straightforward, with buses connecting major cities, but the region close to the border with Burundi is unsafe, with a risk of armed robbery. It's possible to cross Lake Victoria by cargo ship to or from Uganda, and to fix up a similar deal across Lake Nyasa (Lake Malawi) to or from Malawi, but there are no passenger routes across Lake Tanganyika to or from DRC.

Red tape

Visas Required by UK, US, Can, Aus, NZ and SA nationals. Available on arrival at Tanzanian airports and the land border with Kenya (single-entry only). If arriving by land from Burundi, Malawi, Mozambique, Rwanda, Uganda or Zambia, visas must be obtained in advance. Irish citizens do need require a visa.

Nearest consulates Bujumbura; Harare; Kampala; Kigali; Lusaka; Maputo; Nairobi. No consulate in Malawi.

Other consulates London (Ⓦtanzania -online.gov.uk); Melbourne (Ⓦtanzania consul.org); Ottawa (Ⓦtzrepottawa.ca); Perth (Ⓦtanzaniaconsul.com); Pretoria (Ⓦtanzania.org.za); Washington, DC (Ⓦtanzaniaembassy-us.org).

Togo

Area 57,000 square kilometres
Capital Lomé
Population 7 million
Language French (official); Ewe,
Kabyé, more than thirty others
Religion Traditional (especially
Vodun, or voodoo), Christian, Muslim
Government Presidential
democracy, supported by military

Independence April 27, 1960
(from France)
Best time to go Dec–Feb &
June–Aug (dry seasons, south);
Oct–March (dry season, north)
Country code +228
Currency West African CFA Franc
(XOF) US$1: CFA506
Minimum daily budget $30

Which do you want first, the good news or the bad? The Togolese are welcoming to visitors, and have a history of close links with Europe, especially France. Togo (see map, p.288) has good food and a great climate (Lomé is in a moderately dry enclave and the hill country inland is wonderfully mild) and the whole country packs a diverse range of scenery into a small area – forests and hilly cocoa plantations in the southeast and grasslands with rocky outcrops in the north. And there's tremendous cultural diversity too, with cosmopolitan French-speaking Togolese in the capital, Vodun priests in the southern villages and traditionalist Tamberma people living a subsistence lifestyle in their fortress-like homes in the northeast.

The bad news is that Togo has been through heavy political weather in the last two decades: opposition to the post-independence dictator led to political repression, and further violent upheavals followed his death and the appointment by the military of his son as the new president. Togo is crawling towards democratic reform, but still has a long way to go compared with most of its neighbours. This shouldn't affect your travels, but it's still worth checking the news in advance.

Main attractions

● **Lomé** More like a provincial city than a capital, Lomé has survived its chaotic recent history and is still an enjoyable place with exceptional bars and restaurants. The daytime action is all around the Grand Marché, while evening sees the city fragmenting into neighbourhoods of bars and street-food vendors selling steamed cassava, *agouti*

Mean temperatures and rainfall

	Jan	Feb	Mar	Apr	May	Jun	Jul	Aug	Sep	Oct	Nov	Dec
Lomé												
max °C	31	31	32	31	31	29	27	27	28	30	31	31
min °C	23	24	25	24	24	23	23	22	23	23	23	23
rainfall mm	15	24	52	118	145	224	71	8	35	61	28	10

(a large rodent), *djekoumé* (chilli chicken), guinea fowl and *wagashi* (fried cheese) among many other dishes. Don't pass up the chance to visit the Marché des Féticheurs, West Africa's biggest animal parts emporium, presided over by fetish priests and their followers.

● **Lake Togo** With sandy beaches and good swimming and watersports, Lake Togo is a popular weekend getaway from Lomé. The main base is the relaxing village of Agbodrafo on the south shore, which has good hotels and plenty of pirogues to ferry you across the lake to the historic voodoo town of Togoville.

● **Tamberma country** At one time under the constant threat of raids by slavers from Abomey (see p.232), the Tamberma of Togo's remote northeast developed a striking, fortress-like house architecture that guaranteed their security and later their insulation from colonialism and modern ways. You have to make a little effort to bypass the tourist version of local culture: make for the village of Nadoba where a youth association offers guides and rents outs bicycles.

● **Missahohé Forest & Mont Klouto** A dramatic road snakes up through this dense forest, sometimes tunnelling beneath the trees. Built by the Germans before World War I, when they ruled "Togoland" (as it was known before the French took over), it climbs to within a thirty-minute hike of the summit of Mont Klouto (741m). The views into Ghana are sublime, and the area is renowned for its super-abundance of beautiful butterflies.

● **Akloa Falls** Fifty years ago, this sacred area was off-limits to outsiders. Today, you reach these spectacular, 30m falls along a wonderful forest trail. You'll still need to pay tribute to Mammy Wada, the spirit guardian of the falls,

in the form of an entrance ticket. Don't forget your bathing costume.

● **Aledjo** This welcoming northern village is impressively sited on a high ridge, with panoramic views. Ask to be shown the *Rocher de la Morte*, a rocky outcrop where witches were once thrown off the cliff, and the tree to which the executioner was secured to prevent him being pulled off as well.

Routes in and out

The only international airport, at Lomé, isn't well connected. If you can't fly direct, use neighbouring Accra or Cotonou as arrival points. Overland, the routes from Ouagadougou in Burkina Faso and Niamey in Niger are reasonable, and serviced by regular buses. The chaotic main border crossing for Ghana is at Aflao, 2km west of Lomé city centre. There are more relaxed crossings with Ghana on less frequented routes further north. Between Togo and Benin, the main crossing is Hilakondji, a fairly efficient border post midway between Lomé and Cotonou.

Red tape

Visas Required by UK, Ire, US, Can, Aus, NZ and SA nationals. Seven-day single-entry visa available on arrival.

Nearest consulates Accra. The French consulate in Cotonou also issues visas. There's no consulate in Burkina Faso or Niger.

Other consulates Ottawa (☎+1 613 238 5916); Paris (☎+33 1 43 80 12 13); Washington, DC (☎+1 202 234 4212). Visas can also be obtained from the following French consulates: Johannesburg (🌐consulfrance-jhb.org); Sydney (🌐ambafrance-au.org).

Tunisia

Area 164,418 square kilometres
Capital Tunis
Population 10.4 million
Languages Arabic and French (both official); Berber dialects
Religion Muslim
Government Presidential republic; in practice authoritarian
Independence March 20, 1956
(from France)
Best time to go March–June & Sept–Oct for Tunis and the beaches; Nov–Feb for southern and inland regions
Country code +216
Currency Tunisian dinar (TND); US$1: TD1.5
Minimum daily budget US$30

An easy hop from Europe and infinitely more tourist-friendly than neighbouring Algeria and Libya, Tunisia has been attracting the interest of adventurers for millennia. Over time, the native Berbers have seen a cavalcade of civilizations and settlers. The Phoenicians built Carthage; the Romans razed and replaced it, bringing roads, temples, olive groves and a thoroughly impressive colosseum. Later, the Arabs and Ottoman Turks brought Islam and Islamic architecture, and the French brought a new language and a colonial administration. Today, sun-seeking European holiday-makers come and go all year round, drawn by Mediterranean beaches which remain just the right side of over-developed.

Compact, but with more than enough appeal to compensate for its small size, Tunisia is a hospitable place to start a North African adventure, and it can be good value, too, particularly if you visit on a cheap holiday flight or package. It's easy to get around by driving, booking tours or taking buses, trains or *louages* (shared taxis), and you can get a good overview of the highlights in as little as two weeks.

Once you've torn yourself away from the beach resorts, there are World-Heritage-listed Roman and Phoenician ruins to discover, beautiful mosques, tangled souks and intriguing architectural curiosities, such as *ghorfas* (multi-storey mud-built grain stores which look like hobbit-houses) and the underground refuges of the Berbers. Some of these heritage sites are used as striking backdrops to annual music and theatre festivals.

In the south, you can get a vivid taste of the Sahara, with camels trekking across curvaceous dunescapes and eager tour guides escorting movie nerds to the sandy remains of *Star Wars* sets.

Mean temperatures and rainfall

	Jan	Feb	Mar	Apr	May	Jun	Jul	Aug	Sep	Oct	Nov	Dec
Tunis												
max °C	14	16	18	21	24	29	32	33	31	25	20	16
min °C	6	7	8	11	13	17	20	21	19	15	11	7
rainfall mm	64	51	41	36	18	8	3	8	33	51	48	61

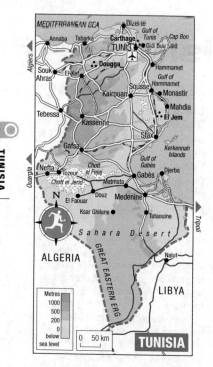

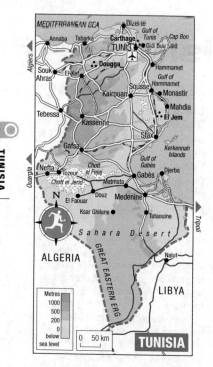

In fact, Tunisia is quite a hotspot for set-jetters: its desert landscapes and splendid coastal fortresses have also served as locations for *The English Patient*, *Raiders of the Lost Ark* and *Monty Python's Life of Brian*.

Main attractions

● **Tunis** The cosmopolitan capital is built upon many layers of history. While the city centre's mishmash of modern and French colonial style may underwhelm you, the thousand-year-old medina is one of Tunisia's most absorbing – a riot of noise, aromas and commercial bustle. In the city's smoky cafés and restaurants, you can choose between sipping French-style coffee or Maghrebian mint tea, munching on an

eggy *brik*, diving into a steaming plate of spicy couscous, sampling haute cuisine or drawing on a shisha. On the western fringe of town is the superb Musée National du Bardo, a palace housing the finest collection of antiquities on the Mediterranean, including an unrivalled array of Roman mosaics.

● **Carthage and Sidi Bou Saïd** Beautifully located on the coast near central Tunis are the tattered remains of Carthage. This Phoenician colony, founded around 800 BC, was torn to pieces by the Romans, who went on to make it their largest North African city. Despite harsh treatment at the hands of the original Vandals and other marauders, its eroded foundations and patched-up columns exude gravitas. Also on this coast is the idyllic suburb of Sidi Bou Saïd, with gorgeous whitewashed villas and bougainvillea-draped courtyards.

● **El-Jem** The third-century Colosseum of El-Jem, once the focal point of the city of Thysdrus and the third largest arena in the Roman world, is still impressive today: it's considered the most significant Roman monument in Africa. One side is an exposed honeycomb of arches, chambers and passageways where wild animals and gladiators once prowled or cowered. The other side features some rather over-restored seating, a blunder you're likely to forgive if you're here for the Festival International de Musique Symphonique (July–Aug), when orchestras take to the stage. Near the Colosseum is a good archeology museum, with well-preserved mosaics and vivid displays on Roman life.

● **Dougga** Just over 100km southwest of Tunis, the picturesque Roman town of Thugga, now Dougga, is deep enough in the countryside to have escaped urban encroachment and annihilation

384

by pillagers. Its golden columns stand out beautifully against its open, pastoral setting, which is green in spring, ochre for the rest of the year. The most admired building is the Capitol, but there are also a couple of dozen other temples, tombs, baths and an elegant open-air amphitheatre, built in 168 AD, in which classical dramas are staged (July–Aug).

● **The east coast** Southeast of Tunis, the coast curves gracefully around the wide Gulf of Hammamet, passing Kélibia, an unpretentious town with a disproportionately chunky fort, and Hammamet, a holiday hotspot with Tunisia's busiest beach. Further south are two places which featured in *Monty Python's Life of Brian*: the lively resort of Sousse, which has a decent beach, a historic medina and a first-rate archeology museum, and Monastir, dominated by its mighty Islamic fortress. Next is the charming resort of Mahdia, whose unspoilt old town is accessed via a legendary stone gateway. The large town of Sfax, 275km south of Tunis, has one of the finest (and least touristy) working medinas in North Africa, its lively lanes winding between beautiful Islamic buildings.

● **Djerba** This popular beach retreat, the supposed home of *The Odyssey's* lotus eaters, is a Mediterranean island connected to the mainland by a ferry or a causeway that dates back to Roman times. Scattered with palms, fortifications and squat minarets, Djerba (or Jerba) has attractively wild coastal stretches, while its main town, Houmt Souq, contains echoes of the Greek Islands in its fish market and its whitewashed domes, squares and facades with blue doors and shutters.

● **Matmâta and the ksour** Inland from Djerba, Matmâta lies at the heart of a region that's a must for *Star Wars*

fans, as several sequences were filmed here. Its architecture is another pull: the Berbers escaped invaders here by hiding out in homes in underground pits, their chambers connected by a labyrinth of passageways. Some of these are now guesthouses. Further south are the striking hilltop *ghorfas* of Tataouine, Douiret, Guermessa and Ksar Ouled Soltane. Chenini, with its whitewashed mosque, is one of the most beautiful of these *ksour* (fortified villages).

● **Douz and the Grand Erg Oriental** West of Matmâta, set against undulating dunes, is Douz, a gateway to the Sahara where you can go camel-trekking or desert-biking. This small settlement reverberates with drumming and pageantry during the annual Festival of the Sahara (Nov–Dec). To explore the desert in more depth, you can join a 4WD camping expedition south to the oasis of Ksar Ghilane.

● **Tozeur** With a beautiful setting, deep in the western interior, the fourteenth-century town of Tozeur is worth the six-hour road trip (or short flight) from Tunis. Its old quarter, Ouled el-Hadef, features many buildings with yellow facades made of handmade bricks set in intricate geometric patterns, and its private museum, the Musée Dar Cheraït, is a palace stuffed with treasures including grand furniture and Tunisian bridal jewellery. Day-trips by jeep take tourists to visit remote desert settlements and mountain oases and to Mos Espa, a set created for *Star Wars: The Phantom Menace*.

Also recommended

● **Tabarka and the north coast** The Mediterranean resort of Tabarka, near the Algerian border, is a favourite of Tunisians and Algerians. Its attractive seafront has a Genoese fort, a long curve of sandy beach and a clutch of lively cafés, The long-running Tabarka Jazz Festival (July–Aug), attracts large crowds of locals and features African jazz, latin and *raï* bands, including big names. East of Tabarka is Cap Serrat, where a splendid headland overlooks a clean and quiet sandy beach. Beyond this is Bizerte a port with a waterfront kasbah (fortress) and fine medina architecture, and Cap-Blanc, the northernmost tip of Africa.

● **El-Kef** The imposing, honey-coloured Byzantine kasbah of El-Kef (or Le Kef) perches on Jebel Dyr hill close to the Algerian border, west of Tunis, with the old town tumbling down before it. A stroll around the stepped and cobbled streets of the walled city is an enchanting experience.

● **Kairouan** For a taste of authentic Tunisia, this town is well worth a short stay. Its status as one of the holiest sites in the Islamic world means that, despite its unpromising location on a sun-baked plain around 150km south of Tunis, it doesn't need to work hard to attract reverent visitors. Its serene focus, the Great Mosque (all of which but the Prayer Hall is open to non-Muslims), built in 836 AD, stands in a charming blue and white medina with splendid Aghlabid architecture and a long tradition of carpet-making.

● **Hammams** A visit to the local hammam (public baths and steam room) for a soak and a massage is a weekly ritual for most Tunisians, and visitors are usually welcome. Some, especially in

Tunis, are exclusively for either males or females; others have different hours for men and women.

Routes in and out

International flights land at Carthage Airport (Tunis), Djerba-Zarzis and Habib Bourguiba (Monastir). The southern region close to the Algeria border can be unsafe (there is a risk of kidnap) and should only be visited with permission from the Tunisian authorities and in the company of an approved guide or tour operator. The border with Algeria may be closed at short notice. Overland travel between Libya and Tunisia is more straightforward.

Red tape

Visas Required by Aus, NZ and SA nationals. Available on arrival. UK/Ire citizens do not require a visa for a stay of up to three months; US/Can citizens do not need a visa for a stay of up to four months.

Nearest consulates Algiers; Cairo; Rabat. The consulate in Tripoli does not normally issue visas to foreigners.

Other consulates Edgecliff, NSW (☎+61 2 9327 1258, ✉constunsyd @bigpond.com); London (☎020 7584 8117, ✉london@tunisianembassy .co.uk); Ottawa (☎+1 613 237 0330); Pretoria (☎+27 12 342 6282); Tokyo (☎+81 3 3511 6622, ✉tunisia.or.jp); Washington, DC (☎+1 202 862 1850).

Uganda

Area 236,000 square kilometres	**Independence** Oct 9, 1962 (from UK)
Capital Kampala	**Best time to go** Dec–Feb & June–Aug (dry seasons)
Population 33 million	
Languages English and Swahili (official); Ganda, Nyankore, Soga and more than thirty others	**Dialling code** +256
	Currency Uganda Shilling (UGX) US$1: Ush2250
Religion Large majority Christian; Muslim and traditional minorities	**Minimum daily budget** US$90 (for a ten-day stay including gorilla-tracking)
Government Presidential democracy	

Uganda is East Africa's great secret – a country of welcoming people, historic kingdoms, glacier-capped mountains and Rousseau-esque rainforests, lakes and waterfalls, with a slew of wonderful national parks to boot. From the visitor's perspective, with its gorilla-tracking and the foremost rainforest tourism in Africa, as well as classic safari parks and adrenaline sports, Uganda is only missing a sea coast, and even on that score the Ssese islands are compensation. The country undoubtedly deserves far more visitors than it currently receives: the next few years are likely to see a tourism boom if security stays as good, generally, as it is today.

The country certainly had a promising start, but for decades suffered indescribably at the hands of despots. When the British built the railway line from Mombasa in the 1890s, Kenya

and its Rift Valley were in the way. Uganda, a country described by the young Winston Churchill as the "Pearl of Africa", was the target destination, and the railway was Britain's response to fears that Germany would become established there and seize control of the headwaters of the Nile. Ultimately, Britain's divisive indirect government in Uganda, which co-opted the Baganda people as stooges of empire by giving them special status, also placed restrictions on the country's colonization and led to rapid social change in the south, especially in the towns.

The first 25 years of independence were not a happy period. The first prime minister, Milton Obote, deploying a mix of cod socialism and thuggery, was unable to get a grip on the country. His army chief of staff, Idi Amin, kicked him out in 1971, expelled the entire Asian

Mean temperatures and rainfall

	Jan	Feb	Mar	Apr	May	Jun	Jul	Aug	Sep	Oct	Nov	Dec
Kampala												
max °C	28	28	27	26	26	25	25	26	27	27	27	27
min °C	18	18	18	18	17	17	17	16	17	17	17	17
rainfall mm	45	62	128	177	148	73	46	86	90	95	124	100

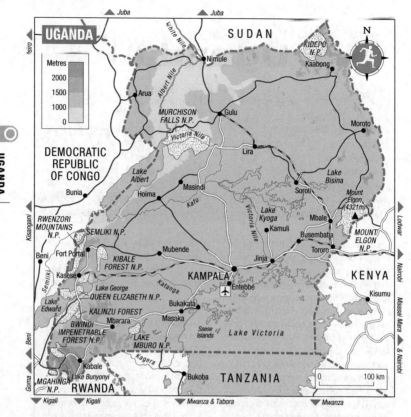

population and went on to indulge his taste for terror for a full eight years, murdering hundreds of thousands of Ugandans. As the country's infrastructure disintegrated, Amin started a diversionary war with Tanzania which led swiftly to his overthrow and exile. An even worse period followed, in which Obote returned to power and faced an internal rebellion in which thousands were massacred. Only when the rebels' National Resistance Movement was finally successful under Yoweri Museveni did peace return.

President Museveni did a great deal to heal the wounds, restoring most of the old kingdoms, welcoming back Ugandan Asians, freeing the media, rebuilding

the infrastructure and running the best anti-HIV programme in Africa. But after 25 years in power, the old man is still there, and that's now a problem in itself – though not for the USA, for whom he is a key ally.

Over the past two decades, Uganda has been embroiled in the huge regional war in Democratic Republic of Congo over mineral rights, provided the bulk of the peace-keeping troops for Somalia, and faced the "Christian-apocalyptic" guerrillas of the Lord's Resistance Army in northern Uganda. The LRA rebels, with their kidnapped child soldiers and sex slaves, have now been driven into DRC and Central African Republic, making virtually the whole country safe for the first time since independence.

Main attractions

● **Kampala** The gentlest and safest big city in East Africa, spreading across a hilly landscape, Kampala is also in many ways the most impressive, with its sprouting high-rises and malls. You're bound to pass through at least once, so make the most of the ethnographic collections at the National Museum, the city's art galleries and nightlife and a fantastic range of restaurants. Sadly, several traditional buildings at the city's premier cultural attraction, the Kasubi tombs – the royal tombs of the Baganda kings – were destroyed by fire in 2010. Restoration work is planned.

● **Bwindi Gorilla-tracking** The evocatively named Bwindi Impenetrable Forest, a rugged mountain jungle, is home to the most habituated groups of mountain gorillas in Africa. There are four groups, which just twenty-four visitors per day, in groups of eight, are permitted to visit (one group gets a break from the social whirl each day). As in Rwanda, tracking gorillas in Bwindi is expensive ($500 for the day), highly controlled and a big commitment: you can book up to two years ahead. Getting close to the gorillas is an indescribable experience, and the feeling of connection is palpable, but Bwindi is not just about gorillas: the forest is an ancient bio-diversity hotspot and will keep any amateur naturalist dribbling with enthusiasm for its extraordinarily rich fauna and flora.

● **Queen Elizabeth National Park** This, the busiest safari park in Uganda, under formal protection for more than eighty years, has a greater variety of large mammals than any other. Several thousand elephants, hundreds of lions, chimpanzees at close range and rare sitatunga antelope are just the standouts, together with six hundred species of birds. QENP also offers spectacular landscapes, including savanna and lakeshore, swamps and crater lakes, the 30km Kazinga channel, on which you can take game-viewing and birdwatching boat trips, and the stunning, forest-filled Kyambura Gorge, where chimp-tracking takes place. On the Ishasha plains in the far south, the local lions have taken to tree-climbing – a highly photogenic, learned behaviour that also occurs at Kidepo and in other East African parks.

● **Jinja and the Victoria Nile** The Nile starts its 6000km journey to the Mediterranean at Jinja, on the north shore of Lake Victoria, where, already 300m wide, it rushes out of the lake, through the Nalubale (Owen Falls) dam, between banks of greenery and over churning rapids. White-water rafting has become hugely popular on the Victoria Nile, with 50km of river to navigate, including no less than four Grade 5 rapids. Other activities – kayaking, river boarding, bungee jumping, quad-biking and riding – are now available too, together with a growing range of backpackers' lodges and camps.

● **Murchison Falls National Park** The biggest park in Uganda was in dire straits in the 1970s and 1980s, when rebels and government forces used it as a larder and poachers reduced the elephants from 15,000 to fewer than 1000. Today, it's triumphantly in the ascendant and easily Uganda's best safari destination. Named after the chasm in the wall of the Rift Valley where the Nile thunderously drops into Lake Albert, the park has it all: plains game and lions, chimp-tracking, amazing birdlife (more than 450 species, including shoebill storks), large numbers of hippos and huge crocodiles, and boat trips to view the falls.

● **Kibale Forest National Park and Kasenda lakes** A sanctuary of dense mountain rainforest in the foothills of the Rwenzoris near Fort Portal, Kibale is East Africa's best location for monkeys, with twelve species, and one of the best places in Africa to see chimpanzees in the wild. Chimp-tracking walks set off twice daily, and chimps are seen more often than not, usually foraging high in the canopy. West of the park, the Kasenda crater lakes are a chain of two dozen, ranging from a kilometre across to not much bigger than a football pitch, with excellent hiking and birdwatching opportunities.

● **Semliki National Park** Wherever you go in Uganda, natural beauty and scenic splendour are all around, but Semliki N.P. (not to be confused with Semliki Wildlife Reserve to the northeast) is outstanding. Tucked into a corner of the country between the DRC border and the Rwenzori range looming above it to the south, this is the place to experience the Congo rainforest without crossing the border. Many Semliki birds and mammals are found nowhere else in the country. Other attractions near the park include the hot springs at Sempaya and, with discretion, the village of Ntandi, whose Basua ("Pygmy") inhabitants came here in the 1920s from the then-Belgian Congo. They welcome visitors and are gradually organizing themselves to host and guide tourists.

● **Kidepo National Park** Despite its remote location in a border region notorious for cattle rustling and tribal conflict, Kidepo – a great plain of grasslands, surrounded by mountains and traced by streams – is now safe and very much worth the trip. In the southern part of the park, the richest area for plains animals, you'll be treated to elephants, buffalo, tree-climbing lions, Uganda's only cheetahs, and the park's remarkable range of birdlife – more than 460 species, including the black variety of the magnificent crowned crane.

Also recommended

● **Entebbe** The old colonial capital – and site of the country's international airport – sprawls lazily across a finger of land pointing south into Lake Victoria. Excellent lakeshore backpacker lodges and hotels offer a good alternative to Kampala, and the botanical gardens are a lovely spot for a few hours between flights.

● **Lake Bunyonyi** Had it with hippos? No longer impressed with lurking crocs whenever you want to swim? Bunyonyi, a high-altitude lake with impeccable budget-tourism credentials, is for you. Located near Kabale, in the southwest corner of the county, this bilharzia-free, island-scattered lake is perfect for lazy swims and a bit of R & R from the rigours of African travel.

● **Mgahinga Gorilla National Park** Contiguous with Rwanda's Parc National des Volcans and DRC's Parc National des Virunga, tiny Mgahinga protects a host of mountain forest animals – and a somewhat peripatetic population of mountain gorillas. When these are in Rwanda, golden monkey tracking and visits to the park's caves and peaks are the order of the day. A new Batwa nature trail is run by the local "Pygmy" community.

● **Mount Elgon National Park** This colossal extinct volcano straddles the Kenyan border northeast of Tororo. Unlike Mount Kenya, and even less like the crowded slopes of Kilimanjaro, you'll usually have Mount Elgon (4321m) and its weird and wonderful Afro-Alpine plant life to yourself. Be prepared for cold weather (the warm springs at the top are a good prize) and beautiful views, and climb slowly to acclimatize.

● **Mabamba Swamp** Just west of Kampala, this will be on your itinerary already if you're a birder: it's the one place in the country where you can pretty much guarantee an encounter with the most ridiculous, prehistoric-looking bird in the world – the shoebill stork – usually from a small dugout, as it's poled through the reeds.

● **Rwenzori Mountains National Park** Mount Kilimanjaro (5893m) and Mount Kenya (5199m) – freestanding peaks of volcanic origin – might be higher, but the "Mountains of the Moon" are the highest *range* of mountains in Africa (Margherita peak is 5109m). Forming the Congo-Nile watershed, the rugged peaks are often wet or icy, and you'll need to be fit and well prepared.

● **Ssese Islands** An archipelago of more than eighty islands and islets set in the bath-warm waters of Lake Victoria, the Sseses are an unexpected delight close to Entebbe, with sandy bays and superb birdlife, and a number of very nice places to stay, from backpacker lodges to luxury camps.

Routes in and out

Uganda's only international airport is Entebbe, 35km south of Kampala on the lakeshore. There are good air links with the rest of East Africa but flights to other parts of the continent and beyond Africa are likely to be via Nairobi or Addis. Uganda's overland routes are straight-forward to Kenya, Tanzania and Rwanda, and increasingly straightforward to Juba in South Sudan. Routes into DRC are open, but insecure: seek local advice before crossing.

Red tape

Visas Required by UK, Ire, US, Can, Aus, NZ and SA nationals. Available on arrival.

Nearest consulates Dar es Salaam; Khartoum; Kigali; Nairobi.

Other consulates Canberra (☎+61 2 6286 1234, ✉ugandahc@velocitynet.com.au); London (🌐ugandahigh commission.co.uk); Ottawa (🌐ugandahighcommission.com); Pretoria (🌐uganda.org.za); Washington, DC (🌐ugandaembassy.com).

Zambia

Area 752,614 square kilometres
Capital Lusaka
Population 12.9 million
Language English (official); various tribal languages
Religion Christian; Muslim and Hindu minorities
Government Presidential republic

Independence Oct 24, 1964 (from UK)
Best time to go Aug–Oct (late dry season) for wildlife; Aug–Dec (late dry and early rainy season) for birds.
Country code +260
Currency Zambian kwacha (ZMK); US$1: ZK5100
Minimum daily budget US$40

If you like the idea of a rugged, back-to-basics safari, exploring pristine bush on foot, watching lions stalk their prey or marvelling at hippos honking and wallowing in a broad, brown river, then Zambia may well fit the bill. This under-rated nation has some of the finest guides in the business, as skilled at inter-preting the intricacies of insect behaviour as at tracking down and pointing out big game. It also has magnificent national parks: Kafue and South Luangwa are among the best places to see leopards in Africa, and Lower Zambezi is superb for elephants, hippos and wild dogs.

Most remarkable of all, there will be times when it feels as if you're the only tourist for miles – an experience you rarely, if ever, get to savour in the busier wildlife-watching areas of Kenya, Tanzania and South Africa. In Zambia, the only place which ever gets at all congested with visitors is Livingstone, which lies within earshot of the mighty curtain of water that is Victoria Falls.

Unlike some of its neighbours, Zambia has been more or less at peace for decades, making its towns relaxed places to spend time. The nation's poverty, however, means that in much of the country the infrastructure is basic. Distances are long and the roads can be arduous, making hopping around by light aircraft by far the fastest – and sometimes the cheapest – option.

For a real adventure, visit in the rainy season (Dec–April). At this time, unsealed roads may be impassable and many camps are closed, particularly in the north, but those fly-in camps that lie on reasonably high ground and are set up for river trips come into their own. The rains bring vivid new life, sights and sounds to the bush, with flowers blooming, butter-flies in full flight, youngsters (including buffalo calves, zebra foals, antelope

Mean temperatures and rainfall

Lusaka	Jan	Feb	Mar	Apr	May	Jun	Jul	Aug	Sep	Oct	Nov	Dec
max °C	26	26	26	26	25	23	23	25	29	31	29	27
min °C	17	17	17	15	12	10	9	12	15	18	18	17
rainfall mm	231	191	142	18	3	0	0	0	0	10	91	150

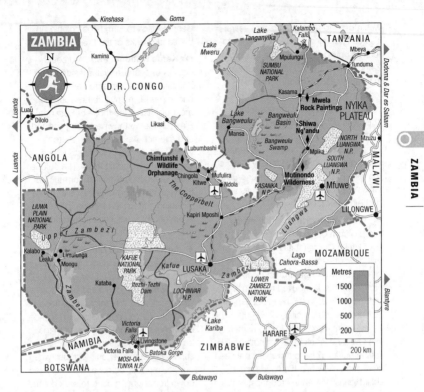

fawns and warthog piglets) scampering around and birds in colourful breeding plumage singing their little hearts out. All this activity makes a green or "emerald" season safari quite unlike anything the dry season can deliver.

Main attractions

● **Victoria Falls** Africa's widest and most spectacular waterfall, named Mosi-oa-Tunya ("the Smoke That Thunders") by the locals, is breathtaking. When the Zambezi is in full flood (March–May), the experience of visiting the falls is more about hearing the roar and feeling the spray than actually seeing anything, such is the density of the vapour clouds thrown up from the foot of the Batoka Gorge as the river tumbles over.

Zambia shares the Falls with Zimbabwe, with the Zambezi marking the border, and the view from each bank is quite different, so it's worth experiencing both – you can cross via the Victoria Falls Bridge. On the Zambian side, you can stand very close to the roar of the water: in the dry season, it's even possible to reach Livingstone Island, near the lip of the falls, and plunge into the Devil's Pool, a natural jacuzzi right on the edge.

● **Livingstone** Founded at an old Zambezi crossing point, Livingstone has had its ups and downs. In the early 1900s, it was given a grand layout and was destined to be a major stopover on Cecil Rhodes' ambitious Cape-to-Cairo railway, but the line was never completed; it briefly flowered as capital of Northern Rhodesia, but dwindled after the capital was moved to Lusaka. In recent years, it's been booming once more thanks to tourists opting to see Victoria Falls from Zambia rather than Zimbabwe. Staying in swanky resorts, elegant riverside lodges or simple guesthouses and camps, you can enjoy the adventure activities held on either side of the border, including white-water rafting, zip-lining, bungee jumping, kayaking and microlighting through the musky spray of the falls. Birders will love the river cruises, which may offer sightings of kingfishers and African finfoots.

● **White-water rafting** With rapids ranging from beginner's level to Grade 5, the Batoka Gorge (at its best Aug–Jan), just downstream from Victoria Falls, is among the world's top rafting locations. No experience is required to join a trip, as you'll be in the hands of expert guides, but you definitely need guts – the most violent rapids don't have names like Overland Truck Eater for nothing. The rafting outfits close for business between April and July, when the floods are at their highest – even the toughest of them won't brave the Zambezi in full spate.

● **South Luangwa National Park** Truly one of Africa's greatest national parks, South Luangwa offers all the ingredients of a classic safari – a superb choice of lodges offering game drives, night drives and walking safaris in the company of first-class guides – but with a thrillingly remote flavour. Lions, leopards, elephants and buffalo share the grasslands and miombo woodland with an abundance of giraffes, kudus, zebras and waterbuck, and rhinos, poached out in the 1980s, are now being reintroduced. Luangwa's birdwatching is unbeatable, with the chance to see rarities such as pale-billed hornbills and African pittas. Come August, there's a colourful flurry of wings when carmine bee-eaters flock in from

Central Africa to form large colonies in the sandy banks of the Luangwa River.

● **Kafue National Park** You could just about squeeze Wales inside Kafue, Zambia's largest protected area. It encompasses many habitats, but the most distinctive are those of Busanga Plains in the north, where flat grasslands and miombo woodlands are dotted with island-like clumps of date palms, sausage trees and fig trees. The Lufupa River keeps the plains lush for much of the year, attracting large herds of game including buffalo, red lechwe, puku, zebra and blue wildebeest, trailed by wild dogs, lions and cheetahs.

● **Lower Zambezi National Park** Ancient leadwood and ebony trees shade the grasslands of the Lower Zambezi Valley, where colourful saddle-billed storks pick their way through the flood channels. As you potter along in a canoe, elephants may loom over you from the banks. The game-viewing is particularly superb in September and October, when buffalo, impalas, zebras and elands head down from higher ground to seek out the last remaining grazing of the dry season, and elusive animals such as leopards may be seen drinking at the river's edge. Some of Zambia's most attractive and appealing bush lodges are found here.

● **Lusaka** Though not exactly pretty, the Zambian capital has plenty of character, with larger-than-life markets, enjoyable nightlife and intriguing art galleries which showcase paintings and sculptures by the city's contemporary artists.

● **Kasanka National Park** Every October, up to eight million straw-coloured fruit bats converge on this small park to gorge themselves on wild fruit – an awesome sight. Several rivers flow through, and shy sitatunga antelopes, crocodiles and hippos lurk in the wetlands, while a huge variety of birds are regular visitors.

● **Bangweulu Swamp** With almost as rich a wetland ecosystem as Botswana's Okavango Delta, the soggy terrain around Lake Bangweulu is a favourite with water-loving birds. A highlight is the shoebill stork, a rare, beaky species often seen between March and May, when the floodwaters are high. Another memorable sight, is of thousand-strong herds of black lechwe antelope splashing through the reedy wetlands. It was at Bangweulu that a fever got the better of David Livingstone; there's a monument to him in the forest fringing the swamp.

● **Shiwa Ng'andu** In 1921, Edwardian eccentric Sir Stewart Gore-Browne created an aristocratic idyll in the North Rhodesian bush by building a substantial Tuscan-style manor house, north of Mpika, and living off the land. The estate, which remains in the Gore-Browne family, is still a working farm, with the house open to the public as a unique safari lodge (Wshiwangandu.com) – much like staying in a grand but cosy stately home.

● **Liuwa Plain National Park** It's quite a slog to reach this park, which is out in the far west and only accessible in the dry months (June–Nov), but if you visit towards the end of this time you'll witness a huge gathering of grazers including zebras, tsessebes and wildebeest, drawn here by the new season's fresh grass.

● **Traditional festivals** The colourful Ku-omboka cultural festival, usually held in April, is the Lozi people's opportunity to mark their homeward migration from the Zambezi floodplain to higher ground. A huge royal barge is paddled through the wetlands south of Liuwa Plain, with much thrashing of oars and beating of drums, to be greeted with feasting and jubilation. Each July, the Luunda people of northwest Zambia venerate their ancestors and celebrate their cultural heritage at Unutomboko, a two-day feast of grand rituals and performances accompanied by thundering drums and lengthy speeches.

● **Nyika Plateau** The natural extension of Malawi's Nyika National Park is an expanse of grassy highlands, sprinkled in January and February with soft-coloured wildflowers including gladioli, irises, proteas and orchids.

● **Chimfunshi Wildlife Orphanage** Chimpanzees are not native to Zambia, so if you'd like to see some during your trip, this sanctuary (Wchimfunshi.org .za) near Chingola is the place. It's not geared towards tourism, but you can visit with permission.

Routes in and out

There are international airports at Lusaka, Livingstone, Ndola and Mfuwe. The easiest overland routes are to and from South Africa via Zimbabwe; the other borders are open but can be slow to negotiate, with infrequent public transport. It's inadvisable to travel in the northern regions of Zambia near Democratic Republic of Congo or close to the borders with Angola or Mozambique, where there's a risk of landmines.

Red tape

Visas Required by UK, US, Can, Aus and NZ nationals. Available on arrival but if travelling overland by public transport, you must obtain a visa in advance. Irish and SA citizens do not require a visa.

Nearest consulates Dar es Salaam; Gaborone; Harare; Lilongwe; Luanda; Pretoria (Wzambiapretoria.net); Windhoek.

Other consulates London (Wzambiahc.org.uk); Ottawa (Wzambiahighcommission.ca); Tokyo (T+81 3 3491 0121, Eemb @zambia.or.jp); Washington, DC (Wzambiaembassy.org).

Zimbabwe

Area 390,580 square kilometres
Capital Harare
Population 12.5 million
Languages English, Shona and Ndebele (official); various others
Religion Majority syncretic (part Christian, part traditional)
Government Presidential republic; in practice authoritarian
Independence April 18, 1980 (from UK)

Best time to go Aug–Oct (late dry season) for wildlife-watching; Nov–April (rainy season) for green landscapes
Country code +263
Currency US dollar (USD); UK pound, euro, SA rand and Botswana pula also accepted; Zimbabwean dollar (ZWL) no longer in active use
Minimum daily budget US$55

Ever stoical in the face of misfortune, Zimbabweans have been claiming that their troubled nation is on the mend for some time. Now that an uneasy political equilibrium has been achieved and the laughable Zimbabwean dollar scrapped, setting economic wheels back in motion, their claims are beginning to look more realistic. Tensions remain, however, and you'd be wise to exercise a degree of caution when planning a visit, particularly if you intend to explore much beyond the relatively safe haven of Victoria Falls.

Once hailed as an African success story, Zimbabwe has been torn to pieces by President Robert Mugabe, whose crimes include the thuggish execution of a laudable ambition – to redistribute land such that its benefits are not longer the exclusive preserve of a white minority. Blighted by violence, unrest and hyperinflation, Zimbabwe's infrastructure neared total disintegration in the early 2000s and tourism virtually dried up.

Despite the drawn-out crisis, Zimbabwe's awe-inspiring wildlife areas have fared better than they might – you'll almost certainly see elephants, hippos, lions, buffalo, zebras and giraffes here, and you may also encounter leopards and wild dogs. And some attractions, such as the magnificent Victoria Falls, are much more enjoyable without the milling crowds. Many of the hotels and safari lodges retain an endearingly old-fashioned atmosphere, from the colonial splendour of the *Victoria Falls Hotel*, where classic prints, photographs and hunting trophies line the walls, to rugged bush camps where your accommodation really is a tent – not a hotel room

Mean temperatures and rainfall

	Jan	Feb	Mar	Apr	May	Jun	Jul	Aug	Sep	Oct	Nov	Dec
Harare												
max °C	26	26	26	26	23	21	21	23	26	28	27	26
min °C	16	16	14	13	9	7	7	8	12	14	16	16
rainfall mm	196	178	117	28	13	3	0	3	5	28	97	163

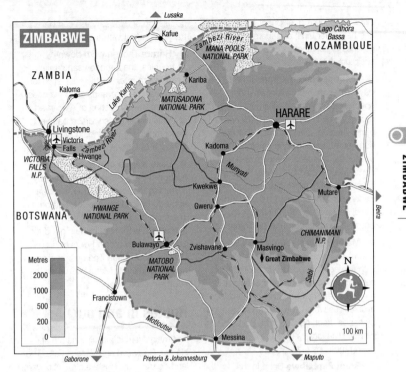

dressed up as a tent – and everything stops for sundowners at sunset.

Main attractions

● **Victoria Falls** Not merely a Zimbabwean highlight, but a wonder to rival any in Africa, the mighty Falls will leave you inspired, exhilarated and, if you visit when the river is highest (March–May), soaked to the skin. As the Zambezi plummets 100m into the narrow Batoka Gorge, spray shoots up in rainbow-filled clouds, visible for miles, ensuring that the tiny, lush Victoria Falls National Park opposite the cataracts remains spangled with raindrops all year round. Zimbabwe shares the falls with Zambia, but while you can get closer to the cataracts on the (easily accessible)

Zambian side, Zimbabwe offers more viewpoints and better views.

● **Victoria Falls town** Pleasantly old-fashioned Vic Falls became a mini-republic of tourism during the worst of Zimbabwe's troubles – it was the only place where the hotels still had steady bookings. The Zambezi is the main attraction – the smooth upper sections for canoeing and cruising, the turbulent lower sections for world-class white-water rafting (best Aug–March), and the Falls in between. While the bars and campsites aren't as stuffed with hard-partying rafters, zip-liners and bungee jumpers as they used to be (many base themselves in Livingstone, in neighbouring Zambia, instead), adrenaline activities still draw travellers – and afternoon tea on the terrace at the *Victoria Falls Hotel* is as elegant as ever. Other popular activities include horseriding, elephant-back safaris and helicopter trips, and there are several galleries of curvaceous Shona stone sculpture in town.

● **Hwange National Park** In better days, this was one of Africa's most spectacular conservation areas, but in recent years it has suffered from chronic under-funding. Despite this, it still has huge numbers of elephants along with antelopes, baboons, big cats and wild dogs. Mechanized boreholes destroy all illusions of this being an untouched wilderness, but at least it's vast, with a real sense of space. Thrillingly, it's possible to canter around on horseback.

● **Mana Pools National Park** Best known as a walking safari destination, with fine scenery and good chances of seeing lions, elephants and buffalo, this park also features beautiful Zambezi riverscapes which you can explore by canoe, keeping watch for pods of hippos. The lodges here are closed during the rains (Jan–March).

● **Great Zimbabwe** Deep in the interior, the remains of Zimbabwe's eleventh-century imperial capital, abandoned in the fifteenth century, were first analysed by European archeologists in the 1900s, prompting a fundamental revision of accepted thinking on African culture. It's thought the city was a hub of a trade route which carried gold and ivory all the way to the Far East. The site consists of chunky stone walls among which impressive artefacts including soapstone monoliths and intricately carved ivory objects were found.

● **Matobo National Park** A commanding landscape of *dwalas* – bulky domes and boulders of lichen-painted granite – makes this a beautiful region to explore. Its many rock art sites hint at age-old secrets of the San Bushmen, and leopard tracks are often seen in the sand. The park has a healthy population of rhinos, which can be tracked on foot with a guide.

● **Harare** Though worn down by its troubles, the Zimbabwean capital manages to retain a little sophistication, with pleasant, jacaranda-lined avenues, an impressive collection of African art at the National Gallery of Zimbabwe, good music venues and, in April, a lively annual arts festival, HIFA (Ⓦhifa.co.zw).

● **Lake Kariba and Matusadona National Park** A reservoir created by damming the Zambezi River, Kariba is home to crocodiles, tigerfish and bream. The calm water, scattered with islands and edged with woodland, is good for canoeing, birdwatching or relaxing on board a houseboat. The best section for game-watching is Matusadona, on the southern shore.

Routes in and out

The main international airports are at Harare, Bulawayo and Victoria Falls. The land border crossings are straightforward. The most common overland route to Zimbabwe by public transport is to travel by bus from Jo'burg to Harare.

Red tape

Visas Required by UK, Ire, US, Can, Aus and NZ nationals. Available on arrival, but some nationalities (including Canadians) must obtain visas in advance. SA nationals do not require a visa (free entry stamp issued on arrival).

Nearest consulates Gaborone; Lusaka; Maputo; Pretoria (Ⓣ+27 12 342 5125, Ⓔzimpret@lantic.net); Windhoek.

Other consulates Canberra (Ⓣ+61 2 6286 2281, Ⓔzimbabwe1@iimetro.com .au); London (Ⓣ020 7836 7755); Ottawa (Ⓦzimottawa.com); Washington, DC (Ⓦzimbabwe-embassy.us).

First-Time Africa

Directory

Tour operators and travel agents

Businesses and organizations marked with a 🏃 are the ones we consider to offer "responsible tourism" or "ethical" or "fair trade" travel to their clients. With few benchmarks and no industry-wide international standards, this tag is a very rough indication of those organizations that are as interested in the communities and environments they work in as their bottom line. Apologies in advance to any organizations that feel they should be given the same recognition (or that we have omitted to list through oversight or ignorance). We have only listed businesses and organizations that we recommend, but omission does not imply rejection.

Africa specialist operators

🏃 **&Beyond** UK Ⓦandbeyondafrica .com. Luxury safari and adventure tours in East and southern Africa, with an emphasis on conservation and sustainability.

Aardvark Safaris UK Ⓦaardvarksafaris .co.uk. Committed and enthusiastic tailor-made Africa specialists who spend a lot of time getting to know the high-end lodges they work with in East and southern Africa.

🏃 **African Pro-poor Tourism Development Centre (APTDC)** Kenya Ⓦpropoortourism-kenya.org. Not-for-profit safaris and eco-tours designed to empower marginalized communities in Kenya.

Africa Select UK Ⓦafricaselect.com. Tailor-made safaris, in East and southern Africa, with some interesting suggestions – such as a fitness holiday on the shores of the Indian Ocean.

Africa Sky UK Ⓦafricasky.co.uk. Very well-established and knowledgeable agent-operator with a helpfully clear website and a host of East and southern African offerings, most of them responsible and mid-priced.

Africa Travel Resource UK Ⓦafricatravel resource.com. Quirky travel company with a liberally illustrated website offering hundreds of lodges and camps in East and southern Africa.

African Adventure Company US Ⓦafrica -adventure.com. One of the best agencies in the business, offering many options across the continent.

African Horizons US Ⓦafricanhorizons .com. Decent range of well-priced safaris with flexible departures.

African Portfolio US Ⓦonsafari.com. Highly regarded US/Zimbabwean outfit offering customizable packages in East and southern Africa.

African Safari Consultants US Ⓦsafariconsultants.com. Wide range of clearly presented and well-priced options from budget to top-end.

African Travel Specialists Aus Ⓦafrican travel.com.au. Well-established agent, part of the Four Corners Travel Group, with an excellent reputation, experienced staff, and offerings to more than twenty countries.

African Wildlife Safaris Aus Ⓦafricanwild lifesafaris.com.au. Upmarket lodge- and camp-based safaris.

🏃 **Africa's Eden** Ⓦafricas-eden.com. Recommended Dutch tour operator, covering CAR, Gabon and São Tomé & Príncipe.

🏃 **Amahoro Tours** Rwanda Ⓦamahoro .may95.com. Community-based tourism and eco-tourism in Rwanda and DRC, including gorilla safaris.

Ashanti African Tours UK Ⓦashantiafrican tours.com. Culture and wildlife (especially birdwatching) tours in Ghana with highly motivated local staff.

Baobab Travel UK Ⓦbaobabtravel.com. Tailor-made responsible travel, with a strong cultural bent.

Batafon Arts UK Ⓦbatafonarts.co.uk. Drumming and dancing holidays in Guinea and The Gambia.

Bicycle Africa US Ⓦibike.org/bikeafrica. Easy-going small-group cycling tours visiting many parts of Africa.

Born Free Safaris US Ⓦbornfreesafaris .com. Plain-speaking safari operator established in the 1970s, with a what-you-see-is-what-you-get approach and good-value safaris on offer.

Calabash Tours South Africa ⓦcalabashtours.co.za. South African ethical township and shebeen tours in Nelson Mandela Bay (Port Elizabeth) and East London.

The Cape Verde Experience UK ⓦcapeverdeexperience.co.uk. Cape Verde beach holidays and island-hopping tours.

Cape Verde Travel UK ⓦcapeverdetravel .com. The original Cape Verde specialists, Cape Verde Travel pre-dates the charter flight era, and offers a good variety of options, including some unusual places to stay.

Classic Safari Company Aus ⓦclassic safaricompany.com.au. Tailor-made tours and safaris ranging across more than half the continent.

Conservancy Safaris Namibia ⓦkcs -namibia.com.na. Groundbreaking luxury camping safari company owned by rural Namibian communities and run by expert conservationists.

Expert Africa UK ⓦexpertafrica.com. Africa specialists (part of Sunvil) with a good range of ethical trips on offer.

Extreme-Safari UK ⓦextreme-safari.com. London- and Diani-based adventure and adrenaline sports company specializing in East Africa and the Indian Ocean.

Fulani Travel UK ⓦfulanitravel.co.uk. Innovative West Africa specialist with a range of tours including visits to festivals.

The Gambia Experience UK ⓦgambia .co.uk. Gambia specialist (part of Serenity Holidays) with a strong commitment to the country.

Gamewatchers Safaris Kenya ⓦporini.com. Kenyan conservancy safaris enabling the Maasai to benefit directly from tourism.

Gane & Marshall UK ⓦganeand marshall.co.uk. Africa specialists, with strong activity tour options and excellent responsible travel credentials. Founders of Charity Challenge (see box, p.409).

Good Earth Tours US ⓦgoodearthtours .com. Very good value safaris, in East and South Africa.

GSE-Ecotours UK ⓦgse-ecotours .com. Village homestay holidays in half a dozen Kenyan locations, aiming to give a lift to the local economy while supporting conservation and sustainability.

Hidden Gambia UK ⓦhiddengambia.com. Unique, customized tours of coastal and upriver Gambia.

IntoAfrica UK ⓦintoafrica.co.uk. Fairly traded tours in Kenya and Tanzania, providing genuine insights while having minimum negative impact on people and environment.

Ker & Downey US ⓦkerdowney.com. Renowned and much-commended upmarket travel company, offering a select range of East African destinations.

Micato Safaris US ⓦmicato.com. Multi-award-winning, upmarket Kenyan-American tour operator with a variety of well-run East and southern African trips.

Natural High Safaris UK ⓦnatural highsafaris.com. Very cool consul-tancy, safari-planner and booking agent, with highly experienced staff, specializing in the safari lands.

Premier Tours US ⓦpremiertours .com. Environmentally sound upmarket safaris in Eastern and southern Africa.

Rainbow Tours UK ⓦrainbowtours .co.uk. Many excellent eco options with East and southern Africa figuring heavily, along with Sierra Leone.

Safari Consultants UK ⓦsafari-consultants .co.uk. Long-established and very personal Africa specialists creating tailor-made trips.

Sahara Overland UK ⓦsahara-overland .com. Highly adventurous self-drive escorted tours by 4WD or motorbike into the heart of the Sahara, especially Algeria, Niger and Libya.

The Senegal Experience UK ⓦ senegal .co.uk. Serenity Holidays' Senegalese trips.

Theobald Barber UK ⓦtheobaldbarber .com. Bespoke safari-planner, offering a very personalized service.

Tourism in Ethiopia for Sustainable Future Alternatives (TESFA) @community-tourism-ethiopia.com. Trekkers' homestay network, run by rural communities.

Tribes Travel UK @tribes.co.uk. Fair trade travel company founded on impeccable responsible tourism principles · and covering a wide range of African destinations.

West Africa Discovery UK @westafricadiscovery.co.uk. One of the few companies specializing in West Africa, with unusual tours and a strong responsible travel ethos.

Wilderness Safaris SA @wilderness -safaris.com. Award-winning luxury safari company specializing in southern African trips with a strong conservation element.

Birdwatching and wildlife tour operators

Avian Adventures UK @avianadventures .co.uk. Tempting range of small-group birdwatching trips to The Gambia and Senegal.

Birding Africa SA @birdingafrica.com. Leading specialist, covering sixteen sub-Saharan nations.

Birdfinders UK @birdfinders.co.uk. Expertly guided birdwatching tours, including trips to nine African countries.

Blue O Two UK @blueotwo.com. Red Sea scuba-diving company that has won awards for its responsibly run liveaboard trips.

Congo Wildlife Adventures Can @congowildlifeadventures.com. Canadian-Congolese company offering visits to Nouabalé-Ndoki National Park in Congo Republic and Dzanga-Sangha National Park in CAR. Co-directed by a gorilla habituation team zoologist.

Naturetrek UK @naturetrek.co.uk. Natural history holidays, including eighteen African countries, led by experts.

Ornitholidays UK @ornitholidays.co .uk. Birdwatching in East, West and southern Africa.

Regaldive UK @regal-diving.co.uk. Diving trips include Egypt, Sudan, Tanzania, Mozambique and South Africa.

Wildlife Worldwide UK @wildlife worldwide.com. Tailor-made trips for wildlife enthusiasts and packages including Gabon, Ethiopia and Madagascar.

Overland tour operators

Absolute Africa UK @absoluteafrica.com. Budget overland operator with trips in East and southern Africa.

Acacia African Adventures UK @acacia -africa.com. Expensive, but good-value overland operator.

African Trails UK @africantrails.co.uk. Well-regarded budget overland operator with a transcontinental range of tours.

Bukima Adventure UK/Aus/NZ/Can @bukima.com. A wide range of good value overland adventure trips.

Dragoman Overland UK @dragoman.com. Highly experi- enced responsible tourism operator offering extended overland journeys in purpose-built expedition vehicles.

Kumuka Expeditions UK @kumuka.com. Large overland truck operator with a very wide range of African tours.

General agents/operators with Africa trips

Adventure World Australia Aus/NZ
ⓦadventureworld.com.au. Agents for many overland operators.

Adventures Abroad US/Can/UK
ⓦadventures-abroad.com. Adventure specialists, with a good programme of small-group two- to four-week tours in more than twenty African countries, led by expert tour leaders.

Audley UK ⓦaudleytravel.com. Highly respected operator offering tailor-made trips to more than a dozen East and southern African countries organized by expert agents who have travelled in Africa.

Backroads US ⓦbackroads.com. Cycling and hiking trips in Morocco, South Africa and Botswana.

Cazenove & Loyd UK ⓦcazenoveandloyd .com. Intelligently designed, entirely tailor-made, private tours and safaris relying on clients who know what they're looking for.

ElderTreks US/Can ⓦeldertreks.com. Small-group, escorted adventures for the over-50s in more than twenty African countries.

Exodus UK ⓦexodus.co.uk. Environmentally and culturally sensitive adventure operator taking small groups on overland trips to 22 countries.

Explore Worldwide UK ⓦexplore.co.uk. Interesting selection of small-group cultural tours, treks, cultural tours and safaris, covering nearly thirty countries.

Footloose Adventure Travel UK ⓦfootlooseadventure.co.uk. Enthusiastic responsible travel company, offering a selection of treks and safaris.

Geographic Expeditions US ⓦgeoex.com. High-end private tours and small group trips with a responsible ethic.

Guerba UK ⓦguerba.co.uk. Part of Intrepid Travel, this is one of the best adventure travel specialists, with a great deal of African experience; options include overland trips to Timbuktu and the Festival au Désert in Mali.

The Imaginative Traveller UK ⓦimaginative-traveller.com. Adventure holidays including twenty African countries.

Journeys International US ⓦjourneys -intl.com. Award-winning eco-tourism operator visiting twenty African countries, including unusual destinations such as Algeria and Togo.

Mountain Madness US ⓦmountain madness.com. Seattle-based adventure travel firm, offering climbs in Kenya and Tanzania.

Mountain Travel Sobek US ⓦmtsobek .com. Adventure travel specialists with trips to take you well off the beaten track, getting around by a mixture of 4WD, hiking, river and camel.

Nature Expeditions International US ⓦnaturexp.com. Good value, flexible educational tours in East and southern Africa, with optional lectures on wildlife, natural history and culture. Good for older kids and teens.

On The Go Tours UK ⓦonthegotours .com. Lively and competitively priced range of East and southern African tours, from no-frills Kenya to family tours in Botswana and gorilla visits in Uganda.

Responsible Travel UK ⓦresponsible travel.com, US ⓦresponsiblevacation .com. Pioneering UK-based travel agent that screens the holidays it sells and offers a good range of wildlife, nature and community voluntourism options.

Steppes Travel UK ⓦsteppestravel.co.uk. Innovative travel planners with a personal approach, specializing in tailor-made trips based in luxury lodges.

Tim Best Travel UK ⓦtimbesttravel.com. Eco-luxurious holiday company with a great reputation for delivering off-the-beaten-track arrangements in twenty African countries.

Wild Frontiers SA ⓦwildfrontiers.com. An excellent range of mid-priced tours to East and southern Africa.

Wild Frontiers UK ⓦwildfrontiers.co.uk. No connection with the previous company, this outfit offers highly adventurous tours, including trips to Algeria, DRC and Djibouti.

D

DIRECTORY

Wilderness Travel US ⓦwildernesstravel .com. A wide array of upmarket vacations in little visited destinations, including a cruise of the length of the west coast.

Discount flight agents

Africa Travel Centre UK ⓦafricatravel .co.uk. Helpful and resourceful.

North South Travel UK ⓦnorthsouth travel.co.uk. Friendly and competitive discount flight agency, with one very big trump card: all its profits support grassroots development projects, principally in Africa.

STA Travel International ⓦstatravel.co .uk. Specialists in flights and tours for students and under-26s, though others are catered for.

Trailfinders UK/Ire/Aus ⓦtrailfinders.com. One of the best-informed and most efficient agents for independent travellers.

Travel Cuts US/Can ⓦtravelcuts.com. Popular, long-established student travel organization.

USIT Ireland ⓦusit.ie. Student and youth specialists.

World Express Travel UK ⓦworld expresstravel.co.uk. Consolidators for Kenya Airways, Brussels Airlines and Ethiopian Airlines.

Sea travel

A Ferrry.co.uk UK ⓦaferry.co.uk. Detailed listings and booking links of ferry services from southern Europe to North Africa.

International Wildlife Adventures US ⓦwildlifeadventures.com. Alluring, upmarket culture and nature cruises along the coasts of West, Central and southern Africa.

Volunteer and work-placement travel

The volunteer travel listings below are arranged into three groups: for-profit travel companies specializing in gap years and voluntary placements; organizations that do the same but have a not-for-profit or

charitable status; and international NGOs that recruit professional people or train graduates for specific assignments. All are especially recommended for their engagement with the local environment and/or community.

Voluntourism travel companies

African Conservation Experience UK ⓦconservationafrica.net. Huge range of general and specialist wildlife and conservation placements and courses for all ages, mostly in South Africa's safari belt.

African Impact SA ⓦafricanimpact.com. Excellent variety of wildlife and community voluntourism opportunities in Kenya, Mozambique, South Africa, Tanzania, Zambia and Zimbabwe, plus the chance to book an internship with a South African marine research centre, winery or film company.

All Africa Volunteers SA ⓦallafrica volunteers.com. Voluntourism placements incorporating taster experiences of working in animal sanctuaries, orphanages, craft projects and natural history research programmes for the course of 10–20 days.

Amanzi Travel UK ⓦamanzitravel.co.uk. Agent offering a good range of voluntourism and adventure holidays in East and southern Africa.

AV UK ⓦaventure.co.uk. Gap year and team-building projects aimed at students, graduates or older travellers, in Kenya, Malawi, South Africa, Tanzania and Uganda, lasting three to sixteen weeks.

Aviva SA ⓦaviva-sa.com. Voluntourism opportunities, working with underprivileged children and endangered wildlife, plus field guide and photography courses.

Camps International UK ⓦcamps international.com. Wildlife conservation and community projects and expeditions, from ten days to three months, for school groups, gap-year students and adults in Kenya, Uganda and Tanzania, mostly with a coastal or mountain theme.

Edge of Africa SA ⓦedgeofafrica.com. Award-winning, ethical volunteering company running wildlife, sports, medical and community projects in South Africa; placements last two or four weeks.

Global Vision International UK ⓦgvi .co.uk. Major voluntourism company operating worldwide and currently offering placements and courses in Ghana, Cameroon, Madagascar, the Seychelles and many East and southern African countries; from one week to two years.

Hands up Holidays UK ⓦhandsupholidays .com. Comfortable 4–17 day adventure holidays with a volunteering element; destinations include Ethiopia, Ghana, Libya, Malawi, Morocco and Tanzania.

i to i UK ⓦi-to-i.com/gap-year-africa.html. Voluntourism travel agent with plenty of experience and a wide range of African options.

N/a'an ku sê ⓦnaankuse.com. Namibian lodge and wildlife sanctuary which offers placements, including medical internships at a clinic set up by the owners to provide

Charity fundraising travel

The best-known operator is 🐾 **Charity Challenge** (ⓦcharitychallenge.com), which in Africa organizes fundraising trips in Ethiopia, Kenya, Tanzania and South Africa. Other operators include **Action Challenge** (ⓦactionchallenge.com) and **Ultimate Challenges** (ⓦutccharitychallenges.co.uk).

The following links should prove helpful in evaluating your chosen charity:

Charity Facts ⓦcharityfacts.org. Useful background about charities, fundraising, admin costs and the like.

Intelligent Giving ⓦintelligentgiving.com. Good advice on charities, volunteering, charity challenges and sponsorship.

emergency care for Bushmen, whose nearest hospital is over 100km away.

PAWS (People and Wildlife Solutions) ⓦpawsnamibia.org. Namibian voluntourism project, maintaining a game reserve as part of the AfriCat Foundation's cheetah rehabilitation programme.

Projects Abroad ⓦprojects-abroad.co.uk. Volunteer work placements around the world, including Ethiopia, Ghana, Morocco, Senegal, South Africa, Tanzania and Togo.

Tribe Wanted ⓦtribewanted.com. Experimental community living project on the Sierra Leone coast; participants share tasks such as gardening, feeding livestock or construction.

Volunteer Africa 32° South SA ⓦvolunteerafrica.co.za. Voluntourism opportunities in South Africa, including an acclaimed project which teaches computer skills to township kids; most ask you to stay at least four weeks.

Voluntours SA ⓦvoluntours.co.za. Respected source of placements in South Africa, Mauritius and Madagascar (one to ten weeks) including dolphin research,

sports coaching and building solar cookers.

Worldwide Experience UK ⓦworldwide experience.com, part of Southern Africa Travel (ⓦsouthernafricatravel.co.uk). Good range of wildlife placements and courses in South Africa (two to twelve weeks), plus helping at a colobus monkey sanctuary in Kenya and community work in Malawi.

Non-profit voluntourism organizations

American Field Service US ⓦafs .org. Intercultural exchange programme founded in 1915 "to create a more just and peaceful world". In Africa, you can volunteer in Tunisia, Egypt, Ghana and South Africa.

Azafady ⓦmadagascar.co.uk. Award-winning UK charity and Malagasy NGO, enabling you to work as a health assistant, language teacher or lemur researcher for two to ten weeks.

Biosphere Expeditions UK ⓦbiosphere -expeditions.org. Highly professional conservation experience company, currently offering two-week placements on a predator conservation project in Namibia. Non-profit.

Blue Ventures UK ⓦblueventures.org. Marine conservation voluntourism in southwest Madagascar; three to twelve weeks with scuba training included if required. All profits go to its sister charity.

BUNAC UK ⓦbunac.org. Community work placements in Ghana and South Africa, from five weeks to eight months. Not-for-profit members club.

Community Projects Africa UK ⓦcommunityprojectsafrica.org. Charity working in association with Charity Challenge (see box, p.409) in Ethiopia, South Africa and Tanzania, offering opportunities for fundraising travel and community visits.

Earthwatch UK ⓦearthwatch.org. Superb selection of wildlife research expeditions lasting 11–22 days. Current African options give you close contact with charismatic species such as elephants, penguins or meerkats. Non-profit.

Responsible tourism resources

If you're concerned about the impact of tourism in Africa, consult some of the following organizations. Travel companies specializing in responsible holidays and travel experiences are listed on pp.401–411.

African Travel and Tourism Association (ATTA) Ⓦ atta.travel. Campaigns to advance tourism in Africa; members include accommodation and activity companies.

Fair Trade in Tourism South Africa (FTTSA) Ⓦ fairtourismsa.org.za. Promotes sustainable tourism development and operates an accreditation scheme.

Imvelo Responsible Tourism Awards Ⓦ imveloawards.co.za. South African award scheme for hotels, reserves and travel companies.

Responsible Tourism Awards Ⓦ www.responsibletourismawards.com. Global award scheme; African tourism businesses regularly beat the competition.

Responsible Tourism Partnership Ⓦ responsibletourismpartnership.org. Works to support the development of responsible tourism businesses and initiatives.

Tourism Concern Ⓦ tourismconcern.org.uk. Fights exploitation in tourism. Publications include *The Ethical Travel Guide*.

Tourism for Tomorrow Awards Ⓦ tourismfortomorrow.com. Scheme which recognizes best practice in sustainable tourism, worldwide; recent winners and finalists have included Botswana Tourism, Wilderness Safaris and Namibia's conservancies.

The Travel Foundation Ⓦ thetravelfoundation.org.uk. Charity set up to take effective action on sustainable tourism.

Frontier UK Ⓦ frontier.ac.uk. Schools and conservation placements in Ghana, Madagascar and Tanzania.

People and Places UK Ⓦ travel-people andplaces.co.uk. Responsible voluntourism company that takes great care to match applicants with projects that will make the best use of their skills. Destinations include The Gambia, Madagascar, Mozambique, South Africa and Swaziland. Profits to charity.

TurtleWill US Ⓦ turtlewill.org/volunteer _projects.html. Placements available on two-week volunteer-funded medical programmes in Mali and Niger.

Volunteers for Peace US Ⓦ vfp.org. A long list of African countries is included

for voluntary placement and workcamp referrals. You pay a registration fee (US$300) and annual membership (US$30), and all other fees are paid to the in-country partner organization.

Voluntary work NGOs

Australian Volunteers International Ⓦ australianvolunteers.com.

CUSO-VSO (North America) Ⓦ cuso -vso.org.

Peace Corps US Ⓦ peacecorps.gov.

VSO (Voluntary Service Overseas) UK Ⓦ vso.org.

Worldwide Veterinary Service UK Ⓦ wvs .org.uk.

Festivals

Algeria

Festival du Raï d'Oran; Oran, dates vary Algeria's foremost festival of Raï music. Ⓦ bit.ly/FestivRai.

Angola

Carnaval Luanda; Feb/March.
Mukanda Southeast Angola; Nov. See p.230.

Benin

Quintessence International Film Festival Ouidah, Jan ⓦfestival-ouidah.org.

Vodun Day Nationwide; Jan 10 Celebrating the voodoo religion.

Assumption Day Dassa-Zoumé and Savalou; Aug 15 Pilgrimages and yam festivals.

Botswana

Kuru Traditional Dance & Music Festival D'Kar; Aug Celebration of San (Bushman) musical culture.

Maitisong Festival Gaborone; March/April ⓦmaitisong.org. Music, dance and theatre.

Maun Festival Maun; April/May.

Burkina Faso

Festival Jazz Ouagadougou & Bobo-Dioulasso; April/May ⓦjazz.zcp.bf.

Festival des Masques et des Arts (FESTIMA) Dédougou; March of even-numbered years ⓦfestima.org.

Festival Panafricain du Cinéma (FESPACO) Ouagadougou; Feb/March of odd-numbered years.

Nuits Atypiques de Koudougou (NAK) Koudougou; Nov/Dec ⓦnak.bf. Music, theatre and dance.

Semaine Nationale de la Culture Bobo-Dioulasso; March/April in even-numbered years ⓦsnc.gov.bf.

Waga Hip Hop Ouagadougou & Bobo-Dioulasso; Oct ⓦwagahiphop .com.

Burundi

Burundi International Film Festival Bujumbura; Aug ⓦburundifilmcenter.org.

Cameroon

Grass-cutting ceremony Bafut; end April Mass rethatching of the palace of the local *fon* (king) followed by a huge public party.

Les Rencontres Théâtrales Internationales du Cameroun (RETIC) Yaoundé; Nov ⓦreticfestival.net. International drama and dance festival.

Cape Verde

Carnaval Mindelo, São Vicente (main event) and all the other island capitals; Feb/March See p.249.

Festival Baía das Gatas São Vicente; Aug Festival of rock and traditional music ⓦmindelo.info.

Central African Republic

Bangui Hip Hop Festival Bangui, Dec ⓦbit.ly/BanguiHipHop.

Chad

Fête National Ndjamena and nation-wide, 1 Dec The so-called Freedom and Democracy Day, commemorating the overthrow of dictator Hissène Habré in 1990.

Comoros & Mayotte

Médina Festival Mutsamudu (Nzwani); May, June or July Indian Ocean music festival.

Congo Republic

Festival Panafricain de Musique (FESPAM) Brazzaville; Aug ⓦwww .fespam.net.

Côte d'Ivoire

Carnaval de Bouaké Bouaké; Feb/March.

Democratic Republic of Congo

Festival de Jazz de Kinshasa Kinshasa; June ⓦwww.ccf-kinshasa.org. Three nights of concerts.

Djibouti

Fest'Horn Djibouti city; Dec Horn of Africa music festival.

Egypt

Moulid of Sayyid Ahmad al-Badawi Tanta; Oct See p.271.

Christian and Muslim calendars

Most countries have **public holidays** to mark their date of independence and usually observe public holidays from the Christian and Islamic calendars. In countries where the Monday to Friday or Monday to Saturday work week is the norm, when an anniversary or holiday date falls on a Sunday, the following Monday is usually declared a public holiday.

Christian and other holidays

1 Jan New Year's Day
Carnival/Mardi Gras/Shrove Tuesday 8 March 2011, 21 Feb 2012, 12 Feb 2013
Palm Sunday 17 April 2011, 1 April 2012, 24 March 2013
Good Friday 22 April 2011, 6 April 2012, 29 March 2013
Easter Monday 25 April 2011, 9 April 2012, 1 April 2013
1 May Labour Day
25 Dec Christmas Day
26 Dec Boxing Day

Islamic festivals: approximate dates

The Islamic calendar dates from 622 AD, the Year of the Hijra when the prophet fled from Mecca to Medina (dates measured with respect to this are denoted AH, thus the year 1432 AH began on 7 December 2010 AD). It uses a lunar system that divides the Islamic year into twelve months of 29 or 30 days (totalling 354 days). The dates of Islamic festivals therefore shift forward, by roughly eleven days each year, relative to the Gregorian calendar. The twelve Muslim months, in calendar order, are: Muharram, Safar, Rabia al-Awwal (Rabia I), Rabia al-Thany (Rabia II), Jumada-al-Awwal (Jumada I), Jumada al-Thany (Jumada II), Rajab, Sha'aban, Ramadan, Shawwal, Dhu al Qi'dah and Dhu al-Hijjah.

The Gregorian dates given below are approximate, as the Islamic months begin when the new moon is sighted. Muslim month dates are given in parentheses.

	2011	2012	2013
Maulidi/Mouloud (12th Rabia I)	16 Feb	5 Feb	24 Jan
Beginning of Ramadan (1st Ramadan)	1 Aug	20 Jul	9 July
Id al-Fitr/Id al-Saghir (1st Shawwal)	31 Aug	19 Aug	8 Aug
Tabaski/Id al-Adha/ Id al-Kabir (10th Dhu'l Hijja)	7 Nov	26 Oct	15 Oct
New Year (1st Moharem)	27 Nov	15 Nov	5 Nov
Ashoura (10th Moharem)	6 Dec	24 Nov	14 Nov

Equatorial Guinea

Cultural renaissance nationwide; various dates Ⓦ bit.ly/EqGuinCulture. Equatorial Guinea's Ministry of Information, Tourism & Culture has a list of events.

Eritrea

Eritrean Orthodox Christmas (Leddet)
7 Jan.
Meskel (Finding of the True Cross)
27 Sept.
Timket (Epiphany) 19 Jan.

Ethiopia

The Ethiopian Orthodox Church follows the Julian calendar of twelve months of thirty days and a thirteenth of five days (six in a leap year). To convert dates, see Ⓦ members.shaw.ca/ethiocal.

Enkutatash (New Year) Addis Ababa, highlands and nationwide; 11 Sept.

Meskel (Finding of the True Cross) Addis Ababa, highlands and nationwide; 27 Sept Processions of torch-bearers mark

413

this ancient symbolic commemoration of the finding of Jesus' cross by St Helena in the fourth century.

Timket (Epiphany) Lalibela, highlands, nationwide; 19 Jan Highlight of the Orthodox calendar celebrating Jesus' baptism. See p.280.

Victory of Adowa Nationwide; 2 March Public holiday marking the Italian army's defeat in 1896.

Gabon

Festival Gabao Libreville; June Ⓦfestivalgabao.com. Gabon's national hip-hop festival.

The Gambia

Kartong Festival Kartong; Jan Ⓦkartong festival.org. See p.286.

Korité (Id al-Fitr) Nationwide; Muslim calendar The feast at the end of the month of Ramadan.

Roots Homecoming Festival and Kanilai International Cultural Festival Kanilai; May/June Ⓦwww.rootsgambia.gm; Ⓦstatehouse.gm. See p.286.

Ghana

Aboakye Winneba; May Groups of hunters compete to capture a live antelope and present it to their chief.

Adae Kumasi; roughly every sixth Sunday (check details locally) Meet the Asantehene (King of Asante) at his elaborate court receptions.

Dzimbenti/Bugum Northern Region; Jan Fire festival tied to the agricultural cycle, including processions of torch-bearers.

Homowo Festival Accra region; Aug or Sept Ga harvest festival with processions, dancing and drumming.

Oguaa Fetu Cape Coast; first Saturday of Sept Major coastal festival lasting several days – a combination of ancient festivals marking the yam harvest and the resumption of sea fishing with the marking of the arrival of the Europeans.

Guinea

Festival de Guinée Conakry; April/May Ⓦfestagg.com. African music festival.

Festival International Koras et Cordes Conakry; Dec Ⓦnuits-metis.org. Festival of West African acoustic music – a *kora* fan's paradise.

Guinea-Bissau

Carnaval Bissau; Feb/March.

Kenya

Agricultural shows Nationwide, various dates Ⓦask.co.ke.

International Camel Derby Maralal; Aug.

Maulidi Coastal towns, especially Lamu; Usually Feb/March. The Prophet Muhammad's birthday.

Lesotho

Horse races Semonkong; winter.

Morija Arts & Cultural Festival Morija; Oct Ⓦmorijafest.com.

Liberia

Liberia Peace and Cultural Festival Monrovia; Dec Ⓦbit.ly/LPCFest. Liberian and West African musicians and other artists.

National Unification Day Nationwide; 14 May National public holiday in commemoration of lives lost and put on hold in the years of civil strife.

Libya

Ghadames International Festival Ghadames; Sept/Oct Berber and Tuareg culture and music festival.

Madagascar

Alahamady Be (Malagasy New Year) Nationwide; March Three days of ceremonies, song and dance.

Donia Festival Nosy Be; May/June Ⓦfestival-donia.com. Traditional music and dance.

Famadihana Antananarivo and Fianarantsoa provinces; June–Sept

Exhumation and reburial ceremonies, with feasting.

Madajazzcar Antananarivo; Oct ⓦmadajazzcar.mg. International jazz festival.

Malawi

Lake of Stars Festival Lake Malawi; Sept ⓦlakeofstars.org. See p.315.

Mali

Dogon Dama festivals Dogon country; variable Mask dances traditionally performed at funerals, more usually now enacted for tourist groups.

Dogon Sigui Festival Dogon country; 2027 ⓦdogoncountry.com. Held every sixty years, the Sigui (commemorating the death of the first Dogon ancestor), is a major African event cycle, expected to last several years, with frequent processions of mask-wearing dancers moving from village to village.

Festival au Desert Timbuktu; early Jan ⓦfestival-au-desert.org. Tuareg music and arts festival, with West African and overseas guest artists.

Festival sur le Niger Ségou; early Feb ⓦfestivalsegou.org. Music and arts festival.

Mauritania

Festival International des Musiques Nomades Nouakchott; April ⓦmusiquesnomades.com. Festival of nomadic music.

Guetna Adrar region; July–Aug Festival of the date harvest.

Mauritius

Festival International Kreol Pailles; Dec Festival of Creole music.

Morocco & Western Sahara

Festival of World Sacred Music Fès; June ⓦfesfestival.com. See p.330.

Gnawa and World Music Festival Essaouira; June ⓦfestival-gnaoua.net. See p.330.

International Arts Festival Asilah; Aug Moroccan fine arts festival.

Wedding Festival Imilchil; Sept Huge traditional Berber market and marriage fair where singles are encouraged to find a match – now very touristy but highly photogenic.

Mozambique

Carnaval Quelimane; Feb/March.

Namibia

Maharero Day (Red Flag Day) Okahandja; Sunday before 23 Aug Festive commemoration honouring Herero Chief Samuel Maharero, leader of the anti-German revolt of 1904.

Oktoberfest Windhoek and nationwide; Oct Bavarian-style beer and sausage fest.

Windhoek Carnival (WIKA) Windhoek; April ⓦwww.skw.com.na/wika Masked ball, parades, concerts and beer.

Niger

Bianou (Muslim New Year) Agadez and nationwide; Muslim calendar (starts a week after Tabaski) A week or three of turn-of-the-year dances and festivities.

Cure Salée In-Gall; Sept Pastoralists converge with their herds on large salt flats for an annual "salt cure", punctuated by partying and dramatic beauty contests for unmarried men and women.

Nigeria

Argungu Fishing Festival Argungu, Feb/March Three days of festivities culminating with a mass hand-fishing competition in the Sokoto River.

Egungun Yorubaland; April, May or June Yoruba ancestor festival, with exhilarating drumming and dancing.

Igue Benin City; Dec Procession of the Oba of Benin.

Ogun Yorubaland; June–Aug Yoruba festival in honour of the god of iron, with singing, dancing and drumming.

Sekiapu River and Cross River states; Oct Masquerades, regattas and a great deal of merriment.

Réunion

Kaloobang St-Denis; Oct ⓦkaloobang
.re. International music festival, with fringe
events (Kaloobang OFF) taking place in the
capital's bars.

Manapany Surf Festival Manapany-les-
Bains; Sept ⓦmanapanysurfestival.com.
Surf competitions and good sounds.

Rwanda

Pan-African Festival of Dance (FESPAD)
Kigali; Aug ⓦfespad.org.

Rwanda Film Festival Nationwide; March
ⓦhillywood.org.

São Tomé & Príncipe

Bienal de Arte e Cultura São Tomé
Capital; June/July of even-numbered years.

Catholic saints' days Nationwide; various
dates.

Senegal

Abéné Festival Abéné; Jan ⓦalnaniking
.co.uk. Festival of Senegalese and Gambian
musicians.

Blues du Fleuve Podor, variable dates
ⓦbaabamaal.tv. Senegalese festival run by
singing star Baaba Maal in his home town.

DAK'ART Dakar; even-numbered years,
May ⓦbiennaledakar.org. Contemporary art
from across the continent.

Fanals Saint Louis; end Dec Night-time
parades featuring paper lanterns (*fanals*)
harking back to the early decades of
French colonialism.

Kafountine carnival Kafountine; Feb/
March Music festival held around mardi
gras time.

Korité (Id al-Fitr) Nationwide; Muslim
calendar The feast at the end of the month
of Ramadan.

Magal Touba; 48 days after the Islamic
New Year Huge pilgrimage of the Mouride
Sufi brotherhood to the burial place of its
founder, combining ascetic multitudes and
crass commercialism.

Saint Louis International Jazz Festival
Saint Louis; May ⓦsaintlouisjazz.com.

**Traditional Casamance and Bassari
festivals** Southern Senegal; mostly at the
end of the dry season, or early rains
(April–June) Initiations, ritual battles,
dances, wrestling matches and partying.

Seychelles

Festival Kreol Victoria, Mont Fleuri and
Au Cap; Oct ⓦseychelles.net/kreolfst. The
islands' main national cultural festival.

Sierra Leone

Freetown Film Festival Lumley Beach;
Dec ⓦfreetownfilmfestival.com.

New Year's Day Picnic Kabala; 1 Jan
Mass exodus from town to Gbawuria Hill.

South Africa

Arts Alive Johannesburg; Sept–Oct
ⓦartsalive.co.za. Jo'bug's biggest
arts event.

Bomvu Cultural Drumming Festival
Coffee Bay, Wild Coast; July ⓦbomvu
backpackers.com. Five-day drumming
and dance marathon; anyone can
take part.

Cape Town International Jazz Festival
Cape Town; April ⓦwww.capetownjazz
fest.com. See p.365.

Cape Town Minstrel Carnival Cape Town;
1–2 Jan.

Cape Town Pride Cape Town; Feb/March
ⓦcapetownpride.co.za.

Durban International Film Festival
Durban; June.

Hermanus Whale Festival Hermanus;
Sep ⓦwhalefestival.co.za. Whale-watching,
concerts and family events.

Mother City Queer Project Cape Town;
Dec ⓦmcqp.co.za. See p.369.

National Arts Festival Grahamstown; July
ⓦnafest.co.za.

**Out in Africa Gay & Lesbian Film
Festival** Nationwide; various dates
ⓦoia.co.za.

Splashy Fen Music Festival Underberg;
April ⓦwww.splashyfen.co.za.
See p.369.

Sudan

Id al-Adha Khartoum and nationwide; Muslim calendar The favourite holiday to make the hajj pilgrimage to Mecca. Every family that can afford to kills a goat or sheep.

Swaziland

Incwala Lobamba; Dec See p.375.

Umhlanga Lobamba; Aug/Sept See p.375.

Tanzania

Bulabo dance contests Bujora, near Mwanza; June Rival dance societies of the Sukuma tribe compete to pull the biggest crowd.

Bullfights Kengeja, Pemba; Sept–Feb Throwback to Portuguese rule. The roped, short-horned bulls involved are not killed.

East African Art Biennale Dar es Salaam; Nov/Dec of odd-numbered years only Contemporary art.

Festival of the Dhow Countries Zanzibar; July ⓦziff.or.tz. Zanzibar's International Film Festival.

Mwaka Kogwa Makunduchi, Zanzibar; July ⓦmzuri-kaja.or.tz/mwaka.html. Stick fights (enacted with banana stems) and ceremonial hut-burning followed by feasting and dancing, all introduced by Zoroastrians in the tenth century, celebrating the passing of the Persian new year.

Sauti za Busara Zanzibar; Feb ⓦbusaramusic.org. See p.378.

Togo

Ayiza Ewe country; second Sat of Aug Ewe harvest festival, celebrated with a bean-feast.

Epe Ekpe (or Yékéyéké) Glidji; mid-Sept Week-long Vodun (voodoo) celebration.

Evala Kara; July Traditional wrestling and initiation ceremonies.

Tunisia

Festival International du Sahara de Douz Douz; Nov ⓦfestivaldouz.org.tn. Desert arts, belly dancing and folklore.

International Festival of Carthage Carthage; July/Aug Tunisia's premier arts festival.

Lag B'Omer Djerba; May Pilgrimage to La Ghriba synagogue on the thirty-third day after the start of Passover.

Uganda

Amakula Kampala; May ⓦamakula.com. International film festival.

Imbalu Mbale and around; even-numbered years, Aug Mass circumcision of Bagisu boys.

Kwetu Fest Ntinda, near Kampala; dates vary ⓦndere.com. Ugandan and international biennial festival of development theatre.

Zambia

Ku-omboka Barotseland; Feb/March ⓦbarotseland.com. See p.395.

Lwiindi Ceremony Mukuninot, near Victoria Falls; July Sacrifices to bring rain, followed by singing, dancing and feasting.

Umotomboko Ceremony Kazembe, west of Lake Bangweulu; July See p.395.

Zimbabwe

Harare International Festival of the Arts (HIFA) Harare; April ⓦwww.hifa.co.zw. Major festival of national and international arts.

INTWASA Bulawayo; Sept ⓦwww.intwasa.org.zw. Arts festival.

Zimbabwe International Film Festival (ZIFF) Harare and nationwide; Aug/Sept ⓦwww.ziff.co.zw.

Websites

Africa

The Atlantic Slave Trade ⓦhitchcock.itc
.virginia.edu/slavery. Remarkably detailed
archive of images, with excellent
accompanying text.

Human Rights Watch ⓦhrw.org/en
/africa. Essential source: find out about the
countries you're visiting.

Project Gutenberg: Africa Bookshelf
ⓦbit.ly/GutenbergAfrica. Wonderful
download resource of out-of-copyright
books.

Sahara Overland ⓦsahara-overland.com.
Excellent site with up-to-date information.

The Story of Africa ⓦbbc.in/BBCStory
ofAfrica. Exceptional BBC World Service
radio production, with extensive notes.

African music

African music stations ⓦshoutcast.com
/radio/African. Get your ears in tune before
you go.

Afropop Worldwide ⓦafropop.org. New
York-based radio show and online musical
treasure trove.

**Nick's African Tape & Record Imports
(Natari)** ⓦnatari.com. UK-based CD
and cassette store. If it's not available to
download or in your local music emporium,
it's probably here.

Songlines ⓦsonglines.co.uk. World music
magazine with excellent Africa coverage.

Algeria

Algeria.com ⓦalgeria.com. Comprehensive
information.

Algerian National Tourist Office
ⓦalgeriantourism.com.

Angola

**Embassy of the Republic of Angola
(Washington DC)** ⓦangola.org. Includes
national news, tourist and general
information.

Kissama Foundation ⓦkissama.org.
Conservation news.

Benin

Hotels Benin ⓦen.hotels-benin.com. Run
by a Benin-based tour operator.

Le Matinal ⓦactubenin.com. News and
features from the national daily paper.

Mami Wata ⓦmamiwata.com. Vodun
religious philosophy.

Botswana

Botswana Tourism Board
ⓦbotswanatourism.co.bw. Offical info,
including news and events.

**Community-based Natural Resources
Management** ⓦcbnrm.bw. IUCN (World
Conservation Union) site covering sustain-
able conservation and development.

**Government of the Republic of
Botswana** ⓦgov.bw. Includes visitor information on national parks and reserves.

Survival: Bushmen ⓦsurvivalinternational
.org/tribes/bushmen. News from Survival's
long-running human rights campaign on
behalf of the Kalahari Bushmen.

Burkina Faso

Faso News ⓦfasonews.net. Burkinabè
news portal. In French.

L'Indépendant ⓦindependant.bf.
Outspoken news and forum. In French.

**L'Office National du Tourisme
Burkinabè** ⓦontb.bf. National tourist
office, in French.

Burundi

Burundi Bwacu ⓦburundibwacu.info.
French-language news and analysis.

Rugamba Netpress ⓦnetpress.bi.
Campaigning French-language news site.

Cameroon

Camnet ⓦcamnet.cm. Service provider
and info portal, including tourist information.

Cameroon News ⓦcameroonnews.com.
English-language news.

Fédération Camerounaise de Football
ⓦfecafootonline.com. Practically a national

religion, football is one of the country's most unifying forces.

Four Museums in Cameroon
Ⓦmuseumcam.org. Useful site for cultural background.

WWF Cameroon Ⓦbit.ly/WWFCameroon. Useful site for wildlife enthusiasts (WWF has a major programme in the country).

Cape Verde

CaboVerde.com Ⓦcaboverde.com. Unofficial tourist site – chaotic but informative.

ECaboverde Ⓦecaboverde.com. Anybody can upload photos of the islands here – great for local flavour.

República de Cabo Verde Ⓦgoverno.cv. Government site; includes national news.

Virtual Cape Verde Ⓦvirtualcapeverde.net. Useful portal stuffed with links to visa info, news, radio stations and more.

Central African Republic

CAR Online Ⓦcentrafricaine.info. The official government site.

Dzanga-Sangha Reserve Ⓦdzanga -sangha.org. Informative and comprehensive coverage.

Chad

Ial Tchad Ⓦialtchad.com. General site, with useful information.

Parc National de Zakouma Ⓦzakouma .com.

Zakouma Elephants Ⓦbit.ly /ZakoumaElephants. 2006 National Geographic film by J. Michael Fay and Michael Nichols.

Comoros & Mayotte

Comores-Online Ⓦcomores-online.com. Useful portal with links to local media and an "encylopaedia" of general information on the islands. In French.

Comores Tourisme Ⓦtourisme.gouv.km. Official tourist information (in French).

Mayotte Tourisme Ⓦmayotte-tourisme .com. Offical tourist information (in French).

Congo Republic

Congo-Site Ⓦcongo-site.net. Essential government-funded portal with links to all things Congo (in French).

République du Congo Ⓦpresidence.cg. Official site from the President's office, with general country information (in French).

Côte d'Ivoire

Côte d'Ivoire Tourisme Ⓦtourismeci.org. Official tourist board site.

Friends of Côte d'Ivoire Ⓦfriendsofcotedivoire.org. Community site for returned Peace Corps volunteers and US-based Ivoirians.

Fraternité Matin Ⓦfratmat.info. FratMat is the paper owned by the ruling coalition.

Democratic Republic of Congo

DRC National Tourism Office (Montreal) Ⓦrdcongotourisme.webs.com. Official site with basic information in English and further details in French.

Virunga National Park Ⓦgorilla.cd. General information and fundraising initiatives relating to the park and its gorillas.

Djibouti

Djiboutian Sightings Ⓦdjiboutian .happyhost.org. Online gallery of historic maps, photos, stamps and documents.

Office National du Tourisme de Djibouti Ⓦoffice-tourisme.dj. Official tourist information (in French).

RTD Ⓦrtd.dj. National radio and television channel, with news clips.

Egypt

Egyptian Museum, Cairo Egyptian Tourist Office Ⓦegypt.travel. Impressive site with plenty to keep you busy, from magazine-style articles to language tips.

Tour Egypt Ⓦtouregypt.net. Detailed visitor information from an association of travel companies specializing in Egypt.

Travellers in Egypt Ⓦtravellersinegypt.org. Fascinating articles on Egyptology and the history of Egyptian travel and exploration.

Equatorial Guinea

Embajada Guinea Ecuatorial (London) Ⓦembarege-londres.org. Embassy site, with basic visitor information (in Spanish).

Guinea-Ecuatorial.net Ⓦguinea-ecuatorial .net. Portal with links to national news (in Spanish).

Eritrea

Asmarino Ⓦasmarino.com. Independent online magazine for those interested in social and political change.

Dehai Ⓦdehai.org. Busy national and regional news portal.

Eritrea: Adventure and Hospitality Ⓦeritrea.be. Detailed travel guide by an enthusiast who visits every year.

Eritrea Ministry of Tourism Ⓦshaebia.org /mot. Basic tourist information.

Ethiopia

Best Ethiopia Ⓦbestethiopia.com. Tourism highlights and listings.

Ethiopian Tourist Commission Ⓦtourismethiopia.org. The Ministry of Culture and Tourism's promotional site.

Ethiopian church icons Ⓦnmafa.si.edu /exhibits/icons/index.html. Gallery of examples from the National Museum of African Art.

Ethiopia Hotel Guide Ⓦethiopiahotelguide .com. Useful reservations and planning resource.

Survival: Omo Valley tribes Ⓦsurvivalinternational.org/tribes/omovalley. Omo pages of the campaigning organization Survival.

Gabon

Embassy of Gabon in South Africa Ⓦwww.gabonembassy.org.za. Embassy site with general country information.

GabonArt Ⓦgabonart.com. No-expense-spared showcase for Gabonese culture and traditions, including a superb "virtual museum". In French.

Le Gabon Ⓦlegabon.org. Official national website with a beautiful multimedia "travel diary" section introducing cultural attractions and national parks.

The Gambia

Asset Ⓦasset-gambia.com. Small, locally owned tourism businesses including independent guesthouses and eco-lodges.

Gambia Tourism Authority Ⓦvisitthegambia.gm. Upbeat and accessible official info.

Gambia Tourist Support Ⓦgambiatouristsupport.com. Huge, thoughtful compilation of visitor-friendly information on what makes The Gambia and its people tick.

Ghana

Ghana Review Ⓦghanareview.com. News coverage.

Ghana Tourist Board Ⓦtouringghana.com.

GhanaWeb Ⓦghanaweb.com. Major portal, with news links, directory and classifieds.

International Council of Museums: Ghana Ⓦghana.icom.museum. Basic information about Ghana's museums.

No Worries Ghana Ⓦnoworriesghana .com. Practical expat and visitor information from the North American Women's Association.

Guinea

Aminata Ⓦaminata.com. First port of call for news and comment.

Foutapédia Ⓦfoutapedia.org. All things Fula (Peulh) and Fouta Djalon.

Friends of Guinea Ⓦfriendsofguinea.org. US Peace Corps-related site with good links and info.

Radio Kankan Ⓦradio-kankan.com. Best of the local radio services, with a lively website (news, links, music news) and live streaming.

Guinea-Bissau

BBC World Routes: Guinea-Bissau Ⓦbit.ly/Guinea-Bissau-Music. Excellent radio documentary on the country's infectious music.

Guinee-Bissau.net ⓦguinee-bissau.net. Detailed tourist information and a good picture gallery, in French.

Kenya

Kenya Tourist Board ⓦmagicalkenya.com.

Kenya Wildlife Service ⓦkws.go.ke. National parks information (doesn't cover reserves).

Kwani? ⓦkwani.org. Kenya's pre-eminent literary website.

Nation Group ⓦnationmedia.com. Several papers, including the *Nation*, plus radio and TV.

The Rough Guide to Kenya ⓦtherough guidetokenya.blogspot.com. News and updates from the author of the *Rough Guide to Kenya*, and co-author of this book.

Traditional music & cultures of Kenya ⓦbluegecko.org/kenya. Superb encyclopedia of text and music files.

You Missed This ⓦkumekucha.blogspot .com. Scurrilous and entertaining rants and scoops.

Wildlife Direct ⓦwildlifedirect.org. Conservation network, including more than fifty blogs from the field in Kenya.

Lesotho

Lesotho Tourism Development Corporation ⓦltdc.org.ls. Decent official site with hotel and restaurant listings.

See Lesotho ⓦseelesotho.com. Handy visitor information from a pony-trekking lodge.

Liberia

The Analyst ⓦanalystliberia.com. "Liberia's most analytical newspaper", featuring up-to-date news and good editorials.

Friends of Liberia ⓦfol.org. Ex-Peace Corps volunteers site – excellent links.

Sliding Liberia ⓦslidingliberia.com. Beautifully crafted website featuring the DVD of the same title: "A story of war, peace and surfing".

Surfing at Robertsport ⓦbit.ly /SurfingLiberia. Useful 2010 report from SurfersVillage.com.

Libya

General People's Committee for Tourism ⓦlibyan-tourism.com. Official visitor information.

Libyaonline.com ⓦlibyaonline.com. Portal with notes on historic sites, music, sport and culture.

Society for Libyan Studies ⓦbritac.ac.uk /institutes/libya. News, publications and London lectures relating to recent archeological research.

Madagascar

Madagascar ⓦwbur.org/special /madagascar. Beautifully assembled by the Boston University media channel, this special feature on the island's rich biodiversity and culture has great articles, photos, audio and video.

Madagascar National Parks ⓦparcs -madagascar.com. A wealth of practicalities to help you plan a widlife and nature tour.

Office National du Tourisme de Madagascar ⓦmadagascar-tourisme.com. Official visitor information.

Wild Madagascar ⓦwildmadagascar .org. Attractive site presenting a mass of information, mostly relating to flora, fauna and habitats.

Malawi

The Cichlid Fishes of Lake Malawi ⓦmalawicichlids.com. Page after page of information on Malawi's famous freshwater fish – and puzzles, too.

Friends of Malawi ⓦfriendsofmalawi.org. Created by ex-volunteers (mostly American), with a "Learn about Malawi" section full of useful cultural background and practical tips.

Malawi Tourism ⓦmalawitourism.com. Official visitor information.

Mali

Kidal.info ⓦkidal.info. Lively and informative site devoted to the Kidal region, with an excellent forum.

421

MaliWeb Ⓦmaliweb.net. News, views, links and listings, in French.

Ministere de l'Artisanat et du Tourisme Ⓦle-mali.com/omatho. Official tourism and hotel site.

Ségou Tourist Office Ⓦtourisme-segou.com.

Visit Gao Mali Ⓦisitgaomali.com. Perhaps the most comprehensive English-language online resource for travellers to Mali, focusing on a lot more than Gao.

Mauritania

SU Mauritania Ⓦbit.ly/StanUniMauritania. Stanford University's annotated links for Mauritania. A good place to start.

Mauritania.mr Ⓦmauritania.mr. Decent French information site, though with a strong official line.

TerreMauritanie.com Ⓦterremauritanie .com. Tourism site with up-to-date information on accommodation options, in French.

Mauritius

Mauritian Wildlife Foundation Ⓦmauritian-wildlife.org. Conservation NGO that looks after Ile aux Aigrettes and the island's rare bats, birds and reptiles.

Mauritius Tourism Promotion Authority Ⓦmauritius.net. Official visitor information.

Mauritius Delight Ⓦmauritiusdelight.com. Features about the island, including things to do.

Rodrigues Tourist Office Ⓦtourism -rodrigues.mu. Official visitor information for Rodrigues Island.

Morocco & Western Sahara

ASVDH Ⓦasvdh.net/english. Website of the Sahrawi Association of Victims of Grave Human Rights Violations.

City of Fes Ⓦvillefes.com. Official portal for Fes.

Jewish Morocco Ⓦrickgold.home .mindspring.com. Interesting and detailed coverage of the country's ancient and still surviving Jewish culture.

Moroccan National Tourist Office Ⓦvisitmorocco.com.

Morocco Blogs Ⓦmoroccoblogs.com. Very useful links and posts.

Tangier American Legation Museum Ⓦlegation.org. Fascinating site, with useful links.

Mozambique

Flora of Mozambique Ⓦmozambiqueflora .com. Nature notes with photos – huge lists of plant and insect species are included.

Iluminando Vidas Ⓦiluminandovidas .org. Inspiring images from an exhibition of Mozambican photography.

Ministério de Turismo Ⓦvisitmozambique .net. Official visitor information.

Rádio Mozambique Ⓦrm.co.mz. Live broadcasts and a daily feed of national news and features (in Portuguese).

Namibia

Namibia Community-Based Tourism Ⓦnacobta.com.na. Trust that issues an occasional newsletter on cultural tourism.

The Namibian Ⓦnamibian.com.na. Independent newspaper reporting on national and Pan-African affairs.

Namibia Tourism Board Ⓦnamibiatourism .com.na.

Namibia Wildlife Resorts Ⓦnwr.com .na. Details of state-owned lodges and campsites in Namibia's national parks.

Travel Namibia Ⓦtravelnamibiamag.com. Online version of an occasional magazine, published in the UK.

Niger

Agadez Niger Ⓦagadez-niger.com. Excellent photo and video site dedicated to northern Niger, with a potentially useful forum for intending Niger travellers.

Friends of Niger Ⓦfriendsofniger.org. Site of current and former US Peace Corps volunteers with info and links.

Libération-Niger Ⓦliberation-niger.com. Website of Libération-Niger, a reputable weekly French-language independent news and opinion magazine.

Temoust @temoust.org. French-based website of the *Temoust: Tuareg Survival* organization, covering culture and news.

Tuareg Fotogalerie @moula-moula.de. Rich and rewarding photo-site, in German, devoted to the Nigérien Sahara.

Nigeria

1930s Southeast Nigeria @bit.ly/SENigeriaArt. Remarkable archive of photos of arts and culture from Igbo-land and around.

African Legacy @bit.ly/AfricanLegacy. Short cut to some of Nigeria's most under-rated (and under-visited) archeological sites.

Lagos Live @lagoslive.com. An excellent online guide for visitors to Lagos.

NaijaBlog @naijablog.blogspot.com. Stay in touch with all that matters in the fields of culture and politics with this much-read blog.

Nigerian Field Society @nigerianfield.org. Founded in 1930, the NFS is dedicated to the human and natural history of West Africa, in particular of Nigeria. An excellent site for background and contacts.

NigeriaWorld @nigeriaworld.com. The latest news from Nigeria, with headline stories and features.

Réunion

Guide to Réunion Island @reunionisland.fr. English-language tourist information site.

Ile de La Réunion @reunion.fr. Detailed French government tourist information.

Reunion Island @reunion.runweb.com. Good tourism and cultural information.

Sakifo @sakifo.com. One of the island's best music festivals.

Rwanda

Birding Rwanda @rwandabirdingguide.blogspot.com. Ruhengeri-based blogger with a wealth of observations.

Dian Fossey Gorilla Fund @gorillafund.org. Main site devoted to the country's gorillas.

Leave None to Tell the Story: Genocide in Rwanda @hrw.org/reports/1999/rwanda. The genocide, its background and aftermath, in cold text.

Rwanda Development Board @rwandatourism.com. Official tourism site.

São Tomé & Príncipe

São Tomé e Príncipe @saotome.st. Brief, digestible visitor information with photos for added flavour.

São Tomé e Príncipe Tourism Portal @turismo-stp.org. Official visitor information.

Senegal

Au Sénégal @au-senegal.com. Good general website.

Senegal online @senegal-online.com. Plenty of practical and cultural information, as well as good links.

Senegalese government @gouv.sn. A useful resource.

Senegalese Tourist Office @senegal-tourism.com. Senegalese tourist office in the USA, based in Atlanta, GA.

Tourisme Sénégal @tourisme-senegal.com. Official site of the Ministry of Tourism and Crafts.

Seychelles

Nature Seychelles @natureseychelles.org. Wildlife, nature and conservation news from a local NGO.

Seychelles Tourism Board @seychelles.travel. Official visitor information.

Virtual Seychelles @virtualseychelles.sc. Attractive, government-funded portal for national news and information, with good sections on island culture and the natural environment.

Sierra Leone

National Tourist Board @visitsierraleone.org. The main site for up-to-date information, straddling the tourist-local divide. Useful forum.

Patriotic Vanguard @thepatrioticvanguard.com. User-friendly news and opinion site.

Sierra Leone High Commission, UK @slhc-uk.org.uk. Useful starting place.

Sierra Leone Web @sierra-leone.org. Masses of archived news and cultural articles, including some fascinating old documents.

South Africa

Coast to Coast Ⓦ coastingafrica.com. Crammed with handy travel information for backpackers.

Mail and Guardian Ⓦ mg.co.za. Award-winning site from one of Africa's most respected newspapers.

Music.org.za Ⓦ music.org.za. The inside track on South Africa's buzzing music scene.

South African National Parks Ⓦ sanparks.org. The full lowdown, including entry fees, activities, accommodation and internships.

South Africa Tourism Ⓦ southafrica.net. Superbly comprehensive official visitor information.

Rage Ⓦ rage.co.za. Online magazine with its finger on the pulse of urban culture, covering South African music, art, nightlife and street style.

Wavescape Ⓦ wavescape.co.za. Where to surf, with webcams to keep an eye on the action.

Sudan

Eyes on Darfur Ⓦ eyesondarfur.org. Amnesty International's Darfur site.

South Sudan Nation Ⓦ southsudannation.com. Secession and Independence movement.

Sudan Artists Gallery Ⓦ sudanartists.org. Impressive online gallery of works by Sudanese artists, mostly based in the US.

Sudan Update Ⓦ sudanupdate.org. Reliable news and analysis.

Swaziland

Swaziland National Trust Commission Ⓦ sntc.org.sz. Excellent, detailed coverage of cultural topics and nature reserves.

Swaziland Tourism Authority Ⓦ welcometoswaziland.com. Official visitor information.

The blog for this guide

For travel updates, news links and general information, check out Ⓦ firsttimeafrica.blogspot.com.

Tanzania

Serengeti Ⓦ serengeti.org. News, issues and practicalities regarding this breathtaking national park.

Tanzania National Parks Ⓦ tanzaniaparks.com. Essential reference for those planning to hit the safari circuit.

Tanzania Tourist Board Ⓦ tanzaniatouristboard.com. Official visitor information.

Zanzibar.net Ⓦ zanzibar.net. General site with a mixed bag of visitor-friendly articles.

Togo

Republic of Togo Ⓦ republicoftogo.com. The best Togo website, with political and economic news, plus a range of country information.

Togolese tourist office Ⓦ togo-tourisme.com.

Voodoo and West Africa's Spiritual Life Ⓦ n.pr/VoodooRadio. Radio Expeditions from NPR and National Geographic, including good coverage of Vodun.

Tunisia

Tunisia.com Ⓦ tunisia.com. Lively portal for visitors, with a whole page on Tunisia's *Star Wars* locations.

Tunisia Online Ⓦ tunisiaonline.com. Official portal introducing local media, historic sites, national parks and news.

Tunisian National Tourist Office Ⓦ cometotunisia.co.uk. Official visitor information, attractively presented.

Uganda

Music Uganda Ⓦ musicuganda.com. Lively coverage of the contemporary scene.

New Vision Ⓦ newvision.co.ug. News and features from one of Uganda's better newspapers (majority government-owned).

Tourism Uganda Ⓦ visituganda.com.

Travel Uganda Ⓦ traveluganda.co.ug. Wide-ranging travel information.

Uganda Community Tourism Association Ⓦ ucota.org.ug. Cultural immersion and eco-tourism.

Uganda Wildlife Authority ⓦuwa.or.ug. Full parks details.

Zambia

South Luangwa Conservation Society ⓦslcs-zambia.org. Wildlife news and links to the region's many excellent camps and safari companies.

Travel Zambia ⓦtravelzambiamag.com. Online version of an occasional magazine, published in the UK.

Zambian Ornithological Society ⓦwattledcrane.com. Activities, events and tick lists for keen birders.

Zambia Tourist Board ⓦzambiatourism .com. Official visitor information presented in excellent detail.

Zimbabwe

Travel Zimbabwe ⓦtravelzimbabwemag .com. Online version of an occasional magazine, published in the UK.

Zimbabwe National Parks and Wildlife ⓦzimparks.com. Everything you need to know about visiting the national parks, including fees and places to stay.

Zimbabwe Tourism Authority ⓦzimbabwe tourism.co.zw. Official visitor information.

Magazines and advice

Africa Centre ⓦafricacentre.org.uk. Long-established London cultural and community centre.

Africa Confidential ⓦafrica-confidential .com. Subscription-only fortnightly newsletter, unsurpassed for inside information.

Bwana Mitch ⓦsafarilinks.de. Up-to-date safari information for East and southern Africa.

Focus on Africa ⓦbbc.in/FocusonAfrica. Consistently well-written and intriguing coverage in this BBC magazine.

Fodors forums ⓦbit.ly/FodorsAfrica. Upmarket, with mostly North American users.

Getaway South African domestic tourism and destination coverage – especially strong on eastern and southern Africa.

Routard Forums ⓦbit.ly/Routardforums. Forums on the *Guide du Routard* website

that are particularly useful for French-speaking countries.

Thorn Tree forums ⓦbit.ly/LPforums. Wide-ranging threads on the *Lonely Planet* website, mostly appealing to adventurous, low-budget travellers.

Travel Africa ⓦtravelafricamag.com. Very strong magazine for wildlife and safari destinations without ignoring lesser-known attractions.

Trip Advisor forums ⓦbit.ly /TA-Africaforums. Huge numbers of country-by-country threads, mostly appealing to mid-market travellers.

Virtual Tourist ⓦbit.ly/VT-Africaforums. Useful, country-by-country threads with an adventurous bent.

Wanderlust ⓦwanderlust.co.uk. Highly respected magazine, with excellent Africa coverage.

Books

General guidebooks and series

African Historical Dictionaries ⓦscarecrowpress.com. For in-depth knowl-edge, this is what you need. Scarecrow

have a title on every African country covering names, places and events in detail.

Heinemann African Writers Series AWS titles were in the vanguard of African fiction publishing in English and reached 359 titles before concluding in 2003. Some are still

425

available. Those titles that are out of print can be found in libraries and secondhand bookstores.

The Rough Guide to West Africa The most comprehensive and detailed guide available, covering fifteen countries.

The Rough Guide to World Music: Vol 1 Africa & the Middle East Detailed articles covering most African countries, plus hundreds of potted artist biographies and CD reviews.

General Africa

Guy Arnold *Africa: A Modern History*. Comprehensive political and social coverage, including – unusually – North Africa, from the 1960s to the end of the twentieth century, with the blame for Africa's problems focusing on outside interference.

Stephen Belcher *African Myths of Origin*. Wonderful array of seventy origin myths from sub-Saharan Africa – a very immediate way of opening doors into Africa's many regional cultures.

Steve Bloomfield *Africa United: How Football Explains Africa*. Highly readable account of a footy fan and journalist's relationship with thirteen African countries, following the thread of football to greater understanding.

T.C. Boyle *Water Music*. Lengthy, captivating, and at times outrageously funny fictionalization of Mungo Park's explorations of West Africa. Essential *in situ* reading for those long roadside waits.

Cheik Anta Diop *Precolonial Black Africa*. The Senegalese academic, who died in 1986, asserted that Western as well as African civilization began in Africa, specifically in Upper Egypt.

Richard Dowden *Africa: Altered States, Ordinary Miracles*. Extended essays covering two dozen countries with the thoughtful, humane engagement of this respected journalist and director of the Royal African Society.

Jens Finke *Chasing the Lizard's Tail: By Bicycle Across the Sahara*. Entertaining and insightful travelogue, recounting Rough Guide author Finke's journey from Morocco to a sudden end in Banjul.

Aidan Hartley *The Zanzibar Chest: A Story of Life, Love, and Death in Foreign Lands*. Beautifully written, if at times gruelling; a blend of family and war reporter's memoir – the Anglo-Kenyan author covered Rwanda, Burundi, Somalia and Ethiopia for Reuters.

Tim Jeal *Stanley: the Impossible Life of Africa's Greatest Explorer*. Fascinating and frequently revealing biography that re-evaluates a complex personality, incorporating research from a mass of previously unstudied papers. Jeal has also written the classic biography of Livingstone.

Jonathan Kingdon *The Kingdon Pocket Guide to African Mammals*. Deservedly the most popular handbook, in accessible, game-viewing format, with identification illustrations and distribution maps for each species.

Mary Kingsley *Travels in West Africa*. Extraordinary account of travels by a freethinking explorer between Sierra Leone and Angola in 1893–4 – part anthropological research, part plant and animal collecting – including an espousal of cultural relativism that was far ahead of its time.

Martin Meredith *The State of Africa/The Fate of Africa*. UK and US editions of a continent-wide modern history that focuses on bad leadership as the most significant cause of Africa's problems.

Tom Phillips *Africa: the Art of a Continent*. Outstanding, sumptuously illustrated and critically written coverage of the entire continent, ranging from ancient times to the modern day, from masks to rock art, from jewellery to textiles.

Fran Sandham *Traversa*. Highly entertaining account of a trans-African walk, from Swakopmund in Namibia to Bagamoyo in Tanzania, accompanied by the author's reflections on Livingstone and other explorers.

Paul Theroux *Dark Star Safari*. Wryly amusing account of a Cairo to Cape journey that you might put aside until after you've returned, lest Theroux' masterfully written but miserable interpretation of Africa's every aspect should put you off going in the first place.

Camilla Toulmin *Climate Change in Africa*. The biggest issue facing the continent – hit by the double whammy of structural poverty and the droughts, floods and famines caused by factors beyond its control – laid bare by the director of the International Institute for Environment and Development.

Algeria

Paul Bowles *The Sheltering Sky*. Set in the Sahara, this disturbing novel of misanthropic travellers and marital breakdown in a terrifying environment is full of Bowles' evocative and unnervingly acute observations of the desert landscape.

Aziz Chouaki *The Star of Algiers*. How do you cope with living in the shadow of the mosque while dreaming of musical stardom? Chouaki's tautly drawn protagonist, Kabyle singer Moussa Massy, shows how, and how that works out. A highly recommended read for a first visit to Algeria.

Isabelle Eberhardt *The Nomad: the Diaries of Isabelle Eberhardt*. One of the nineteenth century's most exceptional adventurers, Eberhardt moved from Geneva to Algeria with her radical mother, who died soon after. Dressed as a man, she travelled the country, smoked *kif* and mixed freely with Algerians. She died in a flash flood in Ain Sefra, in the northern Sahara, aged 27.

Jeremy Keenan *Sahara Man: Travelling with the Tuareg*. London-based political scientist who has lived with the Tuareg in southern Algeria. His outspoken views on the role of the US as agent provocateur – as described in his 2009 book, *The Dark Sahara: America's War on Terror in Africa* – deserve to be more widely broadcast.

Angola

José Eduardo Agualusa *The Book of Chameleons*. Delightfully original magical-realist novel set in contemporary Angola, narrated by a gecko.

Ryszard Kapuscinski *Another Day of Life*. Impressions of Angola's "sloppy, dogged and cruel" civil war from the great journalist's three-month assignment in Luanda, in 1975.

Pedro Rosa Mendes *Bay of Tigers*. Travelogue from a Portuguese journalist who sets out to explore southern Africa's two war-torn lusophone countries, Angola and Mozambique.

Benin

Annie Caulfield *Show Me the Magic: Travels around Benin by Taxi*. Amusing and revealing account of a hectic trip around the country from the back of a battered Peugeot taxi, with a control-freak driver, Isidore.

Bruce Chatwin *The Viceroy of Ouidah*. The first book you should read on Benin – a gripping, fictionalized account of the life of a Brazilian slave-trader.

Christophe Henning and Hans Oberlander *Voodoo: Secret Power in Africa*. One of the Taschen imprint's sumptuous coffee-table books – strong images, with anecdote-based text from the author/photographers who travelled the country.

Botswana

Peter Allison *Don't Run, Whatever You Do*. Cheerful, irreverent safari anecdotes from one of the Okavango Delta's top guides and raconteurs.

Alexander McCall Smith *The No.1 Ladies' Detective Agency*. Hugely popular series of light-hearted novels about Botswana's first ever female private investigator, the endearingly patriotic Mma Precious Ramotswe.

Laurens van der Post *The Lost World of the Kalahari*. Passionate account of van der Post's encounters with the San Bushmen of the Central Kalahari in the 1950s.

Will Randall *Botswana Time*. Likeable portrait of remote rural life, through the eyes of a young Brit who serves a short stint as headmaster of a village school.

Norman Rush *Whites* and *Mating*. Beautifully observed novels about tangled human relationships, written by an

American Pulitzer nominee who got to know Botswana as a Peace Corps volunteer.

Robyn Scott *Twenty Chickens for a Saddle*. A woman in her twenties recalls her eccentric girlhood in 1980s, post-colonial Botswana, and muses on shifting attitudes to race across the generations.

Burkina Faso

Thomas Sankara *Thomas Sankara Speaks*. Collection of the revolutionary's speeches – worth dipping into to see where the revolution was supposed to be going.

Malidoma Patrice Some *Of Water and the Spirit*. The autobiography of a Dagari man born in the 1950s, who fell into the hands of Jesuit missionaries when he was four and didn't return to his roots until adulthood. Descriptions of his tribal initiation and unusual experiences of shamanism invite comparison with Carlos Castaneda.

Burundi

Tracy Kidder *Strength in What Remains*. True story by a Pulitzer prize-winning journalist of medical student refugee Deogratias's life in New York, and his former life in Burundi, and eventual return there.

Peter Uvin *Life After Violence: A People's Story of Burundi*. Interviews with Burundians from many walks of life in Zed Books' "African Arguments" series.

Nigel Watt *Burundi: Biography of a Small African Country*. Engaging and thorough new introduction to the land, its people and history.

Cameroon

Calixthe Beyala *Your Name Shall be Tanga* and *The Sun Hath Looked Upon Me*. Beyala is an emerging name in West African fiction; her heroes are women forced to act against poverty and injustice in patriarchal societies.

Gerald Durrell *The Overloaded Ark, The Bafut Beagles* and *A Zoo in My Luggage*. Durrell's animal-collecting exploits in the (then) British Cameroons are delightfully recounted and still funny. But it's hard to

recognize the present town of Mamfé – even less Bafut – in his misty, gin-soaked pictures.

Ndeley Mokoso *Man Pass Man!* A string of darkly funny short stories. The subject of the title tale – maraboutic meddling on the football pitch – was rumoured to account for Cameroon's success in the 1990 World Cup.

Dervla Murphy *In Cameroon with Egbert*. Entertaining account of the travel writer's horseback adventures with her daughter.

Ferdinand Oyono *Houseboy*. Oyono was one of the first satirical writers of the colonial period. *The Old Man and the Medal* is less caustic, but equally effective in its criticism both of colonial insensitivity and blind adherence to tradition.

Cape Verde

Basil Davidson *The Fortunate Isles*. Readable history by a British academic who specialized in Portuguese Africa.

Central African Republic

André Gide *Travels in the Congo* (translated from *Voyage au Congo*). The French government envoy and naturalist visited the territory of Oubangui-Shari in 1925. His readable descriptions of French slave labour are revealing of how little has really changed for the rural population.

Pierre Sammy-Mackfoy *The Blue Butterfly and the Daughter of the Devil*. The Centrafrican teacher and writer (and sometime government media enforcer) explores the conflict between tradition and modernity.

Louis Sarno *Song from the Forest: My Life Among the Ba-Benjelle Pygmies*. New Jerseyan Sarno's account of his life with the forest people of CAR – he married a Ba-Benjelle woman and has studied their society and music for more than 25 years.

Jacqueline Woodfork *Culture and Customs of the Central African Republic*. Very useful starting point for exploring CAR's society and arts.

Chad

Joseph Brahim Seïd *Told by Starlight in Chad*. One of the country's few writers to have been successful overseas, the late Seïd's fictionalized account of his childhood achieved great acclaim in France.

Comoros and Mayotte

Jean Fasquel *Mayotte, les Comores et la France*. With little available in print, this short analysis of the eternal triangle between France, the French département of Mayotte and the neighbouring independent Republic of the Comoros is a good start for French-speaking visitors.

Congo Republic

Romain Gary *The Roots of Heaven* (*Les Racines du Ciel*). Winner of the 1956 Prix Goncourt, this insightful novel tells of one man's struggle to save the elephants of French Equatorial Africa from extinction.

Redmond O'Hanlon *Congo Journey*. This spirited memoir of a Congolese journey is a modern adventure travel classic.

Côte d'Ivoire

Ahmadou Kourouma *The Suns of Independence* and *Waiting for the Wild Beasts to Vote*. Intense novels, full of wild imagery and suspended reality. Kourouma, who died in 2003, was a northerner who spent much of his life opposing Houphouët-Boigny's dictatorship.

Susan M. Vogel *Baule: African Art/Western Eyes*. A readable examination of the Baule (Baoulé) world view – expressed through sacred as well as workaday objects. Generously illustrated.

Democratic Republic of Congo

Tim Butcher *Blood River*. Butcher sets off along the route of Stanley's 1874–77 expedition down the Congo. A best-selling travel memoir, full of gung-ho detail.

Joseph Conrad *Heart of Darkness*. Conrad's brilliant, short tale of colonialism at its most brutal and ruthless was based on material gathered during his own travels in Central Africa in 1890.

Adam Hochschild *King Leopold's Ghost*. History of the Congo Free State at the turn of the twentieth century when, during rubber fever, millions died at the hands of white officials. A readable, though chilling, companion to *Heart of Darkness*.

Barbara Kingsolver *The Poisonwood Bible*. Superb page-turner of an American novel about the tribulations of a missionary family living in remotest Zaire in the 1960s.

Jeffrey Tayler *Facing the Congo*. The author braves drama, corruption and danger while attempting to canoe the entire navigable length of the Congo.

Michela Wrong *In the Footsteps of Mr Kurtz*. Engrossing portrayal of Mobutu's last days as a champagne-quaffing despot from a foreign correspondent who has covered Africa for Reuters and the BBC.

Djibouti

Elmore Leonard *Djibouti*. 2010 novel from the American thriller writer. A documentary film-maker with a fascination for modern-day pirates sets out to track some of them down.

Egypt

Mark Collier and Bill Manley *How to Read Egyptian Hieroglyphs*. Clear, step-by-step instructions have made this a best-seller.

George Hart *Ancient Egyptian Gods and Goddesses*. Handy pocket reference guide illustrated with colour photos of paintings, papyri and sculptures.

Ewald Lieske and Robert Myers *Coral Reef Guide: Red Sea*. Top-quality guide to everything that swims, scampers and wriggles in Egypt's underwater world.

Naguib Mahfouz *The Cairo Trilogy: Palace of Desires; Palace Walk; Sugar Street*. Mahfouz, a Nobel Prize winner and the father of the modern Egyptian novel, writes elegantly about his home country. This, his greatest epic, follows the lives of a Cairo family from the Revolution of 1919 to the end of World War II.

The Rough Guide to Egypt Frequently updated, this is the most practical and up-to-date guide available, with extensive background coverage.

Nawal el-Saadawi *Woman at Point Zero*. Hard-hitting novel, written in the 1970s, from a political activist and feminist who is not afraid to tackle taboo subjects such as prostitution and female genital mutilation.

Anthony Sattin *The Pharaoh's Shadow*. Sattin travels through Egypt at the turn of the millennium, intrigued by a nation that is both obsessed with its historic glories and traditions and gripped by the potential of the modern world.

Equatorial Guinea

Robert Klitgaard *Tropical Gangsters*. Entertaining insights from a consultant on economic reform. His subtitle, *One Man's Experience with Development and Decadence in Deepest Africa*, sums up his wry despair.

Adam Roberts *The Wonga Coup*. Roberts pieces together the details of Simon Mann's 2004 plot to overthrow the government, seize control of the oil industry and pocket billions of dollars – a coup attempt in which Mark Thatcher was, allegedly, entangled.

Eritrea

Anne Alders *Eritrean Beauty*. Superb portraits of ordinary Eritreans from a talented Dutch photographer.

Michela Wrong *I Didn't Do It for You*. How Eritrea has coped with being used and abused by Italy, Britain, the US, the Soviet Union and Ethiopia.

Hannah Pool *My Fathers' Daughter*. Pool, a *Guardian* journalist who was adopted from an Eritrean orphanage as a baby and grew up in Manchester, travels to Eritrea to trace the family she never knew she had (the second father of the title), and witness the poverty that could so easily have been her own.

Ethiopia

Peter Gill *Famine and Foreigners: Ethiopia Since Live Aid*. Written by the first foreign journalist to cover the 1984 Korem famine, this 25-years-later report coolly looks at development and the legacy of Live Aid, and the role of the new foreigners, the Chinese.

Ryszard Kapuscinski *The Emperor: Downfall of an Autocrat*. Fascinating and tightly written account of the last days of Emperor Haile Selassie in 1974, as perilously relayed at the time to the author by court insiders.

Dervla Murphy *In Ethiopia with a mule*. One of Murphy's earliest African journeys, an entertaining account of an adventure undertaken more than forty years ago, through imperial Ethiopia.

Gabon

Jan Brokken *The Rainbird*. Brokken, a Dutch journalist, treks through Gabon, spicing his account with lively anecdotes and tales of explorers and missionaries.

Michael Nichols and Mike Fay *The Last Place on Earth*. Pricey but inspirational book about ardent environmentalist Fay's Megatransect Expedition in which he surveyed the uncharted rainforests of west Central Africa on foot, with National Geographic photographer Nichols in tow.

The Gambia

Clive Barlow *Birds of The Gambia and Senegal*. Birdwatchers' bible.

Dayo Forster *Reading the Ceiling*. Debut novel about the consequences of pivotal life choices from a Gambian woman who now lives in Kenya. Full of the atmosphere of West Africa.

Alex Haley *Roots*. Wide-ranging saga in which an African American traces his family back to The Gambia. The novel includes an imaginative depiction of colonial West Africa during the slave-trading years.

David Penney *Wildlife of The Gambia*. Useful new field guide with clear photos.

Ghana

Manu Herbstein *Ama: A Story of the Atlantic Slave Trade*. Winner of the 2002 Commonwealth Writers' Prize first book award, South African Herbstein's novel recounts the story of a young Dagomba woman's experiences of the transatlantic slave trade.

Ayi Kwei Armah *The Beautyful Ones Are Not Yet Born*. Politics, greed and corruption in newly independent Africa, seen through the life of a railway clerk. More recently, a compelling historical novel, *The Healers*, is set in the Asante Empire at the time of its demise.

John Miller Chernoff *Hustling Is Not Stealing and Exchange is not Robbery*. Unique, funny, and in places almost unbearably poignant reportage – the verbatim stories of a bar girl, related to Chernoff in the late 1970s and rendered with breathtaking skill and honesty.

William St Clair *The Grand Slave Emporium: Cape Coast Castle and the British Slave Trade*. A highly readable new study illuminating the history of Cape Coast Castle and the British role in the slave trade.

Thierry Secretan *Going into Darkness: Fantastic Coffins from Africa*. Coffee-table coffin portraits – the extraordinary lifestyle-in-death caskets (sardine for fisherman, Merc for businessman) of the Ga in Accra.

Guinea

Alioum Fantouré *Tropical Circle*. Novel about Guinea between the end of World War II and the reign of terror.

Mamadou Kouyaté *Sundiata: An Epic of Old Mali*. Slim but fascinating griot's history of the Mali Empire, the epicentre of which was near Siguiri, in Guinea.

Camara Laye *The African Child*. One of the best-known books by an African writer, these memoirs of a privileged rural childhood in Kouroussa are a homage to the author's parents.

Guinea-Bissau

Basil Davidson *No Fist is Big Enough to Hide the Sky: The Liberation of Guiné and Cape Verde*. Enthusiastic, quirky account of the war of liberation against

the Portuguese, and its aftermath: a rosy picture, tarnished by subsequent events.

Toby Green *Meeting the Invisible Man*. Story of a surreal journey with a Senegalese photographer, much of it through Guinea-Bissau, in search of magic powers – an account that flips unnervingly between dusty banality and a parallel world of magic and spells.

Walter Rodney *A History of the Upper Guinea Coast 1545–1800*. An Afrocentric history dealing in depth with the area the Portuguese moved into and providing a mass of fascinating material on its social complexity.

Kenya

David Anderson *Histories of the Hanged: Testimonies from the Mau Mau Rebellion in Kenya*. Shocking study of Britain's response to the Mau Mau anti-colonial uprising of the 1950s.

Karen Blixen *Out of Africa*. First published in 1937, Blixen's account of her life on her Ngong Hills coffee farm between the wars is an intense read – lyrical, introspective, sometimes obnoxiously and intricately racist, but worth pursuing and never super-ficial, unlike Sydney Pollack's film.

Corinne Hoffmann *The White Masai*. Equally ridiculed and revered, an extraor-dinary account, effectively a journal, of a Swiss woman's extended love affair with a Samburu man, and her life in Barsaloi in the 1990s.

John Le Carré *The Constant Gardener*. The spymaster turns his hand to a whodunnit, in which a campaigner against the misdeeds of Big Pharma is raped and murdered. Her husband, a British diplomat, starts his own investigation.

The Rough Guide to Kenya Longest-established and most detailed and comprehensive guide to Kenya, now in its ninth edition.

Ngugi wa Thiong'o The contribution of the dominant figure of modern Kenyan literature is enormous, and delving in to his oeuvre is rewarding if not always easy. Try *Secret*

Lives for short stories, *Weep Not, Child* for a glowing early novel or *Petals of Blood* for the mature Ngugi – a richly satisfying detective story that is also a saga of wretchedness and struggle.

M.G. Vassanji *The In-between World of Vikram Lall*. Remarkable epic – winner of the 2003 Giller Prize for Canadian fiction – of multiple alienations and the power of corruption in a world of competing moralities. Lall is the chief protagonist, a Ugandan Asian exiled to Canada having been named Kenya's most corrupt man.

Michela Wrong *It's Our Turn to Eat: The Story of a Kenyan Whistle Blower*. "To eat" is a Kenyan euphemism for helping yourself to what doesn't belong to you. Wrong's jaw-dropping account narrates the story of what happened when anti-corruption czar John Githongo tried to do his job.

Lesotho

Mpho 'M'atsepo Nthunya *Singing Away the Hunger*. Moving and uplifting memoir, written by a woman from a poor but proud Basotho community.

Thomas Mofolo *Chaka*. Originally written in Sotho but available in English translation, this is considered one of Africa's best historical novels. It's a compelling take on the myth and motives of one of the continent's bloodiest leaders, Shaka Zulu.

Liberia

Helene Cooper *The House at Sugar Beach*. Memoir of a Liberian-born, US journalist, revisiting after more than two decades, recounting the violence of her departure and meeting up with her nanny – a "country sister" that the family left behind.

Graham Greene *Journey without Maps*. Acid account of the novelist's walk, in 1935, from Foya to Buchanan, via Ganta – still highly recommended reading. He was accompanied by a cousin, whom he hardly mentions, and a line of porters.

Barbara Greene *Too Late to Turn Back*. Revenge of the cousin: "It sounded fun",

she writes of her decision to go, but it evidently wasn't.

Libya

Ronald Bruce St. John *Libya: From Colony to Independence*. Solid background reading on a country that's now in the process of reinventing itself on the world stage.

Roger Jones *Libya – Culture Smart!* A life raft for those fearful of feeling at sea in matters of custom and etiquette.

Philip Kenrick *Tripolitania*. A well-informed guide to Libya's archeological sites.

Hisham Matar *In the Country of Men*. Set in Tripoli in the late 1970s, this haunting debut novel gives a boy's-eye-view of life under a dictatorship. It won several awards and was shortlisted for the Booker Prize in 2006.

Madagascar

Alison Jolly *Lords and Lemurs*. Travelogue with a scientific slant, from a leading British primatologist who has been studying Madagascan wildlife since the 1960s, and even has a mouse lemur named after her.

Nick Garbutt, Hilary Bradt and Derek Schuurman *Madagascar Wildlife*. Paperback field guide from a team who know the island inside out. Masses of photos and handy tips on visiting the parks and reserves.

Malawi

Samson Kambalu *The Jive Talker*. Confident and refreshing autobiographical material from a Malawian Brit who describes himself as a conceptual artist. Subtitled *How to Get a British Passport*, it smashes stereotypical images of black Africa.

William Kamkwamba *The Boy Who Harnessed the Wind*. The uplifting true story of a young man whose childhood experience of famine and hardship left him determined to boost his community's fortunes in later life. His plan: to build a wind-powered generator.

David Livingstone *A Popular Account of Dr. Livingstone's Expedition*. The celebrated nineteenth-century explorer's own account of journeying along the Zambezi, an expedition beset with disaster, and "discovering" Lake Malawi (or Nyassa, as he called it).

Mali

Maryse Condé *Segu*. An epic historical novel – already a francophone classic before its translation into English – by a Guadeloupian author of Bamana descent, that paints a mesmerizing and unsettlingly graphic portrait of the Ségou empire from 1797 to the middle of the nineteenth century.

Banning Eyre *In Griot Time: An American Guitarist in Mali*. Account of a sojourn spent studying Malian guitar styles under Djelimady Tounkara, brilliantly capturing the flavour of modern Mali through its music.

Seydou Keïta *Seydou Keïta: African Photographs*. An extraordinary collection of black-and-white studio photos of Bamako people from the 1950s to the 1970s – a testament to the richness of African urban culture.

Yambo Ouologuem *Bound to Violence*. By the only Malian writer to have achieved international recognition, an exploration of brutality and deceit in an invented African empire, Nakem – a reminder that African society rests on foundations as bloody and self-destructive as any other.

Anthony Sattin *The Gates of Africa: Death, Discovery and the Search for Timbuktu*. The rough outlines of the explorers' tales are familiar, but it's the detail Sattin weaves in that makes this compelling.

Bettina Selby *Frail Dream of Timbuktu*. Selby's account of her bicycle journey from Niamey to Bamako is beautifully written and covers much more than just the journey – with interest-filled deviations and asides.

Mauritania

Samuel Cotton *Silent Terror*. An all-too-rare investigation of the complex issue of slavery in contemporary Mauritania and Senegal.

Peter Hudson *Travels in Mauritania*. Absorbing travelogue detailing a two-month trek across the country in 1988.

Odette du Puigaudeau *Barefoot in Mauritania*. The author (1894–1991) and her female companion took camels across "the land of death" in the 1930s – a ramble through a Mauritania that hardly knew it existed.

Antoine de Saint-Exupéry *Wind, Sand and Stars*. Not well known in the anglophone world, but a cult hero in France, Saint-Exupéry was a pioneering pilot on the Casablanca–Dakar postal run – and also wrote beautifully.

Ronald Segal *Islam's Black Slaves: The Other Black Diaspora*. Though sometimes dry, this is a powerful overview of modern African slavery, with an emphasis on Mauritania and Sudan.

Mauritius

Malcolm de Chazal *Sens-Plastique*. Available in English translation, a pithy, philosophical novel from arguably the island's greatest twentieth-century writer.

Jean-Marie Gustave Le Clézio *The Prospector*. English translation of *Le Chercheur d'Or*, a coming-of-age story from a Nobel Prize-winning French-Mauritian novelist.

Patrick O'Brian *The Mauritius Command*. Rollicking historical novel about naval adventures, set in the Napoleonic Wars.

Bernardin de Saint-Pierre *Paul et Virginie*. Romantic novel, first published in 1788, that's so central to Mauritian culture that there's a display dedicated to it in the Blue Penny Museum.

Morocco & Western Sahara

Paul Bowles *Travels: Collected Writings, 1950–93*. Fascinating collection from the doyen of Morocco's expat writers, who lived in Tangiers for many decades.

Esther Freud *Hideous Kinky*. Delightfully recounted tale of the author's sojourn in Morocco with her older sister and hippy mum in the late 1960s.

Walter Harris *Morocco That Was*. From the 1890s to 1933, in the last decades of the Sultanate, before the French took over,

Harris was the *Times'* man in Morocco and a close confidante of the royal circle, wittily describing its inner workings. *The Times* could not have wished for a wittier, better connected court correspondent.

Mohammed Mrabet *The Lemon*. The prolific storyteller Mrabet was the protegé of Paul Bowles. This vivid, autobiographical tale of boyhood and adolescence is a good place to start.

The Rough Guide to Morocco The most comprehensive guide available, with extensive background coverage, frequently updated.

Mozambique

Mia Couto *Sleepwalking Land*. English translation of *Terra Sonâmbula*, a superb magical realist debut voted one of the best African novels of the twentieth century; Couto has since won several literary honours.

Lília Momplé *Neighbours*. Contemporary novel set in Maputo, from a writer with a strong social conscience.

Lisa St Aubin de Terán *Mozambique Mysteries*. In 2004, this famous English novelist founded a trade-not-aid project in Ilha de Moçambique, Mossuril and Cabaceiras in northern Mozambique; this is a loving portrait of the region.

Namibia

Neshani Andreas *The Purple Violet of Oshaantu*. Novel about friendships and feelings that transcend accepted traditions, centring on an unhappily married woman who finds herself widowed.

Rupert Isaacson *The Healing Land*. Travelogue that presents a sensitive portrait of the Kalahari Bushmen, written by a young adventurer who has been fascinated by their culture since childhood.

Henno Martin *The Sheltering Desert*. World War II survival story of two German geologists hiding out in the Namib desert and learning to hunt, find water and cope with extreme isolation.

Niger

Carol Beckwith and Marion Van Offelen *Nomads of Niger*. Superbly illustrated essay on the Wodaabé Bororo and the Cure Salée.

Peter Chilson *Riding the Demon: On the Road in West Africa*. Account of a year spent crisscrossing Niger by taxi brousse, getting inside the lives of drivers and passengers – recommended preparatory reading for serious budget travellers.

Ibrahim Issa *Grandes Eaux Noires*. Niger's first novel (published before independence), humorously fictionalizing the travails of Mediterranean explorers south of the Sahara in the second-century BC.

Paul Stoller and Cheryl Oakes *Fusion of the Worlds: an Ethnography of Possession among the Songhay of Niger*, and *In Sorcery's Shadow: a Memoir of Apprenticeship among the Songhay*. Stoller is Niger's Carlos Castaneda – apprenticed to a sorcerer and ingesting hallucinogens.

Nigeria

Chinua Achebe *Things Fall Apart; No Longer at Ease; Arrow of God; A Man of the People*. One of Africa's best-known novelists, Achebe gained international fame with his classic first novel *Things Fall Apart* (1958), which deals with the encounter, at the turn of the last century, of missionaries, colonial officers and an Igbo village.

Chimamanda Ngozi Adichie *Purple Hibiscus* (2005) and *Half of a Yellow Sun* (2007). Winner of the Orange Prize for her second novel, Adichie is in the vanguard of a new generation of Nigerian writers born after the 1967–70 civil war.

Helon Habila *Waiting for an Angel*. Much acclaimed debut novel about the precarious life of a journalist under Abacha's regime. His second novel, *Measuring Time*, explores the life of twins growing up in the 1970s in the northeast.

Karl Maier *This House Has Fallen: Nigeria in Crisis*. An incisive survey by *The Independent*'s former Africa correspondent of the political problems besetting modern Nigeria.

Flora Nwapa *Efuru*. As in her later book *Idu*, the late Flora Nwapa, the first African woman to publish a novel, looks at women's roles – not always in a traditional way – in a society precariously balanced between the traditional and the new.

A.D. Nzemeke and E.O. Erhage (eds) *Nigerian Peoples and Culture*. Highly recommended in-depth cultural history of Nigeria's ethnic groups.

Andrew Rowell *The Next Gulf*. A concise and lively account of the oil industry in Nigeria and its relation to politics and Western interests, published in 2005.

Wole Soyinka *Aké* and *Isara*. Known primarily as a playwright, Soyinka was the first African winner of the Nobel Prize for Literature, in 1986. Soyinka's work is denser and less easy-going than Chinua Achebe's and he is politically more outspoken.

Amos Tutuola *The Palm-Wine Drinkard*. Heavily under the spell of Yoruba oral tradition, this 1952 novel recounts a journey into the "Dead Towns" of the supernatural. It was followed by *My Life in the Bush of Ghosts*.

Ken Wiwa *In the Shadow of a Saint*. Ken Saro-Wiwa's son Ken Wiwa's highly readable account of his complex relationship with his father.

Réunion

Fernand Nathan *Anthologie de la litérature réunionnaise*. Good collection of writing by local authors.

Rwanda

Romeo Dallaire *Shake Hands with the Devil*. Dallaire (commander of the UN Assistance Mission to Rwanda in 1994) tells the story of how his own force – through UN hypocrisy and willful ignorance at the highest levels – was prevented from halting the genocide. A savage indictment of the UN.

Dian Fossey *Gorillas in the Mist*. The story of Fossey's life with the mountain gorillas

– from 1967 to 1980 – is the story of how these remarkable animals, living under constant threat of annihilation, have entered global consciousness.

Philip Gourevitch *We Wish To Inform You That Tomorrow We Will Be Killed With Our Families*. The *New York Times'* journalist interviewed dozens of participants, victims and onlookers of the genocide to produce this essential collection of testimonies and the chilling implication that "never again" will never be enough.

São Tomé & Príncipe

Donald Burness *Ossobo*. English-language essays on the islands' traditional poems and tales, including the story of the mythical ossobo bird.

Miguel Sousa Tavares *Equador*. Historical novel about love, glamour and corruption among colonial plantation owners, available in English; it inspired a hit television mini-series in Portugal.

Senegal

Mariama Bâ *So Long a Letter*. Dedicated to "all women and to men of good will", this is the story of a woman's life shattered by her husband's sudden, second marriage to a younger woman.

Mark Hudson *The Music in My Head*. Energetic, constantly amusing and inventive "world music" novel, incorporating glowing passages of superb descriptive prose. If you're going to Senegal – sorry, "Tekrur" – this is the one for the beach.

Sembène Ousmane (aka Ousmane Sembène) *God's Bits of Wood* and *Xala*. A committed, political and very immediate writer and film-maker who could also be very funny, as in *Xala*, the satirical tale of a wealthy Dakarois' loss of virility. His best is *God's Bits of Wood*, the story of the rail strike of 1947.

Seychelles

Adrian Skerrett *Birds of Seychelles*. Useful field guide, satisfyingly specific to the archipelago.

Thomas P. Peschak *Lost World: The Marine Realm of Aldabra and the Seychelles*. Superb underwater photography from an accomplished marine biologist and conservationist.

Sierra Leone

Daniel Bergner *Soldiers of Light*. One of the best books on the civil war, this subtly explores the obsession with supernatural beliefs held by fighters on both sides. Bergner skilfully juxtaposes the hopes of an American missionary against the despair of a country imploding.

Greg Campbell *Blood Diamonds*. Campbell traces a sticky web of corruption and brutalization that financed the civil war and the conflicts in Sierra Leone's neighbours – and still props up Al-Qaeda.

Aminatta Forna *The Devil that Danced on Water: A Daughter's Memoir*. Forna's deeply affecting account of her return to the Sierra Leone she lived in until the age of ten, and where her politician father was hanged for treason, is tender and excruciatingly painful, as she assesses the war and its roots in the 1960s.

Lansana Gberie *A Dirty War in West Africa: The RUF and the Destruction of Sierra Leone*. A rare work by a Sierra Leonean journalist, Gberie traces the pivotal role played by the diamond trade in the country's history.

Graham Greene *The Heart of the Matter*. Set in Freetown during World War II and touching on the racism and repression then present in the colony, Greene's novel uses the town as a seedy web in which his protagonists struggle.

Gail Haddock *What for Chop Today?* Recollections of a young volunteer doctor in Sierra Leone in the early 1990s, mostly delivered through warm and witty dialogue. Good, light preparatory reading – with dark undertones.

South Africa

Lawrence Anthony *The Elephant Whisperer*. Dramatic decisions and tricky situations abound in this warm-hearted account of the author's efforts to save a herd of "rogue" elephants from being culled.

J.M. Coetzee *In the Heart of the Country* and *Disgrace*. Born in Cape Town, Coetzee was awarded the Nobel Prize for Literature in 2003 and has won the Booker twice. *In the Heart of the Country* (1977) is a searing analysis of colonial attitudes, set on an isolated farm, where an unmarried white woman grapples with conflicting emotions when her father takes a black mistress. In *Disgrace* (1999), a white intellectual has an affair with one of his students and finds himself floundering in the changing moral landscape of post-apartheid South Africa.

Athol Fugard *Tsotsi*. Gangster-turns-good novel set in Sophiatown, Jo'burg, from South Africa's leading playwright. The 2005 film adaptation won an Oscar and a Golden Globe.

Nadine Gordimer *July's People*. Banned under apartheid when it was first published in 1981, this is a complex novel: the setting is an imaginary, futuristic South Africa, where misunderstandings between blacks and whites are so endemic that even the most liberal whites feel vulnerable.

Antjie Krog *Country of My Skull*. A prominent journalist throws the spotlight onto the horrors of apartheid in this fearless account of the Truth and Reconciliation Commission hearings.

Alex La Guma *A Walk in the Night*. Evocative short stories about Cape Town's District Six from a writer who was born there, written before the apartheid government forcibly evicted the residents.

Nelson Mandela *Long Walk to Freedom*. The former president's autobiography: a worldwide best-seller.

Zakes Mda *The Heart of Redness*. Award-winning contemporary fiction, offering sharp-eyed insights into class and cultural differences among black South Africans.

Alan Paton *Cry, the Beloved Country*. A Zulu pastor travels from his rural home to Johannesburg in search of his son, and is shocked by what he finds. One of the greatest South African novels.

The Rough Guide to South Africa The most comprehensive guide available. There's also a *Rough Guide to Cape Town and the Garden Route.*

Dan Sleigh *Islands.* A brilliantly drawn historical novel set in the seventeenth century. As the Dutch East India Company's settlement of the Cape of Good Hope takes shape, colonizers and indigenous Africans come face to face.

Sudan

Richard Cocket *Sudan: Darfur and the Failure of an African State.* The Africa editor of the *Economist* magazine does a formidable job of explaining Sudan on the eve of the referendum in the South, through interviews with a wide range of figures.

Julie Flint and Alex de Waal *Darfur: A New History of a Long War.* The inside story, from journalists who are frequent visitors to the region, of a complex conflict that has entered the world's consciousness like no other African war.

Alan Moorehead *The White Nile* and *The Blue Nile.* Classic. Riveting accounts of the search for the source and European rivalries for control in the region.

George Rodger *Village of the Nubas.* A *Life* magazine photographer on the loose in southern Sudan in 1949. Fascinating photos from a time before contact with the rest of the world had been fully established.

Deborah Scroggins *Emma's War.* Sad and insightful biography of the VSO teacher and aid worker Emma McCune who married SPLA guerrilla leader Riek Machar and died in a pointless car accident. A film version is due.

Swaziland

Peter Dunseith *The Bird of Heaven.* Wizards ride baboons and strike their enemies with lightning in this tale of Swazi magic and ritual.

Richard E. Grant *The Wah-Wah Diaries.* Swaziland's most famous international export weaves together childhood recollections and movie-world gossip in this witty account of the making of his autobiographical film.

Tanzania

Jane Goodall *50 Years at Gombe.* Anniversary memoir from the great chimp expert and conservationist, whose first best-seller was *In the Shadow of Man.*

Abdulrazak Gurnah *Paradise.* Vividly poetic, Booker-shortlisted novel depicting East Africa on the brink of World War I, through the eyes of a boy.

Mitsuaki Iwago *Serengeti.* Series of natural history books with photography so compelling, you'll want to book a safari on the spot.

Henry Morton Stanley *How I Found Livingstone.* Remarkably detailed eyewitness account from the ruthless nineteenth-century explorer.

The Rough Guide to Tanzania Frequently updated, this is the most comprehensive and detailed guide published. Also look out for *The Rough Guide to Zanzibar.*

M.G. Vassanji *The Book of Secrets.* Compelling mystery novel exploring the roles of Tanzania's Asian community during the colonial years.

Togo

Fauziya Kassindja *Do They Hear You When You Cry?* Kassindja fled Togo at the age of 17 to escape genital mutilation and forced marriage, then endured years in US prisons while her landmark political asylum case was being fought.

Tete-Michel Kpomassie *An African in Greenland.* Narrative of a young Togolese explorer on a whimsical journey among the Inuit in the 1960s. Fascinating and entertaining for its insights on Togolese as well as Inuit culture.

George Packer *The Village of Waiting.* Informative and wide-ranging account of the experiences of a Peace Corps volunteer (now journalist and novelist) near Notsé in the early 1980s.

Tunisia

Monia Hejaiej *Behind Closed Doors.* Oral narratives on love and life from women living in Tunis.

Patricia Highsmith *The Tremor of Forgery*. Considered one of Highsmith's best, this 1969 psychological thriller is set in Hammamet. An enjoyably creepy read for the beach.

Susan Raven *Rome in Africa*. Informative background reading for a visit to Tunisia's historic sites.

The Rough Guide to Tunisia Detailed guide to the country, with extensive background coverage, frequently updated.

H.F. Ullmann *Tunisia: Mediterranean Cuisine*. A fine culinary portrait of Tunisia, with mouth-watering recipes from a master chef.

Uganda

Giles Foden *The Last King of Scotland*. Fine old romp with a dark heart: Foden's Whitbread-winning novel is a brilliant examination of charisma as the young (and fictitious) Dr Garrigan is embraced as personal physician by the monstrous and risible dictator Idi Amin.

I. Charles Miller *The Lunatic Express*. Miller narrates the dramatic story of one of the great feats of Victorian engineering – the Uganda Railway from Mombasa to Kampala – adding weight with a broad historical background of East Africa, which helps explain the thinking behind the line.

Tim Allen and Koen Vlassenroot (eds) *The Lord's Resistance Army: Myth and Reality*. The first major work to put the brutal LRA into historical and political perspective – in Uganda's pre- and post-colonial history, in the social changes that have taken place in Acholiland, and in support to the LRA from the Sudanese government.

Moses Isegawa *Abyssinian Chronicles*. Beautifully crafted novel, full of exuberant descriptive enthusiasm and finely wrought characterization, describing an upbringing in Uganda in the turbulent 1970s and 80s.

Zambia

Mark and Delia Owens *Secrets of the Savanna*. The highs and lows of conservation, from a pair of American zoologists

who devoted twelve years to eliminating elephant poaching in North Luangwa.

Christine Lamb *The Africa House: The True Story of an English Gentleman and His African Dream*. A nimble biography of Stewart Gore-Browne of Shiwa Ng'andu fame.

Sheila Siddle *In My Family Tree*. Memoir of a chimp expert, from the co-founder of the Chimfunshi Wildlife Orphanage.

Binwell Sinyangwe *A Cowrie of Hope*. Though written by a man, this carefully crafted novel shows great insight into the dilemmas of a woman from rural Zambia.

Anne Thomson *Wash My Bikini*. Recollections of a Scottish woman who, at the age of 60, signed up for a lengthy stint of VSO work in Zambia.

Zimbabwe

Tsitsi Dangarembga *Nervous Conditions*. Fictionalized memoir of 1960s Rhodesia, in which a young black woman flouts convention by choosing to further her education. Winner of the Commonwealth Writers' Prize in 1988.

Peter Godwin *Fear: The Last Days of Robert Mugabe*. New exposé of the corrupt regime from a Zimbabwean journalist whose earlier works include *When a Crocodile Eats the Sun*, an insightful memoir.

Doris Lessing *The Grass is Singing*. What would drive the servant of a white Rhodesian farmer to murder his master's city-girl wife? Lessing's remarkable first novel (1950), set in the claustrophobic confines of a bushveld community, dissects the hypocrisies of colonialism.

Bookey Peek *Wild Honey*. Entertaining real-life stories from the Stone Hills Wildlife Sanctuary.

Douglas Rogers *The Last Resort*. Highly readable, this combines adventure travelogue, political commentary and family memoir; the author's parents ran Drifters, a game farm and popular backpacker lodge.

Small print and
Index

A Rough Guide to Rough Guides

Published in 1982, the first Rough Guide – to Greece – was a student scheme that became a publishing phenomenon. Mark Ellingham, a recent graduate in English from Bristol University, had been travelling in Greece the previous summer and couldn't find the right guidebook. With a small group of friends he wrote his own guide, combining a highly contemporary, journalistic style with a thoroughly practical approach to travellers' needs.

The immediate success of the book spawned a series that rapidly covered dozens of destinations. And, in addition to impecunious backpackers, Rough Guides soon acquired a much broader and older readership that relished the guides' wit and inquisitiveness as much as their enthusiastic, critical approach and value-for-money ethos.

These days, Rough Guides include recommendations from shoestring to luxury and cover more than 200 destinations around the globe, including almost every country in the Americas and Europe, more than half of Africa and most of Asia and Australasia. Our ever-growing team of authors and photographers is spread all over the world, particularly in Europe, the US and Australia.

In the early 1990s, Rough Guides branched out of travel, with the publication of Rough Guides to World Music, Classical Music and the Internet. All three have become benchmark titles in their fields, spearheading the publication of a wide range of books under the Rough Guide name.

Including the travel series, Rough Guides now number more than 350 titles, covering: phrasebooks, waterproof maps, music guides from Opera to Heavy Metal, reference works as diverse as Conspiracy Theories and Shakespeare, and popular culture books from iPods to Poker. Rough Guides also produce a series of more than 120 World Music CDs in partnership with World Music Network.

Visit www.roughguides.com to see our latest publications.

Rough Guide credits

Text editor: James Smart
Additional editing: Emma Gibbs
Layout: Jessica Subramanian
Cartography: Swati Handoo
Picture editor: Sarah Cummins
Production: Rebecca Short
Proofreader: Susanne Hillen
Cover design: Diana Jarvis, Dan May, Chloë Roberts
Editorial: London Andy Turner, Keith Drew, Edward Aves, Alice Park, Lucy White, Jo Kirby, Natasha Foges, Róisín Cameron, James Rice, Emma Beatson, Kathryn Lane, Monica Woods, Mani Ramaswamy, Harry Wilson, Lucy Cowie, Alison Roberts, Lara Kavanagh, Eleanor Aldridge, Ian Blenkinsop, Joe Staines, Matthew Milton, Tracy Hopkins; **Delhi** Madhavi Singh, Jalpreen Kaur Chhatwal, Jubbi Francis

Design & Pictures: London Scott Stickland, Dan May, Diana Jarvis, Mark Thomas, Nicole Newman, Emily Taylor; **Delhi** Umesh Aggarwal, Ajay Verma, Ankur Guha, Pradeep Thapliyal, Sachin Tanwar, Anita Singh, Nikhil Agarwal, Sachin Gupta
Production: Liz Cherry, Louise Daly, Erika Pepe
Cartography: London Ed Wright, Katie Lloyd-Jones; **Delhi** Rajesh Chhibber, Ashutosh Bharti, Rajesh Mishra, Animesh Pathak, Jasbir Sandhu, Deshpal Dabas, Lokamata Sahu
Marketing, Publicity & roughguides.com: Liz Statham
Digital Travel Publisher: Peter Buckley
Reference Director: Andrew Lockett
Operations Coordinator: Becky Doyle
Publishing Director (Travel): Clare Currie
Commercial Manager: Gino Magnotta
Managing Director: John Duhigg

Publishing information

This second edition published April 2011 by
Rough Guides Ltd,
80 Strand, London WC2R 0RL
11, Community Centre, Panchsheel Park, New Delhi 110017, India
Distributed by the Penguin Group
Penguin Books Ltd,
80 Strand, London WC2R 0RL
Penguin Group (USA)
375 Hudson Street, NY 10014, USA
Penguin Group (Australia)
250 Camberwell Road, Camberwell, Victoria 3124, Australia
Penguin Group (NZ)
67 Apollo Drive, Mairangi Bay, Auckland 1310, New Zealand
Rough Guides is represented in Canada by Tourmaline Editions Inc. 662 King Street West, Suite 304, Toronto, Ontario M5V 1M7
Cover concept by Peter Dyer.
Typeset in Bembo and Helvetica to an original design by Henry Iles.

Printed in Singapore
© Emma Gregg and Richard Trillo 2011
Maps © Rough Guides
No part of this book may be reproduced in any form without permission from the publisher except for the quotation of brief passages in reviews.
448pp includes index
A catalogue record for this book is available from the British Library
ISBN: 978-1-84836-481-3
The publishers and authors have done their best to ensure the accuracy and currency of all the information in **The Rough Guide to First Time Africa**, however, they can accept no responsibility for any loss, injury, or inconvenience sustained by any traveller as a result of information or advice contained in the guide.

1 3 5 7 9 8 6 4 2

Help us update

We've gone to a lot of effort to ensure that the second edition of **The Rough Guide to FT Africa** is accurate and up-to-date. However, things change – places get "discovered", opening hours are notoriously fickle, restaurants and rooms raise prices or lower standards. If you feel we've got it wrong or left something out, we'd like to know, and if you can remember the address, the price, the hours, the phone number, so much the better.

Please send your comments with the subject line "**Rough Guide FT Africa Update**" to ©mail @uk.roughguides.com. We'll credit all contributions and send a copy of the next edition (or any other Rough Guide if you prefer) for the very best emails.

Find more travel information, connect with fellow travellers and book your trip on ®www.roughguides.com

Acknowledgements

Both the authors thank: for sharp-eyed editing Kathryn Lane, Emma Gibbs and especially the tirelessly exacting but always kind James Smart; for skilful picture editing Sarah Cummins; for painstaking proofreading Susanne Hillen; and everyone else at Rough Guides who helped along the way.

From Emma: huge thanks, as ever, to Nathan Pope for sharing the journey.

From Richard: my thanks and appreciation to Teresa, Phoebe, David and Alex for sharing the fun parts and putting up with all the long hours.

Photo credits

Index

Map entries are in colour.

INDEX